西安统计年鉴

XI'AN STATISTICAL YEARBOOK

2014

中英文对照 Chinese/English

中国统计出版社
China Statistics Press

西安市统计局
XI'AN MUNICIPAL BUREAU OF STATISTICS
国家统计局西安调查队
NBS SURVEY OFFICE IN XI'AN

图书在版编目（CIP）数据

西安统计年鉴. 2014 / 西安市统计局, 国家统计局西安调查队编. -- 北京 : 中国统计出版社, 2014.8
ISBN 978-7-5037-7187-3

Ⅰ. ①西… Ⅱ. ①西… ②国… Ⅲ. ①统计资料－西安市－2014－年鉴 Ⅳ. ①C832.411-54

中国版本图书馆CIP数据核字(2014)第182596号

西安统计年鉴—2014

作　　者/ 西安市统计局　国家统计局西安调查队
责任编辑/ 陈越月
装帧设计/ 西安力天世纪品牌策划设计有限公司
出版发行/ 中国统计出版社
地　　址/ 北京市丰台区西三环南路甲6号　邮政编码/100073
电　　话/ 邮购（010）63376909　书店（010）68783171
网　　址/ http://csp.stats.gov.cn
印　　刷/ 西安一印制版有限责任公司
经　　销/ 新华书店
开　　本/ 890mm×1240mm　1/16
字　　数/ 1348千字
印　　张/ 40.25
版　　别/ 2014年8月第1版
版　　次/ 2014年8月第1次印刷
定　　价/ 260.00元

本书附同版本CD-ROM一张，光盘内容以书面文字为准。
如有印装差错，由本社发行部调换。

《西安统计年鉴—2014》编辑部

XI'AN STATISTICAL YEARBOOK-2014
EDITORLAL STAFF

编者说明

一、《西安统计年鉴—2014》系统收录了全市、区县及开发区2013年经济、社会各方面统计数据，以及重要历史年份主要统计数据，是一部全面记载西安市国民经济和社会发展情况的大型连续性统计文献资料和重要工具书。

二、本年鉴正文内容分为二十一个篇章：（一）综合；（二）基本单位；（三）国民经济核算；（四）人口、从业人员与职工工资；（五）固定资产投资；（六）财政；（七）物价指数；（八）人民生活；（九）城市公用事业；（十）环境保护；（十一）农业；（十二）工业；（十三）能源；（十四）建筑业；（十五）运输和邮电业；（十六）国内贸易；（十七）对外经济贸易和旅游；（十八）金融业；（十九）教育和科技；（二十）文化、体育、卫生、社会福利和其他；（二十一）企业调查。同时，为方便读者使用，各篇章前均设有简要说明和主要统计指标，对本篇章的主要内容、资料来源、以及历史变动情况予以简要概述，篇末附有《主要统计指标解释》。

三、本年鉴统计资料的统计标准，按当时国家统计制度执行，有关指标的涵义、口径、范围、计算方法等，在不同时期可能有所不同，使用时请注意。本年鉴国民经济行业分类按GB/T4754—2011标准执行。

四、为便于国内外读者查阅，本年鉴全部内容均采用中英文对照编辑。

五、由于第三次全国经济普查尚未结束，本年鉴中国民经济核算、工业等部分为2013年快报数，指标设置与年报制度有一定差异，个别与年报相关指标数据暂时空缺。

六、本年鉴中的部分指标合计数或相对数由于单位取舍不同产生的计算误差均未作机械调整。

七、本年鉴所使用的计量单位均依据2013年相关统计报表制度。

八、本年鉴使用的符号说明："空白"表示该项统计指标无数据或数据不详；"#"表示其中项；"*"表示另有注解。

感谢社会各界长期以来对《西安统计年鉴》的广泛关注和大力支持。为进一步做好工作，更好地为广大读者服务，希望社会各界提出宝贵意见。

PREFACE

I. Xi'an Statistical Yearbook 2014 is a periodical statistic yearbook which record economic and social development of Xi'an all-around in 2013 and some selected data series in historical important years. With its features of comprehensive and intensive information, this practically provides data covering the situation of social and economic developments in Xi'an.

II. The book contains twenty-one parts, 1.General Survey; 2. Unit; 3.National Economic Account; 4.Population, Employment and Wages; 5.Investment in Fixed Assets; 6.Government Finance; 7.Price Indices; 8.People's Livelihood; 9.Urban Public Utilities; 10.Environmental Protection; 11.Agriculture; 12.Industry; 13. Energy;14.Construction; 15Transportation, Post and Telecommunication Service; 16Domestic Trade; 17.Foreign Trade; and Tourism Finanle 19.Education, Science and Technology 20.Culture, Sports, Public Health, Social Welfare Institutions and Other Social Activities; 21.Enterprises Investigation. Meanwhile,in order to facilitate the reader to use,each chapter provides a brief description and key statistical indicators in 2012,gives a brief overview of this chapter about main contents,data sources and historicel data.After each chapter attached with "Main Statistical Indicators" 。

III. The data of various years in conformity to the statistical standards prescribed by national statistical system of the time. The meaning, scope and calculating method of indicators may have some difference in different periods, which readers must pay attention to. For example, national industries classification is carried out according to standard GB/T4754 -2011.

IV. For the convenience of being consulted by foreigners, the book is Chinese-English bilingual edition.

V. Because the Third National Economic Census has not finished yet, in this yearbook, the part of national economic account and industry was using the data of wall bulletin 2013. There are certain differences in index set between wall bulletin and annual report. And the index related to annual report has to vacancy temporary.

VI. Statistical discrepancies due to rounding are not adjusted automatically in this yearbook.

VII. Unit of measurement are used in this yearbook according to 2013 statistics system.

VIII. Explanations on symbols used in this yearbook:

(Blank) indicates the data not available;

\# indicates the items of the total.

* indicates some other explanatory note.

Here we would like to express our sincere thanks to the people for their concerning and support to the Xi an statistical yearbook. In order to do better and provide better service to readers, we hope that the whole society fields can propose constructive advices.

生产总值(亿元)

Gross Domestic Product (100 million yuan)

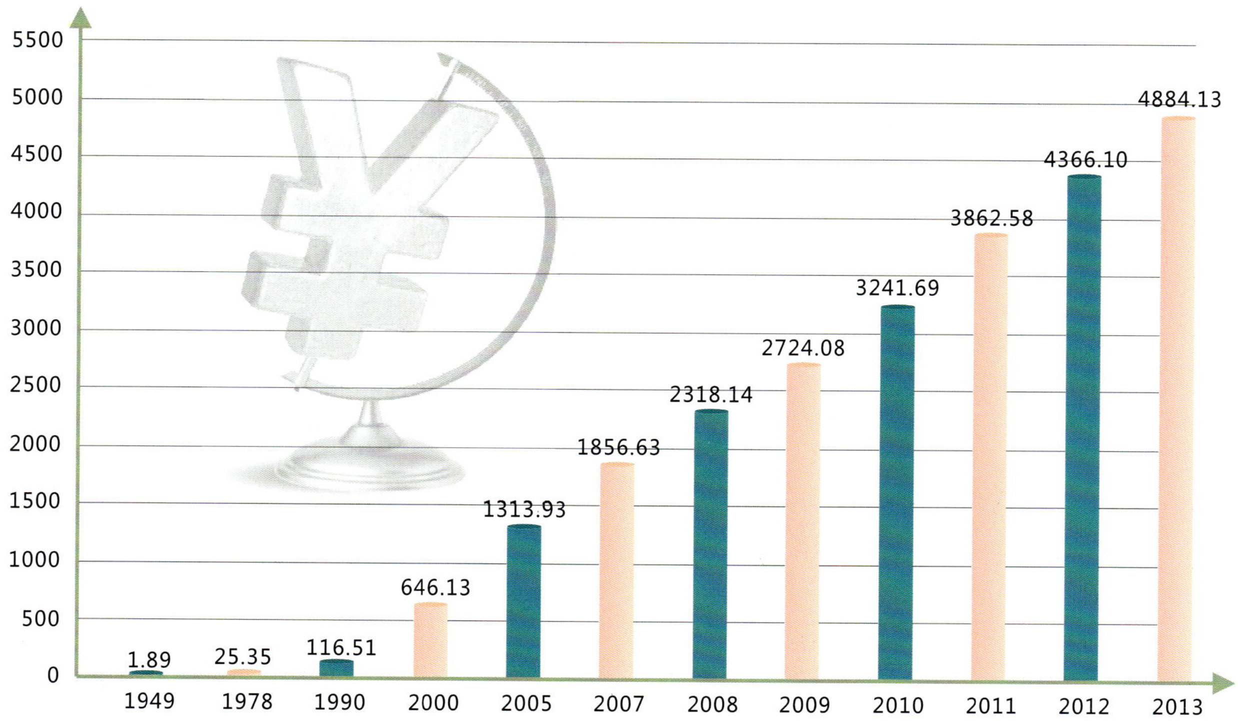

生产总值指数（以上年为100）

Indices of Gross Domestic Product (Preceding year=100)

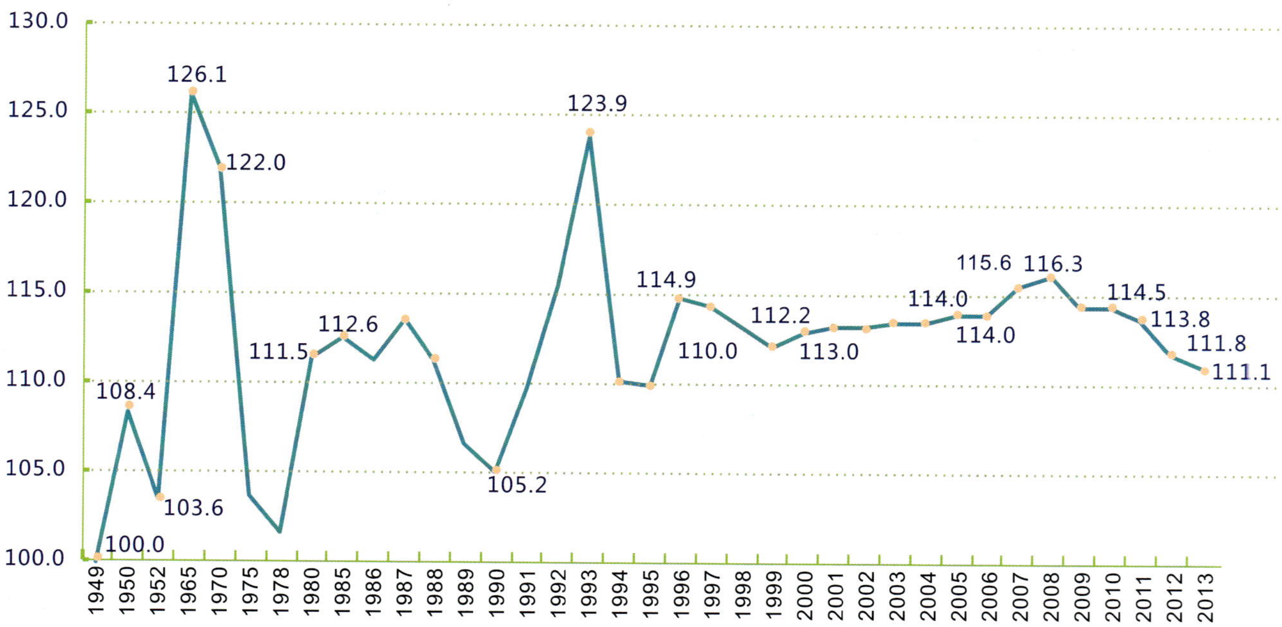

生产总值构成(%)

Composition of Gross Domestic Product (%)

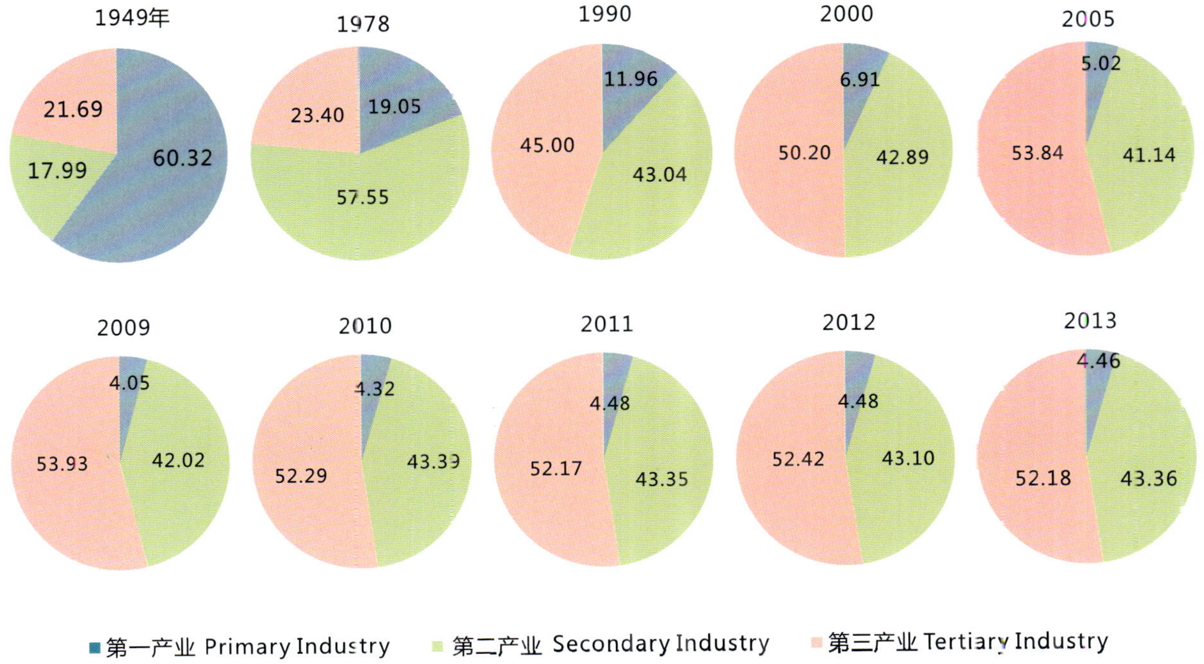

人均GDP(元/人)

Per Capita GDP(yuan/person)

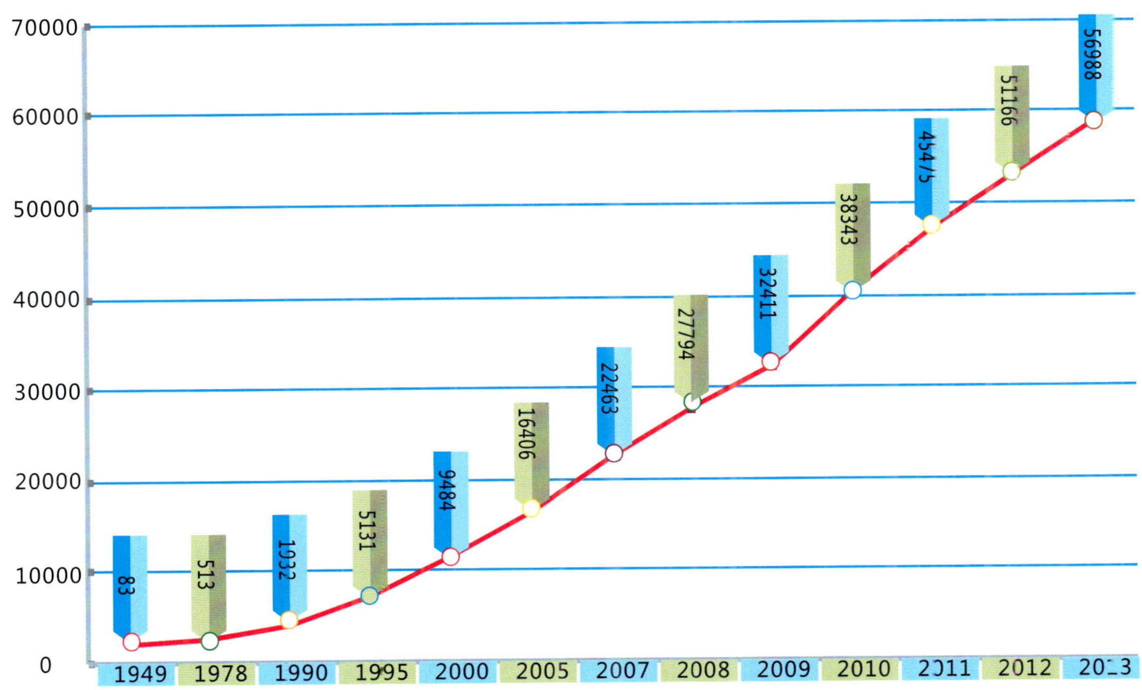

年末常住人口(万人)

Year-end Permanent Population (10000 persons)

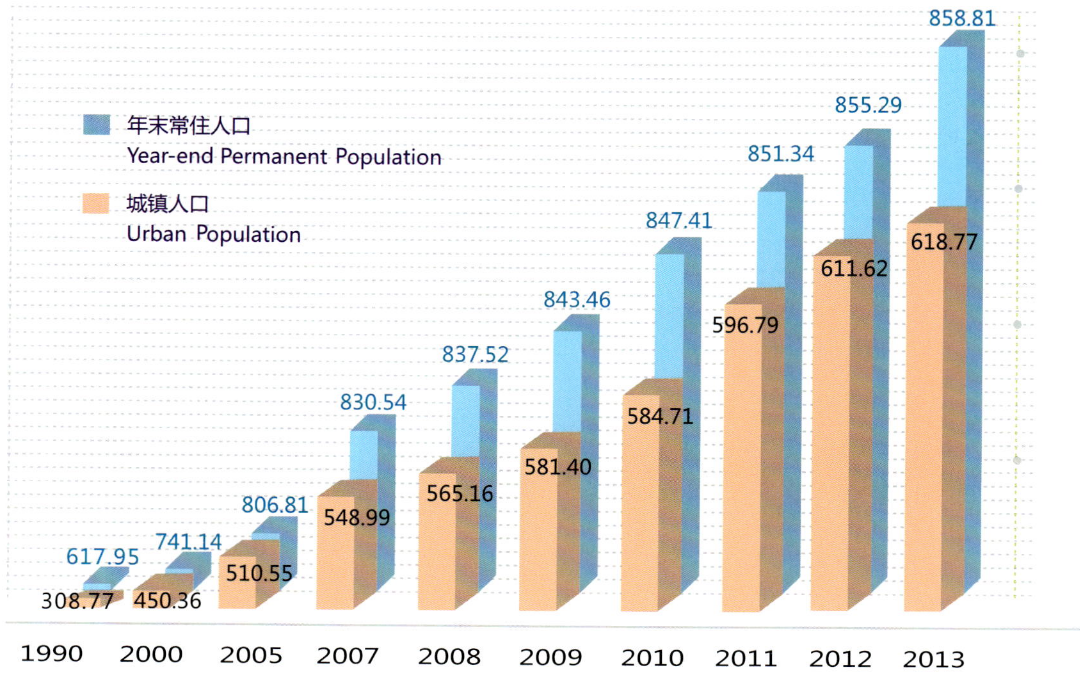

社会从业人数(万人)

Number of Social Laberors(10000 persons)

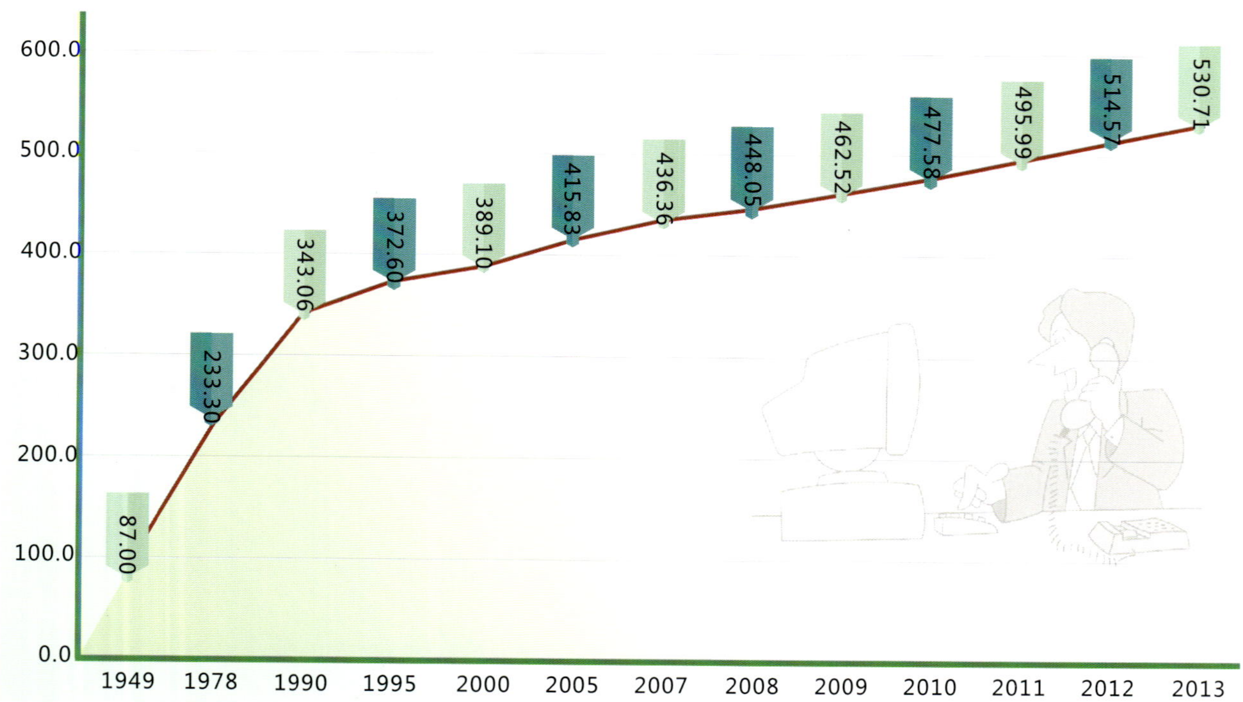

固定资产投资(亿元)

Investment in Fixed Assets(100 million yuan)

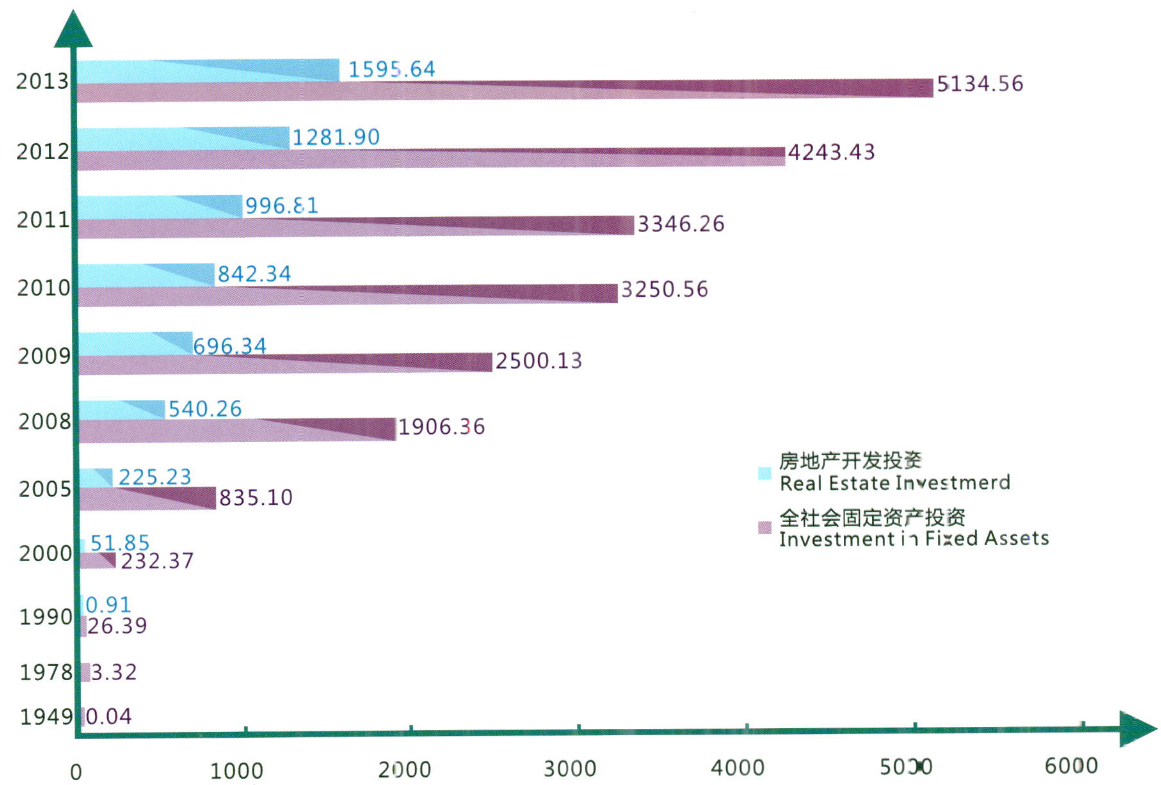

新增固定资产及住宅竣工面积

Newly Increased Fixed Assets and Residenctial Area of Completion

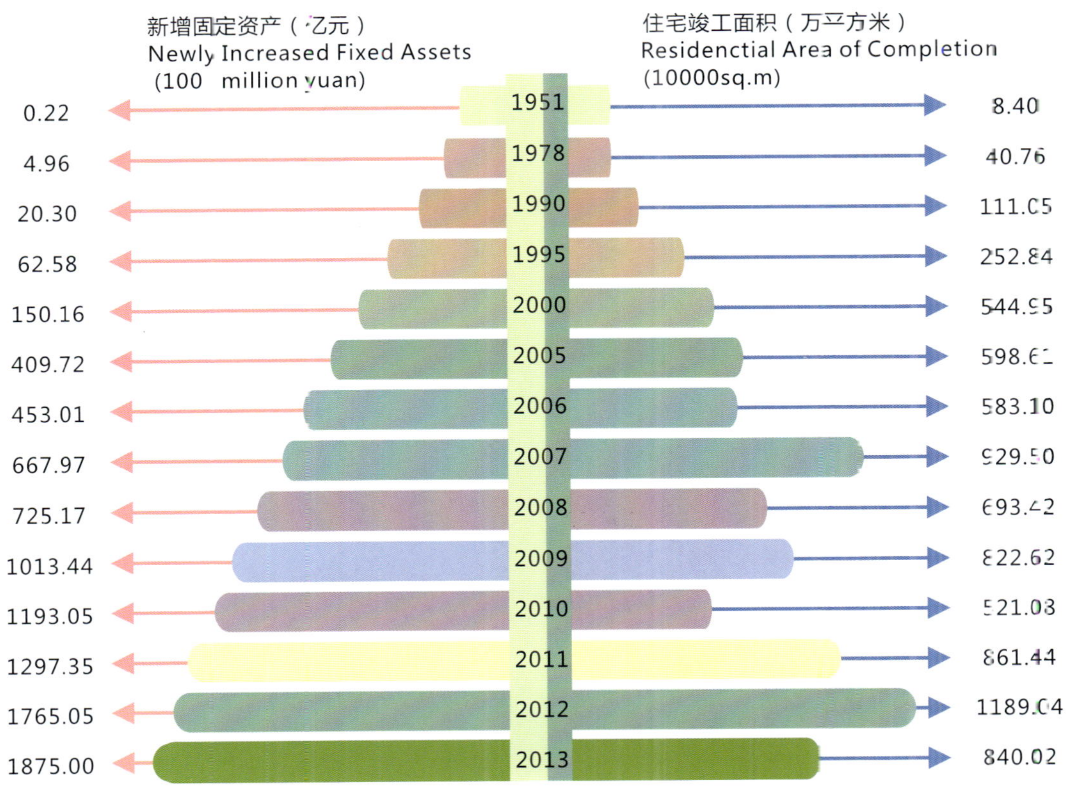

农林牧渔及服务业总产值(亿元)

Gross Output Value of Farming,Forestry, Animal Husbandry, Fishery and Service(100 million yuan)

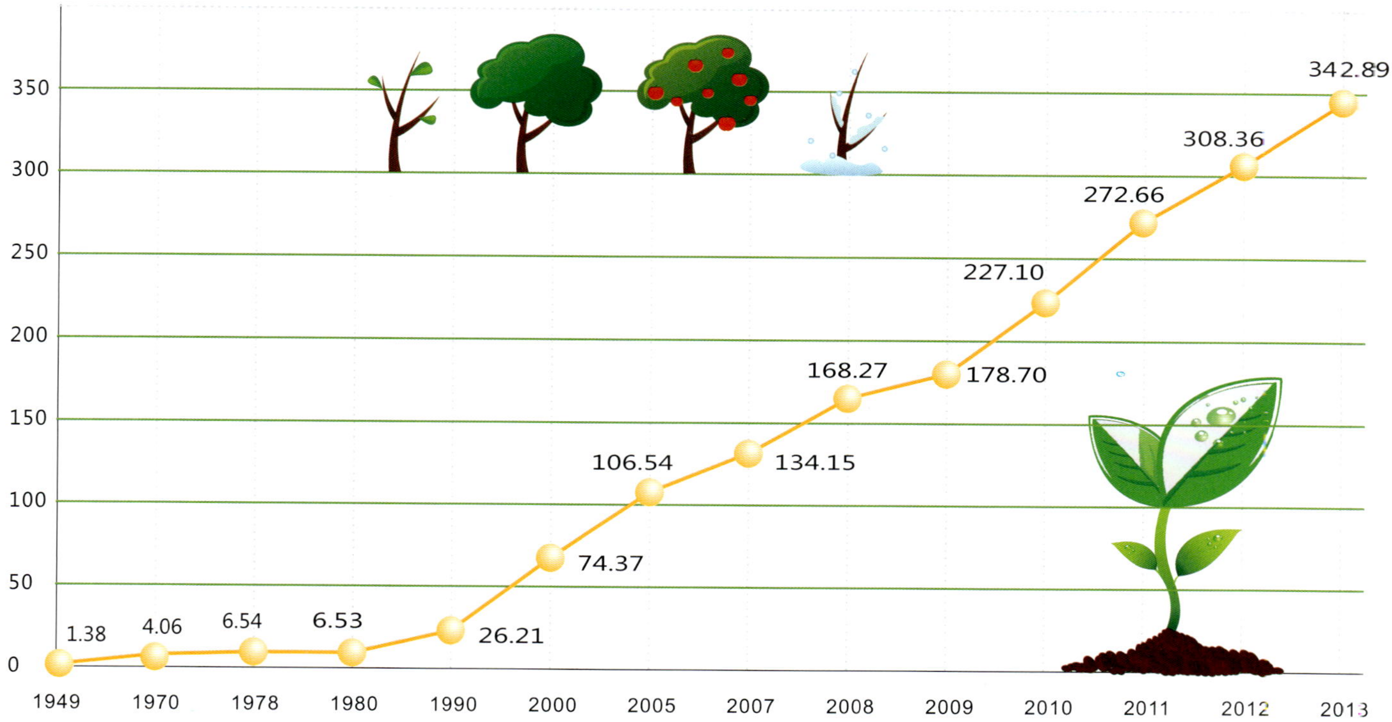

蔬菜产量 (万吨)

Vegetables Product(10000 ton)

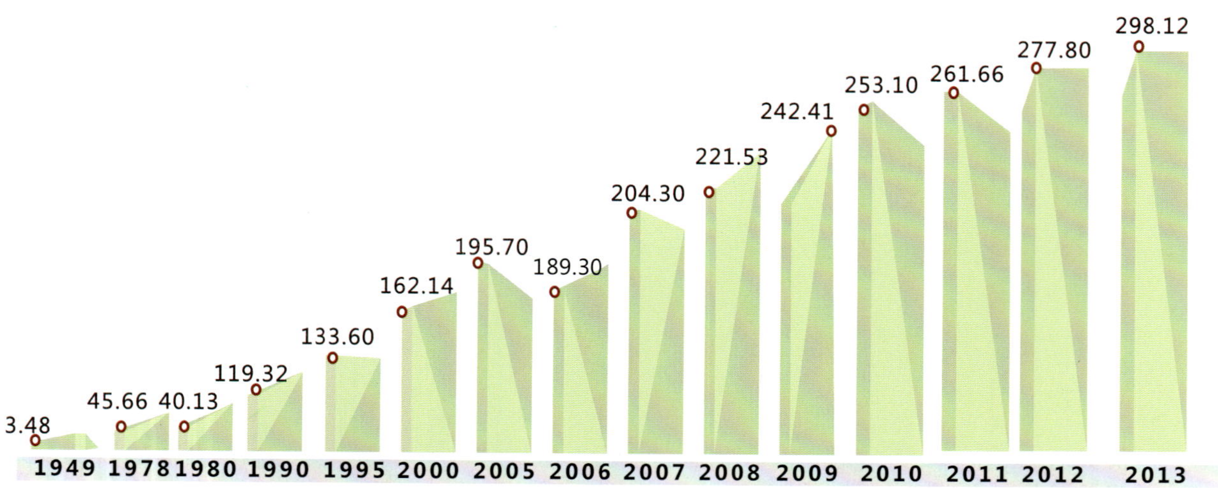

规模以上工业增加值（亿元）

Value Added of Industrial Enterprises Above Designated Size（100 million yuan)

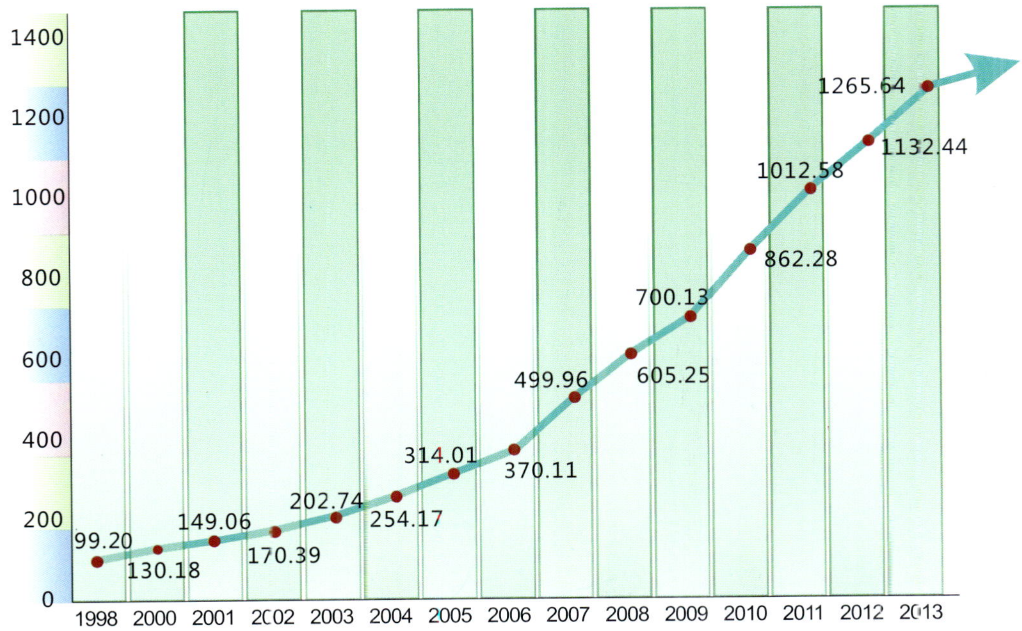

规模以上工业企业主要产品产量

Output of Major Industrial Products Of Industrial Enterprises Above Designated Size

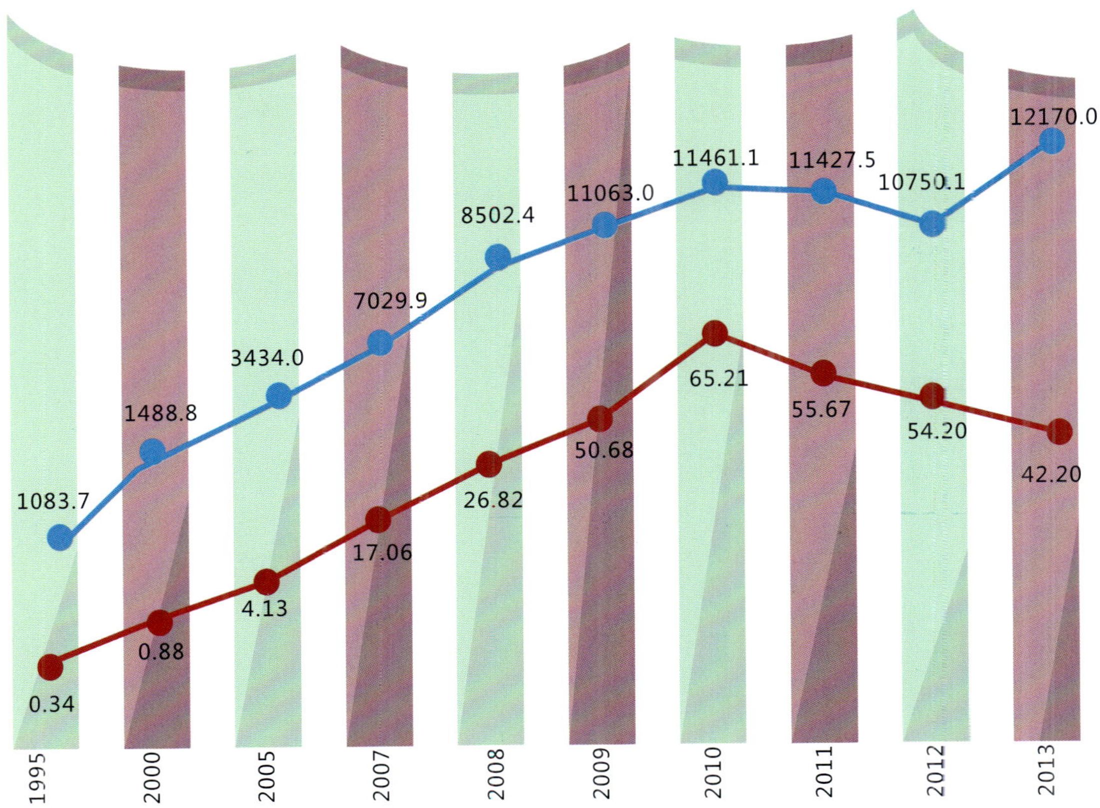

全社会车辆数（万辆）

Possession of Civil Vehicles(10000 unit)

公路里程

Highway Mileage

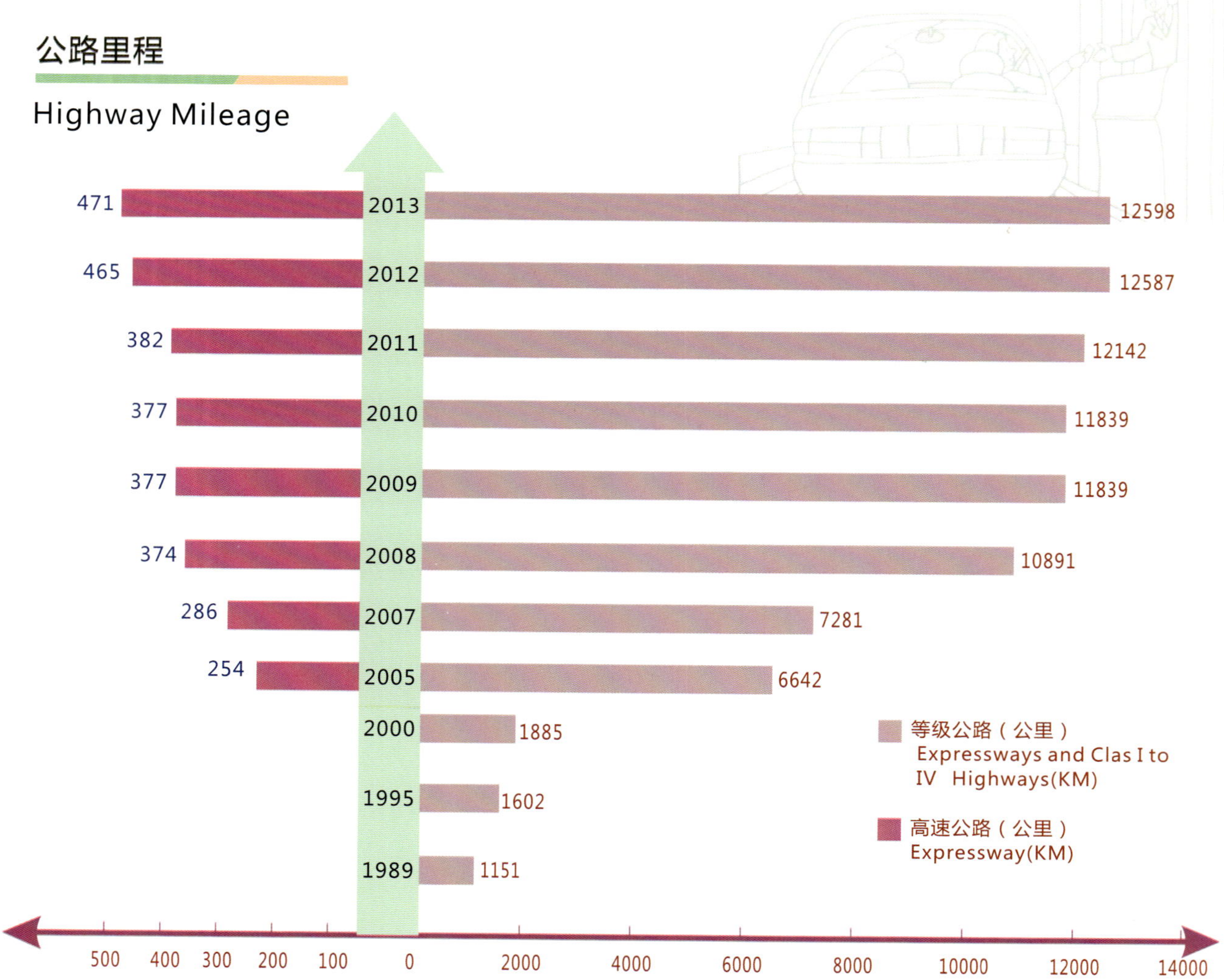

社会消费品零售总额(亿元)

Total Retail Sales of Consumer Goods(100 million yuan)

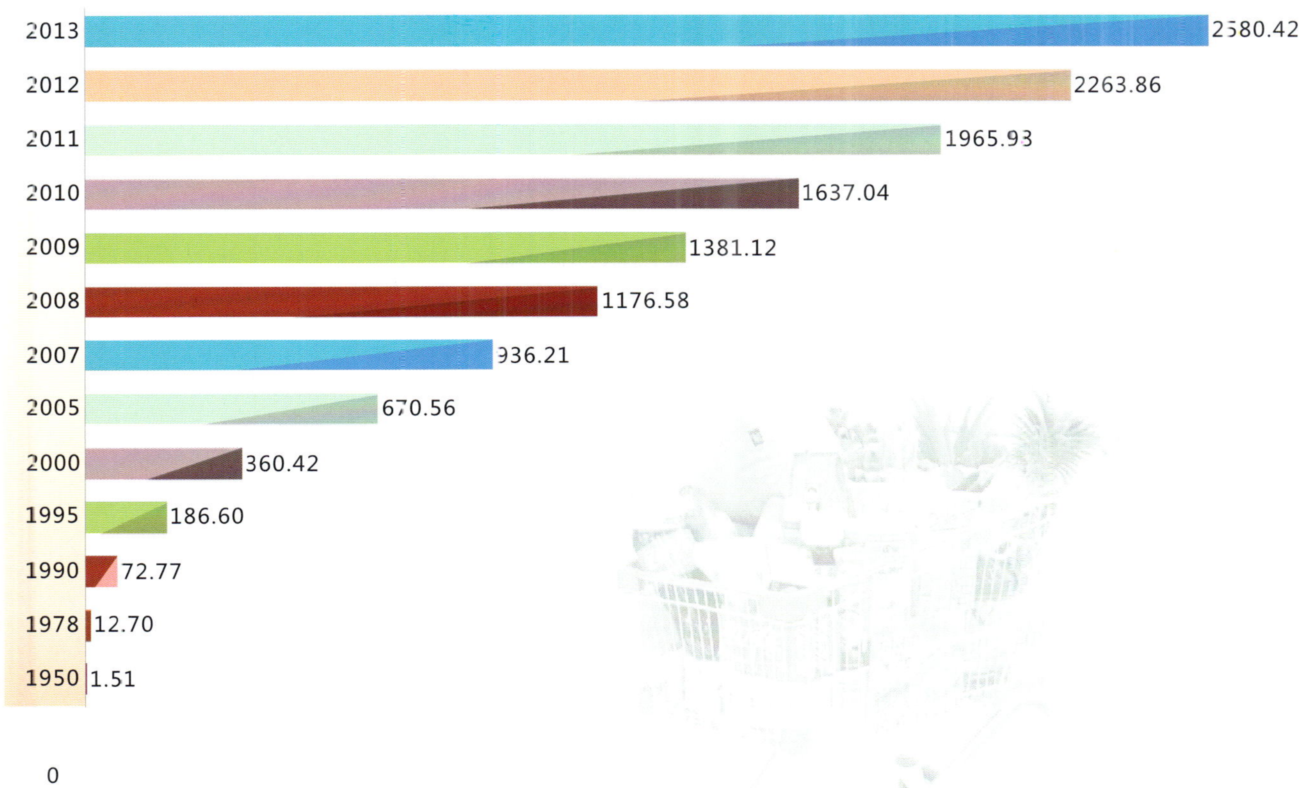

经营网点(个)

Bussiness Network (unit)

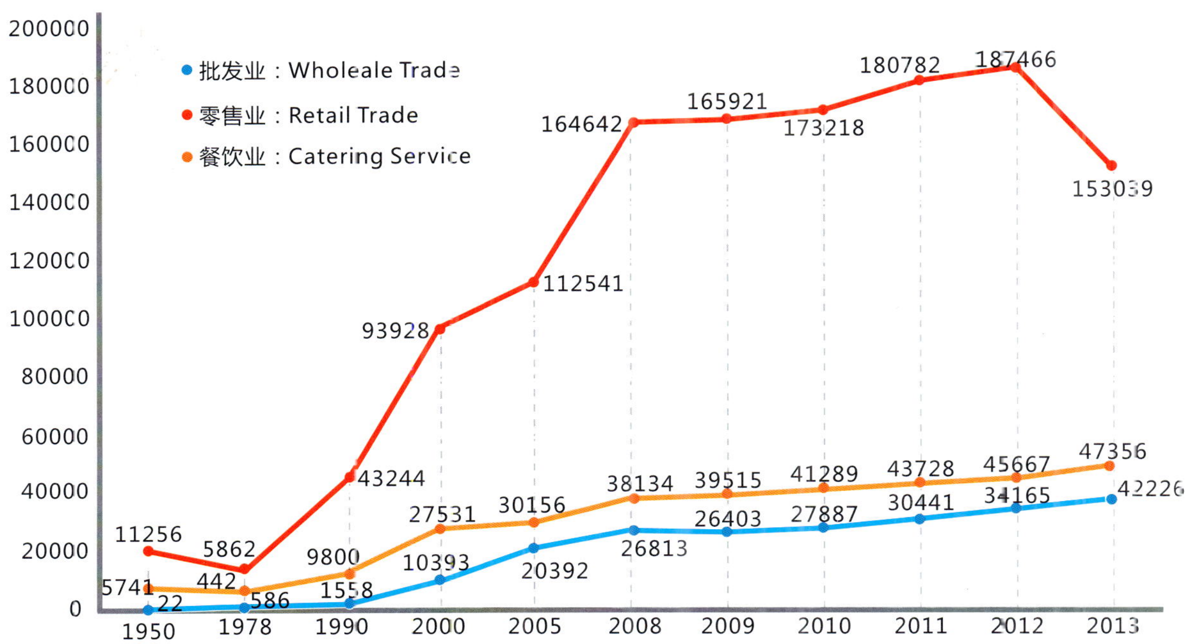

实际利用外商直接投资额（亿美元）

Foreign Direct Investment(USD 100 million)

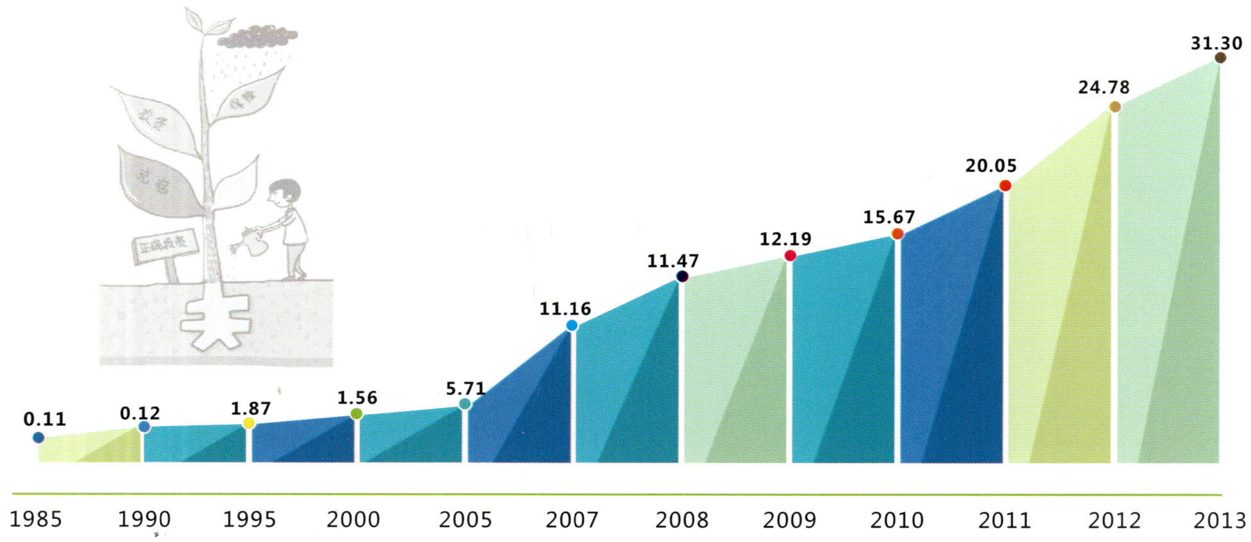

进出口总额（亿美元）

Total Value of Imports and Exports(USD 100 million)

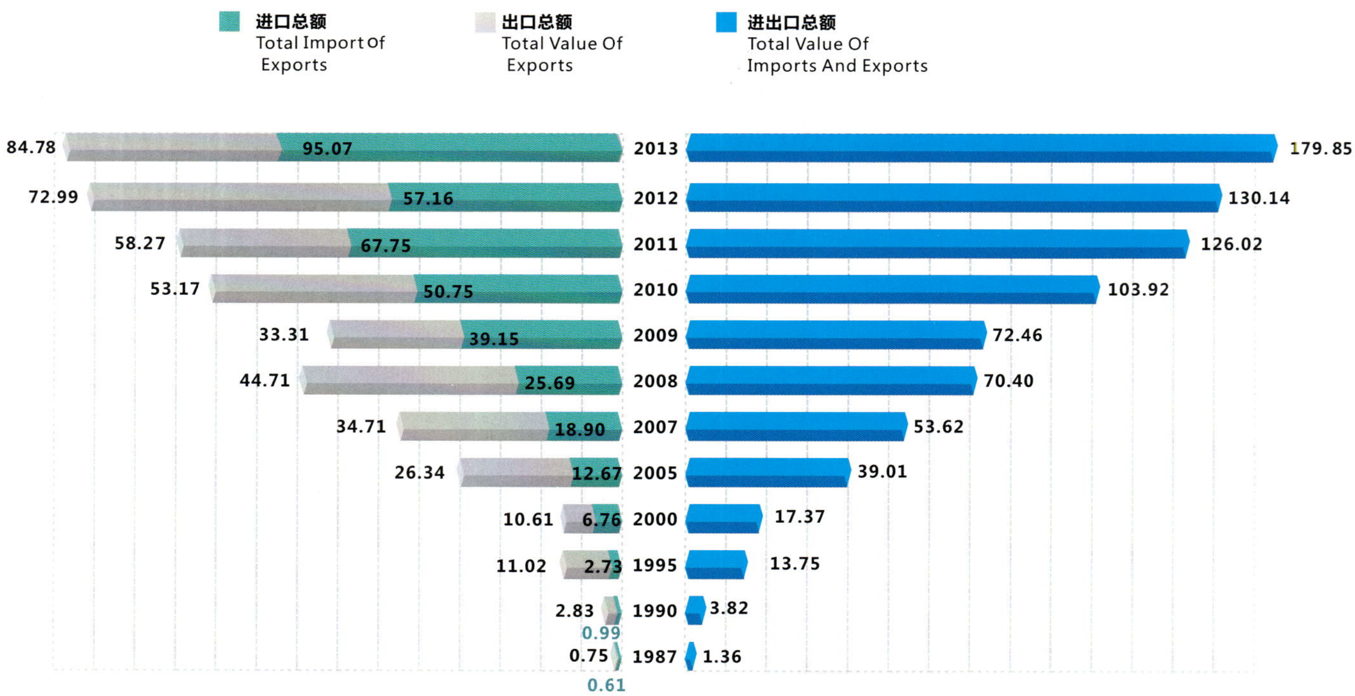

旅游人数及收入

Number of Tourists and Tourism Income

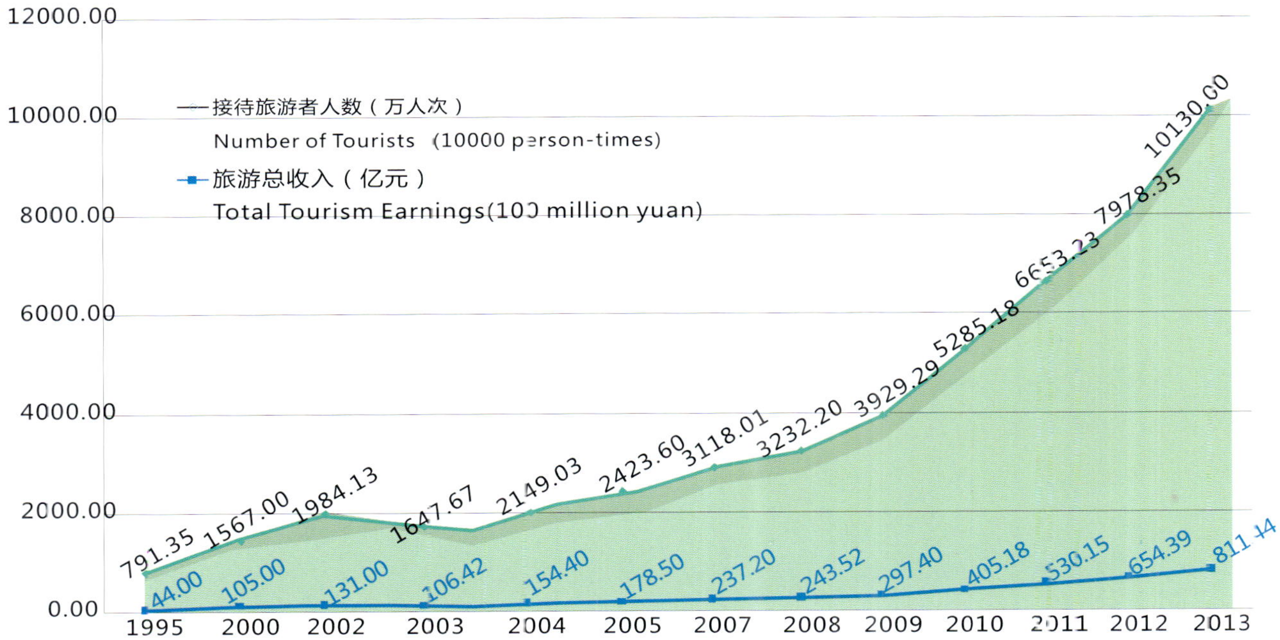

国际旅游人数及收入

Number of International Tourists and Tourism Income

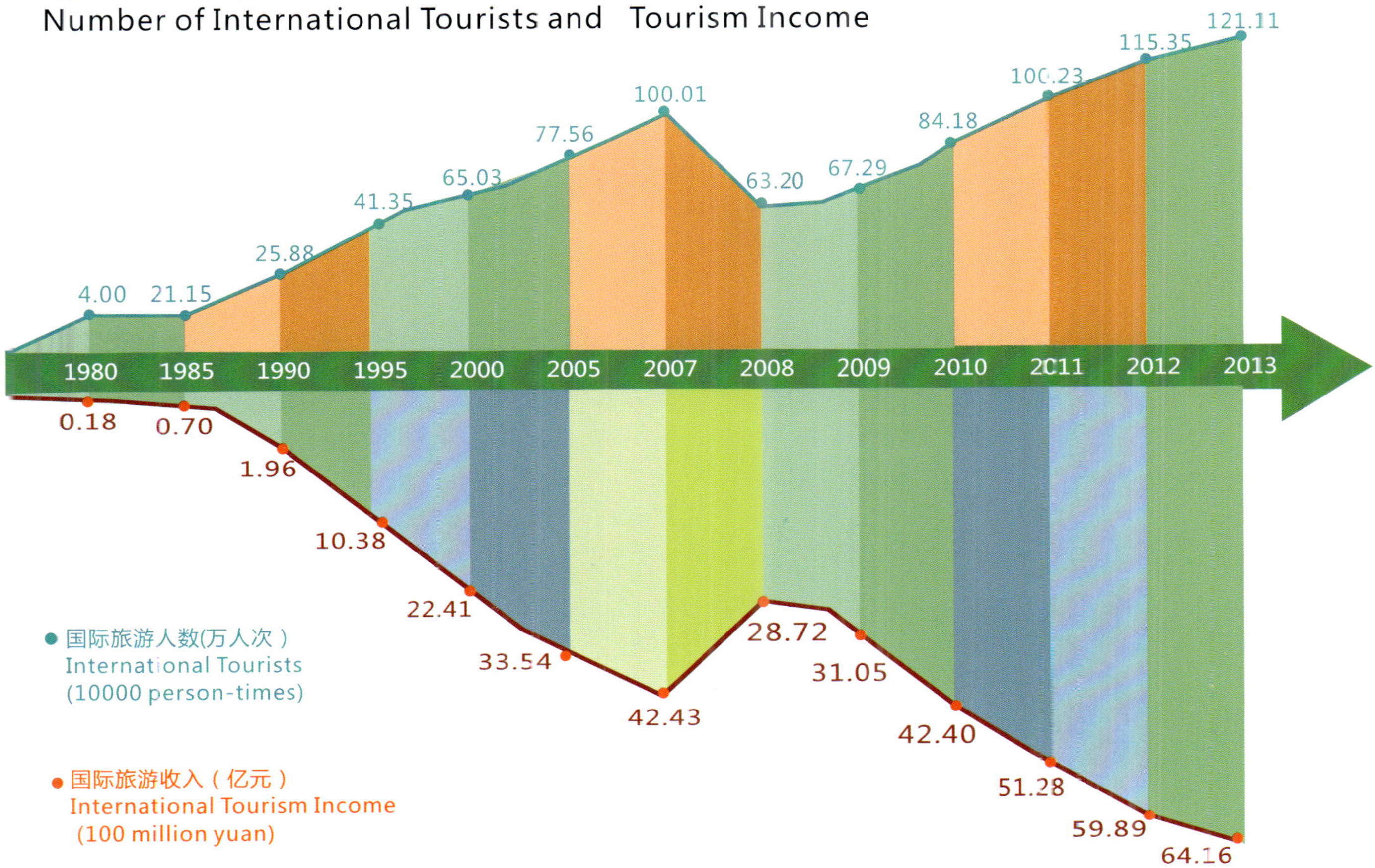

财政收支(亿元)

Govement Revenue and Expenditure(100 million yuan)

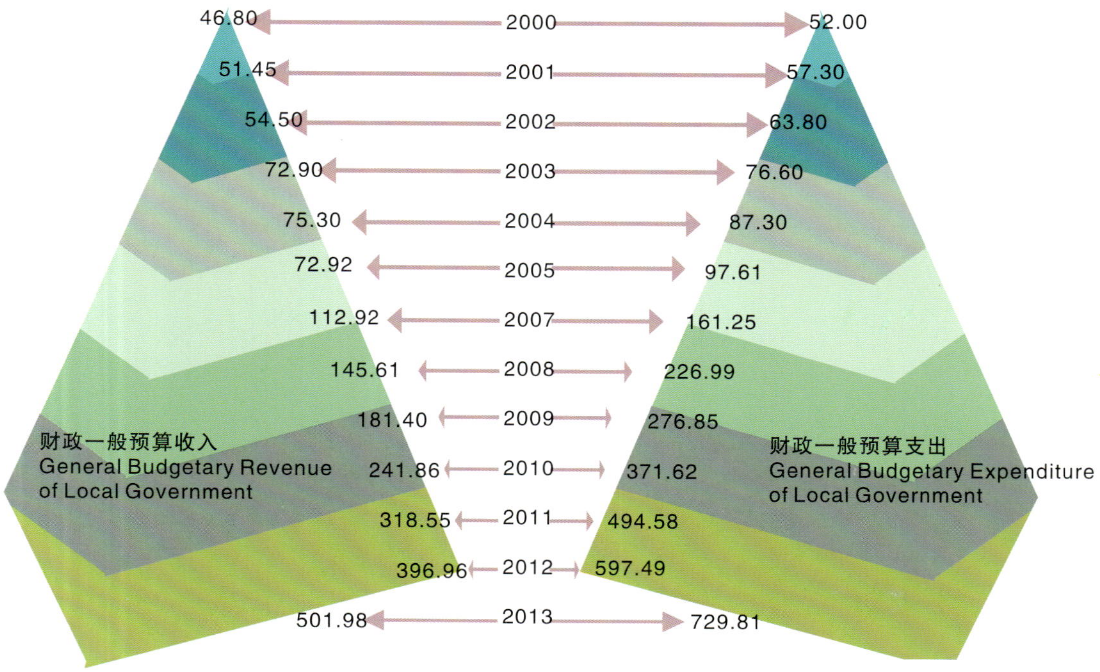

金融机构人民币存贷款年末余额 (亿元)

Year-end Deposit and Loans in Financial Institutions (100 million yuan)

建成区面积（平方公里）

Area of Regions Built-up（sq.km）

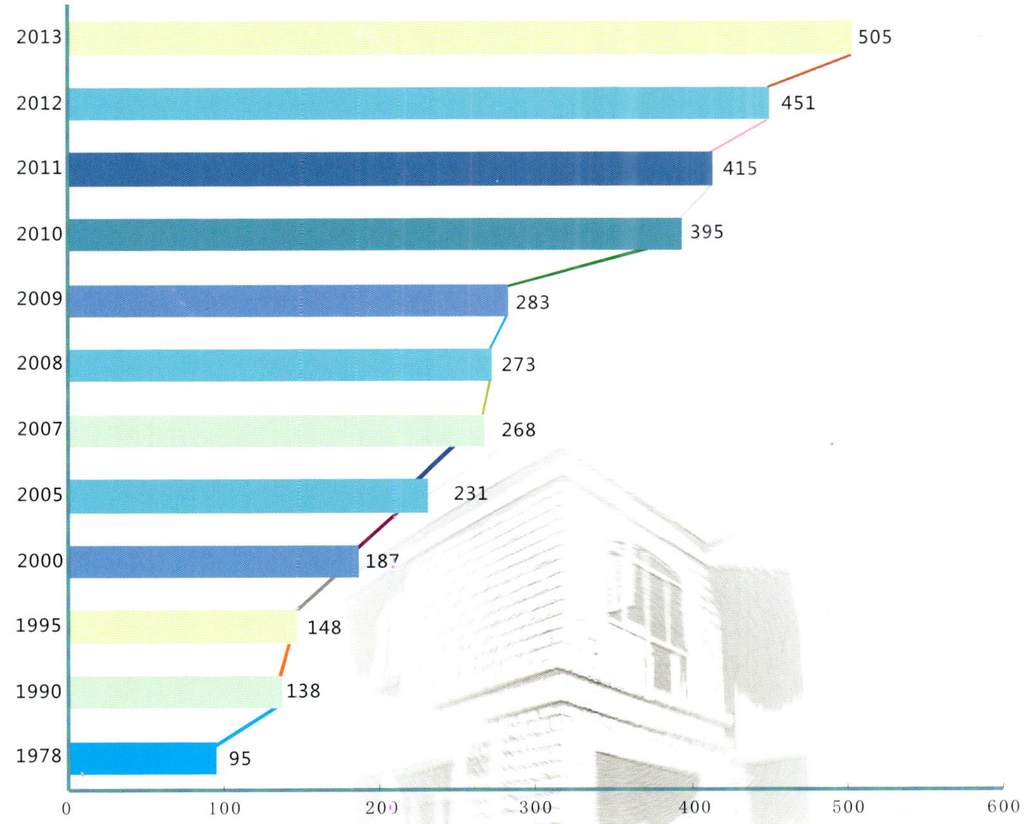

城市公共营运车辆（辆）

City Operating Vehicles(unit)

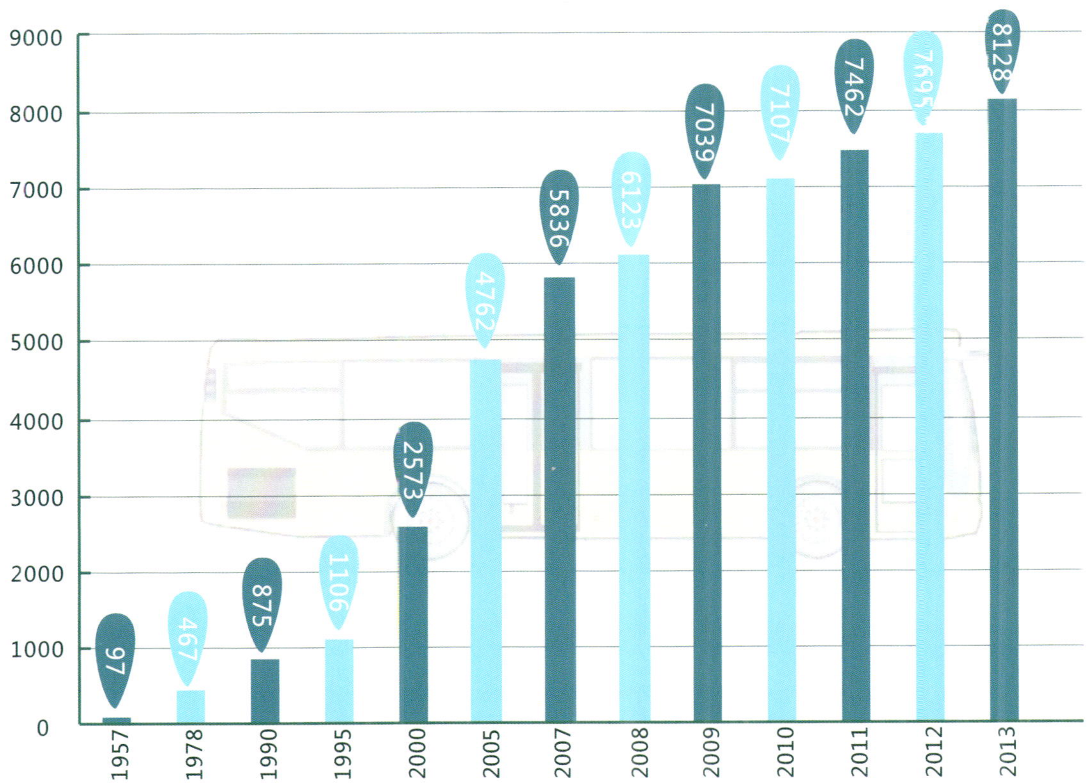

园林绿地面积（公顷）

Total Area of Parks,Gardens and Green Areas（hectares）

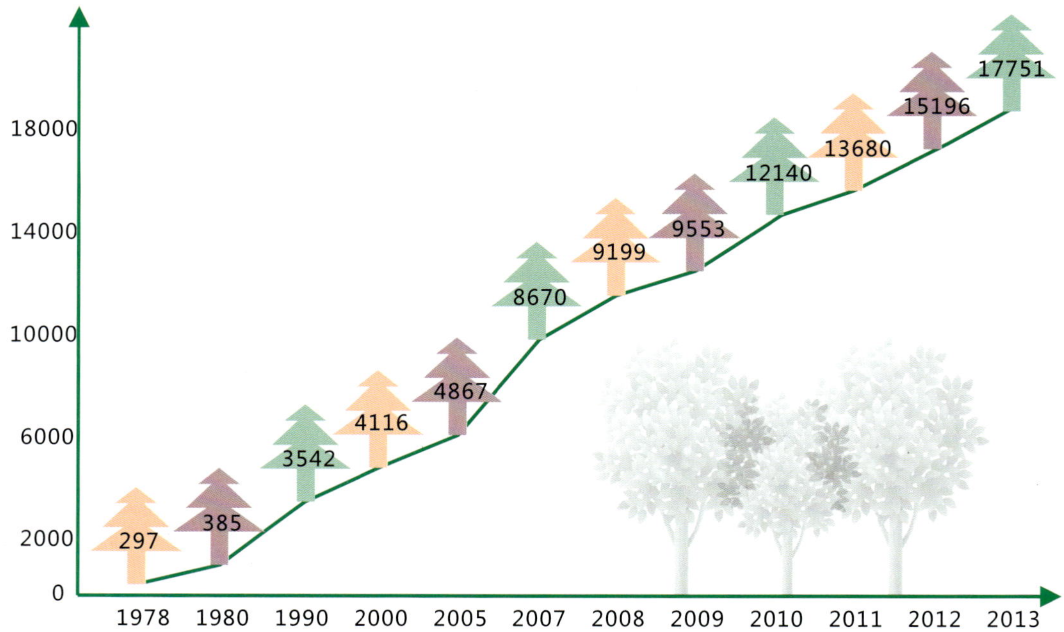

天然气供气总量(万立方米)

Total Natural Gas Supply(10000 cu.m)

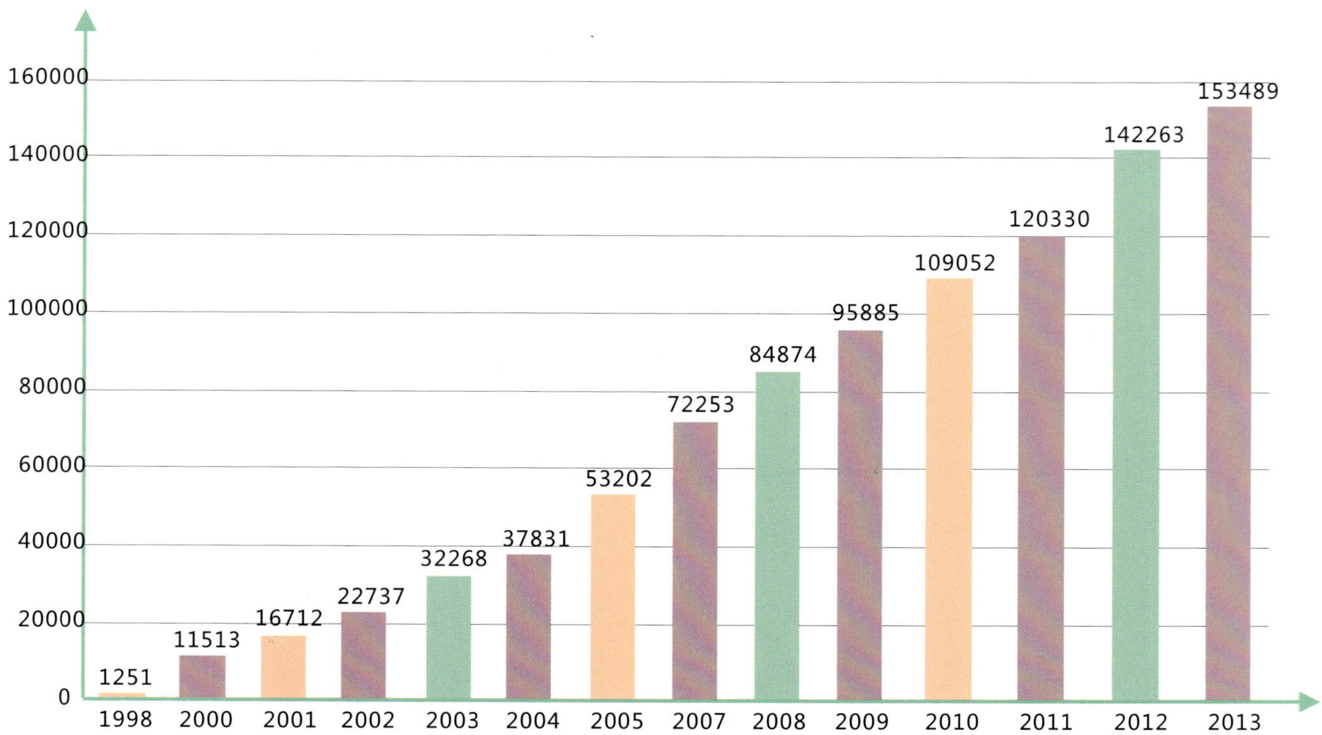

专任教师(万人)

Full-time Teachers (10000 persons)

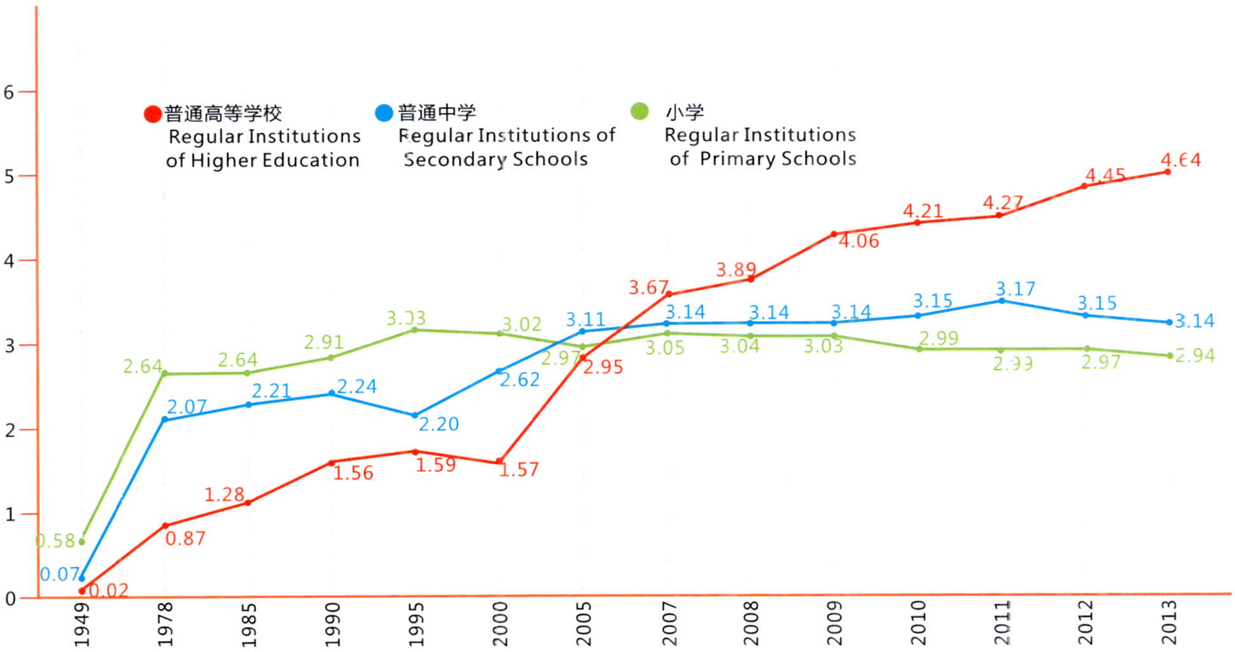

普通教育在校学生（万人）

Total Enrollment of Regular Education (10000 persons)

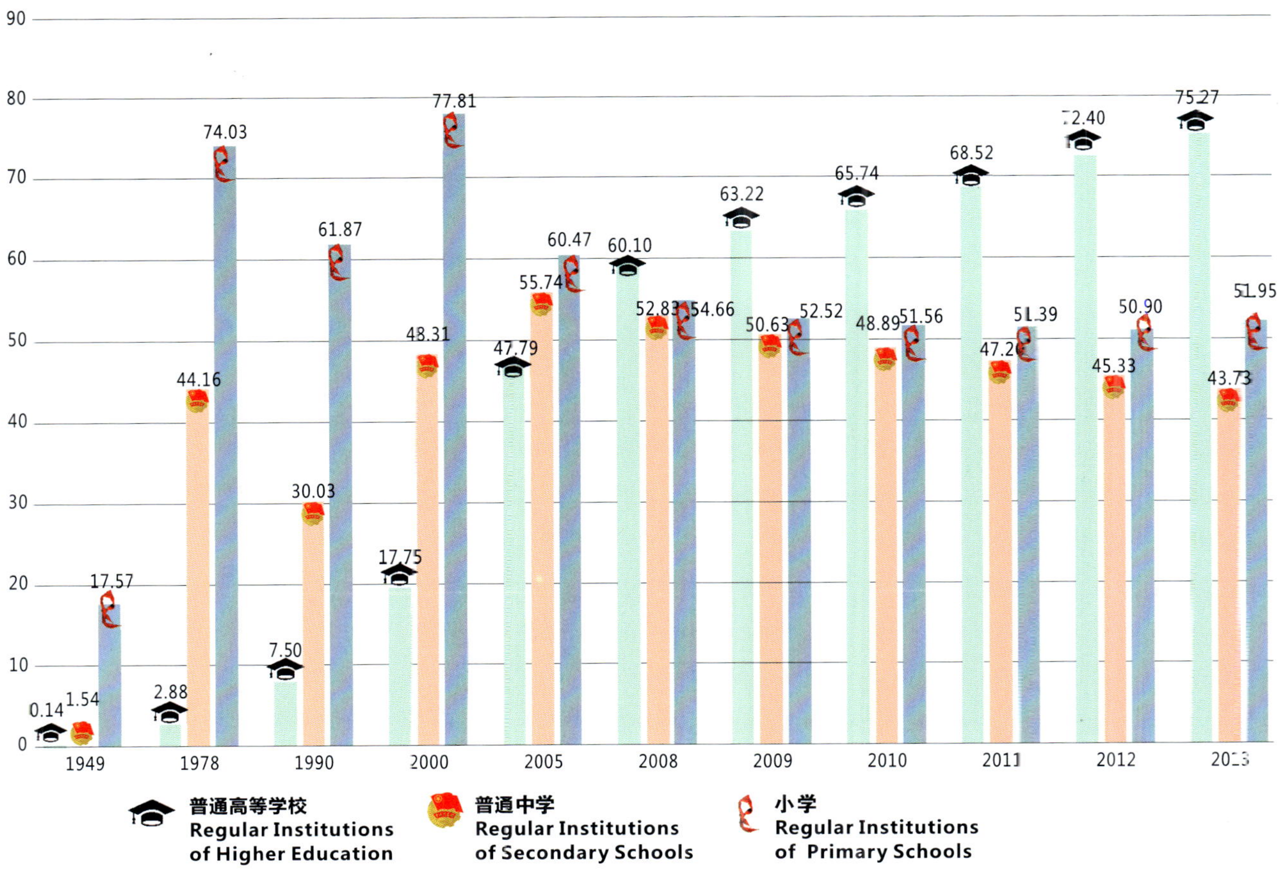

城乡居民收入（元）

The Income of Urban and Rural Residents（yuan）

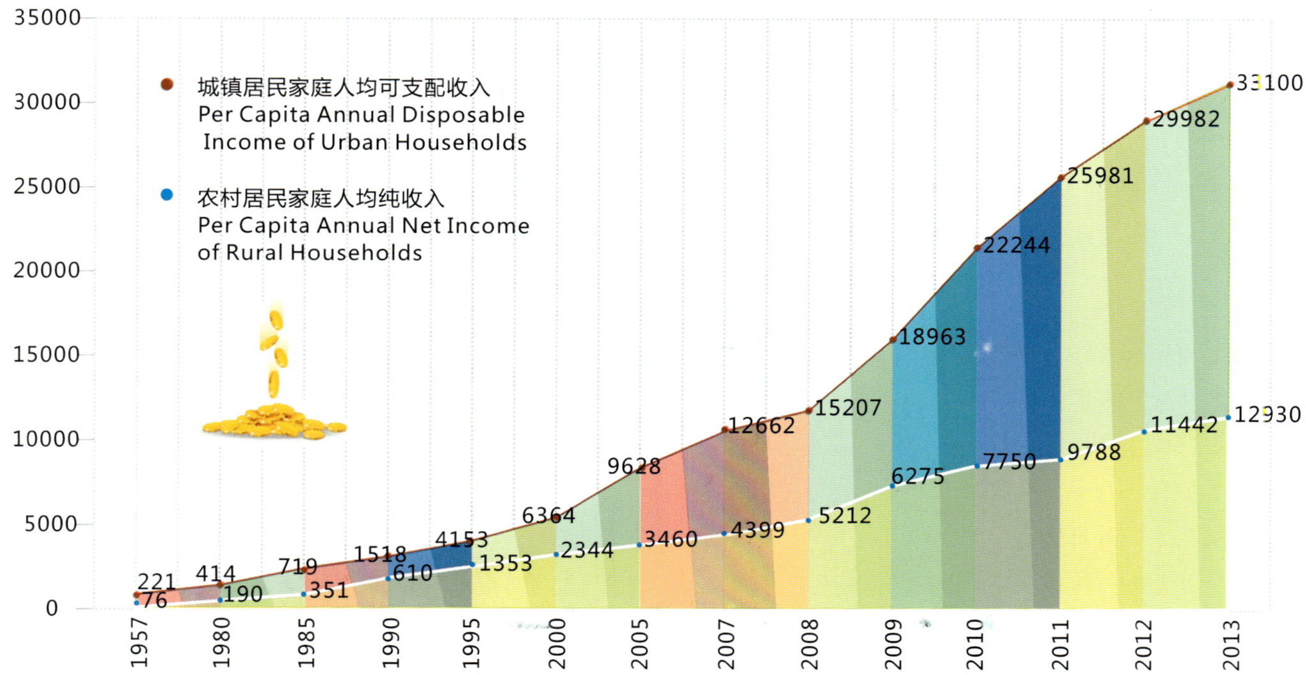

价格指数（以上年价格为100）

Price Indices(the price of preceding year=100)

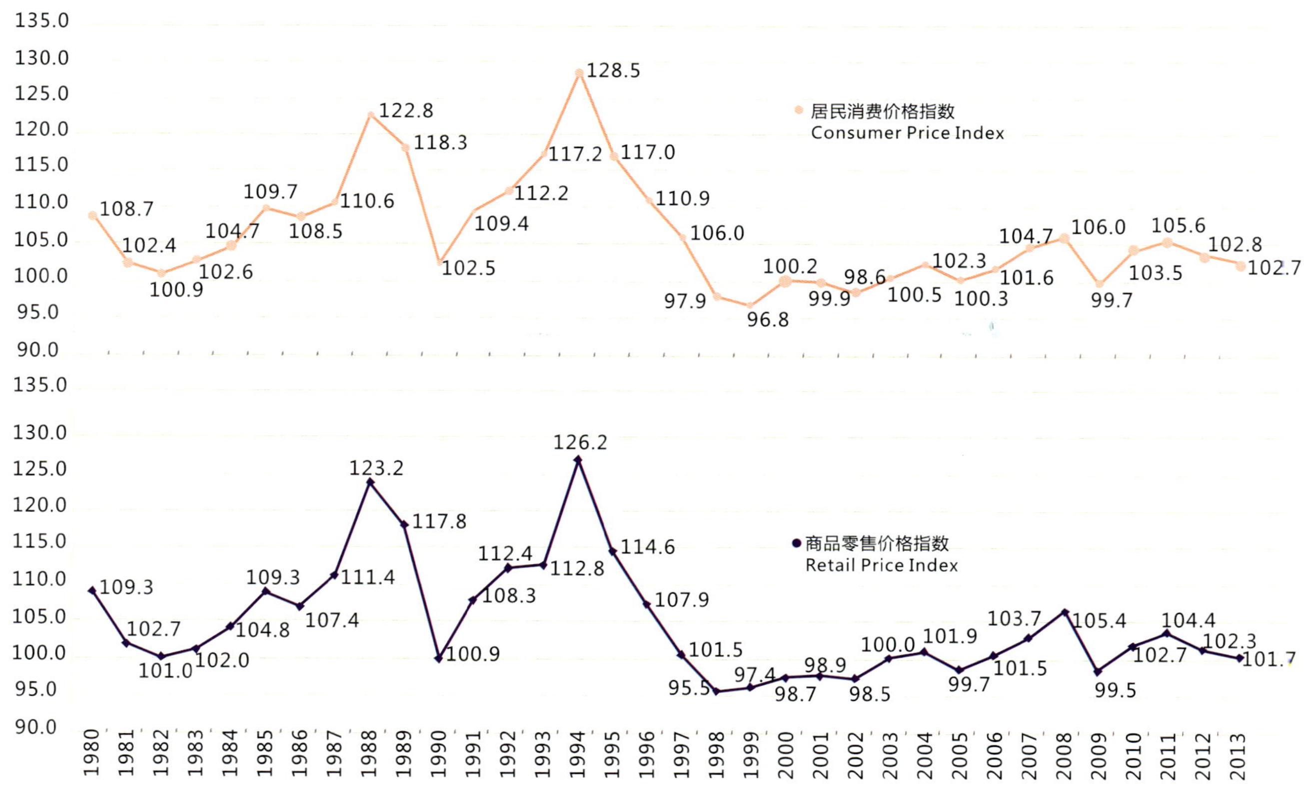

目　录

一、综　合

二、基本单位

三、国民经济核算

四、人口、从业人员与职工工资

五、固定资产投资

六、财　　政

七、物价指数

八、人民生活

九、城市公用事业

十、环境保护

十一、农　　业

十二、工　业

十三、能　源

十四、建筑业

十五、运输和邮电

十六、国内贸易

十七、对外经济贸易和旅游

十八、金融业

十九、教育和科技

二十、文化、体育、卫生、社会福利和其他

二十一、企业调查

CONTENTS

CHAPTER 1 GENERAL SURVEY

CHAPTER 2 BASIC UNIT

CHAPTER 3 NATIONAL ECONOMIC ACCOUNTS

CHAPTER 4 POPULATION,EMPLOYMENT AND WAGES

CHAPTER 5 INVESTMENT IN FIXED ASSETS

CHAPTER 6 GOVERNMENT FINANCE

CHAPTER 7 PRICE INDICES

CHAPTER 8 PEOPLE'S LIVELIHOOD

CHAPTER 9 URBAN PUBLIC UTLITIES

CHAPTER 10 ENVIRONMENT PROTECTION

CHAPTER 11 AGRICULTURE

CHAPTER 12 INDUSTRY

CHAPTER 13 ENERGY

CHAPTER 14 CONSTRUCTION

CHAPTER 15 TRANSPORT, POSTAL AND TELECOMMUNICATION SERVICES

CHAPTER 16 DOMESTIC TRADE

CHAPTER 17 FOREIGN TRADE AND ECONOMIC COOPERATION TOURISM

CHAPTER 18 FINANCIAL LNTERMEDIATION

CHAPTER 19 EDUCATION, SCIENCE AND TECHNOLOGY

CHAPTER 20 CULTURES, SPORTS, SANITATION SOCIAL WELFARE INSTITUTIONS AND OTHER SOCIALACTIVITIES

CHAPTER 21 ENTERPRISES INVESTIGATION

西安市2013年国民经济和社会发展统计公报[1]

西安市统计局　国家统计局西安调查队

2014年3月1日

2013年，面对极为错综复杂的国内外形势，市委、市政府团结带领全市人民，认真贯彻落实党的十八大精神及中、省各项政策部署，坚持稳中求进的工作总基调，努力提高经济运行质量和效益，全市经济社会发展稳中有进、稳中向好。

一、综合

年末全市常住人口858.81万人，其中，男性人口440.98万人，占51.3%；女性人口417.83万人，占48.7%，性别比为105.54（以女性为100，男性对女性的比例）。全年出生人口8.20万人，出生率为9.57‰；死亡人口4.60万人，死亡率为5.37‰。全年净增人口3.52万人，自然增长率为4.20‰。城镇人口618.77万人，占72.05%；乡村人口240.04万人，占27.95%。年末全市户籍总人口806.93万人，比上年增长1.4%。

初步核算，全年生产总值[2]（GDP）4884.13亿元，比上年增长11.1%。其中，第一产业增加值217.76亿元，增长4.8%；第二产业增加值2117.66亿元，增长13.9%；第三产业增加值2548.71亿元，增长9.3%。第一产业增加值占生产总值的比重为4.5%，第二产业增加值比重为43.3%，第三产业增加值比重为52.2%。

全年非公有制经济增加值2548.13亿元，占生产总值的比重为52.2%，比上年提高0.8个百分点。

图1　2009—2013年生产总值及其增长速度

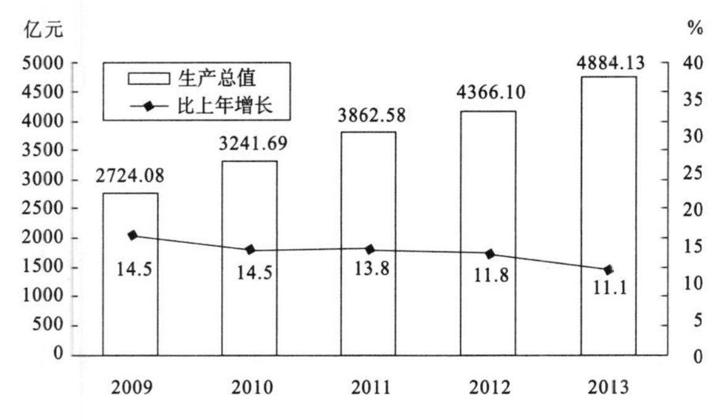

全年居民消费价格比上年上涨2.7%，其中，食品价格上涨4.8%。商品零售价格上涨1.7%。工业生产者出厂价格下降0.5%。工业生产者购进价格下降2.8%。固定资产投资价格上涨0.8%。新建住宅销售价格上涨6.5%。

图2　2013年居民消费价格月度涨跌幅度

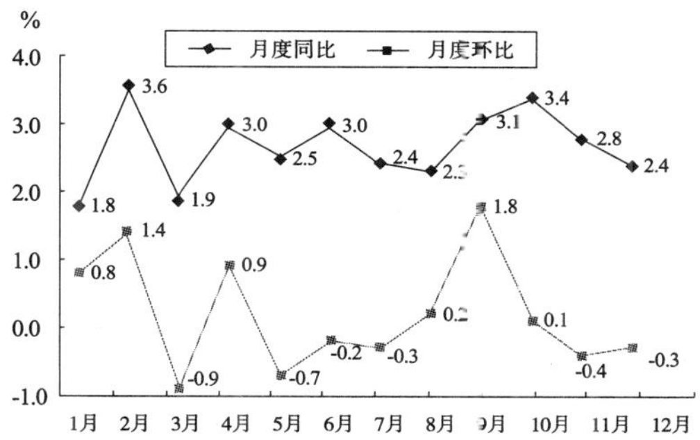

表1　2013年全市居民消费价格比上年涨跌幅度

指　标	涨跌幅度(%)
居民消费价格	2.7
食　品	4.8
其中：粮食	6.1
烟　酒	0.7
衣　着	4.0
家庭设备用品及维修服务	4.0
医疗保健和个人用品	1.9
交通和通信	-2.4
娱乐教育文化用品及服务	1.5
居　住	2.0

全年城镇新增就业12.58万人，城镇失业人员再就业5.05万人，就业困难人员实现再就业1.61万人。年末城镇登记失业率为3.4%。

全年财政总收入902.76亿元，比上年增长19.9%。地方财政一般预算收入501.98亿元，增长26.5%，其中，营业税、增值税、企业所得税和个人所得税分别增长2.2%、12.9%、12.1%和20.9%。全年地方财政一般预算支出729.81亿元，比上年增长22.1%，其中，医疗卫生支出增长21.4%，农林水事务支出增长10.7%，教育支出增长5.1%，社会保障和就业支出增长15.0%，一般公共服务支出下降1.9%，节能环保支出增长30.9%。

二、农业

全年粮食播种面积567.87万亩，比上年下降0.8%；油料播种面积7.67万亩，下降0.4%；蔬菜播种面积99.89万亩，增长2.1%；棉花播种面积2.57万亩，下降51.4%。全年粮食产量183.12万吨，比上年下降4.9%，其中，夏粮83.60万吨，下降12.7%；秋粮99.52万吨，增长2.8%。

表2　2013年全市主要农产品产量

产品名称	单位	产　量	比上年增长（%）
油 料	万吨	1.00	-2.0
蔬 菜	万吨	298.12	7.3
园林水果	万吨	95.19	2.1
肉 类	万吨	15.74	3.8
奶 类	万吨	65.77	-1.3
禽 蛋	万吨	13.54	4.2
大牲畜年末存栏数	万头	21.18	-0.03
猪年末存栏数	万头	96.57	-0.03
羊年末存栏数	万只	27.37	-3.8
家禽年末存栏数	万只	1172.61	-0.4

三、工业和建筑业

全年全部工业增加值1484.63亿元，比上年增长14.5%。规模以上工业增加值1265.64亿元，增长15.4%。在规模以上工业中，轻工业增加值299.44亿元，增长14.7%；重工业增加值966.20亿元，增长15.6%。

图3　2013年规模以上工业增加值增速（累计同比）

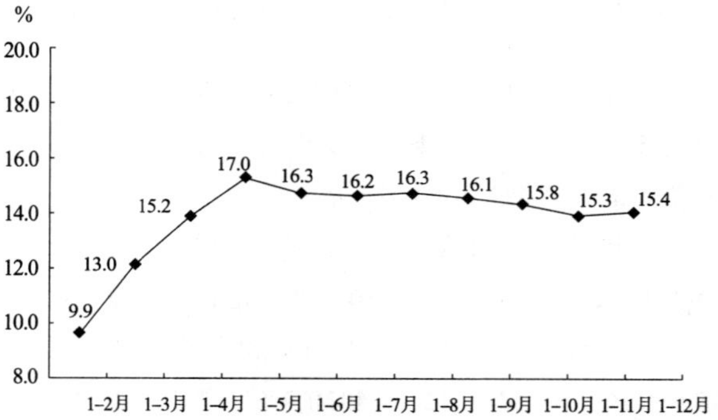

全年规模以上工业中，农副食品加工业增加值比上年增长14.5%，通用设备制造业增长4.9%，专用设备制造业增长14.1%，汽车制造业增长20.7%，铁路、船舶、航空航天和其他运输设备制造业增长13.2%。六大高耗能行业[3]增长16.3%，其中，非金属矿物制品业增长11.8%，化学原料及化学制品制造业增长34.6%，有色金属冶炼及压延加工业增长15.0%，黑色金属冶炼及压延加工业增长3.1%，电力、热力的生产和供应业增长16.9%，石油加工、炼焦及核燃料加工业增长10.2%。

表3　2013年全市工业产品产量

产品名称	计量单位	产　量	比上年增长（%）
发电量	亿千瓦小时	184.48	-1.8
原油加工量	万吨	213.11	-1.9
乳制品	万吨	133.24	7.1
液体乳	万吨	121.72	5.1
商品混凝土	万立方米	2606.10	14.7
机制纸	万吨	15.98	-42.1
交流电动机	万千瓦	574.96	29.8
饲料	万吨	102.51	25.9
合成洗涤剂	万吨	11.72	1.0
水泥	万吨	391.06	-25.5
风机	万台	0.15	10.9
汽车	万辆	42.15	21.1
其中：轿车	万辆	31.70	21.1
高压开关板	面	16844.00	-18.4
变压器	万千伏安	12170.00	13.2
电力电缆	万千米	1.06	-9.5
气体压缩机	万台	416.12	-30.0
电子元件	亿只	3.78	4.4

全年规模以上工业企业经济效益综合指数为247.14，比上年提高25.5个百分点。规模以上工业企业主营业务收入4011.73亿元，增长14.8%。实现利润总额181.82亿元，增长42.7%。

全年建筑业增加值633.03亿元，比上年增长12.2%。全年具有资质等级的总承包和专业承包建筑企业416家。

图4 2009—2013年建筑业增加值及其增长速度

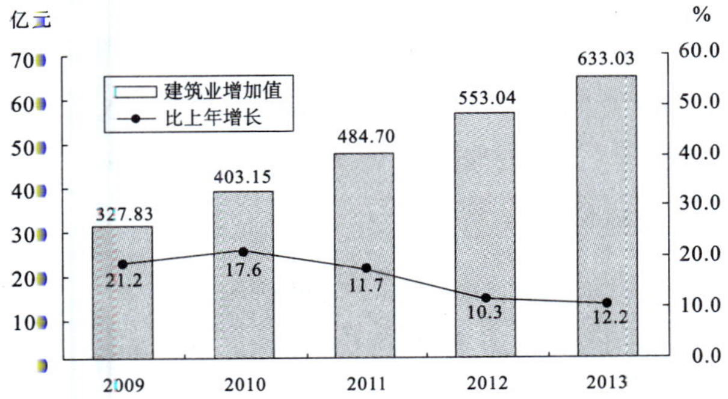

四、固定资产投资

全年全社会固定资产投资5134.56亿元，比上年增长21.0%，扣除价格因素，实际增长20.0%。其中，固定资产投资（不含农户）5055.23亿元，增长21.3%；农户投资79.33亿元，增长2.4%。

图5　2013年固定资产投资（不含农户）增速（累计同比）

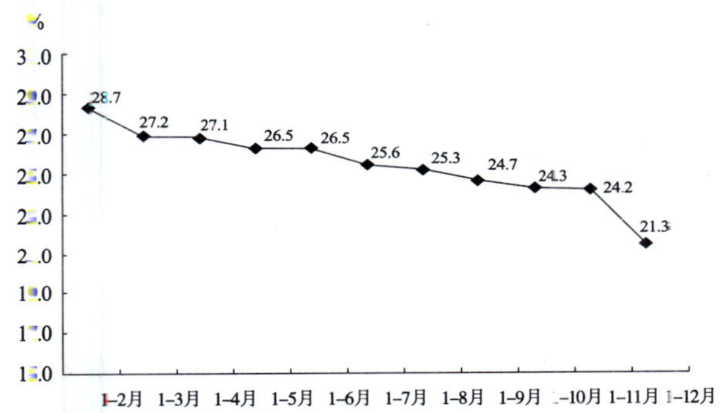

在固定资产投资（不含农户）中，第一产业投资73.15亿元，比上年下降26.4%；第二产业投资983.09亿元，增长46.3%，其中，工业投资868.57亿元，增长50.2%；第三产业投资3998.99亿元，增长17.8%。

表4　2013年重点行业固定资产投资及其增长速度

行 业	投资额（亿元）	比上年增长（%）
农、林、牧、渔业	83.54	-15.9
制造业	687.14	42.5
交通运输、仓储及邮政业	282.98	-3.4
信息传输、软件和信息技术服务业	47.79	-30.5
批发和零售业	138.60	14.5
科学研究和技术服务业	74.00	6.2
水利、环境和公共设施管理业	463.79	42.4
教育	70.27	7.9
卫生和社会工作	73.14	23.7
公共管理、社会保障和社会组织	66.61	-39.4

全年房地产开发投资1595.64亿元，比上年增长24.5%。房屋施工面积10454.27万平方米，增长5.1%，房屋竣工面积795.35万平方米，下降25.2%。

表5　2013年房地产开发主要指标完成情况

指 标	单位	绝对量	比上年增长（%）
房地产开发投资	亿元	1595.64	24.5
#住宅	亿元	1241.47	22.7
房屋施工面积	万平方米	10454.27	5.1
#住宅	万平方米	8461.71	2.0
#新开工面积	万平方米	2586.21	-9.2
#住宅	万平方米	1940.68	-16.1
房屋竣工面积	万平方米	795.35	-25.2
#住宅	万平方米	663.20	-26.6

五、国内贸易

全年社会消费品零售总额2548.02亿元，比上年增长14.0%，扣除价格因素，实际增长12.1%。按经营地统计，城镇消费品零售额2473.74亿元，增长14.1%，乡村消费品零售额74.28亿元，增长8.1%。按消费形态统计，商品零售额2324.18亿元，增长15.4%；餐饮收入额223.84亿元，增长0.7%。

图6　2013年社会消费品零售总额增速（累计同比）

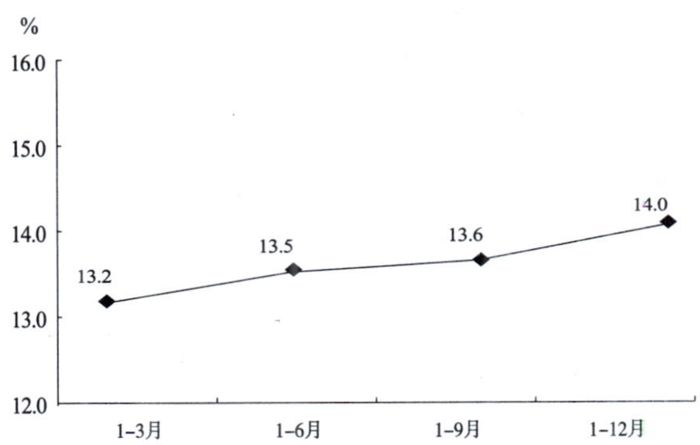

在限额以上企业商品零售额中，粮油、食品、饮料、烟酒类零售额比上年增长12.6%，服装、鞋帽、针、纺织品类增长18.6%，体育、娱乐用品类增长0.9%，书报杂志类增长28.2%，日用品类增长2.6%，家用电器和音像器材类增长27.6%，通讯器材类增长8.0%，家具类增长44.8%，金银珠宝类增长17.0%，汽车类增长13.2%。

六、对外经济

全年进出口总额179.82亿美元，比上年增长

38.2%。其中，出口84.76亿美元，增长16.1%；进口95.06亿美元，增长66.3%。

图7 2009—2013年进出口总额及其增长速度

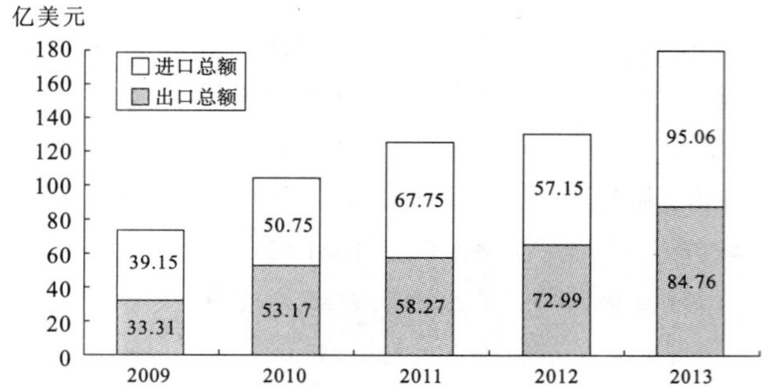

在进出口总额中，加工贸易进出口73.93亿美元，增长82.5%，占进出口总额的41.1%；一般贸易进出口66.80亿美元，下降2.9%，占进出口总额的37.1%。

主要进出口商品中，机电产品出口63.33亿美元，增长28.3%；进口71.19亿美元，增长68.2%。农产品出口4.80亿美元，下降10.5%；进口0.95亿美元，增长56.4%。矿产品出口2.46亿美元，增长0.02%；进口8.22亿美元，增长16.8%。纺织服装出口1.88亿美元，下降44.5%；纺织服装进口578万美元，增长19.3%。

全年批准外商直接投资项目152个，合同利用外商直接投资25.19亿美元，比上年下降30.1%；实际利用外商直接投资31.30亿美元，增长26.3%。

七、交通、邮电和旅游

全年货物运输总量5.01亿吨，比上年增长11.6%。货物运输周转量647.15亿吨公里，增长8.6%。旅客运输总量3.83亿人次，增长5.9%。旅客运输周转量363.49亿人公里，增长7.3%。

表6 2013年各种运输方式完成货物运输量及其增长速度

指 标	单位	绝对数	比上年增长（%）
货物运输总量	万吨	50118.82	11.6
公路	万吨	49243	11.7
铁路	万吨	857.93	4.0
民航（吞吐量）	万吨	17.89	2.3
货物运输周转量	亿吨公里	647.15	8.6
公路	亿吨公里	416.87	11.8
铁路	亿吨公里	229.25	3.2
民航	亿吨公里	1.03	4.9

表7 2013年各种运输方式完成旅客运输量及其增长速度

指 标	单位	绝对数	比上年增长（%）
旅客运输总量	万人次	38288.99	5.9
公路	万人次	32614	5.6
铁路	万人次	3070.50	4.7
民航（吞吐量）	万人次	2604.49	11.2
旅客运输周转量	亿人公里	363.49	7.3
公路	亿人公里	180.45	5.6
铁路	亿人公里	61.94	1.4
民航	亿人公里	121.10	13.2

年末全市机动车保有量186.21万辆，比上年末增长14.0%，其中，私人汽车保有量141.24万辆，增长20.3%。

全年邮政业务总收入17.71亿元。电信业务总收入131.64亿元，增长13.3%。年末全市固定电话用户304.51万户。移动电话用户2160.67万户，其中，3G移动电话用户[4]666.36万户。

全年接待国内外游客10130万人次，比上年增长27.0%；旅游总收入811.44亿元，增长24.0%。

八、金融

年末全市金融机构本外币存款余额13892.77亿元，比上年增长13.1%。人民币存款余额13763.19亿元，增长13.5%，其中，城乡居民储蓄存款余额5357.05亿元，增长11.9%。金融机构本外币贷款余额10214.78亿元，增长16.0%。人民币贷款余额10023.63亿元，增长16.1%，其中，短期贷款余额2326.63亿元，增长21.3%；中长期贷款余额7385.37亿元，增长15.8%。

全年证券市场各类证券交易总额12845.45亿元，比上年增长45.8%。年末全市拥有上市股份公司29家，上市总股本236.96亿股，总市值1909.29亿元。年末股票市场累计开户数174.76万户，比上年末增长1.8%。

年末全市共有保险公司48家，其中，财产险23家，人寿险25家。保险专业中介机构119家。全年保费收入202.40亿元，比上年增长14.5%，其中，财产险保费收入62.99亿元，增13.1%；人身险保费收入139.41亿元，增长15.1%。全年支付各类赔款给付66.49亿元，比上年增长34.0%，其中，财产险、人身险分别为34.49和32.00亿元，分别比上年增长15.2%和62.7%。

九、教育、科学技术和文化

全市普通高校63所，在校学生87.21万人，毕业生22.35万人，另有研究生培养单位46个，在学研究生

8.[illegible]万人，毕业生2.48万人；普通中学418所，在校学生43.73万人，毕业生15.24万人；小学1291所，在校学生51.95万人，毕业生8.51万人。小学、初中学龄人口入学率分别为99.98%和99.71%。

全年实施市级科技计划项目408项，其中，高新技术专项27项。支持建设农业科技示范园14家，实施区县工业科技引导项目8个。全年技术市场交易额415.67亿元。申请发明专利量23534件，发明专利授权量[illegible]708件。

全市博物馆100个，公共图书馆15个，群众艺术馆2个，文化馆14个，文化站181个。地市广播电视台2座，县级广播电视台6座，电视人口覆盖率和广播人口覆盖率分别达98.85%和99.46%。

全年举办各类群众体育展示表演和竞赛活动共计26[illegible]项次，体育社团举办和承办体育赛事300项次，其中，国际性和全国性赛事40项次。新建城市社区全民健身器材配送工程45个，乡镇农民体育健身工程11个，社区全民健身路径50个。全市新增社会体育指导员[illegible]089名。已有晨晚练点1600个，健身气功站点167个，在册练功人数6118人。

2013年，我市培养输送运动员参加国际、国内各项比赛获得金牌14枚、银牌11枚、铜牌13枚。

十、卫生和社会服务

年末全市共有各类卫生计生机构5692个，其中，医院、卫生院381个。各类卫生计生技术人员7.[illegible]6万人，其中，执业（助理）医师2.40万人。卫生计生机构床位4.79万张。

全市社会福利收养类单位81个，共有床位1.5万张，年末在院人数9468人。年末城市低保对象4.7万户、9.2万人，发放低保金4.4亿元；农村低保对象5.4万户、17.2万人，发放低保金3.2亿元。4522人纳入农村五保供养[5]，发放供养金2725.4万元。全年救助城市医疗困难群众4.1万人次；救助农村医疗困难群众20.2万人次。

十一、人民生活和社会保障

全年城镇居民人均可支配收入33100元，比上年增长10.4%，扣除价格因素，实际增长7.5%；农村居民人均纯收入12930元，比上年增长13.0%，扣除价格因素，实际增长10.0%。城镇居民人均消费性支出23848元，比上年增长11.3%；农村居民人均生活消费支出8780元，增长12.9%。城镇居民人均现住房建筑面积3[illegible].4平方米，农村居民人均拥有住房面积81平方米。

图8 2009—2013年城乡居民收入

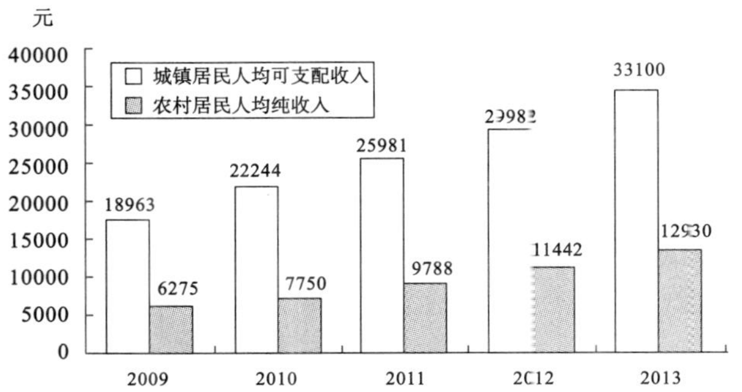

年末全市城镇基本医疗保险参保人数416.63万人；城镇职工养老保险参保人数292.35万人，失业保险参保人数145.58万人；工伤保险参保人数133.85万人，职工生育保险参保人数98.20万人。年末参加农村新型合作医疗的农民人数达402.88万人，实际参合率99.15%。

十二、城市建设、环境和安全生产

全年完成市政公用设施投资297.50亿元。新建人行天桥、地下通道10座，建设公交港湾55处。新建改造绿地广场62个。

全年城市环境空气质量好于国家二级标准（良好）以上的天数138天。二氧化硫年平均浓度为46微克/标立方米，比上年上升15.0%；二氧化氮年平均浓度为57微克/标立方米，上升35.7%；可吸入颗粒物年平均浓度为190微克/标立方米，上升61.0%。全市集中式饮用水源地的水质达标率为100%。区域环境噪声等效声级均值为55.3分贝，道路交通噪声等效声级均值为68.2分贝。

全年共发生各类安全生产事故[illegible]478起，死亡207人，受伤632人，经济损失2826.60万元。

注释：

[1]本公报数据为初步统计数，部分数据因四舍五入的原因，存在着分项与合计不等的情况。

[2]地区生产总值、各产业增加值绝对数按现价计算，增长速度按不变价格计算。

[3]六大高耗能行业分别为：化学原料和化学制品制造业、非金属矿物制品业、黑色金属冶炼和压延加工业、有色金属冶炼和压延加工业、石油加工炼焦和核燃料加工业、电力热力生产和供应业。

[4] 3G是指第三代蜂窝移动通信系统（3rd-generation，简称3G），3G移动电话用户是指报告期末在计费系统拥有使用信息、占用3G网络资源的在网用户。

[5] 农村五保供养是指老年、残疾和未满16周岁的村民，无劳动能力、无生活来源又无法定赡养、抚

养、扶养义务人，或者其法定赡养、抚养、扶养义务人无赡养、抚养、扶养能力的村民，在吃、穿、住、医、葬方面得到的生活照顾和物质帮助。

资料来源：本公报中物价数据来自国家统计局西安调查队；城镇新增就业、登记失业率、社会保障数据来自西安市人力资源和社会保障局；财政数据来自市财政局；进出口数据来自西安海关；利用外资数据来自市商务局；铁路运输数据来自西安铁路局；公路运输数据来自市交通运输局；民航运输数据来自西安咸阳国际机场；机动车数据来自市车管所；邮政业务数据来自市邮政局；电信数据来自中国移动西安分公司、中国电信西安分公司、中国联通西安分公司、陕西铁通西安分公司；旅游数据来自市旅游局；货币金融数据来自中国人民银行西安分行营业管理部；证券数据、保险业数据来自市金融办；教育数据来自市教育局；科技数据来自市科技局；艺术表演团体、公共图书馆、文化馆、广播、电视数据来自市文化广电新闻出版局；博物馆数据来自市文物局；体育数据来自市体育局；卫生、新农合数据来自市卫生局；社会服务、低保和五保供养数据来自市民政局；城市建设数据来自市城乡建设委员会；环境监测数据来自市环境保护局；安全生产数据来自市安全生产监督管理局；其他数据均来自市统计局。

Statistical Communique of Xi'an City on 2013 National Economic and Social Development

Xi'an Municipal Bureau of Statistics and NBS Survey Office in Xi'an

Mar.1st, 2014

In 2013, Faced with a very complicated domestic and international situations, the municipal party committee and municipal government of Xi'an unite and lead the people of the city, conscientiously implement the spirit of the Eighteenth Congress Party People's Congress and the deployment policy of CPC Central Committee and Shaanxi Province, insist on the tone of maintaining stability of overall the work, strive to improve the quality and efficiency of economic operation, The city's economic and social development maintained stability and progress, steady for the better.

I. General Outlook

The resident population of Xi' an city at the end of 2013 was 8.5881million, 4.4098million male and 4.1783 million female, accounted for 51.3 percent and 48.7 percent respectively. The sex ratio was 105.54(granted the female was 100).The born population in the whole year was 82.0 thousand, and the birth rate was 9.57‰.The death population in the whole year was 46.0 thousand, and the death rate was 5.37‰. The net growth of population was 35.2 thousand and the natural growth rate was 4.20‰. The urban population was 6.1877 million, accounted for 72.05 percent; the rural population was 2.4004 million, accounted for 27.95 percent. The total household population was 8.0693 million, up by 1.4 percent by previous year.

In 2013, the gross domestic product (GDP) preliminarily estimated was 488.413 billion Yuan, up by 11.1 percent against the previous year. Analyzed by different industries, the value added of the primary industry was 21.776 billion Yuan, up by 4.8 percent; the value added of the secondary industry was 211.766 billion Yuan, a rise of 13.9 percent; and the value added of the tertiary industry was 254.871 billion Yuan, up by 9.3 percent. The value added of the primary industry accounted for 4.5 percent of the GDP, that of the secondary industry accounted for 43.3 percent, and that of the tertiary industry accounted for 52.2 percent.

The value added of non-public sectors of the economy is 254.813 billion, accounted for the proportion of GDP is 52.2 an increase of 0.8 percent over the previous year.

Table 1 the GDP and Growth Rate between 2009–2013

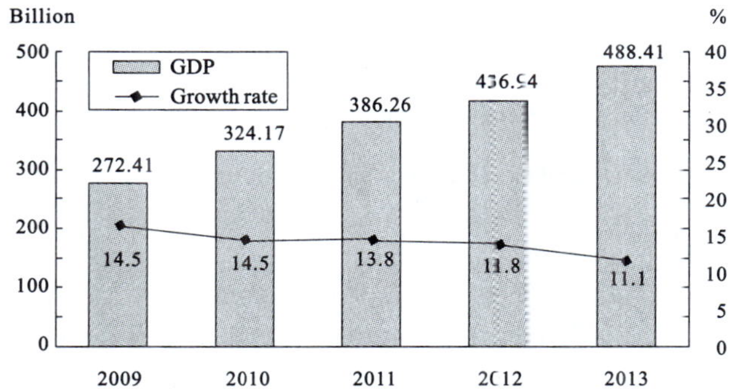

The general level of consumer prices in Xi'an was up by 2.7 percent against the previous year. Of this total, the prices for food went up by 4.8 percent; the retail prices for commodities up by 1.7 percent; the producer prices for manufactured goods went down 0.5 percent; The purchasing prices for manufactured goods went down by 2.8 percent. The fixed asset investment price went up by 0.8 percent and the price of newly founded house increased by 6.5 percent.

Table 2 The rate of increase and decrease of CPI in 2013

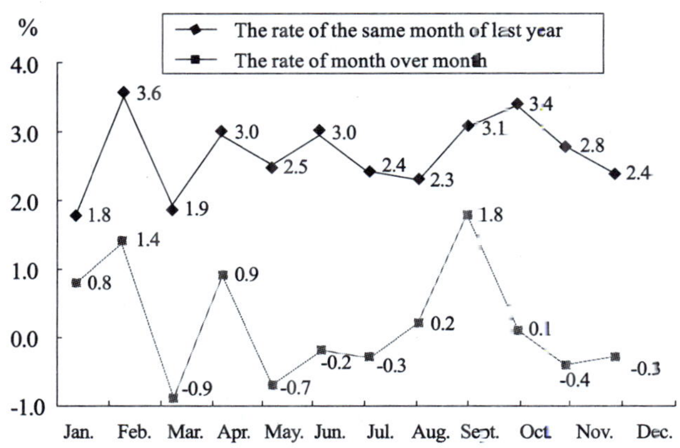

Sheet 1 Up and fall extent of Residents Consumer Price Indices with previous year (2013)

Item	2013(%)
Consumer Price Index	2.7
Food	4.8
#Grain	6.1
Tobacco and liquor	0.7
Clothing	4.0
Household facilities and maintaining services	4.0
Medical, Health and Personal Articles	1.9
Transportation and Communication	-2.4
Recreation, Education and Cultural articles and Services	1.5
Residence	2.0

In 2013, the newly increased employed people in urban areas in Xi'an numbered 125.8 thousand. The number of reemployment of laid-off workers was 50.5 thousand, and the number of reemployment of people who were difficult to find job was 16.1 thousand. The urban unemployment rate through unemployment registration was 3.4 percent at the end of 2013. The financial revenue totaled 90.276 billion Yuan, an increase of 19.9 percent as compared with the previous year. The General Budget Revenue of Regional Finance reached 50.198 billion Yuan, up by 26.5 percent. Of this, business tax, value added tax, income tax of enterprises and individual income tax were up by 2.2 percent, 12.9 percent, 12.1 percent and 20.9 percent respectively. The General Budget Expenditure of Regional Finance totaled 72.981 billion Yuan, up by 22.1 percent. Of this total expenditure, the expenditure on health care was up by 21.4 percent; that on agriculture, forestry and water affairs was up by 10.7 percent; that on education was up by 5.1 percent; that on social security and employment was up by 15.0 percent; that on general public service went down 1.9 percent; that on environmental protection was up by 30.9 percent.

II. Agriculture

In 2013, the sown area of grain was 56.787 thousand hectares, a decrease of 0.8 percent as compared with the previous year; the sown area of oil-bearing crops was 76.7 thousand hectares, a decrease of 0.4 percent; the sown area of vegetables was 998.9 thousand hectares, up by 2.1 percent; the sown area of cotton was 25.7 thousand hectares, a decrease of 51.4 percent. The total output of grain in 2013 was 1.8312 million tons, a decrease of 4.9 percent. Of this, the output of summer crops was 0.8360 million tons, went down by 12.7 percent, and that of the autumn grain was 0.9952 million tons, an increase of 2.8 percent.

Sheet 2 Mail Product of Agriculture Production in 2013

Name of Product	Units	Output	Increase over the last year (%)
Oil	10,000 tons	1.00	-2.0
Vegetable	10,000 tons	298.12	7.3
Fruit	10,000 tons	95.19	2.1
Meat	10,000 tons	15.74	3.8
Milk	10,000 tons	65.77	-1.3
Poultry eggs	10,000 tons	13.54	4.2
Year-end Cattle on hand	10,000 head	21.18	-0.03
Year-end Pig on hand	10,000 head	96.57	-0.03
Year-end Sheep on hand	10,000 head	27.37	-3.8
Year-end Fowl on hand	10,000 head	1172.61	-0.4

III. Industry and Construction

In 2013, the value added by the industrial sector was 148.463 billion Yuan, up by 14.5 percent over the previous year. The value added of industrial enterprises above the designated size was 126.564 billion Yuan, up by 15.4 percent. Of this, the value added of the light industry was 19.944 billion Yuan, up by 14.7 percent; that of the heavy industry was 96.620 billion Yuan, up by 15.6percent.

Table 3 Growth of Above-scale Industrial added Value in 2013

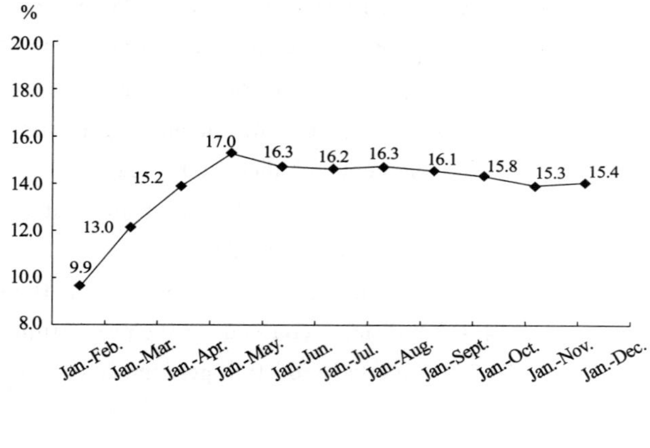

In 2013, of the industrial enterprises above designated size, the growth of value added for processing of food from agricultural products was up by 14.5 percent over the previous year; for manufacture of general machinery up by 4.9 percent; for manufacture of special purpose machinery up by 14.1 percent; for manufacture of car up by 20.7 percent; for manufacture of transport equipment up by 13.2 percent; The growth of the value added for the major six high energy consuming industries were 16.3 percent, of which, that of the manufacture of non-metallic mineral products was 11.8 percent, manufacture of raw chemical materials and chemical products 34.6 percent, smelting and pressing of ferrous metals 15.0 percent, smelting and pressing of non-ferrous metals 3 1 percent, production and supply of electric power and heat power 16.9 percent and 10.2 percent for processing of petroleum, coking, processing of nuclear fuel.

Sheet 3 Output of Major Industrial Products above designated size in Xi' an(2013)

Name of Product	Units	Output	Increase over the last year (%)
Electricity	100 million kilo watt-hour	184.48	-1.8
Crude Oil Processing	10,000 tons	213.11	-1.9
Dairy	10,000 tons	133.24	7.1
Liquid milk	10,000 tons	121.72	5.1
Commercial Concrete	10,000 cubic meter	1606.10	14.7
Machine-made paper and Cardboard	10,000 tons	15.98	-42.1
AC motors	10,000 Kilowatt	574.96	29.8
Feed	10,000 tons	102.51	25.9
Synthetic detergent	10,000 tons	11.72	1.0
Cement	10,000 tons	391.06	-25.5
Draught fan	10,000 units	0.15	10.9
Motor vehicle	10,000 units	42.15	21.1
#Car	10,000 units	31.70	21.1
High voltage switch board	unit	16844.00	-18.4
Transformer	10,000 kilovolt amperes	12170.00	13.2
Electric cable	10,000 Km	1.06	-9.5
Gas compressor	10,000 units	416.12	-30.0
Electronic component	100 million units	3.78	4.4

The composite index on economic benefits of the industrial enterprises above the designated size in 2013 was 247.14, an increase of 25.5 percent over the previous year. The main business income of the industrial enterprises above designated size is 401.173 billion Yuan, up by 14.8 percent over the previous year. The profit was 18.182 billion Yuan, up by 42.7 percent.

Table 4 the value added of construction and growth rate between 2009–2013

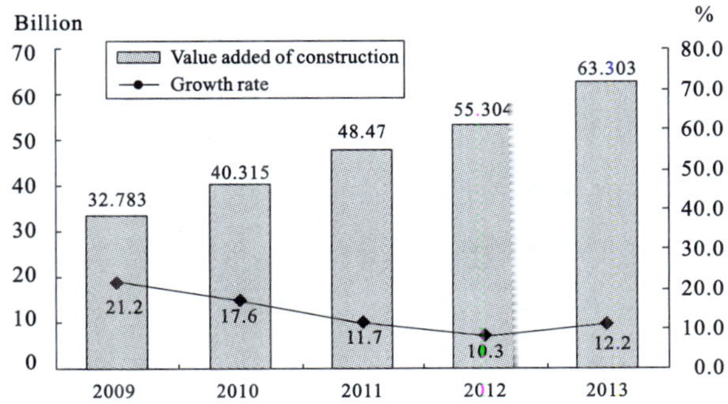

IV. Investment in Fixed Assets

The completed investment in fixed assets of the city in 2013 was 513.456billion Yuan, up by 21.0 percent over the previous year. The real growth was 20.0 percent after deducting the price factors. Of the total investment in urban areas was 505.523 billion Yuan, up by 21.3 percent. Farmers Investment was 7.933 billion Yuan, up by 2.4 percent.

Growth Rate of Fixed Asset Investment (excluding farmers) in 2013

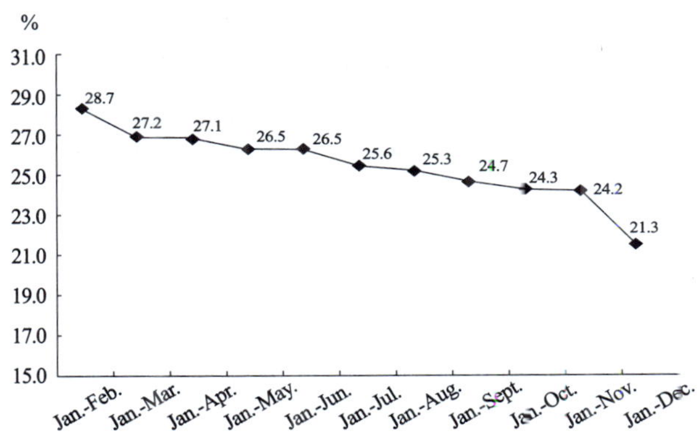

In whole investment, the investment in the primary industry was7.315 billion Yuan, up by 26.4percent against the previous year; in the secondary industry, it was 98.309 billion Yuan, up by 46.3 percent, of which industrial investment was 86.857 billion Yuan, up by 50.2 percent; in the tertiary industry, it was 399.899 billion Yuan, up by 17.8 percent.

Sheet 4 the investment in fixed assets andgrowth rate in Key industries in 2013

Industries	Investment (100 million Yuan)	Growth rate (%)
Agriculture, Forestry, Animal husbandry and fishery	83.54	-15.9
Manufacturing	687.14	42.5
Transportation, storage and postal services	282.98	-3.4
Information transmission, comp uter services and software industry	47.79	-30.5
Wholesale and retail trade	138.60	14.5
Accommodation and catering industry	74.00	6.2
Water Conservancy, environment and public facilities administration industry	463.79	42.4
Education	70.27	7.9
Sanitations, social security and social welfare	73.14	23.7
Public administration and social organizations	66.61	-39.4

In 2013, the investment in real estate development was 159.564 billion Yuan, up by 24.5 percent; housing construction area was 1045.427 million square meters, up by 5.1 percent; the sold area of commercial housing was 79.535 million square meters, decreased by 25.2 percent.

Sheet 5 Mail Indicators of Real estate development and sales in 2013

Item	Units	Absolute Number	ncrease over the last year (%)
Investment in Real Estate Development	100 million Yuan	1595.64	24.5
# Residential Building	100 million Yuan	1241.47	22.7
Floor Space of Commercia l Houses Construction	10,000 sq.m	10454.27	5.1
# Residential Building	10,000 sq.m	8461.71	2.0
#Floor Space of Newly	10,000 sq.m	2586.21	-9.2
Construction			-16.1
# Residential Building	10,000 sq.m	1940.68	
Floor Space of Commercial HousesCompleted	10,000 sq.m	795.35	-25.2
# Residential Building	10,000 sq.m	663.20	-26.6

V. Domestic Trade

In 2013, the total retail sales of consumer goods reached 254.802 billion Yuan, a growth of 14.0 percent over the previous year or a real growth of 12.1 percent after deducting price factors. An analysis on different areas showed that the retail sales of consumer goods in urban areas stood at 247.374 billion Yuan, up by 14.1 percent, and that in rural areas reached 7.428 billion Yuan, up by 8.1 percent. Grouped by consumption patterns, the income of retail sales of commodities was 232.418 billion Yuan, up by 15.4 percent; that of catering industry was 22.384 billion Yuan, up by 0.7 percent.

Table 6 The total retail sales of social consumer goods growth rate

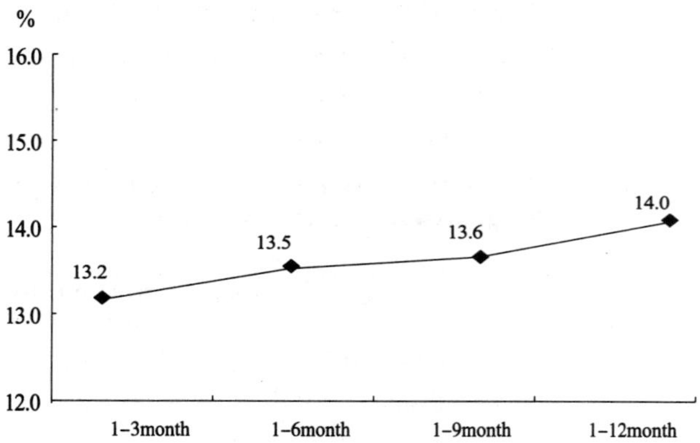

Of the total retail sales by wholesale and retail enterprises above designated size, the sales of food, beverage, wine and cigarette was up by 12.6 percent; clothing, shoes, hats, and needle textiles up by 18.6 percent; sports-recreation up by 0.9 percent; books, newspapers and magazines up by 28.2 percent; daily necessities up by 2.6 percent; electric and electronic appliances for household use and audio-video equipment up by 27.6 percent; telecommunication equipment down by 8.0 percent; furniture increased by 44.8 percent; gold, silver and jewelry up by 17.0 percent and motor vehicles up by 13.2 percent.

VI. Foreign Economic Relations

In 2013, the total value of imports and exports reached 17.982 billion US Dollars, up by 38.2 percent over the previous year. Of this, the value of exports was 8.476 billion US Dollars, up by 16.1 percent, and that of imports was 9.506 billion US Dollars, decreased by 66.3 percent.

Table 7 The total imports and exports and growth rate in 2009–2013

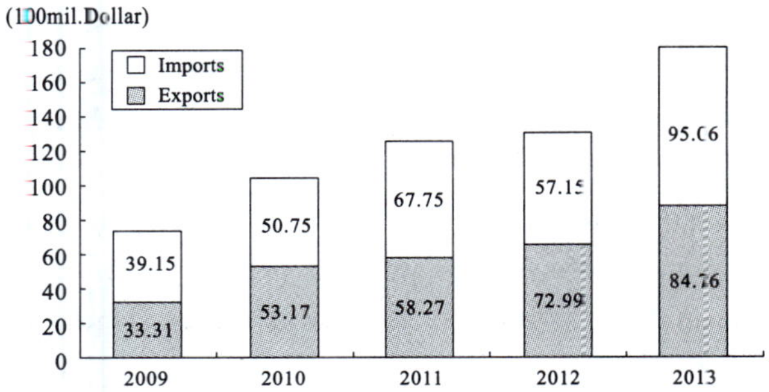

In total imports and exports, the value of processing trade was 7.393 billion US Dollars, up by 82.5 percent, accounted for 41.1 percent of import and export whole value of Xi' an region. The value of imports and exports of general trade was 6.680 billion US Dollars, decreased by 2.9 percent, accounted for 37.1 percent of import and export whole value of Xi' an region.

Of the main import and export commodities, the value of exports of electromechanical products was 6.333 billion US Dollars, an increase of 28.3 percent; that of imports of electromechanical products was 7.119 billion US Dollars, up by 68.2 percent. The value of exports of agricultural product was 0.48 billion US Dollars, a decrease of 10.5 percent; that of imports of agricultural products was 0.095 billion US Dollars, up by 56.4 percent. The value of exports of mineral products was 0.246 billion US Dollars, up by 0.02 percent; that of imports of mineral products was 0.822 billion US Dollars, increased by 16.8 percent. The value of exports of textile products was 0.138 billion US Dollars, a decease of 44.5 percent; that of imports of textile products was 5.78 million US Dollars, up by 19.3 percent.

In 2013, there were 152 Foreign Direct Investment projects approved in Xi'an; the contracted Foreign Direct Investment was 2.519 billion US dollars, a decrease of 30.1 present compared with the previous year; the realized Foreign Direct Investment was 3.130 billion US dollars, up by 26.3 percent.

VII. Transportation, Post, Telecommunications and Tourism

In 2013, the total freight traffic reached 0.501 billion ton, up by 11.6 percent over the previous year. The total goods transportation turnover reached 64.715 billion ton-kilometers, up by 8.6 percent over the previous year. The Total passenger transport reached 0.383 billion, up by 5.9 percent over the previous year. The passenger transport turnover reached 36.349 billion person-kilometers, up by 7.3 percent over the previous year.

Sheet 6 The Total Freight Traffic and growth rate created by Kinds of transport Mode in 2013

Index	Unit	Amount	Growth rate (%)
The Total Freight Traffic	10,000 person	50118.82	11.6
Highway	10,000 person	49243	11.7
Railway	10,000 person	857.93	4.0
Airway	10,000 person	17.89	2.3
Goods Transportation Turnover	billion person-kilometers	647.15	8.5
Highway	billion person-kilometers	416.87	11.3
Railway	billion person-kilometers	229.25	3.2
Airway	billion person-kilometers	1.03	4.9

Sheet 7 The Total Passenger Traffic and growth rate created by Kinds of transport Mode in 2013

Index	Unit	Amount	Growth rate (%)
The Total Passenger Transport	10,000 person	38288.99	5.9
Highway	10,000 person	32614	5.6
Railway	10,000 person	3070.50	4.7
Airway	10,000 person	2604.49	11.2
The passenger transport turnover	billion person-kilometers	363.49	7.3
Highway	billion person-kilometers	180.45	5.6
Railway	billion person-kilometers	61.94	1.4
Airway	billion person-kilometers	121.10	13.2

The total number of motor vehicles for civilian use reached 1862.1 thousand by the end of 2013 up by 14.0 percent, of which private-owned vehicles numbered 1412.4 thousand, up 20.3 percent.

The revenue of post services totaled 1.771 billion Yuan. That of telecommunication services was 13.164 billion Yuan, up by 13.3 percent. At the end of 2013, there were 3.0451 million fixed telephone users; there were 21.6067 million mobile phone users, of which the number of telecom and China Unicom 3G[4] mobile phone was 6663.6 thousand.

The total of domestic tourists was 101.30 million person-times, up by 27.0 percent. The revenue from tourism totaled 81.144 billion Yuan, up by 24.0 percent.

VIII. Financial Intermediation

Savings deposit in RMB and foreign currencies in all items of financial institutions totaled 1389.277 billion Yuan at the end of 2013, an increase of 13.1 percent as compared with the end of the previous year. The savings deposit in RMB stood at 1376.319 billion Yuan, an increase of 13.5 percent, of which the savings deposit of urban and rural residents was 535.705 billion Yuan, up by 11.9 percent. Loans in all items of financial institutions in RMB and foreign currencies reached 1021.478 billion Yuan, an increase of 16.0 percent as compared with the end of the previous year. The loans in RMB stood at 1002.363 billion Yuan, an increase of 16.1 percent, of which the short-term loans totaled 232.663 billion Yuan, up by 21.3 percent, and medium -and- long term loans reached 738.537 billion Yuan, up by 15.8 percent.

The trading volume of stock exchange market was 1284.545 billion Yuan in 2013, an increase of 45.8 percent as compared with the previous year. There were 29 listed companies in Xi'an at the end of 2013 of which the total capital stock was 23.696 billion shares, and the total market value was 190.929 billion Yuan. The were 1.7476 million accounts in stock market at the end of 2013, an increase of 1.8 percent as compared with the end of the previous year.

By the end of 2013, there were 48 insurance institutions, of which the number of property insurance was 23, and that of life insurance was 25. There were 119 intermediary organs of insurance. The received by the insurance companies totaled 20.24 billion Yuan in 2013, up by 14.5 percent. Of this, the revenue from property insurance was 6.299 billion Yuan, up by 13.1 percent; that from life insurance was 13.941 billion Yuan, up by 15.1 percent. In total, insurance companies paid an indemnity worth of 6.649 billion Yuan, up by 34.0 percent over the previous year, of which the worth of property insurance and life insurance were 3.499 billion Yuan and 3.2 billion Yuan respectively, up by 15.2 percent and 62.7 percent respectively.

IX. Education、Science & Technology and Culture

There were 63 general universities and colleges, with 872.1 thousand general tertiary education enrollments, including 223.5 thousand graduates; there were 46 post-graduate training units, with 87.0 thousand students in school and 24.8 thousand graduates. There were 418 general middle schools and high schools, with 437.3 thousand junior high education enrollments and 152.4 thousand graduates; there were 1291 primary schools, with 519.5 thousand primary education enrollments and 85.1 thousand graduates. The enrollment rates for school-age population of primary school and junior high school were 99.98 percent and 99.71 percent respectively.

408 science and technology projects were carried out in 2013 (including 27 projects of high technology). Of this, 14 technology demonstration towns and 8 important direction projects of industry science and technology in districts and counties implemented. The turnover in technology market reached 41.567 billion Yuan. 23534 patents were applied in 2013, including of 3708 patents accredited.

By the end of 2013, there were 100 museums, 15 public libraries, 2 Mass Art Museum, 14 Cultural center, 181 culture stations. There were 2 municipal radio and television stations and 6 county radio and TV station stations. The coverage rate of television broadcasting and radio broadcasting were 98.85 percent and 99.46 percent respectively.

260 mass sports performances and competition activities were organized in 2013, and 300 sports competition were organized and host by sports associations, including 40 international and national sports competition. In 2013, there were 11 fitness projects for township farmers, and 50 public national fitness paths of community built. The number of social sports instructors had increased 1089. There were 1600 sites for morning and evening exercise and 167 sites for fitness Qigong, with 6118 taking part in fitness Qigong.

In 2013, the delegation of Xi'an won 14 gold medals、11 silver medals and 13 bronze medal in the National and international Games.

X. Health and Public Service

At the end of 2013, there were 5692 health institutions in Xi'an, including 381 general hospitals and health centers. There were all 71.6 thousand health care workers, including 24.0 thousand practicing (assistant) doctors. General health centers in Xi'an possessed 47.9 thousand beds.

There were 81 social welfare adoption class units, with a total of 15.0 thousand beds, and 9468 people were in them at the end of the year. There were 47 thousand of urban low-income households, with 92 thousand people, and 440 million Yuan were distributed to them. There were 54.0 thousand of village low-income households, with 172 thousand people, and 320 million Yuan were distributed to them. 4522 people were in the rural five guarantees [5] and 27.25 million Yuan were distributed. 41.0 thousand urban residents and 202 thousand rural residents gained medical relief.

XI. Living Conditions and Social Security

In 2013, the annual per capita disposable income of urban households was 33100 Yuan, growth of 10.4 percent over the previous year, or a real increase of 7.5 percent when the factors of price increase were deducted. And that of rural households was 12930 Yuan, growth of 13.0 percent over the previous year, or a real increase of 10.0 percent. The annual per capita consumer spending of rural households was 23848 Yuan, increase of 11.3 percent, the per capita living expenditure of rural residents was 8780 Yuan, increased by 17.0 percent. The annual per capita building area of urban households was 33.4 square meters, and annual per capita living space of rural households was 81 square meters.

Table 7 Urban and rural resident' s income in 2009–2013

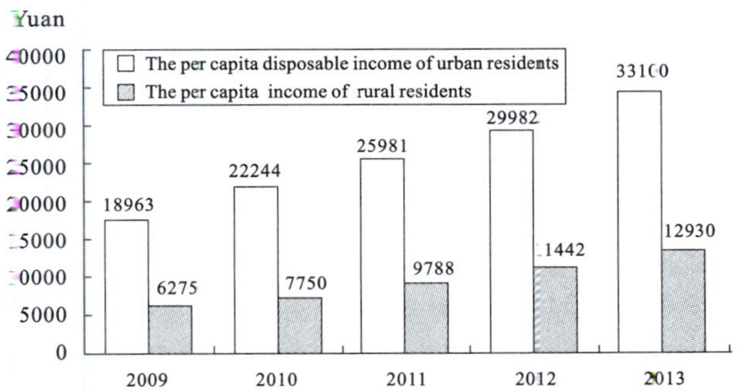

By the end of 2013, a total of 4.1663 million people participated in urban basic health insurance program; a total of 2.2935 million people participated in basic pension program for staff and workers of enterprises; a total of 1.4558 million people participated in unemployment insurance programs; a total of 1.3885 million people participated in work accident insurance; a total of 982.0 thousand people participated in maternity insurance programs for staff and workers. The number of farmers taking part in the new cooperative medical care system in rural areas reached 4.0288 million, with a participation rate of 99.15 percent covered.

XII. Urban Construction, Environment and Work Safety

The total investment of municipal utilities was 29.75 billion Yuan.10 pedestrian bridges, underground passages and 55 bus bays were newly built. In urban areas was newly added 122 green squares were reformed and newly built. In 2013, there were 138 days with air quality better than standard Grade II.The annual mean concentration of Sulfur dioxide, Nitrogen dioxide and respirable particulate matter was 0.046 Mg / cu.m, 0.057 Mg / cu.m and 0.190 Mg / cu.m, a increase by 15.0 percent, 35.7 percent and 61.0 percent. All of water quality of reference water source reached the state standard. The average value of sound level equivalent of regional environmental noises was 55.3 decibel, and the average value of sound level equivalent of transportation noises was 68.2 decibel.

In 2013, various kinds of work accidents amounted to 1478, Of this, there were 207 people dead and 632 people injured, the property losses was 28.27 million Yuan.

Notes:

1. All figures in this Communiqu are preliminary statistics.

2. Gross domestic product (GDP) and value added as quoted in this Communiqu are calculated at current prices, whereas their growth rates are at constant prices.

3. Six highly energy-consuming industries are: manufacture of raw chemical materials and chemical products, manufacture of non-metallic mineral products, smelting and pressing of ferrous metals, smelting and pressing of non-ferrous metals, oil processing, coking and nuclear fuel processing, and production and supply of electricity and heat.

4. 3G refers to the third generation cellular mobile communication system (3rd - generation, referred to as \"3G\'), the 3G mobile phone users refers to those who own using information in the billing system of the final report, and take up the 3G network resources in the network

5. Rural five guarantees is refers to the elderly,disabled,and those under the age of 16 villages, without labor ability, the source of life, and has no fixed support, raising, the obligation of maintenance, or its legal support, raising, the obligation of maintenance support, raising, the villages of bring up ability,who gain help in the care of life and material such as eat,wear, live, medical such as eat, wear, live, medical. and buride.

Data Sources:

In this communiqu , data of price are from NBS Survey Office in Xi'an ;data of newly increased employed people, unemployment rate through unemployment registration and social security are from the Xi'an Municipal Bureau of Human Resources and Social Security; financial data are from the Xi'an Municipal Bureau of Finance; data of imports and exports are from the Xi'an Customs; data of utilizing foreign capital are from the Xi'an Municipal Bureau of Business; data of railway transportation are from the Xi'an Municipal Bureau of Railways; data of highway transportation are from the Xi'an Municipal Bureau of Transport; data of air transport are from the Xi'an-Xian yang International Airport; data of motor vehicles for civilian use are from the Xi'an vehicle administration; data of post services are from the Xi'an Municipal Bureau of post; data of telecommunications are from Xi'an branch of China Mobile China Unicom China Telecom, and Shaanxi CTT; data of tourism are from the Xi'an Tourism Administration; data of monetary and financial are from business management department for Xi'an branch of the People's Bank of China; data of listed companies and insurance are from Xi'an Municipal Finance Office; data of education are from the Xi'an Municipal Bureau of Education; data of technology are from Xi'an Municipal Bureau of Technology; data of art-performing groups, public libraries, culture centers, radio and television are from the Xi'an Municipal Bureau of Culture, Radio, Press and Publication; data of museum are from Xi'an Municipal Bureau of Heritage; data of sports are from the Xi'an Municipal Bureau of Sport; data of health and new cooperative medical care system in rural areas are from the Xi'an Municipal Bureau of Health; data of central heating area and green area are from Xi'an Municipal Urban and Rural Construction Committee; data of sewage treatment in urban and environment monitoring are from the Xi'an Municipal Bureau of Environmental Protection; data of work safety are from the State Administration of Work Safety; all the other data are from Xi'an Municipal Bureau of Statistics.

1 综　合

GENERAL SURVEY

资料整理：张小文　刘　婷

Data management:Zhang Xiacwen　Liu Ting

第一部分　综合

一、简要说明

本章资料主要包括西安市行政区划、自然地理、自然资源、气象、国民经济和社会发展等综合资料，由西安市统计局综合处根据局内各专业处及有关部门统计资料进行整理和编辑。

二、主要指标

生产总值（亿元）	4884.13	比上年增长	11.1%
农林牧渔及服务业总产值（亿元）	342.89	比上年增长	4.9%
规模以上工业增加值（亿元）	1265.64	比上年增长	15.4%
全社会固定资产投资额（亿元）	5134.56	比上年增长	21.0%
社会消费品零售总额（亿元）	2580.42	比上年增长	14.0%
财政一般预算收入（亿元）	501.98	比上年增长	26.5%
财政一般预算支出（亿元）	729.81	比上年增长	22.1%
出口总额（亿美元）	84.78	比上年增长	16.2%
城镇居民人均可支配收入（元）	33100	比上年增长	10.4%
农村居民人均纯收入（元）	12930	比上年增长	13.0%

1　GENERAL SURVEY

Ⅰ.Brief Introduction

This chapter consists of mainly unified data of administrative divisions, natural geography, natural resources, meteorology, national economy and social development of Xi'an city. It is compiled by Integration Division according to the reported data from other divisions of the Xi'an Bureau of Statistics and other departments of the municipal government.

Ⅱ.Major Indicators

		Increase over Preceding Year
Gross Domestic Product (100 mil. Yuan)	4884.13	11.1%
Gross Output Value of Farming, Forestry, Animal, Husbandry and Fishery (100 mil. Yuan)	324.89	4.9%
Gross Industrial Added Value (100 mil. Yuan)	1265.64	15.4%
Investment Fulfilled In Fixed Assets (100 mil. Yuan)	5134.56	21.0%
Total Retail Sales of Consumer Goods (100 mil. Yuan)	2580.42	14.0%
Local Government Revenue (100 mil. Yuan)	501.98	26.5%
Local Government Expenditures (100 mil. Yuan)	729.81	22.1%
Total Value of Exports (USD 100 mil.)	84.78	16.2%
Per Capita Annual Disposable Income of Urban Households (Yuan)	33100	10.4%
Per Capita Net Income of Rural Residents (Yuan)	12930	13.0%

1-1 行政区划（2013年末）

Administrative Division（End of 2013）

单位：个 (unit)

地 区	Region	乡镇及街道办 Township and Urban Subdistrict Office	镇数 Town	街道办事处 Urban Subdistrict Office	村民委员会 Villagers' Committee	社区居委会 Neighbourhood Committee
西安市	**Xi'an**	**178**	**67**	**111**	**2986**	**772**
（一）市辖区	**Urban Districts**	**105**	**2**	**103**	**1376**	**708**
新城区	Xincheng	9		9		105
碑林区	Beilin	8		8		103
莲湖区	Lianhu	9		9	3	131
灞桥区	Baqiao	9		9	223	37
未央区	Weiyang	10		10	99	100
雁塔区	Yanta	8		8	92	119
阎良区	Yanliang	7	2	5	80	23
临潼区	Lintong	23		23	284	41
长安区	Chang'an	22		22	595	49
（二）四县	**Four Counties**	**68**	**65**	**3**	**1501**	**48**
蓝田县	Lantian	22	22		519	9
周至县	Zhouzhi	22	22		376	14
户 县	Huxian	16	16		518	21
高陵县	Gaoling	8	5	3	88	4
（三）沣东新城	**Fengdongxincheng**	**5**		**5**	**109**	**16**

注：本表数据来源市民政局。

1-2 土地面积和常住人口密度（2013年）

Statistics on Land Area and Density of Permanent Population（2013）

地　区	Region	土地面积(2012年末) Area(End of 2012) 绝对数（平方公里）Absolute Value (sq.km)	比重（%）Proportion (%)	常住人口（万人）Total of Permanent Population (10 000 persons)	常住人口密度（人/平方公里）Density of Permanent Population (person/sq.km)
西安市	**Xi 'an**	**10096.81**	**100**	**858.81**	**851**
（一）市区	**Urban Districts**				
新城区	Xincheng	30.13	0.3	59.64	19796
碑林区	Beilin	23.37	0.2	62.23	26623
莲湖区	Lianhu	38.32	0.4	70.43	18378
灞桥区	Baqiao	324.50	3.2	60.50	1864
未央区	Weiyang	264.41	2.6	81.84	3095
雁塔区	Yanta	151.44	1.5	119.29	7877
阎良区	Yanliang	244.55	2.4	28.40	1161
临潼区	Lintong	915.97	9.1	66.81	729
长安区	Chang'an	1588.53	15.7	110.03	693
（二）四县	**Four Counties**				
蓝田县	Lantian	2005.95	19.9	52.07	260
周至县	Zhouzhi	2945.20	29.2	57.24	194
户　县	Huxian	1279.42	12.7	56.32	440
高陵县	Gaoling	285.03	2.8	34.01	1193

注：本表土地面积数据来源市国土资源局，2009年全国第二次土地调查后，土地面积数据变更，但未对外发布使用，从2012年起使用。

1-3 自然状况和资源（2013年）

Nature Conditions and Resources（2013）

指　标	Item	2013
一、自然状况	**Nature Conditions**	
土地总面积（平方公里）	Total Land Area (sq.km)	10096.81
#市区面积	Urban Area	3581.22
气候（市区）	Climate (Urban)	
年平均气温（℃）	Average Annual Temperature (℃)	15.8
年降水量（毫米）	Total Annual Precipitation (mm)	423.9
日照总时数（小时）	Total Sunshine Time (hour)	2190.5
平均风速（米/秒）	Average Wind-speed (m/sec.)	2.3
二、自然资源	**Natural Resources**	
年末实有耕地面积（万亩）	Cultivated Area Year-end (10 000 mu)	366.23
林业用地面积（千公顷）	Area of Forestry (1 000 hectare)	508.39
全市水面面积（万亩）	Whole Water Area (10 000 mu)	9.56
水资源总量（亿立方米）	Total Water Resource (0.1 billion cu.m)	13.87
#天然地表水资源总量	Total Savageness Surface Water Resource	15.61
地下水资源总量（亿立方米）	Total Ground Water Resource (0.1 billion cu.m)	10.76

注：2013年市气象局位于市郊新站启用，本年鉴气象资料为新站监测数据。
全市水面面积包括湖泊、水库、鱼塘、城市段河流面积等
本表数据来源市气象局、林业局、水务局等

1-4 气象情况（2013年）

Climate Condition（2013）

地 区	Region	平均气温（℃）Average Temperature（℃）	日照时数（小时）Sunshine Time (hour)	降水天数（天）Raining days (day)	年降水量（毫米）Total Annual Precipitation (mm)	平均风速（米/秒）Average Wind-speed (m/second)
市 区	Urban Districts	15.8	2190.5	82	423.9	2.3
临潼区	Lintong	15.5	2095.7	73	525.0	1.6
长安区	Chang'an	14.9	1993.2	30	522.3	1.4
蓝田县	Lantian	14.8	2263.0	91	501.9	1.3
周至县	Zhouzhi	14.9	2024.4	92	523.1	1.0
户 县	Huxian	16.0	2174.3	78	535.2	0.6
高陵县	Gaoling	15.7	2189.9	78	395.1	1.6

注：本表数据来源市气象局。

1-5 市区及县各月平均气温（2013年）

Average Temperature of Xi'an and the Districts of each Month(2013)

单位：℃ (℃)

月 份	Month	市区 Urban	临潼 Lintong	长安 Chang'an	蓝田 Lantian	周至 Zhouzhi	户县 Huxian	高陵 Gaoling
一月	January	0.8	0.8	0.3	-0.7	0.5	1.5	0.6
二月	February	4.5	4.5	4.0	3.7	4.3	4.9	4.9
三月	March	13.0	13.6	12.6	12.2	13.1	13.7	13.2
四月	April	16.1	16.2	15.2	14.9	15.7	16.4	16.3
五月	May	21.7	21.6	20.9	21.0	20.7	21.6	21.7
六月	June	27.3	26.9	26.5	26.8	26.3	27.5	27.2
七月	July	27.4	27.2	26.6	26.8	26.2	27.4	27.5
八月	August	28.3	27.2	27.2	28.1	26.8	28.1	28.1
九月	September	22.7	22.0	21.8	22.2	21.2	22.7	22.6
十月	October	16.9	15.8	15.3	16.0	16.1	17.0	16.6
十一月	November	8.4	8.1	7.1	6.7	7.3	8.3	7.8
十二月	December	2.1	1.6	1.2	0.2	0.7	2.6	1.4

注：本表数据来源市气象局

1-6　市区及县各月日照时数（2013年）

Sunshine Duration of Xi'an and the Districts of each Month（2013）

单位：小时　　　　(hour)

月　份	Month	市区 Urban	临潼 Lintong	长安 Chang'an	蓝田 Lantian	周至 Zhouzhi	户县 Huxian	高陵 Gaoling
一月	January	171.9	150.2	174.4	181.5	166.7	220.5	153.5
二月	February	90.8	86.5	73.6	93.8	80.9	98.7	93.7
三月	March	207.5	189.2	176.4	216.9	189.9	215.2	214.3
四月	April	233.9	244.8	199.6	234.3	198.2	217.5	232.0
五月	May	171.4	192.0	157.7	192.4	156.7	159.7	173.4
六月	June	256.9	287.8	254.7	270.4	210.8	232.6	236.3
七月	July	123.3	162.5	160.5	157.8	135.1	163.6	183.1
八月	August	260.5	222.9	227.8	266.7	254.8	252.9	266.4
九月	September	171.1	125.2	135.4	171.5	158.8	169.2	151.4
十月	October	191.4	131.8	176.7	195.1	176.7	189.0	191.2
十一月	November	146.7	145.8	124.1	140.1	136.1	122.6	139.[illegible]
十二月	December	165.1	157.0	132.3	142.5	159.7	132.8	155.0

注：本表数据来源市气象局

1-7　市区及县各月降水天数（2013年）

Precipitation Days of Xi'an and the Districts of each Month（2013）

单位：天　　　　(day)

月　份	Month	市区 Urban	临潼 Lintong	长安 Chang'an	蓝田 Lantian	周至 Zhouzhi	户县 Huxian	高陵 Gaoling
一月	January	1	1	1	3	1	1	1
二月	February	8	7	2	11	7	7	7
三月	March	3	3	1	4	3	3	2
四月	April	5	7	2	6	5	5	6
五月	May	15	15	5	16	16	15	15
六月	June	6	6	3	5	10	6	6
七月	July	15	10	2	15	16	15	15
八月	August	5	3	2	5	6	5	6
九月	September	11	9	4	9	12	7	11
十月	October	4	4	3	6	6	5	5
十一月	November	9	8	5	11	10	9	9
十二月	December							

注：本表数据来源市气象局

1-8 市区及县各月降水量（2013年）

Amount of Precipitation of Xi'an and the Districts of each Month（2013）

单位：毫米 (mm)

月 份	Month	市区 Urban	临潼 Lintong	长安 Chang'an	蓝田 Lantian	周至 Zhouzhi	户县 Huxian	高陵 Gaoling
一月	January	9.0	0.9	0.5	2.3	0.3	0.3	1.2
二月	February	12.4	13.1	8.5	21.2	23.3	24.3	4.3
三月	March	5.5	2.9	1.6	1.6	4.0	3.5	3.4
四月	April	19.3	22.5	9.0	35.3	16.8	19.4	11.1
五月	May	139.6	173.3	16.9	144.3	210.3	159.9	54.0
六月	June	27.0	51.8	56.4	30.9	25.7	28.0	27.9
七月	July	119.3	136.1	24.1	121.8	114.5	174.2	23.8
八月	August	30.5	38.9	7.7	31.3	35.3	30.9	6.1
九月	September	23.1	24.6	13.6	53.5	51.3	28.4	21.7
十月	October	14.5	17.3	12.1	17.3	26.3	30.1	9.2
十一月	November	31.8	43.6	14.5	42.4	15.3	36.2	26.0
十二月	December							

注：本表数据来源市气象局

1-9 市区及县各月平均风速（2013年）

Average Wind Velocity of Xi'an and the Districts of each Month（2013）

单位：米/秒 (m/s)

月 份	Month	市区 Urban Districts	临潼 Lintong	长安 Chang'an	蓝田 Lantian	周至 Zhouzhi	户县 Huxian	高陵 Gaoling
一月	January	1.9	1.3	1.4	0.9	1.0	0.4	1.2
二月	February	1.8	1.4	1.4	1.1	1.0	0.5	1.3
三月	March	2.9	2.0	1.7	1.5	1.4	0.6	2.2
四月	April	2.6	1.8	1.5	1.5	1.1	0.6	1.9
五月	May	2.6	1.7	1.4	1.5	1.1	0.6	1.9
六月	June	2.8	2.1	1.8	1.8	1.4	0.7	[illegible]
七月	July	2.6	1.8	1.6	1.4	1.0	0.6	[illegible]
八月	August	2.8	1.9	1.4	1.5	1.0	0.6	2.3
九月	September	2.3	1.6	1.3	1.5	0.9	0.6	1.7
十月	October	1.9	1.2	1.1	1.2	0.7	0.3	1.2
十一月	November	1.8	1.3	1.3	1.1	0.8	0.5	0.9
十二月	December	1.8	1.2	1.4	1.1	0.9	0.7	1.1

注：本表数据来源市气象局

1-10 国有土地使用权出让、划拨情况

Basic Statistics on Lease and Administrative Allocation of Use Right of State-Owned Land

项　　目	Item	2006	2007	2008	2009	2010	2011	2012	2013
国有土地使用权出让	**Lease of the Use Right of State-owned Land**								
出让地块(宗)	Land leased (item)	316	333	278	297	386	474	581	550
协议	Agreement	225	171	119	100	173	133	80	90
招标	Invitation for Bid		1	3		3			
拍卖	Auction	7	3	5	1	11			
挂牌交易	Listed Transaction	84	158	149	196	199	341	500	460
出让面积（公顷）	Area of Totally Leased Land (hectare)	1208	843	809	1047	1364	1385	1853	2195
土地使用权出让总收入(万元)	**Total Revenue from Leasing of the Use Right(10 000 yuan)**	**156231**	**267666**	**309181**	**284405**	**358098**	**334069**	**218817**	**292945**
国有土地使用权划拨	**Administrative Allocation of the Use Right of State-owned Land**								
划拨地块（宗）	Land Allocated (item)	90	100	102	79	108	253	154	234
划拨面积（公顷）	Area of Land Allocated(hectare)	259	388	455	1721	1027	1426	1617	1986

注：本表数据来源市国土资源局

1-11 国民经济和社会发展总量与速度指标

指　标	Item	总量指标			
		1995	2000	2005	2009
人口与就业	**Population and Employment**				
人口	**Population**				
年底总人口(万人)	Population at the Year-end (10 000 persons)	648.21	688.01	741.73	781.67
非农业	Non-agricultural Population	255.71	285.79	333.14	370.66
农业	Agriculturral Population	392.5	402.22	408.59	411.01
男	Male	334.75	355.18	382.02	399.28
女	Female	313.46	332.83	359.71	382.39
就业	**Employment**				
全社会从业人员数(万人)	Employment(10 000 persons)	372.6	389.1	415.83	462.52
#全部单位在岗职工人数	Number of Employed Staff and Workers	141.17	109.62	119.73	129.62
城镇登记失业人数(万人)	Registered Unemployed in Urban Areas(10 000 persons)	5.92	3.85	8.45	10.02
宏观经济	**Macroeconomic Indicator**				
国民经济核算	**National Accounts**				
生产总值(亿元)	Gross Domestic Product(100 mil. yuan)	330.35	646.13	1313.93	2724.08
第一产业	Primary Industry	41.4	44.65	66.01	110.38
第二产业	Secondary Industry	135.33	277.13	540.5	1144.75
工业	Industry				
第三产业	Tertiary Industry	153.62	324.35	707.42	1468.95
在生产总值中：最终消费	Total Consumption	239.64	413.43	766.62	1403.1
资本形成总额	Total Investment	151.55	287.82	839.01	2281.91
固定资产投资	**Investment in Fixed Assets**				
全社会固定资产投资总额(亿元)	Total Investment in Fixed Assets(100 mil. yuan)	103.42	232.37	835.1	2500.13
按城乡划分：城镇	According to the Division of Urban and Rural：Urban Area	88.5	203.01	776.33	2367.58
#房地产	Real Estate	21.65	51.85	225.23	696.34
农村	Rural Area	14.92	29.36	58.77	132.55
按经济成分划分：国有经济	According to the Division of Economic Component：State-Owned	69.08	159.6	373.7	932.91
集体经济	Collective-Owned	9.78	14.65	59.23	289.91
个体经济	Self-employed Individual	11.13	24.4	79.04	97.86
其他经济	Other	13.43	33.72	323.13	1179.45
财政	**Public Finance**				
财政一般预算收入(亿元)	General Budgetary Revenue of Local Government (100 mil. yuan)	18.21	46.8	72.92	181.4
财政一般预算支出(亿元)	General Budgetary Expenditure of Local Government (100 mil. yuan)	18.42	52	97.61	276.85
物价指数(上年=100)	**Price Indices(preceding year=100)**				
商品零售价格指数	Retail Price Index	114.6	98.7	99.7	99.5
居民消费价格指数	Consumer Price Index	117.0	100.2	100.3	99.7
工业生产者出厂价格指数	Producer Price Indices (PPI) for Manufactured Goods	110.8	99.4	103.9	99.9
利用外资	**Utilization of Foreign Capital**				
利用外资签定协议额(万美元)	Amount of Foreign Capital for Utilization Through Signed Contracts or Agreements(USD 10 000)	28956	54123	121499	60027
外商实际直接投资额(万美元)	Amount of Foreign Capital Actually Utilized (USD 10 000)	18653	15633	57113	121872

注：国民经济核算2004—2008年为全国第二次经济普查修订数据。
2009年及以前年份财政收支为一般预算收支与基金预算收支之和。
由于2010年固定资产投资起报点的变化，指数和平均增长速度为可比口径计算。

Principal Aggregate Indicators on National Economic and Social Development and Their Related Indices and Growth Rates

				速度指标（%） Indices and Growth Rates（%）						
				指数（2013比以下各年） (2013 as percentage of the following years)				平均增长速度 Average Annual Growth Rate		
2010	2011	2012	2013	2000	2005	2010	2012	2001-2005	2006-2010	2011-2013
782.73	791.83	795.98	806.93	117.3	108.8	103.1	101.4	1.5	1.1	1.0
374.64	391.31	392.04	409.82	143.4	123.0	109.4	104.5	3.1	2.4	3.0
408.09	400.52	403.94	397.11	98.7	97.2	97.3	98.3	0.3	-0.02	-0.9
393.80	402.52	397.58	408.78	115.1	107.0	102.5	102.8	1.5	0.9	0.8
383.93	389.31	398.40	398.15	119.6	110.7	103.7	99.9	1.6	1.3	1.2
477.58	495.99	514.57	530.71	136.4	127.6	111.1	103.1	1.3	2.8	3.6
130.7	154.33	155.28	183.60	167.5	153.3	140.5	118.2	1.8	1.8	12.0
10.46	10.37	9.60	10.13	263.1	119.9	96.8	105.5	17.0	4.4	-1.1
3241.59	3862.58	4366.10	4884.13	534.5	284.0	141.4	111.1	13.5	15.0	12.2
140.06	173.14	195.59	217.76	200.2	162.2	118.5	104.8	4.3	6.5	5.8
1406.72	1674.31	1881.75	2117.66	611.1	301.4	146.3	113.9	15.2	15.5	13.5
1694.91	2015.13	2288.76	2548.71	520.7	282.5	139.1	109.3	13.0	15.2	11.6
1598.51	1856.91	2092.97								
2835.42	3264.83	3783.10								
3250.56	3346.26	4243.43	5134.56	2789.8	776.3	199.4	121.0	29.2	31.2	25.9
3104.92	3207.97	4107.54	4982.25	3137.3	820.4	205.1	121.3	30.8	31.9	27.1
842.34	996.81	1281.90	1595.64	3078.0	708.6	189.5	124.5	34.1	30.2	23.7
145.64	138.29	135.89	152.31	518.8	259.2	104.6	112.1	14.9	19.9	1.5
1348.76	1204.80	1661.22	1770.84	1400.9	598.3	165.8	106.6	18.5	29.3	18.3
326.44	258.15	194.71	219.88	1894.5	468.6	85.0	112.9	32.2	40.7	-5.3
54.73	74.64	82.72	84.43	437.0	134.9	194.8	102.1	26.5	-7.1	24.9
1520.63	1808.67	2304.78	3059.41	11451.5	1195	253.9	132.7	57.1	36.6	36.4
241.86	318.55	396.96	501.98	1072.6	688.4	207.5	126.5	9.3	27.1	27.6
371.62	494.58	597.49	729.81	1403.5	747.7	196.4	122.1	13.4	30.7	25.2
102.7	104.4	102.3	101.7							
103.5	105.6	102.8	102.7							
102.3	102.5	100.5	99.5							
119689	120083	360264	251874	465.4	207.3	210.4	69.9	17.6	-0.3	28.1
156653	200522	247800	312994	2002.1	548	199.8	126.3	29.6	22.4	26.0

1-11 续表1

指　标	Item	总量指标 1995	2000	2005	2009
产　　业	**Industry**				
农业	**Agriculture**				
耕地面积(万亩)	Cultivated Areas(10 000 hectares)	463.97	443.37	400.17	387.89
乡村劳动力资源总数(万人)	Total Number of Rural Labor Source (10 000 persons)	213.80	240.76	255.93	255.00
农林牧渔及服务业总产值 (亿元)	Gross Output Value of Farming Forestry, Animal Husbandry and Fishery(100 mil yuan)	75.46	74.37	106.54	178.70
主要农产品产量(万吨)	Output of Major Farm Products(10 000 tons)				
粮　食	Grain	175.30	201.90	205.50	218.20
奶　类	Milk	13.29	24.59	42.22	61.82
油　料	Oil-bearing Crops	2.17	1.34	1.16	1.12
蔬　菜	Vegetables	133.60	162.14	195.70	242.41
水　果	Fruits	24.10	34.36	51.29	78.96
肉　类	Meat	12.78	14.76	18.20	12.62
水产品	Aquatic Products	0.85	1.14	0.94	1.30
工业	**Industry**				
全部工业总产值（亿元）	Gross industrial Output Value(100 mil. yuan)	405.90	639.48	1308.56	2827.07
规模以上工业企业主要经济指标	Principal Indicators of Industrial Enterprises of State Ownership and Non-state-owned Above Designated Size (100 mil. yuan)				
工业增加值（亿元）	Value Added of Industrial(100 mil. yuan)		130.18	314.01	700.13
资产总计（亿元）	Total Assets(100 mil. yuan)		958.05	1503.85	2913.56
主营业务收入（亿元）	Revenue from Principal Business(100 mil. yuan)		420.42	980.97	2384.52
利润总额（亿元）	Profits(100 mil. yuan)		16.11	28.72	177.20
从业人员年平均人数（万人）	Annual Average Employers(10 000 persons)		43.25	37.92	43.42
主要工业产品产量	Output of Major Industrial Products				
布(亿米)	Cloth(100 mil.m)	3.03	2.48	2.70	2.22
机制纸及纸板(万吨)	Machine-Made Paper(10 000ton)	36.44	5.47	22.19	47.63
家用电冰箱(万台)	Household Refrigerators(10 000unit)	1.30	0.59	2.54	9.21
发电量(亿千瓦时)	Electricity(100 million kwh)	22.00	19.00	48.00	83.21
钢材(万吨)	Steel Products(10 000ton)	31.44	10.00	24.02	110.51
汽车(万辆)	Motor Vehicle (10 000 units)	0.30	0.90	4.10	50.70
建筑业	**Construction**				
建筑业企业从业人数(人)	Number of Employed Persons(person)		136718	158311	461080
建筑业总产值(亿元)	Gross Output Value(100 mil. yuan)	42.55	105.93	326.65	1296.58
房屋建筑施工面积 (万平方米)	Floor Space of Buildings under Construction (10 000 sq.m)	601.70	793.30	1801.20	3947.01
房屋建筑竣工面积 (万平方米)	Floor Space of Buildings Completed (10 000 sq.m)	177.15	336.80	569.01	1209.88

continued 1

2010	2011	2012	2013	速度指标（%） Indices and Growth Rates（%）						
				指数（2013比以下各年） (2013 as percentage of the following years)				平均增长速度 Average Annual Growth Rate		
				2000	2005	2010	2012	2001-2005	2006-2010	2011-2013
383.32	377.10	369.91	366.23	82.6	91.5	95.5	99.0	-2.0	-9.0	-1.5
256.36	260.97	259.06	257.96	107.1	100.8	100.6	99.6	1.2	0.04	0.2
227.10	272.66	308.36	342.89	207.0	165.0	118.5	104.9	4.6	6.8	5.8
221.70	182.04	192.55	183.12	90.7	89.1	82.6	95.1	0.4	1.5	-6.2
63.37	64.80	66.64	65.77	267.5	155.8	103.8	98.7	11.4	8.5	1.2
1.20	1.17	1.02	1.00	74.6	86.2	83.3	98.0	-1.6	0.7	-5.9
253.10	261.66	277.80	298.12	183.9	152.3	117.8	107.3	3.8	5.3	5.6
84.78	91.14	93.21	95.19	277.1	185.6	112.3	102.1	8.3	10.6	3.9
13.65	14.46	15.17	15.74	106.7	86.5	115.3	103.8	4.2	-5.6	4.9
1.19	1.18	1.40	1.42	124.6	151.1	119.3	101.4	-3.9	5.7	6.1
3562.88	4093.32	4656.08						14.3	21.2	
862.28	1012.58	1132.44	1265.64				15.4			
3592.13	3975.38	4775.92	4948.67	516.5	329.1	137.8	103.6	9.4	19.0	11.3
3011.19	3381.27	3758.56	4011.73	954.2	409.0	133.2	106.7	18.5	25.1	10.0
245.37	172.94	167.77	181.82	1128.6	633.1	74.1	108.4	12.3	53.6	-9.5
47.11	50.42	49.23	45.88	106.1	121.0	97.4	93.2	-2.6	4.4	-0.9
2.38	1.63	1.43	1.40	56.4	51.8	58.8	97.8	1.7	-2.5	-16.2
49.60	49.79	27.61	15.98	292.4	72.1	32.3	57.9	32.3	17.5	-31.4
10.76	7.22	15.77	10.90	1860.1	429.0	101.3	69.2	34.1	33.5	0.4
96.94	95.01	99.48	184.48	971.1	384.4	190.3	98.2	20.4	15.1	23.9
110.77	18.48	31.29	54.26	543.0	226.1	49.0	109.8	19.2	35.8	-21.2
65.21	55.67	54.17	42.15	4688.9	1029.3	64.7	121.1	35.4	73.9	-13.5
539000	372088	391199	577944	422.7	365.1	107.2	147.7	3.0	27.8	2.4
1820.35	1619.09	1874.23	2228.41	2103.7	682.2	122.4	118.9	25.3	41.0	7.0
4592.57	6218.70	7531.07	9753.45	1229.5	541.5	212.4	129.5	17.8	20.6	28.5
1391.91	2392.39	1985.31	2229.97	662.1	391.9	160.2	112.3	11.1	19.6	17.0

1-11 续表2

指 标	Item	总量指标			
		1995	2000	2005	2009
交通运输	**Transportation**				
货运量(万吨)	Freight Traffic(10 000 tons)	9590	6999	12051	30606
铁 路	Railways	3317	3101	540	614
公 路	Highways	6268	3890	11505	29986
民用航空	Civil Aviation	5	8	6	6
客运量(万人次)	Passenger Traffic(10 000 persons-times)	9069	8068	10479	28693
铁 路	Railways	2678	2130	1796	2585
公 路	Highways	6128	5578	8294	25271
民用航空	Civil Aviation	263	360	389	837
邮电通信业	**Post and Telecommunication Services**				
邮电业务总量(亿元)	Total Business Revenue(100 mil. yuan)	7.65	46.16	132.04	298.92
函 件(万件)	Number of Letters Delivered(10 000 pieces)	14647	8230	9526	6128
本地电话局用交换机容量 (万门)	Capacity of Local Office Telephone Exchanges (10 000 line)	58.3	204.8	457.3	441.1
本地电话年末用户(万户)	Local fixed telephone end users (million)	30.79	141.28	321.48	289.10
城市电话用户	Urban Telephone Subscribers	29.95	124.26	271.40	253.28
乡村电话用户	Rural Telephone Subscribers	0.84	17.02	50.08	35.82
移动电话用户(万户)	Number of Mobile Telephone Subscribers (10 000 subscribers)		73.10	419.96	1120.06
互联网年末宽带用户(万户)	Number of Subscribers of Intemet Services (10 000 subscribers)			33.93	116.79
国内贸易	**Domestic Trade**				
社会消费品零售总额 (亿元)	Total Retail Sales of Consumer Goods (100 mil. yuan)	186.60	360.42	670.56	1381.12
对外经济贸易	**Foreign Trade**				
进出口总额(万美元)	Total Exports and Imports(USD 10 000)	137510	173696	390146	724618
出口额	Exports	110163	106062	263441	333114
进口额	Imports	27347	67634	126705	391504
国际旅游	**International Tourism**				
国际旅游者人数(万人次)	Number of International Tourists(10 000 persons)	41.35	65.03	77.56	67.29
国际旅游收入(亿元)	Foreign Exchange Earnings from Tourism (10 000yuan)	10.38	22.41	33.54	31.05
金融业	**Financial Intermediation**				
金融机构（不含外资）人民币存款余额(亿元)	Balance of Deposits in Domestic Funded Financial Institutions (100 mil. yuan)	359.51	1335.63	3599.7	7457.71
金融机构（不含外资）人民币贷款余额 (亿元)	Balance of Loans in Domestic Funded Financial Institutions (100 mil. yuan)	334.50	972.52	2158.10	4436.50
保险公司保费收入(亿元)	insurance premium income (100 million Yuan)	4.70	13.58	44.94	122.11
保险公司赔款支出及各项给付金额 (亿元)	insurance and compensation paid to Amount (100 million Yuan)	1.70	1.39	9.50	25.16

注：2006年铁路数据按新口径统计；
2006年国际互联网络用户改为互联网宽带用户。

continued 2

2010	2011	2012	2013	速度指标（%） Indices and Growth Rates（%）						
				指数（2013比以下各年） (2013 as percentage of the following years)				平均增长速度 Average Annual Growth Rate		
				2000	2005	2010	2012	2001-2005	2006-2010	2011-2013
34323	39231	44924	50119	716.1	415.9	146.0	111.6	11.5	23.3	13.5
706	823	825	858	27.7	158.9	121.5	104.0	-29.5	5.5	6.7
33610	38399	44082	49243	1265.9	428.0	146.5	111.7	24.2	23.9	13.6
7	9	17	18	225.0	300.0	257.1	105.9	-5.6	3.1	37.0
30294	33375	36154	38289	474.6	365.4	126.4	105.9	5.4	23.7	8.1
2781	2861	2919	3071	144.2	171.0	110.4	105.2	-3.4	9.1	3.4
26536	29358	30893	32614	584.7	393.2	122.9	105.6	8.3	26.2	7.1
977	1156	2342	2604	723.3	669.4	266.5	111.2	1.6	20.2	38.6
323.11	200.50	216.20	247.94	537.1	187.8	76.7	114.7	23.4	19.6	-8.4
8176	3061	2769	2856	34.7	30.0	34.9	103.1	3.0	-3.0	-29.6
449.0	441.5	878.3	835.9	408.2	182.8	186.2	95.2	17.4	-0.4	23.0
261.77	270.36	311.02	319.11	225.9	99.3	121.9	102.6	20.9	-4.0	6.8
228.27	238.34	277.43	286.05	230.2	105.4	125.3	103.1	20.4	-3.4	7.8
33.50	32.02	33.59	33.06	194.2	66.0	98.7	98.4	24.1	-7.7	-0.4
1423.08	1614.15	1803.54	2160.67	2955.8	514.5	151.8	119.8	41.9	27.6	14.9
146.18	184.10	202.31	267.05		787.1	182.7	132.0		33.9	22.2
1637.04	1965.98	2263.86	2580.42	715.9	384.8	157.6	114.0	13.2	19.5	16.4
1039273	1260179	1301446	1798534	1035.4	461.0	173.1	138.2	17.6	21.6	20.1
531729	582662	729878	847819	799.4	321.8	159.4	116.2	20.0	15.1	16.8
507544	677517	571568	950715	1405.7	750.3	187.3	166.3	13.4	32.0	23.3
84.18	100.23	115.35	121.11	186.2	156.2	143.9	105.0	3.6	1.7	12.9
42.40	51.28	59.89	64.16	286.3	191.3	151.3	107.1	8.4	4.8	14.8
8863.36	10350.80	12044.68	13665.89	1023.2	379.6	154.2	113.5	21.9	19.7	15.5
6420.72	7496.25	8559.27	9930.04	1021.1	460.1	154.7	116.0	17.3	24.4	15.6
129.38	162.57	173.21	202.41	1490.5	450.4	156.4	116.9	27.0	23.6	16.1
26.39	37.14	47.55	66.49	4783.5	699.9	252.0	139.8	46.9	24.8	36.1

1-11 续表3

指 标	Item	总量指标			
		1995	2000	2005	2009
教育、科技、文化	**Education, Science and Technology and Culture**				
教育	**Education**				
专任教师数(人)	Full-time Teachers(person)				
#普通高等学校	Institutions of Higher Education	15914	15679	29498	40605
普通中等专业教育学校	Regular Specialized Secondary Schools	2533	3172	2130	1720
普通中等教育学校	Regular Secondary Education Schools	21984	26230	31094	31415
小 学	Primary Schools	30270	30215	29647	30334
在校学生数(万人)	Students Enrollment(10 000 person)				
#普通高等学校	Institutions of Higher Education	11.67	19.41	53.06	70.31
普通中等专业教育学校	Regular Specialized Secondary Schools	3.74	6.02	6.16	7.44
普通中等教育学校	Regular Secondary Education Schools	32.32	48.31	55.74	50.63
小 学	Primary Schools	79.36	77.81	60.47	52.52
科技	**Science and Technology**				
高新技术企业(个)	Hi-tech Enterprises (unit)				
企事业单位累计授权专利数（件）	Accumulated patents awarded(unit)	3164	6139	11670	23962
文化	**Accumulated patents awarded(unit)**				
图书馆总藏量(千册件)	Total Collections in Library (1000 Volume-time)	2830	3214	3671	4324
文化馆、站（个)	Cultural Centers or Stations (unit)	201	251	192	197
电视节目制作时间(小时)	Time for TV Programs Production(hour)	5738	11871	27377	27131
家庭、生活、环境	**Family, People's Livelihood and Environment**				
家庭	**Family**				
家庭总户数 (万户)	Total Number of Households(10 000 household)	171.25	187.08	203.04	221.51
城镇居民平均每户家庭人口(人)	Average Household Size in Urban Areas(person)	3.88	2.99	2.93	2.84
农村居民平均每户家庭人口(人)	Average Household Size in Rural Areas(person)	4.60	4.30	4.22	4.07
婚姻	**Marriages and Divorces**				
结婚(对)	Register Number of Marriages(couple)	47236	46415	49962	88138
离婚(对)	Number of Divorces(couple)	4296	5161	12747	15796
居住	**Housing**				
城镇居民人均现住房总建筑面积(平方米)	Per Capita Total Building Area of Urban Residents' Houses(sq.m)	13.05	14.82	16.38	28.40
农村居民人均居住面积(平方米)	Per Capita Net Floor Space of Rural Residents(sq.m)	21.77	28.31	36.73	56.73

注：2008年及以前图书馆总藏量为图书馆藏书量。
2005年以前城镇居民人均现住房总建筑面积为城镇人均住房使用面积。

continued 3

2010	2011	2012	2013	速度指标（%） Indices and Growth Rates（%）						
				指数（2013比以下各年） (2013 as percentage of the following years)				平均增长速度 Average Annual Growth Rate		
				2000	2005	2010	2012	2001-2005	2006-2010	2011-2013
42098	42734	44487	46436	296.2	157.4	110.3	104.4	13.5	7.4	3.3
1845	1723	1595	1474	46.5	69.2	79.9	92.4	-7.7	-2.8	-7.2
31506	31675	31526	31419	119.8	101.0	99.7	99.7	3.5	0.3	-0.1
29944	29900	29651	29421	97.4	99.2	98.3	99.2	-0.4	0.2	-0.6
73.30	76.60	80.73	83.97	432.6	158.3	114.6	104.0	22.3	6.7	4.6
6.75	6.11	5.43	4.66	77.3	75.6	69.0	85.7	0.7	1.9	-11.6
48.89	47.20	45.33	43.73	90.5	78.5	89.4	96.5	2.9	-2.6	-3.7
51.56	51.39	50.85	51.95	66.8	85.9	100.8	102.2	-4.9	-3.1	0.3
827	978	917	1026			124.1	111.9			7.5
31999	41273	53118	69368	1130.0	594.4	216.8	130.6	13.7	22.4	29.4
4465	4907	6123	6647	206.8	181.1	148.9	108.6	2.7	4.0	14.2
197	196	197	198	78.9	103.1	100.5	100.5	-5.4	0.6	-0.2
29626	43925	30091	46614	392.7	170.3	157.3	154.9	18.2	1.6	16.3
226.71	234.34	239.54	245.53	131.2	120.9	108.3	102.5	1.7	2.2	2.7
2.81	2.83	2.76	2.73	91.3	93.2	97.2	98.9	-0.4	-0.8	-1.0
3.94	3.97	4.09	4.09	95.1	96.9	103.8	100.0	-0.4	-1.6	1.3
83645	94398	89877	89136	192.0	178.4	106.6	99.2	1.5	10.9	2.1
19060	19421	18579	20304	393.4	159.3	106.5	109.3	19.8	8.4	2.1
28.70	28.90	32.98	33.43	225.6	204.1	116.5	101.4	2.0	11.9	5.2
66.73	67	78	81	286.1	220.5	121.4	103.8	5.3	12.7	6.7

1-11 续表4

指 标	Item	总量指标			
		1995	2000	2005	2009
生活	**People's Livelihood**				
城镇居民人均可支配收入(元)	Per Capita Annual Disposable Income of Urban Households (yuan)	4153	6364	9628	18963
农村居民人均纯收入(元)	Per Capita Net Income of Rural Residents(yuan)	1353	2344	3460	6275
城乡储蓄人民币存款余额(亿元)	Savings Deposit of Urban and Rural Households (100 mil. yuan)	230.63	675.83	1716.76	3084.20
工资	**Wages and Welfare**				
在岗职工工资总额(亿元)	The Gross Salary of Workers (100 mil. yuan)	67.23	101.68	211.14	439.74
城镇非私营单位从业人员年平均工资(元)	Aunual Average Wage of Stuff and Workers in Urban Non-privite Enterprises(yuan)	4763	9179	17728	34032
卫生	**Health Care**				
医院、卫生院(个)	Number of Hospitals(unit)	368	426	479	415
执业（助理）医师（人）	Licensed (Assistant) Doctors (person)	18846	18750	17730	19284
医院、卫生院床位数(张)	Number of Hospital Beds(unit)	28265	28697	30087	34904
市政建设	**City Construction**				
自来水供应量(万立方米)	Volume of Tap Water Supply(10 000 cu.m)	35885	30273	35776	38307
自来水供水管道长度(公里)	Length of Water Supply Pipelines(km)	1066	2237	2315	1985
城市天然气供气量 (万立方米)	Volume of Natural Gas Supply in Urban Areas (10 000 cu.m)	8419	11513	53202	95885
公交运营汽(电)车总数(辆)	Total Number of Public Buses and Trolley Buses(unit)	977	2573	4762	7039
道路长度(公里)	Length of Paved Roads(km)	835	975	1382	2296
园林绿地面积(公顷)	Areas of Green Land(hectare)	5603	4116	4867	9553
环境、灾害	**Environment and Disaster**				
工业废水排放量(万吨)	Volume of Waste Water up to the Standard for Discharge(10 000 tons)	12479	9145	16969	13168
火灾发生数(起)	Number of Fire Disasters(case)	426	1040	2664	1485
火灾事故损失额（万元）	Fire Loss(10 000 yuan)	742.1	472.4	1565.5	1850.6
交通事故发生数（起）	Number of Traffic Accidents(case)	3065	4099	4903	2702
交通事故损失额（万元）	Loss of Traffic Accidents(10 000 yuan)	1103.2	1116.1	2024.4	851.7

continued 4

				速度指标（%） Indices and Growth Rates（%）						
				指数（2013比以下各年） (2013 as percentage of the following years)				平均增长速度 Average Annual Growth Rate		
2010	2011	2012	2013	2000	2005	2010	2012	2001-2005	2006-2010	2011-2013
22244	25981	29982	33100	520.1	343.8	148.8	110.4	8.6	18.2	14.2
7750	9788	11442	12930	551.6	373.7	166.8	113.0	8.1	17.5	18.6
3641.09	4155.65	4787.03	5357.05	792.7	312.0	147.1	111.9	20.5	16.2	13.7
501.76	629.35	742.16	987.80	971.5	467.8	196.9	133.1	15.7	18.9	25.3
37870	41679	44533	49350	537.6	278.4	130.3	110.8	14.1	16.4	9.2
412	368	376	381	89.4	79.5	92.5	101.3	2.4	-3.0	-2.6
18763	21551	23051	23885	127.4	134.7	127.3	103.6	-1.1	1.1	8.4
36796	37264	40585	44190	154	146.9	120.1	108.9	1.0	4.1	6.3
41089	38934	45792	51372	169.7	143.6	125.0	112.2	3.4	2.8	7.7
2416	2721	3208	3385	151.3	146.2	140.1	105.5	0.7	0.9	11.9
109052	120330	142263	153489	1333.2	288.5	140.7	107.9	35.8	15.4	12.1
7107	7462	7695	8128	315.9	170.7	114.4	105.6	13.1	8.3	4.6
2662	2755	3119	3387	347.4	245.1	127.3	108.6	7.2	14.0	8.4
12140	13680	15196	17751	431.3	364.7	146.2	116.8	3.4	20.1	13.5
13840	13148	10224	8973	98.1	52.9	64.8	87.8	13.2	-4.0	-13.5
1825	1920	2568	4062	390.6	152.5	222.6	158.2	20.7	-7.3	30.6
2224.2	1587.2	2793.7	3011.9	637.6	192.4	135.4	107.8	27.1	7.3	10.6
2323	2264	2446	2252	54.9	45.9	96.9	92.1	3.6	-13.9	-1.0
736.6	611.9	1011.1	1143.9	102.5	56.5	155.3	113.1	12.6	-18.3	15.8

1-12 国民经济和社会发展结构指标

Structural Indicators on National Economic and Social Development

单位: % (%)

指标	Item	2000	2005	2008	2009	2010	2011	2012	2013
人口与就业	**Population and Employment**								
人口	**Population**								
农业与非农业结构	Structure								
农业	Agriculture	58.46	55.09	52.88	52.58	52.14	50.58	50.75	49.21
非农业	Non-Agriculture	41.54	44.91	47.12	47.42	47.86	49.42	49.25	50.79
性别结构	Sexual Structure								
男	Male	51.62	51.50	51.22	51.08	50.95	50.83	49.95	50.66
女	Female	48.38	48.50	48.78	48.92	49.05	49.17	50.05	49.34
就业	**Employment**								
从业人员产业结构	Industrial Structure								
第一产业	Primary Industry	37.78	32.78	28.50	26.40	25.65	24.41	22.33	20.81
第二产业	Secondary Industry	27.57	27.46	29.10	28.45	29.65	30.51	31.55	28.55
第三产业	Tertiary Industry	34.65	39.76	42.40	45.15	44.70	45.08	46.12	50.64
宏观经济	**Macro Economy**								
国民经济核算	**National Accounting**								
生产总值产业结构	Industrial Structure								
第一产业	Primary Industry	6.91	5.02	4.46	4.05	4.32	4.48	4.48	4.46
第二产业	Secondary Industry	42.89	41.14	42.34	42.02	43.39	43.35	43.10	43.36
第三产业	Tertiary Industry	50.20	53.84	53.20	53.93	52.29	52.17	52.42	52.18
生产总值支出结构	Structure of Gross Domestic by Expenditures								
最终消费	Total Consumption	63.99	58.35	51.02	51.51	49.31	48.07	47.93	
资本形成总额	Total Investment	44.55	63.85	79.28	83.77	87.47	84.52	86.65	
货物和服务净出口	Net Export of Goods and Services	-8.54	-22.20	-30.30	-35.28	-36.78	-32.60	-34.58	
投 资	**Investment**								
全社会固定资产投资结构	Structure of Total Investment in Fixed Assets								
城乡结构	Urban and Rural Composition								
城镇	Urban Area	87.36	92.96	93.72	94.70	95.52	95.87	96.80	97.03
#房地产	Real Estate	22.31	27.00	28.34	27.85	25.91	29.79	30.21	31.08
农村	Rural Area	12.64	7.04	6.28	5.30	4.48	4.13	3.20	2.97
经济成分结构	Registion Status Composition								
国有经济	State-owned Enterprises Investment	68.68	44.75	36.45	37.31	41.49	36.00	39.15	34.49
集体经济	Collective-owned Enterprises Investment	6.30	7.09	12.95	11.60	10.04	7.71	4.59	4.28
个体经济	Self-employed Individual	10. 50	9.46	2.65	3.91	1.68	2.23	1.95	1.64
其他经济	Other	14.51	38.69	47.95	47.18	46.78	54.05	54.31	59.58

1-12 续表1 continued 1

单位:% (%)

指标	Item	2000	2005	2008	2009	2010	2011	2012	2013
财 政	**Government Finance**								
财政收入结构	Structure of Government Revenue								
#中 央	Central Government	31.94	58.30	39.49	39.68	37.28	35.78	32.37	30.80
地 方	Local Governments	68.06	41.70	44.87	45.32	47.36	49.02	52.71	55.60
产 业	**Industrial**								
农 业	**Agriculture**								
农林牧渔及服务业总产值结构	Structure of Gross Output Value of Farming,Forestry,Animal Husbandry, Fishery and Service								
农 业	Farming	69.23	61.69	56.85	59.42	63.36	63.42	62.69	53.38
林 业	Forestry	1.14	1.23	1.13	1.27	1.18	1.27	2.02	2.34
牧 业	Animal Husbandry	28.58	30.96	33.52	30.56	27.72	27.68	26.60	25.19
渔 业	Fishery	1.05	0.69	0.66	0.66	0.56	0.55	0.65	0.66
农林牧渔服务业	Farming,Forestry,Animal Husbandry and Fishery		5.43	7.84	8.09	7.18	7.09	8.04	8.42
工 业	**Industry**								
工业总产值经济类型结构	Structure of Gross Output Value of Industry by Registion Status								
国有经济	State-owned Enterprises	43.00	45.21	52.26	51.07	51.52	50.46	52.20	
集体经济	Collective-owned Enterprises	32.76	5.16	1.85	1.38	1.22	0.92	0.81	
其他经济类型	Others	24.24	49.63	45.89	47.55	47.26	48.62	46.99	
工业总产值轻重结构	Structure of Gross Output Value of Industry by Ligth Industry and Heavy Industry								
轻工业	Light Industry	48.81	31.17	25.17	23.47	22.01	21.97	21.95	
重工业	Heavy Industry	51.19	68.83	74.83	76.53	77.99	78.03	78.05	
工业总产值规模结构	Structure of Gross Output Value of Industry by Size of Enterprises								
大型企业	Large Enterprises	36.29	35.46	43.85	43.54	42.11	41.15	48.46	
中型企业	Medium-sized Enterprises	5.14	24.67	20.96	21.88	23.96	15.17	13.41	
小型企业	Small Enterprises	58.57	39.87	35.19	34.58	33.93	43.68	38.13	

注：本表2008年以后财政收入结构中地方指地方财政一般预算收入。

1–12 续表2 continued 2

单位: % (%)

指 标	Item	2000	2005	2008	2009	2010	2011	2012	2013
建筑业	**Construction**								
建筑业总产值结构	Structure of Gross Output Value of Construction Industry								
房屋建筑业	Building Construction	9.28	34.05	29.80	25.50	24.63	36.81	43.03	43.03
土木工程建筑业	Civil Engineering Construction	88.50	56.59	59.14	67.14	68.61	53.75	47.57	47.86
建筑安装业	Installation of Construction					4.39	6.70	6.49	5.86
建筑装饰和其他建筑业	Decoration and others	2.22	9.36	11.06	7.36	2.37	2.74	2.91	3.25
交通运输业	**Transportation**								
客运量结构	Structure of Freight Traffic								
铁 路	Railways	26.40	17.14	10.11	9.01	9.18	8.57	8.07	8.02
公 路	Highways	69.14	79.15	87.45	88.07	87.59	87.96	85.45	85.18
民用航空	Civil Aviation	4.46	3.71	2.44	2.92	3.23	3.46	6.48	6.80
货运量结构	Structure of Freight Traffic								
铁 路	Railways	44.30	26.92	2.20	2.01	2.06	2.10	1.84	1.71
公 路	Highways	55.58	73.04	97.78	97.97	97.92	97.88	98.13	98.25
民用航空	Civil Aviation	0.12	0.04	0.02	0.02	0.02	0.02	0.04	0.04
国内贸易	**Domestic Trade**								
社会消费品零售总额结构	Composition of Retail Sales of Consumer Goods								
城镇	Urban Area	87.99	90.17	90.43	90.49	95.91	97.08	96.97	96.96
农村	Rural Area	12.01	9.83	9.57	9.51	4.09	2.92	3.03	3.04
国际旅游	**International Tourism**								
国际旅游人数结构	Structure of Tourists								
外国人	Foreigners	84.03	84.91	84.78	87.81	86.97	88.43	87.91	88.26
华侨及港澳台同胞	Overseas Chinese and Compatriots form Hong Kong, Macao and Taiwan	15.97	15.09	15.22	12.19	13.03	11.58	12.08	11.74
教育文化、卫生、人民生活	**Education and Culture，Health Care，People's Livelihood**								
教 育	**Education**								
在校学生结构	Structure of Student Enrollment								
#普通高等学校	Institutions of Higher Education	12.44	28.48	30.53	31.54	32.60	29.74	31.00	33.15
普通中等专业教育学校	Regular Specialized Secondary Schools	3.84	3.33	3.71	3.32	3.02	2.37	2.08	1.84
普通中等教育学校	Regular Secondary Education Schools	30.93	29.89	24.17	22.70	21.74	18.32	17.40	17.26
小学	Primary Schools	49.89	32.45	25.03	23.56	22.95	19.95	19.52	20.51

1-12 续表3 continued 3

单位: % (%)

指　标	Item	2000	2005	2008	2009	2010	2011	2012	2013
专任教师结构	Full-time Teachers by Type								
#普通高等学校	Institutions of Higher Education	19.89	29.93	31.63	31.90	32.47	31.97	32.96	33.91
普通中等专业教育学校	Regular Specialized Secondary Schools	4.02	2.16	1.55	1.35	1.42	1.29	1.18	1.08
普通中等教育学校	Regular Secondary Education Schools	33.21	31.55	25.53	24.68	24.30	23.70	23.36	22.95
小学	Primary Schools	38.34	30.08	24.68	23.83	23.10	22.37	21.97	21.49
人民生活	**People's Livelihood**								
城镇居民消费结构	Consumption Structure of Urban Residents								
食　品	Food	36.46	37.04	36.40	32.43	31.29	31.29	32.48	32.44
衣　着	Clothing	8.13	9.03	10.25	10.98	11.11	12.27	12.17	12.02
家庭设备用品及服务	Household facilities,Articles and Services	11.33	4.73	6.33	7.28	7.56	8.11	7.87	7.80
医疗保健	Health Care	7.23	9.45	9.67	9.65	9.50	9.00	8.52	7.99
交通和通信	Transportation and Communication	6.93	9.67	10.37	11.33	12.06	12.81	14.26	14.01
教育文化娱乐服务	Recreation,Education and Culture Articles	13.74	17.18	14.35	14.34	14.66	14.27	14.33	14.17
居　住	Residence	11.23	9.10	8.81	8.86	9.33	8.26	8.47	7.82
杂项商品和服务	Articles for Daily Use and Others	4.95	3.80	3.82	5.13	4.49	4.00	1.91	3.76
农村居民消费结构	Consumption Structure of Rural Residents								
食品消费支出	Food	36.63	36.34	36.95	35.81	32.54	31.89	33.83	32.96
衣　着	Clothing	6.65	6.11	6.52	6.40	6.55	7.20	7.42	7.87
居　住	Residence	21.41	17.76	19.39	19.47	24.41	23.92	21.91	19.82
家庭设备用品及服务	Household facilities,Articles and Services	5.47	5.11	7.02	6.97	6.53	7.10	7.46	7.76
医疗保健	Health Care	6.93	8.19	8.05	8.50	8.54	8.65	8.85	8.41
交通和通讯	Transportation and Communication	4.21	8.19	7.84	9.83	8.45	9.01	10.19	9.86
文化娱乐用品及服务	Recreation,Education and Culture Articles	14.49	16.15	12.43	11.13	11.20	10.43	10.20	10.56
其它商品及服务	Articles for Daily Use and Others	4.21	2.15	1.80	1.89	1.78	1.80	0.14	2.77
卫　生	**Health Care**								
卫生技术人员结构	Medical Technical Personnel by Types								
执业（助理）医师	Licensed（Assistant） Doctors	44.82	41.96	38.09	37.34	33.16	35.17	34.46	33.58
注册护士	Registered Nurses	34.29	33.14	36.23	39.05	40.01	40.87	41.61	42.13
药　师	Junior Paramedics	8.31	7.30	5.74	5.45	5.36	5.10	5.05	4.99
技　师	Technicians	5.21	5.33	6.68	6.49	8.11	5.91	5.91	5.75
其　他	Others	7.37	12.27	13.26	11.67	13.36	12.95	12.97	13.55

1-13 国民经济和社会发展比例和效益指标

指　标	Item	1995
人口与就业	**Population and Employment**	
人口	**Population**	
出生率(‰)	Birth Rate(‰)	11.95
死亡率(‰)	Death Rate(‰)	4.98
自然增长率(‰)	Natural Growth Rate(‰)	6.79
就业	**Employment**	
就业者负担人口	Dependency Ratio	1.7
三次产业就业者比例	Employment Ratio by Type of Industry	
(以第一产业为100)	(Employment in primary industry=100)	100
第一产业	Primary Industry	71.5
第二产业	Secondary Industry	71.4
第三产业	Tertiary Industry	3.1
城镇登记失业率(%)	Unemployment Rate in Urban Areas(%)	
宏观经济	**Macro Economy**	
国民经济核算	**National Accounting**	
三次产业增加值比例	Ratio of Value-added by Type of Industry	
(以第一产业为100)	(Employment in primary industry=100)	
第一产业	Primary Industry	100
第二产业	Secondary Industry	326.9
第三产业	Tertiary Industry	371.1
全社会劳动生产率(元／人)	Overall Labor Productivity(yuan/person)	8963
第一产业	Primary Industry	2698
第二产业	Secondary Industry	12404
第三产业	Tertiary Industry	14488
人均生产总值(元)	Per Capita GDP(yuan)	5131
固定资产投资	**Investment in Fixed Assets**	
全社会固定资产投资相当于生产总值比例(%)	Proportion of Investment in fixed Assets to GDP(%)	31.3
房屋建筑面积竣工率(%)	Rate of Floor Space of Buildings Completed in Construction(%)	33.4
固定资产交付使用率(%)	Rate of Fixed Assets Completed in Capital Construction and Put into Use(%)	70.7
建设项目建成投产率(%)	Rate of Projects Completed in Capital Construction and Put into Use(%)	43.7
财政	**Finance**	
财政总收入相当于生产总值比例(%)	Proportion of Local Government Revenue to GDP(%)	5.5
一般预算支出相当于生产总值比例(%)	Proportion of Local Government Expenditures to GDP(%)	5.6
利用外资	**Utilization of Foreign Capital**	
外商实际直接投资额相当于利用外资协议金额比例(%)	Proportion of Foreign Capital Actually Used to Total Amount of Foreign Capital for Utilization by Signed Contracts or Agreements (%)	64.4

注：本表财政收入数据2009年及以前为一般预算财政收入和基金收入之和。

Indicators on Proportions and Efficiency in National Economic and Social Development

2000	2004	2005	2006	2007	2008	2009	2010	2011	2012	2013
13.07	9.19	9.58	9.98	10.00	10.15	10.08	9.73	9.71	10.13	9.57
5.96	5.87	5.16	5.46	5.48	5.57	5.63	5.34	5.38	5.57	5.37
7.11	3.32	4.42	4.52	4.52	4.58	4.45	4.39	4.33	4.56	4.20
1.8	1.8	1.8	1.8	1.9	1.9	1.9	1.8	1.7	1.7	1.6
100	100	100	100	100	100	100	100	100	100	100
73.0	78.8	83.8	85.9	93.8	101.9	107.7	124.0	125.0	141.3	137.2
91.7	100.1	121.3	126.5	133.5	148.6	171.0	183.3	184.7	206.5	243.3
3.4	4.3	4.3	4.3	4.3	4.2	4.3	4.2	3.9	3.5	3.4
100	100	100	100	100	100	100	100	100	100	100
620.7	792.1	818.8	916.6	947.7	948.8	1037.1	1004.4	967.0	962.1	972.5
726.4	938.8	1071.7	1168.2	1202.5	1192.0	1330.8	1210.1	1163.9	1170.2	1170.4
16367	27069	31837	36730	43252	52422	59832	68965	79349	86410	93451
2960	4174	4747	5191	6148	7921	8830	11452	14530	16578	19325
25443	43199	47853	56073	64851	76899	87452	102992	112851	119979	134947
24024	37040	44024	48938	56870	67031	73674	80267	91908	99315	100728
9484	15294	16406	18890	22463	27794	32411	38343	45475	51166	56988
36.0	58.7	65.8	72.4	81.4	82.2	91.8	100.3	86.6	97.2	105.1
42.0	24.4	28.1	26.1	29.0	16.9	16.0	6.9	10.0	8.7	13.2
74.0	42.8	52.8	46.6	49.8	40.5	42.8	38.4	40.4	42.4	37.1
44.2	41.5	54.2	47.0	40.6	53.3	72.5	53.9	54.9	56.1	56.1
7.3	7.8	6.6	6.5	7.1	10.9	12.2	15.8	16.8	17.2	13.5
8.0	8.1	8.1	9.1	9.9	14.5	15.4	11.5	12.8	13.7	14.9
28.38	35.24	47.01	45.18	77.49	97.05	203.03	130.9	167.0	68.8	124.3

1-13 续表1

指　　标	Item	1995
能　源	**Energy**	
单位生产总值能耗降低率（%）	Decreasing Rate of Energy Consumption per Unit GDP(%)	
规模以上工业单位工业增加值能耗降低率（%）	Decreasing Rate of Energy Consumption per Unit Industrial value-added of Industry Above Designated Size(%)	
单位生产总值电耗降低率（%）	Decreasing Rate of Electricity Consumption per Unit GDP(%)	
产　业	**Industries**	
农业	**Agriculture**	
人均耕地面积(公顷)	Per Capita Cultivated Land(hectare)	0.08
农业从业者人均耕地面积(公顷)	Cultivated Land per Agricultural Laborer(hectare)	0.2
每公顷耕地农业机械总动力(千瓦)	Total Power of Agricultural Machinery per Hectare of Cultivated Land(kw)	5.23
每公顷耕地化肥施用量(公斤)	Chemical Fertilizer Consumption per Hectare of Cultivated Land(kg)	536
每公顷耕地生产的农业总产值(元)	Agricultural Output Value per Hectare of Cultivated Land(yuan)	24396
每个农林牧渔及服务业劳动力农产品生产量(公斤)	Output of Farm Products per Farming,Forestry,Animal Husbandry,Fishery and Service Husbandry and Fishery Laborer (kg)	
粮食	Grain	1150
蔬菜	Vegetables	877
禽蛋	Poultry Eggs	93
肉类	Meat	84
水产品	Aquatic Products	6
每公顷播种面积农产品产量(公斤)	Output of Farm Crops per Hectare of Sown Area(kg)	
粮食	Grain	3806
油料	Oil-bearing Crops	1753
蔬菜	Vegetables	34800
工业	**Industrial**	
规模以上工业企业经济效益	**Economic Benefit of Industrial Enterprises above Designated Size**	
总资产贡献率（%）	Ratio of Total Assets to Industrial Output Value (%)	
资产负债率（%）	Assets-Liability Ratio (%)	
流动资产周转次数（次/年）	Rate of Annual Turnover Working Capitals(times/year)	
成本费用利润率（%）	Ratio of Profits to Cost (%)	
产品销售率（%）	Proportion of Industrial Products Sold(%)	
全员劳动生产率（元/人）	Overall Labor Productivity (yuan/person)	
建筑业	**Construction**	
机械装备率(元／人)	Value of Machinery per Laborer(yuan/person)	5990
产值利润率(%)	Ratio of Per-tax Profits to Gross Output Value (%)	3.5
全员劳动生产率(元／人)(按总产值计算)	Overall Labor Productivity(yuan/person) (in terms of gross output value per employee)	37689
邮电通信业	**Post and Communication Services**	
电话普及率(含移动电话）(部/百人)	Access to Telephones, National(include mobilphone) (set/100 persons)	7.9
移动电话普及率(部/百人)	Access to Mobilphones (set/100 persons)	0.48

continued 1

2000	2004	2005	2006	2007	2008	2009	2010	2011	2012	2013
			4.15	5.75	6.65	5.56	2.06	3.56	3.51	3.57
			3.04	12.56	13.43	10.48	12.18	15.44	10.52	17.69
			4.48	6.94	6.93	5.33	1.00	4.43	2.92	2.26
0.07	0.07	0.07	0.06	0.06	0.06	0.06	0.06	0.06	0.06	0.06
0.2	0.19	0.22	0.23	0.25	0.21	0.21	0.22	0.22	0.22	0.23
6.78	7.93	8.39	8.63	8.99	10.41	10.12	10.48	11.5	12.1	12.73
654	780	794	819	843	867	891	922	953	987	982
25161	35862	39937	43261	51351	64593	69106	88869	108457	125041	140441
1382	1392	1493	1569	1433	1695	1792	1901	1567	1700	1688
1110	1287	1421	1536	1549	1752	1990	2171	2253	2452	2748
95	84	86	92	74	86	96	106	108	115	125
101	122	132	145	77	91	104	117	124	134	145
8	7	7	7	9	10	11	10	10	12	13
4342	4656	4796	5025	4452	5102	5206	5349	4764	5045	4337
1526	1758	1821	1880	1934	2008	1956	2004	1988	1987	1956
37797	35002	35231	35916	33677	35723	38344	39667	40475	42607	44767
	6.9	8.4	7.8	10.2	8.6	11.3	12.2	8.6	7.7	7.9
65	65.2	65	64.3	64.6	62.6	61.1	57.6	57.7	59.4	58.9
1.0	1.2	1.3	1.4	1.6	1.5	1.7	1.7	1.5	1.5	1.4
4.2	5.0	3.1	5.5	7.3	4.6	8.1	8.8	5.2	4.5	4.7
97.1	97.9	97.5	98.2	96.8	96.1	97.6	97.1	97.4	96.7	95.2
29496	66752	82815	97561	129705	150641	161289	188483	194105	230032	264324
6805	13240	13332	13502	9079	12026	11928	9461	28669	12216	10339
3.4	4.4	4.8	4.5	5.2	6.0	6.3	4.4	4.4	2.8	2.6
74347	163414	206337	241887	203994	226669	285854	321340	334172	479232	354419
31.2	88.8	100.0	111.1	117.9	124.7	167.1	199.0	221.3	247.2	288.7
10.62	48.29	56.62	66.99	80.02	88.09	132.79	168.00	189.58	210.87	251.59

1–13 续表2

指　　标	Item	1995
国内贸易	**Domestic Trade**	
人均批发零售和住宿餐饮业消费品零售额(元)	Per Capita Retail Sales of Wholesale,Retail Trade and Accommodation Catering Trade (yuan)	1979
对外经济贸易	**Foreign Trade**	
进出口总额相当于生产总值比例(%)	Proportion of Total Imports & Exports to GDP(%)	34.76
国际旅游	**International Tourism**	
每一来华游客花费(元)	Expenditure per International Tourist in China(yuan)	2511
金融业	**Finance and Insurance**	
金融机构存款相当于生产总值比例(%)	Bank Deposits as Percentage of GDP(%)	108.83
金融机构贷款相当于生产总值比例(%)	Bank Loans as Percentage of GDP(%)	101.26
教育、科技、文化	**Education, Science and Technology and Culture**	
教育	**Education**	
毕业率(%)	Graduation Rate(%)	
小学	Primary Schools	
初中	Junior Schools	
学校教师负担系数	Student-teacher Ratio(in percentage)	
高等学校	Colleges and Universities	6.83
中等学校	Secondary Schools	14.42
小学	Primary Schools	26.22
文化	**Culture (unit)**	
每百万人有艺术表演团体(个)	Number of Troupes per Million Persons(unit)	3.39
每百万人有公共图书馆(个)	Number of Public Libraries per Million Persons(unit)	2.31
家庭、生活、环境	**Family, People's Livelihood and Environment**	
家庭	**Family**	
城市居民家庭	Urban Households	
平均每户就业面（%）	Percentage of Employees Per Household (%)	55.9
每一就业者负担人数(人)	Persons Supported by Each Laborer (person)	1.79
农村居民家庭	Rural Households	
平均每一劳动力负担人口（人）	Persons Supported by Each Laborer(person)	1.58
卫生	**Health Care**	
每万人医院数、卫生院(个)	Number of Hospitals per 10 000 Persons(unit)	0.6
每万人医生数(人)	Number of Doctors per 10 000 Persons(person)	29.1
每万人医院、卫生院床位数(张)	Number of Hospital Beds per 10 000 Persons(unit)	43.6
市政建设	**City Construction**	
城市自来水普及率(%)	Percentage of Households with Access to Tap Water(%)	
城市用气普及率(%)	Percentage of Households with Access to Tap Gas (%)	
人均公园绿地面积(平方米)	Public Green Areas per 10 000 Persons(hectare)	3.8

continued 2

2000	2004	2005	2006	2007	2008	2009	2010	2011	2012	2013
4027	7859	8795	9437	10932	13840	16432	19363	23145	26529	30108
22.25	23.29	24.79	22.01	22.21	21.97	18.17	21.20	20.56	18.74	22.45
3445	4212	4324	4353	4242	4544	4614	5037	5116	5192	5298
206.71	277.73	283.41	275.92	259.8	264.31	279.84	278.99	267.98	275.87	279.8
150.51	186.17	169.91	159.11	152.16	149.22	166.65	203.30	194.07	196.04	203.31
							100.4	100.2	100.2	99.82
							99.7	100.6	98.7	99.27
12.38	16.69	17.99	17.36	16.97	17.13	17.32	17.41	17.92	18.15	18.08
17.34	18.78	18.47	20.51	19.99	18.97	18.27	17.78	16.91	16.43	15.07
25.75	21.71	20.38	19.78	18.61	17.99	17.32	17.22	18.06	17.15	17.66
3.20	3.03	2.56	2.31	2.16	2.15	2.13	1.53	3.52	2.22	2.10
2.18	2.07	2.02	1.82	1.31	1.79	1.78	1.77	1.76	1.75	1.75
45.73	48.80	47.44	48.30	47.77	47.87	53.2	53.7	54.8	54.0	54.6
2.19	2.05	2.11	2.07	2.09	2.09	1.88	1.86	1.83	1.85	1.83
1.57	1.56	1.6	1.59	1.57	1.5	1.5	1.5	1.5	1.5	1.5
0.57	0.4	0.59	0.58	0.55	0.52	0.49	0.49	0.43	0.44	0.44
25.3	20.4	21.98	21.89	20.79	21.57	22.86	22.14	25.31	26.95	27.81
38.72	39.1	37.29	37.49	37.11	39.40	41.38	43.42	43.77	47.45	51.45
98.95	99.09	99.00	99.09	100.01	111.22	100.00	98.77	99.95	100.00	100.00
81.51	91.20	91.30	92.62	98.60	97.66	98.15	97.02	97.46	98.19	98.68
5.12	5.03	5.63	7.59	7.61	7.80	7.90	9.11	9.89	10.22	10.70

1-14 平均每天主要社会经济活动

指　　标	Item	1995	2000
一、每天创造的财富	**Daily Production**		
生产总值(万元)	Gross Domestic Product(10 000 yuan)	9050.7	17702.2
第一产业	Primary Industry	1134.3	1223.3
第二产业	Secondary Industry	3707.7	7592.6
工业	Industry	3082.2	5984.7
建筑业	Construction	625.5	1608
第三产业	Tertiary Industry	4208.8	8886.3
#交通运输、仓储及邮政业	Transport, Storage, Post & Telecommunication Services	674	1709.3
批发和零售业	Wholesale and Retail Trade		
住宿和餐饮业	Hotels and Catering Services		
财政总收入(万元)	Total Government Revenue(10 000 yuan)	498.8	1304
财政一般预算支出(万元)	Government General Budgetary Expenditures(10 000 yuan)	504.7	1274.1
粮食(吨)	Grain(ton)	4801.0	5532.0
奶类(吨)	Milk(ton)	364	674
蔬菜(吨)	Vegetables(ton)	3660	4442
肉类(吨)	Meat(ton)	350	404
水产品(吨)	Aquatic Products(ton)	23	31
布(万米)	Cloth(10 000 m)	83	77
发电量(万千瓦小时)	Electricity(10 000 kwh)	610	534
钢材(吨)	Steel(ton)	861	274
汽车(辆)	Motor Vehicle(unit)	8	25
二、每天消费量	**Daily National Consumption**		
最终消费(万元)	Final Consumption Expenditure(10 000 yuan)	6565.5	11326.9
社会消费品零售总额(万元)	Total Retail Sales of Consumer Goods (10 000 yuan)	5112.3	9874.5
三、每天其他经济活动	**Other Daily Economic Activities**		
资本形成总额(万元)	Gross Capital Formation(10 000 yuan)	4152.1	7885.5
#固定资本形成	Fixed Capital Formation		
存货增加	Changes in Stock		
竣工住宅面积(平方米)	Floor Space of Buildings Completed (sq.m)	6927	14930
货运量(万吨)	Freight Traffic(10 000 tons)	26	19
客运量(万人次)	Passenger Traffic(10 000 person-times)	25	22
邮电业务总量(万元)	Business Volume of Postal and Telecommunications Services(10 000 yuan)	210	1265
进出口总额(万美元)	Total Value of Imports and Exports (USD 10 000)	110.2	475.9
出口额	Exports	82.5	290.6
进口额	Imports	27.7	185.3
外商实际直接投资额(万美元)	Foreign Capital Actually Used(USD 10 000)	51.1	42.8
国际旅游人数(人次)	Number of Tourists from Abroad(person-time)	1134	1782
四、每天人口变动和婚姻	**Daily Population Changes and Marriages**		
出　生(人)	Births(person)	211	247
死　亡(人)	Deaths(person)	88	113
结　婚(对)	Marriages(couple)	129	129
离　婚(对)	Divorces(couple)	12	14

注：本表财政收入数据2009年及以前为一般预算财政收入和基金收入之和。

Selected Indicators on Average Daily Social and Economic Activities

2005	2007	2008	2009	2010	2011	2012	2013
35998.1	50866.6	63510.7	74632.3	88813.4	105824.1	119619.2	133811.8
1808.5	2260.6	2834.3	3024.1	3837.3	4743.6	5353.6	5966
14808.2	21423.0	26892.6	31363.0	38540.3	45871.5	51554.8	58018.1
11506.9	16300.0	19764.4	22381.4	27495.1	32592.1	36403.0	
3301.4	5123.0	7128.2	8981.6	11045.2	13279.5	15151.8	
19381.4	27183.0	33783.8	40245.2	46435.9	55209.0	62705.8	69827.7
1816.4	2307.1	2716.7	3030.1	3416.2	4044.9	4597.9	
4032.9	5356.4	6655.1	8028.8	9256.4	11477.8	13323.8	
1381.9	1920.3	2346.6	2576.7	2837.8	3405.2	3754.0	
2300.6	3433.6	6417.8	9080.0	13991.5	17805.0	20632.1	24733.3
2819.6	4771.4	8679.2	11509.0	10181.4	13550.0	16369.6	19994.8
5631	5180	5874	5978	6074	4987	5275	5017
1157	1447	1616	1694	1736	1775	1826	1802
5362	5601	6069	6641	6934	7169	7611	8168
499	280	316	346	374	396	416	431
26	34	34	36	33	32	38	39
74.0	76.7	62.3	60.8	65.2	44.8	39.2	38.4
1316	1946	1964	2280	2656	2603	2726	5055
658	2157	1312	3028	3035	506	857	1488
112	468	734	1389	1787	1525	1484	1156
21003.3	27266.3	32400.3	38441.1	43794.8	50874.2	57341.6	
18371.5	25649.6	32235.1	37838.9	44850.4	53862.5	62023.6	70696.4
22986.6	39766.3	50352.3	62518.1	77682.7	89447.4	103546.6	
20918.4	34795.6	45315.3	58878.9	72237.8	83395.6	97509.0	
2068.2	4970.7	5037.0	3639.2	5444.9	6051.8	5137.5	
16400	25466	18998	22537	12287	23601	24752	23014
33.0	41.4	75.5	83.9	94.0	107.5	123	137
29	34	73	79	83	91	99	105
3618	6213	7256	8190	8852	5495	5924	6793
1068.9	1468.9	1923.9	1985.3	2847.3	3452.5	3565.6	4927.5
721.8	951.0	1225.0	912.6	1456.8	1596.3	1999.7	2322.8
347.1	517.9	703.9	1072.6	1390.5	1856.2	1565.9	2504.7
156.5	305.7	314.4	333.9	429.2	549.4	678.9	357.5
2125	2740	1732	1844	2306	2746	3160	3318
210	226	232	232	225	226	237	225
63	124	127	130	124	125	130	126
137	185	213	241	229	259	246	244
35	43	43	43	52	53	51	56

1-15 各区县国民经济和社会发展主要指标（2013年）

指　标	Item	新城区 Xincheng	碑林区 Beilin
一、年底总人口（常住人口）（万人）	Population at the Year-end Permanent population(10 000 persons)	59.64	62.23
二、生产总值（亿元）	Gross Domestic Product(100 mil. yuan)	471.75	525.76
第一产业	Primary Industry		
第二产业	Secondary Industry	190.16	106.71
工业	Industry		
第三产业	Tertiary Industry	281.59	419.05
三、全社会固定资产投资总额（亿元）	Total Investment in Fixed Assets(100 mil. yuan)	378.67	464.26
#城镇	Urban Area	378.67	464.26
#房地产	Real Estate	79.02	151.01
四、财政一般预算收入（亿元）	Local Financial Revenue(100 mil. yuan)	32.07	39.23
财政一般预算支出（亿元）	Local Financial Expenditure(100 mil. yuan)	28.22	24.05
五、农林牧渔及服务业总产值（万元）	Gross Output Value of Farming Forestry Animal Husbandry and Fishery(10 000 yuan)		
主要农产品产量（万吨）	Output of Major Farm Products(10 000 tons)		
粮食	Grain		
蔬菜	Vegetables		
瓜果	Melon and Fruit		
肉类(吨)	Meat (Ton)		
奶类(吨)	Milk (Ton)		
六、规模以上工业总产值（亿元）	Gross industrial Output Value(100 mil. yuan)		
七、建筑业总产值（亿元）	Gross Output Value(100 mil. yuan)	235.01	524.64
房屋建筑施工面积（万平方米）	Floor Space of Buildings under Construction (10 000 sq.m)	946.8	2803.1
房屋建筑竣工面积（万平方米）	Total Retail Sales of Consumer Goods (100 mil. yuan)	218	728.3
八、社会消费品零售总额（亿元）	Floor Space of Buildings Completed(100 mil. yuan)	450.52	447.04
九、城镇居民人均可支配收入（元）	Per Capita Annual Disposable Income of Urban Households (yuan)	33816	34520
农村居民人均纯收入（元）	Per Capita Net Income of Rural Residents(yuan)		
十、医疗机构数（个）	Number of Health Care Institutions(unit)	280	360
卫生技术人员（人）	Number of Medical Technical Personnel (person)	11248	11105
床位数（张）	Number of Beds(unit)	6988	7202

Principal Indicators of National Economy and Social Development by Region (2013)

莲湖区 Lianhu	灞桥区 Baqiao	未央区 Weiyang	雁塔区 Yanta	阎良区 Yanliang	临潼区 Lintong	长安区 Chang'an	蓝田县 Lantian	周至县 Zhouzhi	户　县 Huxian	高陵县 Gaoling
70.43	60.50	81.84	119.29	23.40	66.81	110.03	52.07	57.24	56.32	34.01
526.68	269.03	601.10	938.75	168.96	226.58	369.15	106.89	87.66	155.24	279.94
	18.32	1.54	2.29	22.01	32.75	34.17	26.40	28.16	27.80	24.32
224.67	157.45	318.24	354.85	94.95	126.49	168.63	40.52	24.30	81.73	228.98
302.01	93.26	281.32	581.61	52.00	67.34	166.35	39.97	35.20	45.71	26.64
583.86	315.69	723.42	1029.24	201.16	196.94	541.53	127.38	115.30	142.41	314.71
583.86	309.16	719.34	1026.08	191.92	183.19	525.85	94.38	91.37	126.40	287.77
220.88	103.88	272.20	593.53	19.27	9.35	93.51	2.74	13.42	10.33	26.50
41.54	20.90	31.37	41.42	10.24	10.30	31.16	3.27	2.86	7.01	11.51
29.05	19.07	20.79	27.38	16.64	27.22	44.76	23.49	24.86	23.61	18.41
	279503	25320	31763	324413	515993	509105	436071	460093	447149	399495
	5.63	0.80		8.54	32.68	35.78	26.46	23.07	30.34	19.82
	27.63	2.87	2.27	71.37	43.08	55.90	15.79	19.18	27.70	32.32
	0.74	0.16		21.92	6.35	7.49	3.62	0.48	5.22	2.41
	7461	2449	826	6746	42865	21383	18352	29028	19360	8979
	65636	7080	960	97187	345243	23219	41104	13248	26386	37685
156.08	78.65	479.63	555.22	22.74	13.92	63.19	8.38	7.50	13.50	69.95
1383.1	118.7	1503.7	2084.7	116.5	81.8	178.8	82.1	63.2	139.3	246.6
302.3	52.3	184.4	327.6	29.7	27.9	68.3	22.0	34.9	31.6	202.6
368.29	64.12	361.73	503.53	30.08	62.71	144.15	45.80	31.01	50.18	21.24
34450	31952	33268	35341	34375	27318	29460	21953	22243	24817	25030
	15203	16455	16724	15212	12160	12695	8833	8870	10899	12167
336	483	278	474	163	485	779	589	474	591	211
9313	4129	4984	12347	1960	2454	4526	1565	2543	3195	1765
5972	2621	3330	8508	1401	2221	3349	1127	1276	2612	1260

主要统计指标解释

行政区划 指国家对行政区域的划分。根据有关法规规定，我国的行政区域划分如下：（1）全国分为省、自治区、直辖市；（2）省、自治区分为自治州、县、自治县、市；（3）自治州分为县、自治县、市；（4）县、自治县分为乡、民族乡、镇；（5）直辖市和较大的市分为区、县；（6）国家在必要时设立的特别行政区。

气候 指地球与大气之间长期能量交换与质量交换所形成的一种自然环境状态，它是多种因素综合作用的结果。气候既是人类生活和生产的环境要素之一，又是供给人类生活和生产的重要资源。气温、降水、湿度等气象要素的多年平均值是用来描述一个地区气候状况的主要参数，而各种气象要素某年、某月的平均值（或总量）则可以反映出该时期天气气候状况的重要特征。

自然资源 指人类可以直接从自然界获得，并用于生产和生活的物质资源。自然资源一般可以分成可再生资源和非再生资源两大类。可再生资源指在较短时间内可以再生、可以循环利用的资源，包括土地资源、水资源、气候资源、生物资源和海洋资源等。非再生资源指在使用后不能再生的资源，包括矿产资源和地热能源。

土地资源 土地指陆地的表层部分，它主要由岩石、岩石的风化物和土壤构成。土地资源按利用类型可以分为农用地、建筑用地和未利用地。农用地包括耕地、园地、林地、牧草地和水面。建筑用地包括居民点及工矿用地、交通用地和水利设施用地。未利用地指农用地和建筑用地以外的土地，包括滩涂、荒漠、戈壁、冰川和石山等。

耕地面积 指经过开垦用以种植农作物并经常进行耕耘的土地面积。包括种有作物的土地面积、休闲地、新开荒地和抛荒未满三年的土地面积。

森林面积 指由乔木树种构成，郁闭度0.2以上（含0.2）的林地或冠 宽度10米以上的林带的面积，即有林地面积。森林面积包括天然起源和人工起源的针叶林面积、阔叶林面积、针阔混交林面积和竹林面积，不包括灌木林地面积和疏林地面积。

林业用地面积 指生长乔木、竹类、灌木、沿海红树林等林木的土地面积，包括有林地、灌木林、疏林地、未成林造林地、迹地、苗圃等。

水资源总量 指评价区内降水形成的地表和地下产水总量，即地表产流量与降水入渗补给地下水量之和，不包括过境水量。

地表水资源量 指评价区内河流、湖泊、冰川等地表水体中可以逐年更新的动态水量，即当地天然河川径流量。

地下水资源量 指评价区内降水和地表水对饱水岩土层的补给量，包括降水入渗补给量和河道、湖库、渠系、渠灌田间等地表水体的入渗补给量。

气温 指空气的温度，我国一般以摄氏度（℃）为单位表示。气象观测的温度表是放在离地面约1.5米处通风良好的百叶箱里测量的，因此，通常说的气温指的是离地面1.5米处百叶箱中的温度。其统计计算方法为：

月平均气温是将全月各日的平均气温相加，除以该月的天数而得。

年平均气温是将12个月的月平均气温累加后除以12而得。

降水量 指从天空降落到地面的液态或固态（经融化后）水，未经蒸发、渗透、流失而在地面上积聚的深度。其统计计算方法为：

月降水量是将全月各日的降水量累加而得。

年降水量是将12个月的月降水量累加而得。

日照时数 指太阳实际照射地面的时间。其统计方法与降水量相同。

平均增长速度 平均增长速度表明社会经济现象在一个较长的时期内逐期平均增长变化的程度，它不能根据各个环比增长速度直接求得，但与平均发展速度之间存在着一定的数量关系：平均增长速度＝平均发展速度－1。

平均发展速度 是一种根据环比发展速度计算的序时平均数,由于各时期对比的基础不同，所以计算平均发展速度不能采用一般的序时平均数的计算方法，计算方法分为水平法和累计法。水平法，又称几何平均法，即将环比发展速度按连乘法用几何平均数公式计算。累计法，也称方程法，根据一段时期内各年发展水平总和与基期水平的关系，列出方程式计算平均发展速度。水平法着重考虑最后一年所达到的发展水平；累计法着重考虑整个时期累计发展水平的总量。

本《年鉴》内所列的平均增长速度，均用“水平法”计算。从某年到某年平均增长速度的年份，均不包括基期年在内。如建国六十年以来的平均增长速度是以1949年为基期计算的，则写为1950-2009年平均增长速度，其余类推。

Explanatory Notes on Main Statistical Indicators

Divisions of Administrative Areas refers to the division of administrative areas by the State. The relative laws stipulate that (1)the whole country is divided into provinces, autonomous regions and municipalities directly under the Central Government;(2)provinces and autonomous regions are further divided into autonomous prefectures, counties, autonomous counties and cities; (3)autonomous prefectures are further divided into counties, autonomous counties and cities; (4)counties and autonomous counties are further divided into townships, ethnic townships and towns; (5)municipalities directly under the Central Government and large cities are divided into districts and counties, (6)the State shall, when necessary, establish special administrative regions.

Climate refers to the natural environmental status formed by the long-term exchange of energy and mass between the earth and the atmosphere, and is the result of interaction of many factors. Climate is both one of the environment factors and also the important resources for living and production activities of the human being. The average values across several years of meteorological factors such as temperature, rainfall and humidity are used as important parameters to describe the climate of a region. while the average values (or total values)of a given year or month of meteorological factors reflect the key characteristics of climate for that period of time.

Natural Resources refer to material resources that could be obtained from the nature by human being and used for production and living. Natural resources in general can be classified as renewable resources and non-renewable resources. Renewable resources refer to resources that could be renewed and recycled during a relatively short period of time, including land resource, water resource, climate resource, biology resource and marine resource. Non-renewable resources include resources that could not be renewed, such as minerals and geothermal resource.

Land Resource Land refers to the surface of the earth, consisting of mainly rocks and its whethering and earth. Land resource can be classified, by its utilization, as land for agriculture, land for construction and unused land. Land for agriculture includes cultivated land, plantation land, forestland, grassland and waters. Land for construction includes land for residential purpose, for manufacturing and mining, for transportation and for water-conservancy projects. Unused land refers to land other than land for agriculture and.construction, including beaches, deserts, Gobi, glaciers and rock mountains.

Area of Cultivated Land refers to area of land reclaimed for the regular cultivation of various farm crops, including crop-cover land, fallow, newly reclaimed land and land laid idle for less than 3 years.

Forest Area refers to the area of trees and bamboo grow with canopy density above 0.2, the area of shrubby tree according to regulations of the government, the area of forest land inside farm land and the area of trees planted by the side of villages, farm houses and along roads and rivers.

Area of Afforested Land refers to area for land for trees bamboo, bushes and mangrove, including forest-covered land, bush-covered land, sparse forest land, land planned for afforestation and nurseries of young trees.

Total Water Resources refers to total volume of water resources measured as run-off for surface water from rainfall and recharge for groundwater in a given area, excluding transit water.

Surface Water Resources refers to total renewable resources which exist in rivers, lakes, glaciers and other collectors from rainfall and are measured as run-off of rivers.

Groundwater Resources refers to replenishment of aquifers with rainfall and surface water.

Temperature refers to the air temperature. China uses centigrade as the unit. The thermometry used for weather observation is put in a breezy shutter, which is 1.5 meters high from the ground. Therefore, the commonly used temperature refers to the temperature in the breezy shutter 1.5 meters away from the ground. The calculation method is as follows:

Monthly average temperature is the summation of average daily temperature of one month divided by the actual days of that particular month.

Annual average temperature is the summation of monthly average of a year divided by 12 months.

Volume of Precipitation refers to the deepness of liquid state or solid state (thawed)water falling from the sky to the ground that has not been evaporated, infiltrated or run off. The calculation method is as follows:

Monthly precipitation is the summation of daily precipitation of a month.

Annual precipitation is the summation of 12 months precipitation of a year.

Sunshine Hours refer to the actual hours of sun irradiating the earth. The calculation method is the same as that of the precipitation.

Average Annual Growth Rate shows the average growth rate of social and economic development during a longer period. It can not be directly calculated by chain based growth rate. The relation is:

Average Annual Growth Rate=Average Speed of Development 1

Average speed of development is the time series average of speed which calculated by chain based.Because the reference bases during the different periods are not same, average speed of development can not be calculated by the general method. Level approach and accumulative approach for calculating average speed of development rate are applied. The "level approach" , or the method of calculating the geometric average, is derived by the formula of geometric average of the chain-based speeds of development, or comparing the level of the last year of the interval with that of the beginning year; the other is called the "accumulative approach" or the "algebraic average" , "equation" method, which is derived by the summation of the actual figure of each year in the interval divided by the figure in the base year. The level approach focuses on the level of the last year, while the accumulative approach emphasizes the aggregate development in the duration.

The average annual growth rates listed in the Yearbook are calculated by the level approach except for the growth rate of investment in fixed assets. The base year is not listed in the duration for which average annual growth rates are computed. For instance, the average annual growth rate of the 60 years since 1949 is shown as the average annual growth rate of 1950-2009 without showing the base year 1949.

2 基本单位

BASIC UNIT

资料整理：王亚丽　张利民　张　奇

Data management:Wang Yali　Zhang Limin　Zhang Qi

第二部分　基本单位

一、简要说明

本章资料主要包括法人单位、产业活动单位和企业一套表调查单位数等资料，为2013年快报数据。由西安市统计局普查中心提供。

二、主要指标

法人单位数（个）	105464	比上年增长　1.4%
产业活动单位数（个）	114916	比上年增长　1.1%
规模以上工业企业数（个）	1002	比上年增长　3.7%
限额以上批发零售住宿餐饮业企业数（个）	1082	比上年增长　0.2%
资质内建筑业企业数（个）	421	比上年增长　6.3%
房地产开发经营企业数（个）	662	比上年增长　1.5%
规模以上服务业企业数（个）	566	比上年增长　0.7%

2　BASIC UNIT

Ⅰ.Brief Introduction

This chapter consists of unified data Enterprises and Industrial Active Units and Investigation Unit in "Enterprises of a table", provided by Xian Bureau of Statistic's Census Centre.

Ⅱ.Major Indicators

		Increase over Preceding Year
Number of Enterprises (unit)	105464	1.4%
Number of Industrial Active Units (unit)	114916	1.1%
Number of Industrial Enterprises above designed size (unit)	1002	3.7%
Number of Enterprises about Wholesale、Retail、Accommodation and Catering above designed size (unit)	1082	0.2%
Number of Qualified Construction Enterprises (unit)	421	6.3%
Number of Real Estate Development Enterprises (unit)	662	1.5%
Number of service Enterprises above designed size (unit)	566	0.7%

2-1 按登记注册类型分法人单位数（2013年）

Impersonal Entities Grouped by Status of Registion（2013）

单位：个 (unit)

分 组	Classify	法人单位数 Number of Enterprises	企业 Enterprises
总 计	**Total**	**105464**	**93207**
#非公有制经济	Non-public sectors of the economy	88019	87158
按登记注册类型分	**Grouped by Status of Registion**		
（一）内资	Domestic Funded Enterprises	104601	92352
国有	State-owned Enterprises	6621	1921
集体	Collective-owned Enterprises	2378	1599
股份合作	Cooperative Enterprises	403	374
联营	Joint Ownership Enterprises	239	213
国有联营	State Joint Ownership Enterprises	32	23
集体联营	Collective Joint Ownership Enterprises	82	74
国有与集体联营	Joint State-collective Ownership Enterprises	20	16
其他联营	Other Joint Ownership Enterprises	105	100
有限责任公司	Limited Liability Corporations	36229	36107
国有独资公司	State Sole Funded Corporations	174	173
其他有限责任公司	Other Limited Liability Corporations	36055	35934
股份有限公司	Share-holding Corporations Limited	1284	1274
私营	Private Enterprises	47322	46682
私营独资企业	Private-funded Enterprises	10966	10522
私营合伙	Private Partnership Enterprises	2191	2113
私营有限责任公司	Private Limited Liability Corporations	31423	31313
私营股份有限公司	Private Share-holding Corporations Ltd.	2742	2734
其他	Other Domestic Funded Enterprises	10125	4177
（二）港、澳、台商投资企业	Enterprises with Funds from Hong Kong, Macao and Taiwan	282	279
与港、澳、台商合资经营	Joint-venture with Funds from Hong Kong,Macao and Taiwan	103	102
与港、澳、台商合作经营	Cooperative Enterprises with Funds from Hong Kong Macau and Taiwan	16	16
港澳台商独资经营	Enterprises with Sole Investment from Hong Kong Macau and Taiwan	145	143
港澳台商投资股份有限公司	Share-holding Corporations Ltd. with funds from Hong Kong, Macao & Taiwan	15	16
其他港澳台商投资	Other Enterprises with Funds from Hong Kong, Macao and Taiwan	2	2
（三）外商投资	Foreign Funded Enterprises	581	576
中外合资经营	Sino-foreign Joint Ventures	229	229
中外合作经营	Sino-Foreign Cooperation Enterprises	21	19
外资企业	Foreign Owned Enterprises	286	283
外商投资股份有限公司	Limited Company Funded by Foreign Investment	40	40
其他外商投资	Other Foreign Funded Enterprises	5	5

2-2 按国民经济行业分法人单位数（2013年）

Impersonal Entities by Sector（2013）

单位：个 (unit)

行　业	Sector	法人单位数 Number of Enterprises	企业 Enterprises
总　计	**Total**	**105464**	**93207**
（一）农、林、牧、渔业	Agriculture,Forestry,Animal Husbandry and Fishery	2237	1783
农业	Farming	1211	960
林业	Forestry	232	205
畜牧业	Animal Husbandry	515	410
渔业	Fishery	30	26
农、林、牧、渔服务业	Services in Support of Agriculture	249	182
（二）采矿业	Mining	319	319
煤炭开采和洗选业	Mining and Washing of Coal	13	13
石油和天然气开采业	Extraction of Petroleum and Natural Gas	28	28
黑色金属矿采选业	Mining of Ferrous Metal Ores	13	13
有色金属矿采选业	Mining of Non-ferrous Metal Ores	39	39
非金属矿采选业	Mining and Processing of Nonmetal Ores	78	78
开采辅助活动	Mining of Other Ores	97	97
其他采矿业	Manufacturing	51	51
（三）制造业	Processing of Food from Agricultural Products	13877	13877
农副食品加工业	Manufacture of Foods	368	368
食品制造业	Manufacture of Beverages	389	389
酒、饮料和精制茶制造业	Manufacture of Tobacco	133	133
烟草制品业	Manufacture of Textile	4	4
纺织业	Manufacture of Textile Wearing Apparel, Footware and Caps	145	145
纺织服装、服饰业	Manufacture of Leather, Fur, Feather and Related Products	180	180
皮革、毛皮、羽毛及其制品和制鞋业	Processing of Timber,Manufacture of Wood,Bamboo,Rattan, its Products and Footwear	37	37
木材加工和木、竹、藤、棕、草制品业	Plam and Straw Products and Straw Products	156	156
家具制造业	Manufacture of Furniture	389	389
造纸及纸制品业	Manufacture of Paper and Paper Products	314	314
印刷和记录媒介复制业	Printing,Reproduction of Recording Media	563	563
文教、工美、体育和娱乐用品制造业	Manufacture of Articles For Culture, Education and Sport Activities	216	216

2-2 续表1 continued 1

单位：个 (unit)

行 业	Sector	法人单位数 Number of Enterprises	企业 Enterprises
石油加工、炼焦和核燃料加工业	Processing of Petroleum, Coking, Processing of Nuclear Fuel	63	63
化学原料和化学制品制造业	Manufacture of Raw Chemical Materials and Chemical Products	704	704
医药制造业	Manufacture of Medicines	389	389
化学纤维制造业	Manufacture of Chemical Fibers	23	23
橡胶和塑料制品业	Manufacture of Rubber and Manufacture of Plastics	408	408
非金属矿物制品业	Manufacture of Non-metallic Mineral Products	1129	1129
黑色金属冶炼和压延加工业	Smelting and Pressing of Ferrous Metals	313	313
有色金属冶炼和压延加工业	Smelting and Pressing of Non-ferrous Metals	157	157
金属制品业	Manufacture of Metal Products	960	960
通用设备制造业	Manufacture of General Purpose Machinery	1606	1605
专用设备制造业	Manufacture of Special Equipment	1467	1467
汽车制造业	Manufacture of Motor Vehicle	170	170
铁路、船舶、航空航天和其他运输设备制造业	Railways,Shipbuilding,Aerospace and Other Transportation Equipment Manufacturing Industry	285	285
电气机械和器材制造业	Manufacture of Electric Equipment and Machinery	1451	1451
计算机、通信和其他电子设备制造业	Manufacture of Communication Equipment, Computers and other Electronic Equipment	1063	1063
仪器仪表制造业	Manufacture of Measuring Instruments and Machinery	524	524
其他制造业	Other Manufacturing	125	125
废弃资源综合利用	Recycling and Disposal of Waste	57	57
金属制品、机械和设备修理业	Metal Products,Machinery and Equipment Repair Industry	89	89
（四）电力、燃气及水的生产供应业	Production and Distribution of Electricity,Gas and Water	265	264
电力、热力生产和供应业	Production and Supply of Electric Power and Heat Power	150	149
燃气生产和供应业	Gas mining and supplying industry	44	44
水的生产和供应业	Production and Supply of Water	71	71
（五）建筑业	Construction	7673	7672
房屋建筑业	Construction of Building	1219	1219
土木工程建筑业	Civil Engineering	1000	1000
建筑安装业	Architectural Installation	1392	1392
建筑装饰和其他建筑业	Architectural Decoration and Other Construction	4062	4061
（六）批发和零售业	Wholesale and Retail Trades	34020	34020

2-2 续表2 continued 2

单位：个 (unit)

行 业	Sector	法人单位数 Number of Enterprises	企业 Enterprises
批发业	Wholesale Trade	18892	18892
零售业	Retail Trade	15128	15128
（七）交通运输、仓储和邮政业	Traffic, Transport, Storage and Post	1690	1659
铁路运输业	Transport Via Railway	29	29
道路运输业	Transport Via Road	986	963
水上运输业	Water Transport	1	1
航空运输业	Air Transport	56	53
管道运输业	Transport Via Pipeline	5	5
装卸搬运和运输代理服务业	Loading, Unloading, Portage and Other Transport Services	338	336
仓储业	Storage	206	203
邮政业	Post	69	69
（八）住宿和餐饮业	Hotels and Catering Services	2938	2926
住宿业	Hotels	1084	1080
餐饮业	Catering Services	1854	1846
（九）信息传输、软件和信息技术服务业	Information Transmission, Computer Services and Software	3356	3337
电信、广播电视和卫星传输服务	Telecom & Other Information Transmission Services	178	176
互联网和相关服务	internet and relevant services	601	598
软件和信息技术服务	Software Industry	2577	2563
（十）金融业	Financial Intermediation	973	944
货币金融服务	Monetary and Financial Services	230	208
资本市场服务	Capital Market Services	380	379
保险业	Insurance	137	135
其他金融业	Other Financial Intermediation	226	222
（十一）房地产业	Real Estate	6295	6267
房地产业	Real Estate	6295	6267
（十二） 租赁和商务服务业	Leasing and Business Services	10389	10152
租赁业	Leasing	780	777
商务服务业	Business Services	9609	9375
（十三）科学研究和技术服务业	Scientific Research, Technical Sevice	4548	4000
研究与试验发展	Research and Experimental Development	360	279
专业技术服务业	Professional Technical Services	2348	2082

2-2 续表3 continued 3

单位：个 (unit)

行业	Sector	法人单位数 Number of Enterprises	企业 Enterprises
科技推广和应用服务业	Services of Science and Technology Exchanges and Promotion	1840	1639
（十四）水利、环境和公共设施管理业	Management of Water Conservancy, Environment and Public Facilities	794	632
水利管理业	Management of Water Conservancy	117	53
生态保护和环境治理业	Environmental Management	93	75
公共设施管理业	Management of Public Facilities	584	503
（十五）居民服务、修理和其他服务业	Services to Households and Other Services	3364	3283
居民服务业	Services to Households	836	785
机动车、电子产品和日用产品修理业	The repair service industry for motor vehicle、electronic	1002	997
其他服务业	Other Services	1526	1501
（十六）教育	Education	2903	321
教育	Education	2903	321
（十七）卫生和社会工作	Health, Social Security	2158	147
卫生	Health	2050	135
社会工作	Social	108	12
（十八）文化、体育和娱乐业	Culture, Sports and Entertainment	1866	1601
新闻和出版业	Journalism and Publishing Activities	148	99
广播、电视、电影和影视录音制作业	Broadcasting, Movies, Television and Audiovisual Activities	259	230
文化艺术业	Cultural and Art Activities	534	383
体育	Sports Activities	124	95
娱乐业	Entertainment	801	793
（十九）公共管理、社会保障和社会组织	Public Management and Social Organizaion	5799	3
中国共产党机关	Organs of Communist Party of China	167	
国家机构	Government Agencies	1541	
人民政协、民主党派	People's Political Consultative Conference and Democratic Parties	27	
社会保障	Social Security	36	2
群众团体、社会团体和其他成员组织	Mass organizations、social groups and other members of the organization	694	1
基层群众自治组织	Grass-roots Mass Self-Government Organizations	3334	
（二十）国际组织	International Organizations		
国际组织	International Organizations		

2-3　按行政区划分法人单位数（2013年）

Impersonal Entities by Region（2013）

单位：个 (unit)

区　县	Region	法人单位数 Number of Enterprises	企业 Enterprises
总　计	**Total**	**105464**	**93207**
新城区	Xincheng	7209	6477
碑林区	Beilin	11554	10887
莲湖区	Lianhu	10692	9986
灞桥区	Baqiao	4500	3820
未央区	Weiyang	16875	16302
雁塔区	Yanta	33875	32756
阎良区	Yanliang	1684	1325
临潼区	Lintong	2376	1374
长安区	Chang'an	5710	4241
蓝田县	Lantian	2310	993
周至县	Zhouzhi	2830	1272
户　县	Huxian	3400	1913
高陵县	Gaoling	2449	1861

2-4 按登记注册类型分产业活动单位数（2013年）

Industrial Active Units by Status of Registion（2013）

单位：个 (unit)

分组	Classify	产业活动单位数 Number of Industrial Active Units	企业 Enterprises
总计	**Total**	**114916**	**99915**
按登记注册类型分	Grouped by Status of Registion		
（一）内资	Domestic Funded Enterprises	113525	98534
国有	State-owned Enterprises	9495	2778
集体	Collective-owned Enterprises	3266	1905
股份合作	Cooperative Enterprises	718	686
联营	Joint Ownership Enterprises	280	255
国有联营	State Joint Ownership Enterprises	39	34
集体联营	Collective Joint Ownership Enterprises	93	83
国有与集体联营	Joint State-collective Ownership Enterprises	24	19
其他联营	Other Joint Ownership Enterprises	124	119
有限责任公司	Limited Liability Corporations	38232	38107
国有独资公司	State Sole Funded Corporations	199	198
其他有限责任公司	Other Limited Liability Corporations	38033	37909
股份有限公司	Share-holding Corporations Limited	2364	2353
私营	Private Enterprises	48725	48077
私营独资企业	Private-funded Enterprises	11160	10710
私营合伙	Private Partnership Enterprises	2251	2173
私营有限责任公司	Private Limited Liability Corporations	32457	32345
私营股份有限公司	Private Share-holding Corporations Ltd.	2857	2849
其他	Other Enterprises	10445	4373

2-4 续表 continued

单位：个 (unit)

分组	Classify	产业活动单位数 Number of Industrial Active Units	企业 Enterprises
（二）港、澳、台商投资企业	Enterprises with Funds from Hong Kong,Macao and Taiwan	475	471
与港、澳、台商合资经营	Joint-venture with Funds from Hong Kong,Macao and Taiwan	135	134
与港、澳、台商合作经营	Cooperative Enterprises with Funds from Hong Kong Macau and Taiwan	35	35
港澳台商独资经营	Enterprises with Sole Investment from Hong Kong Macau and Taiwan	285	282
港澳台商投资股份有限公司	Share-holding Corporations Ltd. with funds from Hong Kong, Macao & Taiwan	18	18
其他港澳台商投资	Other Enterprises with Funds from Hong Kong,Macao and Taiwan	2	2
（三）外商投资	Foreign Funded Enterprises	916	910
中外合资经营	Sino-foreign Joint Ventures	278	278
中外合作经营	Sino-Foreign Cooperation Enterprises	25	23
外资企业	Foreign Owned Enterprises	545	541
外商投资股份有限公司	Limited Company Funded by Foreign Investment	60	60
其他外商投资	Other Foreign Funded Enterprises	8	8

2-5 按国民经济行业分产业活动单位数（2013年）

Industrial Active Units by Sector（2013）

单位：个 (unit)

行业	Sector	产业活动单位数 Number of Industrial Active Units	企业 Enterprises
总计	**Item**	**114916**	**99915**
（一）农、林、牧、渔业	Agriculture,Forestry,Animal Husbandry and Fishery	2247	1793
农业	Farming	1214	963
林业	Forestry	234	207
畜牧业	Animal Husbandry	519	414
渔业	Fishery	30	26
农、林、牧、渔服务业	Services in Support of Agriculture	250	183
（二）采矿业	Mining	335	335
煤炭开采和洗选业	Mining and Washing of Coal	13	13
石油和天然气开采业	Extraction of Petroleum and Natural Gas	31	31
黑色金属矿采选业	Mining of Ferrous Metal Ores	13	13
有色金属矿采选业	Mining of Non-ferrous Metal Ores	39	39
非金属矿采选业	Mining and Processing of Nonmetal Ores	79	79
开采辅助活动	Mining auxiliary activities	109	109
其他采矿业	Mining of Other Ores	51	51
（三）制造业	Manufacturing	14187	14187
农副食品加工业	Processing of Food from Agricultural Products	383	383
食品制造业	Manufacture of Foods	394	394
酒、饮料和精制茶制造业	Alcohol,Beverage and Refined tea industry	139	139
烟草制品业	Manufacture of Tobacco	4	4
纺织业	Manufacture of Textile	149	149
纺织服装、服饰业	Textile, Garments industry	182	182
皮革、毛皮、羽毛及其制品和制鞋业	Processing of Timber,Manufacture of Wood,Bamboo,Rattan, its Froducts and Footwear	38	38
木材加工和木、竹、藤、棕、草制品业	Processing of Timber,Manufacture of Wood,Bamboo,Rattan, Plam and Straw Products	164	164
家具制造业	Manufacture of Furniture	398	398
造纸及纸制品业	Manufacture of Paper and Paper Products	317	317
印刷和记录媒介复制业	Printing,Reproduction of Recording Media	574	574
文教、工美、体育和娱乐用品制造业	Manufacture of Articles For Culture,Education and Sport Activities	218	218

2-5 续表1 continued 1

单位：个　　(unit)

行业	Sector	产业活动单位数 Number of Industrial Active Units	企业 Enterprises
石油加工、炼焦和核燃料加工业	Processing of Petroleum, Coking, Processing of Nuclear Fuel	63	63
化学原料和化学制品制造业	Manufacture of Raw Chemical Materials and Chemical Products	718	718
医药制造业	Manufacture of Medicines	397	397
化学纤维制造业	Manufacture of Chemical Fibers	25	25
橡胶和塑料制品业	Manufacture of Rubber	412	412
非金属矿物制品业	Manufacture of Non-metallic Mineral Products	1149	1149
黑色金属冶炼和压延加工业	Smelting and Pressing of Ferrous Metals	315	315
有色金属冶炼和压延加工业	Smelting and Pressing of Non-ferrous Metals	158	158
金属制品业	Manufacture of Metal Products	977	977
通用设备制造业	Manufacture of General Purpose Machinery	1636	1636
专用设备制造业	Manufacture of Special Equipment	1509	1509
汽车制造业	Manufacture of Motor Vehicle	184	184
铁路、船舶、航空航天和其他运输设备制造业	Railways,Shipbuilding,Aerospace and Other Transportation Equipment Manufacturing Industry	296	296
电气机械和器材制造业	Manufacture of Electric Equipment and Machinery	1474	1474
计算机、通信和其他电子设备制造业	Manufacture of Communication Equipment,Computers and other Electronic Equipment	1090	1090
仪器仪表制造业	Manufacture of Measuring Instruments and Machinery	544	544
其他制造业	Other Manufacturing	128	128
废弃资源综合利用	Recycling and Disposal of Waste	58	58
金属制品、机械和设备修理业	Metal Products,Machinery and Equipment Repair Industry	94	94
（四）电力、燃气及水的生产供应业	Production and Distribution of Electricity,Gas and Water	279	276
电力、热力生产和供应业	Production and Supply of Electric Power and Heat Power	159	156
燃气生产和供应业	Gas mining and supplying industry	46	46
水的生产和供应业	Production and Supply of Water	74	74
（五）建筑业	Construction	8016	8015
房屋建筑业	Construction of Building	1368	1368
土木工程建筑业	Civil Engineering	1048	1048
建筑安装业	Architectural Installation	1431	1431
建筑装饰和其他建筑业	Architectural Decoration and Other Construction	4169	4168
（六）批发和零售业	Wholesale and Retail Trades	36284	36284

2–5 续表2 continued 2

单位：个 (unit)

行业	Sector	产业活动单位数 Number of Industrial Active Units	企业 Enterprises
批发业	Wholesale Trade	19299	19299
零售业	Retail Trade	16985	16985
（七）交通运输、仓储和邮政业	Traffic, Transport, Storage and Post	2103	2048
铁路运输业	Transport Via Railway	32	32
道路运输业	Transport Via Road	1103	1062
水上运输业	Water Transport	4	3
航空运输业	Air Transport	58	55
管道运输业	Transport Via Pipeline	7	7
装卸搬运和运输代理服务业	Loading, Unloading, Portage and Other Transport Services	369	367
仓储业	Storage	221	217
邮政业	Post	309	305
（八）住宿和餐饮业	Hotels and Catering Services	3428	3414
住宿业	Hotels	1183	1178
餐饮业	Catering Services	2245	2236
（九）信息传输、软件和信息技术服务业	Information Transmission, Computer Services and Software	3629	3606
电信、广播电视和卫星传输服务	Telecom & Other Information Transmission Services	299	297
互联网和相关服务	internet and relevant services	626	622
软件和信息技术服务	Software and Information Technology Service	2704	2687
（十）金融业	Financial Intermediation	2539	2491
货币金融服务	Monetary and Financial Services	1482	1447
资本市场服务	Capital Market Services	426	425
保险业	Insurance	392	385
其他金融业	Other Financial Intermediation	239	234
（十一）房地产业	Real Estate	6475	6436
房地产业	Real Estate	6475	6436
（十二）租赁和商务服务业	Leasing and Business Services	10811	10470
租赁业	Leasing	804	801
商务服务业	Business Services	10007	9669
（十三）科学研究和技术服务业	Scientific Research, Technical Sevice and	4745	4121
研究与试验发展	Geologic Prospecting	372	289
专业技术服务业	Professional Technical Services	2434	2154

2-5 续表3 continued 3

单位：个 (unit)

行 业	Sector	产业活动单位数 Number of Industrial Active Units	企业 Enterprises
科技推广和应用服务业	Services of Science and Technology Exchanges and Promotion	1939	1678
（十四）水利、环境和公共设施管理业	Management of Water Conservancy, Environment and Public Facilities	913	650
水利管理业			
生态保护和环境治理业	Ecological protection and environmental governance industry	159	53
公共设施管理业	Management of Public Facilities	95	76
其他服务业	Other Services	659	521
（十五）居民服务、修理和其他服务业	Services to Households and Other Services	3745	3639
居民服务业	Services to Households	1128	1063
机动车、电子产品和日用产品修理业	The repair service industry for motor vehicle、electronic	1030	1025
其他服务业	Other Services	1587	1551
（十六）教育	Education	3570	335
教育	Education	3570	335
（十七）卫生和社会工作	Health, Social Security and Social Welfare	2492	162
卫生	Health	2377	150
社会工作	social work	115	12
（十八）文化、体育和娱乐业	Culture, Sports and Entertainment	1957	1650
新闻和出版业	Journalism and Publishing Activities	166	108
广播、电视、电影和影视录音制作业	Broadcasting, Movies, Television and Audiovisual Activities	268	237
文化艺术业	Cultural and Art Activities	563	385
体育	Sports Activities	144	114
娱乐业	Entertainment	816	806
（十九）公共管理、社会保障和社会组织	Public Management and Social Organizaion	7161	3
中国共产党机关	Organs of Communist Party of China	180	
国家机构	Government Agencies	2733	
人民政协、民主党派	Chinese People's Political Consultative Conference、democratic parties	27	
社会保障	Social Security	49	2
群众团体、社会团体和其他成员组织	Non-Government Organizations, Social Organizations and Religion Organizations	811	1
基层群众自治组织	Grass-roots Mass Self-Government Organizations	3361	
（二十）国际组织	International Organizations		
国际组织	International Organizations		

2-6 按行政区划分产业活动单位数（2013年）

Industrial Active Units by Region（2013）

单位：个 (unit)

区 县	Region	产业活动单位数 Number of Enterprises	企业 Enterprises
总 计	**Total**	**114916**	**99915**
新城区	Xincheng	8077	7156
碑林区	Beilin	12982	12216
莲湖区	Lianhu	11744	10911
灞桥区	Baqiao	4905	4179
未央区	Weiyang	17586	16981
雁塔区	Yanta	35662	34194
阎良区	Yanliang	1894	1481
临潼区	Lintong	3046	1574
长安区	Chang'an	6083	4478
蓝田县	Lantian	3008	1138
周至县	Zhouzhi	3232	1376
户 县	Huxian	3923	2245
高陵县	Gaoling	2774	1986

2-7 按统计机构分企业一套表调查单位数（2013年）

Number of Survey Units by Statistical Agencies of "One Table" (2013)

单位：个 (unit)

区县、开发区	Region	规模以上工业 Industrial Enterprises above designed size	限额以上批发零售住宿餐饮业 Above wholesale and retail accommodation and catering industry	资质内建筑业 Qualified Construction Enterprises	房地产开发经营企业 Real Estate Development Enterprises	规模以上服务业 Service Enterprises above designed size
全市	**Total**	1002	1082	421	662	566
新城区	Xincheng	15	141	34	48	25
碑林区	Beilin	15	165	46	68	82
莲湖区	Lianhu	37	127	37	64	45
灞桥区	Baqiao	127	53	32	35	10
未央区	Weiyang	26	56	28	50	19
雁塔区	Yanta	41	113	100	63	45
阎良区	Yanliang	57	16	16	25	6
临潼区	Lintong	40	18	14	7	10
长安区	Chang'an	33	52	23	38	12
蓝田县	Lantian	24	10	9	10	2
周至县	Zhouzhi	29	12	7	19	8
户　县	Huxian	54	22	6	13	6
高陵县	Gaoling	33	20	7	27	9
高新技术开发区	GaoXin	203	112	20	44	147
经济技术开发区	JingKai	160	119	34	48	80
曲江新区	Qujiang		14	2	44	43
浐灞生态区	Chanba Eco-District		1	0	21	5
阎良国家航空技术产业基地	Aviation Industry Base	16			10	
国家民用航天产业基地	Aerospace Base	18	4	2	17	2
国际港务区	International Trade &Logistic Park	0	0	1	2	5
沣东新城	FengDongXinCheng	51	27	3	9	5
其他	other	23				

2-8 按行政区划分企业一套表调查单位数（2013年）

Number of Survey Units by Region of "One Table" (2013)

单位：个 (unit)

区 县	Region	规模以上工业 Industrial Enterprises above designed size	限额以上批发零售住宿餐饮业 Above wholesale and retail accommodation and catering industry	资质内建筑业 Qualified Construction Enterprises	房地产开发经营企业 Real Estate Development Enterprises	规模以上服务业 Service Enterprises above designed size
全市	**Total**	**1002**	**1082**	**421**	**662**	**566**
新城区	Xincheng	21	141	34	50	26
碑林区	Beilin	16	167	46	69	87
莲湖区	Lianhu	46	127	39	65	47
灞桥区	Baqiao	131	53	33	52	19
未央区	Weiyang	168	198	64	114	103
雁塔区	Yanta	205	232	119	142	221
阎良区	Yanliang	75	16	16	35	6
临潼区	Lintong	40	18	14	7	10
长安区	Chang'an	102	62	27	60	19
蓝田县	Lantian	26	10	9	9	2
周至县	Zhouzhi	29	12	7	19	8
户 县	Huxian	56	22	6	13	6
高陵县	Gaoling	87	24	7	27	12

主要统计指标解释

企业（单位）登记注册类型 是以在工商行政管理机关登记注册的各类企业为划分对象，以工商行政管理部门对企业登记注册的类型为依据，将企业登记注册类型分为内资企业、港澳台商投资企业和外商投资企业三大类。内资企业包括国有企业、集体企业、股份合作企业、联营企业、有限责任公司、股份有限公司、私营公司和其他企业；港澳台商投资企业和外商投资企业分别包括合资经营企业、合作经营企业、独资经营企业和股份有限公司。对不在工商行政管理部门进行登记注册的行政机关、事业单位和社会团体，主要按其经费来源和管理方式进行划分。

国有企业 指企业全部资产归国家所有，并按《中华人民共和国企业法人登记管理条例》规定登记注册的非公司制的经济组织。不包括有限责任公司中的国有独资公司。

集体企业 指企业资产归集体所有，并按《中华人民共和国企业法人登记管理条例》规定登记注册的经济组织。

股份合作企业 指以合作制为基础，由企业职工共同出资入股，吸收一定比例的社会资产投资组建，实行自主经营，自负盈亏，共同劳动，民主管理，按劳分配与按股分红相结合的一种集体经济组织。

联营企业 指两个及两个以上相同或不同所有制性质的企业法人或事业单位法人，按自愿、平等、互利的原则，共同投资组成的经济组织。联营企业包括国有联营企业、集体联营企业、国有与集体联营企业和其他联营企业。

有限责任公司 指根据《中华人民共和国公司登记管理条例》规定登记注册，由两个以上、五十个以下的股东共同出资，每个股东以其所认缴的出资额对公司承担有限责任，公司以其全部资产对其债务承担责任的经济组织。有限责任公司包括国有独资公司以及其他有限责任公司。

股份有限公司 指根据《中华人民共和国公司登记管理条例》规定登记注册，其全部注册资本由等额股份构成并通过发行股票筹集资本，股东以其认购的股份对公司承担有限责任，公司以其全部资产对其债务承担责任的经济组织。

私营企业 指由自然人投资设立或由自然人控股，以雇佣劳动为基础的营利性经济组织。包括按照《公司法》、《合伙企业法》、《私营企业暂行条例》规定登记注册的私营有限责任公司、私营股份有限公司、私营合伙企业和私营独资企业。

其他企业 指上述企业之外的其他内资经济组织。

与港澳台商合资经营企业 指港澳台地区投资者与内地企业依照《中华人民共和国中外合资经营企业法》及有关法律的规定，按合同规定的比例投资设立、分享利润和分担风险的企业。

与港澳台商合作经营企业 指港澳台地区投资者与内地企业依照《中华人民共和国中外合作经营企业法》及有关法律的规定，依照合作合同的约定进行投资或提供条件设立、分配利润和分担风险的企业。

港澳台商独资经营企业 指依照《中华人民共和国外资企业法》及有关法律的规定，在内地由港澳台地区投资者全额投资设立的企业。

港澳台商投资股份有限公司 指根据国家有关规定，经原外经贸部依法批准设立，其中港、澳、台商的股本占公司注册资本的比例达25% 以上的股份有限公司。凡其中港、澳、台商的股本占公司注册资本的比例小于25%的，属于内资企业中的股份有限公司。

中外合资经营企业 指外国企业或外国人与中国内地企业依照《中华人民共和国中外合资经营企业法》及有关法律的规定，按合同规定的比例投资设立、分享利润和分担风险的企业。

中外合作经营企业 指外国企业或外国人与中国内地企业依照《中华人民共和国中外合作经营企业法》及有关法律的规定，依照合作合同的约定进行投资或提供条件设立、分配利润和分担风险的企业。

外资企业 指依照《中华人民共和国外资企业法》及有关法律的规定，在中国内地由外国投资者全额投资设立的企业。

外商投资股份有限公司 指根据国家有关规定，经原外经贸部依法批准设立，其中外资的股本占公司注册资本的比例达25% 以上的股份有限公司。凡其中外资股本占公司注册资本的比例小于25%的，属于内资企业中的股份有限公司。

行政机关、事业单位和社会团体 参照企业登记注册类型，主要按其经费来源和管理方式划分。具体规定如下：

（1）行政机关：包括国家机关和政党机关，原则上均列为“国有”。但有特殊规定的，如供销社等，则列为“集体”。

（2）事业单位：包括经国家机构编制部门和有关业务主管部门批准成立的各类事业单位，不包括实行企业化管理的事业单位。事业单位的划分办法如下：

①由国家财政预算拨款或列入财政预算外资金管理以及经费主要来源于国有主管部门或国有上级单位的事业单位，列为“国有”。

②经费主要来源于集体单位的事业单位，列为“集体”。

③公民个人（或个人合伙）开办的事业单位，列为“私营”。

④上述以外的其他事业单位，如果其经费来源不明确，按管理方式进行归类。

（3）社会团体：包括经民政部门批准成立以及未纳入社会团体管理条例范围的工会、妇联等各类社会团体。社会团体的划分办法如下：

①未纳入民政部社会团体管理条例范围的工会、妇联、共青团、青联、工商联、科协、侨联等社会团体，国家拨款设立的基金会或基金管理组织以及经费主要来源于国有业务主管部门或国有上级单位的社会团体，列为“国有”。

②经费主要来源于集体单位的社会团体，列为“集体”。

③公民个人（或个人合伙）开办的社会团体，划为“私营”。

④上述以外的其他社会团体，如果其经费来源不明确，改按管理方式进行归类。

Explanatory Notes on Main Statistical Indicators

Registration Status of Enterprises Enterprises are classified into 3 categories, namely domestic-funded enterprises, enterprises with investment from Hong Kong, Macau and Taiwan, and enterprises with foreign investment, according to the registration status of an enterprise in industrial and commercial administration agencies. Domestic-funded enterprises include State- owned enterprises, collective-owned enterprises, cooperative enterprises, joint ownership enterprises, limited liability corporations, share-holding corporations Ltd., private enterprises and other enterprises. Included in the enterprises with investment from Hong Kong, Macau and Taiwan and enterprises with foreign investment are joint-venture enterprises, cooperative enterprises, sole investment enterprises and share-holding corporations Ltd. For government agencies, institutions and social organizations which are not registered in industrial and commercial administration agencies, they are classified mainly by their sources of funding and manner of management.

State–owned Enterprises refer to non-corporation economic units where the entire assets are owned by the State and which have been registered in accordance with the Regulation of the People's Republic of China on the Management of Registration of Corporate Enterprises. Not included from this category are solely State-funded corporations in the limited liability corporations.

Collective–owned Enterprises refer to economic units where the assets are owned collectively and which have been registered in accordance with the Regulation of the People's Republic of China on the Management of Registration of Corporate Enterprises.

Cooperative Enterprises refer to a form of collective economic units (enterprises)where capitals come mainly from employees as their shares, with certain proportion of capital from the outside, where production is organized on the basis of independent operation, independent accounting for profits and losses, joint work, democratic management, and a distribution system that integrates remuneration according to work with dividend according to capital share.

Joint Ownership Enterprises refer to economic units established by two or more corporate enterprises or corporate institutions of the same or different ownership, through joint investment on the basis of voluntary participation, equality, and mutual benefits. They include State joint ownership enterprises; collective joint ownership enterprises; joint State-collective enterprises; and other joint ownership enterprises.

Limited Liability Corporations refer to economic units established with investment from 2-50 investors and registered in accordance with the Regulation of the People's Republic of China on the Management of Registration of Corporations, each investor bearing limited liability to the corporation depending on its share of investment, and the corporation bearing liability to its debt to the maximum of its total assets. Limited liability corporations include solely State-funded limited liability corporations and other limited liability corporations.

Share–holding Corporations Ltd. refer to economic units registered in accordance with the Regulation of the People's Republic of China on the Management of Registration of Corporations, with total registered capital divided into equal shares and raised through issuing stocks. Each investor bears limited liability to the corporation depending on the holding of shares, and the corporation bears liability to its debt to the maximum of its total assets.

Private Enterprises refer to profit-making economic units invested and established by natural persons, or controlled by natural persons using employed labour~ Included in this category are private limited liability corporations, private share-holding corporations Ltd., private partnership enterprises and private-funded enterprises registered in accordance with the Company Law, the Law on Partnership Business and Interim Regulations on Private Enterprises.

Other Domestic–funded Enterprises refer to domestic-funded economic units other than those mentioned above.

Joint Venture Enterprises with Funds from Hong Kong, Macau and Taiwan are enterprises established by investors from Hong Kong, Macau and Taiwan with enterprises in the mainland of China in accordance with the Law of the People's Republic of China on Sino-foreign Equity Joint Ventures and other relevant laws, where the establishment of the investment and the sharing of profits and risks are stipulated under joint venture contracts.

Cooperative Enterprises with Funds from Hong Kong, Macan and Taiwan established by investors from Hong Kong, Macau and Taiwan with enterprises in the mainland of China in accordance with the Law of the People's Republic of China on Sino-foreign Contractual Joint Venture and other relevant laws, where the investment or provision of facilities and the sharing of profits and risks are stipulated under cooperative contracts.

Enterprises with Sole (exclusive)Investment from

Hong Kong, Macau and Taiwan refer to enterprises established in the mainland of China with exclusive investment from investors from Hong Kong, Macau and Taiwan in accordance with the Law of the People's Republic of China on Wholly Foreign-owned Enterprises and other relevant laws.

Share–holding Corporations Ltd. with Investment from Hong Kong, Macau and Taiwan refer to share- holding corporations Ltd. established with the approval from the former Ministry of Foreign Trade and Economic Relations in line with relevant State regulations, where the share of investment from Hong Kong, Macau or Taiwan businessmen exceeds 25% of the total registered capital of the corporation. In case the share of investmentfrom Hong Kong, Macau or Taiwan is less than 25% of thetotal registered capital, the enterprise is to be classified as domestic-funded share-holding corporation Ltd.

Joint Venture Enterprises with Foreign Investment refer to enterprises jointly established byforeign enterprises or foreigners with enterprises in themainland of China in accordance with the Law of thePeople's Republic of China on Sino-foreign Equity JointVentures and other relevant laws, where the sharing ofinvestment, profits and risks is stipulated under contract.

Cooperative Enterprises with Foreign Investment refer to enterprises jointly established by foreign enterprises or foreigners with enterprises in the mainland of China in accordance with the Law of the People's Republic of China on Sino-foreign Contractual Joint Venture and other relevant laws, where the investment or provision of facilities and the sharing of profits and risks are stipulated under cooperative contracts.

Enterprises with Sole (exclusive)Foreign Investment refer to enterprises established in the mainland of China with exclusive investment from foreign investors in accordance with the Law of the People's Republic of China on Wholly Foreign-owned Enterprises and other relevant laws.

Share–holding Corporations Ltd. with Foreign Investment refer to share-holding corporations Ltd. established with the approval from the former Ministry of Foreign Trade and Economic Relations in line with relevant State regulations, where the share of investment from foreign investors exceeds 25% of the total registered capital of the corporation. In case the share of foreign investment is less than 25% ofthe total registered capital, the enterprise is to be classified as domestic-funded share-holding corporation Ltd.

Government Agencies, Institutions and Social Organizations are classified into the following categories by source of funds and manner of management taking reference of thc registration status of enterprises:

(1)Government agencies: include State and party agencies, classified in principle as State-owned. There are exceptions, such as supply and marketing cooperatives which are classified as collective-owned.

(2)Institutions: include institutions of various types established with the approval by organization and staffing departments of the government, but exclude institutions where enterprise management system is introduced. Institutions are further classified as follows:

(a)Institutions for which their main budgets are from government budget appropriations or extra-budget funds, or allocated from the budget of their competent government agencies. Such institutions are classified as state-owned.

(b)Institutions for which their budget mainly come from collective units. Such institutions are classified as collective-owned.

(c)Social institutions established by individual or a group of citizens, which are classified as private.

(d)Institutions other than those mentioned above for which their sources of budget are not clear. Such institutions are classified by the manner of management.

(3)Social organizations: include social organizations established with the approval from the Ministry of Civil Affairs, and organizations that are not covered by social organization management regulations such as trade unions, women's federations etc.. Social organizations are further classified as follows:

(a)Social organizations that are not covered by social organization management regulations of the Ministry of Civil Affairs such as trade unions, women federations, communist youth leagues, youth associations, industrial and commerce associations, scientist associations, overseas Chinese associations, etc., foundations and fund management organizations established with funds from the state, and social organizations whose funds mainly come from the budget of their competent government agencies. Such institutions are classified as State-owned.

(b)Social organizations for which their budget mainly come from collective units. Such institutions are classified as collective-owned.

(c)Social organizations established by individual or a group of citizens, which are classified as private.

(d)Social organizations other than those mentioned above for which their sources of budget are not clear. Such organizations are classified by the manner of management.

3 国民经济核算

NATIONAL ECONOMIC ACCOUNTS

资料整理　吴　羽　徐　枫

Data management:Wu Yu Xu Feng

第三部分　国民经济核算

一、简要说明

本章资料包括西安生产总值、构成和指数，分区县生产总值等。根据国家统计局的统一要求，为保持GDP数据的历史可比性，根据国家统计局和陕西省统计局《年度GDP历史数据修订办法》，对2005—2007年度GDP历史数据进行了修订；人均GDP按户籍人口计算，2005年以后按常住人口计算。资料由西安市统计局国民经济核算处提供。

二、主要指标

生产总值（亿元）	4884.13	比上年增长	11.1%
第一产业	217.76	比上年增长	4.8%
第二产业	2117.66	比上年增长	13.9%
第三产业	2548.71	比上年增长	9.3%
人均生产总值（元/人）	56988	比上年增长	10.6%

3　NATIONAL ECONOMIC ACCOUNTS

Ⅰ.Brief Introduction

The data in this chapter consists of composition and indices of the GDP in Xi'an and GDP by region, etc. According to the request of National Bureau of Statistic, in order to keep the history GDP data comparable, the GDP of 2005 – 2007 had been adjusted based on Adjusting Method of yearly GDP released by National Bureau of Statistic and Shaan'xi Provincial Bureau of Statistic. Per capital GDP had been calculated on register population, and after 2005 was calculated on permanent population. Data in this chapter is provided by National Economic Accounting Division of the Xi'an Bureau of Statistics.

Ⅱ.Major Indicators

		Increase over Preceding Year
Gross Domestic Product(100 mil. yuan)	4884.13	11.1%
Primary Industry	217.76	4.8%
Secondary Industry	2117.66	13.9%
Tertiary Industry	2548.71	9.3%
Per Capita Gross Domestic Product (yuan/person)	56988	10.6%

3-1 主要年份生产总值

Gross Domestic Product in Representative Years

(本表按当年价格计算)　　　　(Data in the table are calculated at current prices)

单位：亿元　　　　(100 million yuan)

年份 Year	生产总值 Gross Domestic Product	第一产业 Primary Industry	第二产业 Secondary Industry	第三产业 Tertiary Industry	人均生产总值 (元/人) Per Capita GDP (yuan/person)
1952	3.37	1.59	0.88	0.90	135
1965	12.76	2.62	7.22	2.92	323
1970	17.76	3.13	10.96	3.67	412
1975	21.33	4.14	12.63	4.56	448
1978	25.35	4.83	14.59	5.93	513
1980	31.66	4.73	18.69	8.24	623
1983	35.89	5.22	20.14	10.53	674
1984	44.14	7.45	24.17	12.52	817
1985	57.58	8.76	30.83	17.99	1049
1986	65.78	9.59	33.86	22.33	1178
1987	80.16	10.73	37.69	31.74	1409
1988	99.22	11.47	46.58	41.17	1711
1989	109.38	12.78	48.91	47.69	1851
1990	116.51	13.94	50.15	52.42	1932
1991	136.14	17.17	57.06	61.91	2224
1992	164.85	18.78	69.22	76.85	2662
1993	229.56	22.58	110.88	96.10	3661
1994	289.82	31.68	128.27	129.87	4563
1995	330.35	41.40	135.33	153.62	5131
1996	406.95	46.94	161.63	198.38	6246
1997	488.82	51.33	197.97	239.52	7424
1998	525.85	51.91	216.32	257.62	7906
1999	577.29	45.53	243.35	288.41	8599
2000	646.13	44.65	277.13	324.35	9484
2001	734.86	45.87	312.90	376.09	10628
2002	826.68	47.77	353.58	425.33	11831
2003	946.66	50.72	407.38	488.56	13341
2004	1102.39	60.21	476.92	565.26	15294
2005	1313.93	66.01	540.50	707.42	16406
2006	1538.94	70.44	645.65	822.85	18890
2007	1856.63	82.51	781.94	992.18	22463
2008	2318.14	103.45	981.58	1233.11	27794
2009	2724.08	110.38	1144.75	1468.95	32411
2010	3241.69	140.06	1406.72	1694.91	38343
2011	3862.58	173.14	1674.31	2015.13	45475
2012	4366.10	195.59	1881.75	2288.76	51166
2013	4884.13	217.76	2117.66	2548.71	56983

注：2005年以后人均GDP按平均常住人口计算，根据全国第二次经济普查结果，对2005-2007年生产总值及人均GDP进行了修订。

3-2 主要年份生产总值指数（上年＝100）

Indices of Gross Domestic Product in Representative Years(preceding year = 100)

(本表按可比价格计算) (Data in the table are calculated at constant prices)

年 份	Year	生产总值 Gross Domestic Product	第一产业 Primary Industry	第二产业 Secondary Industry	第三产业 Tertiary Industry	人均生产总值 (元/人) Per Capita GDP (yuan/person)
1952		103.6	92.2	137.5	123.7	
1965		126.1	134.1	133.0	106.7	
1970		122.0	109.4	140.0	100.1	
1975		103.8	92.6	107.1	107.5	
1978		101.7	101.6	99.4	108.2	
1980		111.5	83.3	119.7	116.5	
1985		112.6	107.5	111.8	116.9	
1986		111.4	107.7	108.4	118.8	
1987		113.6	100.8	109.1	126.6	
1988		111.4	81.2	115.5	114.7	
1989		106.7	103.0	104.5	110.8	
1990		105.2	103.0	102.5	109.6	
1991		109.8	118.6	108.6	108.6	108.2
1992		115.6	109.4	118.1	115.0	114.3
1993		123.9	112.5	142.7	108.4	122.3
1994		110.3	98.4	110.6	113.2	108.8
1995		110.0	104.5	112.1	108.6	108.5
1996		114.9	106.8	118.8	111.7	113.5
1997		114.4	109.1	116.7	112.4	113.2
1998		113.3	106.5	117.5	108.8	112.1
1999		112.2	97.4	115.7	110.1	111.2
2000		113.0	103.5	115.1	111.5	111.4
2001		113.1	102.5	115.3	112.6	111.4
2002		113.3	103.1	115.0	113.0	112.1
2003		113.5	101.8	117.5	111.2	111.7
2004		113.5	106.7	115.9	112.0	111.7
2005		114.0	107.5	112.3	116.3	112.2
2006		114.0	107.1	113.7	114.9	112.9
2007		115.6	104.5	115.7	116.4	113.9
2008		116.3	107.6	116.4	116.9	115.3
2009		114.5	106.3	114.0	115.5	113.7
2010		114.5	106.9	118.0	112.5	113.8
2011		113.8	106.7	114.9	113.4	113.2
2012		111.8	106.0	111.8	112.2	111.3
2013		111.1	104.8	113.9	109.3	110.6
平均每年增长	**Yearly Average Growth Rates**					
“一五”时期	**The First Five-Year Plan Period**	**15.8**	**5.9**	**37.7**	**16.9**	
“二五”时期	**The Second Five-Year Plan Period**	**2.0**	**-3.7**	**2.5**	**8.4**	
1963--1965年	**Readjust Period**	**14.2**	**16.1**	**23.4**	**0.3**	
“三五”时期	**The Third Five-Year Plan Period**	**7.1**	**0.1**	**11.7**	**5.4**	
“四五”时期	**The Fourth Five-Year Plan Period**	**5.0**	**4.0**	**5.3**	**5.0**	
“五五”时期	**The Fifth Five-Year Plan Period**	**6.0**	**-0.7**	**6.5**	**10.1**	
“六五”时期	**The Sixth Five-Year Plan Period**	**10.7**	**7.9**	**10.4**	**12.9**	
“七五”时期	**The Seventh Five-Year Plan Period**	**9.6**	**-1.3**	**7.9**	**15.9**	
“八五”时期	**The Eighth Five-Year Plan Period**	**13.8**	**8.5**	**17.8**	**10.7**	**12.3**
“九五”时期	**The Ninth Five-Year Plan Period**	**13.6**	**4.6**	**16.8**	**10.9**	**12.3**
“十五”时期	**The Tenth Five-Year Plan Period**	**13.5**	**4.3**	**15.2**	**13.0**	**11.8**
“十一五”时期	**The Eleventh Five-Year Plan Period**	**15.0**	**6.5**	**15.5**	**15.2**	**13.9**

注：根据全国第二次经济普查结果，对2005-2007年生产总值指数进行了修订。

3–3 主要年份生产总值指数（1952年=100）

Indices of Gross Domestic Product in Representative Years(1952= 100)

(本表按可比价格计算)　　(Data in the table are calculated at constant prices)

年　份 Year	生产总值 Gross Domestic Product	第一产业 Primary Industry	第二产业 Secondary Industry	第三产业 Tertiary Industry
1952	100.0	100.0	100.0	100.0
1965	341.6	173.3	1048.3	329.2
1970	431.6	174.3	1821.0	428.6
1975	614.2	211.9	2362.5	547.9
1978	678.7	231.3	2560.8	643.8
1980	821.4	204.2	3237.2	885.2
1983	988.4	222.5	3846.2	1154.4
1984	1213.6	278.2	4748.8	1388.7
1985	1366.8	299.1	5310.6	1532.4
1986	1523.1	322.3	5756.7	1928.9
1987	1730.0	324.9	6280.6	2441.6
1988	1926.3	263.7	7256.6	2801.2
1989	2054.8	271.6	7583.1	3104.6
1990	2162.5	279.7	7772.7	3403.6
1991	2374.4	331.7	8441.2	3696.3
1992	2744.8	362.9	9969.1	4250.7
1993	3400.8	408.2	14225.9	4607.8
1994	3751.1	401.8	15733.8	5216.0
1995	4126.2	419.9	17637.6	5664.6
1996	4741.0	448.5	20953.5	6327.4
1997	5423.7	489.3	24452.7	7112.0
1998	6145.1	521.1	28731.9	7737.9
1999	6894.8	507.6	33242.8	8519.4
2000	7791.1	525.4	38262.5	9499.1
2001	8811.7	538.5	44116.7	10696.0
2002	9983.7	555.2	50734.2	12086.5
2003	11331.5	265.2	59612.7	13440.2
2004	12861.3	603.1	69091.1	15053.0
2005	14661.9	648.3	77589.3	17506.6
2006	16714.6	694.3	88219.0	20115.1
2007	19322.1	725.5	102069.4	23414.0
2008	22471.5	780.6	118808.8	27371.0
2009	25730.0	829.8	135442.0	31613.5
2010	29460.9	950.1	155081.1	36197.5
2011	33513.2	1013.8	178177.0	41045.6
2012	37469.9	1074.6	199290.7	46062.0
2013	41629.1	1126.2	226992.1	50345.8

3-4 主要年份生产总值构成

Composition of Gross Domestic Product in Representative Years

(本表按当年价格计算)　　(Data in the table are calculated at current prices)

单位:%　　(%)

年　份	Year	生产总值 Gross Domestic Product	第一产业 Primary Industry	第二产业 Secondary Industry	第三产业 Tertiary Industry
1952		100	47.18	26.11	26.71
1965		100	20.53	56.58	22.89
1970		100	17.62	61.71	20.67
1975		100	19.41	59.21	21.38
1978		100	19.05	57.55	23.40
1980		100	14.94	59.03	26.03
1985		100	15.21	53.54	31.25
1986		100	14.58	51.47	33.95
1987		100	13.39	47.02	39.59
1988		100	11.56	46.95	41.49
1989		100	11.68	44.72	43.60
1990		100	11.96	43.04	45.00
1991		100	12.61	41.91	45.48
1992		100	11.39	41.99	46.62
1993		100	9.84	48.30	41.86
1994		100	10.93	44.26	44.81
1995		100	12.53	40.97	46.50
1996		100	11.53	39.72	48.75
1997		100	10.50	40.50	49.00
1998		100	9.87	41.14	48.99
1999		100	7.89	42.15	49.96
2000		100	6.91	42.89	50.20
2001		100	6.24	42.58	51.18
2002		100	5.78	42.77	51.45
2003		100	5.36	43.03	51.61
2004		100	5.46	43.26	51.28
2005		100	5.02	41.14	53.84
2006		100	4.58	41.95	53.47
2007		100	4.44	42.12	53.44
2008		100	4.46	42.34	53.20
2009		100	4.05	42.02	53.93
2010		100	4.32	43.39	52.29
2011		100	4.48	43.35	52.17
2012		100	4.48	43.10	52.42
2013		100	4.46	43.36	52.18
"一五"时期	**The First Five-Year Plan Period**	**100**	**32.88**	**43.92**	**23.20**
"二五"时期	**The Second Five-Year Period**	**100**	**18.08**	**58.63**	**23.29**
1963--1965年	**Readjust Period**	**100**	**19.36**	**55.38**	**25.26**
"三五"时期	**The Third Five-Year Plan Period**	**100**	**18.60**	**57.33**	**24.07**
"四五"时期	**The Fourth Five-Year Plan Period**	**100**	**20.46**	**59.59**	**19.95**
"五五"时期	**The Fifth Five-Year Plan Period**	**100**	**18.41**	**57.69**	**23.90**
"六五"时期	**The Sixth Five-Year Plan Period**	**100**	**16.03**	**55.01**	**28.96**
"七五"时期	**The Seventh Five-Year Plan Period**	**100**	**12.42**	**46.11**	**41.47**
"八五"时期	**The Eighth Five-Year Plan Period**	**100**	**11.44**	**43.52**	**45.04**
"九五"时期	**The Ninth Five-Year Plan Period**	**100**	**9.09**	**41.45**	**49.46**
"十五"时期	**The Tenth Five-Year Plan Period**	**100**	**5.49**	**42.47**	**52.04**
"十一五"时期	**The Eleventh Five-Year Plan Period**	**100**	**4.34**	**42.47**	**53.19**

3-5 各区县生产总值（2013年）

Gross Domestic Product by Region (2013)

单位：亿元 (100 million yuan)

区 县	Region	生产总值 Gross Domestic Product	第一产业 Primary Industry	第二产业 Secondary Industry	第三产业 Tertiary Industry
新城区	Xincheng	471.75		190.16	281.59
碑林区	Beilin	525.76		106.71	419.05
莲湖区	Lianhu	526.68		224.67	302.01
灞桥区	Baqiao	269.03	18.32	157.45	93.26
未央区	Weiyang	601.10	1.54	318.24	281.32
雁塔区	Yanta	938.75	2.29	354.85	581.61
阎良区	Yanliang	168.96	22.01	94.95	52.00
临潼区	Lintong	226.58	32.75	126.49	67.34
长安区	Chang'an	369.15	34.17	168.63	166.35
蓝田县	Lantian	106.89	26.40	40.52	39.97
周至县	Zhouzhi	87.66	28.16	24.30	35.20
户 县	Huxian	155.24	27.80	81.73	45.71
高陵县	Gaoling	279.94	24.32	228.98	26.64

3-6 各区县生产总值指数（2013年）（上年=100）

Indices of Gross Domestic Product by Region (2013) (preceding year = 100)

区 县	Region	生产总值 Gross Domestic Product	第一产业 Primary Industry	第二产业 Secondary Industry	第三产业 Tertiary Industry
新城区	Xincheng	109.0		109.1	109.0
碑林区	Beilin	110.3		112.9	109.7
莲湖区	Lianhu	111.1		111.1	111.0
灞桥区	Baqiao	114.9	105.4	118.3	110.8
未央区	Weiyang	111.6	91.5	113.0	110.2
雁塔区	Yanta	110.1	94.5	113.3	108.3
阎良区	Yanliang	111.5	105.2	114.8	108.9
临潼区	Lintong	111.5	104.8	115.8	107.1
长安区	Chang'an	111.2	104.8	115.4	107.8
蓝田县	Lantian	108.0	104.7	108.8	109.1
周至县	Zhouzhi	109.2	105.6	113.5	108.7
户 县	Huxian	108.2	104.7	108.6	109.2
高陵县	Gaoling	117.8	105.9	119.7	110.2

3-7 各区县生产总值构成（2013年）

Composition of Gross Domestic Product by Region (2013)

单位：%　　(%)

区 县	Region	生产总值 Gross Domestic Product	第一产业 Primary Industry	第二产业 Secondary Industry	第三产业 Tertiary Industry
新城区	Xincheng	100		40.3	59.7
碑林区	Beilin	100		20.3	79.7
莲湖区	Lianhu	100		42.7	57.3
灞桥区	Baqiao	100	6.8	58.5	34.7
未央区	Weiyang	100	0.3	52.9	46.3
雁塔区	Yanta	100	0.2	37.8	62.0
阎良区	Yanliang	100	13.0	56.2	30.8
临潼区	Lintong	100	14.5	55.8	29.7
长安区	Chang'an	100	9.3	45.7	45.0
蓝田县	Lantian	100	24.7	37.9	37.4
周至县	Zhouzhi	100	32.1	27.7	40.2
户 县	Huxian	100	17.9	52.6	29.5
高陵县	Gaoling	100	8.7	81.8	9.5

3-8 主要年份三次产业贡献率

Share of the Contributions of the Three Strata of Industry to the Increase of the GDP in Representative Years

单位：%　　(%)

年份 Year	生产总值 Gross Domestic Product	第一产业 Primary Industry	第二产业 Secondary Industry	第三产业 Tertiary Industry
2006	100	2.5	40.2	57.3
2007	100	1.4	41.4	57.2
2008	100	2.0	41.4	56.6
2009	100	1.7	39.5	58.8
2010	100	1.7	50.7	47.6
2011	100	2.1	47.0	50.9
2012	100	2.1	44.1	53.8
2013	100	1.7	54.7	43.6

3-9 主要年份三次产业拉动率

Contribution of the Three Strata of Industry to GDP Growth in Representative Years

单位：%　　(%)

年份 Year	生产总值 Gross Domestic Product	第一产业 Primary Industry	第二产业 Secondary Industry	第三产业 Tertiary Industry
2006	14.0	0.4	5.7	7.9
2007	15.6	0.2	6.4	9.0
2008	16.3	0.3	6.8	9.2
2009	14.5	0.2	5.7	8.6
2010	14.5	0.3	7.4	6.8
2011	13.8	0.3	6.5	7.0
2012	11.8	0.2	5.2	6.4
2013	11.1	0.2	6.1	4.8

3-10 主要年份非公有制经济增加值

The Added Value of Non-public-owned Economic in Representative Years

年 份 Year	非公有制经济增加值（亿元） the Added Value of Non-public-owned Economic (100 million yuan)	第一产业 Primary Industry	第二产业 Secondary Industry	第三产业 Tertiary Industry	非公有制经济增加值占GDP比重(%) the Added Value of Non-public-owned Economic Percentage to GDP(%)	第一产业 Primary Industry	第二产业 Secondary Industry	第三产业 Tertiary Industry
2005	568.45	20.86	232.66	314.93	43.26	31.60	43.05	44.52
2006	684.66	26.27	279.06	379.33	44.46	37.29	43.22	46.04
2007	854.26	25.25	365.24	463.77	46.01	30.60	46.71	46.74
2008	1103.96	36.42	468.58	598.96	47.62	35.21	47.74	48.57
2009	1327.49	36.32	542.37	748.80	48.73	32.90	47.38	50.98
2010	1611.28	42.66	665.90	902.72	49.70	30.46	47.34	53.26
2011	1952.78	52.93	814.44	1085.41	50.56	30.57	48.64	53.86
2012	2244.25	59.79	902.29	1282.17	51.40	30.57	47.95	56.02
2013	2548.13	61.73	1031.66	1454.74	52.17	28.35	48.72	57.08

主要统计指标解释

生产总值（GDP） 是按市场价格计算的一个地区（或国家）所有常住单位在一定时期内生产活动的最终成果。生产总值有三种表现形态，即价值形态、收入形态和产品形态。从价值形态看，它是所有常住单位在一定时期内生产的全部货物和服务价值超过同期中间投入的全部非固定资产货物和服务价值的差额，即所有常住单位的增加值之和；从收入形态看，它是所有常住单位在一定时期内创造并分配给常住单位和非常住单位的初次收入分配之和；从产品形态看，它是所有常住单位在一定时期内最终使用的货物和服务价值与货物和服务净出口价值之和。在实际核算中，生产总值有三种计算方法，即生产法、收入法和支出法。三种方法分别从不同的方面反映生产总值及其构成。

三次产业 是根据社会生产活动历史发展的顺序对产业结构的划分，产品直接取自自然界的部门称为第一产业，对初级产品进行再加工的部门称为第二产业，为生产和消费提供各种服务的部门称为第三产业。它是世界上较为通用的产业结构分类，但各国的划分不尽一致。

三产业的划分是世界上较为常用的产业结构分类，但各国的划分不尽一致。我国的三次产业划分是：

第一产业：农业（包括农业、林业、畜牧业、渔业和农林牧渔服务业）。

第二产业：工业（包括采矿业，制造业，电力气及水的生产和供应业）和建筑业。

第三产业：除第一、第二产业以外的其他各业。

劳动者报酬 指劳动者因从事生产活动所获得的全部报酬。包括劳动者获得的各种形式的工资、奖金和津贴，既包括货币形式的，也包括实物形式的，还包括劳动者所享受的公费医疗和医药卫生费、上下班交通补贴、单位支付的社会保险费、住房公积金等。

生产税净额 指生产税减生产补贴后的余额。生产税指政府对生产单位从事生产、销售和经营活动以及因从事生产活动使用某些生产要素（如固定资产、土地、劳动力）所 收的各种税、附加费和规费。生产补贴与生产税相反，指政府对生产单位的单方面转移支出，因此视为负生产税，包括政策亏损补贴、价格补贴等。

固定资产折旧 指一定时期内为弥补固定资产损耗按照规定的固定资产折旧率提取的固定资产折旧，或按国民经济核算统一规定的折旧率虚拟计算的固定资产折旧。它反映了固定资产年当期生产中的转移价值。各类企业和企业化管理的事业单位的固定资产折旧是指实际计提的折旧费；不计提折旧的政府机关、非企业化管理的事业单位和居民住房的固定资产折旧是按照统一规定的折旧率和固定资产原值计算的虚拟折旧。原则上，固定资产折旧应按固定资产当期的重置价值计算，但是目前我国尚不具备对全社会固定资产进行重估价的基础，所以暂时只能采用上述办法。

营业盈余 指常住单位创造的增加值扣除劳动者报酬、生产税净额和固定资产折旧后的余额。它相当于企业的营业利润加上生产补贴，但要扣除从利润中开支的工资和福利等。

支出法国内生产总值 是从最终使用的角度反映一个国家（或地区）一定时期内生产活动最终成果的一种方法，包括最终消费支出、资本形成总额及货物和服务净出口三部分。计算公式为：

支出法国内生产总值二最终消费支出+资本形成总额+货物和服务净出口

最终消费支出 指常住单位为满足物质、文化和精神生活的需要，从本国经济领土和国外购买的货物和服务的支出。它不包括非常住单位在本国经济领土内的消费支出。最终消费支出分为居民消费支出和政府消费支出。

居民消费支出 指常住住户在一定时期内对于货物和服务的全部最终消费支出。居民消费支出除了直接以货币形式购买的货物和服务的消费支出外，还包括以其他方式获得的货物和服务的消费支出，即所谓的虚拟消费支出。居民虚拟消费支出包括如下几种类型：单位以实物报酬及实物转移的形式提供给劳动者的货物和服务；住户生产并由本住户消费了的货物和服务，其中的服务仅指住户的自有住房服务和付酬的家庭雇员提供的家庭和个人服务；金融机构提供的金融媒介服务。

政府消费支出 指政府部门为全社会提供的公共服务的消费支出和免费或以较低的价格向居民住户提供的货物和服务的净支出，前者等于政府服务的产出价值减去政府单位所获得的经营收入的价值，后者等于政府部门免费或以较低价格向居民住户提供的货物和服务的市场价值减去向住户收取的价值。

资本形成总额 指常住单位在一定时期内获得减去处置的固定资产和存货的净额，包括固定资本形成总额和存货增加两部分。

固定资本形成总额 指常住单位在一定时期内获得的固定资产减处置的固定资产的价值总额。固定资产是通过生产活动生产出来的，且其使用年限在一年以上、单位价值在规定标准以上的资产，不包括自然资产。可分为有形固定资本形成总额和无形固定资本形成总额。有形固定资本形成总额包括一定时期内完成的建筑工程、安装工程和设备工器具购置（减处置）价值，以及土地改良、新增役、种、奶、毛、娱乐用牲畜和新增经济林木价值。无形固定资本形成总额包括矿藏的勘探、计算机软件等获得减处置。

存货增加 指常住单位在一定时期内存货实物量变动的市场价值，即期末价值减期初价值的差额，再扣除当期由于价格变动而产生的持有收益。存货增加可以是正值，也可以是负值，正值表示存货上升，负值表示存货下降。存货包括生产单位购进的原材料、燃料和储备物资等存货，以及生产单位生产的产成品、在制品和半成品等存货。

货物和服务净出口 指货物和服务出口减货物和服务进口的差额。出口包括常住单位向非常住单位出售或无偿转让的各种货物和服务的价值；进口包括常住单位从非常住单位购买或无偿得到的各种货物和服务的价值。由于服务活动的提供与使用同时发生，一般把常住单位从非常住单位得到的服务作为进口，非常住单位从常住单位得到的服务作为出口。货物的出口和进口都按离岸价格计算。

Explanatory Notes on Main Statistical Indicators

Gross Domestic Product (GDP) refers to the final products at market prices produced by all resident units in a country (or a region) during a certain period of time. Gross domestic product is expressed in three different perspectives, namely value, income, and products respectively. GDP in its value perspective refers to the total value of all goods and services produced by all resident units during a certain period of time, minus the total value of input of goods and services of the nature of non-fixed assets; in other words, it is the sum of the value-added of all resident units. GDP from the perspective of income includes the primary income created by all resident units and distributed to resident and non-resident units. GDP from the perspective of products refers to the value of all goods and services for final demand by all resident units plus the net exports of goods and services during a given period of time. In the practice of national accounting, gross domestic product is calculated from three approaches, namely production approach, income approach and expenditure approach, which reflect gross domestic product and its composition from different angles.

For a region, it is called as Gross Regional Product(GRP) or regional GDP.

Three Strata of Industry Classification of economic activities into three strata of industry is a common practice in the world, although the grouping varies to some extent from country to country. In China economic activities are categorized into the following three strata of industry:

Primary industry refers to agriculture, forestry, animal husbandry and fishery and services in support of these industries.

Secondary industry refers to mining and quarrying, manufacturing, production and supply of electricity, water and gas, and construction.

Tertiary industry refers to all other economic activities not included in the primary or secondary industries.

Compensation of Employees refers to the total payment of various forms to employees for the productive activities they are engaged in. It includes wages, bonuses and allowances, which the employees earn in cash or in kind. It also includes the free medical services provided to the employees and the medicine expenses, transport subsidies and social insurance, and housing fund paid by the employers.

Net Taxes on Production refers to taxes on production less subsidies on production. The taxes on production refers to the various taxes, extra charges and fees levied on the production units on their production, sale and business activities as well as on the use of some factors of production, such as fixed assets, land and labour in the production activities they are engaged in. In contrast to taxes on production, subsidies on production refer to the unilateral government transfer to the production units and are therefore regarded as negative taxes on production. They include subsidies on the loss due to implementation of government policies, price subsidies, etc.

Depreciation of Fixed Assets refers to the depreciation of fixed assets in a given period, drawn in accordance with the stipulated depreciation rate for the purpose of compensating the wear-and-tear loss of the fixed assets or the depreciation of fixed assets imputed in accordance with the stipulated unified depreciation rate in the national economic accounting system. It reflects the value of transfer of the fixed assets in the production of the current period. The depreciation of fixed assets in various enterprises and institutions managed as enterprises refers to the depreciation expenses actually drawn. In government agencies and institutions not managed as enterprises which do not draw the depreciation expenses, as well as for the houses of residents, the depreciation of fixed assets is the imputed depreciation, which is calculated in accordance with the stipulated unified depreciation rate. In principle, the depreciation of fixed assets should be calculated on the basis of the re-purchased value of the fixed assets. However, currently the conditions in China do not facilitate the revaluation of all the fixed assets. Therefore, only the above-mentioned methods can be adopted at present.

Operating Surplus refers to the balance of the value added created by the resident units after deducting the labourers remuneration, net taxes on production and the depreciation of fixed assets. It is equivalent to the business profit of the enterprises plus subsidies to production, but the wages and welfare expenses paid from the profits should be deducted.

GDP by Expenditure Approach refers to the method of measuring the final results of production activities of a country (region) during a given period from the perspective of final uses. It includes final consumption expenditure, gross capital formation and net export of goods and services. The formula for computation is.:

GDP by expenditure approach = final consumption expenditure + gross capital formation + net export of goods and services

Final Consumption Expenditure refers to the total expenditure of resident units for purchases of goods and services from both the domestic economic territory and abroad to meet the needs of material, cultural and spiritual life. It does not include the expenditure of non-resident units on consumption in the economic territory of the country. The final consumption expenditure is broken down into household consumption expenditure and government consumption expenditure.

Household Consumption Expenditure refers to the total expenditure of resident households on the final consumption of goods and services. In addition to the consumption of goods and services bought by the households directly with money, the household consumption expenditure also includes expenditure on goods and services obtained by the households in other ways, i.e. the so-called imputed consumption expenditure, which includes the following: (a) the goods and services provided to households by employers in the form of payment in kind and transfer in kind; (b) goods and services produced and consumed by the households themselves, in which the services refer to the owner-occupied housing and services offered by payed family employees; (c) financial intermediate services provided by financial institution.

Government Consumption Expenditure refers to the consumption expenditure spent for the provision of public services provided by the government to the whole country and the net expenditure on the goods and services provided by the government to households free of charge or at reduced prices. The former equals to the output value of the government services minus the value of operating income obtained by the government departments. The latter equals to the market value of the goods and services provided by the government free of charge or at reduced prices to the households minus the value received by the government from the households.

Gross Capital Formation refers to the fixed assets acquired less disposals and the net value of inventory, thus including gross fixed capital formation and changes in inventories.

Gross Fixed Capital Formation refers to the value of acquisitions less those disposals of fixed assets during a given period. Fixed assets are the assets produced through production activities with unit value above a specified amount and which could be used for over one year. Natural assets are not included. Gross fixed capital formation can be categorized into total tangible fixed capital formation and total intangible fixed capital formation. Total tangible fixed capital formation includes the value of the construction projects and installation projects completed and the equipment, apparatus and instruments purchased (less those disposed) as well as the value of land improved, the value of draught animals, breeding stock and animals for milk, for wool and for recreational purposes and the newly increased forest with economic value. Total intangible fixed capital formation includes the prospecting of minerals and the acquisition of computer software minus the disposal of them.

Changes in Inventories refers to the market value of the change in the physical volume of inventory of resident units during a given period, i.e. the difference between the values at the beginning and at the end of the period minus the gains due to the change in prices. The changes in inventories can have a positive or a negative value. A positive value indicates an increase in inventory while a negative value indicates a decrease in inventory. The inventory includes raw materials, fuels and reserve materials purchased by the production units as well as the inventory of finished products, semi-finished products and work-in-progress.

Net Export of Goods and Services refers to the exports of goods and services subtracting the imports of goods and services. Exports include the value of various goods and services sold or gratuitously transferred by resident units to non-resident units. Imports include the value of various goods and services purchased or gratuitously acquired resident units from non-resident units. Because the provision of services and the use of them happen simultaneously, the acquisition of services by resident units from abroad is usually treated as import while the acquisition of services by non-resident units in this country is usually treated as export. The exports and imports of goods are calculated at FOB.

4 人口、从业人员与职工工资

POPULATION, EMPLOYMENT AND WAGES

资料整理：王义龙　张　静

Data management: Wang Yilong　Zhang Jing

第四部分 人口、从业人员与职工工资

一、简要说明

本章资料包括主要年份人口、分区县户籍和常住人口及变动、从业人员及劳动报酬等。户籍人口数为公安年报数，1991年以前年份市区数未包括临潼、长安。主要数据由西安市统计局人口就业处提供。

二、主要指标

年末户籍人口（万人）	806.93	比上年增长	1.4%
人口自然增长率（‰）	4.20	比上年下降	0.36个千分点
常住人口（万人）	858.81	比上年增长	0.4%
男女性别比（以女性为100）	105.54	比上年下降	0.02个百分点
户籍人口密度（人／平方公里）	798	比上年增加	11人/平方公里
城镇非私营单位在岗职工年平均工资（元）	50797	比上年增长	10.8%

4 POPULATION,EMPLOYMENT AND WAGES

Ⅰ.Brief Introduction

This chapter consists of the data about ragistered population and permanent resident population consequent years, population of all the districts and counties and the correspondent changes, the employed and their wages. The registered population data are from the annual report of the Xi'an Bureau of Public Security, with Lintong, Chang'an not included before 1991. The population data is provided primarily by Population & Employment Office of the Xi'an Bureau of Statistics.

Ⅱ.Major Indicators

		Increase over Preceding Year
Total registered Population of Year-end(10 000 persons)	806.93	1.4%
Natural Growth Rate(‰)	4.20	-0.36 thousands of points
Permanent Population(10 000 persons)	858.81	0.4%
Sex Ratio (Female=100)	105.54	-0.02 percentage points
Density of Population (person/sq.km)	798	11
Aunual Average Wage of Stuff and Workers in Urban Non-privite Enterprises(yuan)	50797	10.8%

4-1 主要年份人口数、人口密度和人口发展情况

Population, Population Density and Population Development in Representative years

单位：万人 (10 000 persons)

年份 Year	总人口 Total population	市区 Urban Area	女性人口数 Number of Female	非农业人口数 Non-Agricultural Population	人口密度（人/平方公里） Density of Population (person/sq.km)	总人口指数（上年为100） Total Population Index (100 for preceding year) 全市 Whole City	市区 Urban Area
1952	252.92	92.42	118.81	57.61	254	102.6	103.1
1965	400.05	179.88	190.72	136.39	401	102.5	103.4
1970	435.12	188.12	210.47	139.12	436	101.9	101.4
1978	498.10	210.15	241.82	159.98	499	101.7	102.7
1980	511.91	221.19	249.26	172.85	513	101.4	102.5
1985	553.11	245.76	268.40	201.90	554	101.6	102.2
1986	563.97	251.80	273.30	205.92	565	102.0	102.5
1987	574.46	257.69	278.12	210.25	575	101.9	102.3
1988	585.85	264.94	283.63	216.99	587	102.0	102.8
1989	597.36	270.80	289.44	222.54	598	102.0	102.2
1990	608.89	275.69	295.29	226.98	610	101.9	101.8
1991	615.48	419.29	298.13	230.85	617	101.1	152.1
1992	623.20	429.54	301.92	236.45	624	101.3	102.4
1993	630.91	435.41	305.30	240.85	632	101.2	101.4
1994	639.45	442.30	309.17	248.35	641	101.4	101.6
1995	648.21	448.65	313.46	255.71	645	101.4	101.4
1996	654.87	454.68	316.60	261.28	653	101.0	101.3
1997	662.06	461.17	320.18	267.52	663	101.1	101.4
1998	668.22	466.31	323.20	271.75	669	100.9	101.1
1999	674.50	463.56	326.12	276.14	676	100.9	99.4
2000	688.01	483.10	332.83	285.79	689	102.0	104.2
2001	694.84	489.88	336.04	292.62	696	101.0	101.4
2002	702.59	497.38	339.51	300.05	704	101.1	101.5
2003	716.58	510.26	346.26	312.88	718	102.0	102.6
2004	725.01	516.30	350.85	318.50	717	101.2	101.2
2005	741.73	533.21	359.71	333.14	734	102.3	103.3
2006	753.11	540.97	365.74	343.78	745	101.5	101.5
2007	764.25	549.19	371.84	353.85	756	101.5	101.5
2008	772.30	554.73	376.76	363.87	764	101.1	101.0
2009	781.67	561.58	382.39	370.66	773	101.2	101.2
2010	782.73	562.65	383.93	374.64	774	100.1	100.2
2011	791.83	568.77	389.31	391.31	783	101.2	101.1
2012	795.98	572.76	398.40	392.04	787	100.5	100.7
2013	806.93	580.60	398.15	409.82	798	101.4	101.4

注：人口部分均为公安年报数据，系户籍人口。1991年以前年份，市区数未包括临潼、长安。

4-2 主要年份人口自然变动情况

Natural Population Movements in Representative Years

单位：万人 (10 000 persons)

年份 Year	出生 Birth 人数 Population	出生率（‰） Birth Rate (‰)	死亡 Death 人数 Population	死亡率（‰） Death Rate (‰)	自然增长率（‰） Natural Growth Rate (‰)	迁入人口 Immigrant population	迁出人口 Emigrant population
1985	8.95	16.30	3.01	5.48	10.82	11.60	8.74
1986	10.14	18.15	2.78	4.97	13.18	11.79	8.39
1987	9.76	17.14	2.83	4.97	12.17	12.58	9.26
1988	9.42	16.24	2.89	4.98	11.26	13.54	8.97
1989	11.78	19.92	3.04	5.13	14.79	12.73	10.15
1990	12.40	20.55	3.45	5.72	14.83	11.82	9.86
1991	8.73	14.25	3.26	5.33	8.92	8.98	6.09
1992	8.98	14.49	3.39	5.48	9.01	13.94	9.54
1993	9.25	14.75	3.37	5.38	9.37	11.50	8.33
1994	8.08	12.71	3.16	4.97	7.74	13.40	8.59
1995	7.69	11.95	3.21	4.98	6.97	14.41	8.85
1996	7.26	11.15	3.41	5.24	5.91	11.94	8.88
1997	6.84	10.38	3.12	4.75	5.63	12.58	8.62
1998	6.40	9.62	3.10	4.66	4.96	10.89	8.36
1999	6.19	9.22	3.88	5.78	3.44	12.58	9.23
2000	8.90	13.07	4.06	5.96	7.11	17.12	9.23
2001	5.11	7.39	2.89	4.19	3.20	15.16	10.83
2002	5.34	7.64	3.08	4.41	3.23	13.90	9.41
2003	6.02	8.48	3.32	4.68	3.80	20.60	9.15
2004	6.63	9.19	4.23	5.87	3.32	15.56	10.19
2005	7.67	9.58	4.13	5.16	4.42	22.61	9.46
2006	8.13	9.98	4.45	5.46	4.52	17.23	11.75
2007	8.27	10.00	4.53	5.48	4.52	19.90	14.01
2008	8.47	10.15	4.65	5.57	4.58	18.49	15.04
2009	8.47	10.08	4.73	5.63	4.45	16.84	13.14
2010	8.23	9.73	4.51	5.34	4.39	14.09	13.50
2011	8.25	9.71	4.57	5.38	4.33	14.21	11.74
2012	8.64	10.13	4.75	5.57	4.56	12.55	13.10
2013	8.20	9.57	4.60	5.37	4.20	10.83	8.60

注：2004年以前为公安年报数据。迁入人口和迁出人口为公安年报数据。2010年出生、死亡、自然增长率根据第六次人口普查数据推算得出。2005-2009、2011-2013年出生、死亡、自然增长率为人口变动抽样调查数据。

4-3 全市及各区县人口数和户数（2013年）

Population and Households by Region（2013）

单位：万人 (10 000 persons)

区 县	Region	总户数（万户） Number of Households (10 000 households)	总人口 Total Population	非农业人口 Non-agriculture	按性别划分Grouped by Sex 男 Male	女 Female	迁入人口(人) Immigrant population (person)	迁出人口(人) Emigrant population (person)
全 市	**Total**	**245.53**	**806.93**	**409.82**	**408.78**	**398.15**	**108268**	**86043**
新城区	Xincheng	17.15	50.69	50.69	25.71	24.98	4052	1595
碑林区	Beilin	21.11	71.32	71.32	36.56	34.76	18715	18820
莲湖区	Lianhu	22.37	65.10	65.10	32.82	32.28	6720	3256
灞桥区	Baqiao	17.66	53.21	24.95	26.21	27.00	5116	2567
未央区	Weiyang	18.23	57.11	42.48	28.43	28.68	10303	7317
雁塔区	Yanta	25.49	81.80	71.83	40.89	40.91	21406	28271
阎良区	Yanliang	7.79	26.01	8.88	13.08	12.93	2163	945
临潼区	Lintong	20.37	71.39	11.97	36.09	35.30	3479	1850
长安区	Chang'an	30.43	103.97	20.35	51.85	52.12	11825	5008
蓝田县	Lantian	18.88	65.20	5.78	33.80	31.40	4622	4822
周至县	Zhouzhi	17.72	68.15	6.40	35.94	32.21	6858	4777
户 县	Huxian	18.38	60.66	12.89	31.31	29.35	5910	4470
高陵县	Gaoling	9.95	32.32	17.18	16.09	16.23	7099	2344

注：本表均为公安年报数据。

4-4　全市及各区县常住人口数和人口变动情况（2013年）

Permanent Population and Population Changes by Region（2013）

区　县	Region	常住人口（万人） Permanent Population (10 000 persons)	城镇 Urban	出生率（‰） Birth Rate（‰）	死亡率（‰） Death Rate（‰）	自然增长率（‰） Natural Growth Rate（‰）
全　市	**Total**	**858.81**	**618.77**	**9.57**	**5.37**	**4.2**
新城区	Xincheng	59.64	59.64	6.35	3.18	3.17
碑林区	Beilin	62.23	62.23	6.68	3.51	3.17
莲湖区	Lianhu	70.43	70.43	6.91	3.76	3.15
灞桥区	Baqiao	60.50	56.52	9.96	5.61	4.35
未央区	Weiyang	81.84	75.32	10.43	5.42	5.01
雁塔区	Yanta	119.29	119.29	9.07	4.88	4.19
阎良区	Yanliang	28.40	15.91	9.51	5.48	4.03
临潼区	Lintong	66.81	21.93	10.68	5.57	5.11
长安区	Chang'an	110.03	62.24	11.09	6.77	4.32
蓝田县	Lantian	52.07	14.56	11.16	6.93	4.23
周至县	Zhouzhi	57.24	17.02	11.92	6.91	5.01
户　县	Huxian	56.32	22.48	10.39	6.17	4.22
高陵县	Gaoling	34.01	21.2	10.32	6.01	4.31

注：本表数据均为人口变动抽样调查数据。

4-5　主要年份常住人口数

Permanent Population in Representative Years

单位：万人　　　　(10 000 persons)

年　份 Year	年末常住人口 Permanent population（year-end）	城镇 Urban	农村 Rural
2000	741.14	450.36	290.78
2005	806.81	510.55	296.26
2006	822.52	530.94	291.58
2007	830.54	548.99	281.55
2008	837.52	565.16	272.36
2009	843.46	581.40	262.06
2010	847.41	584.71	262.7
2011	851.34	596.79	254.55
2012	855.29	611.62	243.67
2013	858.81	618.77	240.04

注：2000年常住人口为普查数据。2010年常住人口为年末常住人口数，根据第六次人口普查数据推算得出。2005-2009、2011-2013年常住人口为人口变动抽样调查数据。

4-6 主要年份社会从业人数

Number of Social Laborers in Representative Years

单位：万人　　　　(10 000 persons)

年份 Year	合计 Total	一、按城乡分 Grouped by Urban area and Rural area					二、按三次产业分 Grouped by Industry		
		1.城镇 Urban	国有经济 State-owned Enterprises	集体经济 Collective Enterprises	其他经济 Others	2.乡村 Village	第一产业 Primary Industry	第二产业 Secondary Industry	第三产业 Tertiary Industry
1985	296.80	129.07	96.80	29.07	3.20	167.73	135.89	98.61	62.30
1986	299.45	132.82	101.28	28.43	3.11	166.63	127.46	100.61	71.38
1987	312.16	138.56	104.58	30.72	3.26	173.60	130.36	107.75	74.05
1988	327.76	142.24	106.46	30.73	5.05	185.52	138.87	108.12	80.77
1989	332.65	145.65	108.80	30.44	6.41	187.00	142.21	106.40	84.04
1990	343.06	147.93	110.95	29.78	7.20	195.13	149.64	106.74	86.68
1991	347.65	149.48	111.87	29.80	7.81	198.17	152.24	108.19	87.22
1992	357.51	151.67	113.19	29.97	8.51	205.84	154.75	110.22	92.54
1993	363.70	155.72	112.98	29.77	12.97	207.98	154.02	114.02	95.66
1994	364.56	154.88	113.39	27.97	13.52	209.68	153.51	108.53	102.52
1995	372.60	158.80	113.79	25.58	19.43	213.80	153.39	109.67	109.54
1996	379.29	164.54	113.29	24.82	26.43	214.75	153.43	109.17	116.69
1997	385.14	169.52	112.44	23.52	33.56	215.62	153.23	109.46	122.45
1998	393.95	177.20	106.06	21.50	49.64	216.75	153.00	110.45	130.50
1999	400.43	180.27	105.08	20.50	54.69	220.16	154.64	110.58	135.21
2000	389.10	176.45	103.46	18.40	54.59	212.65	147.03	107.26	134.81
2001	389.30	177.94	100.47	17.10	60.37	211.36	145.09	108.96	135.25
2002	397.16	181.85	100.54	16.90	64.41	215.31	143.04	111.62	142.50
2003	404.92	183.23	94.51	16.78	71.94	221.69	146.67	109.09	149.16
2004	409.57	187.53	93.43	15.41	78.69	222.04	141.81	111.70	156.06
2005	415.83	192.53	93.27	14.47	84.79	223.30	136.31	114.20	165.32
2006	422.15	196.16	84.46	14.41	97.29	225.99	135.10	116.09	170.96
2007	436.36	214.27	90.58	11.88	111.81	222.09	133.33	125.06	177.97
2008	448.05	224.20	90.17	10.60	123.43	223.85	127.87	130.23	189.95
2009	462.52	239.39	90.83	7.63	140.93	223.13	122.13	131.57	208.82
2010	477.58	252.54	94.01	5.48	153.05	225.04	117.27	145.40	214.91
2011	495.99	265.43	91.62	5.33	168.48	230.56	121.05	151.33	223.61
2012	514.57	287.65	95.33	5.10	187.22	226.92	114.92	162.35	237.30
2013	530.71	308.04	86.06	7.29	214.69	222.67	110.45	151.50	268.76

注：第一产业从业人员中包括城镇农林牧渔及服务业企业人员。

4-7 按国民经济行业分从业人数（2013年）

单位：万人

行 业	Sector	合计 Total
总计	**Total**	**530.71**
（一）农、林、牧、渔业	Agriculture ,Forestry,Animal Husbandry and Fishery	110.51
（二）采矿业	Mining	0.15
（三）制造业	Manufacturing	83.27
（四）电力、燃气及水的生产供应业	Production and Distribution of Electricity,Gas and Water	2.45
（五）建筑业	Construction	66.07
（六）批发和零售业	Wholesale and Retail Trades	68.15
（七）交通运输、仓储和邮政业	Traffic,Transport,Storage and Post	33.21
（八）住宿和餐饮业	Hotels and Catering Services	25.19
（九）信息传输、软件和信息技术服务业	Information Transmission,Software and Information Technology Services	12.87
（十）金融业	Financial Intermediation	7.10
（十一）房地产业	Real Estate	8.95
（十二） 租赁和商务服务业	Leasing and Business Services	18.91
（十三）科学研究和技术服务业	Scientific Research and Technical Services	13.83
（十四）水利、环境和公共设施管理业	Management of Water Conservancy, Environment and Public Facilities	2.60
（十五）居民服务、修理和其他服务业	Services to Households, Repairs and Other Services	25.42
（十六）教育	Education	22.38
（十七）卫生和社会工作	Health and Social Work	14.32
（十八）文化、体育和娱乐业	Culture, Sports and Entertainment	3.40
（十九）公共管理、社会保障和社会组织	Public Administration, Social Security and Social Organizations	11.93
（二十）国际组织	International Organizations	

Number of Employed Persons Grouped by Sector（2013）

(10 000 persons)

国有经济 State-owned Enterprises	集体经济 Collective Enterprises	城镇其他经济 Urban Other Enterprises	城镇私营经济及个体劳动者 Urban Private Enterprises and Individual Labors	乡镇劳动者 Villages and Towns Labors
86.06	**7.29**	**105.07**	**109.62**	**222.67**
0.33		0.01	1.69	108.48
0.01		0.05	0.09	
14.95	0.71	29.79	12.16	25.66
0.55	0.03	1.81	0.06	
6.10	4.63	25.38	5.61	24.35
1.34	0.25	10.58	42.68	13.30
12.72	0.06	4.10	1.71	14.62
0.63	0.02	6.62	9.61	8.31
0.18		6.51	5.27	0.91
1.92	0.20	4.02	0.05	0.91
0.97	0.08	4.62	3.28	
0.62	0.81	3.95	9.21	4.32
9.27	0.06	2.79	1.13	0.58
1.44	0.01	0.98	0.17	
0.27	0.31	1.04	15.44	8.36
16.07	0.02	1.48	0.03	4.78
6.60	0.10	0.51	0.15	6.96
1.30		0.82	1.28	
10.79		0.01		1.13

4-8 全部单位从业人员情况（2013年）

单位：人

分　组	Classify	单位从业人员 Employed Persons	女性 Female
总计	**Total**	**1984178**	**698449**
一、按机构类型分组	**Grouped by Organization Type**		
#企业	Enterprises	1568506	508600
机关	Government Units	100271	33177
事业	Public Institutions	298082	148201
二、按国民经济行业分组	**Grouped by Economic Sector**		
（一）农业	Agriculture ,Forestry,Animal Husbandry and Fishery	3347	939
（二）采矿业	Mining	586	58
（三）制造业	Manufacturing	454469	152431
（四）电力、燃气及水的生产供应业	Production and Distribution of Electricity,Gas and Water	23930	7318
（五）建筑业	Construction	361102	43842
（六）批发和零售业	Wholesale and Retail Trades	121611	63748
（七）交通运输、仓储和邮政业	Traffic,Transport,Storage and Post	168746	57053
（八）住宿和餐饮业	Hotels and Catering Services	72760	42296
（九）信息传输、软件和信息技术服务业	Information Transmission,Software and Information Technology Services	66990	24399
（十）金融业	Financial Intermediation	61331	32568
（十一）房地产业	Real Estate	56678	21818
（十二） 租赁和商务服务业	Leasing and Business Services	53838	18667
（十三）科学研究和技术服务业	Scientific Research and Technical Services	121236	31894
（十四）水利、环境和公共设施管理业	Management of Water Conservancy, Environment and Public Facilities	24398	10603
（十五）居民服务、修理和其他服务业	Services to Households, Repairs and Other Services	16132	6943
（十六）教育	Education	175729	94120
（十七）卫生和社会工作	Health and Social Work	72138	44474
（十八）文化、体育和娱乐业	Culture, Sports and Entertainment	21155	9007
（十九）公共管理、社会保障和社会组织	Public Administration, Social Security and Social Organizations	108002	36271
（二十）国际组织	International Organizations		

Basic Facts on All Employed Persons（2013）

(persons)

在岗职工合计 Total Fully Employed Staff and Workers	其他从业人员 Other Employed Persons	单位从业人员平均人数 Average Employment	在岗职工 Staff and Workers	其他从业人员 Other Employed Persons
1835995	**148183**	**2090086**	**1944594**	**145492**
1445678	122828	1669690	1549800	119890
88360	11911	100908	89119	11789
285025	13057	299399	286510	12889
3282	65	3343	3278	65
213	373	567	214	353
439519	14950	506653	491983	14670
22717	1213	26822	25643	1179
281839	79263	396582	319759	76823
118688	2923	120965	118240	2725
164844	3902	176108	172119	3989
65727	7033	73666	66525	7141
66435	555	70636	70107	529
58631	2700	62500	59028	3472
53599	3079	55617	52608	3009
51836	2002	56842	55166	1676
118215	3021	121790	118754	3036
22002	2396	24241	21762	2479
15744	388	16023	15624	399
168400	7329	176853	169723	7130
68880	3258	71013	67806	3207
19500	1655	21144	19492	1652
95924	12078	108721	96763	11958

4-9 国有单位从业人员情况（2013年）

单位：人

分 组	Classify	单位从业人员 Employed Persons	女性 Female
总计	**Total**	**860522**	**330957**
一、按机构类型分组	**Grouped by Organization Type**		
#企业	Enterprises	464267	150203
机关	Government Units	100271	33177
事业	Public Institutions	295197	147032
二、按国民经济行业分组	**Grouped by Economic Sector**		
（一）农业	Agriculture ,Forestry,Animal Husbandry and Fishery	3255	897
（二）采矿业	Mining	53	8
（三）制造业	Manufacturing	149498	53839
（四）电力、燃气及水的生产供应业	Production and Distribution of Electricity,Gas and Water	5512	1487
（五）建筑业	Construction	61031	7497
（六）批发和零售业	Wholesale and Retail Trades	13358	7461
（七）交通运输、仓储和邮政业	Traffic,Transport,Storage and Post	127185	41184
（八）住宿和餐饮业	Hotels and Catering Services	6285	3449
（九）信息传输、软件和信息技术服务业	Information Transmission,Software and Information Technology Services	1824	302
（十）金融业	Financial Intermediation	19151	9482
（十一）房地产业	Real Estate	9690	4016
（十二） 租赁和商务服务业	Leasing and Business Services	6208	2474
（十三）科学研究和技术服务业	Scientific Research and Technical Services	92686	24181
（十四）水利、环境和公共设施管理业	Management of Water Conservancy, Environment and Public Facilities	14448	5941
（十五）居民服务、修理和其他服务业	Services to Households, Repairs and Other Services	2673	824
（十六）教育	Education	160717	85835
（十七）卫生和社会工作	Health and Social Work	66046	40562
（十八）文化、体育和娱乐业	Culture, Sports and Entertainment	12964	5268
（十九）公共管理、社会保障和社会组织	Public Administration, Social Security and Social Organizations	107938	36250
（二十）国际组织	International Organizations		

Basic Facts on Persons Employed by State-owned Units（2013）

(persons)

在岗职工合计 Total Fully Employed Staff and Workers	其他从业人员 Other Employed Persons	单位从业人员平均人数 Average Employment	在岗职工 Staff and Workers	其他从业人员 Other Employed Persons
806011	**54511**	**919949**	**864578**	**55371**
434591	29676	521756	490929	30827
88360	11911	100908	89119	11789
282306	12891	296502	283784	12718
3190	65	3251	3186	55
53		53	53	
144330	5168	191544	186251	5293
5143	369	5545	5174	371
42551	18480	70766	51422	19344
12884	474	13595	13311	284
124994	2191	131730	129455	2275
5911	374	6680	6276	404
1787	37	1796	1757	39
18427	724	19929	19078	851
9380	310	10212	9869	343
6092	116	6189	6063	125
90699	1987	93189	91191	1993
12933	1515	14133	12664	1469
2474	199	2749	2544	205
154936	5781	161960	156201	5759
62861	3185	65013	61879	3134
11506	1458	12958	11505	1453
95860	12078	108657	96699	11958

4-10 城镇集体单位从业人员情况（2013年）

单位：人

分 组	Classify	单位从业人员 Employed Persons	女性 Female
总计	**Total**	**72911**	**15069**
一、按机构类型分组	**Grouped by Organization Type**		
#企业	Enterprises	72136	14648
机关	Government Units		
事业	Public Institutions	775	421
二、按国民经济行业分组	**Grouped by Economic Sector**		
（一）农业	Agriculture ,Forestry,Animal Husbandry and Fishery		
（二）采矿业	Mining		
（三）制造业	Manufacturing	7090	3029
（四）电力、燃气及水的生产供应业	Production and Distribution of Electricity,Gas and Water	306	73
（五）建筑业	Construction	46287	6393
（六）批发和零售业	Wholesale and Retail Trades	2452	913
（七）交通运输、仓储和邮政业	Traffic,Transport,Storage and Post	599	318
（八）住宿和餐饮业	Hotels and Catering Services	249	156
（九）信息传输、软件和信息技术服务业	Information Transmission,Software and Information Technology Services	49	23
（十）金融业	Financial Intermediation	1955	999
（十一）房地产业	Real Estate	773	351
（十二） 租赁和商务服务业	Leasing and Business Services	8102	623
（十三）科学研究和技术服务业	Scientific Research and Technical Services	608	265
（十四）水利、环境和公共设施管理业	Management of Water Conservancy, Environment and Public Facilities	143	49
（十五）居民服务、修理和其他服务业	Services to Households, Repairs and Other Services	3066	1193
（十六）教育	Education	205	133
（十七）卫生和社会工作	Health and Social Work	994	545
（十八）文化、体育和娱乐业	Culture, Sports and Entertainment	33	6
（十九）公共管理、社会保障和社会组织	Public Administration, Social Security and Social Organizations		
（二十）国际组织	International Organizations		

Basic Facts on Persons Employed by Urban Collective-owned Units（2013）

(persons)

		单位从业人员		
在岗职工合计 Total Fully Employed Staff and Workers	其他从业人员 Other Employed Persons	平均人数 Average Employment	在岗职工 Staff and Workers	其他从业人员 Other Employed Persons
70065	**2846**	**73622**	**70813**	**2809**
69332	2804	72846	70079	2767
733	42	776	734	42
6521	569	7131	6564	567
306		317	317	
44844	1443	47181	45816	1365
1885	567	2494	1878	616
599		591	591	
218	31	250	219	31
49		46	46	
1877	78	1929	1854	75
734	39	777	741	36
8097	5	7847	7842	5
600	8	586	578	8
143		143	143	
2999	67	3096	3029	67
205		207	207	
955	39	994	955	39
33		33	33	

4-11 其他经济类型单位从业人员情况（2013年）

单位：人

分 组	Classify	单位从业人员 Employed Persons	女性 Female
总计	Total	1050745	352423
一、按机构类型分组	Grouped by Organization Type		
#企业	Enterprises	1032103	343749
机关	Government Units		
事业	Public Institutions	2110	748
二、按国民经济行业分组	Grouped by Economic Sector		
（一）农业	Agriculture ,Forestry,Animal Husbandry and Fishery	92	42
（二）采矿业	Mining	533	50
（三）制造业	Manufacturing	297881	95563
（四）电力、燃气及水的生产供应业	Production and Distribution of Electricity,Gas and Water	18112	5758
（五）建筑业	Construction	253784	29952
（六）批发和零售业	Wholesale and Retail Trades	105801	55374
（七）交通运输、仓储和邮政业	Traffic,Transport,Storage and Post	40962	15551
（八）住宿和餐饮业	Hotels and Catering Services	66226	38691
（九）信息传输、软件和信息技术服务业	Information Transmission,Software and Information Technology Services	65117	24074
（十）金融业	Financial Intermediation	40225	22087
（十一）房地产业	Real Estate	46215	17451
（十二） 租赁和商务服务业	Leasing and Business Services	39528	15570
（十三）科学研究和技术服务业	Scientific Research and Technical Services	27942	7448
（十四）水利、环境和公共设施管理业	Management of Water Conservancy, Environment and Public Facilities	9807	4613
（十五）居民服务、修理和其他服务业	Services to Households, Repairs and Other Services	10393	4926
（十六）教育	Education	14807	8152
（十七）卫生和社会工作	Health and Social Work	5098	3367
（十八）文化、体育和娱乐业	Culture, Sports and Entertainment	8158	3733
（十九）公共管理、社会保障和社会组织	Public Administration, Social Security and Social Organizations	64	21
（二十）国际组织	International Organizations		

Basic Facts on Persons Employed by Other Units（2013）

(persons)

在岗职工合计 Total Fully Employed Staff and Workers	其他从业人员 Other Employed Persons	单位从业人员平均人数 Average Employment	在岗职工 Staff and Workers	其他从业人员 Other Employed Persons
959919	**90826**	**1096515**	**996738**	**99777**
941755	90348	1075088	975792	99296
1986	124	2121	1992	129
92		92	92	
160	373	514	161	353
288668	9213	307978	299168	8810
17268	844	20960	20152	808
194444	59340	278635	210056	68579
103919	1882	104876	103051	1825
39251	1711	43787	42073	1714
59598	6628	66736	60030	5706
64599	518	68794	68304	490
38327	1898	40642	38096	2546
43485	2730	44628	41998	2630
37647	1881	42806	41261	1545
26916	1026	28015	26985	1030
8926	881	9965	8955	1010
10271	122	10178	10051	127
13259	1548	14686	13315	1371
5064	34	5006	4972	34
7961	197	8153	7954	199
64		64	64	

4-12 主要年份单位从业人员数及工资总额

Number of Employed Persons and Remuneration in Representative Years

年 份 year	单位从业人员 （万人） Number of Employed Persons (10 000 persons)	从业人员工资总额 （亿元） Remuneration of Employed Persons (10 000 yuan)	城镇非私营单位 从业人员平均工资（元） Aunual Average Wage of Employees in Urban Non-privite Units(yuan)
1978	67.19	4.71	713
1980	91.76	7.31	859
1985	127.04	14.17	1148
1986	132.78	16.87	1311
1987	135.48	19.13	1446
1988	137.56	22.81	1702
1989	139.86	25.64	1873
1990	141.55	29.48	2133
1991	142.86	26.88	2276
1992	144.51	30.80	2545
1993	146.03	43.25	2999
1994	142.37	58.87	4172
1995	141.17	67.23	4763
1996	140.60	75.64	5407
1997	138.89	80.83	5785
1998	138.78	82.85	6900
1999	115.88	90.13	7764
2000	112.45	103.80	9179
2001	113.93	123.12	10786
2002	115.77	138.88	12138
2003	116.68	155.95	13504
2004	118.15	184.63	15473
2005	123.66	215.67	17728
2006	125.10	250.87	20475
2007	129.40	319.23	25012
2008	130.85	379.29	29749
2009	135.64	450.48	34032
2010	140.38	520.88	37870
2011	154.33	658.73	41679
2012	165.59	770.86	44533
2013	198.42	1031.46	49350

4-13 全部单位从业人员工资总额（2013年）

Total Wages of All Employed Persons（2013）

单位：万元 （10 000 yuan）

分组	Classify	单位从业人员工资总额 Total Wages of Employment	在岗职工工资总额 Total Wages of Employed Staff and Workers
总计	**Total**	**10314582**	**9877955**
一、按机构类型分组	**Grouped by Organization Type**		
#企业	Enterprises	7976583	7583792
机关	Government Units	509674	492647
事业	Public Institutions	1753603	1722643
二、按国民经济行业分组	**Grouped by Economic Sector**		
（一）农业	Agriculture ,Forestry,Animal Husbandry and Fishery	12255	12176
（二）采矿业	Mining	2712	1019
（三）制造业	Manufacturing	2245530	2199830
（四）电力、燃气及水的生产供应业	Production and Distribution of Electricity, Gas and Water	119774	116970
（五）建筑业	Construction	1566758	1287285
（六）批发和零售业	Wholesale and Retail Trades	451945	446519
（七）交通运输、仓储和邮政业	Traffic,Transport,Storage and Post	953575	943111
（八）住宿和餐饮业	Hotels and Catering Services	217289	207961
（九）信息传输、软件和信息技术服务业	Information Transmission,Software and Information Technology Services	476759	474581
（十）金融业	Financial Intermediation	607122	598688
（十一）房地产业	Real Estate	249339	244649
（十二）租赁和商务服务业	Leasing and Business Services	279147	275994
（十三）科学研究和技术服务业	Scientific Research and Technical Services	849492	838246
（十四）水利、环境和公共设施管理业	Management of Water Conservancy, Environment and Public Facilities	93157	88804
（十五）居民服务、修理和其他服务业	Services to Households, Repairs and Other Services	51380	50535
（十六）教育	Education	1045959	1029250
（十七）卫生和社会工作	Health and Social Work	437455	428960
（十八）文化、体育和娱乐业	Culture, Sports and Entertainment	112489	108377
（十九）公共管理、社会保障和社会组织	Public Administration, Social Security and Social Organizations	542445	525000
（二十）国际组织	International Organizations		

4-13 续表 continued

单位：万元　　　　(10 000 yuan)

分 组	Classify	其他从业人员劳动报酬 Remuneration of Other Employed Persons	城镇非私营单位从业人员平均工资（元） Aunual Average Wage of Employees in UrbanNon-privite Units(yuan)
总计	**Total**	**436627**	**49350**
一、按机构类型分组	**Grouped by Organization Type**		
#企业	Enterprises	387791	47773
机关	Government Units	17027	50509
事业	Public Institutions	30960	58571
二、按国民经济行业分组	**Grouped by Economic Sector**		
（一）农业	Agriculture ,Forestry,Animal Husbandry and Fishery	79	36658
（二）采矿业	Mining	1693	40605
（三）制造业	Manufacturing	45700	44321
（四）电力、燃气及水的生产供应业	Production and Distribution of Electricity, Gas and Water	2804	59955
（五）建筑业	Construction	279473	39507
（六）批发和零售业	Wholesale and Retail Trades	5426	37362
（七）交通运输、仓储和邮政业	Traffic,Transport,Storage and Post	10464	54147
（八）住宿和餐饮业	Hotels and Catering Services	9328	29497
（九）信息传输、软件和信息技术服务业	Information Transmission,Software and Information Technology Services	2178	67495
（十）金融业	Financial Intermediation	8434	97140
（十一）房地产业	Real Estate	4690	44832
（十二） 租赁和商务服务业	Leasing and Business Services	3153	42109
（十三）科学研究和技术服务业	Scientific Research and Technical Services	11246	69951
（十四）水利、环境和公共设施管理业	Management of Water Conservancy, Environment and Public Facilities	4353	38429
（十五）居民服务、修理和其他服务业	Services to Households, Repairs and Other Services	845	32066
（十六）教育	Education	16709	59143
（十七）卫生和社会工作	Health and Social Work	8495	61602
（十八）文化、体育和娱乐业	Culture, Sports and Entertainment	4112	50201
（十九）公共管理、社会保障和社会组织	Public Administration, Social Security and Social Organizations	17445	49893
（二十）国际组织	International Organizations		

4-14 国有单位从业人员工资总额（2013年）

Total Wages of Persons Employed by State-owned Units（2013）

单位：万元 (10 000 yuan)

分组	Classify	单位从业人员工资总额 Total Wages of Employment	在岗职工工资总额 Total Wages of Employed Staff and Workers
总计	**Total**	**4855665**	**4701691**
一、按机构类型分组	**Grouped by Organization Type**		
#企业	Enterprises	2607585	2501479
机关	Government Units	509674	492647
事业	Public Institutions	1734916	1704193
二、按国民经济行业分组	**Grouped by Economic Sector**		
（一）农业	Agriculture ,Forestry,Animal Husbandry and Fishery	12067	11988
（二）采矿业	Mining	221	221
（三）制造业	Manufacturing	731717	716448
（四）电力、燃气及水的生产供应业	Production and Distribution of Electricity, Gas and Water	25159	24358
（五）建筑业	Construction	298451	224723
（六）批发和零售业	Wholesale and Retail Trades	58625	57894
（七）交通运输、仓储和邮政业	Traffic,Transport,Storage and Post	733326	728438
（八）住宿和餐饮业	Hotels and Catering Services	19205	18534
（九）信息传输、软件和信息技术服务业	Information Transmission,Software and Information Technology Services	12755	12655
（十）金融业	Financial Intermediation	180663	176487
（十一）房地产业	Real Estate	37072	36650
（十二） 租赁和商务服务业	Leasing and Business Services	26951	26770
（十三）科学研究和技术服务业	Scientific Research and Technical Services	644880	637853
（十四）水利、环境和公共设施管理业	Management of Water Conservancy, Environment and Public Facilities	55983	53786
（十五）居民服务、修理和其他服务业	Services to Households, Repairs and Other Services	10708	10429
（十六）教育	Education	988374	975029
（十七）卫生和社会工作	Health and Social Work	407660	399400
（十八）文化、体育和娱乐业	Culture, Sports and Entertainment	69010	65135
（十九）公共管理、社会保障和社会组织	Public Administration, Social Security and Social Organizations	542338	524893
（二十）国际组织	International Organizations		

4-14 续表 continued

单位：万元 (10 000 yuan)

分 组	Classify	其他从业人员劳动报酬 Remuneration of Other Employed Persons	城镇非私营单位从业人员平均工资（元） Aunual Average Wage of Employees in UrbanNon-privite Units(yuan)
总计	**Total**	**153974**	**52782**
一、按机构类型分组	**Grouped by Organization Type**		
#企业	Enterprises	106106	49977
机关	Government Units	17027	50509
事业	Public Institutions	30723	58513
二、按国民经济行业分组	**Grouped by Economic Sector**		
（一）农业	Agriculture ,Forestry,Animal Husbandry and Fishery	79	37117
（二）采矿业	Mining		41604
（三）制造业	Manufacturing	15269	38201
（四）电力、燃气及水的生产供应业	Production and Distribution of Electricity, Gas and Water	801	45372
（五）建筑业	Construction	73728	42174
（六）批发和零售业	Wholesale and Retail Trades	731	43122
（七）交通运输、仓储和邮政业	Traffic,Transport,Storage and Post	5388	55707
（八）住宿和餐饮业	Hotels and Catering Services	671	28750
（九）信息传输、软件和信息技术服务业	Information Transmission,Software and Information Technology Services	100	71020
（十）金融业	Financial Intermediation	4176	90653
（十一）房地产业	Real Estate	422	36302
（十二） 租赁和商务服务业	Leasing and Business Services	181	43547
（十三）科学研究和技术服务业	Scientific Research and Technical Services	7027	69201
（十四）水利、环境和公共设施管理业	Management of Water Conservancy, Environment and Public Facilities	2197	39611
（十五）居民服务、修理和其他服务业	Services to Households, Repairs and Other Services	279	38952
（十六）教育	Education	13345	61026
（十七）卫生和社会工作	Health and Social Work	8260	62704
（十八）文化、体育和娱乐业	Culture, Sports and Entertainment	3875	53257
（十九）公共管理、社会保障和社会组织	Public Administration, Social Security and Social Organizations	17445	49913
（二十）国际组织	International Organizations		

4-15 城镇集体单位从业人员工资总额（2013年）

Total Wages of Persons Employed by Urban Collective-owned Units in Towns and Cities（2013）

单位：万元 （10 000 yuan）

分组	Classify	单位从业人员工资总额 Total Wages of Employment	在岗职工工资总额 Total Wages of Employed Staff and Workers
总计	**Total**	**254665**	**247803**
一、按机构类型分组	**Grouped by Organization Type**		
#企业	Enterprises	251380	244610
机关	Government Units		
事业	Public Institutions	3285	3193
二、按国民经济行业分组	**Grouped by Economic Sector**		
（一）农、林、牧、渔业	Agriculture ,Forestry,Animal Husbandry and Fishery		
（二）采矿业	Mining		
（三）制造业	Manufacturing	26596	24734
（四）电力、燃气及水的生产供应业	Production and Distribution of Electricity, Gas and Water	2409	2409
（五）建筑业	Construction	163882	160449
（六）批发和零售业	Wholesale and Retail Trades	5583	4662
（七）交通运输、仓储和邮政业	Traffic,Transport,Storage and Post	2658	2658
（八）住宿和餐饮业	Hotels and Catering Services	768	668
（九）信息传输、软件和信息技术服务业	Information Transmission,Software and Information Technology Services	133	133
（十）金融业	Financial Intermediation	11125	10885
（十一）房地产业	Real Estate	2103	2039
（十二） 租赁和商务服务业	Leasing and Business Services	22252	22246
（十三）科学研究和技术服务业	Scientific Research and Technical Services	3552	3536
（十四）水利、环境和公共设施管理业	Management of Water Conservancy, Environment and Public Facilities	232	232
（十五）居民服务、修理和其他服务业	Services to Households, Repairs and Other Services	7369	7222
（十六）教育	Education	957	957
（十七）卫生和社会工作	Health and Social Work	4934	4861
（十八）文化、体育和娱乐业	Culture, Sports and Entertainment	112	112
（十九）公共管理、社会保障和社会组织	Public Administration, Social Security and Social Organizations		
（二十）国际组织	International Organizations		

4-15 续表 continued

单位：万元 (10 000 yuan)

分 组	Classify	其他从业人员劳动报酬 Remuneration of Other Employed Persons	城镇非私营单位从业人员平均工资（元） Aunual Average Wage of Employees in UrbanNon-privite Units(yuan)
总计	**Total**	**6862**	**34591**
一、按机构类型分组	**Grouped by Organization Type**		
#企业	Enterprises	6770	34508
机关	Government Units		
事业	Public Institutions	92	42327
二、按国民经济行业分组	**Grouped by Economic Sector**		
（一）农、林、牧、渔业	Agriculture ,Forestry,Animal Husbandry and Fishery		
（二）采矿业	Mining		
（三）制造业	Manufacturing	1862	37296
（四）电力、燃气及水的生产供应业	Production and Distribution of Electricity, Gas and Water		75981
（五）建筑业	Construction	3433	34735
（六）批发和零售业	Wholesale and Retail Trades	921	22387
（七）交通运输、仓储和邮政业	Traffic,Transport,Storage and Post		44976
（八）住宿和餐饮业	Hotels and Catering Services	100	30696
（九）信息传输、软件和信息技术服务业	Information Transmission,Software and Information Technology Services		28957
（十）金融业	Financial Intermediation	240	57670
（十一）房地产业	Real Estate	64	27072
（十二） 租赁和商务服务业	Leasing and Business Services	6	28357
（十三）科学研究和技术服务业	Scientific Research and Technical Services	16	60614
（十四）水利、环境和公共设施管理业	Management of Water Conservancy, Environment and Public Facilities		16231
（十五）居民服务、修理和其他服务业	Services to Households, Repairs and Other Services	147	23801
（十六）教育	Education		46251
（十七）卫生和社会工作	Health and Social Work	73	49638
（十八）文化、体育和娱乐业	Culture, Sports and Entertainment		33788
（十九）公共管理、社会保障和社会组织	Public Administration, Social Security and Social Organizations		
（二十）国际组织	International Organizations		

4-16 其他经济类型单位从业人员工资总额（2013年）

Total Wages of Persons Employed by Other Units (2013)

单位：万元 (10 000 yuan)

分 组	Classify	单位从业人员工资总额 Total Wages of Employment	在岗职工工资总额 Total Wages of Employed Staff and Workers
总计	**Total**	**5204252**	**4928462**
一、按机构类型分组	**Grouped by Organization Type**		
企业	Enterprises	5117518	4842703
机关	Government Units		
事业	Public Institutions		
二、按国民经济行业分组	**Grouped by Economic Sector**		
（一）农、林、牧、渔业	Agriculture ,Forestry,Animal Husbandry and Fishery	188	188
（二）采矿业	Mining	2492	799
（三）制造业	Manufacturing	1487213	1458644
（四）电力、燃气及水的生产供应业	Production and Distribution of Electricity, Gas and Water	92206	90203
（五）建筑业	Construction	1104425	902114
（六）批发和零售业	Wholesale and Retail Trades	387737	383963
（七）交通运输、仓储和邮政业	Traffic,Transport,Storage and Post	217091	212015
（八）住宿和餐饮业	Hotels and Catering Services	197318	188760
（九）信息传输、软件和信息技术服务业	Information Transmission,Software and Information Technology Services	463871	461793
（十）金融业	Financial Intermediation	415334	411316
（十一）房地产业	Real Estate	210164	205960
（十二） 租赁和商务服务业	Leasing and Business Services	229945	225979
（一三）科学研究和技术服务业	Scientific Research and Technical Services	201061	196858
（一四）水利、环境和公共设施管理业	Management of Water Conservancy, Environment and Public Facilities	36942	34786
（一五）居民服务、修理和其他服务业	Services to Households, Repairs and Other Services	33303	32884
（一六）教育	Education	56627	53264
（一七）卫生和社会工作	Health and Social Work	24851	24699
（一八）文化、体育和娱乐业	Culture, Sports and Entertainment	43367	43130
（一九）公共管理、社会保障和社会组织	Public Administration, Social Security and Social Organizations	107	107
（二十）国际组织	International Organizations		

4-16 续表 continued

单位：万元 (10 000 yuan)

分 组	Classify	其他从业人员劳动报酬 Remuneration of Other Employed Persons	城镇非私营单位从业人员平均工资（元） Aunual Average Wage of Employees in UrbanNon-privite Units(yuan)
总计	**Total**	**275790**	**47462**
一、按机构类型分组	**Grouped by Organization Type**		
#企业	Enterprises	274915	47602
机关	Government Units		
事业	Public Institutions	146	72620
二、按国民经济行业分组	**Grouped by Economic Sector**		
（一）农、林、牧、渔业	Agriculture ,Forestry,Animal Husbandry and Fishery		20457
（二）采矿业	Mining	1693	48471
（三）制造业	Manufacturing	28569	48290
（四）电力、燃气及水的生产供应业	Production and Distribution of Electricity, Gas and Water	2003	43992
（五）建筑业	Construction	202311	39637
（六）批发和零售业	Wholesale and Retail Trades	3774	36971
（七）交通运输、仓储和邮政业	Traffic,Transport,Storage and Post	5076	49579
（八）住宿和餐饮业	Hotels and Catering Services	8558	29567
（九）信息传输、软件和信息技术服务业	Information Transmission,Software and Information Technology Services	2078	67429
（十）金融业	Financial Intermediation	4018	102193
（十一）房地产业	Real Estate	4204	47092
（十二） 租赁和商务服务业	Leasing and Business Services	2966	53718
（十三）科学研究和技术服务业	Scientific Research and Technical Services	4203	71769
（十四）水利、环境和公共设施管理业	Management of Water Conservancy, Environment and Public Facilities	2156	37071
（十五）居民服务、修理和其他服务业	Services to Households, Repairs and Other Services	419	32721
（十六）教育	Education	3363	38559
（十七）卫生和社会工作	Health and Social Work	162	49662
（十八）文化、体育和娱乐业	Culture, Sports and Entertainment	237	53192
（十九）公共管理、社会保障和社会组织	Public Administration, Social Security and Social Organizations		16688
（二十）国际组织	International Organizations		

4-17 主要年份城镇登记失业人数及失业率

Registered Unemployed Persons and Unemployment Rate in Urban Area in Representative Years

年份 year	城镇登记失业人员数（万人） Real Number of Registered Unemployed Persons (10 000 persons)	城镇登记失业率（%） Registered Unemployment in Urban Area (%)
2002		3.70
2003		4.50
2004	8.29	4.30
2005	8.45	4.30
2006	8.74	4.30
2007	8.77	4.30
2008	9.40	4.20
2009	10.02	4.30
2010	10.46	4.20
2011	10.37	3.90
2012	9.60	3.50
2013	10.13	3.40

主要统计指标解释

人口数 指一定时点、一定地区范围内的有生命的个人的总和。年度统计的年末人口数，指每年12月31日24时的人口数。

常住人口 指实际经常居住在某地区一定时间（半年以上，含半年）的人口。常住人口包括户口在本辖区人也在本辖区居住的人，户口在本辖区之外但在户口登记地半年以上的人，户口待定（无户口和口袋户口）的人，户口在本辖区但离开本辖区半年以下的人。

城镇人口和乡村人口 城镇人口是指居住在城镇范围内的全部常住人口；乡村人口是除上述人口以外的全部人口。

出生率（又称粗出生率） 指在一定时期内（通常为一年）平均每千人所出生的人数的比率，一般用千分率表示。其计算公式为：

出生率＝年出生人数／年平均人数×1000‰

式中：出生人数指活产婴儿，即胎儿脱离母体时（不管怀孕月数），有过呼吸或其他生命现象。年平均人数指年初、年底人口数的平均数，也可用年中人口数代替。

死亡率（又称粗死亡率） 指在一定时期内（通常为一年）一定地区的死亡人数与同期内平均人数（或期中人数）之比，一般用千分率表示。本资料中的死亡率指年死亡率，其计算公式为：

死亡率＝年死亡人数／年平均人数×1000‰

人口自然增长率 指在一定时期内（通常为一年）人口自然增加数（出生人数减死亡人数）与该时期内平均人数（或期中人数）之比，一般用千分率表示。计算公式为：

人口自然增长率＝（本年出生人数—本年死亡人数）／年平均人数×1000‰。

从业人员 指在16周岁及以上，从事一定社会劳动并取得劳动报酬或经营收入的人员。这一指标反映了一定时期内全部劳动力资源的实际利用情况，是研究我国基本国情国力的重要指标。

单位从业人员 指在各级国家机关、政党机关、社会团体及企业、事业单位中工作，取得工资或其他形式的劳动报酬的全部人员。包括在岗职工、再就业的离退休人员、民办教师以及在各单位中工作的外方人员和港澳台方人员、兼职人员、借用的外单位人员和第二职业者。不包括离开本单位仍保留劳动关系的职工。各单位的就业人员反映了各单位实际参加生产或工作的全部劳动力。

城镇私营和个体就业人员 城镇私营就业人员指在工商管理部门注册登记，其经营地址设在县城关镇（含城关镇）以上的私营企业就业人员；包括私营企业投资者和雇工。城镇个体就业人员指在工商管理部门注册登记，并持有城镇户口或在城镇长期居住，经批准从事个体工商经营的就业人员；包括个体经营者和在个体工商户劳动的家庭帮工和雇工。

国有单位 指资产归国家所有的经济组织。包括按《中华人民共和国企业法人登记管理条例》规定登记注册的非公司制的经济组织，以及中央、地方各级国家机关、事业单位和社会团体。

集体单位 指生产资料归集体所有，并按《中华人民共和国企业法人登记管理条例》规定登记注册的经济组织。

其他单位 包括股份合作单位、联营单位、有限责任公司、股份有限公司、港澳台商投资单位以及外商投资单位等其他登记注册类型单位。

在岗职工 指在本单位工作并由单位支付工资的人员，以及有工作岗位，但由于学习、病伤产假等原因暂未工作，仍由单位支付工资的人员。

职工工资总额 指各单位在一定时期内直接支付给本单位全部职工的劳动报酬总额。工资总额的计算原则应以直接支付给职工的全部劳动报酬为根据。各单位支付给职工的劳动报酬以及其他根据有关规定支付的工资，不论是计入成本的还是不计入成本的，不论是按国家规定列入计征奖金税项目的，还是未列入计征奖金税项目的，不论是以货币形式支付的还是以实物形式支付的，均包括在工资总额内。

职工平均工资 指企业、事业、机关单位的职工在一定时期内平均每人所得的货币工资额。它表明一定时期职工工资收入的高低程度，是反映职工工资水平的主要指标。计算公式为：

职工平均工资＝报告期实际支付的全部职工工资总额/报告期全部职工平均人数

城镇登记失业人员 指有非农业户口，在一定的劳动年龄内，有劳动能力，无业而要求就业，并在当地就业服务机构进行求职登记的人员。

城镇登记失业率 指城镇登记失业人数同城镇从业人数与城镇从业人数与城镇登记失业人数之和的比。计算公式为：

$$\text{城镇登记失业率}=\frac{\text{城镇登记失业人数}}{\text{（城镇单位就业人员-使用的农村劳动力-聘用的离退休人员-聘用的港澳台及外方人员）+不在岗职工+城镇私营业主+城镇个体户主+城镇私营企业及个体就业人员+城镇登记失业人数}}\times 100\%$$

Explanatory Notes on Main Statistical Indicators

The annual statistics on total population is taken at midnight, the 31st of December, not including residents in Taiwan province, Hong Kong SAR and Macao SAR and Chinese national residing abroad.

Permanent population refers to the population of actual habitual residence in a certain area six months or over six months. Permanent popul ation include the accounts in this area which are also living in this area, accounts outside this area but with more than half a year of household registration, accounts to be determined including people without accounts or pockets of accounts, and accounts in the area but leaving this area less than six months.

Urban Population and Rural Population Urban population refers to all people residing in cities and towns, while rural population refers to population other than urban population.

Birth Rate (or Crude Birth Rate) refers to the ratio of the number of births to the average population (or mid-period population) during a certain period of time (usually one year), expressed in ‰. Birth rate in the chapter refers to annual birth rate. The following formula is used:

$$\text{Birth Rate}=\frac{\text{Number of Births}}{\text{Annual Average Population}}\times 1000‰$$

Number of births in the formula refers to live births, i.e. when a baby has breathed or showed any vital phenomena regardless of the length of pregnancy.

Annual average population is the average of the number of population at the beginning of the year and that at the end of the year. Sometimes it is substituted by the mid-year population.

Death Rate (or Crude Death Rate) refers to the ratio of the number of deaths to the average population (or mid-period population) during a certain period of time (usually one year), expressed in ‰. Death rate in the chapter refers to annual death rate. The following formula is used:

$$\text{DeathRate}=\frac{\text{Number of Deaths}}{\text{Annual Average Population}}\times 1000‰$$

Natural Growth Rate of Population refers to the ratio of natural increase in population (number of births minus number of deaths) in a certain period of time (usually one year) to the average population (or mid-period population) of the same period, expressed in ‰. The following formula is applied:

Natural Growth Rate of Population =(Number of Births-Number of Deaths)/Annual Average Population× 1000‰

Employed Persons refer to the ones aged 16 and over who are engaged in gainful employment and thus receive remuneration payment or earn business income. This indicator reflects the actual utilization of total labour force during a certain period of time and is often used for the research on China's economic situation and national power.

Persons Employed in Various Units refer to all the persons working in government agencies of various levels, political and party organizations, social organizations, enterprises and institutions, and receiving wages or other forms of payment. They include fully-employed staff and workers, re-employed retirees, teachers in the schools run by the local people, foreigners and Chinese compatriots from Hong Kong, Macao and Taiwan working in various units, part-time employees, employees of other units working temporarily at current posts, and employees holding the second job, but do not include persons who have left their working units while keeping their labour contract (employment relation) unchanged. This indicator reflects the total number of laborers actually engaged in production or other operations in various units.

Persons Employed in Private Enterprises and Self- Employed Individuals in Urban Areas Persons employed in private enterprises refer to the persons employed in the private enterprises which have been registered at the departments of industrial and commercial administration for which the business operation are situated at a county town (i.e. a town where the county government is located), or at urban areas with administrative hierarchy higher than a county town. The self-employed individuals in urban areas refer to persons who hold the certificates of residence in urban areas or have resided in the urban areas for a long time and have been registered at the departments of industrial and commercial administration and approved to be engaged in individual industrial or commercial business, including self-employed persons as well as helpers and hired labourers who work in individual households.

State-owned Units refer to economic units whose assets are owned by the state, including non-corporation units registered according to Regulation of the People's Republic of China on the Registration of Enterprises and

Corporations, state organs, institutions and social organizations at the central-level and local levels.

Collective–owned Units refer to economic units registered according to Regulation of the People's Republic of China on the Registration of Enterprises and Corporations where the means of production are collectively owned.

Units of Other Types of Ownership refer to units registered with other types of ownership, including cooperative units, joint ownership units, limited liability corporations, share holding corporations, units funded by entrepreneurs from Hong Kong, Macao, and Taiwan, and foreign- funded units.

Employed Staff and Workers refer to persons who work in, and receive wages from their working units, including persons who have their work posts but are temporarily absent from work for reasons of study or on sick, injury or maternal leave and still receive wages from their working units.

Total Wage Bill refers to the total remuneration payment to employed persons in various units during a certain period of time. The calculation of total wage bill is based on the total remuneration payment to employed persons . Therefore, all the wages and salaries and other payments to employed persons are included in the total wage bill regardless of sources, reckoning the cost of production or not, category, listing as items of premium taxation or not, and forms, paying in cash or in kind.

Average Wage refers to the average wage in money terms per person during a certain period of time for employed persons in enterprises, institutions, and government agencies, which reflects the general level of wage income during a certain period of time and is calculated as follows:

$$\text{AverageWage} = \frac{\text{TotalWage Billof Employed Personsat Reference Time}}{\text{Average Number of Persons Employedat Reference Time}}$$

Registered Unemployed Persons in Urban Areas refer to the persons with non-agricultural household registration at certain working ages (16 years old to retirement age), who are capable of working, unemployed and willing to work, and have been registered at the local employment service agencies to apply for a job.

Registered Unemployment Rate in Urban Areas refers to the ratio of the number of the registered unemployed persons to the sum of the number of persons employed in various units (minus the employed rural labour force, re-employed retirees, and Hong Kong, Macao, Taiwan or foreign employees), laid-off staff and workers in urban units, owners of private enterprises in urban areas, owners of self-employed individuals in urban areas, employees of private enterprises in urban areas, employee of self-employed individuals in urban areas, and the registered unemployed persons in urban areas. The formula is as follows:

$$\text{Registered Unemployment rate in urban areas} = \frac{\text{numberof registered urban unemployed persons}}{\begin{array}{c}\text{number of persons employed in}\\ \text{urbanunits-employed rurallabour force}\\ \text{re-employed retirees - HongKong,}\\ \text{Macao,Taiwan or foreign employees}\\ \text{+ laid-off staff and workers+owners of}\\ \text{urban private Enterprises+ owners of}\\ \text{urbanself-employed Individuals + employees}\\ \text{ofurbanprivate Enterprises+employees of}\\ \text{urbanself- employed Individuals+ registered}\\ \text{unemployed persons in urbanareas}\end{array}} \times 100\%$$

5 固定资产投资

INVESTMENT IN FIXED ASSETS

资料整理：令润翠　康　敏
Data management:Ling Runcui Kang Min

第五部分　固定资产投资

一、简要说明

本章资料主要包括全社会固定资产投资、城镇投资、房地产开发投资、城乡集体固定资产投资和城乡私人建房投资以及分区县情况，由西安市统计局固定资产投资处提供。

二、主要指标

全社会固定资产投资（亿元）	5134.56	比上年增长	21.0%
#国有经济单位	1770.84	比上年增长	6.6%
集体经济单位	219.88	比上年增长	12.9%
#城镇投资	4982.25	比上年增长	21.3%
#房地产开发	1595.64	比上年增长	24.5%
全市新增固定资产（亿元）	1875.00	比上年增长	6.2%
全市竣工住宅面积（万平方米）	840.02	比上年下降	29.4%

5　INVESTMENT IN FIXED ASSETS

Ⅰ.Brief Introduction

This chapter consists of primarily the data on fixed asset investment, investment of urban units, real estate development investment, urban and rural area collective fixed asset investment, urban and rural area private housing investment and the classified data of the districts and the counties on real estate development investment, provided by Fixed Asset Investment Division of the Xi'an Bureau of Statistics.

Ⅱ.Major Indicators

		Increase over Preceding Year
Investment Fulfilled In Fixed Assets(100 mil. Yuan)	5134.56	21.0%
State-owned Enterprises	1770.84	6.6%
Collective-owned Enterprises	219.88	12.9%
Investment of Urban Units	4982.25	21.3%
Real Estate Development	1595.64	24.5%
Investment Fulfilled Newly Increased FixedAssets(100 mil. yuan)	1875.00	6.2%
Total Floor Space of Building Completed(10 000 sq.m)	840.02	-29.4%

5-1 主要年份按城乡分全社会固定资产投资

Total Investment in Fixed Assets in the Whole Country by Rural and Urban Areas in Representative Years

单位：亿元 (100 million yuan)

年 份 Year	全社会固定资产投资合计 Total	城镇 Urban Area	房地产开发 Real Estate	农村 Rural Area
1979	4.08	3.01	0.00	1.07
1980	6.12	4.48	0.00	1.64
1981	5.59	4.56	0.00	1.03
1982	9.49	8.02	0.00	1.47
1983	10.46	9.17	0.00	1.29
1984	12.89	10.69	0.00	2.20
1985	18.44	14.44	0.00	4.00
1986	22.15	18.54	0.00	3.61
1987	27.05	23.15	0.00	3.90
1988	29.14	24.43	0.00	4.71
1989	28.30	23.85	0.00	4.45
1990	26.39	23.10	0.91	3.29
1991	30.76	25.55	2.01	5.21
1992	38.48	32.85	3.32	5.63
1993	75.06	66.65	7.39	8.41
1994	85.57	73.47	12.02	12.10
1995	103.42	88.50	21.65	14.92
1996	114.38	96.98	24.66	17.40
1997	116.90	95.17	24.68	21.73
1998	154.80	138.68	38.21	16.12
1999	197.31	172.64	44.30	24.67
2000	232.37	203.01	51.85	29.36
2001	287.72	256.95	67.42	30.77
2002	338.15	307.24	79.37	30.91
2003	478.10	445.74	124.82	32.36
2004	646.69	612.03	169.67	34.66
2005	835.10	776.33	225.23	58.77
2006	1066.62	971.84	285.76	94.78
2007	1435.33	1340.59	387.33	94.74
2008	1906.36	1786.60	540.26	119.76
2009	2500.13	2367.58	696.34	132.55
2010	3250.56	3104.92	842.34	145.64
2011	3346.26	3207.97	996.81	138.29
2012	4243.43	4107.54	1281.90	135.89
2013	5134.56	4982.25	1595.64	152.31

5-2 主要年份按经济成分划分全社会固定资产投资

Total Investment in Fixed Assets in the Whole Country by Registion Stares in Representative Years

单位：亿元 (100 million yuan)

年 份 Year	合计 Total	国有经济 State-owned	集体经济 Collective-owned	个体经济 Self-employed Individual	其他经济 Others
1985	18.44	13.96	1.36	3.12	
1986	22.15	18.05	0.97	3.13	
1987	27.05	22.18	1.50	3.37	
1988	29.14	23.72	1.86	3.56	
1989	28.30	23.22	1.46	3.62	
1990	26.39	22.21	1.44	2.74	
1991	30.76	24.42	2.26	4.08	
1992	38.48	32.04	1.45	4.99	
1993	75.06	59.66	3.03	6.55	5.82
1994	85.57	64.71	4.14	10.09	6.63
1995	103.42	69.08	9.78	11.13	13.43
1996	114.38	80.66	8.73	12.50	12.49
1997	116.90	77.46	10.21	15.11	14.12
1998	154.80	113.07	7.89	10.59	23.25
1999	197.31	136.50	13.62	16.22	30.97
2000	232.37	159.60	14.65	24.40	33.72
2001	287.72	175.58	14.67	38.57	58.90
2002	338.15	200.06	13.70	44.68	79.71
2003	478.10	264.83	22.33	73.43	117.51
2004	646.69	329.14	40.06	48.95	228.54
2005	835.10	373.70	59.23	79.04	323.13
2006	1066.62	401.14	110.68	107.33	447.47
2007	1435.33	476.78	207.08	183.09	568.38
2008	1906.36	694.89	246.89	50.43	914.15
2009	2500.13	932.91	289.91	97.86	1179.45
2010	3250.56	1348.76	326.44	54.73	1520.63
2011	3346.26	1204.80	258.15	74.64	1808.67
2012	4243.43	1661.22	194.71	82.72	2304.78
2013	5134.56	1770.84	219.88	84.43	3059.41

注：集体经济：包括城镇集体和农村集体。
　　个体经济：包括私营个体投资及城镇工矿区私人建房和农村私人建房。

5-3 主要年份按产业分全市固定资产投资

Total Investment in Fixed Assets in the Whole City by Three Strata of Industry in Representative Years

单位：亿元　　　　　　　　　　　　　　　　　　　　　　　　(100 million yuan)

年 份 Year	合计 Total	第一产业 Primary Industry	第二产业 Secondary Industry	工业 Industry	第三产业 Tertisry Industry
1979	3.01	0.06	1.24	1.20	1.71
1980	4.48	0.06	2.09	1.99	2.33
1981	4.56	0.11	2.10	1.83	2.35
1982	8.02	0.04	4.07	3.63	3.91
1983	9.17	0.11	4.97	4.41	4.09
1984	10.69	0.19	4.56	3.99	5.94
1985	14.44	0.18	7.22	6.45	7.04
1986	18.54	0.16	8.98	8.37	9.40
1987	23.15	0.19	11.81	11.26	11.15
1988	24.43	0.15	11.95	11.20	12.33
1989	23.85	0.13	11.94	11.50	11.78
1990	23.10	0.25	11.03	10.59	11.82
1991	25.55	0.27	12.48	11.95	12.80
1992	32.85	0.10	15.60	14.73	17.15
1993	66.65	0.07	24.50	22.44	42.08
1994	73.47	0.03	27.04	25.85	46.40
1995	88.50	0.14	28.80	27.71	59.56
1996	96.98	0.13	25.96	24.24	70.89
1997	95.17	0.24	23.65	21.66	71.28
1998	138.68	0.48	35.33	29.86	102.87
1999	172.64	0.94	39.88	36.40	131.82
2000	203.01	0.76	57.21	54.37	145.04
2001	256.95	0.86	63.31	61.28	192.78
2002	307.24	4.29	74.34	68.45	228.61
2003	445.74	3.34	83.25	78.41	359.15
2004	612.03	3.38	97.69	95.67	510.96
2005	776.33	5.26	144.25	140.44	626.82
2006	971.84	10.04	213.43	206.48	748.37
2007	1340.59	10.20	297.53	286.61	1032.86
2008	1786.60	23.75	369.74	356.12	1393.11
2009	2367.58	24.46	458.44	442.70	1884.68
2010	3104.92	39.83	556.10	498.62	2508.99
2011	3207.97	43.10	474.73	390.30	2690.14
2012	4165.99	99.34	671.92	578.17	3394.73
2013	5055.23	73.15	983.09	868.57	3998.99

5-4 全市固定资产投资（2013年）

Total Investment in Fixed Assets in the Whole City （2013）

单位：万元 (10 000 yuan)

指 标	Item	合计 Total	房地产开发 Real Estate
一、本年完成投资（万元）	**Investment Completed This Year(10 000 yuan)**	**50552171**	**15956418**
#住宅	Residential Buildings	13793145	12414728
（一）按登记注册类型分	**Grouped by Registion Status**		
内资	Domestic Funded Enterprises	46775595	14776173
国有	State-owned Enterprises	17389763	1230921
集体	Collective-owned Enterprises	1992102	236480
股份合作	Cooperative Enterprises	203633	129373
联营	Joint Ownership Enterprises	47298	1135
国有联营	State Joint Ownership Enterprises	39636	
集体联营	Collective Joint Ownership Enterprises	3080	
国有与集体联营	Joint State-collective Ownership Enterprises	3447	
其他联营	Other Joint Ownership Enterprises	1135	1135
有限责任公司	Limited Liability Corporations	16833846	9325033
国有独资公司	State-funded Corporations	278941	98725
其他有限责任公司	Other Limited Liability Corporations	16554905	9226308
股份有限公司	Stock Limited Corporation	1063476	229989
私营	Private Enterprises	6921220	3426074
私营独资	Private -funded Enterprises	1201167	229327
私营合伙	Private Limited Liability Corporations	205082	40576
私营有限责任公司	Private Limited Liability Corporations	5172259	3006670
私营股份有限公司	Private Share Holding Corporations	342712	149501
其他	Other	2324257	197168
港澳台商投资	Enterprises Funded by Hong Kong, Macao and Taiwan	785425	598153
与港澳台合资经营	Joint-venture Enterprises	182216	55541
与港澳台合作经营	Cooperative Enterprises	17811	17811
港澳台独资	Wholly Funded from Hong Kong,Macao and Taiwan	570318	524801
港澳台投资股份有限公司	Share-holding Corporations Ltd.	5180	
其他港澳台投资		9900	

5-4 续表1 continued 1

单位：万元 (10 000 yuan)

指　标	Item	合计 Total	房地产开发 Real Estate
外商投资	Foreign Owned Enterprises	2991151	582092
中外合资经营	Joint-venture Enterprises	504277	137302
中外合作经营	Cooperation Enterprises	152857	152857
外资企业	Foreign Funded Enterprises	1909825	291933
外商投资股份有限公司	Share-holding Corporations Ltd. With Foreign Funds	367279	
其他外商投资	Foreign Investment	56913	
（二）按隶属关系分	**Grouped by Jurisdiction of Management**		
中央	Central	2239168	593042
省属	Provincial	4125178	952420
市属	Municipal	44187825	14410956
（三）按建设性质分	**Grouped by Type of Construction**		
新建	New Construction	26063028	
扩建	Expansion	1232264	
改建和技术改造	Reconstruction	3183300	
（四）按构成分	**Grouped by Composition**		
1. 建筑工程	Construction Projects	37912532	12112708
2. 安装工程	Installment Projects	3760115	1645349
3. 设备、工器具购置	Purchasing of Equipment and Instruments	4861642	195443
4. 其他费用	Others	4017882	2002918

5-4 续表2 continued 2

单位：万元 (10 000 yuan)

指　标	Item	合计 Total	房地产开发 Real Estate
二、构成(%)	**Proportion (%)**		
（一）按登记注册类型分组	**Grouped by Status**		
#国有经济	State-owned	35.0	8.3
集体经济	Collective-owned	4.5	2.9
（二）按隶属关系分组	**Grouped by Jurisdiction of Management**		
中央	Central	4.4	3.7
省属	Provincial	8.2	6.0
市属	Municipal	87.4	90.3
（三）按建设性质分	**Grouped by Type of Construction**		
新建	New Construction	51.6	
扩建	Expansion	2.4	
改建和技术改造	Reconstruction	6.3	
（四）按构成分	**Grouped by Composition of Funds**		
1. 建筑工程	Construction Projects	75.0	75.9
2. 安装工程	Installation Projects	7.4	10.3
3. 设备、工器具购置	Purchasing of the Equipment and Instruments	9.6	1.2
4. 其他	Others	7.9	12.6
三、本年新增固定资产（万元）	**Newly Increase in Fixed Assets(10 000 yuan)**	**18750016**	**3344120**
四、房屋面积（万平方米）	**Floor Space (10 000 sq.m)**		
本年施工房屋面积	Floor Space of Buildings Under Construction This Year	14749.84	10454.27
住宅	Residential Buildings	9497.96	8461.71
本年竣工房屋面积	Floor Space of Buildings Completed This Year	1118.69	795.35
住宅	Residential Buildings	840.02	663.20
五、竣工房屋价值（万元）	**Value of the Building Completed (10 000 yuan)**	**3676334**	**2796284**
住宅	Residential Buildings	2766149	2226442

5-5 按国民经济行业分全市固定资产投资（2013年）

Investment in Fixed Assets in the Whole City by Sector（2013）

单位：万元 (10 000 yuan)

行　业	Sector	2013
本年完成固定资产投资（万元）	**Grouped by Sector (10 000 yuan)**	**50552171**
（一）农、林、牧、渔业	Agriculture,Forestry,Animal Husbandry and Fishery	835356
（二）采矿业	Mining	120248
（三）制造业	Manufacturing	6871365
农副食品加工业	Processing of Food from Agricultural Products	159686
食品制造业	Manufacture of Foods	105547
酒、饮料和精制茶制造业	Wine, soft drinks and refined tea industry	18853
烟草制品业	Tobacco Processing	13830
纺织业	Textile Industry	68084
纺织服装、服饰业	Textile, apparel industry	17460
皮革、毛皮、羽毛及其制品和制鞋业	Leather, Fur, Feather (eiderdown) and Their Products Industry	9200
木材加工和木、竹、藤、棕、草制品业	Timber Processing,Bamboo,Cane,Palm Fiber and Straw Products	46541
家具制造业	Furniture Manufacturing	117642
造纸及纸制品业	Papermaking and Paper products	37173
印刷和记录媒介复制业	Printing,Record Medium Reproduction	142677
文教、工美、体育和娱乐用品制造业	Culture, education, Craft art, sports and entertainment goods manufacturing industry	8502
石油加工、炼焦和核燃料加工业	Petroleum Refining, Ccoke Making and Nuclear Fuel Processing Industry	19863
化学原料和化学制品制造业	Raw Chemical Materials and Chemical Products	207349
医药制造业	Medical and Pharmaceutical Products	107682
化学纤维制造业	Chemical Fiber	15065
橡胶和塑料制品业	Rubber and plastic products industry	109981
非金属矿物制品业	Nonmetal Mineral Products	266211
黑色金属冶炼和压延加工业	Smelting and Pressing of Ferrous Metals	36900
有色金属冶炼和压延加工业	Smelting and Pressing of Nonferrou Metals	212641
金属制品业	Metal Products	376028

5-5 续表1 continued 1

单位：万元 (10 000 yuan)

行 业	Sector	2013
通用设备制造业	General Equipment Manufacturing Industry	461584
专用设备制造业	Special Purpose Equipment	514129
汽车制造业	Automotive Manufacturing	593358
铁路、船舶、航空航天和其他运输设备制造业	Railroad, Marine, Aerospace and other Transportation Equipment Manufacturing	497263
电气机械和器材制造业	Electric Equipment and Machinery	420591
计算机、通信和其他电子设备制造业	Communication Equipment, Computer and Other Electronic Equipment Manufacturing Industry	1901023
仪器仪表制造业	Instrument Manufacturing Industry	218277
其他制造业	Other Manufacturing	166569
废弃资源综合利用	Comprehensive Utilization of waste Resources	1050
金属制品、机械和设备修理业	Metal Products, Machinery and Equipment Repair Industry	606
（四）电力、燃气及水的生产供应业	Production & Supply of Electricity,Gas & Water	1714792
（五）建筑业	Construction	1145155
（六）批发和零售业	Wholesale and Retail Trades	1386014
（七）交通运输、仓储和邮政业	Transport, Storage and Post	2829830
（八）住宿和餐饮业	Hotels and Catering Services	687210
（九）信息传输、软件和信息技术服务业	Information Transmission,Computer Service and Software	477923
（十）金融业	Financial Intermediation	242626
（十一）房地产业	Real Estate	25383305
（十二） 租赁和商务服务业	Leasing and Business Services	929105
（十三）科学研究和技术服务业	Scientific Research,Technical Service and Geologic Prospecting	740029
（十四）水利、环境和公共设施管理业	Management of Water Conservancy, Environment and Public Facilities	4637901
（十五）居民服务、修理和其他服务业	Services to Households, repairs and other services	126923
（十六）教育	Education	702722
（十七）卫生和社会工作	Health and social work	731425
（十八）文化、体育和娱乐业	Culture, Sports and Entertainment	324272
（十九）公共管理、社会保障和社会组织	Public administration, social security and social organizations	665970
（二十）国际组织	International Organizations	

5-6 主要年份按资金来源及建设性质分全市固定资产投资

Total Investment in Fixed Assets in the Whole City by Sources of Funds and Type of Construction in Representative Years

单位：万元 (10 000 yuan)

指标	Item	1995	2000	2001	2002	2003	2004	2005
一.投资总额(万元)	**Total Investment (10 000 yuan)**	**884994**	**2030122**	**2569496**	**3072442**	**4457381**	**6120324**	**7763283**
（一）按资金来源分	Grouped by Funds Source							
1. 国家预算内投资	State Budgetary Funds	69185	160982	256403	355960	365263	436496	728885
2. 国内贷款	Domestic Loans	216565	432282	672379	666146	1219234	1565246	1257175
3. 债券	Bonds	873	32460	6753	766	3278		
4. 利用外资	Utilization of Foreign Funds	80792	31622	54907	15192	47509	47401	40583
5. 自筹资金	Self-raising Funds	385047	875352	1121502	1392915	1733132	2629720	4001700
6. 其他资金	Others	132532	497424	457552	641463	1088965	1441461	1734940
（二）按构成分	Grouped by Composition of Funds							
1. 建筑安装工程	Construction and Installation Projects	527220	1404184	1698777	2119151	3067309	4127677	5086664
2. 设备、工器具购置	Purchasing of Equipment and Instruments	233730	382495	452602	552251	577240	708988	1021079
3. 其它费用	Others	124044	243443	418117	401040	812832	1283659	1655540
（三）按建设性质分	Grouped by Type of Construction							
#新建	New Construction	210926	533058	723957	874392	1294032	1874116	2907551
扩建	Expansion	180210	542510	581138	868603	1102914	1169537	1208430
改建	Reconstruction	157457	263657	344879	343184	447944	670229	782953
二.房屋施工面积（万平方米）	**Floor Space Under Construction (10 000sq.m)**	**1070.58**	**1702.58**	**1767.13**	**2396.89**	**2716.18**	**3177.36**	**4030.38**

5-6 续表1 continued 1

单位：万元 (10 000 yuan)

指标	Item	2006	2007	2008	2009	2010	2011	2012	2013
一.投资总额(万元)	**Total Investment (10 000 yuan)**	**9718418**	**13405920**	**17865977**	**23675759**	**31049184**	**32079666**	**41659924**	**50552171**
（一）按资金来源分	Grouped by Funds Source								
1. 国家预算内投资	State Budgetary Funds	677145	670592	1555809	2562756	1649563	1480412	1851860	1439721
2. 国内贷款	Domestic Loans	1631689	1619218	2162957	3301919	4288663	3546561	4023452	4146647
3. 债券	Bonds								11356
4. 利用外资	Utilization of Foreign Funds	165390	183422	261325	144124	126802	89047	135147	182153
5. 自筹资金	Self-raising Funds	5538393	8565573	12771844	15776565	18279153	19400468	28680236	36446760
6. 其他资金	Others	1705801	2367115	1114042	1890395	6705003	7563178	6969229	8325534
（二）按构成分	Grouped by Composition of Funds								
1. 建筑安装工程	Construction and Installation Projects	6486233	9165668	12864657	16337466	21690205	25553161	34268466	41672647
2. 设备、工器具购置	Purchasing of Equipment and Instruments	1409589	1858720	2024631	2619783	3094336	1911180	3311375	4861642
3. 其它费用	Others	1822596	2381532	2976689	4718510	6264643	4615325	4080083	4017882
（三）按建设性质分	Grouped by Type of Construction								
#新建	New Construction	3511432	5123975	6356716	8567540	14292899	16077747	21651399	26063028
扩建	Expansion	1101740	994841	2118013	3054929	2649749	1956527	1685922	1232264
改建	Reconstruction	1099304	1548130	1921664	2738799	2620997	2155112	2810903	3183300
二.房屋施工面积（万平方米）	**Floor Space Under Construction (10 000sq.m)**	**4589.39**	**5759.28**	**6570.94**	**9571.25**	**11166.19**	**12353.11**	**14093.91**	14749.84

5-7 主要年份市属固定资产投资

Investment In Fixed Assets of Municipal Units in Representative Years

单位：万元 (10 000 yuan)

指 标	Item	1995	2000	2001	2002	2003	2004	2005	2006
一、投资总额	**Total Investment**	**432451**	**1263023**	**1539717**	**1848833**	**2978747**	**4355271**	**5788693**	**7835681**
#房地产开发	Real Estate	171291	473787	566557	702233	1114809	1492693	2062940	2641871
按经济类型分	Grouped by Type of Enterprises								
国有经济	State-owned Enterprises	258545	890546	894700	1006245	1586057	1884524	2198836	2591184
集体经济	Collective-owned Enterprises	5720	52893	62895	63877	142849	257226	258327	363909
其他经济	Others	168186	319584	582122	778711	1249841	2213421	3331530	4880588
二、新增固定资产	**Newly Increased Fixed Assets**	**273324**	**953173**	**1159980**	**1295389**	**1812099**	**1962795**	**3011104**	**3495179**
三、房屋竣工面积	**Floor Space of the Building**	**202.52**	**509.48**	**535.98**	**537.44**	**631.89**	**606.23**	**767.70**	**914.80**
（万平方米）	**Completed(10 000sq.m)**								
#住宅	Residential Buildings	143.30	373.51	396.01	331.45	387.82	388.79	436.43	432.43

5-7 续表1 continued 1

单位：万元 (10 000 yuan)

指 标	Item	2007	2008	2009	2010	2011	2012	2013
一、投资总额	**Total Investment**	**10555849**	**14648360**	**19063075**	**25474854**	**26820029**	**35875223**	**44187825**
#房地产开发	Real Estate	3515719	4938202	6575526	8020893	9001953	11655613	14410956
按经济类型分	Grouped by Type of Enterprises							
国有经济	State-owned Enterprises	2972840	4480627	6527566	9306901	8750285	12264895	12847731
集体经济	Collective-owned Enterprises	1366567	1646111	1614290	2253851	1897980	1932578	2148977
其他经济	Others	6216442	8521622	10921219	13914102	16171764	21677750	29191117
二、新增固定资产	**Newly Increased Fixed Assets**	**5279938**	**6488364**	**8380033**	**10423906**	**10663882**	**15376910**	**16019776**
三、房屋竣工面积	**Floor Space of the Building**	**1343.88**	**987.05**	**1359.46**	**668.49**	**1002.82**	**1450.29**	**975.03**
（万平方米）	**Completed(10 000sq.m)**							
#住宅	Residential Buildings	734.05	602.69	727.41	448.46	531.38	1069.61	760.87

5-8 市属固定资产投资（2013年）

Investment in Fixed Assets of Municipal Units（2013）

单位：万元 (10 000 yuan)

指　标	Item	城镇 Urban Area	房地产开发 Real Estate
一、本年完成投资	**Investment Completed This Year**	**44187825**	**14410956**
#住宅	Residential Buildings	12381649	11112742
（一）按登记注册类型分	**Grouped by Registion Status**		
内资	Domestic Funded Enterprises	40422217	13230711
国有	State-owned Enterprises	12644783	856268
集体	Collective-owned Enterprises	1958234	236480
股份合作	Cooperative Enterprises	187663	113403
联营	Joint Ownership Enterprises	47298	1135
国有联营	State Joint Ownership Enterprises	39636	
集体联营	Collective Joint Ownership Enterprises	3080	
国有与集体联营	Joint State-collective Ownership Enterprises	3447	
其他联营	Other Joint Ownership Enterprises	1135	1135
有限责任公司	Limited Liability Corporations	15499785	8232548
国有独资公司	State-funded Corporations	163312	26975
其他有限责任公司	Other Limited Liability Corporations	15336473	8205573
股份有限公司	Stock Limited Corporation	920441	229989
私营	Private Enterprises	6858866	3363720
私营独资	Private -funded Enterprises	1201167	229327
私营合伙	Private Limited Liability Corporations	205082	40576
私营有限责任公司	Private Limited Liability Corporations	5109905	2944316
私营股份有限公司	Private Share Holding Corporations	342712	149501
其他	Other	2305147	197168
港澳台商投资	Enterprises Funded by Hong Kong, Macao and Taiwan	785425	598153
与港澳台合资经营	Joint-venture Enterprises	182216	55541
与港澳台合作经营	Cooperative Enterprises	17811	17811
港澳台独资	Wholly Funded from Hong Kong,Macao and Taiwan	570318	524801
港澳台投资股份有限公司	Share-holding Corporations Ltd.	5180	
其他港澳台投资	Investment From Hongkong,Macao,Taiwan	9900	
外商投资	Foreign Owned Enterprises	2980183	582092
中外合资经营	Joint-venture Enterprises	498990	137302
中外合作经营	Cooperation Enterprises	152857	152857
外资企业	Foreign Funded Enterprises	1909825	291933

5-8 续表1 continued 1

单位：万元 (10 000 yuan)

指 标	Item	城镇 Urban Area	房地产开发 Real Estate
外商投资股份有限公司	Share-holding Corporations Ltd. With Foreign Funds	361598	
其他外商投资	Foreign Investment	56913	
（二）按建设性质分	**Grouped by Type of Construction**		
新建	New Construction	23407460	
扩建	Expansion	1095671	
改建和技术改造	Reconstruction	2675282	
（三）按构成分	**Grouped by Composition**		
建筑工程	Construction Projects	34379029	11015547
安装工程	Installment Projects	3161897	1526519
设备、工器具购置	Purchasing of Equipment and Instruments	3133711	195043
其他费用	Others	3513188	1673847
二、本年完成投资额构成(%)	**the Constitution of Compeleted Investment this year (%)**		
（一）按登记注册类型分组	**Grouped by Status**		
# 国有经济	State-owned	29.1	5.1
集体经济	Collective-owned	4.9	2.6
（二）按建设性质分	**Grouped by Type of Construction**		
新建	New Construction	53	
扩建	Expansion	2.5	
改建和技术改造	Reconstruction	6.1	
（三）按构成分	**Grouped by Composition of Funds**	0	
建筑工程	Construction Projects	77.8	76.4
安装工程	Installation Projects	7.2	10.6
设备、工器具购置	Purchasing of the Equipment and Instruments	7.1	1.4
其他	Others	3	11.6
三、本年新增固定资产（万元）	**Newly Increase in Fixed Assets**	**16019776**	**3184359**
四、房屋面积（万平方米）	**Floor Space (10 000 sq.m)**		
本年施工房屋面积	Floor Space of Buildings Under Construction This Year	13155.3	9460.58
#住宅	Residential Buildings	8487.99	7612.91
本年竣工房屋面积	Floor Space of Buildings Completed This Year	975.03	763.28
#住宅	Residential Buildings	760.87	637.94
五、竣工房屋价值（万元）	**Value of the Building Completed**	**3355415**	**2666301**
#住宅	Residential Buildings	2508154	2114074

5-9 按国民经济行业分市属固定资产投资（2013年）

Investment in Fixed Assets of Municipal Units by Sector （2013）

单位：万元 (10 000 yuan)

行 业	Scetor	2013
本年完成固定资产投资	**Grouped by Sector**	**44187825**
（一）农、林、牧、渔业	Agriculture,Forestry,Animal Husbandry and Fishery	835356
（二）采矿业	Mining	120248
（三）制造业	Manufacturing	6102396
农副食品加工业	Processing of Food from Agricultural Products	159686
食品制造业	Manufacture of Foods	105547
酒、饮料和精制茶制造业	Wine, soft drinks and refined tea industry	14046
烟草制品业	Tobacco Processing	13830
纺织业	Textile Industry	68084
纺织服装、服饰业	Textile, apparel industry	17460
皮革、毛皮、羽毛及其制品和制鞋业	Leather, Fur, Feather (eiderdown) and Their Products Industry	9200
木材加工和木、竹、藤、棕、草制品业	Timber Processing,Bamboo,Cane,Palm Fiber and Straw Products	46541
家具制造业	Furniture Manufacturing	117642
造纸及纸制品业	Papermaking and Paper products	37173
印刷和记录媒介复制业	Printing,Record Medium Reproduction	21980
文教、工美、体育和娱乐用品制造业	Culture, education, Craft art, sports and entertainment goods manufacturing industry	8502
石油加工、炼焦和核燃料加工业	Petroleum Refining, Ccoke Making and Nuclear Fuel Processing Industry	13228
化学原料和化学制品制造业	Raw Chemical Materials and Chemical Products	202949
医药制造业	Medical and Pharmaceutical Products	102395
化学纤维制造业	Chemical Fiber	15065
橡胶和塑料制品业	Rubber and plastic products industry	109981
非金属矿物制品业	Nonmetal Mineral Products	265211
黑色金属冶炼和压延加工业	Smelting and Pressing of Ferrous Metals	36900
有色金属冶炼和压延加工业	Smelting and Pressing of Nonferrou Metals	212641
金属制品业	Metal Products	265845

5-9 续表1 continued 1

单位：万元 (10 000 yuan)

行业	Scetor	2013
通用设备制造业	General Equipment Manufacturing Industry	461584
专用设备制造业	Special Purpose Equipment	473050
汽车制造业	Automotive Manufacturing	526630
铁路、船舶、航空航天和其他运输设备制造业	Railroad, Marine, Aerospace and other Transportation Equipment Manufacturing	374386
电气机械和器材制造业	Electric Equipment and Machinery	288580
计算机、通信和其他电子设备制造业	Communication Equipment, Computer and Other Electronic Equipment Manufacturing Industry	1815393
仪器仪表制造业	Instrument Manufacturing Industry	150642
其他制造业	Other Manufacturing	166569
废弃资源综合利用	Comprehensive Utilization of waste Resources	1050
金属制品、机械和设备修理业	Metal Products, Machinery and Equipment Repair Industry	606
（四）电力、燃气及水的生产供应业	Production & Supply of Electricity,Gas & Water	969634
（五）建筑业	Construction	720271
（六）批发和零售业	Wholesale and Retail Trades	1289616
（七）交通运输、仓储和邮政业	Transport, Storage and Post	2183018
（八）住宿和餐饮业	Hotels and Catering Services	669530
（九）信息传输、软件和信息技术服务业	Information Transmission,Computer Service and Software	269407
（十）金融业	Financial Intermediation	77415
（十一）房地产业	Real Estate	23334398
（十二） 租赁和商务服务业	Leasing and Business Services	865179
（十三）科学研究和技术服务业	Scientific Research,Technical Service and Geologic Prospecting	394209
（十四）水利、环境和公共设施管理业	Management of Water Conservancy, Environment and Public Facilities	4342647
（十五）居民服务、修理和其他服务业	Services to Households, repairs and other services	109251
（十六）教育	Education	533913
（十七）卫生和社会工作	Health and social work	524387
（十八）文化、体育和娱乐业	Culture, Sports and Entertainment	289401
（十九）公共管理、社会保障和社会组织	Public administration, social security and social organizations	557549
（二十）国际组织	International Organizations	

5-10 按资金来源及建设性质分市属固定资产投资（2013年）

Investment in Fixed Assets of Municipal Units by Sources of Funds and Type of Construction（2013）

单位：万元 (10 000 yuan)

指　标	Item	2013
投资总额	**Total Investment**	**44187825**
一、按资金来源分	Grouped by Funds Sources	
1. 国家预算内资金	State Budgetary Funds	1109176
2. 国内贷款	Domestic Loans	3363741
3. 债券	Bonds	2457
4. 利用外资	Utilization of Foreign Funds	180578
5. 自筹资金	Self-raising Funds	32195974
6. 其他资金	Others	7335899
二、按建设性质分	**Grouped by Type of Construction**	
#新建	New Construction	23407460
扩建	Expansion	1095671
改建	Reconstruction	2675282
三、按构成分	**Grouped by Composition of Funds**	
1. 建筑工程	Construction Project	34379029
2. 安装工程	Installation Projects	3161897
3. 设备、工器具购置	Purchasing of Equipment and Instruments	3133711
4. 其他费用	Others	3513188
四、房屋施工面积（万平方米）	Floor Space of Buildings Under Construction (10 000 sq.m)	**13155.30**

5-11　全市固定资产投资资金来源（2013年）

Source of Funds for Total Fixed Assets Investment of Whole City（2013）

单位：万元　　　　　　　　　　　　　　　　　　　　　　　　(10 000 yuan)

指　标	Item	城镇 Urban Area	房地产开发 Real Estate
一、本年资金来源合计	**Total of Sources of Funds This Year**	**63761741**	**24237997**
1. 上年末结余资金	Balance of Last Year	7042634	5509776
2. 本年资金来源小计	Subtotal Funds This Year	56719107	18728221
(1) 国家预算资金	State Budgetary Funds	1602626	
(2) 国内贷款	Domestic Loans	4709149	2504820
(3) 债券	Bonds	12920	
(4) 利用外资	Utilization of Foreign Funds	203540	74400
(5) 自筹资金	Self-raising Funds	40737575	8112540
(6) 其他资金来源	Others	9453197	8036461
二、本年各项应付款合计	**Total Sums of Money to be Paid This Year**	**4274483**	**3016268**

5-12　全市固定资产投资效果（2013年）

Achievements of Total Assets Investment of Whole City（2013）

指　标	Item	城镇 Urban Area	房地产开发 Real Estate
一、建设项目投产率（%）	**Rate of Projects Put Into use(%)**	**56.1**	
施工项目个数（个）	Number of Constructing Projects (unit)	2367	
本年投产项目个数（个）	Number of Projects Put into Use (unit)	1328	
二、固定资产交付使用率（%）	**Rate of Fixed Assets Put into Use(%)**	**37.1**	**21.0**
本年新增固定资产（亿元）	Newly Increased Fixed Assets This Year(100 million yuan)	1875.00	334.41
本年完成投资（亿元）	Investment Completed This Year (100 million yuan)	5055.22	1595.64
三、建设周期（年）	**Construction Period (year)**	**3.4**	**4.9**
计划总投资（亿元）	Total Planned Investment(100 million yuan)	17139.19	7800.29
本年完成投资（亿元）	Investment Completed This Year (100 million yuan)	5055.22	1595.64
四、房屋建筑面积竣工率（%）	**Completion Rate of Buildings (%)**	**13.2**	**13.1**
本年施工房屋面积（万平方米）	Floor Space of the Constructing Buildings This Year (10 000 sq.m)	14749.84	10454.27
本年竣工房屋面积（万平方米）	Floor Space of the Buildings Completed This Year (10 000 sq.m)	1118.69	795.35

5-13 分区县、开发区全社会固定资产投资额（2013年）

Investment Fulfilled in Fixed Assets by Region and Development Zone（2013）

单位：亿元 (100 million yuan)

区县、开发区	Region	全社会固定资产投资 Investment Fulfilled In Fixed Assets	城镇投资 Urban Area	房地产 Real Estate	农村集体 Rural Collective-owned Units	农村私人建房 Private Housing in Country
区县	**Region**	**5134.56**	**4982.25**	**1595.64**	**72.98**	**79.33**
新城区	Xincheng	378.67	378.67	79.02		
碑林区	Beilin	464.26	464.26	151.01		
莲湖区	Lianhu	583.86	583.86	220.88		
灞桥区	Baqiao	315.69	309.16	103.88	0.78	5.74
未央区	Weiyang	723.42	719.34	272.20		4.08
雁塔区	Yanta	1029.24	1026.08	593.53		3.16
阎良区	Yanliang	201.16	191.92	19.27	4.54	4.70
临潼区	Lintong	196.94	183.19	9.35	3.70	10.05
长安区	Chang'an	541.53	525.85	93.51		15.68
蓝田县	Lantian	127.38	94.38	2.74	23.42	9.59
周至县	Zhouzhi	115.30	91.37	13.42	12.62	11.31
户　县	Huxian	142.41	126.40	10.33	5.82	10.19
高陵县	Gaoling	314.71	287.77	26.50	22.10	4.83
开发区	**Development Zones**	**2061.41**	**2061.41**	**627.57**		
高新区	GaoXin	532.08	532.08	88.03		
经开区	JingKai	480.87	480.87	96.80		
曲江新区	Qujiang	456.76	456.76	244.81		
浐灞生态区	Chanba Eco-District	227.35	227.35	100.31		
航空基地	Aviation Industry Base	65.34	65.34	10.92		
航天基地	Aerospace Base	90.08	90.08	41.76		
国际港务区	International Trade&Logistic Park	85.32	85.32	2.68		
沣东新城	FengDongXinCheng	123.61	123.61	42.27		

5-14 主要年份全市新增固定资产及房屋竣工面积

Value of Newly Added Fixed Assets and Floor Spaces Completed of Municipal Units in Representative Years

年 份 Year	新增固定资产（亿元） Newly Increased Fixed Assets (10 000 yuan)	房屋竣工面积（万平方米） Floor Space of Buildings Completed (10 000sq.m)	住宅 Residential Buildings
1978	4.96	99.10	40.76
1980	4.64	164.87	100.15
1985	8.62	222.42	129.07
1986	13.40	272.95	155.91
1987	16.72	241.48	119.21
1988	16.82	211.83	102.43
1989	16.58	178.45	87.77
1990	20.30	211.88	111.05
1991	17.86	185.34	95.84
1992	22.33	204.75	112.66
1993	41.70	257.90	144.88
1994	55.37	282.91	184.49
1995	62.58	357.67	252.84
1996	60.04	332.18	249.52
1997	62.88	374.46	286.54
1998	80.23	382.80	275.63
1999	118.92	681.04	550.83
2000	150.16	714.83	544.95
2001	167.77	692.56	502.26
2002	198.97	773.28	486.13
2003	279.44	917.96	578.06
2004	261.95	776.59	498.33
2005	409.72	1131.41	598.61
2006	453.01	1199.45	583.10
2007	667.97	1672.16	929.50
2008	725.17	1113.31	693.42
2009	1013.44	1529.13	822.62
2010	1193.05	775.16	521.08
2011	1297.35	1231.91	861.44
2012	1765.05	1626.25	1189.04
2013	1875.00	1118.69	840.02

5-15 全市按国民经济行业分房屋建筑面积（2013年）

单位：平方米 (sq.m)

行 业	Sector	本年施工房屋面积 Floor Space of Buildings Under Construction This Year	住宅 Residential Residence
总 计	**Total**	**147498351**	**94979562**
（一）农、林、牧、渔业	Agriculture, Forestry, Animal Husbandry and Fishery		
（二）采矿业	Mining	55075	25400
（三）制造业	Manufacturing	76933	
（四）电力、燃气及水的生产供应业	Generation and Supply of Electricity, Production and Supply of Gas and Water	7533284	29294
（五）建筑业	Construction	175226	
（六）批发和零售业	Wholesale and Retail Trades	520830	19080
（七）交通运输、仓储和邮政业	Transportation, Storage and Post	1375085	
（八）住宿和餐饮业	Hotels and Catering Services	703663	49530
（九）信息传输、软件和信息技术服务业	Information Transmission, Computer Service and Software	497585	12000
（十）金融业	Financial Intermediation	545752	
（十一）房地产业	Real Estate	422893	
（十二） 租赁和商务服务业	Leasing and Business Services	127987851	94246021
（十三）科学研究和技术服务业	Scientific Research and Technical Service	1093234	
（十四）水利、环境和公共设施管理业	Management of Water Conservancy, Environment and Public Facilities	1572738	28830
（十五）居民服务、修理和其他服务业	Services to Households, repairs and other services	620389	6000
（十六）教育	Education	69599	
（十七）卫生和社会工作	Health and social work	1697154	202948
（十八）文化、体育和娱乐业	Culture, Sports and Entertainment	1500589	
（十九）公共管理、社会保障和社会组织	Public administration, social security and social organizations	516404	
（二十）国际组织	International Organizations	534067	360459

Floors Space of Buildings Construction of Municipal Units by Sector（2013）

单位：平方米 (sq.m)

本年竣工房屋面积 Floor Space of Buildings Completed This Year	住宅 Residential Residence	本年竣工房屋价值（万元） Value of Buildings Completed (10 000 yuan)	住宅 Residential Residence
11186937	**8400208**	**3676334**	**2766149**
32840	25400	1672	762
69930		5300	
529089		25439	
28216		5460	
1000		300	
54357		25676	
49868	33100	20496	10566
57500	12000	12150	3000
9687366	7963249	3397179	2652200
9636		1700	
500		8000	
36767	6000	6859	1500
160561		37516	
89250		24258	
380057	360459	104329	98121

5-16 分区县、开发区新增固定资产及房屋施工、竣工面积（2013年）

区县、开发区	Region	新增固定资产（亿元）Increased Fixed Assets (100 million yuan)	本年施工房屋面积（万平方米）Floor Space of Buildings Under Construction (10 000sq.m)	住宅 Residencial Buildings
区县	**Region**	**1860.83**	**14749.84**	**9497.96**
新城区	Xincheng	74.00	644.16	535.67
碑林区	Beilin	274.51	1501.25	1131.52
莲湖区	Lianhu	334.46	1358.17	1096.48
灞桥区	Baqiao	69.37	1051.57	742.99
未央区	Weiyang	168.32	3347.53	2379.50
雁塔区	Yanta	225.02	3200.30	1948.51
阎良区	Yanliang	112.35	410.60	163.89
临潼区	Lintong	91.45	204.45	87.78
长安区	Chang'an	195.17	1766.78	848.56
蓝田县	Lantian	107.27	108.06	45.31
周至县	Zhouzhi	43.73	149.77	106.59
户　县	Huxian	48.19	304.42	148.44
高陵县	Gaoling	116.99	702.77	262.74
开发区	**Development Zones**	**348.94**	**5519.31**	**3093.35**
高新区	GaoXin	118.56	1433.54	440.23
经开区	JingKai	88.24	954.25	694.22
曲江新区	Qujiang	36.00	1094.48	796.91
浐灞生态区	Chanba Eco-District	35.27	893.35	539.84
航空基地	Aviation Industry Base	5.45	69.27	29.09
航天基地	Aerospace Base	35.95	740.53	406.36
国际港务区	International Trade&Logistic Park	16.26	22.67	21.25
沣东新城	FengDong Xincheng	13.20	311.22	165.46

Newly Added Fixed Assets and Floor Space of Constructing and Completed Buildings by Region and Development Zone（2013）

本年竣工房屋面积（万平方米）Floor Space of Buildings Completed(10 000 sq.m)	住 宅 Residenctial Buildings	本年竣工房屋价值（亿元）Value of Buildings Completed (100 million yuan)	住宅 Residenctial Buildings	商品房销售面积（万平方米）Floor Space of Houses Sales(sq.m) Houses(10 000sq.m)	商品房销售额（亿元）Sales Income of Commercial Houses(100 million yuan)
1118.69	**840.02**	**367.63**	**276.61**	**1662.75**	**1112.87**
53.66	38.27	13.14	10.06	54.41	38.31
162.18	123.44	65.86	45.93	306.21	192.95
183.02	145.50	66.82	50.25	140.61	94.64
51.25	46.63	14.15	12.36	180.44	100.13
254.81	218.90	86.51	69.95	343.66	212.75
132.25	96.10	47.92	32.03	386.32	341.47
36.89	34.81	8.35	7.90	24.04	11.02
79.67	28.86	7.68	5.38	10.03	4.61
98.99	91.18	42.14	39.35	107.60	76.61
18.29	0.60	3.57	0.15	9.67	3.18
1.80	1.42	0.86	0.45	14.32	5.38
38.01	10.80	8.98	1.85	20.29	8.35
7.87	3.51	1.65	0.95	65.15	23.46
297.02	**242.03**	**117.90**	**92.15**	**707.77**	**537.91**
92.33	66.90	35.33	25.57	94.67	79.51
94.31	78.59	36.73	28.02	205.77	119.72
16.58	8.07	7.77	2.26	213.72	215.19
48.38	47.42	14.74	14.42	154.24	100.00
3.10	2.50	0.90	0.73	3.29	1.30
42.31	38.55	22.43	21.16	21.22	15.03
				3.01	1.86
				11.86	5.30

5-17 全市按行业分施工项目（2013年）

行 业	Sector	本年新增固定资产（万元） Increased Fixed Assets This Year(10 000 yuan)
总计	**Total**	**18750016**
（一）农、林、牧、渔业	Agriculture, Forestry, Animal Husbandry and Fishery	636794
（二）采矿业	Mining	101530
（三）制造业	Manufacturing	2701959
（四）电力、燃气及水的生产供应业	Generation and Supply of Electricity, Production and Supply of Gas and Water	1106903
（五）建筑业	Construction	710094
（六）批发和零售业	Wholesale and Retail Trades	522824
（七）交通运输、仓储和邮政业	Transportation, Storage and Post	895930
（八）住宿和餐饮业	Hotels and Catering Services	318137
（九）信息传输、软件和信息技术服务业	Information Transmission, Computer Service and Software	78197
（十）金融业	Financial Intermediation	97147
（十一）房地产业	Real Estate	7421685
（十二） 租赁和商务服务业	Leasing and Business Services	214127
（十三）科学研究和技术服务业	Scientific Research and Technical Service	368879
（十四）水利、环境和公共设施管理业	Management of Water Conservancy, Environment and Public Facilities	1992241
（十五）居民服务、修理和其他服务业	Services to Households, repairs and other services	120617
（十六）教育	Education	341545
（十七）卫生和社会工作	Health and social work	555845
（十八）文化、体育和娱乐业	Culture, Sports and Entertainment	293734
（十九）公共管理、社会保障和社会组织	Public administration, social security and social organizations	271828
（二十）国际组织	International Organizations	

Construction Project Grouped by Sector in the Whole City（2013）

施工项目个数（个） Number of Constructing Projects (unit)	本年新开工 Newly Started This Year	本年投产项目个数（个） Projects put into Use (unit)
2367	**1476**	**1328**
185	155	150
9	9	8
539	309	301
74	51	48
43	28	25
105	72	59
171	114	109
71	54	43
43	17	15
12	7	4
387	160	141
30	15	12
42	27	18
410	295	255
21	16	14
99	71	45
39	17	24
39	29	23
48	30	34

5-18 主要年份房地产开发投资主要指标

单位：万平方米

指　标	Item	1997	1998	1999	2000
本年完成投资额（亿元）	Investment Completed This Year(100 million yuan)	24.68	38.21	44.30	51.85
本年房屋施工面积	Floor Space of Buildings Under Construction This Year	451.47	678.87	793.46	763.18
#住宅	Residential Buildings	331.16	552.37	649.53	619.85
本年房屋竣工面积	Floor Space of Buildings Completed This Year	135.62	156.17	377.79	321.10
#住宅	Residential Buildings	120.33	133.33	352.28	295.55
本年房屋竣工价值（亿元）	Value of Floor Space of Buildings Completed(100million yuan)	11.96	14.36	38.22	26.94
#住宅	Residential Buildings	9.63	11.00	33.02	22.97
商品房销售面积	Floor Space of Commercialized Buildings sold	78.45	117.11	296.97	212.92
#住宅	Residential Buildings	72.69	108.61	284.95	200.77
商品房销售额（亿元）	Total Sales of Commercialized Buildings(100 million yuan)	12.81	17.74	35.19	32.52
#住宅	Residential Buildings	11.39	15.46	32.35	29.46
商品房预售面积	Floor Space of Commercialized Buildings Presold	26.35	252.02	30.25	253.03
#住宅	Residential Buildings	23.27	246.77	27.34	253.03
商品房空置面积	Floor Space of Vacant Commercialized Buildings	58.71	32.52	62.38	36.41
#住宅	Residential Buildings	50.26	22.81	52.32	24.02
商品房出租面积	Floor Space of Commercialized Buildings Recenting	25.69	1.04	1.88	1.17
#住宅	Residential Buildings	22.87	0.01	0.15	0.02
本年新增固定资产（亿元）	Newly Increased Fixed Assets This Year(100 million yuan)	14.36	19.93	43.10	38.38

Main Indicators of Investment in Real Estate Development in Representative Years

(10 000 sq.m)

2001	2002	2003	2004	2005	2006	2007	2008	2009	2010	2011	2012	2013
67.42	79.37	124.82	169.67	225.23	285.76	387.33	540.26	696.34	842.34	996.81	1281.90	1595.64
743.78	1172.58	1343.12	1633.68	2174.29	2383.56	2915.95	3632.87	5708.63	6697.39	8247.69	9947.89	10454.27
580.43	964.68	943.61	1204.01	1783.36	1890.27	2376.82	3079.13	4901.59	5777.71	7108.27	8294.92	8461.71
316.24	329.71	339.67	380.84	361.62	399.64	483.30	443.96	542.81	463.65	631.03	1063.70	795.35
269.61	290.30	289.56	308.06	316.52	342.15	422.47	412.46	453.49	412.44	564.59	903.82	663.20
37.20	36.93	54.73	73.75	80.58	82.02	101.13	106.50	168.08	145.62	213.29	310.57	279.63
28.62	30.46	44.01	55.58	68.11	65.80	77.13	96.02	137.42	128.69	185.31	260.04	222.64
225.35	252.90	252.74	305.47	497.34	621.50	833.92	760.72	1256.02	1587.81	1778.02	1538.91	1662.75
192.20	237.04	230.28	279.90	476.39	584.06	782.91	715.76	1202.12	1523.24	1674.85	1383.84	1522.50
47.22	51.35	54.29	81.35	171.29	206.15	281.79	296.44	488.55	707.00	1091.31	1017.74	1112.87
35.53	45.46	44.25	71.27	158.03	179.47	251.74	268.92	450.71	661.27	973.71	858.53	976.19
67.44	61.02	52.35	17.60	300.07	423.20	491.07	569.22	1125.44	1510.20	3105.76	2627.73	1787.89
65.20	55.73	49.12	159.10	287.13	408.11	457.54	541.20	1095.17	1452.20	2826.79	2340.69	1597.82
50.82	57.14	63.85	108.52	123.59	112.49	45.42	55.40	40.68	34.32	59.75	102.58	74.59
34.18	44.70	52.34	72.76	99.17	85.89	38.62	35.40	28.73	26.23	45.41	83.78	61.24
9.19	15.75	10.56	11.18	17.32	8.53	10.84	34.94	38.23	28.60	8.01	15.16	15.57
0.10	1.13	5.43	5.78	4.09	3.74	5.36	4.53	6.55	0.70	3.25	4.03	0.73
50.77	48.43	62.13	83.36	92.78	100.22	143.17	124.02	195.71	168.20	25.53	358.03	334.41

5-19 分区县、开发区房地产开发主要指标（2013年）

单位：万元

区县、开发区	Region	企业（单位）个数（个） Number of Enterprises (Unit)	本年完成投资 Investment Completed This Yea	本年新增固定资产 Increased Fixed Assets This Year
区县	**Region**			
新城区	Xincheng	50	779865	152322
碑林区	Beilin	69	1510074	824995
莲湖区	Lianhu	65	2219132	266615
灞桥区	Baqiao	52	1038781	198657
未央区	Weiyang	114	2721970	662309
雁塔区	Yanta	142	5935284	583513
阎良区	Yanliang	35	192692	92619
临潼区	Lintong	7	93517	31175
长安区	Chang'an	60	935128	491609
蓝田县	Lantian	9	27431	2334
周至县	Zhouzhi	19	134190	8640
户　县	Huxian	13	103337	19741
高陵县	Gaoling	27	265017	9591
开发区	**Development Zones**			
高新区	GaoXin	44	880345	446507
经开区	JingKai	48	967957	381406
曲江新区	Qujiang	44	2448080	160778
浐灞生态区	Chanba Eco-District	21	1003118	167663
航空基地	Aviation Industry Base	10	109169	18001
航天基地	Aerospace Base	17	417600	219498
国际港务区	International Trade&Logistic Park	2	26783	
沣东新城	FengDongXinCheng	9	422650	705

Main Indicators of Real Estate Development by Region and Development Zone（2013）

(10 000 yuan)

房屋施工面积（平方米）Floor Space of Buildings Under Constmction(sq.m)	住宅 Residenctial Buildings	房屋竣工面积（平方米）Floor Space of Buildings Completed(sq.m)	住宅 Residenctial Buildings	竣工房屋价值 Value of Buildings Completed	住宅 Residenctial Buildings
6207114	5356686	435302	382672	115046	100590
12599223	10020356	1541034	1192062	637623	448281
11341779	9452209	904901	642464	265014	199148
7626800	6515863	512487	466261	141542	123594
23769060	18781024	1700756	1509353	601679	503831
25179322	19316427	1300379	960976	472958	320262
2218741	1638886	368877	348123	83514	79026
669946	651946	125588	125588	31175	31175
9627859	8103434	967675	911803	416583	393491
458788	428050				
1267951	1065875	18000	14200	8640	4544
919847	858207	43417	43417	13025	13025
2656225	2428173	35093	35093	9475	9475
7421874	4402306	923288	668979	353275	255659
8881502	6942161	943126	785937	367234	280175
10537551	7969083	165835	80741	77696	22507
6250564	5398362	483821	474213	147442	144175
692728	290856	31023	25000	8997	7250
4428154	3681448	400894	385475	219498	211646
226651	212521				
1887663	1654625				

5-20 房地产开发投资主要指标（2013年）

Main Indicators of Investment in Real Estate Development（2013）

单位：万元 (10 000 yuan)

指标	Item	全市合计 Total	#国有 State-owned	市区 Urban Area	市属 Municipal
一、企业（单位）个数（个）	**Number of Enterprises(unit)**	**662**	**51**	**540**	**607**
二、本年完成投资	**Investment Completed This Year**	**1595.64**	**132.96**	**1542.64**	**1441.1**
按工程用途分	Grouped by Function				
住宅	Residential Buildings	1241.47	105.38	1197.18	1111.27
#别墅、高档公寓	Villas and Top-Grade Apartments	29.32	4	28.82	29.32
办公楼	Office Buildings	69.92	7.08	69.78	65.49
商业营业用房	Houses for Business Use	155.31	11.46	148.41	145.42
其他	Others	128.94	9.04	127.27	118.91
三、本年新增固定资产	**Increased Fixed Assets This Year**	**334.41**	**33.5**	**330.38**	**318.44**
四、房屋施工面积（万平方米）	**Floor Space of Buildings Under Construction (10 000 sq.m)**	**10454.27**	**1029.47**	**9923.98**	**9460.58**
#住宅	Residential Buildings	8461.71	797.67	7983.68	7612.91
五、本年房屋竣工面积（万平方米）	**Floor Space of Buildings Completed (10 000 sq.m)**	**795.35**	**79.86**	**785.7**	**763.28**
#住宅	Residential Buildings	663.2	59.74	653.93	637.94
六、本年房屋竣工价值（亿元）		**279.63**	**30.41**	**276.51**	**266.63**
#住宅	Residential Buildings	**222.64**	**22.07**	**219.94**	**211.41**
七、本年商品房屋销售面积（万平方米）	**Floor Space of Commercialized Buildings Sold(10 000 sq.m)**	**1662.75**	**133.76**	**1553.32**	**1497.7**
本年商品房销售额（亿元）	Sales Income of Commercialized Buildings	1112.87	93.94	1072.49	999.91

5-21 商品房销售情况（2013年）

Sales of Commercial Houses（2013）

指　标	Item	全市合计 Total	#国有 State-owned	市区 Urban Area	市属 Municipal
商品房销售面积（平方米）	**Floor Space of Commercialized Buildings Sold(sq.m)**	**16627457**	**1337612**	**15533169**	**14976977**
现房销售面积（平方米）	**Floor Space of Completed Apartment Sales**	**943593**	**57711**	**904039**	**918203**
期房销售面积（平方米）	**Floor Space of Forward Delivery Housing Sales**	**15683864**	**1279901**	**14629130**	**14058774**
住宅	Residential Buildings	15225020	1258944	14154494	13665090
#别墅、高档公寓	Villas and High-grade Apartments	243165		243165	243165
办公楼	Office Buildings	333588	6176	333588	329747
商业营业用房	Houses for Business Use	651733	13789	627971	623925
其他	Others	417116	58703	417116	358215
商品房销售额（万元）	**Sales Income of Commercialized Buildings (10 000 yuan)**	**11128695**	**939382**	**10724906**	**9959057**
现房销售额（万元）	**Floor Space of Completed Apartment Sales**	**514702**	**48450**	**498899**	**488822**
期房销售额（万元）	**Floor Space of Forward Delivery Housing Sales**	**10613993**	**890932**	**10226007**	**9510235**
住宅	Residential Buildings	9761927	842792	9387984	8733701
#别墅高档公寓	Villas and High-grade Apartments	243847		243847	243847
办公楼	Office Buildings	299012	5612	299012	296142
商业营业用房	Houses for Business Use	746816	26456	716970	707941
其他	Others	320940	64522	320940	256273
商品房待售面积（平方米）	**Vacancy of Commercialized Buildings(sq.m)**	**745888**	**82977**	**713432**	**667521**
#待售一年以上（一一三年）	Being Idle for One Year	350491	48890	338205	279910
待售三年以上（含三年）	Being Idle for Three Year	34261	7467	34261	26794
住宅	Residence	612352	62463	582410	542263
#别墅高档公寓	Villas and High-grade Apartments			6770	6770
办公楼	Office Buildings	17705	2708	17705	17705
商业营业用房	Houses for Business Use	79779	13910	77265	75397
其他	Others	36052	3896	36052	32156
商品房出租面积（平方米）	**Floor Space of Commercialized Leased Buildings(sq.m)**	**155696**		**155010**	**155696**
住宅	Residential Buildings	7283		6597	7283
办公楼	Office Buildings	2026		2026	2026
商业营业用房	Houses for Business Use	146387		146387	146387
其他	Others				

5-22 房地产开发投资资金来源（2013年）

Source of Funds for Investment in Real Estate Development（2013）

单位：万元 (10 000 yuan)

指 标	Item	全市合计 Total	#国有 State-owned	市区 Urban Area	市属 Municipal
一.本年资金来源合计	**Total**	**24237997**	**2096804**	**23506864**	**21709024**
1. 上年末结余资金	Balance of Last Year	5509776	615857	5352355	4808632
2. 本年资金来源小计	Total Funds This Year	18728221	1480947	18154509	16900392
(1) 国内贷款	Domestic Loans	2504820	257470	2456852	2326870
#银行贷款	Bank Loan	2351266	257470	2315444	2201266
非银行金融机构贷款	Loans from financial Institutions except Bank	153554		141408	125604
(2) 利用外资	Utilization of Foreign Funds	74400		74400	74400
#外商直接投资	Foreign Direct Investment	74400		74400	74400
(3) 自筹资金	Self-raising Funds	8112540	525395	7869742	7452328
#自有资金	Funds at the disposal of Enterprises	2673123	220915	2564511	2477126
(4) 其他资金	Others	8036461	698082	7753515	7046794
#定金及预收款	Earnest Money and Advance payment	5538530	535432	5400307	4782621
个人按揭贷款	Personal Mortgage loan	2097231	153937	1957848	1888192
二.本年各项应付款合计（万元）	**Total Sums of Money to be Paid This Year**	**3016268**	**356282**	**2844246**	**2739250**
#工程款	Project Fund	1556059	293655	1448521	1356346

5-23 房地产开发经营情况（2013年）

Running of Real Estate Development（2013）

单位：万元 (10 000 yuan)

指 标	Item	全市合计 Total	#国有 State-owned	市区 Urban Area	市属 Municipal
一、资产负债情况	**Assets and Liabilities**				
1. 资产总计	Total Assets	49279347	4909027	47777583	45520175
2. 负债总计	Total Liabilities	40535713	3998485	39188379	37376517
3. 所有者权益合计	Total Creditor's Equity	8743634	910542	8589203	8143658
#实收资本	Held Capital	6284857	533671	6123509	5863713
二、损益及分配情况	**Profit or Loss and the Distribution**				
1. 主营业务收入	Revenue from Principal Business	10966488	814786	10552599	10256863
土地转让收入	Revenue of Land Transferred	6800	1000	6800	6300
商品房屋销售收入	Revenue of Commercial Houses Sold	10632486	721994	10219088	10001963
房屋出租收入	Revenue of Houses Leased	84755	5006	84629	80775
其他收入	Other Revenue	242447	86785	242082	167825
2. 主营业务成本	Cost of Principal Business	7831708	544134	7519474	7274202
3. 主营业务税金及附加	Taxes and Other Charges on Principal Business	888310	48866	860291	843159
4. 其他业务利润	Other Business Profit	14966	1865	14912	13131
5. 销售费用	Sales Expenditures	343126	30563	324936	315514
6. 管理费用	Management Cost	378768	30912	351903	349647
#税金	Tax	21976	1670	21362	20065
7. 财务费用	Fiscal Expenditure	116073	3532	113362	103200
#利息支出	Interest Exchange	103295	17646	101850	79181
8. 营业利润	Operating Profit	1301583	161577	1274518	1262149
投资收益	Investment Revenue	15411	7765	15405	13327
营业外收入	Non-business Revenue	9233	2532	9219	8827
营业外支出	Non-business Expenditures	23835	1393	23366	23153
9. 利润总额	Total Profit	1296627	162768	1270018	1257469
10. 应付职工薪酬	Salary Payable	239936	31354	228683	218361

主要统计指标解释

全社会固定资产投资 是以货币形式表现的在一定时期内全社会建造和购置固定资产的工作量以及与此有关的费用的总称。该指标是反映固定资产投资规模、结构和发展速度的综合性指标，又是观察工程进度和考核投资效果的重要依据。全社会固定资产投资按登记注册类型可分为国有、集体、联营、股份制、私营和个体、港澳台商、外商、其他等。

城镇固定资产投资 指城镇各种登记注册类型的企业、事业、行政单位及个体户进行的计划总投资500万元及500万元以上的建设项目投资和房地产开发投资。县城及以上区域内发生的投资，县及县以上各级政府及主管部门直接领导、管理的建设项目和企业事业单位的投资均为城镇固定资产投资。

房地产开发投资 指各种登记注册类型的房地产开发公司、商品房建设公司及其他房地产开发法人单位和附属于其他法人单位实际从事房地产开发或经营活动的单位统一开发的包括统代建、拆迁还建的住宅、厂房、仓库、饭店、宾馆、度假村、写字楼、办公楼等房屋建筑物和配套的服务设施，土地开发工程（如道路、给水、排水、供电、供热、通讯、平整场地等基础设施工程）的投资；不包括单纯的土地交易活动。

农村投资 包括在农村区域范围内进行固定资产投资活动的企业、事业、行政单位及农户投资。

固定资产投资的资金来源 根据固定资产投资的资金来源不同，分为国家预算资金、国内贷款、利用外资、自筹资金和其他资金。

（1）国家预算资金：包括一般预算、政府性基金预算、国有资本经营预算和社保基金预算等资金。

（2）国内贷款：指报告期固定资产投资单位向银行及非银行金融机构借入的用于固定资产投资的各种国内借款，包括银行利用自有资金及吸收的存款发放的贷款、上级主管部门拨入的国内贷款、国家专项贷款、地方财政专项资金安排的贷款、国内储备贷款、周转贷款等。

（3）利用外资：指报告期收到的用于固定资产建造和购置的境外资金（包括设备、材料、技术在内）。包括对外借款（外国政府、国际金融组织贷款、出口信贷、外国银行商业贷款、对外发行债券和股票）、外商直接投资及外商其他投资。不包括我国自有外汇资金（国家外汇、地方外汇、留成外汇、调剂外汇和中国银行自有资金发行的外汇贷款等）。计算利用外资时，需要折算成人民币，折算中所使用的外汇汇率按现汇计算，即按使用外汇时的汇率计算。

（4）自筹资金：指固定资产投资单位报告期收到的，由各地区、各部门及企、事业单位筹集用于固定资产投资的预算外资金，包括中央各部门、各级地方和企、事业单位的自筹资金。

（5）其他资金：指在报告期收到的除以上各种资金之外其他用于固定资产投资的资金，包括企业或金融机构通过发行各种债券筹集到的资金、社会集资、个人资金、无偿捐赠的资金及其他单位拨人的资金等。

固定资产投资按国民经济行业分 根据现有企业、事业、行政单位和建设项目建成投产后的主要产品种类或主要用途及社会经济活动性质来确定国民经济行业。一般情况下，一个建设项目或一个企业、事业单位只能属于一种国民经济行业。

固定资产投资按隶属关系分 是按建设单位或企业、事业、行政单位的主管上级机关确定的。

（1）中央：是指中共中央、人大常委会和国务院各部、委、局、总公司以及直属机构直接领导的建设项目和企业、事业、行政单位。这些单位的固定资产投资计划由国务院各部门直接编制和下达，建设中所需物资、主要设备以及建设中的问题都由中央有关部门安排和解决。

（2）地方：是由省（自治区、直辖市）、地区（州、盟、省辖市）、县（旗、县级市）三级政府及业务主管部门直接领导和管理的建设项目、企业、事业、行政单位。地方项目还包括不隶属以上各级政府及主管部门的建设项目和企业、事业单位，如外商投资企业和无主管部门的企业等。

固定资产投资按建设性质分 根据整个建设项目情况来确定。建设项目的性质一般分为新建、扩建、改建和技术改造、单纯建造生活设施、迁建、恢复、单纯购置。房地产开发单位、农户投资不划分建设性质。

（1）新建：一般指从无到有开始建设的企业、事业和行政单位或建设项目。有的单位原有基础很小，经过建设后新增的固定资产价值超过该企、事业、行政单位原有固定资产价值（原值）三倍以上的也应作为新建。

（2）扩建：指在厂内或其他地点，为扩大原有产品的生产能力（或效益）或增加新的产品生产能力，而增建主要的生产车间（或主要工程）、分厂、独立的生产线。行政、事业单位在原单位增建业务用房（如学校增建教学用房、医院增建门诊部、病房等）也作为扩建。

现有企、事业单位为扩大原有主要产品生产能力或增加新的产品生产能力，增建一个或几个主要生产车间（或主要工程）、分厂，同时进行一些更新改造工程的，也应作为扩建。

（3）改建和技术改造：指现有企业、事业单位，对原有设施进行技术改造或更新（包括相应配套的辅助性生产、生活福利设施）的建设项目。现有企业、事业单位为适应市场变化的需要，而改变企业的主要产品种类（如军工企业转产民用品等）的建设项目，应作为改建。原有产品生产作业线由于各工序（车间）之间能力不平衡，为填平补齐充分发挥原有生产能力而增建不增加本企业主要产品设计能力的车间，也应作为改建。技术改造是指企业、事业单位在现有基础上，用先进的技术代替落后的技术，用先进的工艺和装备代替落后的工艺和装备，以改变企业落后的技术经济面貌，实现以内涵为主的扩大再生产，达到提高产品质量、促进产品更新换代、节约能源、降低消耗、扩大生产规模、全面提高社会经济效益的目的。技术改造具体包括以下内容：机器设备和工具的更新改造；生产工艺改革、节约能源和原材料的改造；厂房建筑和公共设施的改造；劳动条件和生产环境的改造等。

固定资产投资按构成分 固定资产投资活动按其工作内容和实现方式分为建筑安装工程，设备工具器具购置和其他费用三个部分。

（1）建筑安装工程（建筑安装工作量）：指各种房屋、建筑物的建造工程和各种设备、装置的安装工程。包括各种房屋建造工程；各种用途设备基础和各种工业窑炉的砌筑工程及金属结构工程；为施工而进行的各种准备工作和临时工程以及完工后的清理工作等；铁路、道路的铺设，矿井的开凿及石油管道的架设等；水利工程；防空地下建筑等特殊工程；列入房屋工程预算内的暖气、卫生、通风、照明、煤气等设备的价值及装设油饰工程；列入建筑工程预算内的各种管道（蒸汽、压缩空气、石油、给排水等管道）、电力、电讯电缆导线等的敷设工程；以及各种机械设备的安装工程；为测定安装工程质量，对设备进行的试运工作；房地产开发单位进行的商品房屋开发建设工程、土地开发工程。

在建筑安装工程中，不包括被安装设备本身的价值。

（2）设备工具器具购置：指建设单位或企、事业单位购置或自制的，达到固定资产标准的设备、工具、器具的价值。新建单位及扩建单位的新建车间，按照设计或计划要求购置或自制的全部设备、工具、器具，不论是否达到固定资产标准均计入“设备工具器具购置”中。

（3）其他费用：指在固定资产建造和购置过程中发生的，除上述几项内容以外的各种应分摊计入固定资产的费用。

施工项目 指报告期内所有施工的建设项目个数，包括本年新开工的项目和以前年度开工在本年继续施工的建设项目。凡是报告期内施过工的建设项目，不论施工时间长短，均作为施工项目统计。施工项目个数可以反映一定时期固定资产投资的实际规模，与同期全部建成投产项目个数相比，可以从建设速度的角度反映固定资产投资的效果。

全部建成投产项目 指报告期内按设计文件规定的全部生产能力（或效益）建成投产，经验收合格交付使用的建设项目。

新增生产能力（或工程效益） 指通过固定资产投资活动而增加的设计能力（或工程效益）。主要指标包括建设规模、本年施工规模、自开始建设累计新增生产能力（或工程效益）、本年新增生产能力（或工程效益）等。

建设规模 指建设项目或工程设计文件中规定的全部设计能力（或工程效益）。包括已经建成投产和尚未建成投产的工程的生产能力（或工程效益）。

本年施工规模 指报告期内施工的单项工程的设计能力（或工程效益），即全部建设规模中在本年正式施工的部分。

自开始建设累计新增生产能力（或工程效益） 指自开始建设至本年底止建成投产的全部单项工程累计的新增生产能力（或工程效益）。

本年新增生产能力（或工程效益） 指在本年度内按照新增生产能力（或工程效益）的计算条件和标准，实际建成投入生产或交付使用的生产能力（或工程效益）。

施工房屋面积 指报告期内施工的全部房屋（包括地下室、半地下室以及配套房屋）建筑面积。包括本期新开工的面积和上期开工跨入本期继续施工的房屋面积，以及上期已停建在本期恢复施工的房屋面积。本期竣工和本期施工后又停缓建的房屋，其建筑面积仍计入本期房屋施工面积中。

竣工房屋面积 指在报告期内房屋建筑按照设计要求已经全部完工，达到住人和使用条件，经验收鉴定合格（或达到竣工验收标准），可正式移交使用单位的各栋房屋建筑面积的总和。

新增固定资产 指报告期内交付使用的固定资产价值。包括本年内建成投入生产或交付使用的工程投资和达到固定资产标准的设备、工具、器具的投资及有关应摊入的费用。该指标是表示固定资产投资成果的价值指标，也是反映建设进度，计算固定资产投资效果的重要指标。

项目建成投产率 指一定时期内全部建成投产项目个数与同期施工项目个数的比率。该指标是从建设单位建设速度的角度反映投资效果的指标。

固定资产交付使用率 指一定时期新增固定资产与同期完成投资额的比率。该指标是反映固定资产动用速度，衡量建设过程中宏观投资效果的综合指标。由于新增固定资产是较长时期内形成的结果，而投资额则是当年完成的，因此，该指标一般适宜于反映较长时期内固定资产的动用情况。

商品房销售面积 指报告期内出售商品房屋的合同总面积（即双方签署的正式买卖合同中所确定的建筑面积）。由现房销售建筑面积和期房销售建筑面积两部分组成。

商品房销售额 指报告期内出售商品房屋的合同总价款（即双方签署的正式买卖合同中所确定的合同总价）。该指标与商品房销售面积同口径，由现房销售额和期房销售额两部分组成。

经济适用房 指根据经济适用房计划安排建设的政策性住宅。经济是指房屋建筑造价和销售价格低于一般商品住宅；适用是指适合中低收入家庭购买使用。经济适用房主要是由地方政府统一下达投资计划，房地产公司开发，对外销售；用地一般采用行政划拨或招标投标方式，免收土地出让金；对各种经批准的收费减半征收，开发利润不超过3%；销售价格实行政府指导价。该指标可以分析房地产投资结构，反映中低收入家庭商品住宅的供求平衡情况。

Explanatory Notes on Main Statistical Indicators

Total Investment in Fixed Assets in the Whole Country refers to the volume of activities in construction and purchases of fixed assets of the whole country and related fees, expressed in monetary terms during the reference period. It is a comprehensive indicator which shows the size, structure and growth of the investment in fixed assets, providing a basis for observing the progress of construction projects and evaluating results of investment. Total investment in fixed assets in the whole country includes, by type of ownership, the investment by State-owned units, collective-owned units, joint ownership units, share-holding units, private units individuals as well as investments by entrepreneurs from Hong Kong, Macao and Taiwan, foreign investors and others.

Urban Investment in Fixed Assets refers to construction projects involving a total planned investment of 5000 000 yuan and over by enterprises of various types of ownership, institutions, administrative units and individuals in urban areas, investment in real estate development. In other words, all investments that take place in county towns and urban areas, investment in construction projects under the direct leadership and management of government agencies at and above county levels and investments by enterprises and institutions at and above county levels are covered in urban investment in fixed assets.

Investment in Real Estate Development refers to investment by real estate development companies, commercialized buildings construction companies and other real estate development units of various types of ownership in the construction of buildings, such as residential buildings, factory buildings, warehouses, hotels, guesthouses, holiday villages, office buildings, and the complementary service facilities and land development projects, such as roads, water supply, water drainage, power supply, heating supply, telecommunications, land leveling and other infrastructural projects. It does not include activities in pure land transactions.

Investment in Rural Areas refers to investment in fixed assets by enterprises, institutions, administrative units and households in rural areas.

Sources of Funds for Investment in Fixed Assets are categorized as funds from the State budget, domestic loans, foreign investment, self-raised funds, and others, depending on the sources of investment.

(1) Fund from the State budget consists of budgetary appropriation and loans from the State budget. More specifically, it includes, from the budget of the central government, capital construction fund (operation fund and non-operational fund), special expenses, loans from repayment, discount fund, expenses on innovation and trial production of new products, expenses on urban construction, expenses on temporary construction from business departments, development fund for less developed areas, as well as local budgetary fund transferred from the central budget.

(2) Domestic loans refer to loans of various forms borrowed by investing units from banks and non-bank financial institutions during the reference period for the purpose of investment in fixed assets, including loans issued by banks from their self-owned funds and deposit, loans appropriated by higher authorities, special loans by government, loans arranged by local government from special funds, domestic reserve loan, and working loan.

(3) Foreign investment refers to overseas funds received during the reference period for the construction and purchase of investment in fixed assets (covering equipment, materials and technology) including foreign borrowings (loans from foreign governments and international financial institutions, export credit, commercial loans from foreign banks, issue of bonds and stocks overseas), foreign direct investment and other foreign investments. Excluded from this category is capital in foreign exchanges owned by China (foreign exchanges owned by the central and local governments, foreign exchanges retained by enterprises, foreign exchanges by enterprises through the regulating mechanism, loans in foreign exchanges issued by the Bank of China with its own fund, etc). In calculating the utilization of foreign capital, foreign currencies are converted into Chinese Renminbi applying the current exchange rate when the foreign capitals are actually used.

(4) Self-raised funds refer to extra-budgetary funds for investment in fixed assets received during the reference period by investing units from central government ministries, local governments, enterprises and institutions, including their self-raised funds.

(5) Others refer to funds for investment in fixed assets received from sources other than those listed above, including capital raised through issuing bonds by

enterprises or financial institutions, funds raised from individuals and through donations, and funds transferred from other units.

Investment in Fixed Assets by Sector The classification of construction projects by sector is determined by enterprises, institutions, administrative units and the major products or the purpose of the projects of existing enterprises, institutional and administrative units when they are put into production or use, and by the nature of their social economic activities. In general, one project or one enterprise or institution can only be classified into one sector.

Investment in Fixed Assets by Jurisdiction of Management refers to the classification of investment by the competent authorities under which investment is made by construction units, enterprises, institutions or administrative units.

(1) Central investment refers to the investment in projects or by enterprises, institutions or administrative units which are under the direct leadership and management of the State Council and of the national commissions, ministries, agencies and State-owned large corporations. Various ministries and departments of the State Council prepare and implement plans for investment in fixed assets by those departments, and arrange and ensure the supply of materials and key equipment required for the projects.

(2) Local investment refers to the investment in projects or by enterprises, institutions or administrative units which are under the direct leadership and management of departments under the provincial, prefecture and county governments. Also included are projects by foreign-invested enterprises and enterprises without competent managing authorities.

Investment in Fixed Assets by Type of Construction Construction projects in general can be classified, by the type of construction, into new construction, expansion, reconstruction and technical transformation, purely construction of living facilities, moving, restoration and purely purchasing. However, investment by type of construction is not applied to investment by real-estate development units and investment by rural households.

(1) New construction in general refers to construction projects, which start from scratch, of enterprises, institutions, administrative agencies. In case the size of the existing unit is quite small, and the value of newly added fixed assets is more than three times of the original value, the expansion will be considered as new construction.

(2) Expansion refers to construction of new major production workshop, branch factory or independent production line within a factory or in other locations, for the purpose of increasing the production capacity (or improving efficiency) or adding new production capacity. Newly constructed accommodation for the operation of institutions and administrative organizations (such as newly constructed buildings for teaching in schools, buildings for clinics or wards in hospitals, etc.) are also classified as expansion.

Also included in expansion are investments by existing enterprises or institutions in building major production line(s) or branch factory(ies) along with some work on innovation, for the purpose of expanding the production capacity of original products or producing new products.

(3) Reconstruction and technical transformation refers to construction projects by existing enterprises or institutions in innovation or technical transformation of the old facilities (including auxiliary production equipment and welfare facilities). Also considered as reconstruction is the construction of new workshops by the existing enterprises or institutions to change the variety of products to meet the market demand (such as the production of civil products by defence industries), or to bring the designed production capacity into full play through a more balanced production process on production lines. Technical transformation refers to replacement of old technology or equipment by new technology or equipment, in order to expand the reproduction through improvement of technology contents in production, to improve product quality, to promote new products to save energy,to reduce consumption, to expand the production scale and to improve overall social-economic efficiency. Contents of technical transformation include: updating of machinery, equipment and tools; reforming production process by using energy or materials saving technology; construction of factory workshops and transformation of public facilities; improvement of working conditions and environment, etc.

Investment in Fixed Assets by Structure By their

contents and the mode of implementation, investment activities are classified into 3 categories, i.e. construction and installation, purchase of equipment and instrument, and other expenses.

(1) Construction and installation (work volume of construction and installation) refers to the construction of houses and buildings and the installation of various kinds of equipment and instruments. They include construction of houses; equipment foundations, industrial kilns and stoves, and metal structure work; preparation works and temporary works for project construction, and clearing up works post project construction; pavement of railways and roads, drilling of mines and putting up of oil pipes; construction of water conservancy; construction of underground air-raid shelters and construction of other special projects; value of equipment for heating, sanitation, ventilation, lighting, gas, painting, etc. that are covered by the budget of housing projects; laying out of various pipelines (for steam, compressed air, petroleum, tap water and sewage) and wiring and cabling for electric power and for communications; installation of various machinery and equipment; testing operation for pre- testing the quality of installation projects, and land and other development work conducted by real estate developers for commercialized housing.

The value of equipment installed is itself not included in the value of construction and installation projects.

(2) Purchase of equipment and instruments refers to the total value of equipment, tools, and instruments purchased or self-produced which come up to the cut-off point for fixed assets by the construction units or investing enterprises or institutions. Equipment, tools and instruments purchased or self-produced for new workshops by newly established or expanded units are categorized as "purchase of equipment and instruments" no matter whether they come up to the cut-off point for fixed assets.

(3) Other expenses refer to expenses arising during the construction or purchase of fixed assets other than those mentioned above.

Projects under Construction refer to number of all projects with construction activities newly started in current year or left-over from the previous year in the reference period. All projects that have construction activities undertaken during the reference period are reported as projects under construction irrespective of the length of construction work. The number of projects under construction can reflect the actual size of investment in fixed assets during a given period, and when compared with the number of projects completed and put into use during the same period, it demonstrates the results of investment in fixed assets from the angle of the speed of the construction.

Projects Completed and Put into Use refer to projects have been completed in accordance with the design documents, resulting in forming production capacity (efficiency) and have been checked and accepted after relevant tests, and have been formally delivered for use.

Newly Increased Production Capacity (or Project Efficiency) refers to the increase in design capacity (or project efficiency) through investment in fixed assets. The main indicators include: construction scale, scale of projects under construction in current year, the accumulated newly increased production capacity (project efficiency) since the start of the projects and the newly increased production capacity (project efficiency) of current year.

Construction Scale refers to the total designed production capacity (project efficiency) of the construction projects in accordance with the design document, including those have been put into operation and those that have not been completed.

Scale of Projects under Construction in Current Year refers to the designed production capacity (project efficiency) of a single project under construction in the reference period, i.e. the part of the total scale of project which is officially under construction in current year.

The Accumulated Newly Increased Production Capacity (project efficiency) since the Start of the Projects refers to the accumulated newly increased production capacity of all the single projects which have been put into use from the beginning of the projects till the end of current year.

The Newly Increased Production Capacity (project efficiency) of Current Year refers to the production capacity (project efficiency) that has been completed and put into operation in current year according to the calculation conditions and standards on newly increased production capacity (project efficiency).

Floor Space of Buildings under Construction refers to the total floor space of all the buildings (including basement, semi-basement and auxiliary buildings), including the effective area and the area occupied by the structure. This indicator is one of the important indicators in physical terms to reflect the scale and accomplishment of the construction industry and also an important basis for monitoring the progress, Calculating the cost, analyzing the efficiency and studying the supply of building materials in relation to the construction projects.

Floor Space Completed refers to the floor space of all buildings completed in the reference period, which have been appraised and accepted (or come up to the designed standards) and have been transferred to owner units.

Newly Increased Fixed Assets refer to the value of fixed that has been put into use, including investment in projects that have been completed and put into operation in current year and the investment in equipment, tools and appliance that meet the standard of fixed assets and fees that should be apportioned. This is an indicator that demonstrates the results of investment in fixed assets in monetary terms, and an important indicator to reflect the speed of construction and to calculate the efficiency of investment.

Rate of Construction Projects Completed and Put into Use refers to the ratio of the number of construction projects completed and put into use in a certain period of time to the number of projects under construction in the same period. This reflects the investment efficiency from the perspective of the speed of projects construction.

Rate of Projects of Fixed Assets Completed and Put into Operation refers to the ratio of the newly increased fixed assets to the total investment made in the same period. This is a comprehensive indicator reflecting the speed of the employment of fixed assets and the investment efficiency at the macro-level. As the newly increase fixed assets is the result of a long period while the investment is completed in the current year, this indicator is expected to be used to reflect the employment of fixed assets over a long period of time.

6 财 政

GOVERNMENT FINANCE

资料整理：刘 婷
Data management:Liu Ting

第六部分　财政

一、简要说明

本章资料主要包括地方财政收入、支出总额构成及分区县情况，由西安市统计局综合处根据西安市财政局提供资料整理。

二、主要指标

财政总收入（亿元）	902.76	比上年增长	19.9%
一般预算收入（亿元）	501.98	比上年增长	26.5%
一般预算支出（亿元）	729.81	比上年增长	22.1%

6　GOVERNMENT FINANCE

Ⅰ.Brief Introduction

This chapter consists of primarily data on regional revenue, expenditure of the municipal government, regional revenue and expenditure of the districts and the counties. The data are provided by the Xi'an Bureau of Finance and are compiled by Integration division of the Xi'an Bureau of Statistics.

Ⅱ.Major Indicators

		Increase over Preceding Year
Total Government Revenue(100 mil. Yuan)	902.76	19.9%
General Budgetary Revenue(100 mil. Yuan)	501.98	26.5%
Ordinary Budgetary Expenditures(100 mil. Yuan)	729.81	22.1%

6-1 主要年份地方财政一般预算收入及支出

General Budgetary Local Government Revenue and Expenditure in Representative Years

单位：亿元 (100 million yuan)

年 份 Year	地方财政一般预算收入 General Budgetary Revenue of Local Government	地方财政一般预算支出 General Budgetary Expenditure of Local Government
2000	46.80	52.00
2001	51.45	57.30
2002	54.50	63.80
2003	72.90	76.60
2004	75.30	87.30
2005	72.92	97.51
2006	85.89	119.22
2007	112.92	161.25
2008	145.61	226.99
2009	181.40	276.35
2010	241.86	371.62
2011	318.55	494.58
2012	396.96	597.49
2013	501.98	729.81

注：本表数据来源：市财政局。

6-2 财政收入（2013年）

Government Revenue（2013）

单位：万元 （10 000 yuan）

指　　标	Item	2013
财政总收入	**Total Government Revenue**	**9027646**
#一般预算收入	**General Budgetary Revenue**	**5019751**
一、税收收入	**Total Tax Revenue**	**3760879**
1. 增值税	Value-added Tax	340792
2. 营业税	Business Tax	1316407
3. 企业所得税	Corporate Income Tax	318163
4. 企业所得税退税	Return for Corporate Income Tax	
5. 个人所得税	Individual Income Tax	110885
6. 资源税	Resource Tax	1780
7. 固定资产投资方向调节税	Tax on Adjustment of the Orientation of Investment in Fixed Assets	
8. 城市维护建设税	City Maintenance and Construction Tax	283104
9. 房产税	House Property Tax	126257
10. 印花税	Stamp Tax	85816
11. 城镇土地使用税	Urban Land Use Tax	73114
12. 土地增值税	Land Appreciation Tax	328866
13. 车船税	Tax on the Use of Vehicles and Ships	57247
14. 耕地占用税	Farm Land Occupatian Tax	336021
15. 契税	Deed Tax	382427
16. 其他税收收入	Other Tax Revenue	
二、非税收入	**Total Non-tax Revenue**	**1258872**
1. 专项收入	Special Program Receipts	169726
2. 行政性收费收入	Charge of Adminnistrative and Institutional Units	637777
3. 罚没收入	Penalty Receipts	130448
4. 国有资本经营收入	State-owned Assets Profit	3655
5. 国有资源（资产）有偿使用收入	Revenue for the use of State-owned Assets (Resources)	299435
6. 其他收入	Other Revenue	17831
政府性基金收入	**Governmental Fund Revenue**	**5143428**

注：本表数据来源：市财政局。

6-3 地方财政支出（2013年）

Government Expenditures（2013）

单位：万元　　　　（10 000 yuan）

指　标	Item	2013
一、政府性基金支出	**Governmental Fund Revenue Expenditure**	**5085857**
二、一般预算支出	**General Budgetary Expenditure**	**7298119**
1.一般公共服务支出	Expenditure for General Public Services	672202
2.国防支出	Expenditure for National Defense	5729
3.公共安全支出	Expenditure for Public Security	347712
4.教育支出	Expenditure for Education	1135398
5.科学技术支出	Expenditure for Science and Technology	78976
6.文化体育与传媒支出	Expenditure for Cultural, sports and the media	208268
7.社会保障和就业支出	Expenditure for Social Safety Net and Employment Effort	779773
8.医疗卫生支出	Expenditure for Medical and Health Care	503387
9.节能环保支出	Expenditure for Energy Saving and Environment Protection	185110
10.城乡社区事务支出	Expenditure for Urban and Rural Community Affairs	1502365
11.农林水事务支出	Expenditure for Agriculture, Forestry and Water Conservancy	499357
12.交通运输支出	Expenditure for Transportation	329989
13.资源勘探电力信息等事务支出	Expenditure for Mining ,Electricity and Information	367325
14.商业服务业等事务支出	Expenditure for Commerce and Services	107572
15.金融监管等事务支出	Expenditure for Financial Supervision	30405
16.地震灾后恢复重建支出	Expenditure for Post-earthquake Recovery and Reconstruction	
17.国土资源气象等事务支出	Expenditure for Land Recources and Meteorological Affairs	37422
18.住房保障支出	Expenditure for Housing Support	374717
19.粮油物资管理事务支出	Material Reserves Management Affairs Spending	18127
20.储备事务支出	Expenditure for Reserve	
21.国债还本付息支出	Expenditure for National Debt and Interest(10 000yuan)	63429
22.其它支出	Other Expenditure	50856

注：本表数据来源：市财政局。

6-4 各区县、开发区财政一般预算收入（2013年）

General Budgetary Revenue by Region and Development Zone（2013）

单位：万元 （10 000 yuan）

区县、开发区	Region	一般预算收入 General Budgetary Revenue	税收收入 Tax Revenue	增值税 Value Added Tax	营业税 Business Revenue	企业所得税 Corporate Income Tax
合计	**Total**	**5019751**	**3760879**	**340792**	**1316407**	**318163**
市本级合计	**Sum of city level**	**680119**	**369039**	**32124**	**52882**	**54709**
区、县合计	**Region**	**2828867**	**2149896**	**197774**	**894920**	**162639**
新城区	Xincheng	320736	170446	15459	69907	31709
碑林区	Beilin	392335	288392	36772	126282	34529
莲湖区	Lianhu	415439	266901	35617	124006	17679
雁塔区	Yanta	414186	338552	26616	160167	28382
灞桥区	Baqiao	208989	189108	7994	80240	4495
未央区	Weiyang	313703	262196	23797	124122	13793
阎良区	Yanliang	102426	83567	7010	15947	2492
临潼区	Lintong	102977	95967	11979	18079	5867
长安区	Chang'an	311607	249606	11316	94166	18871
蓝田县	Lantian	32724	20845	1406	11666	331
周至县	Zhouzhi	28567	24094	1447	12572	237
户　县	Huxian	70107	57591	9779	21276	1594
高陵县	Gaoling	115071	102631	8582	36490	2660
开发区合计	**Sum of Development Zones**	**1510765**	**1241944**	**110894**	**368605**	**100815**
高新区	GaoXin	733642	520870	70334	134050	58902
经开区	JingKai	304473	272397	31678	90806	21009
曲江新区	Qujiang	285442	277665	2104	93878	14082
浐灞生态区	Chanba Eco-District	104504	96656	1991	28950	3682
航空基地	Aviation Industry Base	30245	24615	688	9836	1106
航天基地	Aerospace Base	6534	6190	504	1944	92
国际港务区	International Trade&Logistic Park	20749	20344	153	7086	342
沣东新城	FengDongXinCheng	25176	23207	3442	2055	1600

注：本表数据来源：市财政局。

6-4 续表1 continued 1

单位：万元　　　　(10 000 yuan)

区县、开发区	Region	税收收入 Tax Revenue 个人所得税 Individual Income Tax	资源税 Resource Tax	城市维护建设税 City Maintenance and Construction Tax	耕地占用税 Farm Land Occupation Tax	契税 Deed Tax	其他各项税收收入 Other Tax Revenue
合计	**Total**	**110885**	**1780**	**283104**	**336021**	**382427**	**671300**
市本级合计	**Sum of city level**	**24453**		**41127**		**93213**	**70531**
区、县合计	**Region**	**55740**	**1777**	**155011**	**308472**	**50254**	**323309**
新城区	Xincheng	6190		14475	736		31970
碑林区	Beilin	15816		23355			51538
莲湖区	Lianhu	8104		25532	359		55604
雁塔区	Yanta	10801		24306	44837		43443
灞桥区	Baqiao	1481		11928	60292		22678
未央区	Weiyang	4216	1	22763	26946		46558
阎良区	Yanliang	2401		3940	29959	11422	10396
临潼区	Lintong	1566	2	7896	39650	3292	7636
长安区	Chang'an	3677	10	9015	63000	19845	29706
蓝田县	Lantian	125	265	1273	2515	1281	1983
周至县	Zhouzhi	86	1453	1104	3990	1130	2075
户　县	Huxian	407	46	4147	9704	3922	6716
高陵县	Gaoling	370		5277	26484	9362	12906
开发区合计	**Sum of Development Zones**	**30692**	**3**	**86966**	**27549**	**238960**	**277460**
高新区	GaoXin	21856		46134	21500	70800	97294
经开区	JingKai	5261	2	23833		46828	52930
曲江新区	Qujiang	1712		10187		79497	76205
浐灞生态区	Chanba Eco-District	670		3097		28832	29384
航空基地	Aviation Industry Base	441		1292		3226	8026
航天基地	Aerospace Base	73		624		1531	1422
国际港务区	International Trade&Logistic Park	70		745		6705	5243
沣东新城	FengDongXinCheng	609	1	1054	6049	1491	6906

6-4 续表2

单位：万元

区县、开发区	Region	非税收入 Non-tax Revenue	专项收入 Special Program Receipts	行政事业性收费收入 Charge of Adiministrative and Institutional Units
合计	**Total**	**1258872**	**169726**	**637777**
市本级合计	**Sum of city level**	**311080**	**60933**	**100641**
区、县合计	**Region**	**678971**	**68237**	**353574**
新城区	Xincheng	150290	6183	5859
碑林区	Beilin	103943	10070	86598
莲湖区	Lianhu	148538	10989	125577
雁塔区	Yanta	75634	10365	51172
灞桥区	Baqiao	19881	4817	3306
未央区	Weiyang	51507	11519	4100
阎良区	Yanliang	18859	1087	15992
临潼区	Lintong	7010	3014	1115
长安区	Chang'an	62001	3318	43354
蓝田县	Lantian	11879	746	6745
周至县	Zhouzhi	4473	708	1278
户　县	Huxian	12516	2470	4535
高陵县	Gaoling	12440	2951	3943
开发区合计	**Sum of Development Zones**	**268821**	**40556**	**183562**
高新区	GaoXin	212772	20581	175247
经开区	JingKai	32076	10977	91
曲江新区	Qujiang	7777	4330	1690
浐灞生态区	Chanba Eco-District	7848	1629	4514
航空基地	Aviation Industry Base	5630	555	1961
航天基地	Aerospace Base	344	266	41
国际港务区	International Trade&Logistic Park	405	315	
沣东新城	FengDongXinCheng	1969	1903	18

continued 2

(10 000 yuan)

罚没收入 Penalty Receipts	国有资本经营收入 State-owned Assets Profit	国有资源(资产)有偿使用收入 The Revenues of the Compensation for the Use of State-owned Resoures(Assants)	其他收入 Other Income	基金收入 Fund Revenue
130448	**3655**	**299435**	**17831**	**5143428**
92593		**39128**	**17785**	**691483**
33883		**223231**	**46**	**1060093**
5639		132609		2066
3049		4226		3454
3059		8913		237339
2775		11322		2697
981		10777		273507
1896		33992		18082
788		992		8500
1590		1245	46	37692
3595		11734		247999
2294		2094		22510
1819		668		33434
2277		3234		42145
4121		1425		130668
3972	**3655**	**37076**		**3391852**
1301		15643		695791
689		20319		370544
1210		547		1005286
668	755	282		463358
65	2900	149		244232
15		22		29697
12		78		234932
12		36		348012

6-5 各区县、开发区财政一般预算支出（2013年）

单位：万元

区县、开发区	Region	一般预算支出 Ordinary Budgetary Expenditures	一般公共服务支出 General Public Services	国防支出 Expenditure for National Defense	公共安全支出 Expenditure for Public Safety
合计	**Total**	**7298119**	**672202**	**5729**	**347712**
市本级合计	**Sum of city level**	**2914903**	**184150**	**3223**	**150526**
区、县合计	**Region**	**3275586**	**341924**	**2256**	**176627**
新城区	Xincheng	282246	30286	226	18321
碑林区	Beilin	240507	28160	422	19418
莲湖区	Lianhu	290525	37136	311	19169
雁塔区	Yanta	273763	28919	171	20089
灞桥区	Baqiao	190742	18929	214	13271
未央区	Weiyang	207918	25298	194	16953
阎良区	Yanliang	166351	24098		7390
临潼区	Lintong	272237	26857		10227
长安区	Chang'an	447642	41726	279	16654
蓝田县	Lantian	234919	14687	164	8633
周至县	Zhouzhi	248567	16989	55	8900
户县	Huxian	236117	22286	115	10470
高陵县	Gaoling	184052	26553	105	7132
开发区合计	**Sum of Development Zones**	**1107630**	**146128**	**250**	**20559**
高新区	GaoXin	486844	36214	250	9884
经开区	JingKai	212460	30012		3382
曲江新区	Qujiang	204956	36437		1298
浐灞生态区	Chanba Eco-District	82162	20603		450
航空基地	Aviation Industry Base	30628	6486		2080
航天基地	Aerospace Base	9512	4439		
国际港务区	International Trade&Logistic Park	23946	2345		
沣东新城	FengDongXinCheng	57122	9592		3465

注：本表数据来源：市财政局。

Ordinary Budgetary Expenditures by Region and Development Zone（2013）

（10 000 yuan）

教育支出 Expenditure for Education	科学技术支出 Expenditure for Science and Technology	文化体育与传媒支出 Expenditure for Culture,Sport and Media	社会保障和就业支出 Expenditure for Social Safety Net and Employment Effort	医疗卫生支出 Expenditure for Medical and Health Care	节能环保支出 Expenditure for Energy Saving and Environment Protection
1135398	**78976**	**208268**	**779773**	**503387**	**185110**
288892	**42134**	**84150**	**363195**	**204504**	**124914**
776216	**22003**	**47492**	**405182**	**294226**	**38000**
51249	2150	454	26565	7830	282
45783	2657	1138	44860	11426	1680
69210	2208	1880	36524	14518	3022
50646	2115	1499	38660	20366	965
57419	1319	1463	28028	18529	2680
50907	1735	15442	24208	15258	1092
37183	1165	1564	18161	14021	3106
71326	1563	5146	29375	34743	5634
98483	3371	4751	43052	50147	3096
62397	173	3182	31148	29895	2708
81191	424	3217	30431	30149	5121
60593	1644	4490	32380	27668	3864
39829	1479	3266	21790	19676	4750
70290	**14839**	**76626**	**11396**	**4657**	**22196**
16679	14789	2801	1611	156	2152
10902	50	100	608		3119
12871		68291		70	6600
6608		254			3013
675			120		1517
200					450
620		4096			3206
21735		1084	9057	4431	2139

6-5 续表1

单位：万元

区县、开发区	Region	一般预算支出 Ordinary Budgetary Expenditures 城乡社区事务支出 Expenditure for Urban and Rural Community Affairs	农林水事务支出 Expenditure for Agriculture,Foresty Water Conservancy	交通运输支出 Expenditure for Industry,Commerce and Banking	资源勘探电力信息等事务支出 Expenditure for Mining,Electricity and Information
合计	**Total**	**1502365**	**499357**	**329989**	**367325**
市本级合计	**Sum of city level**	**470585**	**132743**	**268958**	**148619**
区、县合计	**Region**	**630393**	**355811**	**60831**	**16553**
新城区	Xincheng	137589	201	684	326
碑林区	Beilin	78760	244	576	300
莲湖区	Lianhu	95784	237	464	849
雁塔区	Yanta	99592	4095	1085	461
灞桥区	Baqiao	14395	26272	2235	337
未央区	Weiyang	43168	4764	2481	358
阎良区	Yanliang	25670	19858	2454	4448
临潼区	Lintong	13679	60807	3479	674
长安区	Chang'an	73398	63408	22718	1447
蓝田县	Lantian	16478	53624	5202	2529
周至县	Zhouzhi	9272	49591	4311	170
户县	Huxian	9797	44717	6871	3027
高陵县	Gaoling	12811	27993	8271	1627
开发区合计	**Sum of Development Zones**	**401387**	**10803**	**200**	**202153**
高新区	GaoXin	198252	200		174369
经开区	JingKai	107563	345		4882
曲江新区	Qujiang	58678	8322		150
浐灞生态区	Chanba Eco-District	24838			11112
航空基地	Aviation Industry Base	10320	220		9210
航天基地	Aerospace Base	580	220	200	2428
国际港务区	International Trade&Logistic Park	98			
沣东新城	FengDongXinCheng	1058	1496		2

continued 1

(10 000 yuan)

商业服务业等事务支出 Expenditure for Commerce and Services	金融监管等事务支出 Expenditure for Financial Supervision	国土资源气象等事务支出 Expenditure for Land Recources and Meteorological Affairs	住房保障支出 Expenditure for Housing Support	粮油物资管理事务支出 Material Reserves Management Affairs Spending
107572	**30405**	**37422**	**374717**	**18127**
49356	**29452**	**6020**	**262158**	**15268**
19142	**196**	**22044**	**53175**	**2859**
157		660	5225	
1756		666	2577	6
3392	18	631	5051	3
395		2172	2523	9
226		582	4668	110
2070		1559	2324	
1038	139	1870	2795	311
2417	14	1014	4075	214
3940		5020	15258	557
299	25	1077	1510	403
557		1696	1359	303
2023		1527	3970	303
872		3570	1840	640
39074	**757**	**9358**	**59384**	
	109	1130	27545	
26975			9022	
3426	100	1000	7700	
195	548	6009	8472	
			375	
8428		573	4290	
50		646	1980	

6-5 续表2 continued 2

单位：万元　　　　　　　　　　　　　　　　　　　　　　　　　　　　　　　　　　　(10 000 yuan)

区县、开发区	Region	一般预算支出 Ordinary Budgetary Expenditures		基金支出
		国债还本付息支出 Expenditure for National Debt and Interst	其他支出 Other Expenditure	Fund Expenditure
合计	**Total**	**63429**	**50856**	**5085857**
市本级合计	**Sum of city level**	**61325**	**24731**	**806685**
区、县合计	**Region**	**1914**	**8742**	**1132511**
新城区	Xincheng	41		19012
碑林区	Beilin	78		16294
莲湖区	Lianhu	43	75	169760
雁塔区	Yanta	1		21845
灞桥区	Baqiao	52	13	281701
未央区	Weiyang	97	10	21318
阎良区	Yanliang	153	927	15833
临潼区	Lintong	203	790	58918
长安区	Chang'an	207	130	265597
蓝田县	Lantian	146	639	29259
周至县	Zhouzhi	440	4391	45207
户县	Huxian	228	144	43407
高陵县	Gaoling	225	1623	144360
开发区合计	**Sum of Development Zones**	**190**	**17383**	**3146661**
高新区	GaoXin		703	631818
经开区	JingKai		15500	355804
曲江新区	Qujiang	13		955103
浐灞生态区	Chanba Eco-District		60	435748
航空基地	Aviation Industry Base			229105
航天基地	Aerospace Base		620	29723
国际港务区	International Trade&Logistic Park	90	200	203919
沣东新城	FengDongXinCheng	87	300	305441

主要统计指标解释

财政收入 指国家财政参与社会产品分配所取得的收入，是实现国家职能的财力保证。主要包括：

（1）各项税收：包括国内增值税、国内消费税、进口货物增值税和消费税、出口货物退增值税和消费税、营业税、企业所得税、个人所得税、资源税、城市维护建设税、房产税、印花税、城镇土地使用税、土地增值税、车船税、船舶吨税、车辆购置税、关税、耕地占用税、契税、烟叶税等。

（2）非税收入：包括专项收入、行政事业性收费、罚没收入和其他收入。

财政支出 指国家财政将筹集起来的资金进行分配使用，以满足经济建设和各项事业的需要。主要包括：

（1）一般公共服务：指政府提供基本公共管理与服务的支出，包括人大事务、政协事务、政府办公厅（室）及相关机构事务、发展与改革事务、统计信息事务、财政事务、税收事务、审计事务、海关事务、人力资源事务、纪检监察事务、人口与计划生育事务、商贸事务、知识产权事务、工商行政管理事务、国土资源事务、海洋管理事务、测绘事务、地震事务、气象事务、民族事务、宗教事务、港澳台侨事务、档案事务、共产党事务、民主党派事务及工商联事务、群众团体事务、彩票事务等。

（2）外交：指政府外交事务支出，包括外交行政管理、驻外机构、对外援助、国际组织、对外合作与交流、边界勘界联检等方面的支出。

（3）国防：指政府用于国防方面的支出，包括用于现役部队、预备役部队、民兵、国防科研事业、专项工程、国防动员等方面的支出。

（4）公共安全：指政府维护社会公共安全方面的支出，包括武装警察、公安、国家安全、检察、法院、司法行政、监狱、劳教、国家保密、缉私警察等。

（5）教育：指政府教育事务支出，包括教育行政管理、 前教育、小 教育、初中教育、普通高中教育、普通高等教育、初等职业教育、中专教育、技校教育、职业高中教育、高等职业教育、广播电视教育、留 生教育、特殊教育、干部继续教育、教育机关服务等。

（6）科 技术：指用于科 技术方面的支出，包括科 技术管理事务、基础研究、应用研究、技术研究与开发、科技条件与服务、社会科 、科 技术普及、科技交流与合作等。

（7）文化教育与传媒：指政府在文化、文物、体育、广播影视、新闻出版等方面的支出。

（8）社会保障和就业：指政府在社会保障与就业方面的支出，包括社会保障和就业管理事务、民政管理事务、财政对社会保险基金的补助、补充全国社会保障基金、行政事业单位离退休、企业改革补助、就业补助、抚恤、退役安置、社会福利、残疾人事业、城市居民最低生活保障、其他城镇社会救济、农村社会救济、自然灾害生活救助、红十字事务等。

（9）医疗卫生：指政府医疗卫生方面的支出，包括医疗卫生管理事务支出、医疗服务支出、医疗保障支出、疾病预防控制支出、卫生监督支出、妇幼保健支出、农村卫生支出等。

（10）环境保护：指政府环境保护支出，包括环境保护管理事务支出、环境监测与监察支出、污染治理支出、自然生态保护支出、天然林保护工程支出、退耕还林支出、风沙荒漠治理支出、退牧还草支出、已垦草原退耕还草、能源节约利用、污染减排、可再生能源和资源综合利用等支出。

（11）城乡社区事务：指政府城乡社区事务支出，包括城乡社区管理事务支出、城乡社区规划与管理支出、城乡社区公共设施支出、城乡社区住宅支出、城乡社区环境卫生支出、建设市场管理与监督支出等。

（12）农林水事务：指政府农林水事务支出，包括农业支出、林业支出、水利支出、扶贫支出、农业综合开发支出等。

（13）交通运输：指政府交通运输和邮政业方面的支出，包括公路运输支出、水路运输支出、铁路运输支出、民用航空运输支出、邮政业支出等。

（14）工业商业金融等事务：指政府对工业、商业及金融等方面的支出，包括采掘业支出、制造业支出、建筑业支出、工业和信息产业监管支出、国有资产监管支出、商业流通事务支出、金融业监管支出、旅游业管理与服务支出等。

中央财政收入和地方财政收入 指按现行分税制财政体制划分的中央本级收入和地方本级收入。属于中央财政的收入包括关税，进口货物增值税和消费税，出口货物退增值税和消费税，消费税，铁道部门、各银行总行、各保险公司总公司等集中交纳的营业税和城市维护建设税，增值税75%部分，纳入共享范围的企业所得税60%部分，未纳入共享范围的中央企业所得税、中央企业上交的利润，个人所得税60%部分，车辆购置税，船舶吨税，证券交易印花税97%部分，海洋石油资源税，中央非税收入等。属于地方财政的收入包括营业税（不含铁道部门、各银行总行、各保险公司总公司集中交纳的营业税），地方企业上交利润，城市维护建设税（不含铁道部门、各银行总行、各保险公司总公司集中交纳的部分），房产税，城镇土地使用税，土地增值税，车船税，耕地占用税，契税，烟叶税，印花税，增值税25%部分，纳入共享范围的企业所得税40%部分，个人所得税40%部分，证券交易印花税3%部分，海洋石油资源税以外的其他资源税，地方非税收入等。

中央财政支出和地方财政支出 指根据政府在经济和社会活动中的不同职责，划分中央和地方政府的责权，按照政府的责权划分确定的支出。中央财政支出包括一般公共服务，外交支出，国防支出，公共安全支出，以及中央政府调整国民经济结构、协调地区发展、实施宏观调控的支出等。地方财政支出包括一般公共服务，公共安全支出，地方统筹的各项社会事业支出等。

Explanatory Notes on Main Statistical Indicators

Government Revenue refers to income for the government finance through participating in the distribution of social products. It is the financial guarantee to ensure government functioning. The contents of government revenue include the following main items:

(1) Various tax revenues, including domestic value added tax (VAT), domestic consumption tax, VAT and consumption tax from imports, VAT and consumption tax rebate for exports, business tax, corporate income tax, individual income tax, resource tax, city maintenance and construct tax, house property tax, stamp tax, urban land use tax, land appreciation tax, tax on vehicles and boat operation, ship tonnage tax, vehicle purchase tax, tariffs, farm land occupation tax, deed tax, and tobacco leaf tax, etc.

(2) Non-tax revenue, including special program receipts, charge of administrative and institutional units, penalty receipts and others non-tax receipts.

Government Expenditure refers to the distribution and use of the funds which the government finance has raised, so as to meet the needs of economic construction and various causes. It includes the following main items:

(1) Expenditure for general public services: It refers to the spending on the basic public management and services which provided by governments, including the expense on affairs of People' s Congress, affairs of People' s Political Consultative Conference, affairs of government general office and relative institutions, affairs of development and reform, affairs of statistics, affairs of finance, affairs of taxation, affairs of audit, affairs of customs, affairs of human resources and social security, affairs of discipline inspection and supervision, affairs of population and family planning, affairs of commerce and trade, affairs of intellectual property, affairs of administration for industry and commerce, affairs of land and resources, affairs of oceanic administration, affairs of surveying and mapping, affairs of earthquake, ethnic affairs, religious affairs, affairs of Hong Kong, Macao, Taiwan, and Overseas Chinese, affairs of archives administration, affairs of Chinese Communist Party, affairs of democratic parties and federation of industry and commerce, affairs of mass organization, and affairs of lottery, etc.

(2) Expenditure for foreign affairs: It refers to the spending of government on foreign affairs, including the expense on administration of foreign affairs, missions overseas, external assistance, international organizations, foreign cooperation and communication, surveying and joint inspection on borderline, etc.

(3) Expenditure for national defence: It refers to the spending of government on national defence, including the expense on active force, reserve force, militia, scientific research on national defence, special projects, mobilization of national defence, etc.

(4) Expenditure for public security: It refers to the spending of government on maintaining social and public security, including the expense on armed police force, public security, state security, prosecution, courts, justice, prison, labour education and rehabilitation protection of state secrecy, anti-smuggling police, etc.

(5) Expenditure for education: It refers to the spending of government on education, including the expense on the administration of education, pre-primary education, primary education, secondary education, high school education, regular higher education, primary vocational education, secondary vocational education, technical school education, vocational high school education and higher vocational education, radio and television education, student abroad education, special education, on the job training of cadres, education authorities services, etc.

(6) Expenditure for science and technology: It refers to the spending of government on science and technology (S&T), including the expense on the administration of S&T, basic research, applied research, research and development, conditions and services of S&T, popularization of social science, science and technology, exchanges and cooperation of S&T, etc.

(7) Expenditure for culture, sport and media: It refers to the spending of government on culture, cultural heritage, sports, radio, film, television, press and publication, etc.

(8) Expenditure for social safety net and employment effort: It refers to the spending of government on social safety net and employment,

including the expense on administration of social safety net and employment, civil affairs, budgetary subsidy on the social insurance funds, subsidy on National Social Security Fund, retirees of administrative units andinstitutions, subsidy on enterprise reform, subsidy on employment effort, pension, placement of ex-serviceman, social welfare, the handicapped undertakings, the system of cost of living allowances for urban residents, other urban social relief, rural social relief, living relief of natural disasters, affairs of Red Cross Society, etc.

(9) Expenditure for medical and health care: It refers to the spending of government on medical and health care, including the expense on administration of medical and health care, medical services, health care, disease prevention and control, health inspection and supervision, women and children's health, rural health care, etc.

(10) Expenditure for environment protection: It refers to the spending of government on environment protection, including the expense on administration of environment protection, environment monitoring and supervision, pollution control, natural ecology protection, project of virgin forests protection, reforesting farmland, controlling the sources of dust storms, returning pastureland to grassland, returning pastureland to grassland, returning cultivated land to grassland, energy conservation, emissions reduction, comprehensive utilization of renewable energy and resources, etc.

(11) Expenditure for urban and rural community affairs: It refers to the spending of government on urban and rural community affairs, including the expense on administration of urban and rural community, planning and management of urban and rural community, public facilities of urban and rural community, housing of urban and rural community, sanitation of urban and rural community, management and supervision on the construction market, etc.

(12) Expenditure for agriculture, forestry and water conservancy: It refers to the spending of government on agriculture, forestry and water conservancy, including the expense on agriculture, forestry, water conservancy, poverty alleviation, comprehensive agricultural development, etc.

(13) Expenditure for transportation: It refers to the spending of government on transportation and postal services, including the expense on road transportation, waterway transportation, railway transportation, civil aviation transportation, and postal services.

(14) Expenditure for industry, commerce and banking: It refers to the spending of government on industry, commerce and banking, including the expense on mining, manufacturing, construction, industry and information technology supervision and administration, State-owned assets supervision and administration, commerce and circulation affairs, financial intermediation supervision and administration, tourism administration and service, etc.

Revenue of the Central Government and Revenue of the Local Governments refers to the revenue collected by the Central Government and that by the local governments as defined by the decentralized taxation system. In accordance with this system, the revenue of the Central Government includes tariff, VAT and consumption tax from imports, VAT and consumption tax rebate for exports, consumption tax, business tax and city maintenance and construct tax from the Ministry of Railways, head offices of banks, head offices of insurance company, which are handed over to the government in a centralized way, 75% of the value added tax, 60% the share part of the corporate income tax, unshared part of corporate income tax of the central enterprises, profit handed in by the central enterprises, 60% of individual income tax, vehicle purchase tax, ship tonnage tax, 97% of stamp tax on securities transactions, resource tax on the offshore petroleum resources. The revenue of the local governments includes business tax (excluding the part of the Ministry of Railways, head offices of banks, head offices of insurance company, which are handed over to the government in a centralized way), profit handed in by the local enterprises, city maintenance and construct tax (excluding the part of the Ministry of Railways, head offices of banks, head offices of insurance company, which are handed over to the government in a centralized way), house property tax, urban land use tax, land appreciation tax, tax on vehicles and boat operation, farm land occupation tax, deed tax, and tobacco leaf tax, stamp tax, 25% of the value added tax, 40% the share part of the corporate income tax, 40% of individual income tax, 3% of stamp tax on securities transactions, resource tax other than the tax on offshore petroleum resources, local non-tax revenue, etc.

Expenditure of the Central Government and Expenditure of the Local Governments according to the different functions of the Central Government and local governments in economic and social activities, the rights of affairs administration are demarcated between those of the Central Government and those of local governments; and the classification of the expenditure between the Central Government and local governments are made on the basis of the classification of the rights of affairs administration between them. The expenditure of the Central Government includes the expenditure for general public services, expenditure for foreign affairs, expenditure for public security, and the expenditure of the Central Government for adjusting the national economic structure; coordinating the development among different regions; and exercising macroeconomic regulation. The expenditure of the local governments includes mainly the expenditure for general public services, expenditure for public security, and expenditures for social development which are planed by local governments, etc.

7 物价指数

PRICE INDICES

资料整理：李碧生　王　晶　王　茹
Data management:Li Bisheng WangJing WangRu

第七部分　物价指数

一、简要说明

本章资料主要包括居民消费、商品零售、工业生产者出厂、工业生产者购进、土地交易、　地产销售、租赁以及固定资产投资和建筑安装工程等价格指数，由国家统计局西安调查队提供。

二、主要指标

商品零售价格总指数（上年=100）	101.7	比上年下降	0.5个百分点
居民消费价格总指数（上年=100）	102.7	比上年下降	0.1个百分点

7　PRICE INDICES

Ⅰ.Brief Introduction

This chapter consists of primarily data on consumer price indices, retail price indices, producer price indices for industrial products,purchasing price indices for industrial products,land deal, real estate selling, leasing, fixed asset investment and construction installation projects, provided by Fixed Asset NBS Survey Office in Xi'an.

Ⅱ.Major Indicators

		Increase over Preceding Year
Retail Price Index(the price preceding year=100)	101.7	−0.5 percentage points
Consumer Price Index(the price preceding year=100)	102.7	−0.1 percentage points

7-1 主要年份各种价格指数

Price Indices in Representative Years

（以上年价格为100） (the price of preceding year= 100)

年 份 Year	居民消费价格指数 Consumer Price Index	商品零售价格指数 Retail Price Index	工业生产者出厂价格指数 Producer Price Indiees (PPI) for Industrial Producers	工业生产者购进价格指数 Industrial Purchasing Indices （IPI） for Industrial Producers	固定资产投资价格指数 Price Index for Investment in Fixed Assets
1980	108.7	109.3			
1981	102.4	102.7			
1982	100.9	101.0			
1983	102.6	102.0			
1984	104.7	104.8			
1985	109.7	109.3			
1986	108.5	107.4			
1987	110.6	111.4			
1988	122.8	123.2			
1989	118.3	117.8			
1990	102.5	100.9			
1991	109.4	108.3			
1992	112.2	112.4			
1993	117.2	112.8	102.5	104.3	
1994	128.5	126.2	132.2	115.0	
1995	117.0	114.6	110.8	113.1	
1996	110.9	107.9	100.7	103.8	
1997	106.0	101.5	98.6	102.5	
1998	97.9	95.5	94.4	97.5	
1999	96.8	97.4	97.5	96.9	100.8
2000	100.2	98.7	99.4	102.4	102.1
2001	99.9	98.9	99.3	101.0	101.3
2002	98.6	98.5	98.2	98.4	101.2
2003	100.5	100.0	101.5	105.3	102.4
2004	102.3	101.9	102.7	110.4	103.3
2005	100.3	99.7	103.9	109.6	102.4
2006	101.6	101.5	103.2	106.1	102.0
2007	104.7	103.7	101.9	106.2	103.5
2008	106.0	105.4	103.7	108.5	110.5
2009	99.7	99.5	99.9	100.7	97.9
2010	103.5	102.7	102.3	106.3	103.8
2011	105.6	104.4	102.5	108.8	105.4
2012	102.8	102.3	100.5	97.2	101.9
2013	102.7	101.7	99.5	97.2	100.8

注：本表数据来源国家统计局西安调查队

7-2 居民消费价格指数（2013年）

Residents Consumer Price Indices (2013)

(以上年价格为100) (the price of preceding year=100)

指　标	Item	2013
居民价格消费总指数	**Consumer Price Index**	**102.7**
非食品价格指数	Non-foodstuff Price Index	101.6
服务项目价格指数	Price Index of Service	102.0
工业品价格指数	Ex-factory Price Indices of Industrial Products	101.4
扣除食品烟酒和能源价格指数	Price Index with Food,Tobacco,Liquor and Energy Excluded	101.7
扣除鲜菜鲜果总指数	Price Index with Fresh Vegetables and Fruits Excluded	102.6
消费品价格指数	Price Index of Consumer Goods	102.9
一、食品	**Food**	**104.8**
1. 粮食	Grain	106.1
2. 淀粉及制品	Starches and Processed Products	105.3
3. 干豆类及豆制品	Beans and Bean Products	111.2
4. 油脂	Oil or Fat	100.0
5. 肉禽及其制品	Meat,Poultry and Processed Products	104.2
6. 蛋	Eggs	109.1
7. 水产品	Aquatic Products	101.8
8. 菜	Vegetables	106.2
9. 调味品	Flavouring	102.8
10. 糖	Carbohydrate	101.4
11. 茶及饮料	Tea and Beverages	102.8
12. 干鲜瓜果	Dried and Fresh Melons and Fruits	100.4
13. 糕点饼干面包	Cake,Biscuit and Bread	101.3
14. 液体乳及乳制品	Milk and Its Product	108.1
15. 在外用膳食品	Dining Out	106.1
16. 其他食品	Other Food	100.7
二、烟酒	**Tobacco and Liquor**	**100.7**
1. 烟草	Tobacco	100.1
2. 酒	Liquor	101.8
三、衣着	**Clothing**	**104.0**
1. 服装	Garments	103.6
2. 衣着材料	Clothing Material	100.0
3. 鞋袜帽	Footgear and Hats	104.6
4. 衣着加工服务费	Clothing Manufacturing Services	112.3

注：本表数据来源国家统计局西安调查队

7-2 续表 continued

(以上年价格为100) (the price of preceding year=100)

指 标	Item	2013
四、家庭设备用品及维修服务	**Household facilities,Articles and Services**	**104.0**
1. 耐用消费品	Durable Consumer Goods	102.3
2. 室内装饰品	Interior Decorations	100.8
3. 床上用品	Bed Articles	103.2
4. 家庭日用杂品	Daily Use Household Articles	102.7
5. 家庭服务及加工维修服务	Household Service and Maintenance Renovation	117.0
五、医疗保健和个人用品	**Health Care and Personal Articles**	**101.9**
1. 医疗保健	Health Care	102.1
(1) 医疗器具及用品	Medical Instrument Articles	100.0
(2) 中药材及中成药	Traditional Chinese Medicine	106.5
(3) 西药	Western Medicine	100.1
(4) 保健器具及用品	Health Care Appliances and Articles	100.2
(5) 医疗保健服务	Health Care Services	100.0
2. 个人用品及服务	Personal Articles and Services	101.4
六、交通和通讯	**Transportation and Communication**	**97.6**
1. 交通	Transportation	100.0
(1) 交通工具	Transportation Facility	99.1
(2) 车用燃料及零配件	Fuels and Parts	98.7
(3) 车辆使用及维修费	Fees for Vehicles Use and Maintenance	105.3
(4) 市区公共交通费	Incity Traffic Fare	100.0
(5) 城市间交通费	Intercity Traffic Fare	99.2
2. 通信	Communication	95.1
(1) 通信工具	Telecommunication Facility	79.6
(2) 通信服务	Telecommunication Service	96.9
七、娱乐教育文化用品及服务	**Recreation,Education and Culture Articles**	**101.5**
1. 文娱用耐用消费品及服务	Durable Consumer Goods for Cultural and Recreational Use and Services	94.5
2. 教育	Education	101.5
3. 文化娱乐用品类	Cultural and Recreational Articles	101.5
4. 旅游	Touring	106.8
八、居住	**Residence**	**102.0**
1. 建房及装修材料	Building and Building Decoration Materials	98.0
2. 住房租金	Rental Housing	103.5
3. 自有住房	Private Housing	103.9
4. 水、电、燃料	Water, Electricity and Fuels	102.5

7-3 商品零售价格指数（2013年）

Retail Price Indices (2013)

（以上年价格为100）　　(the price of preceding year= 100)

指　标	Item	2013
商品零售价格总指数	**Retail Price Indices**	**101.7**
一、食品类	**Food**	**105.0**
1. 粮食	Grain	106.4
2. 淀粉及制品	Starches and Processed Products	105.3
3. 干豆类及豆制品	Beans and Bean Products	110.6
4. 油脂	Oil or Fat	100.0
5. 肉禽及其制品	Meat,Poultry and Processed Products	104.2
6. 蛋	Eggs	109.2
7. 水产品	Aquatic Products	102.4
8. 菜	Vegetables	106.2
9. 调味品	Flavouring	102.1
10. 糖	Carbohydrate	100.4
11. 干鲜瓜果	Dried and Fresh Melons and Fruits	100.4
12. 糕点饼干面包	Cake,Biscuit and Bread	101.0
13. 液体乳及乳制品	Milk and Its Product	108.3
14. 在外用膳食品	Dining Out	106.2
15. 其他食品	Other Food and Manufacturing Services	100.7
二、饮料、烟酒	**Beverages,Tobacco and Liquor**	**101.6**
1. 茶及饮料	Tea and Beverages	103.0
2. 烟草	Tobacco	99.8
3. 酒	Liquor	101.8
三、服装、鞋帽	**Garments,Shoes and Hats**	**103.9**
1. 服装	Garments	103.5
2. 鞋袜帽	Footgear and Hats	105.3
3. 其他	Others	95.0
四、纺织品	**Textiles**	**102.4**
1. 衣着材料	Cotton Cloth	100.0
2. 床上用品	Blend Cloth	103.5
五、家用电器及音像器材	**Household Appliances,Music and Video Equipment**	**96.8**
1. 家庭设备	Household facility	99.3
2. 文娱用耐用消费品	Durable Consumer Goods on Cultural and Recreational Use	91.9
3. 专业音像器材类	Music and Video Equipment	100.0

注：本表数据来源国家统计局西安调查队

7-3 续表 continued

(以上年价格为100)	(the price of preceding year= 100)	
指 标	Item	2013
六、文化办公用品	**Cultural and Office Appliances**	**99.8**
七、日用品	**Articles for Daily Use**	**100.6**
1. 日用百货	General Merchandise for Daily Use	99.8
2. 日用杂品	Miscellaneous for Daily Use	103.7
3. 洗涤用品	Daily Use Articles For Washing	100.5
4. 其他日用品	Other Daily Articles	100.4
八、体育娱乐用品	**Sports and Recreation Articles**	**100.3**
1. 体育用品	Sports Goods	100.1
2. 娱乐用品	Receration Goods	100.4
九、交通通信用品	**Transportation and Communication Goods**	**97.1**
1. 交通运输机械	Transportation Machinery	98.7
2. 通信器材	Communication Machinery	85.3
十、家具	**Furniture**	**107.3**
十一、化妆品	**Cosmetics**	**102.0**
十二、金银珠宝	**Gold,Silver and Jewelry**	**89.7**
十三、中西药品及医疗保健用品	**Traditional Chinese and Western Medicines And Health Care Articles**	**101.4**
1. 医疗器具及用品	Medical Apparatus and Article	100.0
2. 中药材及中成药	Traditional Chinese Medicinal Materials and Medicines	105.9
3. 西药	Western Medicine	100.1
4. 保健器具及用品	Health Care Apparatus and Article	99.9
十四、书报杂志及电子出版物	**Books,Newspapers,Magazines and Electronic Publications**	**100.7**
1. 教材及参考书	Teaching Materials and Reference Books	100.7
2. 书报杂志	Books, Newspapers and Magazines	100.0
3. 电子音像制品	Electronic Audio-video Products	102.3
十五、燃料	**Fuel**	**99.2**
1、煤炭及制品	Coal and Its Products	98.2
2、石油及制品	Oil and Its Products	99.3
十六、建筑材料及五金电料	**Building Materials and Hardware**	**97.6**
1. 建筑装潢材料	Building Decoration Materials	96.9
2. 五金电料	Hardware	100.1

7-4 主要年份工业生产者出厂价格指数

(上年价格=100)

类 别	Classify	2000	2002	2003
工业生产者出厂价格指数	**Producer Price Indices（PPI）for Industrial Producers**	**99.4**	**98.2**	**101.5**
按轻重工业分	Grouped by Light Industry and Heavy Industry			
轻工业	Light Industry	97.8	98.4	101.3
以农产品为原料	Using Farm Products as Raw Materials	99.2	98.4	104.5
以非农产品为原料	Using Non-farm Products as Raw Materials	95.5	98.6	99.9
重工业	Heavy Industry	100.8	98.2	101.6
采掘	Mining & Quarrying	97.5	101.3	103.4
原料	Raw Materials	107.7	101.3	111.2
加工	Processing	98.4	97.7	100.1
按用途分	Grouped by Use			
生产资料	Means of Production	100.5	98.0	101.8
采掘	Mining & Quarrying	97.5	101.3	103.4
原料	Raw Materials	106.4	101.0	108.1
加工	Processing	98.7	97.4	100.9
生活资料	Consumer Goods	97.3	99.1	100.5
(1)食品	Food	94.4	101.2	101.0
(2)衣着	Clothing	101.6	100.8	99.4
(3)一般日用品	Articles for Daily Use	96.9	97.9	101.2
(4)耐用消费品	Durable Consumer Goods	95.9	98.1	97.2
按工业部门分	Grouped by Industrial Sector			
1. 冶金工业	Metallurgical Industry	98.2	98.7	103.8
2. 电力工业	Power Industry	109.6	100.0	103.2
3. 煤炭及炼焦工业	Coal and Coking Industry	100.5	106.7	136.8
4. 石油工业	Petroleum Industry	134.2	100.7	118.6
5. 化学工业	Chemical Industry	96.7	99.2	100.2
6. 机械工业	Machine Manufacturing Industry	98.0	97.6	99.8
7. 建筑材料工业	Building Materials Industry	98.5	99.6	99.7
8. 森林工业	Timber Industry	98.9	98.9	100.1
9. 食品工业	Food Industry	94.3	101.1	102.8
10. 纺织工业	Textiles Industry	103.4	94.9	117.3
11. 缝纫工业	Tailoring Industry	103.5	101.1	100.2
12. 皮革工业	Leather Industry	99.2	101.8	98.7
13. 造纸工业	Paper Industry	96.7	95.0	96.9
14. 文教艺术用品工业	Cultural,Educational & Handicrafts Articles	96.4	103.4	97.5
15. 其它工业	Other Industry	104.8	99.4	103.3

注：本表数据来源国家统计局西安调查队

Producer Price Indices (PPI) for Industrial Producers in Representative Years

(the price of preceding year= 100)

2004	2005	2006	2007	2008	2009	2010	2011	2012	2013
102.7	**103.9**	**103.2**	**101.9**	**103.7**	**99.9**	**102.3**	**102.5**	**100.5**	**99.5**
103.4	99.9	100.2	101.8	103.7	100.6	102.5	107.0	100.4	100.7
108.7	97.3	100.1	103.3	106.0	98.9	104.0	109.3	100.3	101.0
100.8	101.2	100.2	100.8	102.1	101.8	101.4	100.9	100.5	99.9
101.9	107.9	105.5	101.9	103.8	99.3	102.2	101.6	100.5	99.2
140.5	107.9	100.6	111.6	122.3	90.0	150.2	102.6	101.8	100.6
109.0	114.2	111.8	104.9	110.8	99.5	108.9	111.2	108.5	95.1
100.6	106.7	104.2	101.2	101.9	99.4	100.8	100.1	99.2	99.9
102.7	105.3	104.2	101.3	103.4	99.3	102.2	101.9	100.3	99.2
140.5	107.9	100.6	111.6	122.3	90.0	150.2	102.6	101.8	100.6
106.6	111.3	111.6	104.8	110.2	99.7	109.0	111.3	108.7	95.2
102.0	104.3	103.0	100.6	102.0	99.3	101.0	100.3	98.9	99.9
102.5	100.4	100.4	103.5	104.7	101.4	102.5	104.5	100.8	100.4
103.6	100.3	100.4	105.3	106.6	100.3	103.3	109.5	101.6	100.9
102.7	102.0	103.3	104.6	105.1	102.7	101.2	111.9	99.4	100.4
101.2	101.3	100.8	100.1	102.7	102.6	101.2	101.5	101.5	99.1
93.3	99.1	99.4	100.7	100.7	103.9	101.9	99.5	99.0	100.9
107.1	103.9	106.5	103.2	104.8	92.0	105.8	116.3	100.7	97.5
104.1	110.6	107.9	105.5	110.0	109.0	101.2	104.7	101.2	100.6
131.4	97.1	95.4	106.8	104.8	101.7	110.6	109.3	101.5	100.0
110.5	121.7	117.6	104.8	115.6	96.7	114.2	108.4	108.2	89.7
100.8	103.2	100.8	101.1	104.1	102.6	100.8	104.2	100.3	99.6
100.6	104.9	103.4	101.0	101.7	99.9	100.9	99.5	99.0	100.0
100.0	98.6	98.9	98.9	101.8	101.9	99.9	100.6	99.6	99.3
100.2	101.6	101.6	101.1	101.1	101.1	101.7	105.2	103.2	103.4
107.5	98.3	99.0	106.1	109.3	98.3	104.3	110.1	101.7	101.0
119.1	89.9	102.4	98.4	99.7	97.5	108.9	107.2	88.7	103.9
103.6	100.8	103.5	104.6	105.1	102.6	101.3	113.4	99.4	100.4
99.6	101.2	100.0	99.0	99.6	99.7	99.6	98.0	99.9	99.9
100.2	101.2	100.0	100.1	104.5	98.4	100.4	103.4	99.2	98.4
96.5	98.1	100.1	99.1	99.2	102.2	99.9	100.7	105.0	97.5
105.0	103.4	105.7	111.4	104.3	99.7	100.5	104.3	101.2	99.6

7-5 主要年份工业生产者购进价格指数

Industrial Purchasing Indices (IPI) for Industrial Producers in Representative Years

(上年价格=100) (the price of preceding year= 100)

指　标	Item	2000	2002	2003	2004	2005	2006
工业生产者购进价格指数	**Industrial Purchasing Indices (IPI) for Industrial Producers**	**102.4**	**98.4**	**105.3**	**110.4**	**109.6**	**106.1**
(一)燃料、动力类	Fuel and Power	105.0	100.9	105.7	109.4	123.5	112.6
(二)黑色金属材料类	Ferrous Metals	102.7	98.5	107.4	117.4	107.6	99.2
#钢材	Steel	103.4	97.9	106.0	114.8	107.5	98.5
(三)有色金属材料和电线类	Non-ferrous Metals and Electric Wires	105.2	96.8	105.8	114.1	107.8	116.5
(四)化工原料类	Raw Chemical Materials	104.6	97.9	102.4	106.3	106.1	101.6
(五)木材及纸浆类	Timber and Paper Pulp	101.2	99.4	101.2	100.3	108.2	111.7
(六)建筑材料及非金属矿类	Building Materials and Non-metal ores	100.3	98.6	99.6	110.4	99.3	100.7
(七)其它工业原材料及半成品类	Other Industrial Raw Materials and Semi-Products	98.8	98.9	102.5	111.2	106.1	104.3
(八)农副产品类	Agricultural Products	100.4	98.2	113.7	112.7	100.9	107.2
(九)纺织原料类	Textile Materials	98.0	90.6	103.4	103.9	97.6	101.5

注：本表数据来源国家统计局西安调查队

7-5 续表 continued

(上年价格=100) (the price of preceding year= 100)

指　标	Item	2007	2008	2009	2010	2011	2012	2013
工业生产者购进价格指数	**Industrial Purchasing Indices (IPI) for Industrial Producers**	**106.2**	**108.5**	**100.7**	**106.3**	**108.8**	**97.2**	**97.2**
(一)燃料、动力类	Fuel and Power	107.0	109.8	105.1	108.6	113.5	102.3	96.8
(二)黑色金属材料类	Ferrous Metals	104.8	111.3	99.2	103.1	102.9	93.4	98.0
#钢材	Steel	104.9	111.7	98.7	103.5	102.9	93.3	98.0
(三)有色金属材料和电线类	Non-ferrous Metals and Electric Wires	110.7	99.1	93.9	113.6	118.9	93.0	94.5
(四)化工原料类	Raw Chemical Materials	105.6	111.4	95.0	103.9	108.1	87.7	90.8
(五)木材及纸浆类	Timber and Paper Pulp	105.9	106.5	102.6	101.1	105.4	100.9	99.2
(六)建筑材料及非金属矿类	Building Materials and Non-metal ores	104.0	104.8	106.8	102.1	102.9	97.4	102.2
(七)其它工业原材料及半成品类	Other Industrial Raw Materials and Semi-Products	108.8	110.6	101.4	108.1	109.4	100.3	98.9
(八)农副产品类	Agricultural Products	107.2	108.9	99.6	106.5	107.4	103.4	100.5
(九)纺织原料类	Textile Materials	100.5	99.8	97.6	104.6	107.0	89.1	97.6

7-6 土地交易价格指数（2013年）

Transactions Price Indices of Land (2013)

(上年价格=100) (the price of preceding year= 100)

指　标	Item	2013
土地交易价格指数	**Transactions Price Indices of Land**	**100.5**
一、居住用地	**Land for Residential Building Use**	**100.7**
（一）经济适用住房用地	Economically Affordable Housing	
（二）商品住宅用地	Commercialized Housing	100.7
1. 普通住宅用地	General Residential Buildings	100.7
2. 高档住宅用地	Luxury Residential Buildings	100.1
二、工业用地	**Land for Industry and Storage Use**	**100.3**
三、商业营业用地	**Land for Business,Tourism and Entertainment**	**100.3**
四、其他用地	**Land for Other Uses**	**100.1**

注：本表数据来源国家统计局西安调查队

7-7 住宅销售价格指数（2013年）

Selling Price Indices of Residential Buildings (2013)

(上年价格=100) (the price of preceding year= 100)

指　标	Item	2013
新建住宅销售价格指数	**Newly Residential Buildings**	**100.8**
一、保障性住房	guaranteed house	
二、新建商品住宅	New commodity residential house	100.9
（一）90平方米及以下	90 square meters and less	100.9
（二）90-144平方米	90-144 square metre	100.8
（三）144平方米以上	144 square meters and more	101
二手住宅销售价格指数	**Second-hand Residential Buildings**	**100.6**
一、90平方米及以下	90 square meters and the following	100.5
二、90-144平方米	90-144 square metre	100.4
三、144平方米以上	144 square meters	100.5

注：本表数据来源国家统计局西安调查队

7-8 住宅租赁和物业服务价格指数（2013年）

Lease and Property Service Price Index（2013）

(上年价格=100) (the price of preceding year= 100)

指 标	Item	2013
住宅租赁价格指数	**Renting Price Indices of Residential Buildings**	**101.2**
一、经济适用住房	Economical Affordable Housing	
二、廉租房	Tenement House	100.0
三、商品住宅	Commercialized Residential Buildings	101.3
（一）普通住宅	General Residential Buildings	101.7
（二）高档住宅	Luxury Residential Buildings	100.0
物业服务价格指数	**Property Services**	**100.0**
一、经济适用住房	Economical Affordable Housing	100.0
二、商品住宅	Commercialized Residential Buildings	100.0
（一）普通住宅	General Residential Buildings	100.0
（二）高档住宅	Luxury Residential Buildings	100.0

注：本表数据来源国家统计局西安调查队

7-9 主要年份固定资产投资价格指数

Price Indices for Investment in Fixed Assets in Representative Years

(上年价格=100) (the price of preceding year= 100)

指 标	Item	2000	2005	2006	2007	2008	2009	2010	2011	2012	2013
固定资产投资价格指数	**Price Indices for Investment in Fixed Assets**	**102.1**	**102.4**	**102.0**	**103.5**	**110.5**	**97.9**	**103.8**	**105.4**	**101.9**	**100.8**
建筑安装、装饰工程	Construction,Installation and Decoration	103.9	102.3	102.6	104.9	114.9	97.1	105.5	107.2	102.6	101.0
设备、工器具购置	Purchase of Equipment and Instruments	97.9	104.5	100.8	100.7	101.0	98.6	100.0	100.6	99.1	99.5
其他费用	Others	100.0	100.5	100.5	100.6	101.9	100.9	100.8	102.8	102.7	101.9

注：本表数据来源国家统计局西安调查队

主要统计指标解释

居民消费价格指数 是反映一定时期内城乡居民所购买的生活消费品和服务项目价格变动趋势和程度的相对数，是对城市居民消费价格指数和农村居民消费价格指数进行综合汇总计算的结果。通过该指数可以观察和分析消费品的零售价格和服务项目价格变动对城乡居民实际生活费支出的影响程度。

商品零售价格指数 是反映一定时期内城乡商品零售价格变动趋势和程度的相对数。商品零售价格的变动与国家的财政收入、市场供需的平衡、消费与积累的比例关系有关。因此，该指数可以从一个侧面对上述经济活动进行观察和分析。

工业生产者出厂价格指数 是反映一定时期内全部工业产品出厂价格总水平的变动趋势和程度的相对数，包括工业企业售给本企业以外所有单位的各种产品和直接售给居民用于生活消费的产品。该指数可以观察出厂价格变动对工业总产值及增加值的影响。

工业生产者购进价格指数 是反映工业企业作为生产投入，而从市场和能源、原材料生产企业购买原材料、燃料和动力产品价格的变动趋势和程度的统计指标，是扣除工业企业物质消耗成本中的价格变动影响的重要依据。

固定资产投资价格指数 是反映一定时期内固定资产投资品及取费项目的价格变动趋势和程度的相对数。固定资产投资额是由建筑安装工程投资完成额、设备工器具购置投资完成额和其他费用投资完成额三部分组成的。编制固定资产投资价格指数应首先分别编制上述三部分投资的价格指数，然后采用加权算术平均法求出固定资产投资价格总指数。

该指数可以准确地反映固定资产投资中涉及的各类投资品和取费项目价格变动趋势和变动幅度，消除按现价计算的固定资产投资指标中的价格变动因素，真实地反映固定资产投资的规模、速度、结构和效益，为国家科学地制定、检查固定资产投资计划并提高宏观调控水平，为完善国民经济核算体系提供科学的、可靠的依据。

Explanatory Notes on Main Statistical Indicators

Consumer Price Indices reflect the trend and degree of changes in prices of consumer goods and services purchased by urban and rural households during a given period. They are obtained by combining Consumer Price Indices of Urban Household and Consumer Price Indices of Rural Household. The Indices enable the observation and analysis of the degree of impact of the changes in the prices of retailed goods and services on the actual living expenses of urban and rural residents.

Retail Price Indices reflect the trend and degree of change in retail prices of commodities during a given period. The change in retail prices of commodities is related to government revenue, the equilibrium of market supply and demand, and the ratio of consumption to accumulation. Therefore, the retail price indices are useful from an oblique perspective for observing and analyzing the changes of the above economic activities.

Producer Price Indices (PPI) for Industrial Producers reflect the trend and degree of changes in general ex-factory prices of all manufactured goods during a given period, including sales of manufactured goods by an industrial enterprise to all units outside the enterprise, as well as sales of consumer goods to residents. It can be used to analyze the impact of ex-factory prices on gross output value and value-added of the industrial sector.

Industrial Purchasing Indices (IPI) for Industrial Producers reflect changes in the level and degree of prices paid by industrial enterprises when they purchase production input such as raw materials, fuels and power from the market or from other energy or raw materials producing enterprises. These indices provide an important basis for measuring the material consumption of industrial enterprises after removing the influence of price changes.

Price Indices for Investment in Fixed Assets reflect the trend and degree of changes in prices of investment goods and projects in fixed assets during a given period. The investment in fixed assets consists of three components, namely the investment in construction and installation, the investment in purchases of equipment and instrument, and the investment in other items. Price indices for investment in fixed assets are calculated as the weighted arithmetic mean of the price indices for the three components of investment in fixed assets.

Removing the factor of price change in the aggregates of investment at current prices, this indicator shows the changes in the prices of commodities and fees involved in the investment of fixed assets, and can be used to observe the actual size, growth, structure, and efficiency of investment in fixed assets and provides reliable and scientific data for government planning, management, decision-making, and further improving the current national accounting system.

8 人民生活

PEOPLE´S LIVELIHOOD

资料整理：冯军魁　赵兰莉　张　叶

Data management:Feng Junkui　Zhao Lanli　Zhang Ye

第八部分　人民生活

一、简要说明

本章资料主要内容包括城乡居民家庭基本情况、主要商品购买数量、耐用消费品拥有数量等，由西安市统计局人口就业处提供。

二、主要指标

城镇居民人均可支配收入（元）	33100	比上年增长	10.4%
城镇居民人均消费性支出（元）	23848	比上年增长	11.3%
农村居民人均纯收入（元）	12930	比上年增长	13.0%
农村居民人均生活消费支出（元）	8780	比上年增长	12.9%

8　PEOPLE'S LIVELIHOOD

Ⅰ.Brief Introduction

Data in this chapter reflects situation of the people's daily life of Xi'an city. It consists of mainly basic condition of urban and rural households, volume of primary commodity purchasing, possession of endurable goods, etc. The data come from Population & Employment Division of the Xi'an Bureau of Statistics.

Ⅱ.Major Indicators

		Increase over Preceding Year
Per Capita Annual Disposable Income of Urban Households (yuan)	33100	10.4%
Per Capita Annual Consumption Expenditure of Urban Households (yuan)	23848	11.3%
Per Capita Living Expenditure Built(yuan)	12930	13.0%
Per Capita Net Income of Rural Residents(yuan)	8780	12.9%

8-1 主要年份城乡居民家庭人均收入及恩格尔系数

Per Capita Annual Income and Engel's Coefficient of Urban and Rural Households in Representative Years

年份 Year	城镇居民家庭人均可支配收入 Per Capita Annual Disposable Income of Urban Households		农村居民家庭人均纯收入 Per Capita Annual Net Income of Rural Households		城镇居民家庭恩格尔系数（%） Engel's Coefficient of Urban Households	农村居民家庭恩格尔系数（%） Engel's Coefficient of Rural Households
	绝对数（元）	指数（1980年=100） Index (preceding year= 100)	绝对数（元） Absoulte number (yuan)	指数（1978年=100） Index (preceding year= 100)		
1978			140			
1980	414		190	135.7	53.3	53.3
1982	479	115.6	254	181.4	55.1	56.7
1983	509	122.9	245	175.0	55.1	58.4
1984	540	130.3	299	213.6	54.9	51.7
1985	719	173.5	351	250.7	49.5	48.5
1986	911	219.8	390	278.6	49.9	47.9
1987	1034	249.7	434	310.0	50.5	50.3
1988	1142	275.6	482	344.3	44.9	47.5
1989	1344	324.3	530	378.6	51.7	48.2
1990	1518	366.5	610	435.7	53.1	49.5
1991	1619	390.9	707	505.0	51.5	46.7
1992	1992	481.0	783	559.3	52.5	50.9
1993	2661	642.5	870	621.4	46.4	46.0
1994	3517	849.1	1078	770.0	45.2	50.1
1995	4153	1002.5	1353	966.4	44.7	50.3
1996	5023	1212.6	1586	1132.9	42.5	49.9
1997	5344	1290.1	1846	1318.6	40.7	49.2
1998	5670	1368.7	2052	1465.7	39.3	42.4
1999	5999	1448.3	2203	1573.6	36.3	39.1
2000	6364	1536.5	2344	1674.3	36.5	36.6
2001	6705	1618.8	2490	1778.6	34.3	33.9
2002	7184	1734.3	2641	1886.4	34.4	31.1
2003	7748	1870.7	2838	2027.1	34.3	37.6
2004	8544	2062.8	3143	2245.0	36.1	35.7
2005	9628	2324.5	3460	2471.4	37.0	36.3
2006	10905	2632.9	3808	2720.0	34.4	36.8
2007	12662	3057.0	4399	3142.1	36.5	38.2
2008	15207	3671.4	5212	3722.9	36.4	37.0
2009	18963	4578.2	6275	4482.3	32.4	35.8
2010	22244	5370.4	7750	5535.7	31.3	32.5
2011	25981	6272.6	9788	6991.4	31.3	31.9
2012	29982	7238.5	11442	8172.9	32.5	33.8
2013	33100	7991.3	12930	9235.7	32.5	33.0

8-2 主要年份城乡居民人民币储蓄存款

Savings Deposit of Urban and Rural Households in Representative Years

单位：亿元 (100 million yuan)

年 份 Year	年末余额 Balance at Ycar-end	指数（上年=100） Index(preccding year=100)
1978	3.72	
1980	5.48	113.0
1982	7.76	122.0
1983	10.02	129.1
1984	14.70	146.7
1985	16.70	113.6
1986	23.10	138.3
1987	32.13	139.1
1988	32.51	101.2
1989	45.78	140.8
1990	62.23	135.9
1991	78.64	126.4
1992	96.09	122.2
1993	124.61	129.7
1994	174.19	139.8
1995	230.63	132.4
1996	394.02	170.8
1997	358.78	91.1
1998	499.68	139.3
1999	586.40	117.4
2000	675.83	115.3
2001	800.86	118.5
2002	988.04	123.4
2003	1210.56	122.5
2004	1432.86	118.4
2005	1716.76	119.8
2006	1950.53	113.6
2007	2002.38	102.7
2008	2513.70	125.5
2009	3084.20	122.7
2010	3641.09	118.1
2011	4155.65	114.1
2012	4787.03	115.2
2013	5357.05	111.9

8-3 各区县城乡居民人均收入

Per Capita Income of Urban and Rural Households by Region

区 县 Region	城镇居民人均可支配收入 Per Capita Disposable Income of Urban Households			农村居民人均纯收入 Per Capita net Income of Rural Households		
	绝对数（元）Absoulte number (yuan)		2013指数（上年＝100） Index(preceding year=100)（2013）	绝对数（元）Absoulte number (yuan)		2013指数（上年＝100） Index(preceding year=100)(2013)
	2012	2013		2012	2013	
全 市 Total	**29982**	**33100**	**110.4**	**11442**	**12930**	**113.0**
新城区 Xincheng	30658	33816	110.3			
碑林区 Beilin	31268	34520	110.4			
莲湖区 Lianhu	31195	34450	110.4			
灞桥区 Baqiao	28688	31952	111.4	13278	15203	114.5
未央区 Weiyang	30103	33268	110.5	14562	16455	113.0
雁塔区 Yanta	31934	35341	110.7	14800	16724	113.0
阎良区 Yanliang	31026	34375	110.8	13403	15212	113.5
临潼区 Lintong	24568	27318	111.2	10685	12160	113.8
长安区 Chang'an	26493	29460	111.2	11107	12695	114.3
蓝田县 Lantian	19957	21953	110.0	7824	8833	112.9
周至县 Zhouzhi	20025	22243	111.1	7733	8870	114.7
户 县 Huxian	22520	24817	110.2	9654	10899	112.9
高陵县 Gaoling	23462	26030	110.9	10673	12167	114.0

8-4 主要年份城镇居民家庭及收支基本情况

指　　标	Item	2001	2002	2003	2004
一、平均每户家庭人口（人）	**Average Household Size(person)**	**3.03**	**3.01**	**3.04**	**2.99**
二、平均每户就业人数（人）	**Average Number of Employed Persons Per Housedhold (person)**	**1.38**	**1.47**	**1.46**	**1.46**
三、平均每户就业面（%）	**Proportion Percentage of Employment Per Housedhold (%)**	**45.60**	**48.80**	**48.00**	**48.80**
四、平均每一就业者负担人数(人)	**Number of Dependents per Emplyee(person)**	**2.19**	**2.05**	**2.08**	**2.05**
五、年人均家庭总收入（元）	**Per Capita Annual Income(yuan)**	**6743.12**	**7670.67**	**8315.13**	**9150.65**
#可支配收入	Disposable Income	6704.86	7183.54	7748.38	8544.03
（一）工资性收入	Income from Wages and Salaries	4288.09	5075.62	5443.21	6050.38
（二）经营性收入	Net Business Income	135.27	159.03	111.83	251.37
（三）财产性收入	Income from Properties	49.35	60.90	194.17	186.95
（四）转移性收入	Income from Transfer	2270.41	2375.12	2565.92	2661.95
六、年人均家庭总支出（元）	**Annual Actual Expenditure Per Capita (yuan)**	**6678.56**	**7819.74**	**8610.43**	**9312.05**
（一）消费性支出	Consumption Expenditure	5815.66	6419.21	6805.30	7427.82
1.食品	Food	2023.91	2205.38	2371.02	2685.10
2.衣着	Clothing	485.93	540.52	574.56	611.03
3.家庭设备用品及服务	Facilities,Articles and Services	628.91	467.36	403.24	493.33
4.医疗保健	Health Care and Medical Services	406.13	535.52	602.31	641.77
5.交通和通信	Transport and Communication Services	453.12	567.96	630.48	688.22
6.教育文化娱乐服务	Education,Receration and Cultural Services	908.07	1126.68	1230.60	1252.55
7.居住	Residence	531.45	783.56	779.32	813.14
8.杂项商品和服务	Miscellaneous Goods and Services	378.14	192.23	213.77	242.68
（二）购房和建房支出	Purchase and Construction Expenditure of Houses	289.31	415.08	532.19	590.33
（三）转移性支出	Transfer Expenditure	573.59	567.81	786.70	768.01
（四）财产性支出	Property Expenditure				
（五）社会保障支出	Social Services Expenditure		417.64	486.24	525.89
七、人均期末手存现金（元）	**Cash Reserves at Hand at the end of Year Per Capita (yuan)**	**550.39**	**587.82**	**810.60**	**882.65**

Basic Conditions of Urban Households in Representative Years

2005	2006	2007	2008	2009	2010	2011	2012	2013
2.93	**2.90**	**2.91**	**2.82**	**2.84**	**2.81**	**2.83**	**2.76**	**2.73**
1.39	**1.40**	**1.39**	**1.35**	**1.51**	**1.51**	**1.55**	**1.49**	**1.49**
47.44	**48.28**	**47.77**	**47.87**	**53.20**	**53.70**	**54.80**	**54 00**	**54.60**
2.11	**2.07**	**2.09**	**2.09**	**1.88**	**1.86**	**1.83**	**1.85**	**1.83**
10387.44	**11708.43**	**13421.45**	**16365.67**	**20299.12**	**23879.86**	**27710.24**	**32031.90**	**35274.53**
9627.89	10905.39	12662.03	15206.89	18963.31	22243.63	25981.45	29982.00	33100.09
6926.28	7622.92	8897.30	10944.90	13562.24	15733.57	18240.83	20937.38	23103.67
163.66	345.70	375.68	410.70	715.99	979.22	1442.33	1842.93	2164.83
193.20	317.87	208.80	241.24	357.26	506.47	639.65	970.37	1131.37
3104.30	3421.94	3939.67	4768.83	5663.63	6660.60	7387.43	8230.72	8874.66
10030.64	**12033.94**	**12257.69**	**14380.69**	**17619.36**	**20597.76**	**23991.29**	**26523.86**	**30553.36**
7899.81	8986.87	10097.95	12015.81	14250.78	16543.21	19305.83	21434.06	23848.14
2926.32	3093.12	3696.57	4374.24	4621.40	5176.55	6041.18	6961.40	7737.83
712.98	783.93	950.50	1232.12	1564.44	1837.40	2368.64	2607.69	2866 82
373.36	582.85	597.11	761.02	1037.98	1250.86	1565.74	1685.77	1859 63
746.67	695.09	847.80	1161.86	1375.57	1572.40	1737.36	1825.84	1905.16
763.56	922.99	1145.90	1246.34	1614.68	1995.20	2472.58	3055.51	3340.16
1357.50	1666.93	1466.55	1724.63	2043.52	2424.51	2753.85	3072.05	3378.50
719.00	946.87	1027.90	1058.11	1262.83	1542.76	1594.54	1815.66	1864.32
300.42	295.09	365.62	457.49	730.36	743.53	771.94	410.14	895.72
722.35	1273.52	524.62	262.31	606.42	639.83	1125.88	853.90	2069.15
745.24	1043.44	933.52	1042.50	1517.15	1907.40	1961.60	2423.51	2749.31
	1.89	9.33	23.30	23.09	53.55	119.38	33.12	42.70
663.24	728.22	692.27	1036.77	1221.92	1453.77	1478.60	1759.27	1843.56
1121.29	**1525.31**	**1563.07**	**1296.10**	**2553.73**	**4727.95**	**6295.60**	**6001.00**	**8828.40**

8-5 城镇居民家庭基本情况(2013年)

Basic Conditions of Urban Households(2013)

指　标	Item	2013
一、人均可支配收入(元)	**Per Capita Disposable Income(yuan)**	**33100.09**
二、家庭人口数(人/户)	**Number of Family Members (Person/Household)**	**2.73**
(一)有收入者人数	Family Members Earning Income	2.08
1.就业人口数	Family Members Employed	1.49
(1)国有经济单位职工人数	Employed by State-Owned Enterprises	0.83
(2)城镇集体经济单位职工人数	Employed by Urban Collective Enterprises	0.05
(3)其他经济类型单位职工人数	Employed by Other Units	0.09
(4)城镇个体或私营企业主人数	Personnel of Urban Individual Business	0.11
(5)城镇个体或私营企业被雇人数	Employed by Self-Employers	0.23
(6)离退休再就业人员数	Re-Employed Resigned and Retired Personnel	0.07
(7)其它就业人员数	Others	0.11
2.离退休人数	Resigned and Retired	0.58
3.其它有收入者人数	Others	0.02
(二)无收入者人数	Family Members Without Income	0.65
三、非家庭人口在家用餐人次数	**None-Family Members Eating At Home**	**4.83**
(人次/户)	**(Person-Times/Household)**	
四、家庭人口在外用餐人次数	**Family Members Eating Outside**	10.01
(人次/户)	**(Person-Times/Household)**	

8-6 城镇居民家庭年人均收入情况（2013年）

Statistics on Per Capita Annual Income of Urban Residents（2013）

单位：元 (yuan)

项　　目	Iterm	总平均 Total
一、家庭总收入	**Total Family Income**	**35275**
#可支配收入	Disposable Income	33100
（一）工薪收入	Income from Wages and Salaries	23104
#工资及补贴收入	Wages and Subsidies	22818
（二）经营净收入	Net Income from Business	2165
（三）财产性收入	Income from Properties	1131
#利息收入	Interest Income	113
出租房屋收入	House Rents	759
（四）转移性收入	Transfer Income	8875
#养老金或离退休金	Pensions	7518
提取住房公积金	Withdrawal of Housing Funds	119
记帐补贴	Book-Keeping Allowances	248
二、出售财物收入	**Income from Sales Of Property**	**84**
（一）出售住房收入	Sales of Housing	74
（二）出售其它物品收入	Sales of Other Properties	10
三、借贷收入	**Income For Savings and Credit**	**13198**

8-7 城镇居民家庭年人均支出情况（2013年）

Statistics on Per Capita Annual Living Expenditure of Urban Households（2013）

单位：元 (yuan)

项　目	Item	总平均 Total
一、家庭总支出	**Total Expenditures**	**30553**
（一）消费支出	Consumption Expenditures	23848
#服务性消费支出	Consumption on Service	6442
1.食品	Food	7737
2.衣着	Clothing	2867
3.家庭设备用品及服务	Household Facilities,Articles and Service	1860
4.医疗保健	Health Care and Medical Service	1905
5.交通和通信	Transport and Communications	3340
6.教育文化娱乐服务	Education,Receration and Cultural Services	3379
7.居住	Residence	1864
8.杂项商品和服务	Miscellaneous Goods and Services	896
（二）购房与建房支出	Expenditures on House Purchasing/Construction	2069
（三）转移性支出	Transfer Expenditures	2750
（四）财产性支出	Property Expenditures	43
（五）社会保障支出	Expenditures on Social Security	1843
二、借贷支出	**Expenditures on Loans and Debts**	**13067**

8-8 城镇居民家庭年人均消费性支出情况（2013年）

Statistics on Per Capita Annual Consumption Expenditure of Urban Households（2013）

单位：元 （yuan）

项目	Item	总平均 Total
消费支出（元）	**Consumption Expenditures**	**23843**
#服务性消费支出	Consumption on services	6442
食品	**Food**	**7738**
一、粮油类	Grains and oil	1029
1.粮食	Grain	652
2.淀粉及薯类	Starches and Tubers	78
3.干豆类及豆制品	Bean and Bean Products	101
4.油脂类	Oil or Fats	198
二、肉禽蛋水产品类	Meat,Poultry,Egg and Aquatic Products	1342
1.肉类	Meat	826
2.禽类	Poultry	136
3.蛋类	Egg	121
4.水产品类	Aquatic Products	259
三、蔬菜类	Vegetables	702
1.鲜菜	Fresh Vegetables	636
2.干菜	Dried Vegetables	48
3.菜制品	Vegetable Products	18
四、调味品	Flavouring	121
五、糖烟酒饮料类	Sugar,Tobacco,Liquor and Beverage	1071
1.糖类	Sugar	73
2.烟草类	Tobacco	424
3.酒类	Liquor	332
4.饮料	Beverage	242
六、干鲜瓜果类	Dried and Fresh Melons &Fruits	784
七、糕点、奶及奶制品	Cakes, Milk and Processed Products	591
1.糕点	Cakes	209
2.奶及奶制品	Milk and Its Products	382
八、其它食品	Other Food	140
九、饮食服务	Catering Services	1958
1.食品加工服务费	Charge for Food Processing Services	1
2.在外饮食	Foods Consumed outside	1957

8-8 续表1 continued 1

单位：元 (yuan)

项 目	Item	总平均 Total
非食品类	**Non-food**	**16110**
一、衣着	**Clothing**	**2867**
（一）服装	Garments	2044
（二）衣着材料	Cloth Materials	18
（三）鞋类	Shoes	679
（四）其它衣着用品	Others	111
（五）衣着加工服务费	Tailoring and Laundering	15
二、家庭设备用品及服务	**Household Facilities,Articles and Services**	**1860**
（一）耐用消费品	Durable Consumer Goods	822
1.家具	Furniture	302
2.家庭设备	Household Facilities	520
（二）室内装饰品	Interior Decorations	48
（三）床上用品	Bed Articles	153
（四）家庭日用杂品	Daily Use Household Articles	727
（五）家具材料	Furniture Materials	29
（六）家庭服务	Household Services	81
三、医疗保健	**Medicine and Medical Services**	**1905**
（一）医疗器具	Medical Appliances and Articles	12
（二）保健器具	Health Care Articles	56
（三）药品费	Medicines	788
（四）滋补保健品	Tonic	209
（五）医疗费	Medical Care Services	813
（六）其他	Others	27
四、交通和通讯	**Transportation ,Post and Telecommumication Services**	**3340**
（一）交通	Trasportation	2351
1.家庭交通工具	Family Vehicles	1322
2.车辆用燃料及零配件	Fuel and Accessories	466
3.交通工具服务支出	Expenditure on Maintenance of Vehicles	208
4.交通费	Transport Servi	355

8-8 续表2 continued 2

单位：元 (yuan)

项　　目	Item	总平均 Total
（二）通信	Telecommunication	989
1.通信工具	Telecommunication Tools	337
2.通信服务	Telecommunication Services	652
五、教育文化娱乐服务	**Recreation,Culture and Education Services**	**3379**
(一)文化娱乐用品	Recreating Goods	666
#体育用品	Sporting Goods	15
#健身器材	Fitness Equipment	7
(二)文化娱乐服务	Recreation and Culture Services	1404
#健身活动	Fitness Activities	44
(三)教育	Education	1309
六、居住	**Residence**	1864
（一）住房	Housing	653
1.租赁房房租	House Renting	95
2.住房装潢支出	Home Decorate Expenditure	386
3.维修用建筑材料	Building Material for Repair	93
4.其他	Others	79
（二）水电燃料及其它	Water,Electricity,Fuel and Others	997
1.水	Water	96
2.电	Electricity	368
3.燃料	Fuel	238
4.取暖费	Heating Cost	261
5.其他	Others	34
（三）居住服务费	Cost on Housing Service	214
1.物业管理费	Housing Management	172
2.维修服务费	Expenditures on House Maintenance	11
3.其它	Others	31
七、杂项商品和服务	**Miscellaneous Commodities and Services**	**895**
（一）杂项商品	Miscellaneous Commodities	670
1.金银珠宝饰品	Jewel	288
2.化妆品	Cosmetics	264
3.其它杂品	Others	81
（二）服务	Services	225
1.旅馆住宿费	Rent for Hotels	39
2.理发洗澡费	Hair-cutting and Bathing	72
3.美容费	Cosmetic	66
4.其它服务	Others	48

8-9 主要年份城镇居民家庭年人均购买主要商品数量

商品名称	Name of Commodities	2003	2004	2005
食用植物油（市斤）	Vegetable Oil(500g)	9.4	9.4	12.3
猪　肉（市斤）	Pork (500g)	13.6	12.5	15.0
牛　肉（市斤）	Beef(500g)	1.5	2.0	2.6
羊　肉（市斤）	Mutton (500g)	1.0	1.1	1.1
鸡（市斤）	Chicken (500g)	4.0	3.5	5.0
鲜　蛋（市斤）	Eggs (500g)	11.9	10.4	14.1
鱼（市斤）	Fish(500g)	5.2	4.3	5.6
鲜　菜（市斤）	Fresh Vegetables (500g)	109.7	113.4	132.5
白　酒（市斤）	Liquor(500g)	1.0	1.4	1.3
果　酒（市斤）	Fruit Wine (500g)	0.2	0.2	0.2
啤　酒（市斤）	Beer (500g)	4.0	4.0	6.5
糕　点（市斤）	Cake(500g)	5.3	5.4	6.6
鲜乳品（市斤）	Fresh Dairy Products (500g)	21.8	20.4	28.0
奶　粉（市斤）	Milk Powder (500g)	0.7	0.7	0.6
服　装(件)	Clothes(unit)	6.5	6.8	6.9
鞋(双)	Shoes(pair)	2.7	2.8	2.8
水（吨）	Water(ton)	28.8	26.5	26.1
电（度）	Electricity (degree)	385.3	435.6	449.5
煤　炭(公斤)	Coal (kg)	45.1	51.4	33.9
罐装液化石油气（公斤）	Liquified Petroleum Gas (kg)	12.2	12.7	9.8
管道天燃气（立方米）	Piping Gas (cu.m)	39.0	38.4	58.2

Per Capita Annual Purchases of Principal Goods in Urban Household in Representative Years

2006	2007	2008	2009	2010	2011	2012	2013
10.1	10.2	11.5	10.2	9.5	9.7	10.0	10.8
13.6	12.8	19.0	12.6	13.1	12.9	13.9	14.7
2.4	1.9	2.1	2.7	3.2	3.3	2.7	3.0
0.8	0.8	0.7	1.0	1.1	1.0	1.0	0.9
3.8	4.1	6.3	4.2	4.4	4.6	4.3	4.1
11.8	11.1	13.2	10.7	11.0	11.1	11.2	11.3
4.6	5.3	6.1	5.0	5.1	5.5	5.1	5.7
110.9	113.9	126.5	111.7	111.7	113.1	118.0	1[illegible]8.5
1.3	1.5	0.9	1.1	1.2	1.1	1.[illegible]	1.3
0.3	0.2	0.2	0.3	0.4	0.4	0.4	0.3
6.3	4.6	3.8	5.2	5.3	4.8	3.8	4.0
5.9	6.5	11.3	8.1	8.2	7.9	8.0	8.0
25.0	25.3	16.9	19.6	20.2	19.7	19.7	20.8
0.5	0.7	0.9	0.6	0.6	0.5	1.0	0.7
7.1	9.0	6.9	8.7	9.2	9.3	10.5	10.8
2.8	2.8	3.2	4.2	3.7	3.9	3.9	3.9
22.9	22.8	22.2	27.1	28.4	27.2	30.4	32.3
444.9	460.6	439.3	523.1	589.9	591.8	606.8	654.3
46.0	66.5	70.4	34.3	30.5	21.9	28.3	18.9
7.5	6.9	8.1	7.5	5.6	4.8	3.4	2.3
46.4	38.8	33.2	45.2	54.2	70.4	77.8	103.3

8-10 城镇居民家庭居住情况（2013年）

Conditions of Dwellings of Urban Households（2013）

住房情况	Accommodation data	2013
一、家庭居住人口数（人/户）	**Number of Persons Per Household(person/household)**	**2.73**
二、现住房总建筑面积（平方米/人）	**Building Area of Living Houses(sq.m/person)**	**33.43**
三、房屋产权（合计）（%）	**Proportion of Property Right of Houses(%)**	**100**
租赁公房	Public Houses Rent	5.92
租赁私房	Private Houses Rent	4.98
原有私房	Originally Self-owned Houses	2.62
房改私房	Present Self-owned Houses	40.04
商品房	Commercial Houses	38.91
其他	Others	7.53
四、住宅建筑式样（合计）（%）	**Proportion of Patterns of Residential Building(%)**	**100**
单栋住宅	Flats With Complete Facilities	2.56
四居室	4 Rooms	2.81
三居室	3 Rooms	38.12
二居室	2 Rooms	48.98
一居室	1 Rooms	3.43
普通楼房	Ordinary Storeyed Building	3.63
平房及其他	Single-storey Houses and Others	0.47
五、装修状况（合计）（%）	**Proportion of Decoration Condition(%)**	**100**
有装修	Decorated	73.35
未装修	Undecorated	26.65
如果装修过，最近一次装修花费（元/户）	Expenditure of Latest Decoration(yuan/household)	30259.85
六、现有住房按市场价估计值（元/户）	**Estimated Market Price of Present Houses(yuan/household)**	**362701.03**
七、租赁房房租（元/户）	**Expenditure of Rent Houses(yuan/household)**	**72.19**
八、现住房房租折算（元/户）	**Rent of Self-owned Houses(yuan/household)**	**1069.93**
九、购房总金额（元/户）	**Total Expenditure on Purchase of Houses(yuan/household)**	**118978.85**
购房实际支出金额	Expenditure on Purchase Practice of Houses	112600.32
十、饮水情况（合计）（%）	**Proportion of Water Drinking(%)**	**100**
自来水	Tap Water	94.08
矿泉水	Mineral Water	2.76
纯净水	Pure Water	2.89
井、河水	Well Water and River Water	0.27
其他	Others	

8-10 续表 continued

住房情况	Accommodation data	2013
十一、用水情况（合计）（%）	**Proportion of Water Use Condition(%)**	**100**
独用自来水	Molophy Use of Tap Water	98.45
公用自来水	Public Tap Water	1.08
井、河水	Well Water and River Water	0.47
其他	Others	
十二、卫生设备（合计）（%）	**Proportion of Sanitary Facilities(%)**	**100**
无卫生设备	Without Sanitary Facilities	0.27
有厕所浴室	With Bathroom and Lavatory	91.39
有厕所无浴室	With Lavatory but without Bathroom	7.06
公用	Common-used Sanitary Facilities	1.28
十三、取暖设备（合计）（%）	**Proportion of Heating Facilities(%)**	**100**
无取暖设备	Without Heating Facilities	4.43
空调设备	Air-conditioner	17.13
暖气	Central Heating	67.7
其他	Others	10.74
十四、炊用燃料使用情况（合计）（%）	**Proportion of Cooking Fuels(%)**	**100**
管道天然气	Pipeline Gas	69.82
罐装液化石油	Liquefied Gas	19
煤炭	Coal	8.05
其他燃料	Others	3.13
十五、除了现住房，还有几处其它住房（套/户）	**Other Living Houses besides Present Living House (unit/househole)**	**0.25**
出租房	Houses for Rent	0.17
偶尔居住房	Houses Seldom Living in	0 06
其它用途房	Houses for other Purposes	0.02

8-11 城镇居民家庭每百户主要耐用消费品年末拥有量

指 标	Commodity Names	2002	2003	2004
摩托车（辆）	Motorcycle (unit)	8.7	10.2	9.1
家用汽车（辆）	Car (unit)	0.3	0.3	0.3
洗衣机（台）	Washing Machine (unit)	97.3	95.7	98.3
电冰箱（台 ）	Refrigerator (unit)	95.7	91.8	91.2
彩色电视机（台）	Color TV Set (unit)	128.3	127.0	134.0
家用电脑（台）	Computer (unit)	19.0	23.9	31.7
组合音响（套）	Hi-Fi System (set)	23.0	22.9	20.0
摄像机（台）	Pick-up Camera (unit)	1.0	1.7	1.1
照相机（架）	Camera (set)	48.0	48.3	44.3
钢琴（架）	Piano (set)	1.7	2.0	2.0
其它中高档乐器（件）	Other High-Grade Musical Instruments (unit)	6.7	5.9	7.1
微波炉（台）	Oven (unit)	39.3	42.2	47.1
空调器（台）	Air Conditioner (unit)	75.0	82.4	92.6
淋浴热水器（台）	Shower(unit)	63.7	70.0	74.9
健身器材（件）	Health Care Equipment (unit)	1.7	2.6	2.9
消毒碗柜（台）	Disinfecting Cupboard(unit)	1.7	4.7	7.1
洗碗机（台）	Dishwasher (unit)			
固定电话（部）	Telephone (unit)	88.0	87.1	85.7
移动电话（部）	Hand Telephone (unit)	48.3	74.4	102.0

Number of Durable Consumer Goods Owned Every 100 Urban Households in Representative Years

2005	2006	2007	2008	2009	2010	2011	2012	2013
8.6	8.9	5.4	7.9	7.6	8.0	8.3	11.0	11.8
0.6	0.9	2.0	4.0	9.0	13.3	16.7	24.3	27.5
101.1	101.1	98.9	95.3	98.8	100.3	100.8	100.4	101.4
90.9	94.4	95.7	89.2	95.0	97.1	97.7	96.5	97.4
134.0	136.0	134.5	119.9	126.7	128.7	129.9	122.5	123.9
20.3	37.1	45.6	54.0	68.8	76.1	82.0	86.2	89.1
34.0	20.6	24.8	19.0	25.2	27.7	28.0	22.7	23.0
3.1	4.3	4.8	7.7	9.7	11.1	11.8	12.0	12.7
49.7	47.7	50.1	39.9	52.1	57.7	62.0	65.3	67.6
1.4	1.7	1.1	2.4	2.4	2.7	2.5	3.0	2.9
11.4	12.9	6.0	4.7	5.3	5.3	5.8	7.4	7.7
52.0	52.9	56.4	52.7	62.1	66.4	68.4	65.2	67.1
99.7	102.9	116.0	104.0	119.7	129.5	135.1	146.7	152.8
110.3	71.4	74.1	70.9	79.9	82.3	84.1	91.8	92.2
6.9	3.4	4.0	4.3	4.8	5.0	5.5	6.6	6.7
29.4	6.0	7.4	5.5	7.8	8.5	8.9	8.6	8.1
		0.6	0.6	0.3	0.8	0.8	1.3	1.3
88.0	79.1	75.2	67.4	72.8	71.5	69.9	60.9	61.4
119.7	144.3	162.3	162.1	185.3	196.4	207.1	226.0	230.0

8-12 主要年份农村居民家庭基本情况

指　标	Item	2001	2002
一、调查户数(户)	**Households Surveyed(household)**	**770**	**770**
二、调查人口(人)	**Residents Surveyed(person)**		
1. 常住人口	Average Number of Permanent Residents	3214	3212
2. 整半劳动力	Average Number Able-bodied and Semi-able-bodied Laborers Per Households	2008	2017
3. 平均每个劳动力负担人口	Persons Supported by Each Laborers	1.6	1.59
三、平均每人全年收入(元)	**Per Capita Annual Income(yuan)**		
1. 总收入	Total Revenue	3185.54	3370.82
2. 纯收入	Net Income	2490.27	2641.44
3. 现金收入	Cash Income	2747	2965.92
4. 可支配收入	Disposable Income	2357.3	2560.58
四、按人均纯收入分组(%)	**Grouped by Per Capita Annual Net Income(%)**		
户数占总户数比重	Percentage of Households		
1000元以下	Below 1000 yuan		11.69
1000-2000元	1000-2000 yuan		28.57
2000-3000元	2000-3000 yuan		27.92
3000-4000元	3000-4000 yuan		15.45
4000-5000元	4000-5000 yuan		5.97
5000元以上	Over 5000 yuan		10.40
五、农民家庭房屋情况	**Rural Household Housing Condition**		
1. 年末人均住房价值(元)	Average Value of Living House Per Capita of Year-end(yuan)	6286.53	6883.06
2. 年末人均住房面积(平方米)	Average Floor Space of Living House Per Capita at Year-end(sq.m)	29.72	32.54
3. 年内人均新建房屋面积(平方米)	Percapita Space of Building Newly Built Within the year (sq.m)	1.81	2.20
4. 年内人均新建房屋价值(元)	Percapita Value of Building Newly Built Within the Year(yuan)	475.33	484.18
六、生活消费支出总计(元)	**Per Capita Living Expenditure Built(yuan)**	**1676.42**	**1782.14**
食品消费支出	Food	567.62	553.78
衣着	Clothing	105.53	115.02
居住	Residence	409.9	444.92
家庭设备用品及服务	Household Facilities,Articles and Services	74.29	83.64
医疗保健	Medical and Health Care Services	115.92	136.18
交通通讯	Transport and Communications	88.83	115.14
文化娱乐用品及服务	Culture,Educational and Recreational Articles and Services	241.31	275.38
其它商品及服务	Other Commodities and Services	73.02	58.08

Basic Indicators of Rural Households In Representative Years

2003	2004	2005	2006	2007	2008	2009	2010	2011	2012	2013
750	**710**	**720**	**700**	**700**	**900**	**940**	**940**	**940**	**930**	**930**
3102	2920	3040	2935	2924	3628	3828	3704	3732	3800	3803
1993	1873	1904	1841	1863	2422	2557	2469	2570	2621	2580
1.56	1.56	1.6	1.59	1.57	1.5	1.5	1.5	1.5	1.5	1 5
3571.71	3889.12	4495.44	4968.93	5605.12	6746.04	7961.26	9737	11910	14087	15936
2837.83	3142.78	3459.6	3808.38	4358.64	5212.14	6275.22	7750	9788	11442	12930
3042.02	3299.16	3940.24	4466.49	4969.58	6249.34	7297.58	9265	11278	13719	15803
2729.88	3021.25	3353.43	3562.8	4167.18	4983.23	6008.41	7369		10727	12083
10.00	5.49	5.14	3.57	2.57	1.89	1.70	1.06			
26.67	22.40	18.33	14.57	7.57	7.33	3.83	2.45			
25.00	28.45	25.00	22.43	15.14	13.78	7.98	5.74			
16.13	19.30	20.70	19.43	21.00	13.00	12.55	6.91			
10.00	9.01	11.94	13.57	17.72	14.00	12.87	11.28			
11.20	15.35	18.89	26.43	36.00	50.00	61.07	72.55			
7354.40	7780.97	9052.3	10878.22	13145.27	20476.11	24500.32	32059	37103	56470	47032
33.90	34.66	36.73	40.05	42.92	54.97	56.73	67	63	78	81
0.98	1.13	1.13	1.82	2 03	1.80	2.62	4	2	3	2
239.47	309.07	365.97	746.64	787.03	784.68	1349.27	2380	1591	2641	2025
1802.75	**2276.65**	**2602.68**	**2708.87**	**3380.8**	**3938.09**	**4771.06**	**5633**	**6705**	**7774**	**8780**
677 03	812.47	945.76	996.75	1289.61	1455.22	1708.35	1833	2138	2630	2894
113.15	133.97	159.09	174.81	205.35	256.92	305.46	369	483	577	691
314.04	478.37	462.21	488.47	768.16	763.44	928.87	1375	1604	1703	1740
98.59	104.93	133.11	152.83	191.26	276.61	332.52	368	476	580	681
128.47	173.89	213.04	216.67	257.14	316.95	405.62	481	580	688	738
143.45	191.89	213.12	236.97	256.27	308.85	469.06	476	604	792	866
296.80	340.88	420.45	387.51	352.98	489.68	531.23	631	699	793	927
31.22	40.25	55.9	54.86	59.53	70.42	89.95	100	121	11	243

8-13 主要年份农村居民家庭人均总收入和纯收入

单位：元

指　标	Item	2005	2006
一、全年总收入	**Annul Total Revenue**	**4495.44**	**4968.92**
1. 工资性收入	Wages Income	1292.69	1498.79
2. 家庭经营收入	Household Business Income	2612.18	2799.09
3. 财产性收入	Property Income	330.42	388.00
4、转移性收入	Transfer Income	260.15	283.04
二、全年纯收入	**Annul Net Income**	**3459.60**	**3808.38**
1. 工资性收入	Wages Income	1292.69	1498.79
2. 家庭经营纯收入	Household Business Net Income	1629.54	1661.13
（1）第一产业收入	Income from Primary Industry	982.81	992.79
（2）第二产业收入	Income from Secondary Industry	143.16	166.34
（3）第三产业收入	Income from Tertiary Industry	503.57	502.00
3. 财产性收入	Property Income	330.42	388.00
4. 转移性收入	Transfer Income	206.95	260.46

Per Capita Annual Total Revenue and Net Income of Rural Households In Representative Years

(yuan)

	2007	2008	2009	2010	2011	2012	2013
	5605.13	**6746.04**	**7961.25**	**9736.93**	**11910**	**14087**	**15935**
	1751.84	2161.42	2587.24	3307.61	4282	4946	5707
	3063.28	3595.63	4109.86	4734.60	5347	6599	7270
	449.52	553.35	738.95	1025.49	1417	1637	1946
	340.49	435.64	525.20	669.23	864	905	1013
	4398.64	**5212.14**	**6275.22**	**7750.35**	**9788**	**11442**	**12930**
	1751.84	2161.42	2587.24	3307.61	4282	4946	5707
	1887.68	2092.35	2469.83	2826.61	3413	4133	4472
	1168.79	1232.01	1431.38	1532.79	1740	1794	1830
	177.99	241.48	257.74	290.73	375	591	626
	540.90	618.86	780.71	1003.09	1298	1743	2016
	449.52	553.35	738.95	1025.49	1418	1637	1946
	309.60	405.02	479.20	590.64	675	726	805

8-14 全市及各区县农村居民家庭人均总收入和纯收入（2013年）

单位：元

指 标	Item	西安市 Xi'an	灞桥区 Baqiao	未央区 Weiyang
一、全年总收入（元）	Annual Total Revenue	**15936**	**22877**	**19377**
1. 工资性收入	Income from Wages and Salaries	5707	7388	7034
2. 家庭经营收入	Income from Household Operations	7270	10903	3922
3. 财产性收入	Income from Properties	1946	3287	6944
4. 转移性收入	Income from Transfers	1013	1299	1477
二、全年纯收入（元）	Annual Net Income	**12930**	**17116**	**16455**
1. 工资性收入	Wages Income	5707	7388	7034
2. 家庭经营纯收入	Household Business Net Income	4472	5379	1608
（1）第一产业收入	Income from Primary Industry	1830	324	
（2）第二产业收入	Income from Secondary Industry	626	872	345
（3）第三产业收入	Income from Tertiary Industry	2016	4183	1263
3. 财产性收入	Property Income	1946	3286	6944
4. 转移性收入	Transfer Income	805	1063	869
三、可支配收入（元）	Disposable Income	**12083**	**16531**	**15736**

Per Capita Annual Total Revenue and Net Income of Rural Households in Whole City and Regions(2013)

(yuan)

雁塔区 Yanta	阎良区 Yanliang	临潼区 Lintong	长安区 Chang'an	蓝田县 Lantian	周至县 Zhouzhi	户 县 Huxian	高陵县 Gaoling
18011	**21422**	**15338**	**13820**	**10046**	**11016**	**14784**	**14228**
6319	4325	6189	6698	4581	3288	5849	5703
3429	15037	7520	5123	4862	6854	8040	6244
7805	920	313	463	21	399	46	1289
458	1140	1316	1536	582	475	849	992
16724	**15212**	**12160**	**12695**	**8833**	**8870**	**10899**	**12167**
6319	4325	6139	6698	4581	3288	5849	5703
2186	8889	4548	4408	3813	4744	4339	4356
	5495	2760	900	1992	3178	1996	1254
1580	984	565	428	528	424	286	502
606	2410	1223	3080	1293	1142	2057	2600
7805	920	313	463	21	398	46	1288
414	1078	1110	1126	418	440	665	820
14299	**14669**	**11395**	**12303**	**8469**	**7900**	**9751**	**11444**

8-15 全市及各区县农村居民家庭基本情况（2013年）

指 标	Item	西安市 Xi'an	灞桥区 Baqiao	未央区 Weiyang
一、调查户数（户）	**Number of Households Surveyed (household)**	**930**	**100**	**80**
二、常住人口（人）	**Permanent Residents(person)**	**3803**	**406**	**335**
6岁及以下	6 Year-old and Below	233	26	31
7-15岁人口	7-15 Year-old	353	40	36
16-60岁人口	16-60 Year-old	2754	299	243
61岁以上人口	61 Year-old and Above	463	41	25
三、整半劳动力(人)	**Able-bodied and Semi-able-bodied Labourer(person)**	2580	278	217
四、常住人口外出从业人数(人)	**Permanent Residents Employed in Other Places Outside(person)**	**515**	**60**	**1**
五、劳动力文化程度(人)	**Labourer Literacy(person)**	**2063**	**240**	**152**
1. 不识字或识字很少	Illiterates or Semi-illiterates	17	1	
2. 小学文化程度	Primary Schools	176	15	2
3. 初中文化程度	Junior Secondary Schools	1151	129	85
4. 高中程度	Senior Secondary Schools	474	54	31
5. 中专程度	Specialized Secondary Schools	98	13	13
6. 大专及以上	Universities and Colleges and Above	147	28	21
六、人均耕地经营面积（亩）	**Area of Cultivated Land Managed per Capita(mu)**	**0.84**	**0.57**	**0.04**

Basic Conditions of Rural Households

in Whole City and Regions(2013)

雁塔区 Yanta	阎良区 Yanliang	临潼区 Lintong	长安区 Chang'an	蓝田县 Lantian	周至县 Zhouzhi	户　县 Huxian	高陵县 Gaoling
80	**80**	**100**	**100**	**90**	**100**	**100**	**100**
306	**335**	**428**	**371**	**331**	**459**	**420**	**412**
21	11	23	22	17	26	20	36
21	34	35	40	37	40	34	36
239	255	313	254	228	339	312	272
25	35	57	55	49	54	54	68
218	217	285	237	240	308	306	274
29		**122**	**37**	**45**	**52**	**83**	**86**
113	**73**	**264**	**182**	**231**	**267**	**305**	**246**
		1	4	2	2	7	
1	2	38	30	21	31	27	9
46	30	157	99	167	122	166	150
32	28	54	30	29	88	62	66
11	12	6	11	7	9	17	9
23	1	8	8	5	15	26	12
	1.10	**1.38**	**0.92**	**1.05**	**1.15**	**0.70**	**0.73**

8-16 全市及各区县农村居民家庭人均全年总支出（2013年）

单位：元

指 标	Item	西安市 Xi'an	灞桥区 Baqiao	未央区 Weiyang
全年总支出（元）	**Annual Total Expenditure**	**12610**	**16607**	**16287**
一、家庭经营费用支出	**Expenditure for Household Business**	**2512**	**4795**	**2011**
#农业支出	Farming	1024	345	
牧业支出	Animal Husbandry	364	333	
二、购置生产用固定资产支出	**Purchasing Productive Fixed Assets**	**251**	**890**	**9**
三、建造生产性固定资产雇工支出	**Expenditure on Labor Hiring on Building of Productive Fixed Assets**	**3**	**8**	
四、税费支出	**Expenditure for Tax and Fee**	**9**	**1**	
五、生活消费支出	**Expenditure for Living Consumption**	**8780**	**10091**	**12940**
六、财产性支出	**Expenditure for Property**	**17**	**25**	
七、转移性支出	**Expenditure for Transfer**	**1038**	**797**	**1327**

8-17 全市及各区县农村居民家庭人均生产情况（2013年）

单位：公斤

指 标	Item	西安市 Xi'an	灞桥区 Baqiao	未央区 Weiyang
粮食产量(公斤)	Output of Grain	452		
#小麦	Wheat	232		
玉米	Corn	209		
大豆	Soybean			
棉花产量	Output of Cotton			
油料产量	Output of Oil-bearing Crops	1		
蔬菜产量	Output of Vegetables	243		
水果产量	Output of Fruits	80	187	

Per Capita Annual Total Expenditure of Rural Households in Whole City and Regions(2013)

(yuan)

	雁塔区 Yanta	阎良区 Yanliang	临潼区 Lintong	长安区 Chang'an	蓝田县 Lantian	周至县 Zhouzhi	户 县 Huxian	高陵县 Gaoling
	15224	**16609**	**14192**	**10165**	**6954**	**9442**	**12458**	**9308**
	825	**6143**	**2743**	**638**	**894**	**1904**	**3211**	**1689**
	1	5977	1137	354	446	1152	351	756
		15	426	72	146	37	2307	5
	6	**7**	**739**	**102**	**281**	**49**	**261**	**21**
			3			**14**		
		5		**1**	**11**	**56**	**5**	**1**
	11926	**9849**	**9736**	**8622**	**5241**	**6412**	**7648**	**6700**
			71	**38**		**22**		
	2467	**605**	**900**	**764**	**527**	**985**	**1332**	**897**

Output of Major Farm Crops Per Capita by Rural Households in Whole City and Regions(2013)

(kg)

	雁塔区 Yanta	阎良区 Yanliang	临潼区 Lintong	长安区 Chang'an	蓝田县 Lantian	周至县 Zhouzhi	户 县 Huxian	高陵县 Gaoling
		1331	1030	676	247	58	530	608
		872	435	325	190		245	284
		459	499	351	57	53	284	324
					8			
		1833	152		1	6	5	577
		15	76			388	28	5

8-18 全市及各区县农村居民家庭人均出售产品情况（2013年）

单位：公斤

指　标	Item	西安市 Xi'an	灞桥区 Baqiao	未央区 Weiyang
粮食	Grain	344	24	
棉花	Cotton			
油料	Oil-bearing Corps	1		
蔬菜	Vegetables	194		
水果	Fruits	107	212	3
肉猪及猪肉	Fattened Hogs & Pork	22		
菜牛及牛肉	Beef Cattle & Beef	1		
菜羊及羊肉	Mutton Sheep & Mutton	1		
蛋类	Poultry Eggs	0		
奶类	Milks	15	31	

8-19 全市及各区县农村居民家庭人均粮食收支情况（2013年）

单位：公斤

指　标	Item	西安市 Xi'an	灞桥区 Baqiao	未央区 Weiyang
一、粮食收入合计	**Total Grain Income**	**551**	**177**	**101**
1. 家庭经营生产	Self-produced	452		
2. 购入	Purchased	99	177	101
3. 借入	Borrowed			
4. 收回借出粮	Grains Taken Back			
5. 其它粮食收入	Other Grain Income			
二、粮食支出合计	**Total Grain Expenditure**	**490**	**202**	**101**
1. 主食用粮	Staple Food	117	98	101
2. 其它生活用粮	Other Living Uses			
3. 出售	Sold Out	344	24	
4. 种籽	Seeds	5	1	
5. 饲料	Fodder	24	79	
6. 借出	Lent Out			
7. 归还借粮	Grains Returned			
8. 其它粮食支出	Other Grain Expenditure			
三、年末粮食结存调查数	**Year-end Grain Deposite Balance**	**212**	**79**	**0**

Per Capita Product Sold by Rural Households in Whole City and Regions(2013)

(kg)

雁塔区 Yanta	阎良区 Yanliang	临潼区 Lintong	长安区 Chang'an	蓝田县 Lantian	周至县 Zhouzhi	户　县 Huxian	高陵县 Gaoling
	789	811	203	855	181	182	414
	1						
				6			
	1807	152		75	39	1	56
	12	82		76	533	28	3
		9		15		179	
	14						
				6			
				3			
	81	32	2	4			1

Per Capita Annual Income and Expenditure of Grains of Rural Households in Whole City and Regions(2013)

(kg)

雁塔区 Yanta	阎良区 Yanliang	临潼区 Lintong	长安区 Chang'an	蓝田县 Lantian	周至县 Zhouzhi	户　县 Huxian	高陵县 Gaoling
83	**1388**	**1108**	**730**	**325**	**140**	**707**	**696**
	1331	1030	676	247	58	530	608
83	57	78	54	78	82	177	88
83	**869**	**947**	**377**	**1150**	**272**	**411**	**501**
83	70	129	170	275	88	105	76
	789	811	202	855	181	182	413
	10	7	5	8	2	6	12
				12	1	118	
0	**335**	**493**	**280**	**379**	**145**	**182**	**192**

8-20 全市及各区县农村居民家庭人均购买商品（2013年）

单位：元

商品名称	Commodity Names	西安市 Xi'an	灞桥区 Baqiao	未央区 Weiyang
一、食品	Food	2111	2426	3239
二、衣着类	Clothing	689	900	1033
三、居住	Residence	1094	1250	1587
四、家用设备和日用品	Household Facilities and Articles	649	623	673
五、交通、通讯类	Transport,post and Telecommunication	584	783	700
六、文教	Cultural and Education	324	227	299
七、医疗保健类	Health Care and Medical Services	205	201	285
八、其他杂项商品	Other Commodities and Services	162	217	355

8-21 全市及各区县农村居民家庭人均主要食品消费量（2013年）

单位：公斤

食品名称	Food Names	西安市 Xi'an	灞桥区 Baqiao	未央区 Weiyang
一、粮食	Grain	117	98	101
#小麦	Wheet	88	43	70
二、油脂类	Oil or Fat	13	11	10
三、蔬菜及菜制品	Vegetable and Its Products	69	87	93
四、瓜果类	Melons and Fruits	13	13	19
五、水果类	Fruits	19	24	31
六、肉禽及制品	Meat,Poultry and Their Products	16	15	22
七、蛋类及蛋制品	Eggs and Its Products	10	8	11
八、奶及奶制品	Milk and Dairy Products	11	10	18
九、酒	Liquor	5	5	5

Per Capita Purchase of Commodities in Rural Households in Whole City and Regions(2013)

(yuan)

雁塔区 Yanta	阎良区 Yanliang	临潼区 Lintong	长安区 Chang'an	蓝田县 Lantian	周至县 Zhouzhi	户 县 Huxian	高陵县 Gaoling
2525	2854	2233	1839	1325	1470	1574	1983
1267	774	615	534	389	502	554	502
747	960	1726	1076	465	1058	1341	563
767	1153	842	512	344	450	742	458
481	744	875	622	380	503	325	424
284	1316	375	138	145	126	234	231
272	90	225	203	161	174	237	208
394	73	118	117	47	133	95	131

Per Capita Average Food Consumption of Rural Households in Whole City and Regions(2013)

(kg)

雁塔区 Yanta	阎良区 Yanliang	临潼区 Lintong	长安区 Chang'an	蓝田县 Lantian	周至县 Zhouzhi	户 县 Huxian	高陵县 Gaoling
83	70	129	170	275	88	105	76
49	48	109	144	212	72	79	63
11	7	41	11	9	7	9	9
72	60	76	69	59	36	58	86
12	22	9	10	4	12	10	21
25	19	17	16	8	13	19	20
18	9	34	15	7	11	14	11
7	7	31	5	5	10	5	6
22	6	14	13	9	5	8	7
10	5	9	6	4	3	2	4

8-22 全市及各区县农村居民家庭每百户耐用消费品年末拥有量（2013年）

指 标	Item	西安市 Xi'an	灞桥区 Baqiao	未央区 Weiyang
大型家具（件）	Large Furnitures (unit)			
洗衣机(台)	Washing Machine(unit)	101	91	101
电风扇（台）	Electric Fan(unit)			
电冰箱（台）	Refrigerator(unit)	83	90	100
空调机（台）	Air Conditioner(unit)	77	66	136
热水器（台）	Water Heater(unit)	65	74	93
自行车(辆)	Bicycle (unit)	119	90	96
摩托车(辆)	Motorcycle(unit)	35	17	1
生活用汽车（辆）	Automobile(unit)	18	18	58
电话机（部）	Telephone (unit)	51	39	63
移动电话（部）	Mobile Phone(unit)	245	244	305
彩色电视机（台）	Color TV Set(unit)	118	106	121
黑白电视机（台）	Black-white TV Set(unit)	2	1	
影碟机（台）	Video Disc Player (unit)	38	54	18
照相机（架）	Camera(set)	30	25	56
家用计算机(台)	Computer(unit)	45	47	80

8-23 全市及各区县农村居民家庭人均住房情况（2013年）

指 标	Item	西安市 Xi'an	灞桥区 Baqiao	未央区 Weiyang
一、年末住房面积（平方米）	**Floor Space of Houses at the End of Year (sq.m)**	**81**	**114**	**162**
二、住房类型（平方米）	**Pattern of Houses(sq.m)**			
1. 楼房面积	Floor Space of Storied Building	45	40	50
2. 砖瓦平房面积	Floor Space of Single-storey Building	12	1	
3. 其它	Others			
三、年末住房价值（元）	**Value of Houses at the End of Year (yuan)**	**47032**	**59063**	**93271**
四、年内新建（购）房屋面积（平方米）	**Floor Space Of Newly-Built Purchased Houses (sq.m)**	**2**	**11**	
年内新建（购）房屋价值（元）	Value of Houses of Newly-Built Purchased (yuan)	2025	10875	

Year-end Possession of Durable Consumer Goods Per 100 Rural Households in Whole City and Regions(2013)

雁塔区 Yanta	阎良区 Yanliang	临潼区 Lintong	长安区 Chang'an	蓝田县 Lantian	周至县 Zhouzhi	户县 Huxian	高陵县 Gaoling
116	100	100	98	93	91	108	112
106	100	82	73	38	60	89	99
170	89	44	55	9	27	90	112
99		57	64	18	62	94	89
80	125	119	133	68	106	200	153
10	54	60	36	22	73	33	37
54	5	8	10	3	10	11	19
89	100	34	22	58	21	52	56
315	128	244	207	183	263	293	266
159	100	79	132	106	123	148	113
10		1	1	3	0	2	
58	10	51	25	24	43	56	34
96	48	7	19	4	6	36	18
113	25	12	45	13	21	55	48

Per Capita Housing Conditions of Rural Households in Whole City and Regions (2013)

雁塔区 Yanta	阎良区 Yanliang	临潼区 Lintong	长安区 Chang'an	蓝田县 Lantian	周至县 Zhouzhi	户县 Huxian	高陵县 Gaoling
222	**36**	**47**	**49**	**42**	**42**	**49**	**84**
54	24	12	42	19	29	47	40
	12	34	6	23	13	2	27
			1				
133226	**12633**	**22308**	**43710**	**30088**	**36172**	**22329**	**41167**
1		**2**	**1**		**1**	**1**	**3**
2093		1536	1104		971	1263	1469

8-24 城镇居民家庭人均体育消费支出情况（2013年）

Statistics on Per capita Sports Consumption Expenditure of Urban Households (2013)

单位：元 (yuan)

指标名称	Item	总平均 The total average
体育消费支出	**Sports consumption expenditure**	**120.40**
一、体育健身活动支出	**Fitness activities**	**40.27**
（一）球类健身活动	Ball fitness activities	2.71
（二）水上健身活动	Water fitness activities	11.87
（三）冰雪类健身活动	Ice Class fitness activities	1.08
（四）操类活动	Exercise activity	9.41
（五）野外拓展活动	To expand the field of activities	2.54
（六）民族传统体育活动	The national tradition sports	0.08
（七）棋牌类活动	Chess activity	1.03
（八）各类体育项目培训	All kinds of sports training	7.96
（九）租赁场地、体育器材	Rental venues, sports equipment	2.91
二、观赏性体育消费	**Spectator sports consumption**	
三、体育用品及体育信息支出	**Sports goods and sports information expenditure**	**80.13**
（一）运动服装、鞋帽类	Sports clothing, shoes and hats	56.01
1、运动服装金额	Sports clothing	25.36
数量（件）	Number (Piece)	0.17
2、运动鞋类金额	Sports shoes	30.03
数量（双）	Number(double)	0.13
3、运动帽类金额	Sports hats	0.52
数量（件）	Number(Piece)	0.01
（二）健身器材	Fitness Equipment	6.52
（三）体育用品	Sports goods	17.42
（四）体育音像制品	Sports of audio and video products	0.05
（五）体育报刊杂志书籍	Sports newspapers and magazines and books	0.13

主要统计指标解释

一、城镇住户

城镇家庭人口 指居住在一起，经济上合在一起共同生活的家庭成员。凡计算为家庭人口的成员其全部收支都包括在本家庭中。

城镇就业面 指就业人口占家庭人口的百分比。

城镇就业者负担人数 指家庭人口与就业人口之比。

城镇家庭总收入 指家庭成员得到的工薪收入、经营净收入、财产性收入、转移性收入之和，不包括出售财物收入和借贷收入。

城镇家庭可支配收入 指家庭成员得到可用于最终消费支出和其它非义务性支出以及储蓄的总和，即居民家庭可以用来自由支配的收入。它是家庭总收入扣除交纳的个人所得税、个人交纳的社会保障支出以及记账补贴后的收入。计算公式为：

可支配收入=家庭总收入—交纳个人所得税—个人交纳的社会保障支出—记账补贴

城镇家庭总支出 指除借贷支出以外的全部家庭支出。包括消费性支出、购房建房支出、转移性支出、财产性支出、社会保障支出。

城镇家庭消费性支出 指家庭用于日常生活的支出，包括食品、衣着、居住、家庭设备用品及服务、医疗保健、交通和通信、娱乐教育文化服务、其他商品和服务等八大类支出。

恩格尔系数 指食物支出金额在消费性总支出金额中所占的比例。计算公式为：

$$恩格尔系数=\frac{食品支出金额}{消费性总支出金额}\times 100\%$$

二、农村住户

农村住户 指农村常住户。农村常住户指长期（一年以上）居住在乡镇（不包括城关镇）行政管理区域内的住户，以及长期居住在城关镇所辖行政村范围内的农村住户。户口不在本地而在本地居住一年及以上的住户也包括在本地农村常住户范围内；有本地户口，但举家外出谋生一年以上的住户，无论是否保留承包耕地都不包括在本地农村住户范围内。

常住人口 指全年经常在家或在家居住6个月以上，而且经济和生活与本户连成一体的人口。外出从业人员在外居住时间虽然在6个月以上，但收入主要带回家中，经济与本户连为一体，仍视为家庭常住人口；在家居住，生活和本户连成一体的国家职工、退休人员也为家庭常住人口。但是现役军人、中专及以上（走读生除外）的在校学生、以及常年在外（不包括探亲、看病等）且已有稳定的职业与居住场所的外出从业人员，不算家庭常住人口。家庭常住人口主要作为计算农村住户平均每人收入、消费和积累水平及分析家庭人口状况的依据。

整、半劳动力 整劳动力指男子18周岁到50周岁，女子18周岁到45周岁；半劳动力指男子16周岁到17周岁，51周岁到60周岁；女子16周岁到17周岁，46周岁到55周岁，同时具有劳动能力的人。虽然在劳动年龄之内，但已丧失劳动能力的人，不应算为劳动力；超过劳动年龄，但能经常参加劳动，计入半劳动力数内。常住人口中的职工，若这些职工为劳动力，就包括在本户的整半劳动力中。

总收入 指调查期内农村住户和住户成员从各种来源渠道得到的收入总和。按收入的性质划分为工资性收入、家庭经营收入、财产性收入和转移性收入。

工资性收入 指农村住户成员受雇于单位或个人，靠出卖劳动而获得的收入。

家庭经营收入 指农村住户以家庭为生产经营单位进行生产筹划和管理而获得的收入。农村住户家庭经营活动按行业划分为农业、林业、牧业、渔业、工业、建筑业、交通运输业邮电业、批发和零售贸易餐饮业、社会服务业、文教卫生业和其他家庭经营。

财产性收入 指金融资产或有形非生产性资产的所有者向其他机构单位提供资金或将有形非生产性资产供其支配，作为回报而从中获得的收入。

转移性收入 指农村住户和住户成员无须付出任何对应物而获得的货物、服务、资金或资产所有权等，不包括无偿提供的用于固定资本形成的资金。一般情况下，是指农村住户在二次分配中的所有收入。

现金收入 指农村住户和住户成员在调查期内得到以现金形态表现的收入。按来源分成工资性收入、家庭经营现金收入、财产性收入、转移性收入。

纯收入 指农村住户当年从各个来源得到的总收入相应地扣除所发生的费用后的收入总和。计算方法：

纯收入＝总收入—税费支出—家庭经营费用支出—生产性固定资产折旧—赠送农村内部亲友支出

纯收入主要用于再生产投入和当年生活消费支出，也可用于储蓄和各种非义务性支出。“农民人均纯收入”是按人口平均的纯收入水平，反映的是一个地区农村居民的平均收入水平。

总支出 指农村住户用于生产、生活和再分配的全部支出。包括家庭经营费用支出、购置生产性固定资产支出、税费支出、生活消费支出、财产性支出和转移性支出。

Explanatory Notes on Main Statistical Indicators

I. Urban Households

Population of Urban Households refer to members of households living and sharing economically together in the urban areas. All the income and expenditure of all the members of such households are included in the income and expenditure of the household.

Proportion of Urban Employment refers to the proportion of employed population to the population of urban households.

Number of Dependents per Urban Employee refers to the ratio between number of persons in an urban household and the number of employed persons.

Total Income of Urban Households refers to the sum of wage and salary; net business income; income from properties; and income from transfers of members of the households. Income from selling of properties and income from borrowing are not included..

Disposable Income of Urban Households refers to the actual income at the disposal of members of the households which can be used for final consumption, other non-compulsory expenditure and savings. This equals to total income minus income tax, personal contribution to social security and subsidy for keeping diaries in being a sample household. The following formula is used:

Disposable income = total household income - income tax - personal contribution to social security - subsidy for keeping diaries for a sampled household

Total Expenditure of Urban Households refers to all expenditure of households except expenditure on lending. It includes expenditure on consumption; on purchasing or building houses; on transfers; on properties; and on social security.

Consumption Expenditure of Urban Households refers to total expenditure of households for consumption in daily life, including expenditure on the eight categories of food; clothing; housing; household appliances and services; health care and medical services; transport and communications; recreation, education and cultural services; and miscellaneous goods and services.

Expenditure of Urban Households on Consumption of Services refers to expenditure of households on various kinds of non-commercial services provided by society.

Engel's Coefficient refers to the percentage of expenditure on food in the total consumption expenditure, using the following formula:

$$\text{Engel's Coefficient} = \frac{\text{expenditure on food}}{\text{total consumption expenditure}} \times 100\%$$

II. Rural Household

Rural Households refer to usual resident households in rural areas. Usual resident households in rural areas are households residing on a long term basis(for more than one year) in the areas under the administration of township governments (not including county towns), and in the areas under the administration of villages in county towns. Households residing in the current addresses for over one year with their household registration in other places are still considered as resident households of the locality. For households with their household registration in one place but all members of the households having moved away to make a living in another place for over one year, they will not be included in the rural households of the area where they are registered, irrespective of whether they still keep their contracted land.

Usual Resident Population refers to persons staying at home regularly or for over 6 months during a year and integrated with the household economically and in terms of living.. Members of the household staying away from the household for over 6 months but keeping a close economic relation with the household by sending the majority of income to the household are regarded as usual resident of the household. Government staff and workers or retirees living as close members of the household are also considered as usual resident. However, servicemen, students of secondary technical schools or schools of higher education and persons with stable jobs and residence outside the household (excluding those visiting relatives or seeking medical service) are not included as resident population of the household. Resident population is used in calculating income, consumption, accumulation on per capita basis of rural households and in analyzing composition of rural households.

Full/Semi Labour Force Full labour force refers to persons capable of work, aged 18-50 for males and 18-45 for females. Semi labour force refers to persons capable of work, aged 16-17 and 51-60 for males and 16-17 and 46-55 for females. Persons at their working ages but not capable of work are not to be included as labour force. Persons not at working ages but participating regularly in work are included in semi labour force. For staff and workers who are usual residents, are included as full or semi labour force of the household if they are in the labour force.

Total Income refers to the sum of income earned from various sources by the rural households and their members during the reference period, and is classified as income from wages and salaries, income from household operations, income from properties and income from transfers.

Income from Wages and Salaries refers to income from labour earned by the members of rural households employed by other units or individuals.

Income from Household Operations refers to income by the rural households as units of production and operation. Operations by rural households are classified according to their economic activities namely agriculture, forestry, animal husbandry, fishery, manufacturing, construction, transportation, post and telecommunications, wholesale, retail and catering, social service, culture, education, health, and other household operations.

Income from Properties refers to the income received as returns by owners of financial assets or tangible non-productive assets by providing capitals or tangible non-productive assets to other institutional units.

Income from Transfers refers to the receipt by rural households and their members of goods, services, capital or rights of assets without giving or repaying accordingly, excluding capital provided to them for the formation of fixed assets. In general, it refers to all income received by rural households through redistribution.

Cash Income refers to income received by rural households and their members in the form of cash during the reference period. It is classified, by source of income, into income from wages and salaries, cash income from household operations, income from properties and income from transfers.

Net Income refers to the total income of rural households from all sources minus all corresponding expenses. The formula for calculation is as follows:

Net income = total income - taxes and fees paid - household operation expenses - taxes and fees depreciation of fixed assets for production - gifts to non-rural relatives

Net income is mainly used as input for reinvestment in production and as consumption expenditure of the year, and also used for savings and non-compulsory expenses of various forms. "Per capita net income of farmers" is the level of net income averaged by population, reflecting the average income level of rural households in a given area.

Total Expenditure refers to total expenses of rural households on production, consumption and redistribution, including expenditure on household operations; purchase of productive fixed assets; taxes and fees; expenses on household consumption; expenses on properties; and expenses on transfers.

9 城市公用事业

URBAN PUBLIC UTILITIES

资料整理：郝 静
Data management:Hao jing

第九部分　城市公用事业

一、简要说明

本章资料主要包括城市供水、供燃气、供热、公共交通、市政设施、市政设施水平、城市规模及用地状况、园林绿地、环境卫生等情况，由西安市统计局社会科技处根据西安市建委、市交通局及地铁办提供的数据整理。

二、主要指标

人均公园绿地面积（平方米）	10.70	比上年同口径增长	4.7%
人均城市道路面积（平方米）	17.85	比上年同口径增长	1.8%
用水普及率（%）	100	比上年同口径增加	持平
燃气普及率（%）	98.68	比上年同口径提高	0.49个百分点

9　URBAN PUBLIC UTILITIES

Ⅰ.Brief Introduction

Data in this chapter reflects basic condition of urban public utilities of Xi'an City. Data on public utilities primarily consist of urban water supply, gas sales, urban heating, public transportation, municipal facilities, level of municipal construction, scale of the city, condition of land utilization, parks, greenbelt and environmental sanitation. Data in this chapter is compiled by Social Science & Technology Division of Xi'an Bureau of Statistics according to the data provided by Committee of Urban Construction of Xi'an, Xi'an Burean of Transportation and Xi'an Metro office.

Ⅱ.Major Indicators

		Increase over Preceding Year
Per Capita Public Green Areas (sq.m)	10.70	4.7%
Per Captia Area of Roads (sq.m)	17.85	1.8%
Water-Consuming Popularization (%)	100	unbiased
Gas-Consuming Popularization (%)	98.68	0.49 percentage points

9–1 城市供水

Urban Water Supply

指　标	Item	2009	2010	2011	2012	2013
年末水厂个数（个）	Number of Water Factory at Year-end (units)	9	9	15	15	15
供水综合生产能力（万立方米/日）	Total Volume of Water Supply (10 000 cu.m/day)	190	197.4	197.4	200.33	195.52
# 地下水	Groundwater	55.3	55.8	54.8	57.04	51.35
年末供水管道总长度（公里）	Length of Water Supply Pipelines at Year-end (kms)	1985	2416	2721	3207.73	3385.33
全年供水总量（万立方米）	Total Annual Volume of Water Supply (10 000 cu.m)	38307	41089	38934	45791.77	51372.07
#全年售水量	Annual Volume of Water Sales	32859	35099	33139	39734.86	44701.26
#生产运营用水	For Productive Use	6414	6267	5484	5334.28	6272.62
居民家庭用水	For Residential Use	18513	20944	19945	24703.73	26138.73
用水人口（万人）	Population with Access to Tap Water (10 000 persons)	357.6	410.9	394.1	406.32	444.35

注：本表数据来源于市建委和市水务局。
2009年部门统计制度变化，年末供水管道总长度和用水人口数调整。
2010年后数据为全市口径，2009年以前数据为市区口径。

9–2 城市供燃气

Gas Supply in Urban Area

指　标	Item	2009	2010	2011	2012	2013
一、天然气	**Natural Gas**					
管道长度（公里）	Total Length of Gas Pipelines (km)	3932	4488	4500	5075.19	6163.39
供气总量（万立方米）	Total Gas Supply(10 000 cu.m)	95885	109052	120330	142262.84	153483.90
#销售气量	Volume of Gas Sales	91336	104055	114955	136530.93	147592.97
#家庭用量	Residential Households	15473	20989	22868	27760.63	3667[illegible].17
用气人口（万人）	Population with Access to Gas (10 000 persons)	285	333	356	371.54	410.56
二、液化石油气	**Liquefied Petroleum Gas**					
供气总量（吨）	Total Gas Supply (tons)	74913	11469	5920	4529.70	6047.90
#销售气量	Volume of Gas Sales		11441	5891	4482.00	5986.20
#家庭用量	Residential Households	46275	7376	4352	4254.00	4945.00
用气人口（万人）	Population with Access to Gas (10 000 persons)	50.5	31.2	28.6	27.44	27.92

注：本表数据来源于市建委。
2010年后数据为全市口径，2009年以前数据为市区口径。

9-3 城市供热

Heating in Urban Area

指　标	Item	2009	2010	2011	2012	2013
供热能力	Heating Capacity					
蒸气（吨/小时）	Steam (tons/hour)	2118	2235	2075	3073.00	4283.00
热水（兆瓦）	Hot Water (megawatts)	11467	3531	4570	5401.90	12691.10
供热总量(万吉焦）	Volume Supplied (10 000 gigajoules)					
蒸气	Steam	1541	1674	1421	1616.98	1667.88
热水	Hot Water	1220	2570	2901	2443.57	2990.38
管道长度（公里）	Length of Pipelines (km)					
蒸气	Steam	209	180	167	187.07	204.33
热水	Hot Water	289	361	500	516.18	608.12
供热面积（万平方米）	Heated Area (10 000sq.m)	5178	6094	6524	8512.84	10980.27
#住宅	Residential Buildings	4325	5009	5226	7328.16	9874.54

注：本表数据来源于市建委。
2010年后数据为全市口径，2009　年以前数据为市区口径。

9-4 城市公共交通

Urban Public Traffic

指　标	Item	2009	2010	2011	2012	2013
运营车辆（辆）	Operating Vehicles (units)	7039	7107	7462	7695	8128
标准运营车辆（标台）	Standard Vehicles (units)	7833	8139	8598	8926	9371
公交客运总量（万人次）	Total of Bus Passenger(10 000 person-times)	161782	162400	175234	175241	174051
公交客运收入（万元）	Bus Passenger Transport Income (10 000 yuan)		129397	141505	135505	146417
出租汽车数（辆）	Number of Taxis (units)	12786	12786	13839	14139	14139
地铁运营线路长度（公里）	Length of Subway Lines in Operation(km)				20	44.68
地铁客运量（万人次）	Total of Subway Passenger(10 000 person-times)				5912	12189.61

注：本表数据来源于市交通局和地铁办。

9-5 市政设施

Municipal Facilities

指 标	Item	2009	2010	2011	2012	2013
一、道路长度（公里）	**Length of Roads (km)**	**2296**	**2662**	**2755**	**3119.30**	**3387.43**
二、道路面积（万平方米）	**Area of Roads (10 000 sq.m)**	**5057**	**5965**	**6259**	**7126.56**	**7931.80**
三、人行道面积（万平方米）	**Area of Sidewalks (10 000 sq.m)**	**1517**	**1834**	**1867**	**2105.31**	**2259.29**
四、桥梁数（座）	**Number of Bridges (units)**	**314**	**347**	**402**	**422**	**432**
#立交桥	Overpasses	71	71	91	97	97
五、路灯盏数（盏）	**Number of Street Lights (units)**	**271444**	**291754**	**311991**	**329881**	**333393**
六、排水管道长度（公里）	**Length of Drainage Pipelines (km)**	**2848**	**3765**	**4043**	**4435.92**	**4629.7**
七、污水年排放量（万立方米）	**Annual Discharge Volume of Sewage (10 000 cu.m)**	**31394**	**34706**	**36673**	**40302.7**	**46186**
八、污水处理厂处理能力（万立方米/日）	**Daily Disposal Capacity of Sewage (10 000 cu.m/day)**	**80**	**106.5**	**111.6**	**128.1**	**153.1**
九、污水年处理量（万立方米）	**Yearly Disposal Capacity of Sewage Disposal Plant (10 000 cu.m)**	**20386**	**25088**	**31512**	**35463**	**41898**
十、防洪堤长度（公里）	**Length of Flood Control Dikes (km)**	**119**	**168**	**168**	**188**	

注：本表数据来源于市建委。
2010年后数据为全市口径，2009年以前数据为市区口径。

9-6 城市设施水平

Urban Municipal Facilities

指 标	Item	2009	2010	2011	2012	2013
一、人均日生活用水量（升）	**Per Capita Daily Consumption of Tap Water For Residential Use (liters)**	**198.4**	**186.2**	**185.2**	**220.96**	**225.78**
二、用水普及率(%)	**Water-Consuming Popularization (%)**	**100**	**98.8**	**100**	**100**	**100**
三、每万人拥有公共交通车辆（标台）	**Number of Public Transport Vehicles Per 10 000 Population (units)**		**13.9**	**14.4**	**14.6**	**15.1**
四、燃气普及率(%)	**Gas-Consuming Popularization (%)**	**98.2**	**97**	**97.5**	**98.19**	**98.68**
五、人均城市道路面积（平方米）	**Per Captia Area of Roads (sq.m)**	**14.8**	**15.4**	**15.9**	**17.54**	**17.85**
六、建成区排水管道密度（公里/平方公里）	**Density of Drainage Pipelines in Developed Areas (km/sq.km)**	**10.1**	**9.5**	**9.7**	**9.83**	**9.17**
七、污水处理率(%)	**Rate of Sewerage Disposal (%)**	**81**	**84**	**85.9**	**89.51**	**90.72**
八、园林绿化	**Afforestation and Parks and Gardens**					
人均公园绿地面积（平方米）	Per Capita Public Green Areas (sq.m)	7.9	9.1	9.9	10.22	10.70
建城区绿地率（%）	Rate of Green Areas in Developed Areas (%)	40.4	29.2	30.9	31.20	32.32
九、生活垃圾无害化处理率(%)	**Rate of No Harm Disposal of Garbage (%)**	**90.3**	**93.9**	**93.7**	**94.93**	**93.95**

注：本表数据来源于市建委。
由于用水人口包括不在城市辖区内但已经使用城市供水的人口，故有些年份用水普及率大于100%。
2010年后数据为全市口径，2009年以前数据为市区口。
每万人拥有公共交通车辆计算数据口径调整，故与往年年鉴数据不可比。

9-7 城市规模及用地情况

City Scale and Land Use

单位：平方公里 (sq.km)

指 标	Item	2009	2010	2011	2012	2013
建成区面积	Area of the Constructed Regions	283	395	415	451.38	504.68
城市建设用地	Land use for Construction	277	336	349	376.39	489.03

注：本表数据来源于市建委。
2010年后数据为全市口径，2009年以前数据为市区口径。

9-8 城市园林绿化

Urban Parks,Gardens and Green Areas in Cities

指 标	Item	2009	2010	2011	2012	2013
一、公园个数（个）	**Number of Parks (units)**	**55**	**68**	**66**	**72**	**81**
二、公园面积（公顷）	**Area of Parks (hectares)**	**1241**	**1335**	**1478**	**1529**	**2406**
三、园林绿地面积（公顷）	**Total Area of Parks,Gardens and Green Areas (hectares)**	**9553**	**12140**	**13680**	**15196**	**17751**
#公园绿地面积	Public Green Areas	2700	3526	3898	4154	4756
四、年末绿化覆盖面积（公顷）	**Coverage Space of Green Areas at year-end (hectares)**	**12059**	**15646**	**17325**	**19017**	**21865**
五、建成区绿化覆盖率（%）	**Coverage of Green Areas in Developed Areas (%)**	**40.4**	**37.5**	**38.96**	**39.53**	**40.29**

注：本表数据来源于市建委。
2006年统计制度变化，"公共绿地面积"改为"公园绿地面积"。
2010年数据为全市口径，2009年以前数据为市区口径。

9-9 城市环境卫生

Urban Environment Sanitation

指　标	Item	2009	2010	2011	2012	2013
清扫面积（万平方米）	Area Under Cleaning Program (10 000 sq.m)	5285	6290	6411	6952	8725
清运生活垃圾（万吨）	Volume of Residential Garbage Disposal	179	237	265	287.32	290.76
	(10 000 tons)					
清运粪便（万吨）	Volume of Excrement and Urine	3	3	4	2.99	2.96
	Disposal (10 000 tons)	1131	1257	1493	1594	1770
公共厕所（座）	Number of Public Lavatories (units)					
市容环卫专用车辆（辆）	Special Vehicles of Environmental	939	1042	1200	1279	1639
	Sanitation (units)					

注：本表数据来源于市建委。
2010年后数据为全市口径，2009年以前数据为市区口径。

9-10 市区及县供水（2013年）

Urban Water Supply (2013)

指　标	Item	西安 Xi'an	市区 City	蓝田 Lantian	周至 ZhouZhi	户县 Huxian	高陵 GaoLing
年末水厂个数（个）	Number of Water Factory at Year-end (units)	15	11	1	1	1	1
供水综合生产能力	Total Volume of Water Supply	195.52	182.6	2.60	1.82	5.50	3.00
（万立方米/日）	(10 000 cu.m/day)						
#地下水	Groundwater	51.35	47.83		1.22	2.00	0.30
年末供水管道总长度	Length of Water Supply Pipelines	3385.33	2937.53	118.92	54.00	89.88	185.00
（公里）	at Year-end (km)						
全年供水总量	Total Annual Volume of Water Supply	51372.07	48445.13	602.06	443.50	1611.38	270.00
（万立方米）	(10 000 cu.m)						
#销售水量	Volume of Water Sales	44701.26	41914.32	580.06	414.50	1542.38	250.00
#生产运营用水	For Productive Use	6272.62	5785.94	53.70	11.40	403.58	18.00
居民家庭用水	For Residential Use	26138.73	24549.43	294.40	350.00	755.00	189.90
用水人口（万人）	Population with Access to Tap Water	444.35	390.92	15.45	7.30	16.70	13.98
	(10 000 persons)						

注：本表数据来源于市建委。
2009年部门统计制度变化，年末供水管道总长度和用水人口数调整。

9-11 市区及县供燃气（2013年）

Gas Supply in Urban Area (2013)

指　标	Item	西安 Xi'an	市区 City	蓝田 Lantian	周至 ZhouZhi	户县 Huxian	高陵 GaoLing
一、天然气	**Natural Gas**						
管道长度（公里）	Total Length of Gas Pipelines (km)	6163.39	5908.40	50.50	33.00	54.50	116.99
供气总量（万立方米）	Total Gas Supply(10 000 cu.m)	153488.90	147043.61	665.45	650.00	1425.00	3704.84
#销售气量	Volume of Gas Sales	147592.97	141244.13	664.00	638.00	1380.00	3666.84
#家庭用量	Residential Households	36671.17	31991.57	601.00	626.00	1243.20	2209.40
用气人口（万人）	Population with Access to Gas (10 000 persons)	410.56	389.91	2.95	1.50	8.62	7.58
二、液化石油气	**Liquefied Petroleum Gas**						
供气总量（吨）	Total Gas Supply (tons)	6047.90	2031.00	1466.40	1170.50	1010.00	370.00
#销售气量	Volume of Gas Sales	5986.20	2020.00	1466.20	1170.00	980.00	350.00
#家庭用量	Residential Households	4945.00	1200.00	1250.00	1165.00	980.00	350.00
用气人口（万人）	Population with Access to Gas (10 000 persons)	27.92	1.01	7.25	5.76	7.50	6.40

注：本表数据来源于市建委。

9-12 市区及县供热（2013年）

Heating in Urban Area (2013)

指　标	Item	西安 Xi'an	市区 City	蓝田 Lantian	周至 ZhouZhi	户县 Huxian	高陵 GaoLing
供热能力	Heating Capacity						
蒸气（吨/小时）	Steam (tons/hour)	4283.00	4053.00			230.00	
热水（兆瓦）	Hot Water (megawatts)	12691.10	5498.10				7193.00
供热总量(万吉焦)	Volume Supplied(10 000 gigajoules)						
蒸气	Steam	1667.88	1634.88			33.00	
热水	Hot Water	2990.38	2744.63				245.75
管道长度（公里）	Length of Pipelines (km)						
蒸气	Steam	204.33	192.33			12.00	
热水	Hot Water	608.12	581.02				27.10
供热面积（万平方米）	Heated Area (10 000sq.m)	10980.27	10579.00			50.00	351.27
#住宅	Residential Buildings	9874.54	9487.54			50.00	337.00

注：本表数据来源于市建委。

9-13 市区及县市政设施（2013年）

Municipal Facilities in Urban Area (2013)

指 标	Item	西安 Xi'an	市区 City	蓝田 Lantian	周至 ZhouZhi	户县 Huxian	高陵 GaoLing
一、道路长度（公里）	**Length of Roads (km)**	**3387.43**	**3081.14**	**71.60**	**36.40**	**114.70**	**83.59**
二、道路面积（万平方米）	**Area of Roads (10 000 sq.m)**	**7931.80**	**7017.19**	**127.06**	**76.40**	**442.08**	**269.07**
三、人行道面积（万平方米）	**Area of Sidewalks (10 000 sq.m)**	**2259.29**	**1989.30**	**55.30**	**33.10**	**92.72**	**88.87**
四、桥梁数（座）	**Number of Bridges (units)**	**432**	**414**	**10**	**2**	**3**	**3**
#立交桥	Crossroads	97	92			3	2
五、路灯盏数（盏）	**Number of Street Lights (units)**	**333393**	**311267**	**1576**	**4555**	**7235**	**8760**
六、排水管道长度（公里）	**Length of Drainage Pipelines (km)**	**4629.7**	**4191.7**	**78.5**	**43.0**	**127.2**	**189.3**
七、污水年排放量（万立方米）	**Annual Discharge Volume of Sewage (10 000 cu.m)**	**46186**	**43868**	**464**	**349**	**1289**	**216**
八、污水处理厂处理能力（万立方米/日）	**Daily Disposal Capacity of Sewage (10 000 cu.m/day)**	**153.1**	**146.5**	**1.5**	**1.1**	**3.0**	**1.0**
九、污水年处理量（万立方米）	**Yearly Disposal Capacity of Sewage Disposal Plant (10 000 cu.m)**	**41898**	**40139**	**351**	**264**	**982**	**162**

注：本表数据来源于市建委。

9-14 市区及县市政设施水平(2013年）

Urban Municipal Facilities in Urban Area (2013)

指 标	Item	西安 Xi'an	市区 City	蓝田 Lantian	周至 ZhouZhi	户县 Huxian	高陵 GaoLing
一、人均日生活用水量（升）	**Per Capita Daily Consumption of Tap Water For Residential Use (liters)**	**225.78**	**241.83**	**92.42**	**151.06**	**160.54**	**41.37**
二、用水普及率(%)	**Water-Consuming Popularization (%)**	**100**	**100**	**100**	**100**	**100**	**100**
三、每万人拥有公共交通车辆（标台）	**Number of Public Transport Vehicles Per 10 000 Population (units)**	**15.1**					
四、燃气普及率（%）	**Gas-Consuming Popularization (%)**	**98.68**	**100.00**	**66.02**	**99.45**	**96.53**	**100.00**
五、人均城市道路面积（平方米）	**Per Captia Area of Roads (sq.m)**	**17.85**	**17.95**	**8.22**	**10.47**	**26.47**	**19.25**
六、建成区排水管道密度（公里/平方公里）	**Density of Drainage Pipelines (km/sq.km)**	**9.17**	**9.89**	**6.54**	**4.30**	**5.37**	**5.41**
七、污水处理率(%)	**Rate of Sewerage Disposal (%)**	**90.72**	**91.50**	**75.65**	**75.64**	**76.18**	**75.00**
八、园林绿化	**Afforestation and Parks and Gardens**						
人均公园绿地面积（平方米）	Per Capita Public Green Areas (sq.m)	10.70	11.20	4.27	13.01	6.29	7.87
建城区绿地率（%）	Rate of Green Areas in Developed Areas(%)	32.32	33.80	28.98	17.10	35.32	17.89
九、生活垃圾无害化处理率(%)	**Rate of No Harm Disposal of Garbage (%)**	**93.95**	**99.86**		**100**		**100**

注：本表数据来源于市建委。

主要统计指标解释

建成区面积 城市行政区内实际已成片开发建设、市政公用设施和公共设施基本具备的区域。对核心城市，它包括集中连片的部分以及分散的若干个已经成片建设起来，市政公用设施和公共设施基本具备的地区；对一城多镇来说，它包括由几个连片开发建设起来的，市政公用设施和公共设施基本具备的地区组成。因此建成区范围，一般是指建成区外轮廓线所能包括的地区，也就是这个城市实际建设用地所达到的范围。

供水综合生产能力 指按供水设施取水、净化、送水、出厂输水干管等环节设计能力计算的综合生产能力。包括在原设计能力的基础上，经挖、革、改增加的生产能力。计算时，以四个环节中最薄弱的环节为主确定能力。

供水管道长度 指从送水泵至用户水表之间所有管道的长度。不包括新安装尚未使用、水厂内以及用户建筑物内的管道。在同一条街道埋设两条或两条以上管道时，应按每条管道的长度计算。

供水总量 指报告期供水企业（单位）供出的全部水量。包括有效供水量和漏损水量。

用水普及率 指报告期末城区内用水人口与总人口的比率。计算公式:

$$用水普及率=\frac{城区用水人口（含暂住人口）}{城区人口+城区暂住人口}\times 100\%$$

供气管道长度 指报告期末从气源厂压缩机的出口或门站出口至各类用户引入管之间的全部已经通气投入使用的管道长度。不包括煤气生产厂、输配站、液化气储存站、灌瓶站、储配站、气化站、混气站、供应站等厂（站）内的管道。

供气总量 指报告期燃气企业（单位）向用户供应的燃气数量。包括销售量和损失量。

燃气普及率 指报告期末城区内使用燃气的人口与总人口的比率。计算公式：

$$燃气普及率=\frac{城区用气人口（含暂住人口）}{城区人口+城区暂住人口}\times 100\%$$

供热能力 指供热企业（单位）向城市热用户输送热能的设计能力。不是热电厂的生产能力。

供热总量 指在报告期供热企业（单位）向城市热用户输送全部蒸汽和热水的总热量。

供热管道长度 指从各类热源到热用户建筑物接入口之间的全部蒸汽和热水的管道长度。不包括各类热源厂内部的管道长度。

供热面积 指供热企业（单位）向城市各类房屋建筑物、构筑物及其附属设施供热的全部建筑面积。

道路长度 指道路长度和与道路相通的桥梁、隧道的长度，按车行道中心线计算。

道路面积 指道路实际铺装面积和与道路相通的广场、桥梁、隧道的铺装面积（统计时， 人行道面积单独统计）。

人行道面积按道路两侧面积相加计算，包括步行街和广场，不含人车混行的道路。

排水管道长度 指所有排水总管、干管、支管、检查井及连接井进出口等长度之和。计算时按单管计算，即在同一条街道上如有两条或两条以上并排的排水管道时，应按每条排水管道的长度相加计算。

绿化覆盖面积 指城市中的乔木、灌木、草坪等所有植被的垂直投影面积。包括公园绿地、防护绿地、生产绿地、附属绿地、其他绿地的绿化种植覆盖面积、屋顶绿化覆盖面积以及零散树木的覆盖面积，不含各类绿地中的水域面积以及没有被植被覆盖的面积（硬化道路、无屋顶绿化的建筑物等）。乔木树冠下重迭的灌木和草本植物不重复计算。

人均城市道路面积 指报告期末城区内平均每人拥有的城市道路面积。计算公式：

$$人均城市道路面积=\frac{城区道路面积}{城区人口+城区暂住人口}$$

建成区排水管道密度 指报告期末建成区排水管道分布的疏密程度，计算公式：

$$排水管道密度=\frac{排水管道长度}{建成区面积}$$

污水处理率 指报告期内污水处理总量与污水排放总量的比率。计算公式：

$$污水处理率=\frac{污水处理总量}{污水排放总量}\times 100\%$$

人均公园绿地面积 指报告期末城区内平均每人拥有的公园绿地面积。计算公式：

$$人均公园绿地面积=\frac{城区公园绿地面积}{城区人口+城区暂住人口}$$

建成区绿地率 指报告期末建成区内绿地面积与建成区面积的比率。计算公式：

$$建成区绿地率\frac{建成区绿地面积}{建成区面积}\times 100\%$$

Explanatory Notes on Main Statistical Indicators

Area of the Constructed Regions refers to developed and built city administrative area where basic municipal utilities and public facilities complete constructed. To core city, it includes part of contiguous centralized and a number of decentralized part where basic municipal utilities and public facilities complete constructed. To a multi-city town, it consists of several contiguous developed and build area where municipal utilities and public facilities with basic composition. Therefore, the range of built-up area, generally refers to the built-up areas in the contour line, which is the actual construction site of the city achieved range

Production Capacity of Water Supply refers to the designed overall production capacity of water facilities, covering the four segments of water collection, purification, conveyance, and out flow through trunk pipelines. Increased capacity through transformation and innovation projects is included as well. The capacity is determined mainly on the weakest of the above-mentioned four segments.

Length of Water Supply Pipelines at Year–end refers to the total length of all the pipelines between the water pumps and the user water meters, excluding pipelines newly installed but not used yet, pipeline in the water factory, and pipeline in the user's buildings.

Volume of Water Supply refers to the total volume of water supplied by water-works(units) during the reference period, including both the effective water supply and loss during the water supply.

Coverage Rate of Urban Population with Access to Tap Water refers to the ratio of the urban population with access to tap water to the total urban population . The formula is :

$$\text{Coverage of urban population with access to tap water} = \frac{\text{Urban population with access to tap water}}{\text{Urban population}} \times 100\%$$

Length of Gas Pipeline refers to the total length of pipelines in use between the outlet of the compressor of gas-work of outlet gas stations and the leading pipe of users , excluding pipelines within gasworks , delivery stations ,LPG storage stations ,refilling stations, gas-mixing stations and supply stations.

Volume of Gas Supply refers to the total volume of gas provided to users by gas-producing enterprises (units) in a year ,including the volume sold and the volume lost .

Coverage Rate of Urban Population with Access to Gas refers to the ratio of the urban population with access to gas to the total urban population at the end of the reference period. The formula is :

$$\text{Coverage rate of urban population with access to gas} = \frac{\text{Urban population with access to gas}}{\text{Urban population}} \times 100\%$$

City Heating capacity in Urban Areas refers to the designed capacity of heating enterprises (units) in supplying heating energy to urban users during the reference period .

City Quantity of Heat Supplied in Urban Areas refers to the total quantity of heat from steam and hot water urban users by heating enterprises (units) during the reference period .

City Length of Urban Heating Pipelines refers to the total length of steam or hot water pipelines for sources of heat to the leading pipelines of the building of the users ,excluding internal pipelines in heat generating enterprises

Heated Area refers to the total structure area of heat supplied to urban constructions, structures and ancillary facilities by heating enterprises (units) during the reference period .

Length of Paved Roads refers to the length of roads with paved surface including bridges and tunnels connected with roads. Length of the roads is measured by the central lines .

Area of Paved Roads refers to the actual pavement area of roads and the actual pavement area of squares, bridges and tunnels connecting to the roads (the area of sidewalk pavements is calculated separately).

The area of sidewalk pavements is the sum of area of roads on sides of road, including pedestrian streets and squares, excluding roads for both pedestrians and vehicles .

Length of exhaust pipelines refers to the total length of all main drain piles ,trunk pipes ,branch pipes

,access manholes ,and connector well entrances and exits ,and so on . The whole length is calculated as of single pipes. Namely ,if there are two or more drain pipes parallel on a street ,the length of every pipe shall be summed .

Total area of green land refers to vertical projection area of all vegetation including trees, shrubs, lawns. Including parks, protective green space, production green space, green subsidiaries, green plants covering area, covering an area other green spaces, green roofs and covering area of scattered trees, excluding kinds of water area in kinds of green area and the area not covered by vegetation(hardened road, building of no green roof). shrubs and herbaceous plants overlap under the canopy of trees do not double counting.

Per Capita Area of Paved Roads refers to the area of urban roads per capita at the end of the reporting period. The formula is :

$$\text{Per capita area of paved roads} = \frac{\text{Area of urban roads}}{\text{Urban population+temporary resident population}}$$

Density of Drainage Pipelines refers to density of drainage pipelines in developed areas at the end of the reporting period .The formula is :

$$\text{Density of drainage pipelines} = \frac{\text{Length of drainage pipelines}}{\text{Ares of developed areas}}$$

Rate of Sewerage Disposal refers to the ratio of waste water disposed with the total discharge of waste water in the reporting period .The formula is:

$$\text{Rate of Sewerage Disposal} = \frac{\text{Waste Water Disposed}}{\text{Total Discharge of Waste Water}} \times 100\%$$

Per Capita Area of Public Green refers to the area of public green areas per capita at end of the reporting period .The formula is :

$$\text{Per capita area of public green} = \frac{\text{Area of public green areas}}{\text{Urban population+temporary resident population}}$$

Coverage of Green Areas in Developed Areas refers to the ratio of green areas in built-up areas with the area of developed areas at the end of reporting period . The formula is:

$$\text{Coverage of green land in developed areas} = \frac{\text{Area of green land in developed aresa}}{\text{Area of developed areas}} \times 100\%$$

10 环境保护

ENVIRONMENT PROTECTION

资料整理：李　炜
Data management: Li　Wei

第十部分　环境保护

一、简要说明

本章资料反映环境保护、工业污染排放及处理利用情况、危险废物集中处置情况、生活及其他污染情况和工业污染治理项目建设情况，由西安市统计局综合处根据西安市环保局提供的数据资料整理。

二、主要指标

工业用水重复利用率（%）	68.31	比上年提高	0.02个百分点
工业固体废物综合利用率（%）	95.43	比上年下降	0.49个百分点
全年环境空气达到二级以上天数（天）	138	比上年减少	168天

10　ENVIRONMENT PROTECTION

Ⅰ.Brief Introduction

This chapter contain information that reflect environment protection, discharge and treatment of industrial pollutant, centralized treatment of dangerous wastes, domestic pollution and other pollution, construction of projects of industrial pollution treatment. Data in this chapter is compiled by General Division of the Xi'an Bureau of Statistics according to the reported data from Environment Protection Administration department of the municipal government.

Ⅱ.Major Indicators

		Increase over Preceding Year
Percentage of Industrial Water Recycled (%)	68.31	0.02percentage points
Percentage of Industrial Solid Waste Utilized (%)	95.43	-0.49percentage points
Days of Air Quality up to the secondarylevels（day）	138	-168

10-1 城市环境保护（2013年）

Urban Environmental Protection (2013)

指　标	Item	2013
一、饮用水环境	**Potable Water Environment**	
全市饮用水水质达标率(%)	Compliance Rate of the City's Potable Water Quality (%)	100
二、大气环境	**Atmospheric Environment**	
1、可吸入颗粒物浓度年平均值(毫克/立方米)	Annual Average Concentration of Particulate Matters(mg/cu.m)	0.190
二氧化硫浓度年平均值	Annual Average Concentration of Sulphur Dioxide	0.046
二氧化氮浓度年平均值	Annual Average Concentration of Nitrogen Dioxide	0.057
2、全年环境空气质量达标天数(天)	Days of Air Quality up to the Standards(days)	138
全年环境空气质量达标率(%)	Annual compliance rate of Ambient Air Quality(%)	37.80
三、声环境	**Voice**	
1、功能区噪声平均值(dB(A))	Average Noise Value of Functional Districts(dB(A))	
0类区	Class 0	52.0
1类区	Class 1	54.0
2类区	Class 2	59.0
3类区	Class 3	63.0
4类区	Class 4	68.0
2、道路交通噪声平均值(dB(A))	Average Noise Value of Road Traffic(dB(A))	68.2
3、区域噪声平均值(dB(A))	Average Noise Value of Region(dB(A))	55.3
四、环境污染治理	**Environmental pollution treatment**	
当年完成环保验收项目环境保护投资（亿元）	Year Completed Investment in Environmental Protection Projects of Environmental acceptance(100 million yuan)	7.6

注：本表数据来源于市环保局。

10-2 主要年份工业“三废”排放及处理利用情况

指　标	Item	2000	2006	2007
一、工业废水排放量（万吨）	**Volume of Waste Water Discharge (10 000 tons)**	**9145**	**16389**	**19069**
工业废水处理量（万吨）	Volume of Industrial Wastewater Disposal (10 000 tons)			
废水治理设施数（套）	Number of Facilities for Treatment of Waste Water (sets)			
二、工业废气排放量（亿立方米）	**Total Volume of Industrial Waste Gas Emission (100 million cu.m)**	**275.97**	**642.51**	**1149.41**
废气治理设施数（套）	Number of Facilities for Treatment of Waste Gas(sets)		466	846
三、工业固体废物产生量（万吨）	**Volume of Industrial Solid Wastes Produced (10 000 tons)**	107	161	193
工业固体废物处置量（万吨）	Volume of Industrial Solid Wastes Treated (10 000 tons)	20	5	6
工业固体废物综合利用量（万吨）	Volume of Industrial Solid Waste Utilized (10 000 tons) in a Comprehensive Way	63	143	171
工业固体废物综合利用率（%）	Percentage of Volume of Industrial Solid Waste Utilized in a Comprehensive Way(%)	58.88	89.07	88.48
四、工业锅炉（台/蒸吨）	**Industrial Boilers (units/tons)**			

注：本表数据来源于市环保局。

2010年全国统一进行了污染源普查动态更新调查工作，“十二五”的环境统计体系与污染源普查体系相衔接，与“十一五”环境统计口径不同。

Discharge and Treatrment of Waste Gas, Water & Solid Wastes in Repersentative Years

2008	2009	2010	2011	2012	2013
18304	**13168**	**13840.00**	**13148.00**	**10223.73**	**8972.97**
		10673.52	12632.38	9089.04	6798.71
		267	314	312	295
1519.18	**737.24**	**791.56**	**1018.46**	**1043.31**	**844.11**
920	852	816	745	649	661
220	246	267.29	279.00	259.14	255.78
5	4.85	3.56	6.00	9.24	9.68
215	241	262	271.00	248.58	244.08
97.78	97.83	98.05	97.30	95.92	95.43
		503/8785	**576/13466**	**567/14565**	**520/14177**

10-3 工业污染排放及处理利用情况（2013年）

Discharge and Treatment of Industrial Pollution (2013)

指　标	Item	2013
一、被调查企业基本情况	**Basic condition of Enterprises investigated**	
1. 企业数（个）	Number of Enterprises (units)	431
2. 工业总产值（亿元）（当年价格）	Gross Industry Output Value (100 millian yuan)	1924.75
3. 工业锅炉数（台/蒸吨）	Industrial Boilers (units/tons)	520/14177
4. 工业炉窑数（座）	Number of Industrial Grates (items)	224
二、工业废水	**Industrial Waste Water**	
1. 工业用水总量（万吨）	Total Volume of Industrial Water (10 000 tons)	44480.28
#新鲜水量	Volume of Fresh Water	14097.66
重复用水量	Volume of Water Recycled	30382.62
2. 工业用水重复利用率（%）	Percentage of Industrial Water Recycled (%)	68.31
3. 废水治理设施数（套）	Number of Facilities for Treatment of Waste Water (sets)	295
4. 废水治理设施处理能力（万吨/日）	Disposal Capacity of Facilities for Treatment of Waste Water (10 000 tons/day)	27.54
5. 废水治理设施运行费用（万元）	Operating Expense of Facilities for Treatment of Waste Water (10 000 yuan)	13312.3
6. 工业废水排放量（万吨）	Volume of Industrial Waste Water Discharged (10 000 tons)	8972.97
三、工业废气	**Industrial Waste Gas**	
1. 煤炭消费量（万吨）	Total Coal Consumption (10 000 tons)	802.49
2. 燃料油消费量（不含车船用）（万吨）	Fuel Oil Consumption (10 000 tons)	1.14
3. 天然气消费量（亿立方米）	Natural Gas Consumption (100 millian cu.m)	1.77
4. 工业废气排放总量（亿立方米）	Total Volume of Industrial Waste Gas Emission (100 millian cu.m)	844.11
5. 废气治理设施数（套）	Number of Facilities for Treatment of Waste Gas (sets)	661
6. 废气治理设施处理能力（万立方米/时）	Disposal Capacity of Facilities for Treatment of Waste Gas (10 000 cu.m./h)	2816.62
7. 废气治理设施设备运行费用（万元）	Operating Expense of Facilities for Treatment of Waste gas(10 000 yuan)	27280.7
8. 二氧化硫去除量（吨）	Volume of Sulphur Dioxide Removed (tons)	146422.12
9. 二氧化硫排放量（吨）	Volume of Sulphur Dioxide Emission (tons)	64664.15
10. 氮氧化物生产量（吨）	Production of nitrogen oxides(tons)	45867.51
11. 氮氧化物排放量（吨）	Nitrogen oxide emissions(tons)	34921.76
12. 烟（粉）尘生产量（吨）	Tobacco (powder) dust production(tons)	1281383.91
13. 烟（粉）尘排放量（吨）	The smoke (powder) dust emissions(tons)	13658.34
四、工业固体废物	**Industrial Solid Waste**	
1. 工业固体废物产生量（万吨）	Volume of Industrial Solid Waste Produced (10 000tons)	255.78
2. 工业固体废物综合利用量（万吨）	Volume of Industrial Solid Waste Utilized (10 000tons)	244.08
3. 工业固体废物综合利用率（%）	Percentage of Industrial Solid Waste Utilized (%)	95.43
4. 工业固体废物贮存量（万吨）	Volume of Industrial Solid Waste Accumulated (10 000tons)	2.02
5. 工业固体废物处置量（万吨）	Volume of Industrial Solid Waste Treated (10 000tons)	9.68
6. 工业固体废物倾倒丢弃量（万吨）	Volume of Industrial Solid Waste Discharged (10 000tons)	0

注：本表数据来源于市环保局。

10-4 城市污水排放及处理情况（2013年）

Discharge and Treatment of City Sewage(2013)

指　标	Item	2013
一、污水处理厂数（座）	**Number of Sewage Treatment Works(units)**	**26**
污水处理厂处理能力（万吨/日）	Daily Disposal Capacity of Sewage(10 000 tons/day)	147.41
二、污水处理	**Sewgae Disposal**	
污水实际处理量（万吨）	Volume of Sewgae Disposal(10 000 tons)	33212.09
生活污水处理量	Volume of Domestic Sewgae Disposal	31038.47
工业污水处理量	Volume of Industrial Sewage Disposal	2173.62
三、再生水	**Recycled water**	
生产量（万吨）	Production(10 000 tons)	1291.97
利用量（万吨）	Utilization(10 000 tons)	1248.27
四、化学需氧量去除量（吨）	**Volume of COD Removed (tons)**	**93919.92**
五、氨氮去除量（吨）	**Volume of Ammonia and Nitrogen Removed(tons)**	**9409.94**
六、总磷去除量（吨）	**Volume of Total Phosphorus Removed(tons)**	**1186.97**
七、污泥生产量（万吨）	**Volume of Sludge Produced(10 000 tons)**	**25.69**
八、污泥处置量（万吨）	**Volume of Sludge Disposal(10 000 tons)**	**25.69**
九、污泥倾倒丢弃量（吨）	**Dumping sludge discards (tons)**	**0**
十、本年运行费用（万元）	**Operating Expense(10 000 yuan)**	**44289.88**

注　本表数据来源于市环保局。

10-5 危险废物（医疗废物）集中处理情况(2013年)

Condition of Collected Dangerous Wastes Treated (2013)

指　标	Item	2013
一、危险废物集中处理（置）厂数（个）	**Number of Colleted Dangerous Wastes Treated Plants(items)**	**1**
二、医疗废物集中处理（置）厂数（个）	**The number of Manufacturing Plants of Medical waste treatment (units)**	**1**
三、危险废物设计处置能力（吨/日）	**Design hazardous waste disposal capacity (tons / day)**	**3363.7**
四、实际处置危险废物量（吨）	**The actual amount of hazardous waste disposal (tons)**	**84970.55**
五、危险废物综合利用量（吨）	**Volume of Dangerous Wastes Utilized in a Comprehensive Way (tons)**	**1390**
六、焚烧残渣流向（千克）	**Flow Direction of Residuum after Burning (kg)**	
1. 焚烧残渣量	Volume of Residuum after Burning	405000.00
2. 焚烧残渣安全填进处理量	Secure landfill disposal incineration residues	405000.00
3. 焚烧飞灰生产量	Fly ash production	70200.00
4. 焚烧飞灰安全填进处理量	Fly ash landfill disposal safety	70200.00
七、当年运行费用（万元）	**Operating Expenses in Current year(10 000 yuan)**	**6809.28**

注：本表数据来源于市环保局。

10-6 生活及其他污染情况(2013年)

Domestic Pollution and Other conditions (2013)

指　标	Item	2013
一、基本情况	**Basic Condition**	
1. 生活天然气消费量（万立方米）	Volume of Living natural gas consumption (10 000 cu.m)	100924
2. 生活用水总是（万吨）	Volume of Living water (10 000 tons)	42676.325
二、污染排放情况	**Discharge of Pollutant**	
1. 城镇生活污水排放量（万吨）	Volume of Urban Domestic Sewage Discharged(10 000 tons)	29134.785
2. 生活污水处理量（万吨）	Volume of Domestic Sewgae Disposal(10 000 tons)	26658.33
3. 生活CDD生产量（吨）	Volume of Life CDD production (tons)	156825.45
4. 生活CDD排放量（吨）	Volume of Life CDD emissions (tons)	62905.53
5. 生活氨氮生产量（吨）	Volume of Ammonia and Nitrogen in Urban Domestic Sewage Produced (tons)	20085.4
6. 生活氨氮排放量（吨）	Volume of Ammonia and Nitrogen in Urban Domestic Sewage Discharged (tons)	10675.46
7. 二氧化硫排放量（吨）	Volume of Domestic and Other Sulphur Dioxide Emission (tons)	33270.66
8. 氨氮化物排放量（吨）	Volume of Ammonia and Nitrogen in Urban Domestic Sewage Discharged (tons)	10950.63
9. 烟尘排放量（吨）	Volume of Soot Emission (tons)	12772.04

注：本表数据来源于市环保局。

10-7 工业污染治理项目建设情况(2013年)

Condition of Anti-Industrial-Pollution Projects (2013)

指　标	Item	2013
一、工业企业数（个）	**Number of Industrial Enterprises (units)**	**18**
二、老工业污染源项目治理本年施工总数（个）	**The total number of construction projects of Old industrial pollution sources control this year(units)**	**11**
#工业废水治理项目	Treatment of Waste Water	4
工业废气治理项目	Treatment of Waste Gas	7
工业固体废物治理项目	Treatmen of Solid Wastes	0
三、老工业污染源项目治理本年竣工总数（个）	**The Total Number of Old Industrial Pollution Control Projects Completed this year(units)**	**12**
#工业废水治理项目	Treatment of Waste Water	8
工业废气治理项目	Treatment of Waste Gas	4
工业固体废物治理项目	Treatmen of Solid Wastes	0
四、老工业污染源治理项目本年完成投资（万元）	**Investment completed in Old industrial pollution control projects this Year(10 000 yuan)**	**46185.43**
#废水治理项目	Treatment of Waste Water	41060.4
废气治理项目	Treatment of Waste Gas	5125.03
固体废物治理项目	Treatmen of Solid Wastes	0
五、老工业污染源治理项目本年投资来源（万元）	**Source of Investment in Old industrial pollution control projects this Year(10 000 yuan)**	
#排污费补助	Pollution Charges Subsidies	0
政府其他补助	Other Government Subsidies	2189.6
企业自筹	Self-raising Funds	43995.83
六、"三同时"项目竣工验收数（个）	**number of "Three simultaneous" project completion and acceptance (a)**	**6**
七、"三同时"竣工验收项目实际环保投资（万元）	**"Three simultaneous" actual environmental investment completed and accepted (10 000 yuan)**	**2415**
八、"三同时"项目废水治理新增处理能力（万吨/日）	**"Three simultaneous"Add processing capacity of wastewater treatment (10 000 tons / day)**	**0.141**
九、"三同时"项目废气治理新增处理能力（万立方米/时）	**"Three simultaneous"Add processing capacity of Exhaust treatment (10 000 cu.m/h)**	**500.01**

注：本表数据来源于市环保局。

"三同时"指建设项目中防治污染的措施，必须与主体工程同时设计，同时施工，同时投产使用。

10-8 各区县、开发区环境保护基本情况（2013年）

区县、开发区	Region	本年完成环保验收项目环保投资额（万元）Investment Completed in accepted Environmental projects this year (10 000 yuan)	工业二氧化硫排放量（吨）Volume of Industrial Sulphur Dioxide Discharged (tons)
全　市	**Total**	**119563.2**	**64664.148**
市本级	city	75956.1	
新城区	Xincheng	1510.8	55.47
碑林区	Beilin	80.0	1678.28
莲湖区	Lianhu	2716.5	3985.93
灞桥区	Baqiao	1658.0	8205.4
未央区	Weiyang	4840.5	1096.93
雁塔区	Yanta	4450.8	1079.66
阎良区	Yanliang	2374.6	1874.14
临潼区	Lintong	3464.7	1548.91
长安区	Chang'an	2944.0	2386.13
蓝田县	Lantian	0	577.25
周至县	Zhouzhi	560.0	261.41
户　县	Huxian	1960.0	6910.84
高陵县	Gaoling	4683.5	652.55
高新开发区	Gaoxinkaifaqu	10662.5	994.76
经济开发区	Jingjikaifaqu	658.5	2396.96
航天基地	Hangtianjidi	979.0	487.66
浐东新城	Fendongxincheng	63.7	30471.86

注：本表数据来源于市环保局。
　　环境统计中污水处理厂个数包含部分大学园区及部分大型小区的污水处理厂。

Condition of Environment Protection by Regions (2013)

工业化学需氧量排放量（吨） Volume of COD Removed (tons)	垃圾处理站数（座） Number of Rubbish Disposal Works (units)	污水处理厂数（个） Number of Sewage Treatment Works (units)
21604.88	**2**	**26**
331.76		
25.23		
1090.2		1
1263.59	1	2
2057.55		3
107.26		2
104.01		1
201.6		2
85.53		7
35.07		2
134.69		1
5203.32		2
159.58	1	1
1495.99		1
700.4		1
8248.34		
360.75		

主 要 统 计 指 标 解 释

工业用水 指工矿企业在生产过程中用于制造、加工、冷却、空调、净化、洗涤等方面的用水，按新水取用量计，不包括企业内部的重复利用水量。

工业废水排放量 指经过企业厂区所有排放口排到企业外部的工业废水量。包括生产废水、外排的直接冷却水、超标排放的矿井地下水和与工业废水混排的厂区生活污水，不包括外排的间接冷却水（清污不分流的间接冷却水应计算在内）。

直接排入海的 指经企业位于海边的排放口，直接排入海的废水量。直接排放指废水经过工厂的排污口直接排入海，而未经过城市下水道或其他中间体，也不受其他水体的影响。

工业废水排放达标量 指报告期内废水中各项污染物指标都达到国家或地方排放标准的外排工业废水量，包括未经处理外排达标的，经废水处理设施处理后达标排放的，以及经污水处理厂处理后达标排放的。

生活污水排放量 指城镇居民每年排放的生活污水。用人均系数法测算。测算公式为：

$$\frac{\text{生活污水}}{\text{排放量}} = \frac{\text{城镇生活污水}}{\text{排放系数}} \times \frac{\text{市镇非}}{\text{农业人口}} \times 365$$

生活污水中化学需氧量（COD）排放量 指城镇居民每年排放的生活污水中的COD的量。用人均系数法测算。测算公式为：

$$\frac{\text{城镇生活污水中}}{\text{COD产生系数}} = \frac{\text{城镇牛活污水}}{\text{中COD排放量}} \times \frac{\text{市镇非}}{\text{农业人口}} \times 365$$

化学需氧量（COD） 指用化学氧化剂氧化水中有机污染物时所需的氧量。COD值越高，表示水中有机污染物污染越重。

工业废气排放量 指报告期内企业厂区内燃料燃烧和生产工艺过程中产生的各种排入大气的含有污染物的气体的总量，以标准状态（273K，101325Pa）计算。测算公式为：

$$\frac{\text{工业废气}}{\text{排放量}} = \frac{\text{燃料燃烧过程}}{\text{中废气排放量}} + \frac{\text{生产工艺过程}}{\text{中废气排放量}}$$

生活及其他SO_2排放量 以生活及其他煤炭消费量和其含硫量为基础，根据以下公式计算：

$$\frac{\text{生活及其他}}{SO_2\text{排放量}} = \frac{\text{生活及其他}}{\text{煤炭消费量}} \times \text{含硫量} \times 0.8 \times 2$$

工业SO_2排放量 指报告期内企业在燃料燃烧和生产工艺过程中排入大气的SO_2总量，计算公式为：

$$\frac{\text{工业}SO_2}{\text{排放量}} = \frac{\text{燃料燃烧过程}}{\text{中}SO_2\text{排放量}} + \frac{\text{生产工艺过程}}{\text{中}SO_2\text{排放量}}$$

工业烟尘排放量 指企业厂区内燃料燃烧过程中产生的烟气中夹带的颗粒物排放量。

生活及其他烟尘排放量 指除工业生产活动以外的所有社会、经济活动及公共设施的经营活动中燃烧所排放的烟尘纯重量。以生活及其他煤炭消费量为基础进行测算。

工业粉尘排放量 指企业在生产工艺过程中排放的能在空气中悬浮一定时间的固体颗粒物排放量。如钢铁企业的耐火材料粉尘、焦化企业的筛焦系统粉尘、烧结机的粉尘、石灰窑的粉尘、建材企业的水泥粉尘等。不包括电厂排入大气的烟尘。

工业固体废物产生量 指报告期内企业在生产过程中产生的固体状、半固体状和高浓度液体状废弃物的总量，包括危险废物、冶炼废渣、粉煤灰、炉渣、煤矸石、尾矿、放射性废物和其他废物等；不包括矿开采的剥离废石和掘进废石（煤矸石和呈酸性或碱性的废石除外）。酸性或碱性废石指采掘的废石其流经水、雨淋水的pH值小于4或pH值大于10.5者。

危险废物 指列入国家危险废物名录或根据国家规定的危险废物鉴别标准和鉴别方法认定的，具有爆炸性、易燃性、易氧化性、毒性、腐蚀性、易传染疾病等危险特性之一的废物。

工业固体废物综合利用量 指报告期内企业通过回收、加工、循环、交换等方式，从固体废物中提取或者使其转化为可以利用的资源、能源和其他原材料的固体废物量（包括当年利用往年的工业固体废物贮存量），如用作农业肥料、生产建筑材料、筑路等。综合利用量由原产生固体废物的单位统计。

工业固体废物综合利用率 指工业固体废物综合利用量占丁业固体废物产生量（包括综合利用往年贮存量）的百分率。计算公式为：

$$\text{工业固体废物综合利用率}=\frac{\text{工业固体废物综合利用量}}{\text{工业固体废物产生量}+\text{综合利用往年贮存量}}\times 100\%$$

工业固体废物贮存量 指报告期内企业以综合利用或处置为目的，将固体废物暂时贮存或堆存在专设的贮存设施或专设的集中堆存场所内的数量。专设的固体废物贮存场所或贮存设施必须有防扩散、防流失、防渗漏、防止污染大气、水体的措施。

工业固体废物处置量 指报告期内企业将固体废物焚烧或者最终置于符合环境保护规定要求的场所，并不再回取的工业固体废物量（包括当年处置往年的工业固体废物贮存量）。处置方式有填埋（其中危险废物应安全填埋）、焚烧、专业贮存场（库）封场处理、深层灌注、回填矿井及海洋处置（经海洋管理部门同意投海处置）等。

工业固体废物排放量 指报告期内企业将所产生的固体废物排到固体废物污染防治设施、场所以外的数量，不包括矿山开采的剥离废石和掘进废石（煤矸石和呈酸性或碱性的废石除外）。

“三废”综合利用产品产值 指报告期内利用“三废”作为主要原料生产的产品价值（现行价）；已经销售或准备销售的应计算产品价值，留作生产自用的不应计算产品价值。

生活垃圾清运量 指报告期内收集和运送到各生活垃圾处理厂（场）和生活垃圾最终消纳点的生活垃圾数量。生活垃圾指城市日常生活或为城市日常生活提供服务的活动中产生的固体废物以及法律行政规定的视为城市生活垃圾的固体废物。包括：居民生活垃圾、商业垃圾、集市贸易市场垃圾、街道清扫垃圾、公共场所垃圾和机关、学校、厂矿等单位的生活垃圾。

生活垃圾无害化处理率 指报告期生活垃圾无害化处理量与生活垃圾产生量的比率。在统计上，由于生活垃圾产生量不易取得，可用清运量代替。计算公式为：

$$\text{生活垃圾无害化处理率}=\frac{\text{生活垃圾无害化处理量}}{\text{生活垃圾产生量}}\times 100\%$$

Explanatory Notes on Main Statistical Indicators

Water Use by Industry refers to new withdrawals of water, excluding reuse of water within enterprises.

Waste Water Discharged by Industry refers to the volume of waste water discharged by industrial enterprises through all their outlets, including waste water from production process, directly cooled water, groundwater from mining wells which does not meet discharge standards and sewage from households mixed with waste water produced by industrial activities, but excluding indirectly cooled water discharged (It should be included if the discharge is not separated from waste water).

Waste Water Directly Discharged into Sea refers to the volume of waste water directly discharged into sea through outlets of enterprises situated by sea without going through municipal sewerage networks or any other intermediates or being affected by any other water bodies.

Industrial Waste Water Meeting Discharge Standards refers to volume of industrial waste water discharge which, with or without treatment, reaches national or local standards with regard to all pollutants.

Urban Non-industrial Waste Water Discharge refers to annual discharge of non-industrial waste water by urban households. It is estimated by per capita coefficient using the formula:

$$\begin{array}{c}\text{Urban non-industrial}\\\text{waste water discharge}\end{array} = \begin{array}{c}\text{urban non-industrial waste}\\\text{water discharge coefficient}\end{array} \times \begin{array}{c}\text{urban non-alagricultur}\\\text{population}\end{array} \times 365$$

Volume of Chemical Oxygen Demand (COD) Generated by Urban Non-industrial Waster Water refers to chemical oxygen demand generated through the annual discharge of non-industrial waste water by urban households. It is estimated as:

$$\begin{array}{c}\text{Volume of chemical oxygen}\\\text{demand (cod) generated}\\\text{by urban non-industrial}\\\text{waster water}\end{array} = \begin{array}{c}\text{Coefficient of COD}\\\text{generated through urban}\\\text{non-industrial waste water}\end{array} \times \begin{array}{c}\text{urban}\\\text{non-agricultura}\\\text{population}\end{array} 1365$$

Chemical Oxygen Demand (COD) refers to the amount of oxygen required when chemical oxidants are used to oxidize organic pollutants in water. A higher value of COD corresponds to more serious pollution by organic pollutants.

Industrial Waste Air Emission refers to the discharge into atmosphere of waste air containing pollutants generated from fuel burning and production processes in enterprises within a given period of time. It is calculated at standard status (273K, 101325Pa) as:

$$\begin{array}{c}\text{Industrial waste}\\\text{air emission}\end{array} = \begin{array}{c}\text{tnoissimehrough}\\\text{fuel burning}\end{array} + \begin{array}{c}\text{tnoissimehrough}\\\text{production process}\end{array}$$

SO_2 Emission through Non-industrial and Other Activities is calculated on the basis of consumption of coal by households and other activities and the sulphur content of coal with the following formula:

$$\begin{array}{c}SO_2\text{ emission}\\\text{through non-}\\\text{industrial and}\\\text{other activities}\end{array} = \begin{array}{c}\text{of coalby}\\\text{households}\\\text{andother}\\\text{activities}\end{array} \times \begin{array}{c}\text{sulphur}\\\text{content}\end{array} \times 0.8 \times 2$$

SO_2 Emission through Industrial Activities refers to volume of sulphur dioxide emission from fuel burning and production process by enterprises during a given period of time. It is calculated as:

$$\begin{array}{c}SO_2\text{ emission}\\\text{through industrial}\\\text{activities}\end{array} = \begin{array}{c}SO_2\text{emIssIon from}\\\text{fuel burning}\end{array} + \begin{array}{c}SO_2\text{ emission from}\\\text{production process}\end{array}$$

Industrial Soot Emission refers to the volume of soot in smoke emitted in the process of fuel burning in the premises of enterprises.

Soot Emission by Consumption and Others refers to the net volume of soot emitted by fuel burning from all social and economic activities and operations of public facilities other than industrial activities. It is calculated on the basis of coal consumption by households and others.

Industrial Dust Emission refers to volume of dust emitted by production process of enterprises and suspended in the air for a given period of time, including dust from refractory material of iron and steel works, dust from coke-screening systems and sintering machines of coke plants, dust from lime kilns and dust from cement production in building material enterprises, but excluding soot and dust emitted from power plants.

Industrial Solid Wastes Produced refers to total volume of solid, semi-solid and high concentration liquid residues produced by industrial enterprises from production process in a given period of time, including hazardous wastes, slag, coal ash, gangue, tailings, radioactive residues and other wastes, but excluding stones stripped or dug out in mining - gangue and acid or alkaline stones not included (a stone is acid or alkaline according to the pH value of the water being below 4 or above 10.5 when the stone is in, or soaked by water).

Hazardous Wastes refers to those included in the national hazardous wastes catalogue or specified as any one of the following properties in the national hazardous wastes identification standards: explosive, ignitable, oxidizable, toxic, corrosive or liable to cause infectious diseases or lead to other dangers.

Industrial Solid Wastes Utilized refers to volume of solid wastes from which useful materials can be extracted or which can be converted into usable resources, energy or other materials by means of reclamation, processing, recycling and exchange (including utilizing in the year the stocks of industrial solid wastes of the previous year). Examples of such utilizations include fertilizers, building materials and road materials. The information shall be collected by the producing units of the wastes.

Rate of Utilization of Industrial Solid Wastes refers to the percentage of industrial solid wastes utilized over industrial solid wastes produced (including stocks of the previous years). It is calculated as:

$$\text{Rate of utilization of industrial solid wastes} = \frac{\text{volume of industrial solid wastes utilized}}{\text{industrial solid wastes produced} + \text{stock of previous years}} \times 100\%$$

Stock of Industrial Solid Wastes refers to the volume of solid wastes placed in special facilities or special sites for purposes of utilization or disposal. The sites or facilities should take measures against dispersion, loss, seepage, and air and water contamination.

Industrial Solid Wastes Disposed refers to the quantity of industrial solid wastes which are burnt or placed ultimately in the sites meeting the requirements for environmental protection and not salvaged or recycled (including disposition in the year of those wastes of previous years). The disposition includes landfill (Safe landfills should be conducted for hazardous wastes), incineration, containment spaces, deep underground disposal, backfill in mining pits and disposal at sea.

Industrial Solid Wastes Discharged refers to the volume of industrial solid wastes discharged by producing enterprises to disposal facilities or to other sites. The wastes exclude stones stripped or dug from mining (gangue and acid or alkaline waste stones not included).

Output Value of Products Made from Waste Gas, Waste Water and Solid Wastes refers to the current value of products with waste gas, waste water and solid wastes as main materials of production. Products sold and ready to sell shall be included while those produced for own use shall not be included.

Consumption Wastes Transported refers to volume of consumption wastes collected and transported to disposal factories or sites. Consumption wastes are solid wastes produced from urban households or from service activities for urban households, and solid wastes regarded by laws and regulations as urban consumption wastes, including those from households, commercial activities, markets, cleaning of streets, public sites, offices, schools, factories, mining units and other sources.

Ratio of Consumption Wastes Treated refers to consumption wastes treated over that produced. In practical statistics, as it is difficult to estimate, the volume of consumption wastes produced is replaced with that transported. It is calculated as:

$$\text{Ratio of consumption wastes treated} = \frac{\text{consumption wastes treated}}{\text{consumption wastes produced}} \times 100\%$$

11 农业

AGRICULTURE

资料整理：张喜兰　马秋娟　薛　丰
Data management:Zhang Xilan　Ma Qiujuan　Xue Feng

第十一部分　农业

一、简要说明

本章资料主要包括农村基本情况、农业生产条件与生产情况、耕地、农林牧渔及服务业产值、主要农产品产量以及各区县农业生产和农村经济效益主要指标，由西安市统计局农村处提供。

二、主要指标

年末耕地面积（万亩）	366.23	比上年下降	1.0%
农林牧渔及服务业总产值（亿元）	342.89	比上年增长	4.9%
农作物播种面积（万亩）	695.53	比上年下降	0.8%
粮食产量（万吨）	183.12	比上年下降	4.9%

11　AGRICULTURE

Ⅰ.Brief Introduction

Data in this chapter reflects basic condition of agriculture production of Xi'an city. It is primarily consist of basic condition of rural area, condition of agriculture production, plow land, production value of farming, forestry, animal husbandry and fishery, gross yield of primary produce and primary indicators of agriculture production and rural area economic performance. The data are provided and compiled by Rural Area Division of the Xi'an Bureau of Statistics.

Ⅱ.Major Indicators

		Increase over Preceding Year
Cultivated Area Year-end(10 000 mu)	366.23	-1.0%
Gross Output Value of Farming, Forestry, Animal Husbandry, Fishery and Service(100 mil. Yuan)	342.89	4.9%
Sown Area of Crops(10 000 mu)	695.53	-0.8%
Grain Output(10 000 tons)	183.12	-4.9%

11-1 主要年份农村户数、人口和劳动力情况

Grass-roots Households, Population and Labor Resources in Rural Area

指 标	Item	2008	2009	2010	2011	2012	2013
一、乡村户数（万户）	**Number of Households (10 000 households)**	**101.02**	**101.00**	**101.43**	**102.59**	**101.92**	**101.37**
二、农村人口和从业人员情况	**Rural Population and Employment**						
1. 乡村劳动力资源总数（万人）	Total Number of Rural Labor Source (10 000 persons)	256.17	255.00	256.36	260.97	259.06	257.96
2. 乡村从业人员数（万人）	Rural Laborers(10 000 persons)	223.85	223.13	225.04	230.55	226.92	222.67
# 女性	Female	103.11	102.76	103.25	109.61	107.63	106.70
#农业	Laborers of Farming	126.46	121.78	116.58	116.15	113.29	108.48
三、自来水受益村数（个）	**Number of Villages Benefited from the Tap Water System(unit)**	**1934**	**2058**	**2184**	**2400**	**2545**	**2650**
四、通汽车村数（个）	**Number of Villages Accessible by motor Vehicles (unit)**	**2996**	**2989**	**2989**	**2978**	**2936**	**2927**
五、通电话村数（个）	**Number of Villages Accessible by Telephone (unit)**	**3086**	**3071**	**3052**	**3033**	**2974**	**2966**

11-2 各区县乡村从业人员数（2013年）

Number of Labours in Families by Region（2013）

单位：万人 (10 000 persons)

区 县	Region	乡村劳动力资源总数 Total Number of Rural Labor Source	乡村从业人员数合计 Rural Laborers Total	#女性 Female	#农林牧渔业 Farming,Forestry Animal Husbandry and Fishery
合 计	**Total**	**257.96**	**222.67**	**106.70**	**108.48**
新城区	Xincheng				
碑林区	Beilin				
莲湖区	Lianhu				
灞桥区	Baqiao	18.78	15.77	6.61	5.36
未央区	Weiyang	12.46	8.26	3.79	2.53
雁塔区	Yanta	7.27	5.50	2.60	0.20
阎良区	Yanliang	10.73	9.52	4.58	4.40
临潼区	Lintong	36.26	31.96	15.18	16.99
长安区	Chang'an	54.33	48.29	20.95	19.27
蓝田县	Lantian	34.13	33.39	21.91	21.18
周至县	Zhouzhi	40.20	32.92	13.83	18.19
户 县	Huxian	33.31	28.48	13.20	16.17
高陵县	Gaoling	10.49	8.58	4.05	4.19

11-3 主要年份耕地面积

Area of Cultivated Land in Representatives Years

单位：万亩 (10 000 mu)

年 份 Year	年末实有耕地面积 Cultivated Area Year-end	水田 Paddy Field	水浇地 Irrigable Land
1970	554.09	18.20	297.05
1975	538.35	20.34	349.13
1978	530.96	16.70	370.46
1980	526.29	17.45	372.96
1985	508.88	17.63	328.10
1990	495.32	17.97	311.91
1992	485.30	16.44	298.19
1993	479.04	14.36	304.49
1994	471.44	13.98	299.58
1995	463.97	17.04	278.01
1996	451.50	14.21	283.76
1997	456.62	11.90	290.49
1998	455.15	11.18	282.23
1999	450.74	11.31	281.96
2000	443.37	10.26	284.04
2001	431.69	9.00	274.73
2002	424.46	7.98	275.96
2003	413.84	6.65	263.75
2004	404.87	6.59	254.04
2005	400.17	5.55	254.04
2006	395.79	5.33	263.75
2007	391.77	4.80	255.95
2008	390.77	4.64	255.36
2009	387.89	4.39	260.71
2010	383.32	4.03	257.43
2011	377.10	3.80	253.46
2012	369.91	3.32	248.97
2013	366.23	2.46	237.39

11-4 各区县耕地面积（2013年）

单位：亩

区 县	Region	年末实有耕地面积 Cultivated Area Year-end	水田 Paddy Field	旱地 Dry Land	水浇地 Irrigable Land
合 计	**Total**	**3662255**	**24632**	**3637623**	**2373908**
新城区	Xincheng				
碑林区	Beilin				
莲湖区	Lianhu				
灞桥区	Baqiao	147597		147597	79450
未央区	Weiyang	20790		20790	20790
雁塔区	Yanta	6511		6511	5260
阎良区	Yanliang	235438		235438	226295
临潼区	Lintong	703094		703094	524551
长安区	Chang'an	653690	21848	631842	332374
蓝田县	Lantian	598179	724	597455	96000
周至县	Zhouzhi	498949	960	497989	361031
户 县	Huxian	570050	1100	568950	500200
高陵县	Gaoling	227957		227957	227957

Area of Cultivated Land by Region (2013)

(mu)

当年增加的耕地面积 Area of Newly Increased Cultivated Land	新开荒地面积 Area of Newly Reclamation of Wasteland	当年减少的耕地面积 Decrease in Cultivated Area in the Year	国家基建占地 Capital Construction	退耕改果、茶、桑面积 Area for Change into Fruit, Tea and Mulberry	退耕造林面积 Area for Change into Woods
9536	**5314**	**57441**	**20920**	**24535**	**6160**
		10068	2400	1800	4800
		1237	852	292	
		1955	1955		
		2465	1653	185	
		1812	996	614	20
138	58	9729	9008	661	60
1374	1051	5495	791	2006	500
7234	4205	20884	1969	17435	780
790		3100	600	1542	
		696	696		

11-5 主要年份农业机械拥有量（年末数）

指标	Item	2005	2006	2007
农用机械总动力（千瓦）	Total Power of Agricultural Machinery(kw)	2239001	2277584	2348856
大中型拖拉机（台）	Large and Medium Tractors(unit)	8415	8963	10431
小型拖拉机（台）	Mini-tractors(unit)	26326	23437	21555
大中型拖拉机配套农具（台）	Number of Large and Medium Tractor Towing Farm Machinery(unit)	19334	18724	23487
小型拖拉机配套农具（台）	Mini-Tractor Towing Farm Machinery (unit)	47883	30439	28780
农用排灌柴油机（台）	Agricultural Diesel Engines(unit)	2219	3547	2709
农用排灌电动机（台）	Agricultural Motors(unit)	79666	76614	84416
农用水泵（台）	Agricultural Water Pump(unit)	77567	73039	80722
节水灌溉类机械（套）	Equipment in Water-saving Irrigation(set)	1290	2656	1991
联合收割机（台）	Combine Harvesters(unit)	4802	5026	5294
自走式机动割晒机（台）	Self-propelled Motorized Swather(unit)	4226	1342	4918
机动脱粒机（台）	Motorized Huller (unit)	13870	5806	11585
农用运输车（辆）	Agricultucal Transporter(unit)	47348	50395	49576

Possession of Agricultural Machinery in Representative Years（Number of year-end）

2008	2009	2010	2011	2012	2013
2712616	2616053	2677334	2890247	2983979	3108354
11092	11479	14675	12585	12987	12927
19036	18406	14194	13008	11471	8971
25125	26575	29215	36209	32166	32662
26984	29039	24393	29624	27869	25353
2670	2691	3309	2639	2891	2509
85349	83243	79462	87461	87056	86216
80462	80174	77367	75426	80982	80575
1728	1799	1710	1733	2106	2218
5390	6155	6718	7854	8502	9114
2174	1220	208	187		
23781	11960	13231	13407	14493	14700
54860	50671	51665	51838	51850	51710

11-6 各区县农业机械拥有量（2013年）

指标	Item	西安市 Xi' an	灞桥区 Baqiao	未央区 Weiyang
农用机械总动力（千瓦）	Total Power of Agricultural Machinery(kw)	3108354	179284	44892
大中型拖拉机（台）	Large and Medium Tractors(unit)	12927	415	145
小型拖拉机（台）	Mini-tractors(unit)	8971	41	10
大中型拖拉机配套农具（台）	Number of Large and Medium Tractor Towing Farm Machinery(unit)	32662	925	490
小型拖拉机配套农具（台）	Mini-Tractor Towing Farm Machinery (unit)	25853	82	10
农用排灌柴油机（台）	Agricultural Diesel Engines(unit)	2509		
农用排灌电动机（台）	Agricultural Motors(unit)	86216	3188	1081
农用水泵（台）	Agricultural Water Pump(unit)	80575	2927	891
节水灌溉类机械（套）	Equipment in Water-saving Irrigation(set)	2218	40	132
联合收割机（台）	Combine Harvesters(unit)	9114	203	40
自走式机动割晒机（台）	Self-propelled Motorized Swather(unit)			
机动脱粒机（台）	Motorized Huller (unit)	14700	50	
农用运输车（辆）	Agricultual Transporter(unit)	51710	3681	500

Possession of Agricultural Machinery by Region（2013）

雁塔区 Yanta	阎良区 Yanliang	临潼区 Lintong	长安区 Chang'an	蓝田县 Lantian	周至县 Zhouzhi	户 县 Huxian	高陵县 Gaoling
92424	187779	578816	533830	302196	423649	494342	271142
48	977	2411	2540	1058	1506	2387	1440
10	496	922	1222	1055	4048	960	207
85	2790	6826	6078	2185	2217	5966	5100
30	1540	3742	4728	4052	7384	3395	890
		73	1409	682	289	56	
520	6384	16973	22971	2923	15721	12735	3720
500	6384	16460	17423	2486	17049	12735	3720
	359	142	1143	63	227	112	
30	727	2156	1664	334	445	2557	958
	1375	4948	975	2025	2423	2374	530
725	2244	14007	7822	4498	8337	4028	5868

11-7 主要年份农业机械化、化肥、水利、水电情况

指标	Item	2000	2005	2007
一、农业机械化水平（万亩）	**Statistics on Agricultural Machinery (10 000 mu)**			
当年机械耕地面积（实际）	Area Ploughed by Tractors	366.81	360.68	361.62
当年机械播种面积（作业）	Seeded Area by Tractors	482.74	485.62	521.36
当年机械收获面积（作业）	Harvest Area by Tractors	272.83	271.77	296.06
二、农用化肥施用量（吨）	**Use of Agricultural Fertilizers and Insecticides(ton)**			
1.按实物量计算合计	Practicality Consumption	697243	749802	762401
氮肥	Nitrogenous Fertilizer	392366	411161	408847
磷肥	Phosphate Fertilizer	155480	161444	160932
钾肥	Potash Fertilizer	31841	34114	34284
复合肥	Compound Fertilizer	78620	115458	124784
2.按折纯法计算合计	Standard Consumption	196343	211790	220251
氮肥	Nitrogenous Fertilizer	102982	107645	109484
磷肥	Phosphate Fertilizer	18658	19368	19311
钾肥	Potash Fertilizer	15921	17055	17141
复合肥	Compound Fertilizer	39313	57009	62398
三、农用塑料薄膜使用量（公斤）	**Plastic Sheet for Agricultural Use(kg)**	**1622198**	**1855383**	**2096169**
四、农用柴油使用量（吨）	**Diesel Oil for Agricultural Use (ton)**	**52706**	**50832**	**50137**
	Pesticide (kg)			
五、农药使用量（公斤）	**Number of Mash Gas Pond Managed**	**1559333**	**1427879**	**1444867**
	by Village Government in Year-end(unit)			
六、农村水利化情况（万亩）	**Irrigation and Water Conservancy (10 000 mu)**			
有效灌溉面积	Effective Irrigation Area	335.97	280.1	276.28
旱涝保收面积	Stable-Harvesting Arable Land	294.06	255.37	247.99
机电排灌面积	Electrical Irrigation Area	249.11	223.74	210.51
七、农村电气化情况	**Rural electrization**			
乡村及村以下办水电站（个）	Hydropower Station in Rural Areas(unit)	67	79	76
装机容量（千瓦）	Installed Power Generation Capacity(kw)	7236	13775	24827
发电量（万千瓦小时）	Generating Capacity (10 000 kwh)	1137.95	2239	10085
已配套机电井（眼）	Electricity Powered Well(unit)	50289	46505	45783

Agricultural Machinery,Chemical Fertilizers,Water Conservancy, Hydropower in Representative Years

2008	2009	2010	2011	2012	2013
404.42	413.70	367.32	427.03	425.40	425.21
539.81	544.86	548.28	507.55	529.99	523.15
313.11	342.82	403.50	413.93	428.28	443.57
767980	776319	781072	785885	807900	794361
413397	414481	397975	398395	414339	401140
157145	153825	152943	151005	151967	152565
34149	33069	37715	38195	43356	39630
132481	142137	158062	163797	198238	201026
225949	230299	235532	239497	243281	239701
112000	112275	108868	110412	113662	109497
18855	18457	18315	18026	18061	18023
17077	16534	17997	18095	21267	18973
66247	71042	78811	81764	90291	93208
2122310	**2141969**	**2450496**	**2533372**	**2683201**	**2678745**
51097	**51346**	**61917**	**61637**	**57451**	**62563**
1465819	**1325459**	**1243105**	**1242773**	**1252490**	**1210060**
274.48	273.17	281.28	262.32	267.84	240.22
249.31	247.60	234.15	214.62	211.31	196.96
211.01	213.42	224.60	200.36	198.66	229.29
76	75	44	44	46	46
24827	25047	22325	22325	78848	80433
10477	10678	7268	7268	26447	19613
47032	46790	44310	40345	33959	

11-8 各区县农业机械化、化肥、水利、水电情况（2013年）

指标	Item	西安市 Xi'an	灞桥区 Baqiao	未央区 Weiyang
一、农业机械化水平（万亩）	**Statistics on Agricultural Machinery (10 000 mu)**			
当年机械耕地面积（实际）	Area Ploughed by Tractors	425.21	15.52	5.08
当年机械播种面积（作业）	Seeded Area by Tractors	523.15	19.58	3.27
当年机械收获面积（作业）	Harvest Area by Tractors	443.57	16.81	2.72
二、农用化肥施用量（吨）	**Use of Agricultural Fertilizers and Insecticides(ton)**			
1.按实物量计算合计	Practicality Consumption	794361	20944	3984
氮肥	Nitrogenous Fertilizer	401140	8459	2462
磷肥	Phosphate Fertilizer	152565	518	332
钾肥	Potash Fertilizer	39630	2105	15
复合肥	Compound Fertilizer	201026	9862	1175
2.按折纯法计算合计	Standard Consumption	239701	8705	1642
氮肥	Nitrogenous Fertilizer	109497	3892	1030
磷肥	Phosphate Fertilizer	18023	63	41
钾肥	Potash Fertilizer	18973	1052	7
复合肥	Compound Fertilizer	93208	3698	564
三、农用塑料薄膜使用量（公斤）	**Plastic Sheet for Agricultural Use(kg)**	2678745	174650	16202
四、农用柴油使用量（吨）	**Diesel Oil for Agricultural Use (ton)**	62563	601	626
	Pesticide (kg)			
五、农药使用量（公斤）	**Number of Mash Gas Pond Managed by Village Government in Year-end(unit)**	1210060	35687	2930
六、农村水利化情况（万亩）	**Irrigation and Water Conservancy (10 000 mu)**			
有效灌溉面积	Effective Irrigation Area	240.22	10.11	3.49
旱涝保收面积	Stable-Harvesting Arable Land	196.96	8.47	2.10
机电排灌面积	Electrical Irrigation Area	229.29	10.11	3.39
七、农村电气化情况	**Rural electrization**			
乡村及村以下办水电站（个）	Hydropower Station in Rural Areas(unit)	46		
装机容量（千瓦）	Installed Power Generation Capacity(kw)	80433		
发电量（万千瓦小时）	Generating Capacity (10 000 kwh)	19613		
已配套机电井（眼）	Electricity Powered Well(unit)			

Agricultural Machinery,Chemical Fertilizers,Water Conservancy, Hydropower by Region （2013）

雁塔区 Yanta	阎良区 Yanliang	临潼区 Lintong	长安区 Chang'an	蓝田县 Lantian	周至县 Zhouzhi	户 县 Huxian	高陵县 Gaoling
	23.62	52.98	107.94	54.79	66.98	53.07	45.23
	29.63	92.80	103.17	66.03	77.85	91.60	39.23
	23.07	92.50	98.37	39.20	45.51	88.00	37.40
441	60389	149600	132155	94730	148741	110138	73239
230	27758	79835	75406	51926	62384	66500	26180
30	12395	43956	25445	19298	16090	16839	17612
81	5150	2703	6345	6107	9025	5062	3037
100	15086	23106	24959	17399	61242	21687	26410
122	21696	39256	30124	36091	46989	32783	22293
29	10588	21077	11696	22520	15324	17885	5456
3	1418	5275	2884	2270	1929	2026	2114
40	2512	1351	3070	2914	4232	2277	1518
50	7178	11553	12474	8387	25504	10595	13205
0	973801	218955	143579	176058	98750	600966	275774
100	2746	12170	14257	9881	3369	10177	8636
20	177183	320235	132790	78043	165108	63280	234784
0.63	21.69	46.51	27.74	9.62	48.64	49.39	22.30
	22.55	46.50	20.31		28.76	47.77	20.50
0.63	20.30	45.59	27.74	7.24	45.36	47.23	21.60
			7	6	27	6	
			5425	14270	56118	4620	
			1861	1042	15646	1064	

11-9 主要年份农林牧渔及服务业总产值及指数

Gross Output Value of Farming,Forestry,Animal Husbandry,Fishery, Service and Related Indices in Representative Years

单位：万元　　(10 000 yuan)

年　份 Year	农林牧渔及服务总产值（现价） Gross Output Value (At current prices)	农业 Farming	林业 Forestry	牧业 Animal Husbandry	渔业 Fishery	农林牧渔服务业 Service of Farming, Forestry, Animal Husbandry and Fishery	指数（上年=100）（可比价） Indices(preceding year= 100) (At cinstant prices)
1970	40617	35965	713	3896	43		111.2
1975	55322	47378	1509	6403	32		93.9
1978	65423	56519	1444	7427	33		104.7
1980	65322	54004	1177	10106	35		85.0
1985	134933	105888	2559	26186	300		106.4
1990	262073	191088	3134	65840	2011		102.5
1992	321155	219160	4225	94045	3725		108.6
1993	387068	261959	5031	115810	4268		112.8
1994	565056	359609	7819	192140	5488		102.4
1995	754597	513348	7185	228598	5466		106.8
1996	786003	552726	7573	219214	6490		102.1
1997	836201	585973	9226	233623	7379		110.3
1998	853279	625465	8146	212045	7623		107.5
1999	739905	530029	8883	194552	6441		100.7
2000	743712	514845	8482	212612	7773		104.3
2001	767511	527160	8427	223861	8063		102.8
2002	797444	539978	11378	238761	7327		103.0
2003	837857	551398	10550	269610	6299		101.5
2004	967946	580798	12773	314517	6728	53130	108.4
2005	1065437	657262	13086	329856	7340	57893	107.7
2006	1141484	686748	15188	346626	7017	85905	107.2
2007	1341450	798163	15845	410213	9051	108178	105.3
2008	1682725	956549	19031	564095	11084	131966	107.8
2009	1787032	1061756	22663	546191	11830	144592	106.5
2010	2270994	1438934	26787	629376	12830	163067	107.4
2011	2726608	1729295	34453	754593	14856	193411	106.6
2012	3083562	1933149	62291	820392	19877	247853	106.0
2013	3428905	2173363	80199	863902	22773	288668	104.9

11-10 主要年份农林牧渔及服务业总产值指数

Related Indices of Gross Output Value of Farming,Forestry,Animal Husbandry,Fishery and Service in Representative Years

年份 Year	农林牧渔及服务业总产值指数（上年=100）（可比价） Indices(preceding year= 100) (At constant prices)	农业 Farming	林业 Forestry	牧业 Animal Husbandry	渔业 Fishery	农林牧渔服务业 Service of Farming, Forestry, Animal Husbandry and Fishery
2005	107.7	108.0	98.7	107.3	112.6	107.9
2006	107.2	106.0	102.5	109.3	104.5	109.4
2007	105.3	106.4	101.3	102.4	106.3	108.7
2008	107.8	107.9	112.2	106.0	100.5	113.7
2009	106.5	105.4	121.3	106.8	107.4	110.2
2010	107.4	108.7	115.2	104.3	92.7	108.9
2011	106.6	108.2	105.7	102.9	102.1	107.7
2012	106.0	105.6	143.0	104.8	113.4	108.5
2013	104.9	104.3	131.3	104.0	110.1	105.9

11-11 主要年份农林牧渔及服务业总产值构成

Gross Output Value and Its Composition of Farming, Forestry, Animal Husbandry,Fishery and Service at Current Price in Representative Years

年份 Year	农林牧渔及服务业总产值(%) Service of Farming, Forestry, Animal Husbandry and Fishery(%)	农业 Farming	林业 Forestry	牧业 Animal Husbandry	渔业 Fishery	农林牧渔服务业 Service of Farming, Forestry, Animal Husbandry and Fishery
2005	100	61.7	1.2	31.0	0.7	5.4
2006	100	60.9	1.3	31.5	0.6	5.7
2007	100	59.5	1.2	30.6	0.7	8.0
2008	100	56.9	1.1	33.5	0.7	7.3
2009	100	59.4	1.3	30.5	0.7	8.1
2010	100	63.3	1.2	27.7	0.6	7.2
2011	100	63.4	1.3	27.7	0.5	7.1
2012	100	62.7	2.0	26.6	0.7	8.0
2013	100	63.4	2.3	25.2	0.7	8.4

11-12 各区县农林牧渔及服务业总产值（2013年）

Gross Output Value of Farming, Forestry, Animal Husbandry, Fishery and Service by Region（2013）

单位：万元 (10 000 yuan)

区 县	Region	农林牧渔及服务业总产值 Gross Output Value	农业 Farming	林业 Forestry	牧业 Animal Husbandry	渔业 Fishery	农林牧渔服务业 Service of Farming, Forestry, Animal Husbandry and Fishery
合 计	**Total**	**3428905**	**2173363**	**80199**	**863902**	**22773**	**288668**
新城区	Xincheng						
碑林区	Beilin						
莲湖区	Lianhu						
灞桥区	Baqiao	279503	204989	2095	43299	3166	25954
未央区	Weiyang	25320	14131	6	7159	2080	1944
雁塔区	Yanta	31763	22068	160	5050		4485
阎良区	Yanliang	324413	238814	655	58096	419	26429
临潼区	Lintong	515993	266339	8296	193116	3257	44985
长安区	Chang'an	509105	347559	3755	111587	6233	39971
蓝田县	Lantian	436071	255639	22928	120230	4101	33173
周至县	Zhouzhi	460093	314083	38647	74649	853	31861
户县	Huxian	447149	292226	2480	103568	1259	47616
高陵县	Gaoling	399495	217515	1177	147148	1405	32250

11-13 各区县农林牧渔及服务业总产值指数和构成（2013年）

Gross Output Value and Its Composition of Farming, Forestry, Animal Husbandry,Fishery and Service at Current Price by Region（2013）

单位：%　　　　(%)

区县	Region	农林牧渔及服务业总产值 Gross Output Value	农业 Farming	林业 Forestry	牧业 Animal Husbandry	渔业 Fishery	农林牧渔服务业 Service of Farming, Forestry, Animal Husbandry and Fishery
全市指数	**Total**	**104.9**	**104.3**	**131.3**	**104.0**	**110.1**	**105.9**
新城区	Xincheng						
碑林区	Beilin						
莲湖区	Lianhu						
灞桥区	Baqiao	105.4	106.1	180.9	100.4	112.3	105.1
未央区	Weiyang	91.2	94.8	46.2	83.2	84.6	104.5
雁塔区	Yanta	93.9	100.4	107.9	68.4		104.8
阎良区	Yanliang	105.2	106.4	104.9	102.5	134.8	101.1
临潼区	Lintong	104.7	105.9	107.7	102.9	115.8	105.0
长安区	Chang'an	104.8	104.7	334.5	103.1	109.0	102.6
蓝田县	Lantian	104.9	100.9	105.3	115.1	119.7	100.8
周至县	Zhouzhi	106.1	103.2	149.7	99.7	112.6	110.8
户县	Huxian	104.9	104.2	134.0	102.7	106.9	114.5
高陵县	Gaoling	106.0	105.6	136.9	106.1	117.3	105.7
全市构成	**Total**	**100**	**63.4**	**2.3**	**25.2**	**0.7**	**8.4**
新城区	Xincheng						
碑林区	Beilin						
莲湖区	Lianhu						
灞桥区	Baqiao	100	73.3	0.7	15.5	1.1	9.3
未央区	Weiyang	100	55.8		28.3	8.2	7.7
雁塔区	Yanta	100	69.5	0.5	15.9		14.1
阎良区	Yanliang	100	73.6	0.2	17.9	0.1	8.1
临潼区	Lintong	100	51.6	1.6	37.4	0.6	8.7
长安区	Chang'an	100	68.3	0.7	21.9	1.2	7.9
蓝田县	Lantian	100	58.6	5.3	27.6	0.9	7.6
周至县	Zhouzhi	100	68.3	8.4	16.2	0.2	6.9
户县	Huxian	100	65.4	0.6	23.2	0.3	10.6
高陵县	Gaoling	100	54.4	0.3	36.8	0.4	8.1

11-14 主要年份农林牧渔及服务业增加值

Value-Added of Farming, Forestry, Animal Husbandry, Fishery and Service in Representative Years

单位：万元 (10 000 yuan)

年 份 Year	农林牧渔及服务业增加值 Farming,Forestry, Animal Husbandry, Fishery and Service	农业 Farming	林业 Forestry	牧业 Animal Husbandry	渔业 Fishery	农林牧渔服务业 Service of Farming, Forestry, Animal Husbandry and Fishery
1995	413981	329662	4413	76746	3160	
2000	446481	336777	4323	101353	4028	
2001	458720	342427	4258	108096	3939	
2002	477691	351358	6419	116591	3323	
2003	458378	312849	5473	137236	2820	
2004	582009	393349	6811	164572	2919	14358
2005	660148	444320	6888	169701	3373	35866
2006	704427	465823	8556	177431	3227	49390
2007	825053	538794	8420	210930	4467	62442
2008	1034471	639071	10592	301305	5598	77905
2009	1103793	698043	11958	303594	5913	84285
2010	1400575	935489	14362	349204	6503	95017
2011	1731398	1161249	18807	428169	7679	115494
2012	1955931	1297824	33973	465476	10115	148543
2013	2177588	1459093	43740	490162	11589	173004

11-15 主要年份农林牧渔及服务业增加值指数

Indices of Value-Added of Farming, Forestry, Animal Husbandry, Fishery and Service in Representative Years

年 份 Year	农林牧渔及服务业增加值指数（上年=100）（可比价） Farming,Forestry,Animal Husbandry,Fishery and Service	农业 Farming	林业 Forestry	牧业 Animal Husbandry	渔业 Fishery	农林牧渔服务业 Service of Farming Forestry, Animal Husbandry and Fishery
2008	107.6	107.6	112.0	105.8	100.0	114.0
2009	106.3	103.6	114.6	111.2	106.3	108.8
2010	106.9	107.9	108.7	104.3	94.0	108.9
2011	106.7	108.1	106.1	102.8	102.7	108.1
2012	106.0	105.6	142.8	104.8	113.4	108.5
2013	104.8	104.3	131.3	104.0	110.1	105.9

11-16 各区县农林牧渔及服务业增加值（2013年）

Value-Added of Farming, Forestry, Animal Husbandry, Fishery and Service by Region（2013）

单位：万元 (10 000 yuan)

年 份 Year	Region	农林牧渔及服务业增加值 Farming,Forestry, Animal Husbandry, Fishery and Service	农业 Farming	林业 Forestry	牧业 Animal Husbandry	渔业 Fishery	农林牧渔服务业 Service of Farming, Forestry, Animal Husbandry and Fishery
合 计	**Total**	**2177588**	**1459093**	**43740**	**490162**	**11589**	**173004**
新城区	Xincheng						
碑林区	Beilin						
莲湖区	Lianhu						
灞桥区	Baqiao	183247	140114	1266	26041	1264	14562
未央区	Weiyang	15404	9037	1	4270	830	1266
雁塔区	Yanta	22874	15856	113	3315		3590
阎良区	Yanliang	220101	164190	336	38951	206	16418
临潼区	Lintong	327531	178313	4635	114005	1949	28529
长安区	Chang'an	341660	264523	2116	46918	4016	24087
蓝田县	Lantian	264031	159844	13306	69620	1785	19476
周至县	Zhouzhi	281566	203384	19944	39591	451	18196
户 县	Huxian	277995	186893	1372	64256	666	24808
高陵县	Gaoling	243179	136939	651	83195	422	21972

11–17　各区县农林牧渔及服务业增加值指数（2013年）

Indices of Value-Added of Farming, Forestry, Animal Husbandry, Fishery and Service by Region（2013）

（上年 =100）（可比价）　　　　(preceding year = 100) (At constant prices)

区　县	Region	农林牧渔及服务业增加值指数 Farming,Forestry,Animal Husbandry,Fishery and Service	农业 Farming	林业 Forestry	牧业 Animal Husbandry	渔业 Fishery	农林牧渔服务业 Service of Farming, Forestry, Animal Husbandry and Fishery
合　计	**Total**	**104.8**	**104.3**	**131.3**	**104.0**	**110.1**	**105.9**
新城区	Xincheng						
碑林区	Beilin						
莲湖区	Lianhu						
灞桥区	Baqiao	105.4	106.0	182.1	100.5	112.1	105.3
未央区	Weiyang	91.6	94.7	33.3	83.2	84.4	104.7
雁塔区	Yanta	94.5	100.4	108.5	68.5		105.0
阎良区	Yanliang	105.2	106.3	105.5	102.6	134.7	101.3
临潼区	Lintong	104.8	105.9	108.4	103.0	115.5	105.2
长安区	Chang'an	104.8	104.7	336.7	103.1	108.7	102.8
蓝田县	Lantian	104.7	100.8	106.0	115.2	119.4	101.0
周至县	Zhouzhi	105.6	103.1	150.6	99.8	112.2	111.0
户　县	Huxian	104.7	104.1	134.8	102.8	106.7	114.7
高陵县	Gaoling	105.9	105.6	137.8	106.2	117.1	105.9

11-18 主要年份农作物播种面积

Sown Areas of Farm Crops In Representative Years

单位：万亩 （10 000mu）

年份 Year	总播种面积 Total Sown Area	粮食 Grain Crops	小麦 Wheat	玉米 Corn	棉花 Cotton	油料 Oil-bearing Crops	蔬菜 Vegetables
1980	835.43	706.35	324.17	273.14	81.23	10.01	24.02
1985	795.41	704.36	378.20	271.14	21.02	8.01	45.03
1990	816.41	731.42	387.20	282.14	15.02	12.00	51.03
1991	820.41	731.37	389.19	283.14	19.01	13.01	47.03
1992	820.65	715.50	384.60	273.60	26.70	16.20	54.60
1993	821.63	713.49	380.40	273.69	17.66	14.34	63.90
1994	821.10	719.00	375.90	272.40	19.70	13.30	59.90
1995	784.74	690.63	370.41	259.55	11.07	18.57	57.59
1996	797.40	709.00	366.30	286.80	7.70	18.30	55.50
1997	755.78	670.83	367.71	248.79	4.50	15.53	59.36
1998	789.99	705.03	370.17	285.45	3.56	14.69	60.95
1999	793.08	709.95	371.94	294.00	2.85	12.74	60.68
2000	784.94	697.55	369.89	283.70	2.48	13.46	64.35
2001	763.16	678.05	359.19	278.57	2.91	11.37	61.77
2002	751.10	655.59	350.64	271.95	2.63	11.40	67.71
2003	737.06	632.55	336.05	261.89	3.38	11.04	69.44
2004	753.83	630.63	311.52	286.50	4.94	9.74	77.55
2005	757.91	642.75	325.10	287.87	5.40	9.51	83.33
2006	769.49	648.00	313.23	307.89	6.09	8.58	87.03
2007	762.38	637.05	306.98	304.13	6.93	7.41	91.07
2008	756.06	630.31	319.39	286.69	6.35	8.59	93.02
2009	757.11	628.69	318.36	285.20	6.45	8.59	94.83
2010	751.74	621.71	317.18	279.93	6.26	8.98	95.71
2011	704.17	573.13	306.39	243.06	5.97	8.33	96.97
2012	701.33	572.50	305.34	242.20	5.00	7.70	97.82
2013	695.53	567.87	298.93	245.64	2.57	7.57	99.89

注：2011年农作物播种面积为陕西省统计局依据(国统字办[2011]68号)文件调整数。

11-19 各区县主要农作物播种面积（2013年）

Sown Areas of Major Farm Crops by Region (2013)

单位：万亩 (10 000 mu)

区县	Region	总播种面积 Total Sown Area	粮食 Grain Crops	小麦 Wheat	玉米 Corn	棉花 Cotton	油料 Oil-bearing Crops	蔬菜 Vegetables	瓜果类 Fruits Class
合计	**Total**	**695.53**	**567.87**	**298.93**	**245.64**	**2.57**	**7.67**	**99.89**	**16.26**
新城区	Xincheng								
碑林区	Beilin								
莲湖区	Lianhu								
灞桥区	Baqiao	27.81	19.82	12.03	7.37	0.08	0.37	7.11	0.43
未央区	Weiyang	4.72	2.95	2.16	0.79			1.72	0.05
雁塔区	Yanta	0.64						0.64	
阎良区	Yanliang	47.80	21.37	11.35	10.00	2.11	0.10	17.76	6.46
临潼区	Lintong	125.29	106.21	58.07	43.48	0.05	1.46	14.85	2.33
长安区	Chang'an	137.48	110.61	58.36	50.96	0.02	1.62	22.18	2.27
蓝田县	Lantian	109.02	96.14	50.38	32.04	0.31	2.20	8.74	1.53
周至县	Zhouzhi	89.68	79.02	39.60	37.54		1.45	9.03	0.18
户县	Huxian	101.31	89.81	45.82	43.03		0.47	9.22	1.81
高陵县	Gaoling	51.78	41.94	21.16	20.43			8.64	1.20

11-20　主要年份农作物产品产量

Yield of Major Farm Crops in Representative Years

单位：万吨　　　　　　　　　　　　　　　　　　　　　　　　　　　　(10 000 ton)

年份 Year	粮食作物 Grain Crops	夏粮 Summer Grain	小麦 Wheat	秋粮 Autumn Grain	稻谷 Rice	玉米 Corn	棉花 Cotton	油料 Oil-bearing Crops	油菜籽 Rapeseeds	蔬菜 Vegetables
1978	132.8	64.2	58.2	68.7	5.1	55.8	2.85	0.09	0.07	45.66
1980	114.4	56.6	52.2	57.8	4.7	47.7	1.97	0.54	0.50	40.13
1981	116.1	78.7	74.3	37.4	3.4	31.5	1.36	0.76	0.75	34.06
1982	148.9	85.6	82.2	63.3	4.9	55.5	2.88	0.51	0.49	53.71
1983	148.1	81.8	79.6	66.3	4.8	58.5	0.85	0.36	0.34	46.99
1984	157.6	82.4	81.0	75.2	5.0	66.5	1.49	0.46	0.29	75.47
1985	150.1	76.1	74.8	74.0	5.1	65.1	0.49	0.75	0.39	86.44
1986	162.4	91.7	90.1	70.7	4.8	61.8	0.44	1.25	0.82	85.84
1987	171.2	87.0	85.2	84.2	5.0	74.3	0.47	1.57	1.22	95.16
1988	158.0	86.8	84.6	71.1	3.8	61.4	0.42	0.89	0.51	113.50
1989	173.6	93.5	91.2	80.2	4.7	70.4	0.55	1.33	0.94	129.32
1990	172.4	91.7	89.7	80.8	5.5	70.4	0.7	1.35	0.94	119.32
1991	178.8	91.1	89.2	87.7	5.0	77.5	0.97	1.20	0.74	117.41
1992	183.4	101.7	99.6	81.7	4.7	72.3	0.74	1.49	0.87	128.12
1993	190.0	101.1	99.0	88.9	4.9	78.6	0.75	1.40	1.00	145.80
1994	157.4	86.9	84.9	70.5	4.5	61.4	0.65	1.08	0.78	135.26
1995	175.3	99.8	97.4	75.5	3.4	67.8	0.29	2.17	1.90	133.60
1996	187.5	80.1	78.4	107.4	3.4	95.6	0.24	1.83	1.55	138.01
1997	190.5	114.3	112.3	76.3	3.5	69.4	0.17	1.86	1.65	142.11
1998	212.7	104.4	104.0	108.3	3.2	99.1	0.14	1.67	1.36	148.87
1999	204.4	95.5	94.4	108.9	2.9	99.7	0.15	1.30	1.00	153.24
2000	201.9	92.6	91.6	109.3	3.1	100.5	0.14	1.34	0.95	162.14
2001	197.1	98.1	97.2	98.9	2.7	91.3	0.17	1.23	0.90	152.80
2002	192.4	94.5	93.5	97.9	2.1	91.6	0.18	1.22	0.84	169.74
2003	176.3	98.2	96.7	78.2	1.6	72.3	0.22	1.13	0.70	169.67
2004	195.8	97.8	96.0	98.0	1.7	91.6	0.40	1.14	0.84	180.96
2005	205.5	100.0	99.1	105.5	1.6	99.3	0.45	1.16	0.89	195.70
2006	193.5	86.0	85.4	107.4	1.4	101.2	0.48	1.08	0.87	189.30
2007	189.1	77.3	76.7	111.8	1.5	105.6	0.59	0.96	0.77	204.30
2008	214.4	105.9	105.6	108.5	0.9	103.0	0.62	1.15	0.95	221.53
2009	218.2	103.0	102.1	115.2	0.9	109.5	0.63	1.12	0.93	242.41
2010	221.7	106.6	105.8	115.1	0.8	108.9	0.60	1.20	1.00	253.10
2011	182.04	90.54	89.68	91.49	0.67	85.3	0.56	1.17	0.95	261.66
2012	192.55	95.73	94.92	96.32	0.57	89.29	0.47	1.02	0.88	277.80
2013	183.12	83.59	82.77	99.52	0.39	91.83	0.25	1.00	0.87	298.12

注：2011年农作物产品产量为陕西省统计局依据（国统字办[2011]70号）文件调整数。

11-21 各区县主要农作物产品产量（2013年）

Yield of Major Farm Crops by Region (2013)

单位：万吨 （10 000 tons）

区 县	Region	粮食作物 Grain Crops	夏粮 Summer Grain	小麦 Wheat	秋粮 Autumn Grain	稻谷 Rice	玉米 Corn
合 计	**Total**	**183.12**	**83.59**	**82.77**	**99.52**	**0.39**	**91.83**
新城区	Xincheng						
碑林区	Beilin						
莲湖区	Lianhu						
灞桥区	Baqiao	5.63	2.91	2.91	2.72		2.62
未央区	Weiyang	0.80	0.50	0.50	0.30		0.30
雁塔区	Yanta						
阎良区	Yanliang	8.54	4.27	4.27	4.27		4.26
临潼区	Lintong	32.68	15.76	15.74	16.92		15.31
长安区	Chang'an	35.78	15.47	15.45	20.30	0.21	19.79
蓝田县	Lantian	26.46	11.93	11.74	14.53	0.15	9.75
周至县	Zhouzhi	23.07	10.28	9.92	12.79	0.03	12.41
户 县	Huxian	30.34	14.00	13.79	16.34		16.24
高陵县	Gaoling	19.82	8.47	8.45	11.35		11.15

11-21 续表 continued

单位：万吨 （10 000 tons）

区 县	Region	棉花 Cotton	油料 Oil-bearing Crops	油菜籽 Rapeseeds	蔬菜 Vegetables	瓜果类 Fruits Class
合 计	**Total**	**0.25**	**1.00**	**0.87**	**298.12**	**48.38**
新城区	Xincheng					
碑林区	Beilin					
莲湖区	Lianhu					
灞桥区	Baqiao	0.01	0.05	0.04	27.63	0.74
未央区	Weiyang				2.87	0.16
雁塔区	Yanta				2.27	
阎良区	Yanliang	0.21	0.01	0.01	71.37	21.92
临潼区	Lintong		0.17	0.16	43.08	6.35
长安区	Chang'an		0.25	0.25	55.90	7.49
蓝田县	Lantian	0.03	0.22	0.22	15.79	3.62
周至县	Zhouzhi		0.21	0.12	19.18	0.48
户 县	Huxian		0.09	0.07	27.7	5.22
高陵县	Gaoling				32.32	2.41

11-22 主要年份农作物单位面积产量

Yield of Farm Crops Per Unit Area in Representative Years

单位：公斤/亩 (kg/mu)

年份 Year	粮食作物 Grain Crops	夏粮 Summer Grain	小麦 Wheat	秋粮 Autumn Grain	玉米 Corn	棉花 Cotton	油料 Oil-bearing Crops	油菜籽 Rapeseeds	蔬菜 Vegetables
1990	236	232	232	241	249	46	103	101	2349
1995	254	263	263	243	261	27	117	128	2320
1996	265	214	214	321	333	32	86	100	2489
1997	284	305	306	257	279	38	76	129	2395
1998	302	278	279	328	347	40	114	121	2443
1999	288	253	254	327	339	52	102	106	2526
2000	289	247	248	338	354	55	102	112	2520
2001	291	270	271	314	328	60	104	113	2474
2002	293	266	267	326	337	70	107	115	2507
2003	279	287	288	269	276	67	102	110	2444
2004	310	308	308	313	320	81	117	129	2333
2005	320	304	305	336	345	84	121	132	2349
2006	299	273	273	323	329	80	125	135	2175
2007	297	250	250	341	347	85	129	132	2245
2008	340	330	331	350	359	97	134	137	2382
2009	347	320	321	375	384	97	131	131	2556
2010	357	333	334	381	389	94	130	131	2644
2011	318	293	293	347	351	95	133	134	2698
2012	336	310	311	367	369	94	132	130	2840
2013	322	277	277	374	374	96	130	125	2985

注：2011年农作物单产为陕西省统计局依据(国统字办[2011]72号)文件调整数。

11-23 各区县主要农作物单位面积产量（2013年）

The Output of Main Crops Per Unit Area by Region (2013)

单位：公斤/亩 (kg/mu)

区县	Region	粮食作物 Grain Crops	夏粮 Summer Grain	小麦 Wheat	秋粮 Autumn Grain	玉米 Corn
合计	**Total**	**322**	**277**	**277**	**374**	**374**
新城区	Xincheng					
碑林区	Beilin					
莲湖区	Lianhu					
灞桥区	Baqiao	284	242	242	350	355
未央区	Weiyang	272	231	231	383	383
雁塔区	Yanta					
阎良区	Yanliang	399	376	376	426	426
临潼区	Lintong	308	271	271	352	352
长安区	Chang'an	323	265	265	389	388
蓝田县	Lantian	275	233	233	324	304
周至县	Zhouzhi	292	254	251	332	331
户县	Huxian	338	301	301	377	377
高陵县	Gaoling	473	400	399	546	546

11-23 续表 continued

单位：公斤/亩 (kg/mu)

区 县	Region	棉花 Cotton	油料 Oil-bearing Crops	油菜籽 Rapeseeds	蔬菜 Vegetables	瓜果类 Fruits Class
合 计	**Total**	**96**	**130**	**125**	**2985**	**2975**
新城区	Xincheng					
碑林区	Beilin					
莲湖区	Lianhu					
灞桥区	Baqiao	66	131	131	3888	1735
未央区	Weiyang				1669	3556
雁塔区	Yanta				3529	
阎良区	Yanliang	96	123	120	4020	3395
临潼区	Lintong	96	118	114	2901	2729
长安区	Chang'an	85	154	154	2520	3283
蓝田县	Lantian	104	100	100	1806	2348
周至县	Zhouzhi		146	123	2124	2680
户 县	Huxian		183	186	3006	2883
高陵县	Gaoling				3739	2012

11-24 设施农业生产情况（2013年）

Agricultural Production Facilities (2013)

指 标	Item	种植面积（亩） planting area (mu)	产量（吨） output(ton)
一、蔬菜	**Vegetables**	**244612**	**1275389**
其中：芹菜	Celery	72561	386621
油菜	Rape	2709	6145
菠菜	Spinach	13682	32801
黄瓜	Cucumber	22353	110335
西红柿	Tomato	25346	109393
辣椒	Chilli	11867	40780
二、瓜果类	**Fruits class**	**101069**	**339707**
其中：草莓	Strawberry	4629	7212
三、花卉苗木	**Flower seedling wood**	**13609**	
四、食用菌	**Edible Fungi**	**2798**	**10898**
五、其他	**Others**	**24273**	
补充资料： 蔬菜大棚个数:93875（个）	Updates. Vegetable shed number (93875unit)		
蔬菜大棚面积:153206（亩）	Vegetables awning area(153206mu)		

11-25 主要年份林业生产情况

Statistics on Forestry in Representative Years

指 标	Item	2000	2005	2008	2009	2010	2011	2012	2013
一 营林情况	**Afforestation**								
当年造林面积合计（万亩）	Build Forestry Areas(10 000 mu)	27.47	16.56	8.76	15.6	16.1	10.42	9.08	12.29
封山育林面积（万亩）	Hill-closeure for Afforestation Areas (10 000 mu)	18.78	18.65	30.19	37.4	55.1	41.3	41.9	44.4
零星四旁植树（万株）	Planting(10 000 plants)	731	1064	952	931	509.2	536.7	579.2	588.3
育苗面积（万亩）	Raise Seedlings Areas(10 000 mu)	2.05	5.99	4.72	3.41	11.95	9.93	11.64	17.37
#本年新育	New Seedling of Current Year	**1.69**	**2.54**	**2.19**	**1.86**	**1.75**	**1.93**	**1.98**	**6.1**
二 主要林产品产量（吨）	**Main Forestry Product(ton)**								
生漆	Lacquer	11	2	6	5	10	4		
核桃	Walnuts	997	3351	4589	4306	7875	13235	15253	18033
板栗	Chinese Chestnut	744	2076	2728	3122	7736	8229	7654	4379
花椒	Pepper	**140**	**525**	**842**	**689**	**1420**	**889**	**879**	**319**
三 村及村以下采伐木材（万立方米）	**Timber Harvested at or below** Village Level (10 000 cu.m)	1.62	1.87	1.23	0.97	3.3	1.39	1.04	0.88

注：2009年迹地更新面积改为更新造林面积；
2010年起，根据统计制度要求，林业统计数据取自林业部门。

11-26 各区县林业生产情况（2013年）

Statistics On Forestry by Region (2013)

区 县	Region	当年造林面积（亩）Build Forestry Areasin in The Year(mu)	零星植树（万株）Planting (10 000 plants)	育苗面积（亩）Raise Seedlings Areas(mu)	核桃产量（吨）Output of Walnuts (ton)	板栗产量（吨）Output of Chinese Chestnut (ton)	村及村以下采伐木材（万立方米）Timber Harvesting at\under Vallage level (10 000 cu.m)
合 计	**Total**	**122925**	**588.3**	**173713**	**18033**	**4379**	**0.88**
新城区	Xincheng						
碑林区	Beilin						
莲湖区	Lianhu						
灞桥区	Baqiao	1230	20	2100	1000		
未央区	Weiyang	15	30				
雁塔区	Yanta		90	3390	100		
阎良区	Yanliang	3300	30	750			
临潼区	Lintong	32190	70		1213	200	
长安区	Chang'an	6120	111	3041	1885	113	
蓝田县	Lantian	45375	80	39000	5600	1800	
周至县	Zhouzhi	23415	75	118632	7905	2242	0.47
户 县	Huxian	10275	82.3	3800	330	24	0.41
高陵县	Gaoling	1005		3000			

11-27 主要年份果业生产情况

Statistics on Fruits in Representative Years

指标	Item	2000	2005	2009	2010	2011	2012	2013
果园面积合计（万亩）	**Areas of Orchards (10 000 mu)**	**47.86**	**55.55**	**71.08**	**74.95**	**74.27**	**76.83**	**78.06**
苹果园	Apple Orchards	12.15	5.96	5.66	3.55	1.53	1.44	1.28
梨园	Pears Orchards	5.79	3.01	2.66	2.27	1.66	1.65	1.68
葡萄园	Grapes Orchards	1.89	3.02	4.59	4.83	4.91	5.46	6.70
桃园	Peach Orchards	3.47	8.66	8.48	7.68	6.87	6.78	6.49
猕猴桃园	Chinese Goosebeery Orchards	16.83	4.33	29.01	34.92	36.97	41.36	41.99
杏园	Apricot Orchards	0.62	2.50	2.97	3.62	3.60	3.59	3.52
柿子园	Presimmons Orchards	1.96	2.69	3.26	3.16	2.83	2.91	2.78
石榴园	Pomegranate Orchards			3.61	3.43	3.38	3.61	3.57
水果产量（吨）	**Output of Fruits (ton)**	**343551**	**512869**	**789587**	**847821**	**911361**	**932054**	**951851**
苹果	Apple	89416	53387	53023	39130	34313	28675	25212
梨	Pears	65459	57059	57929	55122	48026	47463	47618
葡萄	Grapes	16647	30951	56731	64885	69003	75516	92380
桃	Peach	27010	89755	146651	142051	137683	125857	122186
猕猴桃	Chinese Goosebeery	96640	137853	233296	296023	357066	386336	395847
杏	Apricot			55535	48544	34340	57772	55330
柿子	Persimmon			34780	35287	31625	41211	41712
石榴	Pomegranate			42122	40211	34340	32329	30642

11-28 各区县果业生产情况（2013年）

Area and Output of Fruits by Region (2013)

区　县	Region	果园面积（万亩） Area of Orchards(10 000 mu)	水果产量（吨） Output of Fruits(ton)
合　计	**Total**	**78.06**	**951851**
新城区	Xincheng		
碑林区	Beilin		
莲湖区	Lianhu		
灞桥区	Baqiao	7.18	96308
未央区	Weiyang	0.24	5654
雁塔区	Yanta	0.33	5190
阎良区	Yanliang	2.70	65748
临潼区	Lintong	4.89	48116
长安区	Chang'an	5.51	74847
蓝田县	Lantian	8.97	117942
周至县	Zhouzhi	39.69	391500
户、县	Huxian	5.60	92791
高陵县	Gaoling	2.95	53755

11-29 主要年份畜牧业生产情况

Statistics on Livestock Husbandry in Representative Years

指标	Item	2000	2005	2010	2011	2012	2013
一 大牲畜年末总头数（头）	**Large Animals In Stock at Year-end (head)**	260742	322521	216043	212351	211852	211791
# 役畜	Draught Animals	98130	90717	42243	32877	31866	31510
1. 牛	Cattle	256073	320773	215072	211334	210819	210743
# 能繁殖母畜	Female Animals of Reprductive Ability	136626	176445	144012	142977		
# 当年生仔畜	Newborn Livestock in the Year	69015	72163	40052	36093		
#肉牛	Farm Cattle			65447	62127	60233	60165
#奶牛	Dairy Cattle	48164	96498	118747	117149	119888	120836
2. 马（匹）	Horses	736	559	456	496	533	549
3. 驴	Donkeys	476	175	67	71	46	52
4. 骡	Mules	3457	1014	448	450	454	447
二、猪年末头数（头）	**Hogs in Stock Year-end (head)**	1284592	1472869	943183	943987	966018	965683
# 能繁殖的母猪	Female Hogs of Reprductive Ability	93775	123543	106610	101332	103926	103967
三、羊年末只数（只）	**Sheeps and Goats in Stock at Year-end(head)**	421103	532471	294539	295995	284596	273747
1. 山羊	Goats	397121	520354	288738	288346	278738	267382
# 奶山羊	Milch Goats	266525	358733	246442	245118	234643	222546
2. 绵羊	Sheeps	23982	12117	5801	7649	5858	6365
四、家禽年末存栏（万只）	**Poultry in Stock at Year-end (10 000 heads)**	1623.81	1372.56	1034.20	1153.76	1176.73	1172.61
五、年末养蜂箱数（箱）	Honey (box)	20408	24287	22984	17567	17161	17415

11–30 各区县畜牧业生产情况（2013年）

Statistics On Livestock, Animal Husbandry by Region（2013）

区 县	Region	大牲畜年末头数（头）Large Animals In Stock at Year-end (head)	役畜 Draught Animals	牛（头）Cattle (head)	奶牛 Dairy Cattle	马（匹）Horses (head)	驴（头）Donkeys (head)	骡（头）Mutes (head)
合 计	**Total**	**211791**	**31510**	**210743**	**120836**	**549**	**52**	**447**
新城区	Xincheng							
碑林区	Beilin							
莲湖区	Lianhu							
灞桥区	Baqiao	13242	152	13226	12919	16		
未央区	Weiyang	4964		4964	4632			
雁塔区	Yanta	220		220	200			
阎良区	Yanliang	17865		17865	16380			
临潼区	Lintong	72735	7825	72735	64910			
长安区	Chang'an	10998	1136	10310	3921	330		358
蓝田县	Lantian	38908	12314	38908	2592			
周至县	Zhouzhi	32929	9807	32815	2801	79		35
户 县	Huxian	9820	45	9820	5280			
高陵县	Gaoling	10110	231	9880	7201	124	52	54

11–30 续表 continued

区 县	Region	羊（只）Sheep and Goats (head)	山羊 Goats	奶山羊 Milch Goats	家禽（万只）Poultry (10 000 head)	蜂（箱）Honey (box)
合 计	**Total**	**273747**	**267382**	**222546**	**1172.61**	**17415**
新城区	Xincheng					
碑林区	Beilin					
莲湖区	Lianhu					
灞桥区	Baqiao	11426	11426	10201	44.37	330
未央区	Weiyang	1536	1536	1010	5.33	
雁塔区	Yanta				2.50	
阎良区	Yanliang	56838	56838	56838	61.73	580
临潼区	Lintong	80525	80525	80525	267.40	1591
长安区	Chang'an	15056	12485	5326	298.90	4094
蓝田县	Lantian	71079	71079	46731	125.00	
周至县	Zhouzhi	13037	12880	2375	95.58	6435
户 县	Huxian	7026	7026	6819	130.80	4385
高陵县	Gaoling	17224	13587	12721	141.00	

11-31 主要年份畜产品和水产品产量

Output of Livestock Products and Aquatic Products in Representative Years

单位：吨 (ton)

年份 Year	肉类总产量 Output of Meat	猪肉 Pork	牛肉 Beef	羊肉 Mutton	禽肉 Poultry
1990	63273	50646	4667	1931	5885
1991	72268	55086	5623	2162	9062
1992	88994	68134	6468	2460	11290
1993	93420	71274	7249	2220	12174
1994	106691	79433	8298	2350	15681
1995	127815	86513	11251	3731	23948
1996	91468	63750	5402	2578	19324
1997	106597	75381	6672	3468	20596
1998	134152	98974	8788	4710	21424
1999	130124	93859	9827	4147	21963
2000	147571	106137	12066	4766	23760
2001	157277	113353	11900	5153	20540
2002	161092	118634	11516	5394	20515
2003	165860	122759	13241	5180	19682
2004	171545	126404	13641	5874	18493
2005	182046	136503	14031	6106	18803
2006	108634	81199	8267	2841	13417
2007	102191	73254	8589	3111	14075
2008	115352	84654	9840	3335	16060
2009	126182	94490	10142	3677	17190
2010	136501	102296	10854	3875	18338
2011	144631	104816	11860	3645	19390
2012	151711	110506	12079	3697	20046
2013	157449	114288	12143	4035	20817

注：2010年起，根据统计制度要求，水产品产量及养殖面积统计数据取自水务部门。

11-31 续表 continued

单位：吨 (ton)

年 份 Year	奶类产量 Output of Milk	牛 奶 Cow Milk	禽 蛋 Poultry Eggs	蜂蜜（公斤） Honey(kg)	水产品 Output of Aquatic Products	养殖面积（万亩） Water Raise Areas (10 000 mu)
1990	82017	50528	55938	1035392	4259	2.55
1991	91006	57700	90558	1022797	4949	2.63
1992	100080	63586	104970	739275	6015	2.8
1993	111070	73897	125244	662049	7132	2.97
1994	145412	99025	146503	547808	7900	3.1
1995	132909	85753	141227	535891	8517	3.21
1996	133372	86103	138044	613290	8910	3.51
1997	150964	98078	156066	713918	10054	3.46
1998	174099	119719	142519	537304	10480	3.4
1999	209144	145191	135981	541613	11061	3.38
2000	245913	176155	138305	460598	11384	3.35
2001	255437	179977	132303	479839	12480	3.17
2002	288009	202826	134336	497530	12017	3.31
2003	336296	245407	128833	537805	9967	2.48
2004	384319	289564	117597	449765	9721	2.46
2005	422229	327961	118115	421052	9370	2.38
2006	471438	374813	97816	414271	11937	1.6
2007	528037	428462	98140	401761	12402	1.38
2008	589697	475681	108515	503031	12487	1.4
2009	618186	498394	116685	528731	13044	1.52
2010	633663	509178	123793	436759	11850	2.24
2011	647978	509777	125639	217632	11800	2.2
2012	666439	513337	129970	213174	14010	2.95
2013	657748	512796	135382	219344	14200	2.33

11-32 各区县主要畜产品和水产品产量（2013年）

Output of Major Livestock Products and Aquatic Products by Region（2013）

单位：吨 (tou)

区 县	Region	肉类总产量 Output of Meat	猪 肉 Pork	牛 肉 Beef	羊 肉 Mutton	禽 肉 Poultry
合 计	**Total**	**157449**	**114288**	**12143**	**4036**	**20817**
新城区	Xincheng					
碑林区	Beilin					
莲湖区	Lianhu					
灞桥区	Baqiao	7461	5574	757	144	811
未央区	Weiyang	2449	1608	196	9	30
雁塔区	Yanta	826	765	13		48
阎良区	Yanliang	6746	4461	620	612	984
临潼区	Lintong	42865	30251	3550	1610	4320
长安区	Chang'an	21383	14055	597	257	5803
蓝田县	Lantian	18352	10457	3379	985	2786
周至县	Zhouzhi	29028	25078	1941	207	1698
户 县	Huxian	19360	15911	660	75	2296
高陵县	Gaoling	8979	6128	430	137	2041

11-32 续表 continued

单位：吨 (tou)

区 县	Region	奶类产量 Output of Milk	牛 奶 Cow Milk	禽 蛋 Poultry Eggs	蜂蜜（公斤） Honey(kg)	水产品 Output of Aquatic Products	养殖面积（亩） Water Raise Areas (mu)
合 计	**Total**	**657748**	**512796**	**135382**	**219344**	**14200**	**23310**
新城区	Xincheng						
碑林区	Beilin						
莲湖区	Lianhu						
灞桥区	Baqiao	65636	58488	5583	8300	1500	2850
未央区	Weiyang	7080	6950	111		3000	1445
雁塔区	Yanta	960	960	276		50	120
阎良区	Yanliang	97187	65358	7454	15860	202	150
临潼区	Lintong	345243	289035	32574	42920	1835	5175
长安区	Chang'an	23219	18445	41506	71269	4876	6520
蓝田县	Lantian	41104	11824	6534		900	3660
周至县	Zhouzhi	13248	11484	9956	60382	828	2310
户 县	Huxian	26386	22351	14538	20613	804	900
高陵县	Gaoling	37685	27901	16850		205	180

11-33 农业科技、教育情况（2013年）

Agricultural Science and Technology Education（2013）

指标	Item	2013
农业研究开发机构（个）	Agricultural research and development institutions (unit)	245
农业科技人员（人）	Agricultural scientific and technical personnel(persons)	3770
农业科研成果（个）	Agricultural scientific research achievements (unit)	17
农民技能培训人数（万人）	The number of peasants skills training(10000 persons)	19
良种推广面积（万亩）	Thoroughbred promotion area (10000 mu)	567
农业信息站（个）	information station of Agricultural (unit)	3104

11-34 主要年份农产品人均占有量

Per Capita Output of Major Farm Products in Representative Years

单位：公斤/人 (kg/ person)

年份 Year	粮食 Grain	棉花 Cotton	油料 Oil-bearing Crops	猪牛羊肉 Pork Beef and Mutton	禽蛋 Poultry Eggs	奶类 Milk	水果 Fruits	蔬菜 Vegetables
1978	266.7	5.7	0.2	5.4	0.9	3.3	6.8	91.7
1979	288.6	5.2	0.6	6.7	1.0	4.0	5.1	97.3
1980	223.5	3.8	1.1	5.9	1.2	4.1	6.9	78.4
1981	222.9	2.6	1.5	6.6	1.7	4.7	5.8	55.4
1982	281.5	5.5	1.0	4.9	2.7	5.6	5.9	101.6
1983	276.6	1.6	0.7	4.9	3.2	6.5	5.0	37.8
1984	289.4	2.7	0.8	4.8	6.2	8.7	4.8	138.6
1985	271.4	0.9	1.4	6.8	5.7	10.2	7.6	156.3
1986	288.0	0.8	2.2	7.8	6.4	12.1	9.6	152.2
1987	298.0	0.8	2.7	7.3	6.8	13.8	10.6	155.6
1988	269.7	0.7	1.5	8.0	8.9	15.6	11.1	193.7
1989	290.7	0.9	2.2	8.4	7.6	13.1	10.2	216.5
1990	298.7	1.2	2.1	9.4	9.2	14.2	11.5	196.0
1991	290.6	1.6	2.0	10.2	14.7	14.8	11.7	190.8
1992	294.3	1.2	2.4	12.4	16.8	16.2	17.3	205.6
1993	301.2	1.2	2.2	12.8	19.9	17.6	25.9	231.1
1994	246.1	1.0	1.7	14.1	22.9	22.7	28.0	211.5
1995	270.4	0.5	3.4	15.7	21.8	20.5	37.5	206.1
1996	286.3	0.4	3.2	11.0	21.1	20.4	43.9	210.8
1997	287.8	0.3	2.8	12.9	23.6	22.8	43.3	214.7
1998	318.3	0.2	2.5	16.8	21.3	26.1	50.0	222.8
1999	303.0	0.2	1.9	16.0	20.2	31.0	52.7	227.2
2000	293.5	0.2	1.9	17.9	20.1	35.7	49.9	235.7
2001	283.7	0.2	1.8	18.8	19.0	36.8	48.8	219.9
2002	273.8	0.3	1.7	19.3	19.1	41.0	53.5	241.6
2003	246.0	0.3	1.6	19.7	18.0	46.9	53.6	236.8
2004	270.1	0.6	1.6	20.1	16.2	53.0	63.9	249.6
2005	277.1	0.6	1.6	21.1	15.9	56.9	69.1	263.8
2006	256.9	0.6	1.4	12.3	13.0	62.6	73.5	251.4
2007	247.4	0.8	1.3	11.1	12.8	69.1	79.2	267.3
2008	256.0	0.7	1.4	11.7	13.0	70.4	85.6	264.5
2009	258.7	0.7	1.3	12.84	13.83	73.3	93.6	287.4
2010	261.8	0.7	1.4	13.8	14.6	74.8	100.1	298.9
2011	213.8	0.7	1.4	14.1	14.8	76.1	107.1	318.9
2012	225.6	0.6	1.2	14.8	15.2	78.1	109.2	325.6
2013	213.2	0.3	1.2	15.2	15.8	76.6	110.8	347.1

11-35 主要年份农村经济效益指标

Main Indicators of Rural Economic Benefit in Representative Years

年份 Year	每一劳动力创造的 Average Labor Force Production 农林牧渔及服务业总产值（元） Gross Output Value of Farming,Forestry, Animal Husbandry, Fishery and Service (yuan)	粮食（公斤） Grain Crops(kg)	棉花（公斤） Cotton (kg)	油料（公斤） Oil-bearing Crops(kg)	每亩耕地种植业总产值（元） Output of Each Unit of Area Planting(yuan)	每百元物耗生产的总产值（元） Output per 100-Yuan of Material Consumed(yuan)
1978	504.7	1024.6	22.0	0.7	104.3	
1979	549.0	1096.5	19.8	2.3	116.0	
1980	483.1	846.1	14.5	4.0	99.2	
1981	502.8	840.5	9.9	5.5	105.4	
1982	631.5	1058.9	20.5	3.6	139.3	
1983	606.5	1053.2	6.1	2.6	124.1	
1984	850.7	1154.2	10.9	3.4	163.6	
1985	1020.1	1134.6	3.7	5.6	183.1	
1986	1132.2	1236.4	3.4	9.5	204.6	
1987	1280.3	1277.2	3.5	11.7	231.5	
1988	1558.4	1148.0	3.0	6.5	273.2	
1989	1605.3	1231.9	3.9	9.5	295.0	
1990	1766.3	1279.1	5.2	10.0	343.4	233.3
1991	1958.8	1326.6	7.2	8.9	380.4	238.4
1992	2093.7	1360.7	5.5	11.1	451.6	241.8
1993	2528.9	1409.7	5.6	10.4	546.8	240.1
1994	3705.0	1167.8	4.8	8.0	762.8	227.6
1995	4953.0	1300.6	2.2	16.1	1106.5	225.9
1996	5154.8	1391.2	1.8	13.6	1224.2	234.5
1997	5493.0	1413.4	1.3	13.8	1283.3	239.2
1998	5615.9	1578.1	1.0	12.4	1374.3	247.0
1999	4826.5	1516.6	1.1	9.7	1175.9	251.7
2000	5091.5	1498.0	1.0	9.9	1161.1	250.2
2001	5328.5	1462.4	1.3	9.1	1221.1	248.6
2002	5617.4	1427.5	1.3	9.1	1272.0	265.9
2003	5761.2	1308.1	1.6	8.4	1332.4	254.3
2004	6885.4	1452.7	3.0	8.5	1434.6	261.7
2005	7737.9	1524.7	3.3	8.6	1642.3	262.9
2006	8415.5	1435.7	3.6	8.0	1756.9	263.1
2007	10165.6	1403.0	4.4	7.1	2037.3	259.8
2008	13306.4	1695.4	4.9	9.1	2447.9	259.6
2009	14674.3	1791.7	5.1	9.2	2737.9	261.6
2010	19480.7	1901.3	5.1	10.0	3753.4	260.9
2011	23474.6	1567.2	4.9	10.1	4585.8	274.0
2012	27219.4	1699.6	4.2	10.1	5175.7	273.5
2013	31608.7	1688.0	2.3	9.2	5934.5	274.0

主要统计指标解释

农林牧渔业总产值 指以货币表现的农、林、牧、渔业全部产品和对农林牧渔业生产活动进行的各种支持性服务活动的价值总量，它反映一定时期内农林牧渔业生产总规模和总成果。1957年以前的农林牧渔业总产值中包括了厩肥和农民自给性手工业（如农民自制衣服、鞋、袜，自己从事粮食初步加工等）。1958年及以后，林业中增加了村及村以下竹木采伐产值；牧业中取消了厩肥产值；副业中取消了农民自给性手工业产值，增加了村及村以下办的工业产值；渔业中增加了海洋捕捞水产品产值。1980年及以后，在副业中增加了农民家庭兼营工业商品部分的产值。从1984年起村及村以下工业产值划归工业。从1993年起取消副业，将野生动物的捕猎划入牧业，野生植物采集和农民家庭兼营商品性工业划归农业。从2003年起，执行新的国民经济行业分类标准，农林牧渔业总产值中包括了农林牧渔服务业产值。林业中增加了森林采运业产值。农业中取消了家庭兼营商品性工业产值，将野生林产品的采集划归林业。第一次农业普查以后，由于畜牧业产品年报数据与普查数据之间存在一定的差距，根据农业普查结果对畜牧业年报数据进行了修正，对畜牧业产值进行了相应修正。

农林牧渔业总产值的计算方法通常是按农、林、牧、渔业产品及其副产品的产量分别乘以各自单位产品价格求得；少数生产周期较长，当年没有产品或产品产量不易统计的，则采用间接方法匡算其产值；然后将四业产品产值及农林牧渔服务业产值相加即为农林牧渔业总产值。

粮食产量 指全社会的产量。包括国有经济经营的、集体统一经营的和农民家庭经营的粮食产量，还包括工矿企业办的农场和其他生产单位的产量。粮食除包括稻谷、小麦、玉米、高粱、谷子及其他杂粮外，还包括薯类和豆类。其产量计算方法，豆类按去豆荚后的干豆计算；薯类（包括甘薯和马铃薯，不包括芋头和木薯）1963年以前按每4公斤鲜薯折1公斤粮食计算，从1964年开始改为按5公斤鲜薯折1公斤粮食计算。城市郊区作为蔬菜的薯类（如马铃薯等）按鲜品计算，并且不作粮食统计。其他粮食一律按脱粒后的原粮计算。1989年以前全国粮食产量数据主要靠全面报表取得，1989年开始使用抽样调查数据。

棉花产量 指全社会的产量。包括春播棉和夏播棉。产量按皮棉计算。不包括木棉。

油料产量 指全部油料作物的生产量。包括花生、油菜籽、芝麻、向日葵籽、胡麻籽（亚麻籽）和其他油料。不包括大豆、木本油料和野生油料。花生以带壳干花生计算。

水产品产量 指人工养殖的水产品和天然生长的水产品的捕捞量。包括海水的鱼类、虾蟹类、贝类和藻类以及内陆水域的鱼类、虾蟹类和贝类，不包括淡水生植物。水产品产量是通过各级水产和统计部门逐级上报取得数据。1995年及以前，贝类中牡蛎按鲜肉计算；蚶、蛤、蛙按5斤鲜品折1斤计算。1996年以后则统一按鲜品计算。

猪、牛、羊肉产量 指当年出栏并已屠宰、除去头蹄下水后带骨肉（即胴体重）的重量。包括全社会范围内的产量。1996年前为各级逐级上报数据。1996年第一次农业普查以后，由于畜牧业产品年报数据与普查数据之间存在一定的差距，根据普查结果对畜牧业年报数据进行了修正。1999年以后，国家统计局在部分地区开展了猪、牛、羊、禽等主要畜禽品种的抽样调查，并用抽样数据作为国家定案数据使用。未开展抽样调查的地区和品种，仍使用各级统计部门逐级上报数据。2007年，根据第二次农业普查结果，对2000-2006年畜牧业年报数据进行了修正。2008年，建立了主要畜禽监测调查制度，猪、牛、羊、禽等主要畜牧业数据均以抽样调查数为法定数据。

期初（末）畜禽存栏头（只）数 指报告期初（末）农村各种合作经济组织和国营农场、农民个人、机关、团体、学校、工矿企业、部队等单位以及城镇居民饲养的大牲畜、猪、羊、家禽等畜禽的存栏数。数据上报方式及数据调整情况同猪、牛、羊肉产量。

常用耕地 是指耕地总资源中专门种植农作物并经常进行耕种、能够正常收获的土地。包括当年实际耕种的熟地；弃耕、休闲不满三年，随时可以复耕的地；开荒利用三年以上的地。不包括临时种植农作物的坡度在25度以上的陡坡地；在河套、湖畔、库区临时开发的成片或零星土地；也不包括已列为国家和省（区、市）退耕计划但临时耕种的土地。

农作物播种面积 指实际播种或移植有农作物的面积。凡是实际种植有农作物的面积，不论种植在耕地上还是种植在非耕地上，均包括在农作物播种面积中。在播种季节基本结束后，因遭灾而重新改种和补种的农作物面积，也包括在内。它是反映我国耕地面积利用情况的一个重要指标。目前，农作物播种面积料、麻类、烟叶、蔬菜和瓜类、药材和其他农作物九大类。

主要包括粮食、棉花、油料、糖料、麻类、烟叶、蔬菜和瓜类、药材和其他农作物九大类。

有效灌溉面积 指具有一定的水源，地块比较平整，灌溉工程或设备已经配套，在一般年景下，当年能够进行正常灌溉的耕地面积。在一般情况下，有效灌溉面积应等于灌溉工程或设备已经配备，能够进行正常灌溉的水田和水浇地面积之和。它是反映我国耕地抗旱能力的一个重要指标。

农用化肥施用量 指本年内实际用于农业生产的化肥数量，包括氮肥、磷肥、钾肥和复合肥。化肥施用量要求按折纯量计算数量。折纯量是指把氮肥、磷肥、钾肥分别按含氮、含五氧化二磷、含氧化钾的百分之百成份进行折算后的数量。复合肥按其所含主要成分折算。公式为：

折纯量=实物量×某种化肥有效成份含量的百分比

农业机械总动力 指主要用于农、林、牧、渔业的各种动力机械的动力总和。包括耕作机械、排灌机械、收获机械、农用运输机械、植物保护机械、牧业机械、林业机械、渔业机械和其他农业机械【内燃机按引擎马力折成瓦（特）计算、电动机按功率折成瓦（特）计算】。不包括专门用于乡、镇、村、组办工业、基本建设、非农业运输、科学试验和教学等非农业生产方面用的动力机械与作业机械。这个指标的统计数据主要来源于农机部门。

Explanatory Notes on Main Statistical Indicators

Gross Output Value of Agriculture, Forestry, Animal Husbandry and Fishery refers to the total value of products of agriculture, forestry, animal husbandry and fishery, and total value of services in support of agriculture, forestry, animal husbandry and fishery activities. It reflects the total scale and results of agricultural production during a given period. Prior to 1957, China's gross agricultural output value included barnyard manure and handicraft products for self- consumption (clothes, shoes, stockings, and initial grain processing undertaken by peasants). Since 1958, cutting and felling of bamboo and trees by villages and other cooperative organizations under villages have been included in forestry; value of barnyard manure has been excluded from animal husbandry; self consumed handicrafts have not been included from sideline occupations, while the output value of industries run by villages and cooperative organizations under village has been included in sideline occupations; and the output value of fish catches by motor fishing boats has been added to fishery. Since 1980, the value of handicraft products made for sale by individuals in households has been added to sideline occupations. Since 1984, industries run by villages and under villages have been included in the sector of industry. Since 1993, the subdivision of sideline occupations has been cancelled, and the hunting of wild animals has been classified into animal husbandry, and the gathering of wild plants and commodity industry run by rural household have been included in farming. A new industrial classification of economic activities was introduced in 2003. Under the new classification, value of services to agriculture, forestry, animal husbandry and fishery is included in the gross output value of agriculture, value of wood felling and transport is included in forestry, value of industrial output by rural households is not included in agriculture, and the collection of wild forest products is taken from agriculture and included in forestry. The First Agriculture Census of China revealed some discrepancy between the production of animal products from the annual reports and that from the census. According to the result of the First Agriculture census, efforts were made to adjust the output value of animal husbandry to make the figures from the annual reports consistent with the census data.

Gross output value of agrieulture is obtained by multiplying the output of each product or by-product by its price, resulting in the output value of each single item. For a small number of products, annual output of which is not available or difficult to get due to the long production (growing) process involved, the output value is estimated through an indirect approach. The sum of output values of all products of agriculture, forestry, animal husbandry and fishery and services in support to those industries is then equal to the gross output value of agriculture.

Grain Output refers to the total output in the whole country including grains produced by State farms, collective units, rural households, as well as by farms affiliated to industrial and mining enterprises and other production units. Grain includes rice, wheat, corn, sorghum, millet and other miscellaneous grains as well as tubers and beans. Output of beans refers to dry beans without pods. The output of tubers (sweet potatoes and potatoes, not including taros and cassava) are converted into that of grain at the ratio 4:1, i.e. 4 kilograms of fresh tubers were equivalent to 1 kilogram of grain up to 1963. Since 1964 the ratio for conversion has been 5:1. Tubers supplied as vegetables (such as potatoes) in cities and suburbs are calculated as fresh vegetables and their output is not included in the output of grain. Output of all other grains refers to husked grain. Data on grain production before 1989 were obtained through the Comprehensive Statistical Reporting System. Since 1989, data from sample surveys are used.

Cotton Output refers to cotton production in the whole country including cotton planted in spring and in autumn. Output is measured as the weight of ginned cotton. Ceiba is not included.

Output of Oil-bearing Crops refers to the total production of oil-bearing crops of various kinds, including peanuts (dry, in shell), rapeseeds, sesame, sunflower seeds, flax seeds, and other oil-bearing crops. Soybeans, oil-bearing woody plants, and wild oil-bearing crops are not included.

Output of Aquatic Products refers to catches of both artificially cultured and naturally grown aquatic products, including fish, shrimps, crabs and shellfish in sea and inland water as well as seaweed. Freshwater plants are not included. Data on output of aquatic products are reported by aquatic product and statistical agencies level by level. Before 1995, among the shellfish, oyster was counted as fresh meat; 5 kilograms of ark shell, clams and frogs are equivalent to 1 kilogram of fresh aquatic products; they have all been counted as flesh aquatic products since 1996.

Output of Pork, Beef, and Mutton refers to the meat of slaughtered hogs, cattle, sheep and goats with head, feet, and offal taken away. Data refers to the production of the whole country. The First Agricultural Census of China in 1996 revealed some discrepancy between the production of animal products from the annual reports and that from the census. Efforts were made to adjust the output value of animal husbandry to make the figures from the annual reports consistent with the census data. Since 1999, the NBS conducted sample surveys for the major animal husbandry products, such as hogs, cattle, sheep and goats and fowls, and the data from sample surveys are used as national finalized data. Those products, which are not covered by the sample survey, are still reported by statistical agencies level by level. In 2007. the data on animal husbandry from 2000 to 2006 were revised according to the results of the Second Agriculture Census of China. In 2008, A Monitoring and Survey Program was set up on main livestock, the data on the main livestock such as hog, cattle, sheep and poultry became the official data based on the sampling survey.

Number of Livestock or Poultry in Stock at Beginning (or End) of Period refers to the total number of large animals, pigs, sheep, fowls, etc. raised by rural cooperative organizations, State farms, rural individuals, government agencies, schools, industrial and mining enterprises, army, and urban residents at the beginning (or end) of the reference period. Data reporting system and data adjustment are the same as that in the output of pork, beef and mutton.

Regularly Cultivated Land refers to farmland among the total land resources which is exclusively used for farming and is under regular cultivation with harvest in normal years. Included are currently cultivated land, land that has been abandoned or put in idle for less than 3 years and could be re-used for cultivation at any time, and new-claimed land that has been put into cultivation for more than 3 years. Excluded under this category are steep slope land over 25 degrees under temporary cultivation, land (large or small plots) that is claimed along river bends, lake sides or banks of reservoirs, as well as land that has been designated under the "Green for Grain" programmes of the state and provincial governments but is still temporarily under cultivation.

Sown Area of Crops refers to area of transplanted with crops regardless of being land sown or in cultivated area or non-cultivated area. Area of land re-sown due to lso included. This is an important indicator that can reflect the utilization condition of the cultivated land in China. At present, the sown area of crops mainly include the following 9 categories of crops: grain, cotton, oil-bearing crops, sugar crops, flax crops, tobacco, vegetables and melons, medicinal materials and other farm crops.natural disasters is also included. This is an important indicator that can reflect the utilization condition of the cultivated land in China. At present, the sown area of crops mainly include the following 9 categories of crops: grain, cotton, oil-bearing crops, sugar crops, flax crops, tobacco, vegetables and melons, medicinal materials and other farm crops.

Irrigated Area refers to area of land that are effectively irrigated, i.e. relatively level land, where there are water sources or complete sets of irrigation facilities to lift and move adequate water for irrigation purpose under normal conditions. Under normal situations, irrigated area is the sum of watered fields and irrigated fields where irrigation systems or equipment have been installed for regular irrigation purpose. This important indicator reflects drought resistance capacity of the cultivated land in China.

Consumption of Chemical Fertilizers in Agriculture refers to the quantity of chemical fertilizers applied in agriculture in the year, including nitrogenous fertilizer, phosphate fertilizer, potash fertilizer, and compound fertilizer. The consumption of chemical fertilizers is calculated in terms of volume of effective components by means of converting the gross weight of the respective fertilizers into weight containing effective component (e.g. nitrogen content in nitrogenous fertilizer, phosphorous pentoxide contents in phosphate fertilizer, and potassium oxide contents in potash fertilizer). Compound fertilizer is converted in regard to its major components. The formula is:

Volume of effective component= physical quantity × effective component of certain chemical fertilizer (%)

Total Power of Agricultural Machinery refers to total mechanical power of machinery used in agriculture, forestry, animal husbandry and fishery, including machinery for ploughing, irrigation and drainage, harvesting, transport, plant protection, animal husbandry, forestry and fishery and other agricultural machineries. (For the power of internal combustion engines, it is converted from its horsepower into watts while for electric motors the output power is converted into watts.) Machinery employed for non-agricultural purposes, such as the machines used in township-run and village-run industry, construction, non-agricultural transport, scientific experiments and teaching, are not included. Data are mainly from agricultural machinery agencies.

12 工 业

INDUSTRY

资料整理：赵　晖　王风玲　赵　博　陈小兵　李　玫　王　玥
Data management: Zhao Hui Wang Fengling Zhao Bo Chen Xiaobing Li Mei Wang Yue

第十二部分　工业

一、简要说明

本章资料包括规模以上工业企业单位数、总产值、主要经济指标等，由西安市统计局工业处提供。

二、主要指标

规模以上工业企业单位数（个）	1002	比上年增长	3.7%
规模以上工业增加值（亿元）	1265.64	比上年增长	15.4%

12　INDUSTRY

Ⅰ.Brief Introduction

Data in this chapter includes number of industrial enterprises above designated size and gross product, primary economic. Data in this chapter are provided and compiled by Industry Division of the Xi'an Bureau of Statistics.

Ⅱ.Major Indicators

		Increase over Preceding Year
Number of Industrial Enterprises Above Designated Size(item)	1002	3.7%
Value Added of Industry Above Designated Size(100 million yuan)	1265.64	15.4%

12-1 主要年份规模以上工业企业主要经济指标

Main Economic Indicators of all Industrial Enterprises above Designated Size in Representative Years

单位：亿元 (100 million yuan)

年 份 Year	企业单位数（个） Number of Enterprises (unit)	工业总产值（当年价） Gross Industrial Output Value (At Current Prices)	工业增加值（现价） Value-added of Industry	从业人员年平均人数（万人） Annual Average Employed Persons (10 000 persons)
1998	793	350.38	99.20	51.71
1999	770	366.59	106.56	45.64
2000	816	417.97	130.18	43.25
2001	785	482.61	149.06	40.12
2002	771	544.78	170.39	38.48
2003	735	638.66	202.74	36.55
2004	1066	830.06	254.17	38.08
2005	902	981.02	314.01	37.92
2006	904	1187.74	370.11	37.94
2007	937	1577.05	499.96	38.55
2008	1032	2007.85	605.25	40.17
2009	1131	2468.27	700.13	43.42
2010	1126	3130.15	862.28	47.11
2011	891	3552.21	1012.58	50.42
2012	970	4066.31	1132.44	49.23
2013	1002	4497.62	1265.64	45.88

12-1 续表 continued

单位：亿元 (100 million yuan)

年 份 Year	资产合计 Total Assets	负债合计 Total Liabilities	主营业务收入 Revenue from Principal Business	利润总额 Total Profits	利税总额 Total Pre-tax Profits
1998	810.56	548.68	346.84	-1.26	14.82
1999	853.90	577.94	346.26	8.26	27.30
2000	958.05	622.46	420.42	16.11	36.29
2001	1054.36	657.88	451.62	17.97	40.84
2002	1065.76	643.78	541.64	25.43	51.31
2003	1195.69	733.04	645.53	33.82	64.99
2004	1333.91	869.30	812.46	38.57	74.23
2005	1503.85	977.42	980.97	28.72	67.25
2006	1651.67	1062.11	1183.51	61.46	110.23
2007	1940.52	1254.01	1561.25	106.22	168.54
2008	2426.13	1518.86	1928.05	84.89	168.63
2009	2913.56	1779.38	2384.52	177.2	280.68
2010	3592.13	2069.29	3011.19	245.37	373.56
2011	3975.38	2295.49	3381.27	172.94	312.78
2012	4775.92	2835.55	3758.56	167.77	320.57
2013	4948.67	2915.72	4011.73	181.82	321.00

12-2 规模以上工业企业主要工业产品产量（2013年）

Output of Major Industrial Products of Enterprises above Designated Size（2013）

产品名称	Name of Products	2013	比上年增长（%）Increase over Preceding Year (%)
铁矿石成品矿(万吨)	Iron Ore(10 000 ton)	3.3	23.5
发电量(亿千瓦小时)	Electricity Generation Volume(100 million kw.h)	184.5	-1.8
其中：火电	Thermal Power	162.4	-2.5
水力发电	Hydroelectric Power	19.9	4.2
自来水生产量(亿立方米)	Tap Water Production (100 million cu.m)	4.1	9.7
大米(万吨)	Rice (10 000 ton)	4.5	-18.7
小麦粉(万吨)	Wheat Flour (10 000 tons)	130.7	36.7
精制食用植物油(万吨)	Edible Vegetable Oil (10 000 ton)	23.5	-17.5
鲜、冷藏肉（万吨）	Fresh/Frozen Meat(10 000 ton)	1.8	-5.5
配混合饲料(万吨)	Mixed Feed(10 000 ton)	102.5	25.9
方便面(万吨)	Inshunt Noodle(10 000 ton)	8.6	-4.3
乳制品(万吨)	Dairy Products (10 000 ton)	133.2	7.1
其中 ：液体乳(万吨)	Milk	121.7	5.1
饮料酒(万千升)	Beverage Wine (10 000 kiloliter)	44.1	-3.3
其中：白酒（折65度，商品量）	Liquor (as 65 degree, amount of goods)	0.1	5.5
啤酒	Beer	44.0	-3.3
软饮料(万吨)	Soft Beverage (10 000 ton)	250.3	22.7
其中：碳酸饮料类（汽水）	Carbonated Beverage	51.3	14.9
果汁和蔬菜汁饮料	Juice and Fruit Beverage	38.5	12.2
包装饮用水类	Canned Drinking Water	10.3	-6.0
纱(万吨)	Yarn (10 000 ton)	2.7	-21.7
1. 棉纱	Cotton Yarn	0.7	-49.5
2. 棉混纺纱	Blend Fabric	0.5	-27.3
3. 化学纤维纱	Pure Chemical-Fibre Yarn	1.6	3.3
布(亿米)	Cloth (100 million m)	1.4	-2.2
1. 棉布	Cotton Cloth	0.5	4.9
2. 棉混纺布	Blend Fabric	0.2	-14.2
3. 化学纤维布	Pure Chemical-Fibre Cloth	0.7	-2.6
服装（万件）	Garment (10 000 units)	656.7	-35.6
其中：梭织服装	Shuttle-Woven Garment	5.9	195.0

注:本表增长速度基期数据为2013年加报同期数

12-2 续表1 continued1

产品名称	Name of Products	2013	比上年增长（%） Increase over Preceding Year (%)
皮革鞋靴（万双）	Leather Shoes (10 000 pairs)	650.8	-36.1
人造板（万立方米）	Artificial Board (10 000 cu.m)	205.4	18.5
其中：纤维板	Fibre Board	46.4	16.5
家具（件）	Furniture (unit)	450198	31.6
其中：木质家具	Wooden Furniture	70701	-58.7
金属家具		64041	1.5
软体家具	Soft Furniture (inc.: Sofa ,Mattress etc.)	102250	-5.1
机制纸及纸板（外购原纸加工除外）（万吨）	Machine Made Paper(not including processing of procured base paper)(10 000 ton)	16.0	-42.1
纸制品（万吨）	Paper-Made Products (10 000 ton)	4.4	-50.7
其中：瓦楞纸箱	Corrugated Paper	3.9	-53.2
单色印刷（万令）	Monochrom Printed products(10 000 reams)	154.3	7.8
多色印刷品（万对开色令）	Colored Printed products(10 000 reams)	869.7	-3.2
原油加工量（万吨）	Crude Oil Processing (10 000 ton)	213.1	-1.9
汽油（万吨）	Petrol(10 000 ton)	49.0	42.3
柴油（万吨）	Diesel(10 000 ton)	62.6	0.4
燃料油（万吨）	Fuel Oil(10 000 ton)	5.1	-63
石油沥青（万吨）	Petroleum Pitch (10 000 ton)	7.0	-68.8
液化石油气（万吨）	Liquefied Petroleum Gas (10 000 ton)	9.1	35.2
石油焦（万吨）	Petroleum Coke (10 000 ton)	65.8	29.9
化学农药原药(折有效成分100%)(万吨)	Chemical Pesticide(100% effective content)(10 000 ton)	0.4	-5.3
涂料（万吨）	Construction Paint(10 000 ton)	1.6	20.8
合成洗涤剂（万吨）	Synthetic Detergents (10 000 ton)	11.7	1.0
其中：合成洗衣粉（万吨）	Washing Power	3.2	-11.9
化学原料药（万吨）	Chemical Medicine (10 000 ton)	0.4	-18.8
中成药（万吨）	Traditional Chinese Medicine (10 000 ton)	0.3	4.2
化学纤维（万吨）	Chemical Fiber	2.4	-10.8
其中 ：人造纤维（纤维素纤维）（万吨）	Man-made Fiber	2.4	-10.8
塑料制品（万吨）	Plastic Product (10 000 ton)	14.5	40.8
水泥（万吨）	Cement (10 000 ton)	391.1	-25.5

12-2 续表2 continued2

产品名称	Name of Products	2013	比上年增长（%）Increase over Preceding Year (%)
硅酸盐水泥熟料（万吨）	Portland Cement Clinker (10 000 ton)	169.9	10.9
其中：窑外分解窑水泥熟料（万吨）	Outside Decomposition of Kiln Cement Clinker	4.6	-17.2
水泥混凝土电杆（万根）	Cement Pole(10 000 unit)	2.9	-0.4
商品混凝土(万立方米)	Ready-mixed Concrete (10 000 cu.m)	2606.1	14.7
沥青和改性沥青防水卷材（万平方米）	Asphalt and Modified Bitumen Membrane(10 000 sq.m)	1818.2	-14.5
平板玻璃（万重量箱）	Plate Glass (10 000 wt.cases)		
钢化玻璃(万平方米)	Toughened Glass(10 000 sq.m)	23.8	-13.8
日用玻璃制品（万吨）	Glassware(10 000 ton)	0.6	-24.4
钢材（万吨）	Rolled-steel Final Products (10 000 ton)	54.3	9.8
其中：盘条（线材）	Wire Rod	29.6	0.7
无缝钢管	Seamless Steel Pipe	1.0	1.9
其它钢材	Others Rolled-steel Final Products	23.7	30
铁合金（万吨）	Ferroalloy (10 000 ton)	1.0	-16.5
铝材(万吨)	Aluminum Material (10 000 ton)	4.4	3.4
黄金（千克）	Gold (kg)	266.0	-14.7
单晶硅（千克）	Monocrystalline Silicon (kg)	2206830	62.7
工业锅炉（蒸发量吨）	Industrial Boiler steam(ton)	3159.8	115.2
发动机（万千瓦）	Engine (10 000 kw)	161.7	144.1
汽车发动机（万千瓦）	Motor Engine	161.7	144.1
金属切削机床(万台)	Metal-cutting Machines (10 000 unit)	0.4	-22.0
泵(液体泵)(万台)	Pump (Liquid pump)(10 000 unit)	0.2	-41.6
风机（万台）	Fan(10 000 unit)	0.2	10.9
气体压缩机（万台）	Gas Compressor(10 000 unit)	416.1	-30.0
阀门（万吨）	Valves (10 000 ton)	0.1	-29.0
铸铁件（万吨）	Iron Castings (10 000 ton)	1.4	-40.1
铸钢件（万吨）	Steel Castings (10 000 ton)	0.7	-26.8
锻件（万吨）	Forgings (10 000 ton)	0.9	33.7
粉末冶金零件(万吨)	Powder Melallurgy Products(10 000 ton)	0.1	17.1
矿山专用设备（万吨）	Mining Equipment (10 000 ton)	0.7	-13.9

12-2 续表3 continued3

产品名称	Name of Products	2013	比上年增长（%）Increase over Preceding Year (%)
炼油、化工专用设备（万吨）	Oil Refining and Chemical Industry Machine(10 000 ton)	1.4	127.5
金属冶炼设备(冶炼设备)（吨）	Metal Smelting Equipments(ton)	9082	-37.9
金属轧制设备（吨）	Metal-rolling Machine(ton)	7002.1	86.3
混凝土机械（台）	Concrete Machinery(unit)	189	-41.8
印刷专用设备（吨）	Printing Equipment(ton)	6210	-3.7
环境保护专用设备(台、套)	Special Equipment for Environment Protection	113	-21.5
大气污染防治设备	Equipment for Preventing Atmospheric Pollution	89	-7.3
铁路货车（辆）	Freight(unit)	2866	-11
汽车（万辆）	Motor Vehicle(10 000unit)	42.2	21.1
其中：基本型乘用车（轿车）（万辆）	Basic Passenger Vehicles (10 000Cars)	31.7	21.1
①排量≤1升	1.0L and Below Gas Displacement	0.1	0.1
②1升<排量≤1.6升	1.0L- 1.6L Gas Displacement(1.6L included)	31.4	22.2
③排量>1.6升	Displacement of >1.6 Liter	0.2	-50.3
客车	Passenger Vehicles	0.3	-70.3
大型客车（车长>10）	Buses	0.04	-18.6
轻型客车（车长<7）	Large(40seats and above)	0.2	-73
载货汽车	Trucks	10.2	31.1
改装汽车（万辆）	Refit Trucks (10 000 ton)unit)	1.5	39.8
交流电动机（万千瓦）	Alternating Current Motor(10 000kw)	575.0	29.8
变压器（万千伏安）	Transformer(10 000KVA)	12170.0	13.2
高压开关板（面）	High-voltage Switch Panel(unit)	16844	-18.4
低压开关板（万面）	Low-voltage Switch Panel(10 000 unit)	1.7	-37.9
电力电缆(万千米)	Electric Power Cables(10 000 km)	1.1	-9.5
通信及电子网络用电缆(万对千米)	Communication Cables(10 000 pair km)	3.0	152.5
光缆(光纤通讯电缆)（万芯千米）	Cable (Optical Communication Cable) (10 000 Core.km)	398.0	18.9
绝缘制品(吨)	Insulating Products(ton)	3055.0	-41.2
家用电冰箱（万台）	Household refrigerator(10 000 unit)	10.9	-30.8
电子元件（亿只）	Electronic Components(100 million units)	3.8	4.4
工业自动化调节仪表与控制系统（万台、套）	Automatization meter and system (10 000 unit)	15.1	210.5
电工仪器仪表（万台）	Electrical Instrumentation (10 000 sets)	1.5	-31.7
分析仪器及装置（万台、套）	Analysis Instruments and Apparatus(10 000 sets)	3.9	-18.5

12-3 规模以上工业企业分行业工业增加值(2013年)

Value Added of Industrial Enterprises above Designated Size by Sector (2013)

单位:亿元 (100 million yuan)

行　业	Sector	2013
总计	**Total**	**1265.64**
按工业行业大类分	**Grouped by Sector**	
煤炭开采和洗选业	Mining and Washing of Coal	0.83
石油和天然气开采业	Extraction of Petroleum and Natural Gas	
黑色金属矿采选业	Mining and Processing of Ferrous Metal Ores	0.11
有色金属矿采选业	Mining and Processing of Non-ferrous Metal Ores	
非金属矿采选业	Mining and Processing of Nonmetal Ores	
开采辅助活动	Mining Auxiliary Activities	39.08
其他采矿业	Mining of Other Ores	
农副食品加工业	Processing of Food from Agricultural Porducts	53.06
食品制造业	Manufacture of Foods	50.35
酒、饮料和精制茶制造业	Manufacture of Alcohol,Beverages and Tea	33.07
烟草制品业	Manufacture of Tobacco	0.71
纺织业	Manufacture of Textile	6.34
纺织服装、服饰业	Textile, Garments industry	4.49
皮革、毛皮、羽毛及其制品和制鞋业	Manufacture of Leather, Fur, Feather and Related Products	1.30
木材加工和木、竹、藤、棕、草制品业	Processing of Timber, Manufacture of Wood,Plam and Straw Products	4.30
家具制造业	Manufacture of Furniture	2.37
造纸及纸制品业	Manufacture of Paper and Paper Products	4.25
印刷和记录媒介复制	Printing,Reproduction of Recording Media	24.51
文教、工美、体育和娱乐用品制造业	Manufacture of Articles For Cultural,Educational and Sports Activities	6.75
石油加工业、炼焦和核燃料加工业	Processing of Petroleum, Cokeing,Processing of Nuclear and Nuclear Fuel	42.09
化学原料及化学制品制造业	Manufacture of Raw Chemical Materials and Chemical Products	48.05
医药制造业	Manufacture of Medicines	55.59
化学纤维制造业	Manufacture of Chemical Fibers	2.48
橡胶和塑料制品业	Manufacture of Rubber and Plastics	16.59
非金属矿物制品业	Manufacture of Non-metallic Mineral Products	60.90
黑色金属冶炼和压延加工业	Smelting and Pressing of Ferrous Metals	23.83
有色金属冶炼和压延加工业	Smelting and Pressing of Non-ferrous Metals	26.55
金属制品业	Manufacture of Metal Products	38.24
通用设备制造业	Manufacture of General Purpose Machinery	51.66
专用设备制造业	Manufacture of Special Equipment	89.76
汽车制造业	Manufacture of Motor Vehicle	194.02
铁路、船舶、航空航天和其他运输设备制造业	Railways, Shipbuilding,Aerospace and Other Transportation Equipment Manufacturing Industry	97.03
电气机械和器材制造业	Manufacture of Electric Equipment and Machinery	103.22
计算机、通讯和其他电子设备制造业	Manufacture of Communication Equipment, Computers and other Electronic Equipment	38.02
仪器仪表制造业	Manufacture of Measuring Instruments and Machinery	30.40
其他制造业	Manufacture of Other Manufacturing	24.69
废弃资源综合利用业	Recycling and Disposal of Waste	
金属制品、机械和设备修理业	Metal Products,Machinery and Equipment Repair Industry	1.85
电力、热力的生产和供应业	Production and Supply of Electric Power and Heat Power	58.52
燃气生产和供应业	Gas Mining and Supplying Industry	24.87
水的生产和供应业	Production and Supply of Water	5.76

12-4 主要年份规模以上工业企业经济效益指标（2013）

Indicators of Economic Benefit of Industrial Enterprises above Designated Size in Representative Years(2013)

年 份 Year	总资产贡献率 (%) Ratio of Total Assets to Industrial Output Value (%)	资产负债率 (%) Assets-Liability Ratio (%)	流动资产周转次数 (次/年) Rate of Annual Turnover Working Capitals (times/year)	成本费用利润率 (%) Ratio of Profits to Cost (%)	全员劳动生产率 (元/人·年) Overall Labor Productivity (yuan/person·year)	产品销售率 (%) Proportion of Industrial Products Sold (%)
1998		67.7	0.9	-266.1	19185	95.3
1999		67.7	0.9	2.5	22878	95.9
2000		65.0	1.0	4.2	29496	97.1
2001	5.8	62.4	0.9	4.1	38267	96.7
2002	6.2	60.4	1.1	5.1	46940	96.7
2003	7.0	61.3	1.1	5.7	58801	96.3
2004	6.9	65.2	1.2	5.0	66752	97.9
2005	8.4	65.0	1.3	3.1	82815	97.5
2006	7.8	64.3	1.4	5.5	97551	98.2
2007	10.2	64.6	1.6	7.3	129706	96.8
2008	8.6	62.6	1.5	4.6	150641	96.1
2009	11.3	61.1	1.7	8.1	161239	97.6
2010	12.2	57.6	1.7	8.8	188483	97.1
2011	8.6	57.7	1.5	5.2	194105	97.4
2012	7.7	59.4	1.5	4.5	230032	96.7
2013	7.9	53.9	1.4	4.7	264324	96.2

12-5 规模以上工业企业主要经济指标（2013年）

单位：万元

分　组	Classify	企业单位数（个） Number of Enterprises (unit)	亏损企业 Loss Making Enterprises	工业总产值（当年价格） Gross Industrial Output Value (At Current Prices)
总计	**Total**	**1002**	**185**	**44976189**
按登记注册类型分组	**Grouped by Registion Status**			
内资企业	Domestic Investment Enterprises	885	152	37166984
国有	State-owned Enterprises	71	12	9736282
集体	Collective-owned Enterprises	21	1	188035
股份合作	Share-holding Corperative	10	1	183337
联营	Joint Ownership Enterprises	2		10276
有限责任公司	Limited Liability Corporations	472	90	20191345
股份有限公司	Share-holding Corperation Ltd.	62	11	2993387
私营	Private Enterprises	241	37	3825546
其他	Other Domestic Funded Enterprises	6		38776
港澳台商投资	Enterprises with Funds from Hong Kong,Macao and Taiwan	28	14	419957
外商投资	Foreign Funded Enterprises	89	19	7389248
按轻重工业分	**Grouped by Light Industry and Heavy Industry**			
轻工业	Light Industry	275	50	8684949
重工业	Heavy Industry	727	135	36291240
按企业规模分	**Grouped by Size of Enterprises**			
大型企业	Large-size	63	7	24313775
中型企业	Medium-size	160	35	7298827
小型企业	Small-size	779	143	13363587
微型企业	Microenterprise			
按工业行业大类分	**Grouped by Sector**			
煤炭开采和洗选业	Mining and Washing of Coal			

Main Economic Indicators of All Industrial Enterprises above Designated Size (2013)

(10 000yuan)

工业销售产值（当年价） Value of Industry Products Sales (At Current Prices)	出口交货值 Export Delivery Value	从业人员年平均人数（人） Annual Average Employers (person)	资产总计 Total Assets	流动资产合计 Total Working Capitals
43219872	**2332350**	**458778**	**49486698**	**28947311**
35817378	1738751	390340	43933380	26085901
9480287	154353	95753	14246492	7596534
184133		4361	74621	44206
177289		1771	190508	136906
9976		178	11748	10005
19597759	1274019	224886	22850169	14489809
2708321	131181	31035	4297701	2397103
3621835	128521	31957	2218661	1381018
37778	677	399	43480	30220
392770	56454	7250	507014	218896
7009724	537145	61188	5046304	2642514
8347892	312723	68710	5269161	3016412
34871980	2019627	390068	44217537	25930899
23590801	1665022	272247	28956921	17542977
6770336	295432	78327	7976668	5032781
12858735	361896	108204	12553109	6371553

12-5 续表1

单位：万元

分 组	Classify	负债合计 Total Liabilites	营业收入 Total Revenue	主营业务收入 Revenue from Principal Business
总计	**Total**	**29157156**	**40987756**	**40117279**
按登记注册类型分组	**Grouped by Registion Status**			
内资企业	Domestic Investment Enterprises	26204682	34478242	33763735
国有	State-owned Enterprises	9076729	8344157	8084886
集体	Collective-owned Enterprises	47494	184512	184511
股份合作	Share-holding Corperative	147011	142158	142158
联营	Joint Ownership Enterprises	5689	7910	7910
有限责任公司	Limited Liability Corporations	13706925	19965077	19567119
股份有限公司	Share-holding Corperation Ltd.	2070715	2431144	2388083
私营	Private Enterprises	1123602	3366059	3351924
其他	Other Domestic Funded Enterprises	26517	37225	37144
港澳台商投资	Enterprises with Funds from Hong Kong,Macao and Taiwan	261450	330505	325393
外商投资	Foreign Funded Enterprises	2691024	6179009	6028151
按轻重工业分	**Grouped by Light Industry and Heavy Industry**			
轻工业	Light Industry	2718834	7758861	7691288
重工业	Heavy Industry	26438322	33228895	32425991
按企业规模分	**Grouped by Size of Enterprises**			
大型企业	Large-size	16171653	21423580	20930701
中型企业	Medium-size	4593453	5469406	5184707
小型企业	Small-size	8392050	14094770	14001871
微型企业	Microenterprise			
按工业行业大类分	**Grouped by Sector**			
煤炭开采和洗选业	Mining and Washing of Coal			

continued1

(10 000yuan)

营业成本		营业税金及附加		销售费用
	主营业务成本		主营业务税金及附加	
Total Cost	Cost of Principal Business	Taxs and Other Changes	Taxes and Other Charges on Principal Business	Expenses for Sales
35222821	**34172471**	**386248**	**381652**	**1573659**
29834486	28904815	316086	313829	1080864
7258273	6720946	202945	202016	208001
153509	153509	695	694	4559
130310	130310	214	214	5282
7283	7283	20	20	268
17426219	17080106	79066	78034	615076
1976156	1942082	12671	12671	121339
2847850	2835693	20402	20108	126103
34886	34886	73	72	236
272026	268562	3232	3215	41429
5116309	4999094	66930	64608	451366
6275848	6226786	46663	44700	694061
28946973	27945685	339585	336952	879598
18505975	17776350	288517	285541	909361
4479987	4237313	30819	29835	293536
12236859	12158808	66912	66276	370762

12-5 续表2

单位：万元

分 组	Classify	管理费用 Expenses for Management	财务费用 Financial cost	营业利润 Operating Profit
总计	**Total**	**2164189**	**464951**	**1530768**
按登记注册类型分组	**Grouped by Registion Status**			
内资企业	Domestic Investment Enterprises	1894928	437797	1267843
国有	State-owned Enterprises	545421	192886	337892
集体	Collective-owned Enterprises	8288	802	16925
股份合作	Share-holding Corperative	5561	2982	-2459
联营	Joint Ownership Enterprises	291	35	13
有限责任公司	Limited Liability Corporations	1046322	160334	613323
股份有限公司	Share-holding Corperation Ltd.	154439	39926	116268
私营	Private Enterprises	133282	40488	185477
其他	Other Domestic Funded Enterprises	1324	344	404
港澳台商投资	Enterprises with Funds from Hong Kong,Macao and Taiwan	31901	2644	-19609
外商投资	Foreign Funded Enterprises	237360	24510	282534
按轻重工业分	**Grouped by Light Industry and Heavy Industry**			
轻工业	Light Industry	336010	50170	334515
重工业	Heavy Industry	1828179	414781	1196253
按企业规模分	**Grouped by Size of Enterprises**			
大型企业	Large-size	1271129	169546	637556
中型企业	Medium-size	382674	70073	221690
小型企业	Small-size	510386	225332	671522
微型企业	Microenterprise			
按工业行业大类分	**Grouped by Sector**			
煤炭开采和洗选业	Mining and Washing of Coal			

continued 2

(10 000yuan)

利润总额 Total Profits	亏损企业亏损额 Total Loss of Deficit Enterprises	税金总额 Total taxes	应付职工薪酬 Salary Payable	本年应交增值税 Value Added Tax Payable
1818195	**208056**	**1391789**	**3043831**	**1010137**
1497999	150167	1117444	2556794	803514
423272	41630	520350	745826	318334
17189	35	6465	12845	5770
3003	128	1557	5379	1343
13		144	476	124
721438	78683	423123	1471975	345089
138454	19351	69880	181350	57209
193867	10340	95348	137795	75240
763		577	1148	505
-19758	32084	17572	37309	14357
339954	25805	256773	449728	192166
376793	33640	307169	456893	262470
1441402	174416	1084620	2586938	747667
833297	58120	796255	2005953	510714
276366	82910	184826	461099	154990
708532	67026	410708	576779	344433

12-5 续表3

单位：万元

分 组	Classify	企业单位数（个） Number of Enterprises (unit)	亏损企业（个） Loss Making Enterprises	工业总产值（当年价格） Gross Industrial Output Value (At Current Prices)
石油和天然气开采业	Extraction of Petroleum and Natural Gas			
黑色金属矿采选业	Mining and Processing of Ferrous Metal Ores	1	1	3170
有色金属矿采选业	Mining and Processing of Non-ferrous Metal Ores			
非金属矿采选业	Mining and Processing of Nonmetal Ores			
开采辅助活动	Mining Auxiliary Activities	2		217955
其他采矿业	Mining of other Ores			
农副食品加工业	Processing of Food from Agricultural Porducts	48	8	2074648
食品制造业	Manufacture of Foods	33	1	1496332
酒、饮料和精制茶制造业	Manufacture of Alcohol,Beverages and Tea	13	3	857458
烟草制品业	Manufacture of Tobacco	1		8523
纺织业	Manufacture of Textile	15	4	194944
纺织服装、服饰业	Textile, apparel industry	7	1	136219
皮革、毛皮、羽毛及其制品和制鞋业	Manufacture of Leather, Fur, Feather and Related Products, and Shoes	2	1	53791
木材加工和木、竹、藤、棕、草制品业	Processing of Timber, Manufacture of Wood,Plam and Straw Products	4	1	135516
家具制造业	Manufacture of Furniture	9		61881
造纸及纸制品业	Manufacture of Paper and Paper Products	21	2	124662
印刷和记录媒介复制	Printing,Reproduction of Recording Media	20	6	541894
文教、工美、体育和娱乐用品制造业	Manufacture of Articles For Cultural,Educational and Sports Activities	7	1	201808
石油加工业、炼焦和核燃料加工业	Processing of Petroleum, Cokeing,Processing of Nuclear and Nuclear Fuel	8	1	2561442
化学原料及化学制品制造业	Manufacture of Raw Chemical Materials and Chemical Products	52	4	1484561

continued 3

(10 000yuan)

工业销售产值（当年价）Value of Industry Products Sales (At Current Prices)	出口交货值 Export Delivery Value	从业人员年平均人数（人）Annual Average Employers (person)	资产总计 Total Assets	流动资产合计 Total Working Capitals
3170			2155	1666
73829		833	66164	43862
2038466	4102	8241	677376	440126
1410134		8759	515954	293384
910685	135474	6299	907079	445377
8273		260	18518	7123
176805	13429	3763	224720	137911
129347		1571	109466	83520
54963		988	50556	28881
123120		732	118150	62780
56721		990	33015	23104
120880		2627	88104	47132
523384	1036	7762	621733	266584
200328	141776	597	111547	99937
2566470		5789	613982	318606
1436616	172695	20052	1799004	1038878

12-5 续表4

单位：万元

分 组	Classify	负债合计 Total Liabilites	营业收入 Total Revenue	主营业务收入 Revenue from Principal Business
石油和天然气开采业	Extraction of Petroleum and Natural Gas			
黑色金属矿采选业	Mining and Processing of Ferrous Metal Ores	3938	3113	3113
有色金属矿采选业	Mining and Processing of Non-ferrous Metal Ores			
非金属矿采选业	Mining and Processing of Nonmetal Ores			
开采辅助活动	Mining Auxiliary Activities	17116	45849	44791
其他采矿业	Mining of other Ores			
农副食品加工业	Processing of Food from Agricultural Porducts	451490	1734389	1730856
食品制造业	Manufacture of Foods	221194	1321127	1295723
酒、饮料和精制茶制造业	Manufacture of Alcohol,Beverages and Tea	510953	878475	868944
烟草制品业	Manufacture of Tobacco	11562	9166	9037
纺织业	Manufacture of Textile	118497	171107	169720
纺织服装、服饰业	Textile, apparel industry	70615	180325	177960
皮革、毛皮、羽毛及其制品和制鞋业	Manufacture of Leather, Fur, Feather and Related Products, and Shoes	24500	55890	55385
木材加工和木、竹、藤、棕、草制品业	Processing of Timber, Manufacture of Wood,Plam and Straw Products	61284	105016	104648
家具制造业	Manufacture of Furniture	17266	41485	41219
造纸及纸制品业	Manufacture of Paper and Paper Products	46470	118480	118037
印刷和记录媒介复制	Printing,Reproduction of Recording Media	242047	523196	518442
文教、工美、体育和娱乐用品制造业	Manufacture of Articles For Cultural,Educational and Sports Activities	96280	168964	168964
石油加工业、炼焦和核燃料加工业	Processing of Petroleum, Cokeing,Processing of Nuclear and Nuclear Fuel	430655	2377614	2375306
化学原料及化学制品制造业	Manufacture of Raw Chemical Materials and Chemical Products	940906	1451698	1332775

continued 4

(10 000yuan)

营业成本 Total Cost	主营业务成本 Cost of Principal Business	营业税金及附加 Taxs and Other Changes	主营业务税金及附加 Taxes and Other Charges on Principal Business	销售费用 Expenses for Sales
2715	2715	32	32	25
32908	32622	1069	1069	314
1619834	1618041	2581	2547	48865
1064926	1047229	4209	4209	144700
672573	664787	14865	13500	99480
5781	5767	94	94	125
156265	155455	903	865	2626
156363	155715	2787	2785	5771
50224	49803	194	194	1322
97051	96679	346	344	1887
33383	33207	262	262	3435
105492	105218	333	333	2910
393293	387036	4200	4185	13969
158479	158479	311	311	1337
2194365	2192203	152478	152419	12043
1234813	1116073	5023	5004	47755

12-5 续表5

单位：万元

分　组	Classify	管理费用 Expenses for Management	财务费用 Financial cost	营业利润 Operating Profit
石油和天然气开采业	Extraction of Petroleum and Natural Gas			
黑色金属矿采选业	Mining and Processing of Ferrous Metal Ores	550	193	-350
有色金属矿采选业	Mining and Processing of Non-ferrous Metal Ores			
非金属矿采选业	Mining and Processing of Nonmetal Ores			
开采辅助活动	Mining Auxiliary Activities	3578	44	7937
其他采矿业	Mining of other Ores			
农副食品加工业	Processing of Food from Agricultural Porducts	33762	14548	14849
食品制造业	Manufacture of Foods	44208	-2129	58194
酒、饮料和精制茶制造业	Manufacture of Alcohol,Beverages and Tea	30900	6812	46715
烟草制品业	Manufacture of Tobacco	1984	-22	1193
纺织业	Manufacture of Textile	6578	620	3141
纺织服装、服饰业	Textile, apparel industry	6144	2593	4989
皮革、毛皮、羽毛及其制品和制鞋业	Manufacture of Leather, Fur, Feather and Related Products, and Shoes	1696	163	2195
木材加工和木、竹、藤、棕、草制品业	Processing of Timber, Manufacture of Wood,Plam and Straw Products	3073	2898	-263
家具制造业	Manufacture of Furniture	2208	340	1733
造纸及纸制品业	Manufacture of Paper and Paper Products	3660	723	5647
印刷和记录媒介复制	Printing,Reproduction of Recording Media	56129	5835	50965
文教、工美、体育和娱乐用品制造业	Manufacture of Articles For Cultural,Educational and Sports Activities	1853	284	5614
石油加工业、炼焦和核燃料加工业	Processing of Petroleum, Cokeing,Processing of Nuclear and Nuclear Fuel	23457	9297	-15208
化学原料及化学制品制造业	Manufacture of Raw Chemical Materials and Chemical Products	105928	14955	55949

continued 5

(10 000yuan)

利润总额 Total Profits	亏损企业亏损额 Total Loss of Deficit Enterprises	税金总额 Total taxes	应付职工薪酬 Salary Payable	本年应交增值税 Value Added Tax Payable
-350	350	173	134	141
7935		2175	6869	1106
23643	2856	20069	34368	17521
62781	131	32222	50718	28013
53747	12376	42771	56427	29271
1188		863	2680	769
5997	2017	7605	33725	6741
11201	58	6276	7038	3491
2194	112	276	4514	82
1988	12	3413	3129	3069
1717		1339	2663	1077
8059	483	2821	8080	2489
51359	6922	30673	73047	26487
5673	126	1389	2069	1079
-15263	31815	185651	37681	33232
66142	13836	33693	112514	28689

12-5 续表6

单位：万元

分组	Classify	企业单位数（个） Number of Enterprises (unit)	亏损企业（个） Loss Making Enterprises	工业总产值（当年价格） Gross Industrial Output Value (At Current Prices)
医药制造业	Manufacture of Medicines	49	10	1530663
化学纤维制造业	Manufacture of Chemical Fibers	2	1	94269
橡胶和塑料制品业	Manufacture of Rubber and Plastics	31	7	659922
非金属矿物制品业	Manufacture of Non-metallic Mineral Products	98	21	1838151
黑色金属冶炼和压延加工业	Smelting and Pressing of Ferrous Metals	23	5	854919
有色金属冶炼和压延加工业	Smelting and Pressing of Non-ferrous Metals	29	4	1127714
金属制品业	Manufacture of Metal Products	61	7	1431303
通用设备制造业	Manufacture of General Purpose Machinery	63	9	1855467
专用设备制造业	Manufacture of Special Equipment	97	23	2650964
汽车制造业	Manufacture of Motor Vehicle	38	8	8160643
铁路、船舶、航空航天和其他运输设备制造业	Railways,Shipbuilding,Aerospace and Other Transportation Equipment Manufacturing Industry	50	12	4236246
电气机械和器材制造业	Manufacture of Electric Equipment and Machinery	96	17	4345727
计算机、通讯和其他电子设备制造业	Manufacture of Communication Equipment, Computers and other Electronic Equipment	56	13	1654449
仪器仪表制造业	Manufacture of Measuring Instruments and Machinery	35	7	1317494
其他制造业	Manufacture of Other Manufacturing	3	1	36186
废弃资源综合利用业	Recycling and Disposal of Waste			
金属制品、机械和设备修理业	Metal Products,Machinery and Equipment Repair Industry	3		14276
电力、热力的生产和供应业	Production and Supply of Electric Power and Heat Power	15	3	2223740
燃气生产和供应业	Gas Mining and Supplying Industry	7	2	706779
水的生产和供应业	Production and Supply of Water	3	1	82473

continued 6

(10 000yuan)

工业销售产值（当年价）Value of Industry Products Sales (At Current Prices)	出口交货值 Export Delivery Value	从业人员年平均人数（人）Annual Average Employers (person)	资产总计 Total Assets	流动资产合计 Total Working Capitals
1445606	16069	15571	1163398	744191
99810		372	75134	35561
597138	1626	14515	741160	456290
1782517		12423	893766	519103
849431	13344	3489	246755	134573
1024557	50177	8534	985195	535232
1401974	37151	24586	1865970	1102471
1775138	43275	16921	2836746	2204821
2338308	206436	29883	3347890	2286806
7797330	474211	78709	6613186	3734727
4137758	562710	70457	8217743	5405001
4189213	159324	44175	5577595	3914818
1605849	230636	25891	3114037	1906824
1279780	58696	22454	1946791	1212667
36026	183	602	31528	21555
14071		346	20294	16566
2223180		12750	4182724	857323
706522		4827	1478543	437925
82473		3010	190720	80986

12-5 续表7

单位：万元

分　组	Classify	负债合计 Total Liabilites	营业收入 Total Revenue	主营业务收入 Revenue from Principal Business
医药制造业	Manufacture of Medicines	495080	1314196	1312440
化学纤维制造业	Manufacture of Chemical Fibers	11537	99810	99206
橡胶和塑料制品业	Manufacture of Rubber and Plastics	537043	567820	560127
非金属矿物制品业	Manufacture of Non-metallic Mineral Products	457537	1610626	1605122
黑色金属冶炼和压延加工业	Smelting and Pressing of Ferrous Metals	154003	551887	544557
有色金属冶炼和压延加工业	Smelting and Pressing of Non-ferrous Metals	534206	994052	955553
金属制品业	Manufacture of Metal Products	1120227	1293331	1277322
通用设备制造业	Manufacture of General Purpose Machinery	1507183	1642422	1630085
专用设备制造业	Manufacture of Special Equipment	1580477	2270536	2214956
汽车制造业	Manufacture of Motor Vehicle	3856693	7219144	7008334
铁路、船舶、航空航天和其他运输设备制造业	Railways,Shipbuilding,Aerospace and Other Transportation Equipment Manufacturing Industry	5093498	4897031	4848237
电气机械和器材制造业	Manufacture of Electric Equipment and Machinery	2706229	3810838	3698742
计算机、通讯和其他电子设备制造业	Manufacture of Communication Equipment, Computers and other Electronic Equipment	2030985	1741775	1704590
仪器仪表制造业	Manufacture of Measuring Instruments and Machinery	819637	1228472	1205881
其他制造业	Manufacture of Other Manufacturing	18542	36109	35906
废弃资源综合利用业	Recycling and Disposal of Waste			
金属制品、机械和设备修理业	Metal Products,Machinery and Equipment Repair Industry	11797	17727	17717
电力、热力的生产和供应业	Production and Supply of Electric Power and Heat Power	3969696	1666656	1604970
燃气生产和供应业	Gas Mining and Supplying Industry	890506	743816	695894
水的生产和供应业	Production and Supply of Water	97507	95614	82720

continued 7

(10 000yuan)

营业成本 Total Cost	主营业务成本 Cost of Principal Business	营业税金及附加 Taxs and Other Changes	主营业务税金及附加 Taxes and Other Charges on Principal Business	销售费用 Expenses for Sales
740609	739273	12022	12022	338531
81197	80592	434	434	320
477410	475947	3046	2841	23990
1412255	1406716	11104	11103	36360
506496	498909	2294	2293	5414
893786	853616	1836	1819	11579
1103100	1092252	6158	5882	29779
1293715	1285126	10653	10651	56990
1854203	1808066	17411	17204	95367
6492136	6294420	59421	59386	219021
4238969	4204574	17640	17607	85863
3534068	3113802	18849	18848	186179
1479878	1444693	5258	4993	35821
973644	962565	9190	8488	32276
31249	31243	187	187	607
11442	11442	132	132	1359
1438511	1404572	16764	16764	407
600605	571730	3057	2249	22957
81083	71904	1105	596	3775

12-5 续表8

单位：万元

分 组	Classify	管理费用 Expenses for Management	财务费用 Financial cost	营业利润 Operating Profit
医药制造业	Manufacture of Medicines	101958	15055	103546
化学纤维制造业	Manufacture of Chemical Fibers	3077	-128	14566
橡胶和塑料制品业	Manufacture of Rubber and Plastics	20708	8451	32622
非金属矿物制品业	Manufacture of Non-metallic Mineral Products	39050	6955	101434
黑色金属冶炼和压延加工业	Smelting and Pressing of Ferrous Metals	10075	4801	21699
有色金属冶炼和压延加工业	Smelting and Pressing of Non-ferrous Metals	37996	20806	25340
金属制品业	Manufacture of Metal Products	88206	15746	51157
通用设备制造业	Manufacture of General Purpose Machinery	159471	-3369	126950
专用设备制造业	Manufacture of Special Equipment	169578	18282	177079
汽车制造业	Manufacture of Motor Vehicle	293481	38468	133044
铁路、船舶、航空航天和其他运输设备制造业	Railways,Shipbuilding,Aerospace and Other Transportation Equipment Manufacturing Industry	316839	58428	144250
电气机械和器材制造业	Manufacture of Electric Equipment and Machinery	269126	25819	103584
计算机、通讯和其他电子设备制造业	Manufacture of Communication Equipment, Computers and other Electronic Equipment	133012	9483	75813
仪器仪表制造业	Manufacture of Measuring Instruments and Machinery	138940	8319	60244
其他制造业	Manufacture of Other Manufacturing	2623	536	876
废弃资源综合利用业	Recycling and Disposal of Waste			
金属制品、机械和设备修理业	Metal Products,Machinery and Equipment Repair Industry	3275	53	1360
电力、热力的生产和供应业	Production and Supply of Electric Power and Heat Power	10803	159390	38974
燃气生产和供应业	Gas Mining and Supplying Industry	30899	20442	74860
水的生产和供应业	Production and Supply of Water	9364	260	70

continued 8

(10 000yuan)

利润总额 Total Profits	亏损企业亏损额 Total Loss of Deficit Enterprises	税金总额 Total taxes	应付职工薪酬 Salary Payable	本年应交增值税 Value Added Tax Payable
105106	3686	137021	126443	124999
14570	271	4814	4513	4380
34789	1577	16976	34113	14136
105714	6813	57842	60477	46739
22533	9604	12036	19438	9742
35898	4853	10150	45475	8331
62234	3266	26987	158151	21105
135485	2222	65439	160103	54788
222701	34761	81828	207756	64625
191603	6344	181339	418616	121953
184113	11494	58251	548588	40643
124411	14754	131185	298707	112338
94046	20455	29360	168824	24367
71654	5245	55558	224401	47070
1090	337	1119	2767	932
1534		1138	2059	1006
46208	7315	130391	65378	113626
72845	3890	13386	44143	11137
3650	75	5560	18223	4963

12-6 规模以上国有及国有控股工业企业主要经济指标（2013年）

单位：万元

分 组	Classify	企业单位数（个）Number of Enterprises (unit)	亏损企业 Loss Making Enterprises	工业总产值（当年价格）Gross Industrial Output Value (At Current Prices)
总计	**Total**	**209**	**45**	**24836926**
#亏损企业	Deficit Enterprises	45	45	
按轻重工业分	**Grouped by Light Industry and Heavy Industry**			
轻工业	Light Industry	39	12	1431272
重工业	Heavy Industry	170	33	23405654
按企业规模分	**Grouped by Size of Enterprises**			
大型企业	Large-size	42	6	19019300
中型企业	Medium-size	65	18	2590280
小型企业	Small-size	102	21	3227346
微型企业	Microenterprise			
按工业行业大类分	**Grouped by Sector**			
煤炭开采和洗选业	Mining and Washing of Coal			
石油和天然气开采业	Extraction of Petroleum and Natural Gas			
黑色金属矿采选业	Mining and Processing of Ferrous Metal Ores			
有色金属矿采选业	Mining and Processing of Non-ferrous Metal Ores			
非金属矿采选业	Mining and Processing of Nonmetal Ores			
开采辅助活动	Mining Auxiliary Activities	1		183056
其他采矿业	Mining of Other Ores			
农副食品加工业	Processing of Food from Agricultural Porducts	3	1	34551
食品制造业	Manufacture of Foods	5		434636
酒、饮料和精制茶制造业	Manufacture of Alcohol,Beverages and Tea	1		113820
烟草制品业	Manufacture of Tobacco	1		8523
纺织业	Manufacture of Textile	4	2	101175
纺织服装、服饰业	Textile, apparel industry			
皮革、毛皮、羽毛及其制品和制鞋业	Manufacture of Leather, Fur, Feather and Related Products, and Shoes	1		49251
木材加工和木、竹、藤、棕、草制品业	Processing of Timber, Manufacture of Wood,Plam and Straw Products			
家具制造业	Manufacture of Furniture			
造纸及纸制品业	Manufacture of Paper and Paper Products			
印刷和记录媒介复制	Printing,Reproduction of Recording Media	5	2	284176

Economic Indicators of all State-owned and State-holding Share Industrial Enterprises above Designated Size (2013)

(10 000 yuan)

工业销售产值（当年价） Value of Industry Products Sales (At Current Prices)	出口交货值 Export Delivery Value	从业人员年平均人数（人） Annual Average Employers (person)	资产总计 Total Assets	流动资产合计 Total Working Capitals
24199560	**1301263**	**280376**	**35015894**	**20255149**
		23082	2291745	1118687
1548268	18388	18781	1294682	643600
22651292	1282875	261595	33721212	19611549
18597360	1232356	216441	24748490	15523077
2449546	44326	36518	4007914	2545373
3152654	24581	27417	6259490	2186699
38929		131	9035	79200
34483	4101	926	43775	24899
423090		1548	40064	23484
278890		1317	195207	123037
8273		260	18518	7123
97784	13068	2569	149868	90776
50423		845	42449	20941
286984	1036	4375	363774	131921

12-6 续表1

单位：万元

分 组	Classify	负债合计 Total Liabilites	营业收入 Total Revenue	主营业务收入 Revenue from Principal Business
总计	**Total**	**21488516**	**23559922**	**22882389**
#亏损企业	Deficit Enterprises	1675237	2416597	2370683
按轻重工业分	**Grouped by Light Industry and Heavy Industry**			
轻工业	Light Industry	537707	1542202	1518815
重工业	Heavy Industry	20950809	22017720	21363574
按企业规模分	**Grouped by Size of Enterprises**			
大型企业	Large-size	13967758	16245561	15824207
中型企业	Medium-size	2574780	2427967	2223703
小型企业	Small-size	4945978	4886394	4834479
微型企业	Microenterprise			
按工业行业大类分	**Grouped by Sector**			
煤炭开采和洗选业	Mining and Washing of Coal			
石油和天然气开采业	Extraction of Petroleum and Natural Gas			
黑色金属矿采选业	Mining and Processing of Ferrous Metal Ores			
有色金属矿采选业	Mining and Processing of Non-ferrous Metal Ores			
非金属矿采选业	Mining and Processing of Nonmetal Ores			
开采辅助活动	Mining Auxiliary Activities	5041	12072	12072
其他采矿业	Mining of Other Ores			
农副食品加工业	Processing of Food from Agricultural Porducts	25367	32986	32499
食品制造业	Manufacture of Foods	18442	392937	391403
酒、饮料和精制茶制造业	Manufacture of Alcohol,Beverages and Tea	96487	280091	279786
烟草制品业	Manufacture of Tobacco	11562	9166	9037
纺织业	Manufacture of Textile	78811	97722	96847
纺织服装、服饰业	Textile, apparel industry			
皮革、毛皮、羽毛及其制品和制鞋业	Manufacture of Leather, Fur, Feather and Related Products, and Shoes	22947	51917	51412
木材加工和木、竹、藤、棕、草制品业	Processing of Timber, Manufacture of Wood,Plam and Straw Products			
家具制造业	Manufacture of Furniture			
造纸及纸制品业	Manufacture of Paper and Paper Products			
印刷和记录媒介复制	Printing,Reproduction of Recording Media	57515	298804	295393

continued 1

(10 000 yuan)

营业成本 Total Cost	主营业务成本 Cost of Principal Business	营业税金及附加 Taxs and Other Changes	主营业务税金及附加 Taxes and Other Charges on Principal Business	销售费用 Expenses for Sales
20540653	**19673949**	**263272**	**260741**	**647012**
2212687	2173205	156118	155877	32604
1230551	1214168	17313	16803	92756
19310102	18459781	245959	243938	554256
14078066	13414884	228519	226916	524359
2091123	1924617	13374	12555	78137
4371464	4334448	21379	21270	44516
10291	10291	48	48	216
26450	26116	158	158	1175
321886	321581	573	573	42182
219402	219081	10270	10270	16788
5781	5767	94	94	125
95276	94466	689	689	1095
47201	46780	170	170	918
211916	209184	3128	3126	3677

12-6 续表2

单位：万元

分 组	Classify	管理费用 Expenses for Management	财务费用 Financial cost	营业利润 Operating Profit
总计	**Total**	**1428932**	**326356**	**727549**
#亏损企业	Deficit Enterprises	116254	32055	-130224
按轻重工业分	**Grouped by Light Industry and Heavy Industry**			
轻工业	Light Industry	101148	-466	100267
重工业	Heavy Industry	1327784	326822	627282
按企业规模分	**Grouped by Size of Enterprises**			
大型企业	Large-size	1122864	122558	532619
中型企业	Medium-size	183929	38995	26195
小型企业	Small-size	122139	164803	168735
微型企业	Microenterprise			
按工业行业大类分	**Grouped by Sector**			
煤炭开采和洗选业	Mining and Washing of Coal			
石油和天然气开采业	Extraction of Petroleum and Natural Gas			
黑色金属矿采选业	Mining and Processing of Ferrous Metal Ores			
有色金属矿采选业	Mining and Processing of Non-ferrous Metal Ores			
非金属矿采选业	Mining and Processing of Nonmetal Ores			
开采辅助活动	Mining Auxiliary Activities	539	-2	979
其他采矿业	Mining of Other Ores			
农副食品加工业	Processing of Food from Agricultural Porducts	1780	853	2168
食品制造业	Manufacture of Foods	22976	12	5298
酒、饮料和精制茶制造业	Manufacture of Alcohol,Beverages and Tea	4986	-3481	32581
烟草制品业	Manufacture of Tobacco	1984	-22	1193
纺织业	Manufacture of Textile	4646	131	-3710
纺织服装、服饰业	Textile, apparel industry			
皮革、毛皮、羽毛及其制品和制鞋业	Manufacture of Leather, Fur, Feather and Related Products, and Shoes	1347	163	2207
木材加工和木、竹、藤、棕、草制品业	Processing of Timber, Manufacture of Wood,Plam and Straw Products			
家具制造业	Manufacture of Furniture			
造纸及纸制品业	Manufacture of Paper and Paper Products			
印刷和记录媒介复制	Printing,Reproduction of Recording Media	38136	174	37056

continued 2

(10 000 yuan)

利润总额 Total Profits	亏损企业亏损额 Total Loss of Deficit Enterprises	税金总额 Total Pre-tax Profits	应付职工薪酬 Salary Payable	本年应交增值税 Value Added Tax Payable
908428	**107957**	**819506**	**2065387**	**558765**
-107957	107957	205276	155562	49399
109995	6674	70436	156620	53633
798433	101283	749070	1908767	505132
668886	51199	585483	1641668	353567
57327	43459	74177	243017	61622
182215	13299	159846	180702	13856
988		529	935	481
2151	1161	960	3934	799
5689		4428	7369	3854
32829		19788	16390	9518
1188		863	2680	769
-920	1830	5018	30971	4329
2306		170	4034	
36888	1066	22715	53629	19589

12-6 续表3

单位：万元

分 组	Classify	企业单位数（个）Number of Enterprises (unit)	亏损企业 Loss Making Enterprises	工业总产值（当年价格）Gross Industrial Output Value (At Current Prices)
文教、工美、体育和娱乐用品制造业	Manufacture of Articles For Cultural,Educational and Sports Activities			
石油加工业、炼焦和业核燃料加工	Processing of Petroleum, Cokeing,Processing of Nuclear and Nuclear Fuel	2	1	2316776
化学原料及化学制品制造业	Manufacture of Raw Chemical Materials and Chemical Products	14	1	499583
医药制造业	Manufacture of Medicines	5	1	100844
化学纤维制造业	Manufacture of Chemical Fibers	2	1	94269
橡胶和塑料制品业	Manufacture of Rubber and Plastics	4	1	290464
非金属矿物制品业	Manufacture of Non-metallic Mineral Products	6		48256
黑色金属冶炼和压延加工业	Smelting and Pressing of Ferrous Metals	2	1	459443
有色金属冶炼和压延加工业	Smelting and Pressing of Non-ferrous Metals	9	2	490406
金属制品业	Manufacture of Metal Products	11		913695
通用设备制造业	Manufacture of General Purpose Machinery	11	2	1278375
专用设备制造业	Manufacture of Special Equipment	23	7	1223992
汽车制造业	Manufacture of Motor Vehicle	11	2	5108573
铁路、船舶、航空航天和其他运输设备制造业	Railways,Shipbuilding,Aerospace and Other Transportation Equipment Manufacturing Industry	26	5	3791540
电气机械和器材制造业	Manufacture of Electric Equipment and Machinery	15	5	2385473
计算机、通讯和其他电子设备制造业	Manufacture of Communication Equipment, Computers and other Electronic Equipment	20	4	787544
仪器仪表制造业	Manufacture of Measuring Instruments and Machinery	8	2	884702
其他制造业	Manufacture of Other Manufacturing	2	1	21579
废弃资源综合利用业	Recycling and Disposal of Waste			
金属制品、机械和设备修理业	Metal Products,Machinery and Equipment Repair Industry			
电力、热力的生产和供应业	Production and Supply of Electric Power and Heat Power	10	2	2201840
燃气生产和供应业	Gas Mining and Supplying Industry	4	1	647911
水的生产和供应业	Production and Supply of Water	3	1	82473

continued 3

(10 000 yuan)

工业销售产值（当年价）Value of Industry Products Sales (At Current Prices)	出口交货值 Export Delivery Value	从业人员年平均人数（人）Annual Average Employers (person)	资产总计 Total Assets	流动资产合计 Total Working Capitals
2320950		1390	429685	251182
473304	45683	13609	826762	408777
89928		1580	66529	35851
99810		372	75134	35561
286630	1171	12017	565493	350996
47747		1137	46300	31797
459443		710	43785	34944
424414	14770	2755	383917	232670
897515	35352	18152	1523478	924306
1214979	23942	10514	2353274	1854268
998239	126646	14200	1862001	1392855
4964052	411761	43625	4842915	2874168
3707495	504382	66367	7878347	5157653
2355416	103150	31185	4277237	2961738
815493	10087	13968	1883514	1159516
872503	5931	16860	1540787	890393
21419	183	365	11276	8420
2201280		12263	4017253	732418
647614		4326	1334797	356549
82473		3010	190720	30986

12-6 续表4

单位：万元

分　组	Classify	负债合计 Total Liabilites	营业收入 Total Revenue	主营业务收入 Revenue from Principal Business
文教、工美、体育和娱乐用品制造业	Manufacture of Articles For Cultural,Educational and Sports Activities			
石油加工业、炼焦和业核燃料加工	Processing of Petroleum, Cokeing,Processing of Nuclear and Nuclear Fuel	317442	2137513	2137513
化学原料及化学制品制造业	Manufacture of Raw Chemical Materials and Chemical Products	414943	588359	471058
医药制造业	Manufacture of Medicines	35716	79386	79290
化学纤维制造业	Manufacture of Chemical Fibers	11537	99810	99206
橡胶和塑料制品业	Manufacture of Rubber and Plastics	442120	291804	284779
非金属矿物制品业	Manufacture of Non-metallic Mineral Products	33205	45721	45696
黑色金属冶炼和压延加工业	Smelting and Pressing of Ferrous Metals	9776	136675	133372
有色金属冶炼和压延加工业	Smelting and Pressing of Non-ferrous Metals	259291	437320	401417
金属制品业	Manufacture of Metal Products	943204	813493	800076
通用设备制造业	Manufacture of General Purpose Machinery	1270000	1145644	1134051
专用设备制造业	Manufacture of Special Equipment	936142	956331	942385
汽车制造业	Manufacture of Motor Vehicle	2820798	4899521	4737179
铁路、船舶、航空航天和其他运输设备制造业	Railways,Shipbuilding,Aerospace and Other Transportation Equipment Manufacturing Industry	4914544	4516696	4468098
电气机械和器材制造业	Manufacture of Electric Equipment and Machinery	1986940	2009247	1903141
计算机、通讯和其他电子设备制造业	Manufacture of Communication Equipment, Computers and other Electronic Equipment	1379096	935467	928222
仪器仪表制造业	Manufacture of Measuring Instruments and Machinery	631289	826476	806392
其他制造业	Manufacture of Other Manufacturing	5747	20922	20725
废弃资源综合利用业	Recycling and Disposal of Waste			
金属制品、机械和设备修理业	Metal Products,Machinery and Equipment Repair Industry			
电力、热力的生产和供应业	Production and Supply of Electric Power and Heat Power	3847548	1650148	1588462
燃气生产和供应业	Gas Mining and Supplying Industry	815499	698080	650158
水的生产和供应业	Production and Supply of Water	97507	95614	82720

continued 4

(10 000 yuan)

营业成本 Total Cost	主营业务成本 Cost of Principal Business	营业税金及附加 Taxs and Other Changes	主营业务税金及附加 Taxes and Other Charges on Principal Business	销售费用 Expenses for Sales
1989077	1989077	151186	151186	5122
490979	383720	2202	2198	19573
50478	50473	325	325	13215
81197	80592	434	434	320
242881	242073	2191	1986	13161
40617	40608	1504	1504	868
132800	129411	219	219	503
394668	356716	845	845	3274
693321	684265	2906	2906	15932
875300	866726	7862	7862	35653
793782	784061	6685	6628	36955
4373031	4225637	12380	12346	168818
3919379	3885059	16287	16255	78868
1948265	1531887	13604	13604	131651
804879	800636	2309	2044	22792
681215	671160	6572	5957	7039
19210	19203	60	60	264
1425450	1391511	16591	16591	240
564838	535964	2875	2067	17772
81083	71904	1105	596	3775

12-6 续表5

单位：万元

分 组	Classify	管理费用 Expenses for Management	财务费用 Financial cost	营业利润 Operating Profit
文教、工美、体育和娱乐用品制造业	Manufacture of Articles For Cultural,Educational and Sports Activities			
石油加工业、炼焦和业核燃料加工	Processing of Petroleum, Cokeing,Processing of Nuclear and Nuclear Fuel	14216	6517	-29359
化学原料及化学制品制造业	Manufacture of Raw Chemical Materials and Chemical Products	68116	8178	14848
医药制造业	Manufacture of Medicines	5337	122	9979
化学纤维制造业	Manufacture of Chemical Fibers	3077	-128	14566
橡胶和塑料制品业	Manufacture of Rubber and Plastics	11039	5721	16039
非金属矿物制品业	Manufacture of Non-metallic Mineral Products	2144	-131	891
黑色金属冶炼和压延加工业	Smelting and Pressing of Ferrous Metals	2415	900	-537
有色金属冶炼和压延加工业	Smelting and Pressing of Non-ferrous Metals	19130	9555	9077
金属制品业	Manufacture of Metal Products	66043	12781	24272
通用设备制造业	Manufacture of General Purpose Machinery	131755	-8714	106660
专用设备制造业	Manufacture of Special Equipment	83687	3764	88960
汽车制造业	Manufacture of Motor Vehicle	223368	25119	105981
铁路、船舶、航空航天和其他运输设备制造业	Railways,Shipbuilding,Aerospace and Other Transportation Equipment Manufacturing Industry	295162	56522	116263
电气机械和器材制造业	Manufacture of Electric Equipment and Machinery	195093	12507	30286
计算机、通讯和其他电子设备制造业	Manufacture of Communication Equipment, Computers and other Electronic Equipment	85855	14446	3682
仪器仪表制造业	Manufacture of Measuring Instruments and Machinery	99358	5343	22350
其他制造业	Manufacture of Other Manufacturing	810	84	472
废弃资源综合利用业	Recycling and Disposal of Waste			
金属制品、机械和设备修理业	Metal Products,Machinery and Equipment Repair Industry			
电力、热力的生产和供应业	Production and Supply of Electric Power and Heat Power	8860	158198	39011
燃气生产和供应业	Gas Mining and Supplying Industry	27709	17484	76266
水的生产和供应业	Production and Supply of Water	9364	260	70

continued 5

(10 000 yuan)

利润总额 Total Profits	亏损企业亏损额 Total Loss of Deficit Enterprises	税金总额 Total Pre-tax Profits	应付职工薪酬 Salary Payable	本年应交增值税 Value Added Tax Payable
-29359	31815	183231	13169	32046
23791	11441	16266	79490	14068
10089	183	3069	6550	2745
14570	271	4814	4513	4380
17885	69	12248	23650	10262
1258		4113	5209	2609
-413	1637	1204	4219	985
15662	3816	4266	23137	3421
33854		14531	130828	11625
114056	573	49930	129902	42069
129010	17625	35822	113957	29194
126156	5423	98699	241181	86353
155348	8361	46954	528789	30699
44653	2058	90403	227585	76800
14069	11657	9869	100592	7825
32120	1689	41545	186653	35583
470	337	474	1717	414
46112	5728	129564	63970	112973
74328	1142	12473	42111	10406
3650	75	5560	18223	4963

12-7 规模以上股份制工业企业主要经济指标（2013年）

单位：万元

分 组	Classify	企业单位数（个） Number of Enterprises (unit)	亏损企业 Loss Making Enterprises	工业总产值（当年价格） Gross Industrial Output Value (At Current Prices)
总计	**Total**	**747**	**136**	**26612056**
#亏损企业	Deficit Enterprises	136	136	
按轻重工业分	**Grouped by Light Industry and Heavy Industry**			
轻工业	Light Industry	202	36	5010936
重工业	Heavy Industry	545	100	21601120
按企业规模分	**Grouped by Size of Enterprises**			
大型企业	Large-size	37	5	12057198
中型企业	Medium-size	105	21	3846488
小型企业	Small-size	605	110	10708370
微型企业	microenterprise			
按工业行业大类分	**Grouped by Sector**			
煤炭开采和洗选业	Mining and Washing of Coal			
石油和天然气开采业	Extraction of Petroleum and Natural Gas			
黑色金属矿采选业	Mining and Processing of Ferrous Metal Ores	1	1	3170
有色金属矿采选业	Mining and Processing of Non-ferrous Metal Ores			
非金属矿采选业	Mining and Processing of Nonmetal Ores			
开采辅助活动	Mining Auxiliary Activities	2		46072
其他采矿业	Mining of Other Ores			
农副食品加工业	Processing of Food from Agricultural Porducts	39	8	1801322
食品制造业	Manufacture of Foods	25	1	403884
酒、饮料和精制茶制造业	Manufacture of Alcohol,Beverages and Tea	5		166180
烟草制品业	Manufacture of Tobacco			
纺织业	Manufacture of Textile	13	3	186281
纺织服装、服饰业	Textile, apparel industry	7	1	136219
皮革、毛皮、羽毛及其制品和制鞋业	Manufacture of Leather, Fur, Feather and Related Products, and Shoes	1	1	4540
木材加工和木、竹、藤、棕、草制品业	Processing of Timber,Manufacture of Wood,Plam and Straw Products	4	1	135517
家具制造业	Manufacture of Furniture	8		57717
造纸及纸制品业	Manufacture of Paper and Paper Products	13	2	51801

Main Indicators of Share-holding Corporation Industrial Enterprises above Designated Size (2013)

(10 000 yuan)

工业销售产值（当年价） Value of Industry Products Sales (At Current Prices)	出口交货值 Export Delivery Value	从业人员年平均人数（人） Annual Average Employers (person)	资产总计 Total Assets	流动资产合计 Total Working Capitals
25554840	**1583721**	**285451**	**29260383**	**18212427**
		27806	2879783	1658367
4908062	153246	44695	3146190	1818688
20646778	1430475	240756	26114193	16393739
11727057	1209724	162925	17778170	10510825
3541066	120671	52605	4985826	3123459
10286717	253326	69921	6496387	4578143
3170			2155	1666
46972		833	66164	43862
1773083	4101	6142	480648	305677
376394		4955	174414	90693
330633		1950	210278	133141
170851	13429	3625	200530	127753
129347		1571	109466	83520
4540		143	8107	7940
123120		732	118150	62780
53272		990	30205	21492
50646		926	30644	15635

12-7 续表1

单位：万元

分组	Classify	负债合计 Total Liabilites	营业收入 Total Revenue	主营业务收入 Revenue from Principal Business
总计	**Total**	**16845194**	**25406567**	**24952205**
#亏损企业	Deficit Enterprises	2021026	1851160	1800835
按轻重工业分	**Grouped by Light Industry and Heavy Industry**			
轻工业	Light Industry	1638751	4480205	4447086
重工业	Heavy Industry	15206443	20926362	20505119
按企业规模分	**Grouped by Size of Enterprises**			
大型企业	Large-size	10345269	12538076	12291525
中型企业	Medium-size	2752625	3429888	3269883
小型企业	Small-size	3747300	9438603	9390797
微型企业	microenterprise			
按工业行业大类分	**Grouped by Sector**			
煤炭开采和洗选业	Mining and Washing of Coal			
石油和天然气开采业	Extraction of Petroleum and Natural Gas			
黑色金属矿采选业	Mining and Processing of Ferrous Metal Ores	3938	3113	3113
有色金属矿采选业	Mining and Processing of Non-ferrous Metal Ores			
非金属矿采选业	Mining and Processing of Nonmetal Ores			
开采辅助活动	Mining Auxiliary Activities	17116	45849	44791
其他采矿业	Mining of Other Ores			
农副食品加工业	Processing of Food from Agricultural Porducts	316999	1535449	1533326
食品制造业	Manufacture of Foods	77585	322330	317547
酒、饮料和精制茶制造业	Manufacture of Alcohol,Beverages and Tea	101666	327867	327451
烟草制品业	Manufacture of Tobacco			
纺织业	Manufacture of Textile	104237	165561	164174
纺织服装、服饰业	Textile, apparel industry	70615	180325	177960
皮革、毛皮、羽毛及其制品和制鞋业	Manufacture of Leather, Fur, Feather and Related Products, and Shoes	1553	3973	3973
木材加工和木、竹、藤、棕、草制品业	Processing of Timber,Manufacture of Wood,Plam and Straw Products	61284	105016	104648
家具制造业	Manufacture of Furniture	16521	38489	38223
造纸及纸制品业	Manufacture of Paper and Paper Products	18838	49645	49478

continued 1

(10 000 yuan)

营业成本 Total Cost	主营 业务成本 Cost of Principal Business	营业税金 及附加 Taxs and Other Changes	主营业务 税金及附加 Taxes and Other Charges on Principal Business	销售费用 Expenses for Sales
21923047	**21531908**	**110896**	**109845**	**858475**
1763947	1720063	5715	5522	50114
3710142	3684862	30802	30231	287477
18212905	17847046	80094	79614	570998
10924537	10712976	50738	50162	347857
2761581	2623930	20721	20514	220361
8236929	8195002	39437	39169	290257
2715	2715	32	32	25
32908	32622	1069	1069	314
1438303	1437430	2132	2125	41381
262906	259005	1410	1410	24263
248205	247838	10727	10727	26195
150940	150130	897	858	2588
156363	155715	2787	2785	5771
3024	3024	25	25	404
97051	96679	346	344	1887
30733	30558	246	246	3434
45102	45002	106	106	997

12-7 续表2

单位：万元

分 组	Classify	管理费用 Expenses for Management	财务费用 Financial cost	营业利润 Operating Profit
总计	**Total**	**1328155**	**238603**	**900896**
#亏损企业	Deficit Enterprises	115052	35358	-121987
按轻重工业分	**Grouped by Light Industry and Heavy Industry**			
轻工业	Light Industry	202655	25500	212894
重工业	Heavy Industry	1125500	213103	688002
按企业规模分	**Grouped by Size of Enterprises**			
大型企业	Large-size	737029	133180	313621
中型企业	Medium-size	230039	49210	155938
小型企业	Small-size	361087	56213	431337
微型企业	microenterprise			
按工业行业大类分	**Grouped by Sector**			
煤炭开采和洗选业	Mining and Washing of Coal			
石油和天然气开采业	Extraction of Petroleum and Natural Gas			
黑色金属矿采选业	Mining and Processing of Ferrous Metal Ores	550	193	-350
有色金属矿采选业	Mining and Processing of Non-ferrous Metal Ores			
非金属矿采选业	Mining and Processing of Nonmetal Ores			
开采辅助活动	Mining Auxiliary Activities	3578	44	7937
其他采矿业	Mining of Other Ores			
农副食品加工业	Processing of Food from Agricultural Porducts	27743	11347	13803
食品制造业	Manufacture of Foods	11571	1987	19121
酒、饮料和精制茶制造业	Manufacture of Alcohol,Beverages and Tea	11978	-3127	33049
烟草制品业	Manufacture of Tobacco			
纺织业	Manufacture of Textile	6141	622	3405
纺织服装、服饰业	Textile, apparel industry	6144	2593	4989
皮革、毛皮、羽毛及其制品和制鞋业	Manufacture of Leather, Fur, Feather and Related Products, and Shoes	349		-12
木材加工和木、竹、藤、棕、草制品业	Processing of Timber,Manufacture of Wood,Plam and Straw Products	3073	2898	-263
家具制造业	Manufacture of Furniture	1928	340	1682
造纸及纸制品业	Manufacture of Paper and Paper Products	1579	678	1194

continued 2

(10 000 yuan)

利润总额 Total Profit	亏损企业亏损额 Total Loss of Deficit Enterprises	税金总额 Total Pre-tax Profits	应付职工薪酬 Salary Payable	本年应交增值税 Value Added Tax Payable
1039383	**106937**	**582643**	**1779536**	**472799**
-106937	106937	31655	159284	26133
234950	11293	154224	248983	123993
804433	95644	428419	1530553	348806
395476	27793	237394	1138448	187231
188093	33404	125090	281368	104576
455814	45740	220159	359720	180992
-350	350	173	134	141
7935		2175	6869	1106
17064	2857	15644	25205	13522
20699	131	7229	16737	5820
33290		21568	18621	10841
5789	2004	7598	33316	6740
11201	58	6276	7038	3491
-112	112	107	480	82
1988	12	3413	3129	3069
1665		1182	2193	936
1349	483	619	2890	513

12-7 续表3

单位：万元

分组	Classify	企业单位数（个） Number of Enterprises (unit)	亏损企业 Loss Making Enterprises	工业总产值（当年价格） Gross Industrial Output Value (At Current Prices)
印刷和记录媒介复制	Printing,Reproduction of Recording Media	15	3	447797
文教、工美、体育和娱乐用品制造业	Manufacture of Articles For Cultural,Educational and Sports Activities	4	1	167755
石油加工业、炼焦和核燃料加工业	Processing of Petroleum, Cokeing,Processing of Nuclear and Nuclear Fuel	5		1203785
化学原料及化学制品制造业	Manufacture of Raw Chemical Materials and Chemical Products	42	3	1350727
医药制造业	Manufacture of Medicines	38	6	922762
化学纤维制造业	Manufacture of Chemical Fibers	1	1	4530
橡胶和塑料制品业	Manufacture of Rubber and Plastics	22	6	345965
非金属矿物制品业	Manufacture of Non-metallic Mineral Products	83	20	1441611
黑色金属冶炼和压延加工业	Smelting and Pressing of Ferrous Metals	15	3	572948
有色金属冶炼和压延加工业	Smelting and Pressing of Non-ferrous Metals	24	2	945358
金属制品业	Manufacture of Metal Products	43	6	906045
通用设备制造业	Manufacture of General Purpose Machinery	48	8	922037
专用设备制造业	Manufacture of Special Equipment	79	17	1834803
汽车制造业	Manufacture of Motor Vehicle	25	5	5166569
铁路、船舶、航空航天和其他运输设备制造业	Railways,Shipbuilding,Aerospace and Other Transportation Equipment Manufacturing Industry	31	7	3552345
电气机械和器材制造业	Manufacture of Electric Equipment and Machinery	69	13	1406140
计算机、通讯和其他电子设备制造业	Manufacture of Communication Equipment, Computers and other Electronic Equipment	41	7	1003360
仪器仪表制造业	Manufacture of Measuring Instruments and Machinery	27	5	792025
其他制造业	Manufacture of Other Manufacturing	1		14607
废弃资源综合利用业	Recycling and Disposal of Waste			
金属制品、机械和设备修理业	Metal Products,Machinery and Equipment Repair Industry	1		2210
电力、热力的生产和供应业	Production and Supply of Electric Power and Heat Power	7	2	52551
燃气生产和供应业	Gas Mining and Supplying Industry	6	2	486874
水的生产和供应业	Production and Supply of Water	2	1	76549

continued 3

(10 000 yuan)

工业销售产值（当年价）Value of Industry Products Sales (At Current Prices)	出口交货值 Export Delivery Value	从业人员年平均人数（人）Annual Average Employers (person)	资产总计 Total Assets	流动资产合计 Total Working Capitals
439980		5610	478966	195939
166791	125706	352	98741	94071
1204640		314	223634	181099
1308678	170058	17845	1611195	908196
827131	10010	9145	747197	446901
4530		113	26373	4496
285343		2611	182550	115895
1394548		10929	701208	446509
564261		2679	164366	87965
891727	38813	7462	749255	382860
888873	34602	17465	1210091	688764
880821	1506	9590	1040055	810233
1666879	152768	21616	2390121	1682731
4920273	413311	48024	5088819	3043103
3446285	502607	58285	6957762	4633562
1288878	49889	12740	1221376	895729
919352	39315	16851	1905089	1322545
761493	27606	14969	1298160	825218
14607		237	20252	13135
2005		55	3558	1128
52551		1272	463559	202204
486617		2610	1081062	261927
76549		2810	166233	74053

12-7 续表4

单位：万元

分 组	Classify	负债合计 Total Liabilites	营业收入 Total Revenue	主营业务收入 Revenue from Principal Business
印刷和记录媒介复制	Printing,Reproduction of Recording Media	162455	441766	437958
文教、工美、体育和娱乐用品制造业	Manufacture of Articles For Cultural,Educational and Sports Activities	91337	135763	135763
石油加工业、炼焦和核燃料加工业	Processing of Petroleum, Cokeing,Processing of Nuclear and Nuclear Fuel	149151	1014079	1013449
化学原料及化学制品制造业	Manufacture of Raw Chemical Materials and Chemical Products	812272	1246583	1227953
医药制造业	Manufacture of Medicines	330373	695373	694104
化学纤维制造业	Manufacture of Chemical Fibers	1935	4530	3926
橡胶和塑料制品业	Manufacture of Rubber and Plastics	97724	268789	267659
非金属矿物制品业	Manufacture of Non-metallic Mineral Products	393735	1282991	1278556
黑色金属冶炼和压延加工业	Smelting and Pressing of Ferrous Metals	109205	330985	325426
有色金属冶炼和压延加工业	Smelting and Pressing of Non-ferrous Metals	393750	869376	831085
金属制品业	Manufacture of Metal Products	671968	812493	799567
通用设备制造业	Manufacture of General Purpose Machinery	555512	771364	768308
专用设备制造业	Manufacture of Special Equipment	1196222	1622417	1597166
汽车制造业	Manufacture of Motor Vehicle	2908968	5096242	4935510
铁路、船舶、航空航天和其他运输设备制造业	Railways,Shipbuilding,Aerospace and Other Transportation Equipment Manufacturing Industry	4385544	4210680	4173087
电气机械和器材制造业	Manufacture of Electric Equipment and Machinery	706052	1276658	1266236
计算机、通讯和其他电子设备制造业	Manufacture of Communication Equipment, Computers and other Electronic Equipment	1261527	1059823	1028311
仪器仪表制造业	Manufacture of Measuring Instruments and Machinery	740396	794050	778255
其他制造业	Manufacture of Other Manufacturing	12795	15188	15182
废弃资源综合利用业	Recycling and Disposal of Waste			
金属制品、机械和设备修理业	Metal Products,Machinery and Equipment Repair Industry	2514	2005	2005
电力、热力的生产和供应业	Production and Supply of Electric Power and Heat Power	356084	106292	50886
燃气生产和供应业	Gas Mining and Supplying Industry	626386	482060	480580
水的生产和供应业	Production and Supply of Water	88937	89443	76549

continued 4

(10 000 yuan)

营业成本 Total Cost	主营业务成本 Cost of Principal Business	营业税金及附加 Taxs and Other Changes	主营业务税金及附加 Taxes and Other Charges on Principal Business	销售费用 Expenses for Sales
330225	324501	3450	3435	7824
127247	127247	253	253	1167
998515	998222	532	532	4685
1058753	1032874	4236	4216	42974
419279	418379	6061	6061	145805
4168	3564	5	5	112
222895	222257	947	947	13428
1131023	1125496	7050	7049	35476
297909	292339	1864	1863	3149
790786	750818	1495	1478	9243
692810	684344	4141	4141	22689
651566	649227	4520	4519	26998
1321715	1301505	12196	12147	77578
4535012	4384170	13487	13453	177862
3689349	3661427	14715	14682	73763
1089830	1081679	4555	4554	42632
900611	869945	2645	2645	26379
615894	608962	4215	3921	23993
12040	12040	127	127	343
1251	1251	20	20	90
96377	62759	2829	2829	149
390337	390159	715	689	11464
77205	68025	1061	552	3413

12-7 续表5

单位：万元

分 组	Classify	管理费用 Expenses for Management	财务费用 Financial cost	营业利润 Operating Profit
印刷和记录媒介复制	Printing,Reproduction of Recording Media	44806	1480	53439
文教、工美、体育和娱乐用品制造业	Manufacture of Articles For Cultural,Educational and Sports Activities	1143	188	4678
石油加工业、炼焦和核燃料加工业	Processing of Petroleum, Cokeing,Processing of Nuclear and Nuclear Fuel	4320	1781	4245
化学原料及化学制品制造业	Manufacture of Raw Chemical Materials and Chemical Products	87206	12615	54239
医药制造业	Manufacture of Medicines	53305	4286	64949
化学纤维制造业	Manufacture of Chemical Fibers	547	-27	-275
橡胶和塑料制品业	Manufacture of Rubber and Plastics	10928	3892	15918
非金属矿物制品业	Manufacture of Non-metallic Mineral Products	36658	5989	63765
黑色金属冶炼和压延加工业	Smelting and Pressing of Ferrous Metals	7269	2099	17940
有色金属冶炼和压延加工业	Smelting and Pressing of Non-ferrous Metals	27965	15797	21902
金属制品业	Manufacture of Metal Products	60480	7764	28258
通用设备制造业	Manufacture of General Purpose Machinery	41879	6355	34418
专用设备制造业	Manufacture of Special Equipment	114528	12822	76578
汽车制造业	Manufacture of Motor Vehicle	233423	27028	124477
铁路、船舶、航空航天和其他运输设备制造业	Railways,Shipbuilding,Aerospace and Other Transportation Equipment Manufacturing Industry	252735	53106	86748
电气机械和器材制造业	Manufacture of Electric Equipment and Machinery	62838	13123	62465
计算机、通讯和其他电子设备制造业	Manufacture of Communication Equipment, Computers and other Electronic Equipment	79629	12828	34185
仪器仪表制造业	Manufacture of Measuring Instruments and Machinery	99830	9223	32314
其他制造业	Manufacture of Other Manufacturing	1813	451	405
废弃资源综合利用业	Recycling and Disposal of Waste			
金属制品、机械和设备修理业	Metal Products,Machinery and Equipment Repair Industry	568	-23	99
电力、热力的生产和供应业	Production and Supply of Electric Power and Heat Power	6436	6368	-5596
燃气生产和供应业	Gas Mining and Supplying Industry	16462	23616	42515
水的生产和供应业	Production and Supply of Water	8753	267	-1325

continued 5

(10 000 yuan)

利润总额 Total Profit	亏损企业亏损额 Total Loss of Deficit Enterprises	税金总额 Total Pre-tax Profits	应付职工薪酬 Salary Payable	本年应交增值税 Value Added Tax Payable
53513	311	27869	62242	24434
4737	126	734	1219	481
4265		2865	1279	2332
61789	11605	28223	95511	24007
66727	2098	50302	36696	44240
-271	271	5	933	
16732	1202	5663	11414	4715
68144	6425	47051	54109	40002
18634	6736	8436	14401	6573
28967	3816	9447	36066	7969
34390	2599	19261	110927	15120
37785	1141	24061	56766	19542
89023	18933	59689	135802	47542
146487	5240	107368	259481	93915
116825	6707	40560	449994	25877
70510	6930	39293	62951	34740
43852	11760	15606	89582	12961
36421	4933	18706	128389	14786
621		645	1050	518
99		183	317	163
-3340	6132	3058	10682	229
41031	3890	2489	25657	1799
1924	75	5145	17456	4593

12-8 规模以上外商及港澳台商投资工业企业主要经济指标（2013年）

单位：万元

分 组	Classify	企业单位数（个）Number of Enterprises (unit)	亏损企业 Loss Making Enterprises	工业总产值（当年价格）Gross Industrial Output Value (At Current Prices)
总计	**Total**	**117**	**33**	**7809205**
#亏损企业	Deficit Enterprises	33	33	7809205
按轻重工业分	**Grouped by Light Industry and Heavy Industry**			
轻工业	Light Industry	42	12	3175075
重工业	Heavy Industry	75	21	4634130
按企业规模分	**Grouped by Size of Enterprises**			
大型企业	Large-size	15	1	4361520
中型企业	Medium-size	20	7	1967770
小型企业	Small-size	82	25	1479915
微型企业	microenterprise			
按工业行业大类分	**Grouped by Sector**			
煤炭开采和洗选业	Mining and Washing of Coal			
石油和天然气开采业	Extraction of Petroleum and Natural Gas			
黑色金属矿采选业	Mining and Processing of Ferrous Metal Ores			
有色金属矿采选业	Mining and Processing of Non-ferrous Metal Ores			
非金属矿采选业	Mining and Processing of Nonmetal Ores			
开采辅助活动	Mining Auxiliary Activities			
其他采矿业	Mining of Other Ores			
农副食品加工业	Processing of Food from Agricultural Porducts	4		109118
食品制造业	Manufacture of Foods	5		1045764
酒、饮料和精制茶制造业	Manufacture of Alcohol,Beverages and Tea	8	3	691278
烟草制品业	Manufacture of Tobacco			
纺织业	Manufacture of Textile	1	1	8662
纺织服装、服饰业	Textile, apparel industry			
皮革、毛皮、羽毛及其制品和制鞋业	Manufacture of Leather, Fur, Feather and Related Products, and Shoes			
木材加工和木、竹、藤、棕、草制品业	Processing of Timber,Manufacture of Wood,Plam and Straw Products			
家具制造业	Manufacture of Furniture			
造纸及纸制品业	Manufacture of Paper and Paper Products	2		32293
印刷和记录媒介复制	Printing,Reproduction of Recording Media	2	1	31350
文教、工美、体育和娱乐用品制造业	Manufacture of Articles For Cultural,Educational and Sports Activities	1		16071

Economic Indicators of Foreign Fund Industrial Enterprises above Designated Size (2013)

(10 000 yuan)

工业销售产值（当年价） Value of Industry Products Sales (At Current Prices)	出口交货值 Export Delivery Value	从业人员年平均人数（人） Annual Average Employers (person)	资产总计 Total Assets	流动资产合计 Total Working Capitals
7402493	**593599**	**68438**	**5553317**	**2861410**
7402493	593599	5845	839658	415578
2963582	159294	16987	1717966	961643
4438911	434305	51451	3835351	1899767
4185618	309590	44815	3367021	1578611
1788505	166299	8724	883156	530629
1428370	117710	14899	1303140	752170
102947		898	44267	21302
991972		3086	333088	197383
580051	135473	4349	696801	313237
5954		138	12085	6001
31661		295	24323	11901
33129	1036	759	71138	34315
16071	16071	158	7496	4771

12-8 续表1

单位：万元

分组	Classify	负债合计 Total Liabilites	营业收入 Total Revenue	主营 实收资本 Revenue from Principal Business
总计	**Total**	**2952474**	**6509514**	**6353544**
#亏损企业	Deficit Enterprises	560749	427404	420844
按轻重工业分	**Grouped by Light Industry and Heavy Industry**			
轻工业	Light Industry	829223	2832618	2799879
重工业	Heavy Industry	2123251	3676896	3553665
按企业规模分	**Grouped by Size of Enterprises**			
大型企业	Large-size	1852808	4437498	4320240
中型企业	Medium-size	458831	718725	693494
小型企业	Small-size	640835	1353291	1339810
微型企业	microenterprise			
按工业行业大类分	**Grouped by Sector**			
煤炭开采和洗选业	Mining and Washing of Coal			
石油和天然气开采业	Extraction of Petroleum and Natural Gas			
黑色金属矿采选业	Mining and Processing of Ferrous Metal Ores			
有色金属矿采选业	Mining and Processing of Non-ferrous Metal Ores			
非金属矿采选业	Mining and Processing of Nonmetal Ores			
开采辅助活动	Mining Auxiliary Activities			
其他采矿业	Mining of Other Ores			
农副食品加工业	Processing of Food from Agricultural Porducts	4616	70150	68738
食品制造业	Manufacture of Foods	138014	954353	933733
酒、饮料和精制茶制造业	Manufacture of Alcohol,Beverages and Tea	409287	550608	541493
烟草制品业	Manufacture of Tobacco			
纺织业	Manufacture of Textile	5530	5422	5422
纺织服装、服饰业	Textile, apparel industry			
皮革、毛皮、羽毛及其制品和制鞋业	Manufacture of Leather, Fur, Feather and Related Products, and Shoes			
木材加工和木、竹、藤、棕、草制品业	Processing of Timber,Manufacture of Wood,Plam and Straw Products			
家具制造业	Manufacture of Furniture			
造纸及纸制品业	Manufacture of Paper and Paper Products	6783	29550	29550
印刷和记录媒介复制	Printing,Reproduction of Recording Media	49884	28697	28447
文教、工美、体育和娱乐用品制造业	Manufacture of Articles For Cultural,Educational and Sports Activities	4174	16071	16071

continued 1

(10 000 yuan)

营业成本 Total Cost	主营实收资本 Cost of Principal Business	营业税金及附加 Taxs and Other Changes	主营业务税金及附加 Taxes and Other Charges on Principal Business	销售费用 Expenses for Sales
5388335	**5267656**	**70163**	**67823**	**492795**
392905	386853	2987	2981	34366
2173457	2150749	14304	12912	390683
3214878	3116907	55859	54911	102112
3706350	3617595	57164	55023	391859
577983	556221	4394	4287	46238
1104002	1093840	8605	8513	54698
62364	61445	339	312	2353
763240	749444	2640	2640	118150
424368	416949	4138	2773	73285
5194	5194	6	6	38
24248	24248	155	155	325
21083	21009	217	217	1300
15749	15749			77

12-8 续表2

单位：万元

分组	Classify	管理费用 Expenses for Management	财务费用 Financial cost	营业利润 Operating Profit
总计	**Total**	**269260**	**27154**	**262924**
#亏损企业	Deficit Enterprises	43947	16983	-67960
按轻重工业分	**Grouped by Light Industry and Heavy Industry**			
轻工业	Light Industry	113794	19701	109876
重工业	Heavy Industry	155466	7453	153048
按企业规模分	**Grouped by Size of Enterprises**			
大型企业	Large-size	140008	22371	114695
中型企业	Medium-size	53822	-2659	41474
小型企业	Small-size	75430	7442	106755
微型企业	microenterprise			
按工业行业大类分	**Grouped by Sector**			
煤炭开采和洗选业	Mining and Washing of Coal			
石油和天然气开采业	Extraction of Petroleum and Natural Gas			
黑色金属矿采选业	Mining and Processing of Ferrous Metal Ores			
有色金属矿采选业	Mining and Processing of Non-ferrous Metal Ores			
非金属矿采选业	Mining and Processing of Nonmetal Ores			
开采辅助活动	Mining Auxiliary Activities			
其他采矿业	Mining of Other Ores			
农副食品加工业	Processing of Food from Agricultural Porducts	2524	21	2910
食品制造业	Manufacture of Foods	31075	-4112	37764
酒、饮料和精制茶制造业	Manufacture of Alcohol,Beverages and Tea	18922	9939	13667
烟草制品业	Manufacture of Tobacco			
纺织业	Manufacture of Textile	334	-2	-145
纺织服装、服饰业	Textile, apparel industry			
皮革、毛皮、羽毛及其制品和制鞋业	Manufacture of Leather, Fur, Feather and Related Products, and Shoes			
木材加工和木、竹、藤、棕、草制品业	Processing of Timber,Manufacture of Wood,Plam and Straw Products			
家具制造业	Manufacture of Furniture			
造纸及纸制品业	Manufacture of Paper and Paper Products	910	-96	3710
印刷和记录媒介复制	Printing,Reproduction of Recording Media	5726	3378	-1312
文教、工美、体育和娱乐用品制造业	Manufacture of Articles For Cultural,Educational and Sports Activities	207	1	37

continued 2

(10 000 yuan)

利润总额 Total Profits	亏损企业亏损额 Total Loss of Deficit Enterprises	税金总额 Total Pre-tax Profits	应付职工薪酬 Salary Payable	本年应交增值税 Value Added Tax Payable
320196	**57889**	**274345**	**487036**	**206523**
-57889	57889	12337	42741	9356
123702	21252	144443	179336	131530
196494	36637	129903	307700	74993
164275	6921	195648	334401	140625
43656	34033	30727	58144	26440
112265	16935	47971	94492	39458
3357		3124	5828	2814
40739		23631	31633	20991
20456	12376	21203	37807	18430
-12	12	6	393	
5711		1458	1738	1303
-1195	5516	1967	4142	1749
37		482	621	482

12-8 续表3

单位：万元

分组	Classify	企业单位数（个） Number of Enterprises (unit)	亏损企业 Loss Making Enterprises	工业总产值（当年价格） Gross Industrial Output Value (At Current Prices)
石油加工业、炼焦和核燃料加工业	Processing of Petroleum, Cokeing,Processing of Nuclear and Nuclear Fuel	2		192113
化学原料及化学制品制造业	Manufacture of Raw Chemical Materials and Chemical Products	5	1	50048
医药制造业	Manufacture of Medicines	9	4	590035
化学纤维制造业	Manufacture of Chemical Fibers	1		89739
橡胶和塑料制品业	Manufacture of Rubber and Plastics	5	1	26451
非金属矿物制品业	Manufacture of Non-metallic Mineral Products	7	1	304663
黑色金属冶炼和压延加工业	Smelting and Pressing of Ferrous Metals	3	1	75716
有色金属冶炼和压延加工业	Smelting and Pressing of Non-ferrous Metals	3	2	55097
金属制品业	Manufacture of Metal Products	4	1	31272
通用设备制造业	Manufacture of General Purpose Machinery	5		107031
专用设备制造业	Manufacture of Special Equipment	9	3	378011
汽车制造业	Manufacture of Motor Vehicle	5	1	2566079
铁路、船舶、航空航天和其他运输设备制造业	Railways,Shipbuilding,Aerospace and Other Transportation Equipment Manufacturing Industry	7	3	134534
电气机械和器材制造业	Manufacture of Electric Equipment and Machinery	10	3	638136
计算机、通讯和其他电子设备制造业	Manufacture of Communication Equipment, Computers and other Electronic Equipment	10	5	319804
仪器仪表制造业	Manufacture of Measuring Instruments and Machinery	4	1	75768
其他制造业	Manufacture of Other Manufacturing	1	1	4932
废弃资源综合利用业	Recycling and Disposal of Waste			
金属制品、机械和设备修理业	Metal Products,Machinery and Equipment Repair Industry	2		12066
电力、热力的生产和供应业	Production and Supply of Electric Power and Heat Power	1		3268
燃气生产和供应业	Gas Mining and Supplying Industry	1		219906
水的生产和供应业	Production and Supply of Water			

continued 3

(10 000 yuan)

工业销售产值（当年价）Value of Industry Products Sales (At Current Prices)	出口交货值 Export Delivery Value	从业人员年平均人数（人）Annual Average Employers (person)	资产总计 Total Assets	流动资产合计 Total Working Capitals
192113		4085	146744	34347
43334	2083	274	31059	24407
600860	6059	6140	409273	293703
95280		259	48761	31064
23243	456	329	44156	28357
301147		588	169564	60654
80321	13344	387	33436	8292
52508	13454	319	46776	40063
31085	2078	1573	68257	15824
97008	17828	1382	118660	93322
323223	46254	3335	376857	227954
2455014	60900	28506	1427888	620191
123311	52884	792	116289	102106
593031	6630	2215	221861	155653
313506	187958	5046	603504	279218
75694	31091	766	76182	60148
4790		195	5594	2971
12066		291	16736	15438
3268		56	5041	1790
219906		2217	397481	175998

12-8 续表4

单位：万元

分 组	Classify	负债合计 Total Liabilites	营业收入 Total Revenue	主营 实收资本 Revenue from Principal Business
石油加工业、炼焦和核燃料加工业	Processing of Petroleum, Cokeing,Processing of Nuclear and Nuclear Fuel	88318	185363	183685
化学原料及化学制品制造业	Manufacture of Raw Chemical Materials and Chemical Products	25270	24550	24543
医药制造业	Manufacture of Medicines	162249	604748	604260
化学纤维制造业	Manufacture of Chemical Fibers	9602	95280	95280
橡胶和塑料制品业	Manufacture of Rubber and Plastics	26237	14176	14123
非金属矿物制品业	Manufacture of Non-metallic Mineral Products	50365	243612	242657
黑色金属冶炼和压延加工业	Smelting and Pressing of Ferrous Metals	36025	80336	78565
有色金属冶炼和压延加工业	Smelting and Pressing of Non-ferrous Metals	17063	53430	53221
金属制品业	Manufacture of Metal Products	40465	31980	31889
通用设备制造业	Manufacture of General Purpose Machinery	37989	118036	117871
专用设备制造业	Manufacture of Special Equipment	161786	352053	330272
汽车制造业	Manufacture of Motor Vehicle	872893	1692489	1646937
铁路、船舶、航空航天和其他运输设备制造业	Railways,Shipbuilding,Aerospace and Other Transportation Equipment Manufacturing Industry	71656	98410	98315
电气机械和器材制造业	Manufacture of Electric Equipment and Machinery	116789	587895	586472
计算机、通讯和其他电子设备制造业	Manufacture of Communication Equipment, Computers and other Electronic Equipment	310129	310851	307630
仪器仪表制造业	Manufacture of Measuring Instruments and Machinery	30227	76527	75982
其他制造业	Manufacture of Other Manufacturing	2970	4181	4094
废弃资源综合利用业	Recycling and Disposal of Waste			
金属制品、机械和设备修理业	Metal Products,Machinery and Equipment Repair Industry	9284	15722	15712
电力、热力的生产和供应业	Production and Supply of Electric Power and Heat Power	749	3268	3268
燃气生产和供应业	Gas Mining and Supplying Industry	264120	261756	215314
水的生产和供应业	Production and Supply of Water			

continued 4

(10 000 yuan)

营业成本 Total Cost	主营实收资本 Cost of Principal Business	营业税金及附加 Taxs and Other Changes	主营业务税金及附加 Taxes and Other Charges on Principal Business	销售费用 Expenses for Sales
156720	154852	1139	1080	6017
20210	20177	309	309	1331
309571	309135	5942	5942	192087
77028	77028	429	429	207
10531	10514	102	102	579
204853	204853	2376	2376	881
72887	70870	227	227	1632
51594	51392	80	80	1290
25405	25405	138	138	1878
101267	101267	200	200	5301
304621	285150	858	751	8048
1567048	1523698	44869	44869	39238
69914	69913	680	680	2927
547038	546843	1176	1176	14436
274288	272271	1466	1466	3143
52620	52453	136	136	4252
3982	3982	29	29	152
10191	10191	112	112	1269
2053	2053	58	58	105
210268	181571	2342	1560	11494

12-8 续表5

单位：万元

分　组	Classify	管理费用 Expenses for Management	财务费用 Financial cost	营业利润 Operating Profit
石油加工业、炼焦和核燃料加工业	Processing of Petroleum, Cokeing,Processing of Nuclear and Nuclear Fuel	7271	1427	12362
化学原料及化学制品制造业	Manufacture of Raw Chemical Materials and Chemical Products	2734	602	-1745
医药制造业	Manufacture of Medicines	48072	10550	37738
化学纤维制造业	Manufacture of Chemical Fibers	2530	-101	14841
橡胶和塑料制品业	Manufacture of Rubber and Plastics	1601	-133	1516
非金属矿物制品业	Manufacture of Non-metallic Mineral Products	1365	718	33717
黑色金属冶炼和压延加工业	Smelting and Pressing of Ferrous Metals	1565	1604	2420
有色金属冶炼和压延加工业	Smelting and Pressing of Non-ferrous Metals	2339	334	-2610
金属制品业	Manufacture of Metal Products	3543	-49	806
通用设备制造业	Manufacture of General Purpose Machinery	5046	981	5646
专用设备制造业	Manufacture of Special Equipment	27163	1852	11691
汽车制造业	Manufacture of Motor Vehicle	42645	10316	-10246
铁路、船舶、航空航天和其他运输设备制造业	Railways,Shipbuilding,Aerospace and Other Transportation Equipment Manufacturing Industry	9068	540	13856
电气机械和器材制造业	Manufacture of Electric Equipment and Machinery	17624	1524	10827
计算机、通讯和其他电子设备制造业	Manufacture of Communication Equipment, Computers and other Electronic Equipment	13142	-8907	27785
仪器仪表制造业	Manufacture of Measuring Instruments and Machinery	5937	-195	13862
其他制造业	Manufacture of Other Manufacturing	312	28	-338
废弃资源综合利用业	Recycling and Disposal of Waste			
金属制品、机械和设备修理业	Metal Products,Machinery and Equipment Repair Industry	2707	76	1261
电力、热力的生产和供应业	Production and Supply of Electric Power and Heat Power	461	32	559
燃气生产和供应业	Gas Mining and Supplying Industry	14437	-3174	32345
水的生产和供应业	Production and Supply of Water			

continued 5

(10 000 yuan)

利润总额 Total Profits	亏损企业亏损额 Total Loss of Deficit Enterprises	税金总额 Total Pre-tax taxes	应付职工薪酬 Salary Payable	本年应交增值税 Value Added Tax Payable
12287		1611	23455	532
-1709	2232	1490	1814	1181
37520	1587	86585	89027	80644
14841		4809	3579	4380
1567	375	573	1615	471
33607	389	7395	2907	5020
2549	2833	2554	3197	2326
-697	1037	326	2190	246
1972	667	580	5547	441
5772		1734	8229	1534
13999	12151	8334	23087	7583
25559	163	67965	149035	23096
13217	2853	6478	8438	5798
11487	7775	4874	18901	3698
31740	7304	11488	34592	10022
13921	282	3154	8118	3018
-337	337	189	616	159
1435		955	1742	843
559		483	299	425
31814		10897	18486	9337

12-9 规模以上大中型工业企业主要经济指标（2013年）

单位：万元

分 组	Classify	企业单位数（个）Number of Enterprises (unit)	亏损企业 Loss Making Enterprises	工业总产值（当年价格）Gross Industrial Output Value (At Current Prices)
总计	**Total**	**223**	**42**	**31612603**
#亏损企业	Deficit Enterprises	42	42	
按登记注册类型分组	**Grouped by Registion Status**			
内资企业	Domestic Investment Enterprises	188	34	25283313
国有	State-owned	39	7	9176467
集体	Collective-owned	5		32899
股份合作	Share-holding Corperative	1		118575
联营	Joint Ownership			
有限责任公司	Limited Liability Corporations	88	16	12467809
股份有限公司	Share-holding Corperation Ltd.	32	5	2574488
私营	Private Enterprises	22	6	913076
其他	Other Domestic Funded Enterprises	1		
港澳台商投资	Enterprises with Funds from Hong Kong, Macao and Taiwan	7	5	206886
外商投资	Foreign Funded Enterprises	28	3	6122403
按轻重工业分	**Grouped by Light Industry and Heavy Industry**			
轻工业	Light Industry	64	12	5286320
重工业	Heavy Industry	159	30	26326283
按企业规模分	**Grouped by Size of Enterprises**			
大型企业	Large-size	63	7	24313775
中型企业	Medium-size	160	35	7298827
按工业行业大类分	**Grouped by Sector**			
煤炭开采和洗选业	Mining and Washing of Coal			
石油和天然气开采业	Extraction of Petroleum and Natural Gas			
黑色金属矿采选业	Mining and Processing of Ferrous Metal Ores			
有色金属矿采选业	Mining and Processing of Non-ferrous Metal Ores			
非金属矿采选业	Mining and Processing of Nonmetal Ores			
开采辅助活动	Mining Auxiliary Activities	1		206783
其他采矿业	Mining of other Ores			
农副食品加工业	Processing of Food from Agricultural Porducts	6		887772
食品制造业	Manufacture of Foods	9		1151229
酒、饮料和精制茶制造业	Manufacture of Alcohol,Beverages and Tea	6	2	790822
烟草制品业	Manufacture of Tobacco			
纺织业	Manufacture of Textile	4	2	86203
纺织服装、服饰业	Textile, apparel industry	1		52774

Economic Indicators of Large and Medium-sized Industrial Enterprises above Designated Size (2013)

(10 000 yuan)

工业销售产值（当年价）Value of Industry Products Sales (At Current Prices)	出口交货值 Export Delivery Value	从业人员年平均人数（人）Annual Average Employers (person)	资产总计 Total Assets	流动资产合计 Total Working Capitals
30361137	**1960454**	**350574**	**36933589**	**22575758**
		23925	2737038	1303146
24387014	1484566	297035	32683413	20466519
8930825	154171	80092	10472539	6682379
31314		2602	20338	3935
117535		939	144404	107553
12147386	1157945	179015	18302204	11301450
2298640	171809	25137	2922954	1897742
861314	641	9250	808869	464302
			12105	4158
191675	34915	3606	292029	105752
5782449	440974	49933	3958148	2003488
5141634	157770	44067	3631553	2009139
25219503	1802684	306507	33302036	20566619
23590801	1665022	272247	28956921	17542977
6770336	295432	78327	7976668	5032781
61757		702	57129	35942
866068	4101	4157	446990	305378
1094668		5788	390267	242638
844891	135474	5131	866341	425596
85770	13068	2569	155298	89200
48552		1108	70501	57671

12-9 续表1

单位：万元

分组	Classify	负债合计 Total Liabilites	营业收入 Total Revenue	主营业务成本 Revenue from Principal Business
总计	**Total**	**20765106**	**26892986**	**26115408**
#亏损企业	Deficit Enterprises	1915750	2411803	2370914
按登记注册类型分组	**Grouped by Registion Status**			
内资企业	Domestic Investment Enterprises	18453468	21736762	21101676
国有	State-owned	5655324	6137924	5887990
集体	Collective-owned	14373	33287	33287
股份合作	Share-holding Corperative	125677	83894	83894
联营	Joint Ownership			
有限责任公司	Limited Liability Corporations	10976452	13143494	12805370
股份有限公司	Share-holding Corperation Ltd.	1287204	1642517	1604415
私营	Private Enterprises	385708	695522	686596
其他	Other Domestic Funded Enterprises	8730	124	124
港澳台商投资	Enterprises with Funds from Hong Kong, Macao and Taiwan	178254	190179	187114
外商投资	Foreign Funded Enterprises	2133384	4966044	4826620
按轻重工业分	**Grouped by Light Industry and Heavy Industry**			
轻工业	Light Industry	1907659	4832789	4775786
重工业	Heavy Industry	18857447	22060197	21339622
按企业规模分	**Grouped by Size of Enterprises**			
大型企业	Large-size	16171653	21423580	20930701
中型企业	Medium-size	4593453	5469406	5184707
按工业行业大类分	**Grouped by Sector**			
煤炭开采和洗选业	Mining and Washing of Coal			
石油和天然气开采业	Extraction of Petroleum and Natural Gas			
黑色金属矿采选业	Mining and Processing of Ferrous Metal Ores			
有色金属矿采选业	Mining and Processing of Non-ferrous Metal Ores			
非金属矿采选业	Mining and Processing of Nonmetal Ores			
开采辅助活动	Mining Auxiliary Activities	12074	33777	32719
其他采矿业	Mining of other Ores			
农副食品加工业	Processing of Food from Agricultural Porducts	359829	645394	644671
食品制造业	Manufacture of Foods	172052	1074049	1049590
酒、饮料和精制茶制造业	Manufacture of Alcohol,Beverages and Tea	486802	816457	807210
烟草制品业	Manufacture of Tobacco			
纺织业	Manufacture of Textile	84704	85832	84957
纺织服装、服饰业	Textile, apparel industry	53105	100828	100828

continued 1

(10 000 yuan)

营业成本 Total Cost	主营业务成本 Cost of Principal Business	营业税金及附加 Taxs and Other Changes	主营业务税金及附加 Taxes and Other Charges on Principal Business	销售费用 Expenses for Sales
22985962	**22013663**	**319336**	**315376**	**1202897**
2187505	2148972	157551	157312	52689
18701629	17839848	257778	256065	764801
5312817	4779914	187145	186216	199785
30020	30020	116	116	1017
79130	79130	21	21	4338
11410768	11119331	55568	54790	405308
1345936	1315647	9406	9406	102530
522826	515674	5522	5516	51823
132	132			
158016	155076	2291	2285	26605
4126316	4018739	59267	57025	411492
3781109	3737796	37102	35230	547697
19204853	18275867	282233	280147	655199
18505975	17776350	288517	285541	909361
4479987	4237313	30819	29835	293536
22616	22330	1021	1021	98
592662	592576	1575	1570	28481
844367	827568	3564	3564	136151
632657	624934	14354	12989	88386
84337	83527	659	659	609
89250	89250	2481	2481	4834

12-9 续表2

单位：万元

分组	Classify	管理费用 Expenses for Management	财务费用 Financial cost	营业利润 Operating Profit
总计	**Total**	**1653803**	**239619**	**859245**
#亏损企业	Deficit Enterprises	131330	48186	-164458
按登记注册类型分组	**Grouped by Registion Status**			
内资企业	Domestic Investment Enterprises	1459973	219907	703075
国有	State-owned	499970	58260	281621
集体	Collective-owned	1469	141	622
股份合作	Share-holding Corperative	2338	2618	-4550
联营	Joint Ownership			
有限责任公司	Limited Liability Corporations	798771	127012	326286
股份有限公司	Share-holding Corperation Ltd.	118055	14364	41430
私营	Private Enterprises	39266	17512	57785
其他	Other Domestic Funded Enterprises	104		-119
港澳台商投资	Enterprises with Funds from Hong Kong, Macao and Taiwan	19221	2315	-17465
外商投资	Foreign Funded Enterprises	174608	17397	173633
按轻重工业分	**Grouped by Light Industry and Heavy Industry**			
轻工业	Light Industry	224881	33241	201773
重工业	Heavy Industry	1428921	206378	657472
按企业规模分	**Grouped by Size of Enterprises**			
大型企业	Large-size	1271129	169546	637556
中型企业	Medium-size	382674	70073	221690
按工业行业大类分	**Grouped by Sector**			
煤炭开采和洗选业	Mining and Washing of Coal			
石油和天然气开采业	Extraction of Petroleum and Natural Gas			
黑色金属矿采选业	Mining and Processing of Ferrous Metal Ores			
有色金属矿采选业	Mining and Processing of Non-ferrous Metal Ores			
非金属矿采选业	Mining and Processing of Nonmetal Ores			
开采辅助活动	Mining Auxiliary Activities	3039	45	6958
其他采矿业	Mining of other Ores			
农副食品加工业	Processing of Food from Agricultural Porducts	12273	10462	-391
食品制造业	Manufacture of Foods	36906	-3532	50933
酒、饮料和精制茶制造业	Manufacture of Alcohol,Beverages and Tea	21822	6324	47231
烟草制品业	Manufacture of Tobacco			
纺织业	Manufacture of Textile	4196	142	-3708
纺织服装、服饰业	Textile, apparel industry	4893	2355	-2984

continued 2

(10 000 yuan)

利润总额 Total Profits	亏损企业亏损额 Total Loss of Deficit Enterprises	税金总额 Total Pre-tax Profits	应付职工薪酬 Salary Payable	本年应交增值税 Value Added Tax Payable
1109663	**141030**	**981081**	**2467053**	**665704**
-141030	141030	204920	169275	47608
901731	100076	754706	2074509	498640
360332	39569	395007	668449	208790
647		945	4921	829
535		151	2471	130
415844	41044	271285	1219093	216495
64200	18313	54648	135825	45242
59953	1150	32669	43734	27153
220		1	16	1
-18425	25741	9152	19735	6866
226356	15213	217223	372809	160199
235587	21493	238333	346410	203103
874076	119537	742748	2120643	462601
833297	58120	796255	2005953	510714
276366	82910	184826	461099	154990
6948		1645	5934	625
6751		11467	15011	9897
54521		28439	38979	24876
54142	11213	40433	51330	27443
-842	1830	4802	24413	4144
3232		4221	3148	1740

12-9 续表3

单位：万元

分组	Classify	企业单位数（个）Number of Enterprises (unit)	亏损企业 Loss Making Enterprises	工业总产值（当年价格）Gross Industrial Output Value (At Current Prices)
皮革、毛皮、羽毛及其制品和制鞋业	Manufacture of Leather, Fur, Feather and Related Products, and Shoes	1		49251
木材加工和木、竹、藤、棕、草制品业	Processing of Timber,Manufacture of Wood,Plam and Straw Products	1		101689
家具制造业	Manufacture of Furniture			
造纸及纸制品业	Manufacture of Paper and Paper Products	6	1	22113
印刷和记录媒介复制	Printing,Reproduction of Recording Media	10	4	424695
文教、工美、体育和娱乐用品制造业	Manufacture of Articles For Cultural,Educational and Sports Activities			
石油加工业、炼焦和核燃料加工业	Processing of Petroleum, Cokeing,Processing of Nuclear and Nuclear Fuel	1	1	1355197
化学原料及化学制品制造业	Manufacture of Raw Chemical Materials and Chemical Products	9	1	770466
医药制造业	Manufacture of Medicines	14	2	1052190
化学纤维制造业	Manufacture of Chemical Fibers			
橡胶和塑料制品业	Manufacture of Rubber and Plastics	3	1	322130
非金属矿物制品业	Manufacture of Non-metallic Mineral Products	5		277395
黑色金属冶炼和压延加工业	Smelting and Pressing of Ferrous Metals	3	2	331605
有色金属冶炼和压延加工业	Smelting and Pressing of Non-ferrous Metals	6	2	747940
金属制品业	Manufacture of Metal Products	9		771458
通用设备制造业	Manufacture of General Purpose Machinery	6	1	1138579
专用设备制造业	Manufacture of Special Equipment	28	6	1780749
汽车制造业	Manufacture of Motor Vehicle	16	2	7446991
铁路、船舶、航空航天和其他运输设备制造业	Railways,Shipbuilding,Aerospace and Other Transportation Equipment Manufacturing Industry	18	4	3570640
电气机械和器材制造业	Manufacture of Electric Equipment and Machinery	17	3	3122044
计算机、通讯和其他电子设备制造业	Manufacture of Communication Equipment, Computers and other Electronic Equipment	27	6	1208054
仪器仪表制造业	Manufacture of Measuring Instruments and Machinery	8	1	1097258
其他制造业	Manufacture of Other Manufacturing			
废弃资源综合利用业	Recycling and Disposal of Waste			
金属制品、机械和设备修理业	Metal Products,Machinery and Equipment Repair Industry			
电力、热力的生产和供应业	Production and Supply of Electric Power and Heat Power	5		2134383
燃气生产和供应业	Gas Mining and Supplying Industry	2	1	639061
水的生产和供应业	Production and Supply of Water	1		73132

continued 3

(10 000 yuan)

工业销售产值（当年价） Value of Industry Products Sales (At Current Prices)	出口交货值 Export Delivery Value	从业人员年平均人数（人） Annual Average Employers (person)	资产总计 Total Assets	流动资产合计 Total Working Capitals
50423		845	42449	20941
92282		495	104350	57146
20336		1075	17796	5713
413897	1036	6098	550138	225612
1359371		1390	243603	103160
745836	157680	16085	1142792	527416
998735	3891	10600	725588	448165
308841	1171	12089	583379	354346
256952		1761	118217	82063
331574		957	18024	7904
655408	25377	5814	743634	367794
763650	35073	18531	1555098	931384
1072190	41770	10788	2227382	1711497
1510089	194503	21199	2515464	1708425
7102301	472662	74574	6382555	3570043
3499539	492597	66048	7560979	4934063
3054444	141822	34422	4461903	3153084
1202247	200359	21212	2752627	1650282
1074997	39870	18254	1628670	972573
2134383		3634	913099	277037
638804		2568	512273	233060
73132		2680	147044	67621

12-9 续表4

单位：万元

分 组	Classify	负债合计 Total Liabilites	营业收入 Total Revenue	主营业务成本 Revenue from Principal Business
皮革、毛皮、羽毛及其制品和制鞋业	Manufacture of Leather, Fur, Feather and Related Products, and Shoes	22947	51917	51412
木材加工和木、竹、藤、棕、草制品业	Processing of Timber,Manufacture of Wood,Plam and Straw Products	52643	73899	73809
家具制造业	Manufacture of Furniture			
造纸及纸制品业	Manufacture of Paper and Paper Products	16321	23041	23041
印刷和记录媒介复制	Printing,Reproduction of Recording Media	189770	387645	382899
文教、工美、体育和娱乐用品制造业	Manufacture of Articles For Cultural,Educational and Sports Activities			
石油加工业、炼焦和核燃料加工业	Processing of Petroleum, Cokeing,Processing of Nuclear and Nuclear Fuel	193185	1178172	1178172
化学原料及化学制品制造业	Manufacture of Raw Chemical Materials and Chemical Products	550391	765282	650446
医药制造业	Manufacture of Medicines	283174	915208	914473
化学纤维制造业	Manufacture of Chemical Fibers			
橡胶和塑料制品业	Manufacture of Rubber and Plastics	457632	315471	307831
非金属矿物制品业	Manufacture of Non-metallic Mineral Products	68243	172443	169809
黑色金属冶炼和压延加工业	Smelting and Pressing of Ferrous Metals	18249	14822	11514
有色金属冶炼和压延加工业	Smelting and Pressing of Non-ferrous Metals	409838	604202	586246
金属制品业	Manufacture of Metal Products	934812	768445	752789
通用设备制造业	Manufacture of General Purpose Machinery	1136614	1015164	1006594
专用设备制造业	Manufacture of Special Equipment	1113978	1321202	1277557
汽车制造业	Manufacture of Motor Vehicle	3704963	6522994	6322516
铁路、船舶、航空航天和其他运输设备制造业	Railways,Shipbuilding,Aerospace and Other Transportation Equipment Manufacturing Industry	4687002	4275288	4229283
电气机械和器材制造业	Manufacture of Electric Equipment and Machinery	2040889	2499731	2392431
计算机、通讯和其他电子设备制造业	Manufacture of Communication Equipment, Computers and other Electronic Equipment	1873397	1504369	1468724
仪器仪表制造业	Manufacture of Measuring Instruments and Machinery	658698	910674	892488
其他制造业	Manufacture of Other Manufacturing			
废弃资源综合利用业	Recycling and Disposal of Waste			
金属制品、机械和设备修理业	Metal Products,Machinery and Equipment Repair Industry			
电力、热力的生产和供应业	Production and Supply of Electric Power and Heat Power	778959	438762	384593
燃气生产和供应业	Gas Mining and Supplying Industry	323792	292119	245678
水的生产和供应业	Production and Supply of Water	81045	85803	73132

continued 4

(10 000 yuan)

营业成本 Total Cost	主营业务成本 Cost of Principal Business	营业税金及附加 Taxs and Other Changes	主营业务税金及附加 Taxes and Other Charges on Principal Business	销售费用 Expenses for Sales
47201	46780	170	170	918
69190	69190	267	267	1307
21531	21531	25	25	602
284240	277986	3646	3644	10639
1039130	1039130	150807	150807	1342
649111	543286	2530	2530	27563
499548	499107	8596	8596	258725
266644	265199	2157	1951	14627
145857	143303	427	427	14977
14187	10798	61	61	36
551025	530917	763	746	5851
654090	643412	2432	2432	17773
760487	753674	6738	6738	37227
1033406	996453	10286	10085	67811
5886383	5596807	56660	56632	207721
3699459	3667893	15881	15849	70365
2365579	1948405	15234	15234	148735
1308084	1273718	4267	4002	26343
735006	726009	6496	5939	12089
382253	349977	4811	4811	88
233897	205201	2405	1623	16270
73768	64703	1028	527	3328

12-9 续表5

单位：万元

分组	Classify	管理费用 Expenses for Management	财务费用 Financial cost	营业利润 Operating Profit
皮革、毛皮、羽毛及其制品和制鞋业	Manufacture of Leather, Fur, Feather and Related Products, and Shoes	1347	163	2207
木材加工和木、竹、藤、棕、草制品业	Processing of Timber,Manufacture of Wood,Plam and Straw Products	1756	2865	-1486
家具制造业	Manufacture of Furniture			
造纸及纸制品业	Manufacture of Paper and Paper Products	599	324	-40
印刷和记录媒介复制	Printing,Reproduction of Recording Media	48553	3404	42996
文教、工美、体育和娱乐用品制造业	Manufacture of Articles For Cultural,Educational and Sports Activities			
石油加工业、炼焦和核燃料加工业	Processing of Petroleum, Cokeing,Processing of Nuclear and Nuclear Fuel	11866	6088	-31815
化学原料及化学制品制造业	Manufacture of Raw Chemical Materials and Chemical Products	77277	10136	6711
医药制造业	Manufacture of Medicines	70531	11745	65086
化学纤维制造业	Manufacture of Chemical Fibers			
橡胶和塑料制品业	Manufacture of Rubber and Plastics	10527	6992	13698
非金属矿物制品业	Manufacture of Non-metallic Mineral Products	4090	758	6396
黑色金属冶炼和压延加工业	Smelting and Pressing of Ferrous Metals	2335	173	-1999
有色金属冶炼和压延加工业	Smelting and Pressing of Non-ferrous Metals	21509	17065	7865
金属制品业	Manufacture of Metal Products	63823	12101	19719
通用设备制造业	Manufacture of General Purpose Machinery	127348	-7883	93441
专用设备制造业	Manufacture of Special Equipment	125896	11729	134553
汽车制造业	Manufacture of Motor Vehicle	256417	34696	96959
铁路、船舶、航空航天和其他运输设备制造业	Railways,Shipbuilding,Aerospace and Other Transportation Equipment Manufacturing Industry	288086	53935	111019
电气机械和器材制造业	Manufacture of Electric Equipment and Machinery	215918	14857	61477
计算机、通讯和其他电子设备制造业	Manufacture of Communication Equipment, Computers and other Electronic Equipment	107377	7926	49414
仪器仪表制造业	Manufacture of Measuring Instruments and Machinery	107521	6544	39750
其他制造业	Manufacture of Other Manufacturing			
废弃资源综合利用业	Recycling and Disposal of Waste			
金属制品、机械和设备修理业	Metal Products,Machinery and Equipment Repair Industry			
电力、热力的生产和供应业	Production and Supply of Electric Power and Heat Power	3442	30618	16173
燃气生产和供应业	Gas Mining and Supplying Industry	16301	-364	29583
水的生产和供应业	Production and Supply of Water	8156	-49	-500

continued 5

(10 000 yuan)

利润总额 Total Profits	亏损企业亏损额 Total Loss of Deficit Enterprises	税金总额 Total Pre-tax Profits	应付职工薪酬 Salary Payable	本年应交增值税 Value Added Tax Payable
2306		170	4034	
877		2656	1945	2389
-2	226	293	2701	269
43001	6612	26403	64584	22760
-31815	31815	181175	12947	30368
17401	11441	17505	88296	14975
65666	1133	111379	109377	102784
15505	354	11733	23783	9782
10246		8942	9147	8515
-1723	1723	570	4263	508
13417	3816	2273	29005	1527
28927		12543	132231	10111
99172	95	45172	123141	33435
178037	27980	54487	152261	44402
154383	5198	165348	399661	103716
149193	7696	44495	521017	23646
77449	8519	103915	243867	88681
63443	16972	19162	141478	15159
49064	1659	43362	196887	37422
19301		22369	30701	17558
29065	2749	11208	19925	9586
1999		4915	16987	4388

12-10　规模以上工业企业主要经济效益指标（2013年）

行　业	Sector	总资产贡献率（%） Ratio of Total Assets to Industrial Output Value (%)	资产负债率（%） Assets-Liability Ratio (%)
总计	**Total**	**7.9**	**58.9**
按工业行业大类分	**Grouped by Sector**		
煤炭开采和洗选业	Mining and Washing of Coal		
石油和天然气开采业	Extraction of Petroleum and Natural Gas		
黑色金属矿采选业	Mining and Processing of Ferrous Metal Ores	0.7	182.7
有色金属矿采选业	Mining and Processing of Non-ferrous Metal Ores		
非金属矿采选业	Mining and Processing of Nonmetal Ores		
开采辅助活动	Mining Auxiliary Activities	16.2	25.9
其他采矿业	Mining of other Ores		
农副食品加工业	Processing of Food from Agricultural Porducts	9.1	66.7
食品制造业	Manufacture of Foods	19.6	42.9
酒、饮料和精制茶制造业	Manufacture of Alcohol,Beverages and Tea	12.0	56.3
烟草制品业	Manufacture of Tobacco	11.9	62.4
纺织业	Manufacture of Textile	7.6	52.7
纺织服装、服饰业	Textile, apparel industry	17.4	64.5
皮革、毛皮、羽毛及其制品和制鞋业	Manufacture of Leather, Fur, Feather and Related Products, and Shoes	5.8	48.5
木材加工和木、竹、藤、棕、草制品业	Processing of Timber,Manufacture of Wood,Plam and Straw Products	7.3	51.9
家具制造业	Manufacture of Furniture	11.4	52.3
造纸及纸制品业	Manufacture of Paper and Paper Products	12.8	52.7
印刷和记录媒介复制业	Printing,Reproduction of Recording Media	14.6	38.9
文教、工美、体育和娱乐用品制造业	Manufacture of Articles For Cultural,Educational and Sports Activities	11.3	86.3
石油加工、炼焦和核燃料加工业	Processing of Petroleum, Cokeing,Processing of Nuclear and Nuclear Fuel	31.6	70.1

Main Indicators of Economic Benefit of Industrial Enterprises above Designated Size (2013)

流动资产周转率（次）Rate of Annual Turnover Working Capitals (times)	成本费用利润率（%）Ratio of Profits to Cost (%)	工业产品销售率（%）Proportion of Industrial Products Sold (%)	产值利税率（%）Ratio of Output Value to Profits and Tax (%)	每百元固定资产实现利税（元）Profit and Tax per 100 yuan of Fixed Assets (yuan)	每百元销售收入实现利税（元）Profit and Tax per 100 yuan of Sales Revenue (yuan)
1.4	**4.7**	**96.2**	**7.1**		**8.0**
1.9	-10	100.0	-5.6		-5.7
1.1	21.7	33.9	4.6		22.6
4.3	1.4	98.3	2.1		2.5
4.6	5.1	94.2	6.3		7.3
2.0	6.7	106.2	11.3		11.1
0.9	15.1	97.1	24.1		22.7
1.6	3.6	90.7	7.0		8.0
1.9	6.6	95.0	12.8		9.8
2.3	4.1	102.2	4.6		4.5
1.8	1.9	90.9	4.0		5.2
2.1	4.4	91.7	4.9		7.4
2.6	7.2	97.0	8.7		9.2
1.9	11.1	96.6	15.1		15.3
3.1	3.5	99.3	3.5		4.2
8.1	-0.7	100.2	6.7		7.2

12-10 续表1

行　业	Sector	总资产贡献率（%） Ratio of Total Assets to Industrial Output Value (%)	资产负债率（%） Assets-Liability Ratio (%)
化学原料和化学制品制造业	Manufacture of Raw Chemical Materials and Chemical Products	6.6	52.3
医药制造业	Manufacture of Medicines	22.3	42.6
化学纤维制造业	Manufacture of Chemical Fibers	26.1	15.4
橡胶和塑料制品业	Manufacture of Rubber and Plastics	9.4	72.5
非金属矿物制品业	Manufacture of Non-metallic Mineral Products	20.2	51.2
黑色金属冶炼和压延加工业	Smelting and Pressing of Ferrous Metals	15.4	62.4
有色金属冶炼和压延加工业	Smelting and Pressing of Non-ferrous Metals	7.2	54.2
金属制品业	Manufacture of Metal Products	6.0	60.0
通用设备制造业	Manufacture of General Purpose Machinery	7.5	53.1
专用设备制造业	Manufacture of Special Equipment	10.4	47.2
汽车制造业	Manufacture of Motor Vehicle	7.0	58.3
铁路、船舶、航空航天和其他运输设备制造业	Railways,Shipbuilding,Aerospace and Other Transportation Equipment Manufacturing Industry	3.9	62.0
电气机械和器材制造业	Manufacture of Electric Equipment and Machinery	5.4	48.5
计算机、通信和其他电子设备制造业	Manufacture of Communication Equipment, Computers and other Electronic Equipment	4.4	65.2
仪器仪表制造业	Manufacture of Measuring Instruments and Machinery	7.3	42.1
其他制造业	Manufacture of Other Manufacturing	9.7	58.8
废弃资源综合利用	Recycling and Disposal of Waste		
金属制品、机械和设备修理业	Metal Products,Machinery and Equipment Repair Industry	14.3	58.1
电力、热力生产和供应业	Production and Supply of Electric Power and Heat Power	4.7	94.9
燃气生产和供应业	Gas Mining and Supplying Industry	8.0	60.2
水的生产和供应业	Production and Supply of Water	5.5	51.1

continued 1

流动资产周转率（次） Rate of Annual Turnover Working Capitals (times)	成本费用利润率（%） Ratio of Profits to Cost (%)	工业产品销售率（%） Proportion of Industrial Products Sold (%)	产值利税率（%） Ratio of Output Value to Profits and Tax (%)	每百元固定资产实现利税（元） Profit and Tax per 100 yuan of Fixed Assets (yuan)	每百元销售收入实现利税（元） Profit and Tax per 100 yuan of Sales Revenue (yuan)
1.4	5.1	96.8	6.7		7.5
1.9	8.8	94.4	15.8		18.4
3.0	17.4	105.9	20.6		19.5
1.4	6.6	90.5	7.8		9.2
3.3	7.1	97.0	8.9		10.2
4.0	4.3	99.4	4.0		6.3
1.9	3.9	90.9	4.1		4.8
1.2	5.1	98.0	6.2		7.0
0.7	9.0	95.7	10.8		12.3
1.0	10.6	88.2	11.5		13.7
2.1	2.8	95.5	4.6		5.3
1.0	3.9	97.7	5.7		5.0
1.0	3.5	96.4	5.9		6.9
1.0	5.8	97.1	7.5		7.2
1.0	6.3	97.1	9.7		10.5
2.0	3.1	99.6	6.1		6.2
1.1	9.5	98.6	18.7		15.1
1.8	2.9	100	7.9		11.0
1.7	11.3	100	12.2		12.4
1.2	4.3	100	11.2		11.1

主要统计指标解释

工业 指从事自然资源的开采，对采掘品和农产品进行加工和再加工的物质生产部门。具体包括：（1）对自然资源的开采，如采矿、晒盐等（但不包括禽兽捕猎和水产捕捞）；（2）对农副产品的加工、再加工，如粮油加工、食品加工、缫丝、纺织、制革等；（3）对采掘品的加工、再加工，如炼铁、炼钢、化工生产、石油加工、机器制造、木材加工等，以及电力、自来水、煤气的生产和供应等；（4）对工业品的修理、翻新，如机器设备的修理、交通运输工具（如汽车）的修理等。

工业统计调查单位为独立核算法人工业企业。

独立核算法人工业企业指从事工业生产经营活动的单位。独立核算法人工业企业应同时具备以下条件：①依法成立，有自己的名称、组织机构和场所，能够承担民事责任；②独立拥有和使用资产，承担负债，有权与其他单位签订合同；③独立核算盈亏，并能够编制资产负债表。

国有及国有控股企业 指国有企业加上国有控股企业。国有企业（即原全民所有制工业或国营工业）指企业全部资产归国家所有，并按《中华人民共和国企业法人登记管理条例》规定登记注册的非公司制的经济组织。包括国有企业、国有独资公司和国有联营企业。1957年以前的公私合营和私营工业，后均改造为国营工业，1992年改为国有工业，这部分工业的资料不单独分列时，均包括在国有企业内。国有控股企业是对混合所有制经济的企业进行的“国有控股”分类。它是指这些企业的全部资产中国有资产（股份）相对其他所有者中的任何一个所有者占资（股）最多的企业。该分组反映了国有经济控股情况。

本篇涉及的其他企业登记注册类型的解释详见综合篇。

轻工业 指主要提供生活消费品和制作手工工具的工业。按其所使用的原料不同，可分为两大类：（1）以农产品为原料的轻工业，是指直接或间接以农产品为基本原料的轻工业。主要包括食品制造、饮料制造、烟草加工、纺织、缝纫、皮革和毛皮制作、造纸以及印刷等工业；（2）以非农产品为原料的轻工业，是指以工业品为原料的轻工业。主要包括文教体育用品、化学药品制造、合成纤维制造、日用化学制品、日用玻璃制品、日用金属制品、手工工具制造、医疗器械制造、文化和办公用机械制造等工业。

重工业 指为国民经济各部门提供物质技术基础的主要生产资料的工业。按其生产性质和产品用途，可以分为下列三类：（1）采掘（伐）工业，是指对自然资源的开采，包括石油开采、煤炭开采、金属矿开采、非金属矿开采等工业；（2）原材料工业，指向国民经济各部门提供基本材料、动力和燃料的工业。包括金属冶炼及加工、炼焦及焦炭、化学、化工：原料、水泥、人造板以及电力、石油和煤炭加工等工业；（3）加工工业，是指对工业原材料进行再加工制造的工业。包括装备国民经济各部门的机械设备制造工业、金属结构、水泥制品等工业，以及为农业提供的生产资料如化肥、农药等工业。

根据上述划分原则，修理业中以重工业产品为修理作业对象的划为重工业，反之划为轻工业。

工业总产值

（1）定义：

工业总产值是工业企业在一定时期内生产的以货币形式表现的工业最终产品和提供工业性劳务活动的总价值量。它反映一定时间内工业生产的总规模和总水平。

（2）计算原则：

工业生产的原则，即凡是企业在报告期生产的经检验合格的产品，不管是否在报告期销售，均包括在内。

最终产品的原则，即凡是计入工业总产值的产品，必须是本企业生产的经检验合格的，不需要再进行任何加工的最终产品。如果企业有中间产品（半成品）对外销售，则对外销售的中间产品应视为企业的最终产品。

工厂法原则，即工业总产值是以下业企业作为基本计算（核算）单位，即按企业的最终产品计算工业总产值。按这种方法计算的工业总产值，不允许同一产品价值在企业内部重复计算，不能把企业内部各个车间（分厂）生产的成果相加，但允许企业间的重复计算。

（3）内容及计算方法：

1995年全国工业普查对工业总产值（原规定）的内容及计算原则和方法做了某些修订，修订后的工业总产值（新规定）包括三项内容：即本期生产成品价值、对外加工费收入、在制品半成品期末期初差额价值三部分。

本期生产成品价值指企业本期生产，并在报告期内不再进行加工，经检验、包装入库的全部工业成品（半成品）价值合计，包括企业生产的自制设备及提供给本企业在建工程、其他非工业部门和福利部门等单位使用的成品价值。本期生产成品价值为按自备原材料生产的产品的数量乘以本期不含增值税（销项税额）的产品实际销售平均单价计算；会计核算中按成本价格转帐的自制设备和自产自用的成品，按成本价格计算生产成品价值。生产成品价值中不包括用定货者来料加工的成品（半成品）价值。

对外加工费收入指企业在报告期内完成的对外承接的工业品加工（包括用定货者来料加工产品）的加工费收入和对外工业修理作业所取得的加工费收入。对外加工费收入按不含增值税（销项税额）的价格计算，可根据会计"产品销售收入"科目的有关资料取得。

对于本企业对内非工业部门提供的加工修理、设备安装的劳务收入，如果企业会计核算基础较好，能取得这部分资料，而且这部分价值所占比重较大，应包括在对外加工费收入中。

自制半成品在制品期末期初差额价值指企业报告期在制品期末减期初的差额价值，本指标一般可以从会计核算资料中取得。如果会计产品成本核算中不计算半成品、在制品的成本，则总产值中也不包括这部分价值，反之则包括。

（2）工业总产值统计范围变化和计算方法修订情况

1984年以前工业总产值不包括村办工业，村办工业总产值划归农业。1984年以后工业总产值包括村办工业。

1995年工业普查对工业总产值计算方法做了修订，即从1995年始按新修订（新规定）方法计算工业总产值。新规定与原规定的区别如下：

全价与加工费的计算原则不同：新规定为凡自备原材料，不论其生产繁简程度如何，一律按全价计算工业总产值；凡来料加工，允许按加工费计算工业总产值。原规定则视生产加工的繁简程度不同，规定哪些行业按全价，哪些行业按加工费计算工业总产值。

自制半成品、在产品期末期初差额价值的计算原则不同：新规定要求，凡会计产品成本核算时计算了成本的差额价值，总产值中就应包括，否则可不包括；原规定则按生产周期六个月的界限区分，凡生产周期六个月以上的企业，总产值计算中应包括这部分差额价值，否则可不包括。

计算价格不同：新规定按不含增值税（销项税额）的价格计算；原规定则按含增值税（销项税额）的价格计算。

工业增加值 指工业企业在报告期内以货币表现的工业生产活动的最终成果。

工业增加值有两种计算方法：一是生产法，即工业总产出减去工业中间投入加上应交增值税；二是收入法，即从收入的角度出发，根据生产要素在生产过程中应得到的收入份额计算，具体构成项目有固定资产折旧、劳动者报酬、生产税净额、营业盈余，这种方法也称要素分配法。本年鉴中的工业增加值是以收入法计算的。

生产法工业增加值的计算方法为：

工业增加值＝工业总产出–工业中间投入+应交增值税

（1）工业总产出：指工业企业在一定时期内工业生产活动的总成果。工业总产出包括：成品生产价值，对外加工费收入，自制半成品、在产品期末期初差额价值。1995年后用新规定计算的工业总产值代替。

（2）工业中间投入：指工业企业在工业生产活动中消耗的外购物质产品和对外支付的服务费用。服务费用包括支付给物质生产部门（工业、农业、批发零售贸易业、建筑业、运输邮电业）的服务费用和支付给非物质生产部门（如保险、金融、文化教育、科学研究、医疗卫生、行政管理等）的服务费用。工业中间投入的确定须遵循以下原则：必须从外部购入的，并已计入工业总产出的产品和服务价值；必须是本期投入生产，并一次性消耗掉（包括本期摊销的低值易耗品等）的产品和服务价值。

工业中间投入包括直接材料费用、制造费用中的工业中间投入、管理费用中的工业中间投入、销售费用中的工业中间投入和利息支出五部分。

资产总计 指企业拥有或控制的能以货币计量的经济资源，包括各种财产、债权和其他权利。资产按流动性分为流动资产、长期投资、固定资产、无形资产、递延资产和其他资产。该指标根据企业会计"资产负债表"中"资产总计"项目的期末数填列。

流动资产 指企业可以在一年内或者超过一年的一个生产周期内变现或者耗用的资产，包括现金及各种存款、短期投资，应收及预付款项、存货等。

固定资产原价 指企业在建造、购置、安装、改建、扩建、技术改造某项固定资产时所支出的全部货币总额。它一般包括买价、包装费、运杂费和安装费等。

固定资产净值 指固定资产原价减去历年已提折旧额后的净额。计算公式为：

固定资产净值=固定资产原价-累计折旧

负债合计 指企业所承担的能以货币计量，将以资产或劳务偿付的债务，偿还形式包括货币、资产或提供劳务。负债一般按偿还期长短分为流动负债和长期负债。根据会计“资产负债表”中“负债合计”的年末数填列。

所有者权益合计 指企业投资人对企业净资产的所有权。企业净资产为企业全部资产与企业全部负债的差额，包括实收资本、资本公积、盈余公积、未分配利润等。根据会计“资产负债表”中“所有者权益”项的期末数填列。

主营业务收入 指会计“利润表”中对应指标的本年累计数。未执行2001年《企业会计制度》的企业，用“产品销售收入”的本期累计数代替。

主营业务成本 指会计“利润表”中对应指标的本年累计数。未执行2001年《企业会计制度》的企业，用“产品销售成本”的本期累计数代替。

主营业务税金及附加 指会计“利润表”中对应指标的本年累计数。未执行2001年《企业会计制度》的企业，用“产品销售税金及附加”的本期累计数代替。

利润总额 指企业在生产经营过程中各种收入扣除各种耗费后的盈余，反映企业在报告期内实现的盈亏总额，包括营业利润、补贴收入、投资净收益和营业外收支净额。根据会计“利润表”中的对应指标的本期累计数填列。

本年应交增值税 指企业按税法规定，从事货物销售或提供加工、修理修配劳务等增加货物价值的活动本期应交纳的税金。指企业在报告期应交增值税额。计算公式为：

本年应交增值税=销项税额-（进项税额-进项税额转出）-出口抵减内销产品应纳税额-减免税款+出口退税

本年进项税额 指工业企业在报告期内购入货物或接受应税劳务而支付的、准予从销项税额中抵扣的增值税额。

本年销项税额 指工业企业在报告期内销售货物或提供应税劳务应收取的增值税额。

从业人员平均人数 是指报告期内每天拥有的从业人员人数。其计算公式为：

月平均人数=报告月内每天实有人数之和／报告月日历日数

季平均人数=季内各月平均人数之和／3

年平均人数=年内各月平均人数之和／12

总资产贡献率 反映企业全部资产的获利能力，是企业经营业绩和管理水平的集中体现，是评价和考核企业盈利能力的核心指标。计算公式为：

总资产贡献率（%）=（利润总额+税金总额+利息支出）／平均资金总额×100%

公式中：税金总额为产品销售税金及附加与应交增值税之和；平均资产总额为期初期末资产之和的算术平均值。

资产负债率 该指标既反映企业经营风险的大小，也反映企业利用债权人提供的资金从事经营活动的能力。计算公式为：

资产负债率（%）=负债总额／资产总额×100%

资产与负债均为报告期期末数。

流动资产周转次数 指一定时期内流动资产完成的周转次数，反映投入工业企业流动资金的周转速度。计算公式为：

流动资产周转次数：产品销售收入／全部流动资产平均余额

公式中：全部流动资产平均余额为期初和期末的流动资产之和的算术平均值。

成本费用利润率 反映企业投入的生产成本及费用的经济效益，同时也反映企业降低成本所取得的经济效益。计算公式为：

成本费用利润率（%）=利润总额／成本费用总额×100%

公式中：成本费用总额为产品销售成本、销售费用、管理费用、财务费用之和。

产品销售率 该指标反映工业产品已实现销售的程度，是分析工业产销衔接情况，研究工业产品满足社会需求的指标。计算公式为：

产品销售率（%）=工业销售产值／工业总产值（现价）×100%

Explanatory Notes on Main Statistical Indicators

Industry refers to the material production sector which is engaged in the extraction of natural resources and processing and reprocessing of minerals and agricultural products, including (1) extraction of natural resources, such as mining, salt production (but not including hunting and fishing); (2) processing and reprocessing of farm and sideline produces, such as rice husking, flour milling, wine making, oil pressing, silk reeling, spinning and weaving, and leather making; (3) manufacture of industrial products, such as steel making, iron smelting, chemicals manufacturing, petroleum processing, machine building, timber processing; water and gas production and electricity generation and supply; (4)repairing of industrial products such as the repairing of machinery and means of transport (including cars).

In industrial statistics surveys, the units of enquiry are corporate industrial enterprises with independent accounting systems.

Corporate industrial enterprises with independent accounting systems refer to enterprises engaging in industrial production activities, which meet the following requirements: (1) They are established legally, having their own names, organizations, location and able to take civil liability; (2) They possess and use their assets independently, assume liabilities and are entitled to sign contracts with other units; (3) They are financially independent and compile their own balance sheets.

State–owned and State–holding Enterprises refer to state-owned enterprises plus State-holding enterprises. State-owned enterprises (originally known as State-run enterprises with ownership by the whole society) are non-corporate economic entities registered in accordance with the Regulation of the People's Republic of China on the Management of Registration of Legal Enterprises, where all assets are owned by the State. Included in this category are State-owned enterprises, State-funded corporations and State-owned joint-operation enterprises. Joint State- private industries and private industries, which existed before 1957, were transformed into state-run industries since 1957, and into State-owned industries after 1992. Statistics on those enterprises are included in the State- owned industries instead of being grouped them separately. State-holding enterprises are a sub- classification of enterprises with mixed ownership, referring to enterprises where the percentage of State assets (or shares by the State) is larger than any other single share holder of the same enterprise. This sub- classification illustrates the control of the State over a particular industry.

For explanation of enterprises of other types of registration covered in this chapter, please refer to General Survey.

Light Industry refers to the industry that produces consumer goods and hand tools. It consists of two categories, depending on the materials used:

(1) Industries using farm products as raw materials. These are the branches of light industry which directly or indirectly use farm products as basic raw materials, including the manufacture of food and beverages, tobacco processing, textile, clothing, fur and leather manufacturing, paper making, printing, etc.

(2) Industries using non-farm products as raw materials. These are the branches of light industry which use manufactured goods as raw materials, including the manufacture of cultural, educational articles and sports goods, chemicals, synthetic fibre, chemical products for daily use, glass products for daily use, metal products for daily use, hand tools, medical apparatus and instruments, and the manufacture of cultural and office machinery.

Heavy Industry refers to the industry which produces capital goods, and provides various sectors of the national economy with necessary material and technical basis for production. It consists of the following three branches according to the purpose of production or the use of products:

(1) Mining, quarrying and logging industry, which refers to the industry that extracts natural resources, including extraction of petroleum, coal, metal and non-metal ores.

(2) Raw materials industry refers to the industry that provides various sectors of the national economy with raw materials, fuels and power. It includes smelting and processing of metals, coking and coke chemistry, chemical materials and building materials such as cement, plywood, and power, petroleum refining and coal dressing

(3) Manufacturing industry which refers to the industry that processes raw materials. It includes machine-building industries which equip sectors of the national economy; industries producing metal structure and cement products; and industries producing means of agricultural production, such as chemical fertilizers and pesticides.

In accordance with the above principles of classification, the repairing trades, which are engaged primarily in repairing products of heavy industry, are classified as heavy industry while those which are engaged in repairing products of light industry are classified as light industry.

Gross Industrial Output Value

(1) Definition: Gross industrial output value is the total volume of final industrial products produced and industrial services provided during a given period in monetary terms. It reflects the total achievements and overall scale of industrial production during a given period.

(2) Principles for calculation:

Statistics on industrial production follow the principle that all products produced by the enterprises and accepted through quality check during the reference period are to be included no matter whether they are sold or not during the reference period.

Determination of final products follows the principle that all products that are included in the calculation of gross industrial output value are the final products of the enterprise which have been accepted through quality check and require no further processing. If an enterprise has intermediate (semi-finished) products to sell, these intermediate products are considered as the final products of the enterprise.

Gross industrial output value is calculated following the principle of factory approach, i.e. industrial enterprise is used as the basic accounting unit in calculating the gross industrial output value. By this approach, value of the same product is not to be double-counted, and the output value of different workshops (branch factories) within the enterprise should not be added. However, this approach allows the possibility of double counting between enterprises.

(3) Content and method of calculation: The old definition of gross industrial output value was modified during the 1995 National Industrial Census. The revised (new) definition of gross industrial output value consists of 3 components: value of the finished products during the reference period, income from processing for external parties, and value of change in semi-finished products between the end and the beginning of the reference period.

Value of finished products during the reference period: refers to the value of all finished (semi-finished) industrial products that are produced during the reference period without the need for further processing, checked for acceptance, packed and put into the warehouse of the enterprise, including the value of own-produced equipment and the value of products provided to the projects under construction of the enterprise, and to other non-industrial or welfare units. Value of finished products during the reference period is calculated by the quantity of products produced using own materials multiplied by the average unit prices at which products are sold (excluding value-added tax). Own-produced equipment and products produced for own use are valued at cost prices as in the case of enterprise accounting. Value of finished products does not include the value of finished products (semi-finished products) that are produced using the materials from the clients who place the orders.

Income from external processing: refers to income from contracted external processing of industrial products (including processing of industrial products using materials from the clients), and the income from industrial repairing work provided to other parties. Income from external processing is calculated using information from the item "products sales income" in the enterprise accounting at the prices with value-added tax excluded.

For income from services such as processing, repairing and installation of equipment provided to non- industrial units within the enterprise, if the accounting work of the enterprise is good enough to separate it from other records, and the share of such services is significant, it should also be included in the income from external processing.

Value of change in semi-finished products between the end and the beginning of the reference period: refers to the value of change in semi-finished products between the end and the beginning of the reference period, which generally can be obtained from accounting records of enterprises. If the enterprise accounting excludes the cost of semi-finished products, then it should not be included in the gross industrial output value, and the reverse if otherwise.

(4) Changes in the scope and method of calculation of the gross industrial output value

Prior to 1984, the value of rural industry run by villages was classified into agriculture instead of industry Since 1984, it has been included in the gross industrial output value. Method of calculation for the gross industrial output value was modified in the industriaLcensus in 1995. The difference in the new method as compared with the old one is outlined below:

Principle in using full value vs. processing fee: The new method stipulates that all products produced using own materials are to be calculated with full value in reporting the gross industrial output value irrespective of the complexity of production, and for external processing, it allows calculation using processing fee. In the old method, however, the use of full value or processing fee was determined by the degree of complexity of production in different branches of industries.

Principle in determining the value of change in semi-finished products: The new method requires that value of change in semi-finished products should be included in the gross industrial output value if it is included in the accounting record of the enterprise, otherwise it should not be included. In the old method, it is determined by the type of enterprises in terms of production cycle. If the production cycle is over 6 months, the value of change in semi-finished products is included in the gross industrial output value, otherwise it is not.

Difference in prices: The new method uses prices excluding value-added tax in the calculation of gross industrial output value, while the old method used prices including value-added tax.

Value–added of Industry refers to the final results of industrial production of industrial enterprises in money terms during the reference period.

Industrial value-added can be calculated by two approaches: the production approach, i.e. gross industrial output value minus intermediate input plus value-added tax, and the income approach, i.e. income for various factors used in the course of production, including depreciation of fixed assets, remuneration of labourers, net of production tax, and operating surplus. Value-added of industry in the Yearbook is calculated by the income approach as follows:

Value-added of industry = gross industrial output - industrial intermediate input + value-added tax

(1) Gross industrial output: refers to the total achievements of industrial production activities during a given period. Gross industrial output includes value of finished products, income from external processing, and value of change in semi-finished products between the end and the beginning of the reference period. Since 1995, the gross industrial output value obtained by the new method is used in the calculation.

(2) Industrial intermediate input: refers to purchased goods and paid services consumed during the industrial production of enterprises. Fees paid for services include fees paid for the services provided by material production sectors (industry, agriculture, wholesale and retail trade, construction, transport, post and telecommunications) and by non-material production sectors (insurance, banking, culture, education, scientific research, health and medical care, public administration, etc.). The determination of industrial intermediate input follows the principle that the goods and services must be purchased from outside and included in the gross industrial output, and that the goods and services are inputted into production and consumed (include low-value consumables) during the reference period.

Industrial intermediate input includes 5 components, namely direct consumption of materials, industrial intermediate input in manufacturing cost, industrial intermediate input in management cost, industrial intermediate input in marketing cost and expenditure on interest.

Total Assets refer to all economic resources in monetary term, these are owned or controlled by enterprises, including properties, creditor's equity and other economic rights of all forms. Classified by the degree of liquidity, total assets include working capitals, long-term investment, fixed assets, intangible assets, deferred assets and other assets. Data on this indicator can be obtained by the year-end figures of total assets in the Assets and Liability Table of accounting records of enterprises.

Working Capital refers to capital that an enterprise can cash or use during one year or one production cycle that may exceed one year, including cash and savings deposits of various forms, short-term investment, money receivable and prepaid money, inventories, etc.

Original Value of Fixed Assets refers to the total value, in monetary terms, that an enterprise spent on fixed assets, through construction, purchase, installation, transformation, expansion or technical upgrading. Generally, it covers cost of purchase, packing, transportation and installation, etc.

Net Value of Fixed Assets refers to the original value of fixed assets minus depreciation over the years, i.e.:

Net value of fixed assets = original value of fixed assets - cumulative depreciation

Total Liabilities refer to payable liabilities of enterprises that have to be repaid in terms of money, assets or labour services. In terms of payment, it can be divided into liquid liabilities and long-term liabilities. Data on this item is obtained from the ending figures on total liabilities from the Assets and Liability Table from the enterprises.

Total Equity refers to the ownership of net assets of enterprise by its investors. Net assets equal total assets minus total liabilities of the enterprise, including the paid-in capital, accumulation of capital and operating surplus and non-distributed profits. Data are obtained from the ending figures on "total equity" from the "balance sheets".

Revenue from Principal Business refers to the annual accumulation of the corresponding item in the "profit table" of the accountant. For enterprises that do not follow the 2001 Enterprise Accounting Standards, the year-end accumulation of revenue from the sales of products is used as a substitute.

Cost of Principal Business refers to the annual accumulation of the corresponding item in the "profit table" of the accountant. For enterprises that do not follow the 2001 Enterprise Accounting Standards, theyear-end accumulation of cost for the sales of products is used as a substitute.

Tax and Extra Charges from Principal Bosiness refer to the annual accumulation of the corresponding item in the "profit table" of the accountant. For enterprises that do not follow the 2001 Enterprise Accounting Standards, the year-end accumulation of tax and extra charges from the sales of products is used as a substitute.

Total Profits refers to the balance of various incomes minus various spendings in the course of operation, reflecting the total profits and losses of enterprises in reporting period. It includes: operating profits, income from subsidies, net investment income and net income from activities other than operation. Data are obtained from the annual accumulation of the corresponding item in the "profit table" of the accountant.

Value-added Tax Payable in the Current Year refers to the payable tax of enterprises which engaged in selling of goods or providing services that bring added value to the goods, such as processing, repairing, fitting and other activities should be paid according to Tax Law. It refers to the amount of the value-added tax which should be paid by the enterprises during the reference period. The formula is as tollows:

Value-added Tax Payable in the Current Year = tax on sales-(tax on purchase-transferred tax on purchase)- exports deduct tax payable on domestic sales-tax relief+the export tax rebate.

Tax on Purchase in Current Year refers to goods purchased by industrial enterprises or value added tax that should be paid but being granted the right to deduct from the tax on sales.

Tax on Sales in Current Year refers to value added tax on industrial enterprises from sales of goods or taxable services that should be charged value added tax.

Average number of employed persons refers to the number of employee everyday during the reference period, calculated with the following formula:

$$\text{Monthly average Number} = \frac{\text{sum of actual employees everyday in reference month}}{\text{number of calendar dates in reference month}}$$

$$\text{Quarterly average number} = \frac{\text{sum of monthly average number in reference quarter}}{3}$$

$$\text{Annual average number} = \frac{\text{sum of monthly average number in reference year}}{12}$$

Ratio of Profits, Taxes and Interests to Average Assets reflects the profit-making capability of all assets of the enterprise and is a key indicator manifesting the performance and management and evaluating the profit-making potential of the enterprise. It is calculated as

$$\text{Ratio of Profits, Taxes and Interests toAverageAssets(\%)} = \frac{\text{otal profits+ total taxes+ interest payment}}{\text{average assets}} \times 100\%$$

In the above formula, total taxes is the sum of tax and extra charges on the sales of products and value-added tax payable; and average assets is the arithmetic mean of the sum of beginning assets and ending assets.

Ratio of Debts to Assets reflects both the operation risk and the capability of the enterprise in making use of the capital from the creditors. It is calculated as follows:

$$\text{Ratio of Debts toAssets(\%)} = \frac{\text{total debts}}{\text{total assets}} \times 100\%$$

Both assets and debts are figures at the end of the reference period.

Turnover of Working Capital refers to the number of times of turnover of working capital in a given period of time, which reflects the speed of the turnover of working capital of industrial enterprises, and is calculated as follows:

$$\text{Turnover of Working Capital} = \frac{\text{sales revenue of products}}{\text{average balance of total working capital}}$$

In the above formula, average balance of total working capital refers to the arithmetic mean of the sum of working capital at the beginning and at the end of the reference period.

Ratio of Profits to Total Industrial Costs refers to the ratio of profits realized in a given period to the total costs in the same period, which reflects the economic efficiency of input cost and is calculated as follows:

$$\text{Ratio of Profits to Total Industrial Cost (\%)} = \frac{\text{total profits}}{\text{total costs}} \times 100\%$$

Total costs in the above formula are the sum of cost of products sold, marketing cost, management cost and financial cost.

Sales Ratio of Products is an indicator reflecting the actual sale of industrial products, analyzing the production-selling and supply-demand relations. It is calculated as:

$$\text{Sales Ratio of Products (\%)} = \frac{\text{value of industrial sales}}{\text{gross industrial output value (current prices)}} \times 100\%$$

13 能　源

ENERGY

资料整理：张　育　于元英　雷稳强
Data management:Zhang Yu　Yu Yuanying　Lei Wenqiang

第十三部分　能源

一、简要说明

本章资料包括规模以上工业能源购销存情况、全市单位GDP能耗、单位GDP电耗、规模以上工业单位增加值能耗、规模以上工业企业用水情况等，由西安市统计局能源处提供。

二、主要指标

规模以上工业综合能源消费量（万吨标准煤）	642.85	比上年下降	5.01%
单位GDP能耗（吨标准煤/万元）	0.568	比上年下降	3.57%
单位GDP电耗（千瓦时/万元）	557.81	比上年下降	2.26%
规模以上工业单位增加值能耗（吨标准煤/万元）	0.369	比上年下降	17.69%

13 ENERGY

Ⅰ.Brief Introduction

Data in this chapter reflects energy purchases consumption and inventory of industrial enterprises above designated size,energy consumption per unit of GDP in whole city,electricity consumption per unit of GDP,energy consumption per unit of industrial value-added above designated size and statistics on water use of industrial enterprises above designated size. data in this chapter are provided and compiled by Energy Division ransportation Division of the Xi'an Bureau of Statistics.

Ⅱ.Major Indicators

		Increase over Preceding Year
Comprehensive Energy Consumption Above Designated Size(10 000 Tons of Standard Coal)	642.85	-5.01%
Energy Consumption of GDP per Unit (Tons of Standard Coal /10 000 yuan)	0.568	-3.57%
Electricity Power Consumption of GDP per Unit (kilowatt-hour/10 000 yuan)	557.81	-2.26%
Energy Consumption of value added per Unit of Industrial Enterprises Above Designated Size (Tons of Standard Coal/10 000 yuan)	0.369	-17.69%

13-1 主要年份全市及各区县单位GDP能耗

Energy Consumption per Unit of GDP by City (District)

单位：吨标准煤 / 万元　　(ton of SCE/10 000 yuan)

地 区	Region	单位GDP能耗 Energy Consumption Per Unit of GDP									
		GDP按2005年价格计算 GDP are calculated at 2005 constant prices						GDP按2010年价格计算 GDP are calculated at 2010 constant prices			
		2005	2006	2007	2008	2009	2010	2010	2011	2012	2013
西安市	**Xi'an**	**1.030**	**0.987**	**0.930**	**0.869**	**0.820**	**0.803**	**0.633**	**0.610**	**0.589**	**0.568**
新城区	Xincheng	0.828	0.794	0.749	0.705	0.664	0.656	0.524	0.506	0.488	0.476
碑林区	Beilin	0.801	0.768	0.726	0.685	0.644	0.639	0.454	0.437	0.421	0.440
莲湖区	Lianhu	0.942	0.904	0.862	0.794	0.749	0.722	0.543	0.522	0.503	0.485
灞桥区	Baqiao	1.803	1.757	1.648	1.545	1.456	1.394	0.819	0.788	0.759	0.731
未央区	Weiyang	1.026	0.985	0.932	0.870	0.817	0.806	0.678	0.654	0.634	0.612
雁塔区	Yanta	0.929	0.885	0.835	0.787	0.739	0.708	0.541	0.522	0.506	0.473
阎良区	Yanliang	0.831	0.783	0.745	0.700	0.661	0.644	0.516	0.499	0.481	0.464
临潼区	Lintong	1.035	1.004	0.946	0.869	0.829	0.789	0.597	0.576	0.556	0.536
长安区	Chang'an	1.339	1.257	1.187	1.125	1.063	1.041	0.634	0.611	0.589	0.605
蓝田县	Lantian	1.698	1.645	1.579	1.492	1.420	1.446	1.228	1.186	1.146	1.108
周至县	Zhouzhi	1.831	1.786	1.689	1.596	1.508	1.464	1.120	1.083	1.047	1.012
户 县	Huxian	2.532	2.454	2.311	2.133	2.015	1.978	1.307	1.257	1.211	1.168
高陵县	Gaoling	0.953	0.907	0.845	0.798	0.753	0.725	0.567	0.545	0.525	0.507

13-1 续表

continued

地 区	Region	比上年增长(%) Growth Rates over Preceding Year(%)							
		2006	2007	2008	2009	2010	2011	2012	2013
西安市	**Xi'an**	**-4.15**	**-5.75**	**-6.65**	**-5.56**	**-2.06**	**-3.56**	**-3.51**	**-3.57**
新城区	Xincheng	-4.15	-5.67	-5.79	-5.80	-1.15	-3.51	-3.50	-3.50
碑林区	Beilin	-4.18	-5.44	-5.65	-5.95	-0.91	-3.89	-3.50	-3.50
莲湖区	Lianhu	-4.07	-4.60	-7.93	-5.65	-3.58	-3.84	-3.60	-3.61
灞桥区	Baqiao	-2.54	-6.20	-6.24	-5.80	-4.20	-3.81	-3.62	-3.64
未央区	Weiyang	-3.97	-5.44	-6.63	-6.05	-1.31	-3.60	-3.60	-3.60
雁塔区	Yanta	-4.71	-5.64	-5.80	-6.08	-4.18	-3.61	-3.61	-3.60
阎良区	Yanliang	-5.77	-4.80	-6.08	-5.62	-0.61	-3.38	-3.50	-3.50
临潼区	Lintong	-3.03	-5.73	-8.16	-4.58	-4.81	-3.52	-3.51	-3.51
长安区	Chang'an	-6.15	-5.53	-5.22	-5.50	-2.08	-3.60	-3.63	-3.63
蓝田县	Lantian	-3.13	-4.01	-5.50	-4.84	-2.06	-3.39	-3.40	-3.30
周至县	Zhouzhi	-2.46	-5.43	-5.51	-5.50	-2.06	-3.30	-3.30	-3.30
户 县	Huxian	-3.07	-5.85	-7.70	-5.50	-2.99	-3.85	-3.60	-3.62
高陵县	Gaoling	-4.85	-6.85	-5.50	-5.70	-3.82	-3.93	-3.52	-3.54

13-2 主要年份全市及各区县单位GDP电耗

Electricity Consumption per Unit of GDP by City and District

单位：千瓦时 / 万元 (kw. h/10 000 yuan)

地 区	Region	单位GDP电耗 Energy Consumption Per Unit of GDP									
		GDP按2005年价格计算 GDP are calculated at 2005 constant prices						GDP按2010年价格计算 GDP are calculated at 2010 constant prices			
		2005	2006	2007	2008	2009	2010	2010	2011	2012	2013
西安市	**Xi'an**	**963.34**	**920.19**	**856.29**	**796.92**	**754.45**	**761.98**	**615.07**	**587.77**	**570.64**	**557.81**
新城区	Xincheng	740.68	714.54	624.76	590.40	544.38	529.86	450.10	417.16	385.27	379.83
碑林区	Beilin	578.78	557.34	536.48	520.04	477.09	469.01	376.07	337.21	318.44	318.65
莲湖区	Lianhu	735.51	697.56	677.92	635.02	590.14	567.40	489.95	451.03	423.38	395.12
灞桥区	Baqiao	1606.69	1534.34	1483.26	1367.56	1275.24	1309.49	968.39	895.00	822.64	788.68
未央区	Weiyang	1112.49	1055.75	1007.35	936.19	940.23	921.64	723.10	686.76	690.61	695.55
雁塔区	Yanta	1043.36	998.03	871.48	814.97	776.04	827.95	684.87	654.82	631.32	603.70
阎良区	Yanliang	632.75	620.65	574.19	535.33	517.29	497.13	398.54	398.71	377.18	358.56
临潼区	Lintong	1019.71	997.91	952.62	878.57	792.07	780.29	601.65	587.27	561.04	532.45
长安区	Chang'an	1055.34	996.57	910.94	844.84	774.85	797.92	590.44	621.09	609.14	612.04
蓝田县	Lantian	1135.17	1104.82	1087.11	1010.23	992.80	1031.64	754.15	684.77	604.04	618.21
周至县	Zhouzhi	815.19	788.52	756.79	714.80	709.39	688.20	537.35	607.54	684.76	731.20
户 县	Huxian	848.39	824.19	810.60	773.10	742.15	769.32	636.22	628.20	586.37	587.68
高陵县	Gaoling	1065.50	972.08	828.71	726.45	638.98	651.46	509.28	438.84	384.44	377.69

注：GDP为第二次经济普查调整后数据。

13-2 续表

continued

地 区	Region	比上年增长(%) Growth Rates over Preceding Year(%)							
		2006	2007	2008	2009	2010	2011	2012	2013
西安市	**Xi'an**	**–4.48**	**–6.94**	**–6.93**	**–5.33**	**1.00**	**–4.43**	**–2.92**	**–2.26**
新城区	Xincheng	-3.53	-12.57	-5.50	-7.80	-2.67	-7.32	-7.65	-1.69
碑林区	Beilin	-3.70	-3.74	-3.06	-8.26	-1.69	-10.33	-5.57	-7.64
莲湖区	Lianhu	-5.16	-2.82	-6.33	-7.07	-3.85	-7.94	-6.13	-6.68
灞桥区	Baqiao	-4.50	-3.33	-7.80	-6.75	2.69	-7.58	-8.08	-4.13
未央区	Weiyang	-5.10	-4.59	-7.06	0.43	-1.98	-5.03	0.08	0.49
雁塔区	Yanta	-4.34	-12.68	-6.49	-4.78	6.69	-4.39	-4.16	-1.37
阎良区	Yanliang	-1.91	-7.49	-6.77	-3.37	-3.90	0.04	-5.40	-4.93
临潼区	Lintong	-2.14	-4.54	-7.77	-9.85	-1.49	-2.39	-4.47	-5.10
长安区	Chang'an	-5.57	-8.59	-7.26	-8.28	2.98	5.19	-1.92	-5.75
蓝田县	Lantian	-2.67	-1.60	-7.07	-1.73	3.91	-9.20	-11.79	2.35
周至县	Zhouzhi	-3.27	-4.02	-5.55	-0.76	-2.99	13.06	12.71	6.78
户 县	Huxian	-2.85	-1.65	-4.63	-4.00	3.66	-1.26	-6.66	0.22
高陵县	Gaoling	-8.77	-14.75	-12.34	-12.04	1.95	-13.83	-12.40	-1.76

13-3 主要年份全市及各区县规模以上工业企业单位工业增加值能耗

Energy Consumption Per Unit of Industrial Value Added above Designated Size by City and District

单位：吨标准煤 / 万元 (ton of SCE/10 000 yuan)

地 区	Region	单位工业增加值能耗 Energy Consumption Per Unit of Industrial Value Added									
		工业增加值按2005年价格计算 VAI are calculated at 2005 constant prices						工业增加值按2010年价格计算 VAI are calculated at 2010 constant prices			
		2005	2006	2007	2008	2009	2010	2010	2011	2012	2013
西安市	**Xi'an**	**1.220**	**1.100**	**1.092**	**0.915**	**0.800**	**0.703**	**0.593**	**0.502**	**0.449**	**0.369**
新城区	Xincheng	0.822	0.798	0.716	0.663	0.420	0.379	0.329	0.361	0.338	0.326
碑林区	Beilin	0.876	0.846	0.782	0.763	0.293	0.246	0.115	0.073	0.067	0.059
莲湖区	Lianhu	0.861	0.832	0.775	0.639	0.269	0.232	0.226	0.207	0.191	0.157
灞桥区	Baqiao	3.029	2.871	2.446	2.078	2.072	2.032	1.447	1.106	1.074	0.926
未央区	Weiyang	1.030	1.000	0.876	0.770	1.008	0.936	0.786	0.651	0.675	0.572
雁塔区	Yanta	1.358	1.308	1.123	1.000	0.578	0.414	0.359	0.341	0.242	0.190
阎良区	Yanliang	0.876	0.849	0.761	0.625	0.354	0.271	0.255	0.209	0.194	0.180
临潼区	Lintong	1.031	0.992	0.882	0.715	0.644	0.371	0.203	0.165	0.140	0.126
长安区	Chang'an	1.370	1.300	1.208	1.087	0.725	0.698	0.366	0.323	0.183	0.131
蓝田县	Lantian	2.579	2.515	2.133	2.084	3.670	3.487	2.534	2.087	1.484	1.399
周至县	Zhouzhi	1.946	1.900	1.891	1.842	0.364	0.336	0.257	0.237	0.202	0.176
户 县	Huxian	7.467	7.168	5.857	4.910	4.514	4.036	3.570	3.135	2.974	2.494
高陵县	Gaoling	0.966	0.905	0.719	0.693	0.239	0.221	0.223	0.189	0.169	0.137

注：本表2005—2010年(工业增加值按2005年价格)统计范围为主营业务收入500万元及以上的法人工业企业；2010—2013年(工业增加值按2010年价格)统计范围为主营业务收入2000万元及以上的法人工业企业。
能源消耗按当量值计算。

13-3 续表

continued

地 区	Region	比上年增长(%) Growth Rates over Preceding Year(%)							
		2006	2007	2008	2009	2010	2011	2012	2013
西安市	**Xi'an**	**-3.04**	**-12.56**	**-13.43**	**-10.48**	**-12.18**	**-15.44**	**-10.52**	**-17.69**
新城区	Xincheng	-2.92	-10.26	-7.38	-2.68	-9.69	9.68	-6.44	-3.48
碑林区	Beilin	-3.42	-7.59	-2.45	-0.44	-15.89	-36.63	-8.39	-11.42
莲湖区	Lianhu	-3.47	-6.91	-17.61	0.89	-13.63	-8.19	-8.02	-17.73
灞桥区	Baqiao	-5.22	-14.79	-15.04	0.29	-1.92	-23.61	-2.90	-13.78
未央区	Weiyang	-2.91	-10.63	-12.15	-15.20	-7.18	-17.17	3.64	-15.15
雁塔区	Yanta	-3.68	-14.14	-10.98	-13.98	-28.43	-4.88	-28.97	-21.78
阎良区	Yanliang	-3.05	-10.42	-17.83	-18.36	-23.44	-18.11	-6.83	-7.41
临潼区	Lintong	-3.82	-11.06	-18.99	3.05	-42.41	-18.32	-15.27	-10.29
长安区	Chang'an	-5.11	-4.06	-10.05	-18.68	-3.67	-11.88	-43.40	-28.21
蓝田县	Lantian	-2.48	-15.18	-2.29	-3.39	-5.00	-17.63	-28.90	-5.71
周至县	Zhouzhi	-2.38	-0.48	-2.62	-12.27	-7.71	-7.56	-14.72	-12.91
户 县	Huxian	-4.01	-18.29	-16.17	-18.48	-10.58	-12.19	-5.13	-16.16
高陵县	Gaoling	-6.32	-20.52	-3.56	-18.90	-7.65	-15.26	-10.91	-18.63

13-4 主要年份全社会用电量

Electricity Consumption of the Whole Society in Representative Years

单位：万千瓦时 (10 000 kw. h)

行 业	Sector	2000	2008	2009	2010	2011	2012	2013
总 计	**Total**	**732373**	**1605089**	**1724067**	**1993751**	**2167453**	**2352571**	**2554679**
行业用电量合计	Total of Industry of Electricity	599855	1293574	1358483	1499903	1590486	1706859	1854696
按产业分	**Grouped by Sector**							
1. 第一产业	Primary Industry	77579	127054	99083	108720	117984	109086	110405
2. 第二产业	Secondary Industry	354245	724852	766029	883259	910360	932622	991202
3. 第三产业	Tertiary Industry	168031	441668	493371	507924	562142	665151	753089
按国民经济行业分	**Grouped by Industry**							
一、农、林、牧、渔、水利业	Agriculture ,Forestry,Animal Husbandry and Fishery	77579	127054	99083	108720	117984	109086	110405
二、工业	Industry	345175	696291	724920	838317	859796	875018	920024
1. 轻工业	Light Industry	152125	182176	167144	177362	183766	175392	170246
2. 重工业	Heavy Industry	193050	514115	557776	660955	676030	699626	749778
三、信息传输、计算机服务和软件业	Information Transmission,Computer Service and Software		26680	29328	30760	33191	37444	39551
四、建筑业	Construction	9070	28561	41108	44942	50564	57605	71179
五、交通运输、仓储及邮政业	Traffic,Transport, Storage and Post	22904	56614	62031	58509	66684	69633	78722
六、公共事业及管理组织	Public Utilities and Management Organization		165024	177409	154074	164473	207271	240866
七、商业、住宿和餐饮业	Commercial,Hotels and Catering Services		111676	122203	148418	166558	199970	228117
八、金融、房地产、商务及居民服务业	Finance,Real Estate,Business Affairs and Households Services		81674	102400	116163	131236	150832	165833
九、城乡居民生活用电	Electricity Consumption of Urban and Rural Residents	132518	311515	365585	493848	576966	645713	699982
1. 乡村	Rural	31281	63072	99941	142059	169898	197937	216148
2. 城市	City	101237	248443	265644	351789	407068	447776	483834

注：本表数据来源西安市供电局

13-5　规模以上工业企业能源购进、消费及库存（2013年）

Energy Purchases Consumption and Inventory of Industrial Enterprises above Designated size（2013）

能源名称	Name	年初库存量 Stock (year-beginning)	购进量 实物量 Quantity	Purchases 金额(万元) Sum (10 000 yuan)
原煤(吨)	Raw Coal (ton)	745573	10311962	4987421
洗精煤(吨)	Washed Coal(ton)	147	1109	759
其他洗煤(吨)	Other Washed Coals(ton)			
煤制品（吨）	Briquettes(ton)	139	3543	2574
焦炭(吨)	Coke(ton)	354	8276	14824
其他焦化产品(吨)	Other Coking Products(ton)	1035	2000	3450
焦炉煤气（万立方米）	Other Gases(10 000cu.m)			
天然气（气态）（万立方米）	Natural Gas(10 000cu.m)	68	25142	543597
液化天然气（液态）（万立方米）	Liquefied Natural Gas (Liquid)(10 000cu.m)	13	15	97
原油(吨)	Crude Oil(ton)	42538	2149733	12145995
汽油(吨)	Gasoline(ton)	658	32400	268530
煤油(吨)	Kerosene(ton)	961	15325	107245
柴油(吨)	Diesel Oil(ton)	1411	66020	530404
燃料油(吨)	Fuel Oil(ton)	36	1100	5753
液化石油气(吨)	LPG(ton)		634	4357
其它石油制品(吨)	Other Petroleum Products(ton)	44	2912	35312
热力(百万千焦)	Heat (1 million kilo-joule)		8870096	404477
电力(万千瓦时)	Electricity(10 000kwh)		668320	4780156
其他燃料（吨标准煤）	Other Fuels(ton of SCE)	20	2230	7294
能源合计(吨标准煤)	Total Energy(ton of SCE)			

13-5 续表 continued

能源名称	Name	消费量 Consumption 合计 Total	工业生产消费 Industrial Production Consume	用于原材料 as Raw Material	非工业生产消费 Non-industrial Production Consume	年末库存 Stock (year-end)
原煤(吨)	Raw Coal (ton)	10311449	10217052	17599	94397	735547
洗精煤(吨)	Washed Coal(ton)	1256	1256			
其他洗煤(吨)	Other Washed Coals(ton)					
煤制品（吨）	Briquettes(ton)	3593	3067		526	74
焦炭(吨)	Coke(ton)	8364	8364			65
其他焦化产品(吨)	Other Coking Products(ton)	2920	2920			115
焦炉煤气（万立方米）	Other Gases(10 000cu.m)					
天然气（气态）（万立方米）	Natural Gas(10 000cu.m)	25117	24614	7549	503	25
液化天然气（液态）（万立方米）	Liquefied Natural Gas (Liquid)(10 000cu.m)	15	11		4	
原油(吨)	Crude Oil(ton)	2131055	2131055			61216
汽油(吨)	Gasoline(ton)	33086	29032	134	4054	402
煤油(吨)	Kerosene(ton)	14703	14696		7	1579
柴油(吨)	Diesel Oil(ton)	66547	65295	5351	1252	963
燃料油(吨)	Fuel Oil(ton)	1105	1105			31
液化石油气(吨)	LPG(ton)	647	622		25	
其它石油制品(吨)	Other Petroleum Products(ton)	2922	2922			33
热力(百万千焦)	Heat (1 million kilo-joule)	11878805	10622837		1255968	
电力(万千瓦时)	Electricity(10 000kwh)	751732	734284		17448	
其他燃料（吨标准煤）	Other Fuels(ton of SCE)	2225	2225			25
能源合计(吨标准煤)	Total Energy(ton of SCE)	12022674	11872616		150058	

13-6 规模以上工业企业分行业主要能源品种消费量（2013年）

Major Energy Consumption above Designated Size by Sector (2013)

行　业	Sector	原煤 (吨) Raw Coal (ton)	天然气 (万立方米) Natural Gas(10 000 cu.m)	原油 (吨) Crude Oil (ton)
总 计	**Total**	**10311449**	**25117**	**2131055**
煤炭开采和洗选业	Coal Mining and Dressing			
石油和天然气开采业	Petroleum and Natural Gas Extraction			
黑色金属矿采选业	Ferrous Metals Mining and Dressing			
有色金属矿采选业	Nonferrous Metals Mining and Dressing			
非金属矿采选业	Nonmetal Minerals Mining and Dressing			
开采辅助活动	Ancillary activities for mining	338	129	
其他采矿业	Other Mining Industry			
农副食品加工业	Agricultural Products and Non-stable Food Processing Industry	184574	15	
食品制造业	Food Production	87454	455	
酒、饮料和精制茶制造业	Wine, soft drinks and refined tea industry	128577	949	
烟草制品业	Tobacco Processing	15		
纺织业	Textile Industry	2152		
纺织服装、服饰业	Textile, apparel industry			
皮革、毛皮、羽毛及其制品和制鞋业	Leather, Fur, Feather (eiderdown) and Their Products Industry			
木材加工和木、竹、藤、棕、草制品业	Timber Processing,Bamboo,Cane,Palm Fiber and Straw Products	5870		
家具制造业	Furniture Manufacturing	107		
造纸及纸制品业	Papermaking and Paper products	63459		
印刷和记录媒介复制业	Printing,Record Medium Reproduction	443	219	
文教、工美、体育和娱乐用品制造业	Culture, education, Craft art, sports and entertainment goods manufacturing industry	65		
石油加工、炼焦和核燃料加工业	Petroleum Refining, Ccoke Making and Nuclear Fuel Processing Industry	23764	178	2131052
化学原料和化学制品制造业	Raw Chemical Materials and Chemical Products	76448	610	
医药制造业	Medical and Pharmaceutical Products	40770	654	
化学纤维制造业	Chemical Fiber			
橡胶和塑料制品业	Rubber and plastic products industry	121713	9	
非金属矿物制品业	Nonmetal Mineral Products	299003	42	
黑色金属冶炼和压延加工业	Smelting and Pressing of Ferrous Metals	12950	3454	
有色金属冶炼和压延加工业	Smelting and Pressing of Nonferrou Metals	2751	609	
金属制品业	Metal Products	51592	426	
通用设备制造业	General Equipment Manufacturing Industry	8860	125	
汽车制造业	Automotive Manufacturing	20057	539	
专用设备制造业	Special Purpose Equipment	53534	4103	
铁路、船舶、航空航天和其他运输设备制造业	Railroad, marine, aerospace and other transportation equipment manufacturing	219887	883	
电气机械和器材制造业	Electric Equipment and Machinery	16575	2093	
计算机、通信和其他电子设备制造业	Communication Equipment, Computer and Other Electronic Equipment Manufacturing Industry	2976	601	
仪器仪表制造业	Instrument manufacturing industry	576	227	
其他制造业	Other manufacturing	220		
废弃资源综合利用	Comprehensive utilization of waste resources			
金属制品、机械和设备修理业	Metal products, machinery and equipment repair industry			
电力、热力生产和供应业	Electric Power, Heating Power Generating and Supplying Industry	8886719	1	
燃气生产和供应业	Gas Mining and Supplying Industry		8533	
水的生产和供应业	Water Processing and Supplying Industry		262	

13-6 续表 continued

行 业	Sector	汽油(吨) Gasoline (ton)	柴油(吨) Diesel Oil (ton)	热能(百万千焦) Heat (million kilo joule)	电力(万千瓦时) Electricity (10 000 kwh)
总 计	**Total**	**33086**	**66547**	**11878805**	**751732**
煤炭开采和洗选业	Coal Mining and Dressing				
石油和天然气开采业	Petroleum and Natural Gas Extraction				
黑色金属矿采选业	Ferrous Metals Mining and Dressing				
有色金属矿采选业	Nonferrous Metals Mining and Dressing				
非金属矿采选业	Nonmetal Minerals Mining and Dressing				
开采辅助活动	Ancillary activities for mining	143	1099		519
其他采矿业	Other Mining Industry				
农副食品加工业	Agricultural Products and Non-stable Food Processing Industry	1669	1806	1198305	26593
食品制造业	Food Production	769	555	379782	16269
酒、饮料和精制茶制造业	Wine, soft drinks and refined tea industry	291	647	217152	20315
烟草制品业	Tobacco Processing	24		10510	216
纺织业	Textile Industry	71	19	362340	23849
纺织服装、服饰业	Textile, apparel industry	45	1		716
皮革、毛皮、羽毛及其制品和制鞋业	Leather, Fur, Feather (eiderdown) and Their Products Industry	37		9983	200
木材加工和木、竹、藤、棕、草制品业	Timber Processing,Bamboo,Cane,Palm Fiber and Straw Products	87			6307
家具制造业	Furniture Manufacturing	154	128		941
造纸及纸制品业	Papermaking and Paper products	223	98	794379	6891
印刷和记录媒介复制业	Printing,Record Medium Reproduction	532	268	80547	9106
文教、工美、体育和娱乐用品制造业	Culture, education, Craft art, sports and entertainment goods manufacturing industry	96	7		842
石油加工、炼焦和核燃料加工业	Petroleum Refining, Ccoke Making and Nuclear Fuel Processing Industry	7691	288		46053
化学原料和化学制品制造业	Raw Chemical Materials and Chemical Products	584	767	794887	24346
医药制造业	Medical and Pharmaceutical Products	1097	104	167680	13243
化学纤维制造业	Chemical Fiber	17	10	678008	2973
橡胶和塑料制品业	Rubber and plastic products industry	473	3068	2205	22063
非金属矿物制品业	Nonmetal Mineral Products	1358	28091	64818	46754
黑色金属冶炼和压延加工业	Smelting and Pressing of Ferrous Metals	119	78		20816
有色金属冶炼和压延加工业	Smelting and Pressing of Nonferrou Metals	426	228	347579	36185
金属制品业	Metal Products	1102	371	987457	20435
通用设备制造业	General Equipment Manufacturing Industry	899	313	9682	10830
汽车制造业	Automotive Manufacturing	3248	5663	87214	26007
专用设备制造业	Special Purpose Equipment	4176	8961	569566	94516
铁路、船舶、航空航天和其他运输设备制造业	Railroad, marine, aerospace and other transportation equipment manufacturing	2330	3438	318035	54491
电气机械和器材制造业	Electric Equipment and Machinery	1917	825	1102810	42661
计算机、通信和其他电子设备制造业	Communication Equipment, Computer and Other Electronic Equipment Manufacturing Industry	517	116	607057	42205
仪器仪表制造业	Instrument manufacturing industry	1814	7611	130025	6461
其他制造业	Other manufacturing	31	215		367
废弃资源综合利用	Comprehensive utilization of waste resources				
金属制品、机械和设备修理业	Metal products, machinery and equipment repair industry	83			64
电力、热力生产和供应业	Electric Power, Heating Power Generating and Supplying Industry	126	1675	2958784	114245
燃气生产和供应业	Gas Mining and Supplying Industry	687	79		5820
水的生产和供应业	Water Processing and Supplying Industry	250	18		8341

13-7 规模以上工业企业分行业综合能源消费量（2013年）

Comprehensive Energy Consumption by Sector above Designated Size （2013）

单位：吨标准煤 (ton of SCE)

行 业	Scetor	2013	比上年增长(%) Increase over Preceding Year (%)
总 计	**Total**	**6428451**	**-5.0**
煤炭开采和洗选业	Coal Mining and Dressing		
石油和天然气开采业	Petroleum and Natural Gas Extraction		
黑色金属矿采选业	Ferrous Metals Mining and Dressing	112	30.7
有色金属矿采选业	Nonferrous Metals Mining and Dressing		
非金属矿采选业	Nonmetal Minerals Mining and Dressing		
开采辅助活动	Ancillary activities for mining	87100	0.4
其他采矿业	Other Mining Industry		
农副食品加工业	Agricultural Products and Non-stable Food Processing Industry	164734	-37.3
食品制造业	Food Production	102612	4.2
酒、饮料和精制茶制造业	Wine, soft drinks and refined tea industry	137519	2.2
烟草制品业	Tobacco Processing	534	10.1
纺织业	Textile Industry	39386	-8.3
纺织服装、服饰业	Textile, apparel industry	953	-41.3
皮革、毛皮、羽毛及其制品和制鞋业	Leather, Fur, Feather (eiderdown) and Their Products Industry	634	-26.7
木材加工和木、竹、藤、棕、草制品业	Timber Processing,Bamboo,Cane,Palm Fiber and Straw Products	12073	10.4
家具制造业	Furniture Manufacturing	1646	15.8
造纸及纸制品业	Papermaking and Paper products	53258	-45.6
印刷和记录媒介复制业	Printing,Record Medium Reproduction	17875	-2.2
文教、工美、体育和娱乐用品制造业	Culture, education, Craft art, sports and entertainment goods manufacturing industry	1181	49.5
石油加工、炼焦和核燃料加工业	Petroleum Refining, Ccoke Making and Nuclear Fuel Processing Industry	400865	-0.2
化学原料和化学制品制造业	Raw Chemical Materials and Chemical Products	112300	-5.3
医药制造业	Medical and Pharmaceutical Products	60123	-14.9
化学纤维制造业	Chemical Fiber	26814	-7.6
橡胶和塑料制品业	Rubber and plastic products industry	61159	9.4
非金属矿物制品业	Nonmetal Mineral Products	314498	5.4
黑色金属冶炼和压延加工业	Smelting and Pressing of Ferrous Metals	88211	-19.6
有色金属冶炼和压延加工业	Smelting and Pressing of Nonferrou Metals	69158	13.7
金属制品业	Metal Products	86467	-10.6
通用设备制造业	General Equipment Manufacturing Industry	19266	0.6
汽车制造业	Automotive Manufacturing	67427	12.7
专用设备制造业	Special Purpose Equipment	202875	-2.1
铁路、船舶、航空航天和其他运输设备制造业	Railroad, marine, aerospace and other transportation equipment manufacturing	215944	-1.9
电气机械和器材制造业	Electric Equipment and Machinery	133300	2.3
计算机、通信和其他电子设备制造业	Communication Equipment, Computer and Other Electronic Equipment Manufacturing Industry	66491	13.6
仪器仪表制造业	Instrument manufacturing industry	27614	12.7
其他制造业	Other manufacturing	967	-9.3
废弃资源综合利用	Comprehensive utilization of waste resources		
金属制品、机械和设备修理业	Metal products, machinery and equipment repair industry	180	-19.9
电力、热力生产和供应业	Electric Power, Heating Power Generating and Supplying Industry	3721952	-5.1
燃气生产和供应业	Gas Mining and Supplying Industry	121768	6.8
水的生产和供应业	Water Processing and Supplying Industry	11455	0.6

13–8 规模以上工业企业用水情况（2013年）

Statistics on Water Use of Industrial Enterprises above Designated Size（2013）

指　标	Item	取水量（万立方米）Water Use (10 000 cu.m)	支付费用的取水量（万立方米）Paid WaterUse (10 000 cu.m)	取水支付金额（万元）Money Paid for Water Use (10 000 yuan)	外供水量（万立方米）Outward Water Supply (10 000 cu.m)
合　计	**Total**	**67435**	**56382**	**86009**	**46803**
1. 陆地地表水	Surface Water	37035	36933	28273	12
其中：陆地湖咸水	Land lake Salt water	871	871	1132	
2. 地下水	Ground-water	17402	9266	25423	437
其中：地下咸水	Ground-Salt water	1303	1300	3186	
3. 自来水	Tap Water	11864	9108	30918	46354
4. 其他水	Other Water	1134	1075	1395	
其中：雨水收集利用	Rain Water Collected				
海水淡化水					
再生水(中水)	Reclaimed Water	1129	1074	1259	

13-9 规模以上工业企业分行业用水情况（2013年）

Volume of Water Use of Industrial Enterprises above Designated Size by Sector（2013）

行　业	Sector	取水量（万立方米）Water Use (10 000 cu.m)	支付费用的取水量 Paid Water Use
总　计	**Total**	**67435**	**56382**
煤炭开采和洗选业	Coal Mining and Dressing		
石油和天然气开采业	Petroleum and Natural Gas Extraction	8425	8425
黑色金属矿采选业	Ferrous Metals Mining and Dressing	11	
有色金属矿采选业	Nonferrous Metals Mining and Dressing		
非金属矿采选业	Nonmetal Minerals Mining and Dressing		
开采辅助活动	Ancillary activities for mining	894	894
其他采矿业	Other Mining Industry	0	
农副食品加工业	Agricultural Products and Non-stable Food Processing Industry	227	211
食品制造业	Food Production	346	311
酒、饮料和精制茶制造业	Wine, soft drinks and refined tea industry	904	810
烟草制品业	Tobacco Processing	95	87
纺织业	Textile Industry	121	119
纺织服装、服饰业	Textile, apparel industry	18	18
皮革、毛皮、羽毛及其制品和制鞋业	Leather, Fur, Feather (eiderdown) and Their Products Industry	2	2
木材加工和木、竹、藤、棕、草制品业	Timber Processing,Bamboo,Cane,Palm Fiber and Straw Products	2	2
家具制造业	Furniture Manufacturing	3	2
造纸及纸制品业	Papermaking and Paper products	280	268
印刷和记录媒介复制业	Printing,Record Medium Reproduction	64	64
文教、工美、体育和娱乐用品制造业	Culture, education, Craft art, sports and entertainment goods manufacturing industry	2	2
石油加工、炼焦和核燃料加工业	Petroleum Refining, Ccoke Making and Nuclear Fuel Processing Industry	220	189
化学原料和化学制品制造业	Raw Chemical Materials and Chemical Products	662	493
医药制造业	Medical and Pharmaceutical Products	400	399
化学纤维制造业	Chemical Fiber	25	25
橡胶和塑料制品业	Rubber and plastic products industry	237	236
非金属矿物制品业	Nonmetal Mineral Products	255	121
黑色金属冶炼和压延加工业	Smelting and Pressing of Ferrous Metals	33	27
有色金属冶炼和压延加工业	Smelting and Pressing of Nonferrou Metals	163	162
金属制品业	Metal Products	32	28
通用设备制造业	General Equipment Manufacturing Industry	85	84
汽车制造业	Automotive Manufacturing	284	238
专用设备制造业	Special Purpose Equipment	1020	978
铁路、船舶、航空航天和其他运输设备制造业	Railroad, marine, aerospace and other transportation equipment manufacturing	719	719
电气机械和器材制造业	Electric Equipment and Machinery	532	529
计算机、通信和其他电子设备制造业	Communication Equipment, Computer and Other Electronic Equipment Manufacturing Industry	327	324
仪器仪表制造业	Instrument manufacturing industry	196	196
其他制造业	Other manufacturing	47	44
废弃资源综合利用	Comprehensive utilization of waste resources		
金属制品、机械和设备修理业	Metal products, machinery and equipment repair industry	1	1
电力、热力生产和供应业	Electric Power, Heating Power Generating and Supplying Industry	3907	3903
燃气生产和供应业	Gas Mining and Supplying Industry	30	23
水的生产和供应业	Water Processing and Supplying Industry	46866	36448

13-9 续表 continued

行 业	Scetor	取水支付金额（万元）Maney Paid for Water Use (10 000 yuan)	外供水量（万立方米）Outward Water Supply (10 000 cu.m)
总 计	**Total**	**86009**	**46803**
煤炭开采和洗选业	Coal Mining and Dressing		
石油和天然气开采业	Petroleum and Natural Gas Extraction	25932	
黑色金属矿采选业	Ferrous Metals Mining and Dressing		
有色金属矿采选业	Nonferrous Metals Mining and Dressing		
非金属矿采选业	Nonmetal Minerals Mining and Dressing		
开采辅助活动	Ancillary activities for mining	2709	
其他采矿业	Other Mining Industry		
农副食品加工业	Agricultural Products and Non-stable Food Processing Industry	257	
食品制造业	Food Production	918	
酒、饮料和精制茶制造业	Wine, soft drinks and refined tea industry	2758	
烟草制品业	Tobacco Processing	323	
纺织业	Textile Industry	413	10
纺织服装、服饰业	Textile, apparel industry	56	
皮革、毛皮、羽毛及其制品和制鞋业	Leather, Fur, Feather (eiderdown) and Their Products Industry	7	
木材加工和木、竹、藤、棕、草制品业	Timber Processing,Bamboo,Cane,Palm Fiber and Straw Products	5	
家具制造业	Furniture Manufacturing	9	
造纸及纸制品业	Papermaking and Paper products	963	
印刷和记录媒介复制业	Printing,Record Medium Reproduction	245	
文教、工美、体育和娱乐用品制造业	Culture, education, Craft art, sports and entertainment goods manufacturing industry	4	
石油加工、炼焦和核燃料加工业	Petroleum Refining, Ccoke Making and Nuclear Fuel Processing Industry	507	
化学原料和化学制品制造业	Raw Chemical Materials and Chemical Products	1008	164
医药制造业	Medical and Pharmaceutical Products	1320	4
化学纤维制造业	Chemical Fiber	50	
橡胶和塑料制品业	Rubber and plastic products industry	529	
非金属矿物制品业	Nonmetal Mineral Products	280	
黑色金属冶炼和压延加工业	Smelting and Pressing of Ferrous Metals	94	
有色金属冶炼和压延加工业	Smelting and Pressing of Nonferrou Metals	468	2
金属制品业	Metal Products	83	
通用设备制造业	General Equipment Manufacturing Industry	329	
汽车制造业	Automotive Manufacturing	2088	5
专用设备制造业	Special Purpose Equipment	3383	
铁路、船舶、航空航天和其他运输设备制造业	Railroad, marine, aerospace and other transportation equipment manufacturing	2388	1
电气机械和器材制造业	Electric Equipment and Machinery	1988	
计算机、通信和其他电子设备制造业	Communication Equipment, Computer and Other Electronic Equipment Manufacturing Industry	1208	
仪器仪表制造业	Instrument manufacturing industry	685	1
其他制造业	Other manufacturing	167	5
废弃资源综合利用	Comprehensive utilization of waste resources		
金属制品、机械和设备修理业	Metal products, machinery and equipment repair industry	7	
电力、热力生产和供应业	Electric Power, Heating Power Generating and Supplying Industry	6879	
燃气生产和供应业	Gas Mining and Supplying Industry	84	
水的生产和供应业	Water Processing and Supplying Industry	27865	46611

主要统计指标解释

能源消费总量 指一定时期内，地区各行业和居民生活消费的各种能源的总和。该指标是观察能源消费水平、构成和增长速度的总量指标。能源消费总量包括原煤和原油及其制品、天然气、电力等，不包括低热值燃料、生物质能和太阳能等的利用。能源消费总量分为终端能源消费量、能源加工转换损失量和能源损失量三部分。

（1）终端能源消费量：指一定时期内，全国生产和生活消费的各种能源在扣除了用于加工转换二次能源消费量和损失量以后的数量。

（2）能源加工转换损失量：指一定时期内，全国投入加工转换的各种能源数量之和与产出各种能源产品之和的差额。该指标是观察能源在加工转换过程中损失量变化的指标。

（3）能源损失量：指一定时期内，能源在输送、分配、储存过程中发生的损失和由客观原因造成的各种损失量，不包括各种气体能源放空、放散量。

工业生产能源消费 指工业企业为进行工业生产活动所消费的能源。

非工业生产能源消费 指在工业企业能源消费中，除“工业生产能源消费”以外的能源消费，即非工业生产用能和工业企业附属的不从事工业生产活动的非独立核算单位用能。

运输工具消费 指在厂区内、外进行交通运输活动的交通运输工具所消费的能源。

能源加工转换投入 能源的加工转换是指为了特定的用途，将一种能源（一般为一次能源），经过一定的工艺，加工或转换成另外一种能源（一般为二次能源）。能源加工转换的投入即能源加工、转换消费。

一次能源 是指自然界中以现成形式存在，不经任何改变或转换的天然能源资源，即从自然界直接取得并不改变其形态和品位的能源。如原煤、原油、天然气、核燃料、植物燃料、风能、水能、太阳能、地热能、海洋能、潮汐能等。

二次能源 是指为了满足生产工艺和生活的特定需要以合理利用能源，将一次能源直接或间接加工转换产生的其它种类和形式的人工能源。如原煤加工产出的洗煤；由煤炭加工转换产出的焦炭，煤气；由原油加工产出的汽油、煤油、柴油、燃料油、液化石油气、炼厂干气等；由煤炭、石油、天然气转换产出的电力。

综合能源消费量　报告期内工业企业在工业生产活动中实际消费的各种能源的总和净值。计算综合能源消费量时，需要先将使用的各种能源折算成标准燃料后再进行计算。

单位生产总值能耗 指一定时期内，一个国家或地区每生产一个单位的生产总值所消耗的能源。计算公式为：

单位生产总值能耗=能源消费总量／生产总值

单位生产总值电耗 指一定时期内，一个国家或地区每生产一个单位的生产总值所消耗的电力。计算公式为：

单位生产总值电耗=全社会用电量／生产总值

单位工业增加值能耗 指一定时期内，一个国家或地区每生产一个单位的工业增加值所消耗的能源。计算公式为：

单位工业增加值能耗=工业能源消费量／工业增加值

Explanatory Notes on Main Statistical Indicators

Total Energy Consumption refers to the total consumption of energy of various kinds by the production sectors and the households in the country in a given period of time. It is a comprehensive indicator to show the scale,composition and pace of increase of energy consumption. Total energy consumption includes that of coal,crude oil and their products,natural gas and electricity. However,it does not include the consumption of fuel of low calorific value, bio-energy and solar energy. Total energy consumption can be divided into three parts: end-use energy consumption; loss during the process of energy conversion; and energy loss.

(1) End-use Energy Consumption: It refers to the total energy consumption by the production sectors and the households in the country (region) in a given period of time. It does not include the consumption during the conversion of primary energy into secondary energy and the loss in the process of energy conversion.

(2) Loss During the Process of Energy Conversion: It refers to the total input of various kinds of energy for conversion, minus the total output of various kinds of energy in the country in a given period of time. It is an indicator to show the loss that occurs during the process of energy conversion.

(3) Energy Loss: It refers to the total of the loss of energy during the course of energy transport, distribution and storage and the loss caused by any objective reason in a given period of time. The loss of various kinds of gas due to gas discharges and stocktaking is not included.

Industry Consumption Energy refers to the volume of energy consumed by Industrial enterprises for industrial production activities.

Non-industry Consumption Energy refers to the energy consumed by industrial enterprises except for industrial production activities,means that energy consumed by non-industry production and not independent accounting units which was not engaged in industrial production activities affiliated to industrial enterprises.

Vehicle Energy refers to the energy consumed by vehicles which carried out transport activities in and out of factories.

Energy Processing Conversion Devoted energy processing conversion refers to for specialized application, a source of energy (normally primary energy), after a certain technology, processed or converted to another kind of energy (normally secondary energy). The input of energy conversion processing that is energy processing, and conversion consumption.

Primary Energy Source refers to natural energy resources as found naturally in the form of ready-made,without any change or conversion,as energy obtaineddirectly from natural and not change its shape and grade,such as raw coal, crude oil, natural gas, nuclear fuel, plantfuel, wind energy, water energy, solar energy,geothermalenergy, oceanic energy, tidal energy and so on.

Secondary Energy refers to other types and formsof artificial energy which was processed and conversed from primary energy sources directly or indirectly, in order to meet the specific needs in production process and life to use energy more effectively. Such as washing coalprocessed from raw coal; coke and coal gas processed andtransformed from raw coal; gasoline, kerosene, diesel oil, fuel oil, liquefied petroleum gas, dry gas refinery processed from crude oil; electric power conversed from coal, oil and natural gas.

Comprehensive energy consumption refers to the total and net energy actually consumed in industrial production activities by industrial enterprises in the reference period. When calculated the volume of consumption of comprehensive energy, should converted sorts of energy which was used into standards fuel firstly.

Energy Consumption per Unit of GDP refers to the energy consumption per unit of Gross Domestic Product in a country or the Gross Regional Product in a region in the same reference period. The formula is:

$$\text{Energy Consumption per Unit of GDP} = \frac{\text{Total Energy Consumption}}{\text{Gross Domestic Product}}$$

Electricity Consumption per Unit of GDP refers to the electricity consumption per unit of Gross Domestic Product in a country or the Gross Regional Product in a region in the same reference period. The formula is:

$$\text{Electricity Consumption per Unit of GDP} = \frac{\text{Total Electricity Consumption}}{\text{Gross Domestic Product}}$$

Energy Consumption per Unit of Industrial Value-added refers to the energy consumption per unit of industrial value-added in a country or region in the same reference period. The formula is:

$$\text{Energy Consumption per Unit of Industrial Value-added} = \frac{\text{Total Energy Consumption}}{\text{Industrial Value-added}}$$

14 建筑业

CONSTRUCTION

资料整理：陈海生

Data management:Chen Haisheng

第十四部分　建筑业

一、简要说明

本章资料主要包括建筑业基本情况、建筑业施工企业生产情况和财务状况，由西安市统计局固定资产投资处提供。

二、主要指标

企业个数（个）	420	比上年增长	6.0%
建筑业总产值（亿元）	2228.41	比上年增长	18.9%
#国有及国有控股企业	1702.08	比上年增长	24.7%
房屋建筑竣工面积（万平方米）	2229.97	比上年下降	12.3%
房屋建筑面积竣工率(%)	22.9	比上年下降	3.4个百分点

14　CONSTRUCTION

Ⅰ.Brief Introduction

This chapter consists of primarily the data basic situation of the construction industry, production situation and financial situation of the construction enterprises, provided by Fixed Asset Investment Division of the Xi'an Bureau of Statistics.

Ⅱ.Major Indicators

		Increase over Preceding Year
Number of Enterprises(item)	420	6.0%
Total Output Value of Construction(100 mil. yuan)	2228.41	18.9%
State-owned Or State Holding Majority Shares	1702.08	24.7%
Floor Space of Buildings Completed(10 000 sq.m)	2229.97	-12.3%
Rate of Floor Space of Buildings Completed(%)	22.9	-3.4 percentage points

14-1 主要年份建筑业总产值

Total Output Value of Construction in Representative Years

单位：万元 (10 000 yuan)

年份 Year	建筑业总产值 Total Output Value of Construction	国有及国有控股 State-owned Or State Holding Majority Shares	集体企业 Collective-owned Enterprises
2000	1059250	788704	143709
2001	1148091	918169	154749
2002	1334713	850278	153482
2003	1771126	1199911	134010
2004	2444242	2016792	165922
2005	3266535	2766785	195111
2006	4164782	3482016	235493
2007	6047524	4326279	325658
2008	9151199	6761190	4601423
2009	12965787	10672178	471533
2010	18203450	15203874	583928
2011	16190888	12783270	794189
2012	18742273	13647046	968291
2013	22284063	17020790	1548721

注：1996年以后建筑业年报统计范围由往年的县及县以上（含县级建制镇）各种经济类型的建筑企业，改为具有建筑业资质等级四级及四级以上的各种经济类型的建筑施工企业；2002年改为具有建筑业资质等级的各种经济类型的建筑施工企业。
本表资料含劳务分包企业。

14-2 全市建筑施工总承包企业基本情况（2013年）

Basic situation of Construction General contracting business in whole city(2013)

指　　标	Item	合计 Total	国有及国有控股 State-owned Or State Holding Majority Shares
企业单位数（个）（施工总承包）	Number of Enterprises (unit) (Overall Contractor For Construction)	283	87
#二级以上企业（施工总承包）	First and Second Class Enterprise	221	76
计算劳动生产率的平均人数（人）施工总承包）	Average Number of Employed Persons in Calculation of Labor Productivity (person) (Overall Contractor For Construction)	577345	438090
#二级以上企业（施工总承包）	First and Second Class Enterprise	566624	435963
建筑业总产值（亿元）（施工总承包）	Total Output Value of Construction(100 million yuan) (Overall Contractor For Construction)	2046.22	1612.06
#二级以上企业（施工总承包）	First and Second Class Enterprise	2006	1595
全员劳动生产率 按总产值计算(元/人)	Overall Labor Productivity Calculated by Total Output Value(yuan/person)	354419	369770

14-3 施工总承包和专业承包建筑企业生产情况（2013年）

分 组	Classify	签订的合同额（万元）Contract Value (10 000 yuan)
总计	**Total**	**52369381**
#国有及国有控股	State-Owned and State Holding Majority Shares	43323212
一、按登记注册类型分	**Grouped by Registion Status**	
内资	Domestic Investment Enterprises	51723753
国有企业	State-owned Enterprises	6428697
集体企业	Collective-owned Enterprises	1962072
股份合作企业	Share-holding Corperative Enterprises	9043
联营企业	Joint Ownership Enterprises	27342
有限责任公司	Limited Liability Corporations	38525763
股份有限公司	Share-holding Corperation Ltd.	1179226
私营企业	Private Enterprises	3591610
其他企业	Others	
港澳台商投资企业	Enterprises with Funds from Hong Kong,Macao and Taiwan	223
外商投资企业	Enterprises with Foreign Investment	645405
二、按国民经济行业分	**Grouped by Sector**	
房屋建筑业	Building Engineering Construction	18853785
土木工程建筑业	Civil Engineering Construction	30756258
建筑安装业	Installation of Construction	1820442
建筑装饰和其他建筑业	Architectural decoration and other Construction	938895
三、按隶属关系分	**Grouped by Administrative Relationship**	
中央	Central	29718603
地方	Region	22650778
四、按企业资质等级分	**Grouped by Class of Enterprises**	
1. 施工总承包	Overall Contractor for Construction	49498153
#特级	Special Class	12081937
一级	First Class	33055527
二级	Second Class	3405903
2. 专业承包	Special Contractor	2871228
#一级以上	First Class	1836719

Main Indicators on Overall Constructing Contractors and Professional Contractors by Registration Status（2013）

建筑业总产值（万元）Total Output Value of Constrution (10 000 yuan)	建筑工程产值 Output Value of Constrution	安装工程产值 Output Value of Installation	其他产值 Others	计算劳动生产率的平均人数（人）Average Number of Employed Persons in Calculation of Labour Productivity(person)	期末从业人员数（人）Number of Employment at Year-end (person)	工程技术人员 Technical Personnel	企业总产值（万元）Total Output Value of Enterprises (10 000 yuan)
22284063	**19902349**	**1972662**	**409052**	**623857**	**577944**	**66152**	**24129898**
17020790	15688391	1038535	293864	453239	409122	44781	18706246
21989070	19607356	1972662	409052	614796	568778	65249	23833387
3232229	2891132	297288	43809	79877	79478	6533	3254670
1088445	914929	157445	16070	45674	47072	5718	1122379
8950	8950			33	33	25	8950
22353	22264	89		805	599	113	22353
14950827	13478485	1171598	300744	403655	358955	42272	16641728
528717	488533	40184		13156	13808	1964	530801
2157549	1803062	306058	48429	71596	68833	3624	2252505
150	150			16	16	6	150
294843	294843			9045	9150	897	296362
9589469	8692072	687607	209790	306366	297491	33573	9703396
10665127	10039363	464808	160956	272940	238005	26953	12322653
1305121	613175	658432	33514	28387	26122	3302	1324267
724346	557739	161815	4793	16164	16326	1324	779583
9894574	9293431	494678	106466	269720	234332	25603	11562477
12389489	10608918	1477985	302586	354137	343612	40549	12567421
20462188	18800220	1265418	396551	577345	533428	61097	22231108
2184180	2076565	63390	44225	39386	22476	4380	3704431
15556393	14514310	911914	130169	453914	428506	44518	15762257
2319585	1931618	225325	162642	73324	71901	10089	2349389
1821875	1102129	707245	12501	46512	44516	5055	1893791
1119751	831288	280439	8024	22807	21329	3239	1135427

14-3 续表

分组	Classify	房屋建筑施工面积（平方米） Number of Projects under Constrution (sq.m)	本年新开工 Beginning Projects in this year
总计	**Total**	**97534510**	**32655161**
#国有及国有控股	State-Owned and State Holding Majority Shares	68029261	20935164
一、按登记注册类型分	**Grouped by Registion Status**		
内资	Domestic Investment Enterprises	97534510	32655161
国有企业	State-owned Enterprises	13873516	5222544
集体企业	Collective-owned Enterprises	9607776	4669616
股份合作企业	Share-holding Corperative Enterprises		
联营企业	Joint Ownership Enterprises	16176	16176
有限责任公司	Limited Liability Corporations	59017323	18037161
股份有限公司	Share-holding Corperation Ltd.	2579329	839278
私营企业	Private Enterprises	12440390	3870386
其他企业	Others		
港澳台商投资企业	Enterprises with Funds from Hong Kong,Macao and Taiwan		
外商投资企业	Enterprises with Foreign Investment		
二、按国民经济行业分	**Grouped by Sector**		
房屋建筑业	Building Engineering Construction	90544144	30982910
土木工程建筑业	Civil Engineering Construction	6937113	1636851
建筑安装业	Installation of Construction	53253	35400
建筑装饰和其他建筑业	Fitting and Decoration Others		
三、按隶属关系分	**Grouped by Administrative Relationship**		
中央	Central	24281853	7015354
地方	Region	73252657	25639807
四、按企业资质等级分	**Grouped by Class of Enterprises**		
1. 施工总承包	Overall Contractor for Construction	95506549	32032762
#特级	Special Class	6908107	2367605
一级	First Class	74981336	24224697
二级	Second Class	12001855	4866546
2. 专业承包	Special Contractor	2027961	622399
#一级以上	First Class	616300	104000

continued

房屋建筑 竣工面积 （平方米） Floor Space of Buildings Completed (sq.m)	自有机械设备 年末净值 （万元） Net Value of Mechanical Equipment owned by Constructions Enterprises at Year-end(10 000 yuan)	自有机械设备 年末总台数 （台） Number of Mechanical Equipment Owned By Construction Enterprises at Year-end(unit)	自有机械设备 年末总功率 （千瓦） Total Power of Mechanical Equipment Owned by Construction Enterprises at Year-end(kw)
22299737	**597558**	**139041**	**3397466**
14321194	482706	50203	2541448
22299737	589297	138565	3326950
3284427	77762	19157	526968
3118845	27062	44206	229726
	52	7	528
	5373	1778	7229
11981450	419687	48549	2065877
541015	12537	1210	82631
3374000	46823	23658	413991
	8262	476	70516
21234815	130196	98374	790192
1025822	442553	32701	2202891
39100	6569	4570	266186
	18241	3396	138197
3497841	377975	27865	1787561
18801896	219584	111176	1609905
21880568	557768	133243	2985150
1418776	100174	9616	528880
16883375	394436	74361	2073277
3184757	55463	46761	335053
419169	39791	5798	412316
102000	34271	4106	234169

14-4 施工总承包和专业承包建筑业企业财务状况（2013年）

单位：万元

指　标	Item	总　计 Total
一、年初存货	**Stocks at the beginning of year**	**3383109**
二、期末资产负债	**Total Assets and Liabilities of the final**	
流动资产合计	Total Circulating Funds	19085747
#应收工程款	Receivable Project Money	4605259
#存货	Stock	3927902
固定资产合计	Fixed Assets	1521369
固定资产原价	Original Value of Fixed Assets	2440617
累计折旧	Accumulative Total Depreciation	1210620
#本年折旧	Depreciation Within the Year	244516
在建工程	Projects Under Construction	194338
资产总计	Total Assets	22836933
流动负债合计	Total Liquid Liabilities	16665100
#应付帐款	Accounts Payable	6953109
非流动负债合计	Total Non-Liquid Liabilities	1188500
负债合计	Total Liabilities	17982860
所有者权益合计	Owner Rights and Interests	4854073
#实收资本	Actual Capital Hold	3767704
三、损益及分配	**Profit or Loss and the Distribution**	
营业收入	Total Revenue	24985547
#主营业务收入	Revenue from Principal Business	24894416
营业成本	Total Cost	22850737
#主营业务成本	Cost of Principal Business	22694671
营业税金及附加	Taxs and Other Changes	777009
#主营业务税金及附加	Taxs and Other Changes on Principal Business	773526
其他业务利润	Profits from Other Operation	20619
销售费用	Sale Expenses	61303
管理费用	Managenment Expenses	700716
财务费用	Financial Expenses	107195
营业利润	Business Profits	574473
利润总额	Total Profits	585597
四、人工成本	**Cost of Labor**	
应付职工薪酬	Salary Payable	2905964

Financial Status of Overall Constructing Contractors and Professional Contractors (2013)

(10 000 yuan)

国有及国有控股 State-Owned and State Holding Majority Shares Enterprises	中央企业 Enterprises Central	省属企业 Province Enterprises	市属企业 Municipal Enterprises
2606545	**2040769**	**462017**	**880323**
15072105	10604582	3256008	5225158
3705575	2095363	1174429	1335467
2857911	2137253	553544	1237105
1048562	780345	218328	522696
1934108	1500480	312544	627593
1023604	806518	149903	254198
215019	176881	29053	38582
99891	67653	46610	80074
18007366	12882204	3771893	6182836
13847037	9993024	2879749	3792328
6191783	4490849	1265218	1197042
1076541	890435	79379	218686
14923588	10883463	2960394	4139004
3083778	1998741	811500	2043832
2288015	1414735	701420	1651550
20376873	13815611	5336044	5833892
20300880	13773387	5315280	5805748
18852940	12770874	4987488	5092375
18713961	12747872	4944964	5001835
622077	418885	164855	193270
619166	418063	163095	192367
16480	14446	3005	3169
21435	13560	1910	45833
528114	370022	112354	218340
70608	42681	15954	48560
366275	278644	57490	238339
375786	287970	57433	240194
2248493	1327815	719983	858167

14-5 劳务分包建筑业企业基本情况（2013年）

Basic Statistic on Enterprises of Work Subcontractors（2013）

单位：万元 (10 000 yuan)

指标	Item	2013
一、期末资产负债	**Total Assets and Liabilities of the final**	
固定资产原价	Value of Fixed Assets	43
本年折旧	Depreciation In The Year	6
资产总计	Total Assets	2015
负债合计	Total Liabilities	1436
实收资本	Paid in Capital	579
二、损益及分配	**Profit or Loss and the Distribution**	
营业收入	Total Revenue	1555
#主营业务收入	Revenue from Principal Business	1538
营业成本	Total Cost	1332
#主营业务成本	Cost of Principal Business	1195
营业税金及附加	Taxs and Other Changes	48
#主营业务税金及附加	Taxs and Other Changes on Principal Business	48
其他业务利润	Profits from Other Operation	
销售费用	Sale Expenses	
管理费用	Managenment Expenses	157
财务费用	Financial Expenses	
营业利润	Business Profits	24
利润总额	Total Profits	

14-6 各区县建筑业主要经济指标（2013年）

Main Indicators of Construction Enterprises by Region（2013）

区县	Region	企业个数(个) Number of Enterprises (unit)	总产值(万元) Total Output Value (10 000 yuan)	计算劳动生产率的平均人数(人) Average Number of Employed Persons in Calculation of Labor Productivity(person)	全员劳动生产率(万元/人) Overall Labor Productivity (10 000 yuan/person)	利税总额(万元) Total Pre-tax Profits (10 000 yuan)
新城区	Xincheng	34	2350114	54491	43	75879
碑林区	Beilin	45	5246441	99771	53	208563
莲湖区	Lianhu	34	1560773	49626	32	47452
灞桥区	Baqiao	30	786542	21732	36	39705
未央区	Weiyang	65	4796314	182617	26	182330
雁塔区	Yanta	121	5552179	122971	45	175094
阎良区	Yanliang	16	227407	10456	22	6818
临潼区	Lintong	14	139183	6041	23	3280
长安区	Chang'an	27	631854	24333	26	21465
蓝田县	Lantian	9	83769	3717	23	1662
周至县	Zhouzhi	7	74997	3545	21	2559
户县	Huxian	6	135029	6393	21	4589
高陵县	Gaoling	7	699462	38164	18	27488

14-7 各区县建筑业房屋施工及竣工面积（2013年）

Floor Space of Buildings under Construction & Completed by Region（2013）

区 县	Region	房屋建筑施工面积（万平方米）Floor Space under Construction (10 000sq.m)	本年新开工面积 Newly Started This Year	房屋建筑竣工面积（万平方米）Floor Space of Buildings Completed (10 000sq.m)	竣工房屋价值（亿元）Value of Buildings Completed (100 million yuan)
新城区	Xincheng	946.80	314.90	218.00	35.30
碑林区	Beilin	2803.10	943.70	728.30	140.60
莲湖区	Lianhu	1388.10	297.50	302.30	56.90
灞桥区	Baqiao	118.70	56.30	52.30	6.40
未央区	Weiyang	1503.70	483.40	184.40	30.80
雁塔区	Yanta	2084.70	680.60	327.60	49.50
阎良区	Yanliang	116.50	41.00	29.70	5.20
临潼区	Lintong	81.80	49.00	27.90	4.30
长安区	Chang'an	178.80	75.50	68.30	12.50
蓝田县	Lantian	82.10	17.20	22.00	2.60
周至县	Zhouzhi	63.20	29.10	34.90	5.00
户 县	Huxian	139.30	48.60	31.60	5.10
高陵县	Gaoling	246.60	229.00	202.60	33.50

14-8 各区县建筑业企业主要经济效益指标（2013年）

Main Economic Benefit Indicators on Construction Enterprises by Region（2013）

区　县	Region	人均利润总额（元/人）Per Profit (yuan/person)	人均利税（元/人）Per Pre-tax Profits (yuan/person)	人均竣工产值（元/人）Per Output Value of Buildings Completed (yuan/person)	人均施工面积（平方米/人）Per Floor Space of Buildings Under Construcyion (sq.m/person)	人均竣工面积（平方米/人）Per Floor Space of Buildings Completed (sq.m/person)
新城区	Xincheng	6003	13925	164894	174	40
碑林区	Beilin	7485	20904	204680	281	73
莲湖区	Lianhu	5115	9562	171327	280	61
灞桥区	Baqiao	6661	18270	386027	55	24
未央区	Weiyang	8086	9984	42170	82	10
雁塔区	Yanta	16572	14320	198030	170	27
阎良区	Yanliang	5000	6521	80088	111	28
临潼区	Lintong	3277	5429	85196	136	46
长安区	Chang'an	6759	8821	89358	74	28
蓝田县	Lantian	26949	4471	97891	221	59
周至县	Zhouzhi	10118	7218	152827	178	99
户　县	Huxian	1898	7179	91944	218	49
高陵县	Gaoling	12690	7203	87765	65	53

14-8 续表 continued

区　县	Region	产值利润率（%）Ratio of Profits to Output Value (%)	产值利税率（%）Ratio of Pre-tax Profits to Output Value (%)	资产利润率（%）Ratio of Profits to Assets (%)	资产利税率（%）Ratio of Pre-tax Profits to Assets（%）	资产负债率（%）Ratio of Debts to Assets（%）
新城区	Xincheng	1.4	3.2	1.5	3.4	85.3
碑林区	Beilin	1.4	4.0	1.4	4.0	81.9
莲湖区	Lianhu	1.6	3.0	1.7	3.1	79.4
灞桥区	Baqiao	1.8	5.0	1.5	4.2	84.6
未央区	Weiyang	3.1	3.8	2.6	3.2	82.6
雁塔区	Yanta	3.7	3.2	3.5	3.0	77.4
阎良区	Yanliang	2.3	3.0	2.8	3.6	64.8
临潼区	Lintong	1.4	2.4	3.4	5.6	50.0
长安区	Chang'an	2.6	3.4	3.0	4.0	75.2
蓝田县	Lantian	12.0	2.0	28.1	4.7	69.9
周至县	Zhouzhi	4.8	3.4	7.9	5.6	61.0
户　县	Huxian	0.9	3.4	1.9	7.4	62.6
高陵县	Gaoling	6.9	3.9	8.3	4.7	5.0

主要统计指标解释

建筑业统计单位 指从事房屋、构筑物建造和设备安装活动的法人企业。建筑业法人企业应具有建筑业资质并能够独立核算，同时其应具备以下条件：①依法成立，有自己的名称、组织机构和场所，能够承担民事责任；②独立拥有和使用资产，承担负债，有权与其他单位签订合同；③独立核算盈亏，能够编制资产负债表。

建筑业总产值 是以货币形式表现的建筑业企业在一定时期内生产的建筑业产品和提供的服务的总和。建筑业总产值包括：

（1）建筑工程产值：指列入建筑工程预算内的各种工程价值。

（2）安装工程产值：指设备安装工程价值，不包括被安装设备本身的价值。

（3）其他产值：建筑业总产值中除建筑工程、安装丁程以外的产值。包括房屋构筑物修理产值、非标准设备制造产值、总包企业向分包企业收取的管理费以及不能明确划分的施工活动所完成的产值。

a. 房屋构筑物修理产值：指房屋和构筑物修理所完成的产值，但不包括被修理房屋、构筑物本身价值和生产设备的修理价值。

b. 非标准设备制造产值：指加工制造没有定型的非标准生产设备的加了费和原材料价值（如化工厂、炼油厂用的各种罐、槽，矿井生产统一使用的各种漏斗、三角槽、阀门等）以及附属加工厂为本企业承建工程制作的非标准设备的价值。

建筑业增加值 指建筑业企业在报告期内以货币形式表现的建筑业生产经营活动的最终成果。

从2004年第一次全国经济普查开始，建筑业现价增加值按生产法和分配法（收入法）两种方法计算，以收入法的计算结果为准，即从收入的角度出发，根据生产要素在生产过程中应得的收入份额计算。具体计算方法：经济普查年度建筑业增加值按照《经济普查年度GDP核算方案》计算，非经济普查年度建筑业增加值按照们≥经济普查年度GDP核算方案》计算。

房屋建筑施工面积 指在报告期内施过工的全部房屋建筑面积，包括本期新开工的房屋面积、上期施工跨入本期继续施工的房屋面积、上期停　建在本期恢复施工的房屋面积、本期竣工的房屋面积及本期施丁后又停　建的房屋面积。

房屋建筑竣工面积 指在报告期内房屋建筑按照设计要求全部完工，达到了使用条件，经验收鉴定合格，正式移交使用单位的房屋建筑面积。

Explanatory Notes on Main Statistical Indicators

Statistical Unit in the Construction Industry refers to a corporate enterprise engaged in the construction of buildings and structures and in the installation of equipment. A corporate construction enterprise should have qualification certificates with independent accounting system, and should meet the following 3 requirements: a) being set up in line with relevant legal basis, having its full name, organization and location, and capable of taking civil liabilities; b) independently possessing and using its assets and assuming its liabilities, and entitled to sign contracts with other institutions; and c) making independent accounts of its profits and losses, and capable of compiling its own balance sheet.

Gross Output Value of Construction refers to total of construction products and services, expressed in money terms, produced or rendered by construction and installation enterprises during a given period of time. It includes:

(1)Output value of construction projects: the value of projects covered by the project budgets;

(2) Output value of installation projects: the value of the installation of equipment, (excluding the value of the equipment to be installed);

(3)Other output values: the output value of construction industry apart from that of construction projects and installation projects. It includes: output value of repair of buildings and structures; output value of non-standard equipment manufacturing; overhead expenses received by contracted enterprises from the sub-contracted enterprises and the completed output value of construction activities for which there is no clear definition.

a. Output value of repair of buildings and structures: the value created through the repairs of buildings or structures. It does not include the value of buildings or structures being repaired and the value of the repair of production equipment;

b. Output value of manufactured non-standard equipment: the value of non-standard production equipment, including raw materials and manufacturing cost, made for the construction project (i.e., chemical plant; kettles or tanks used by refineries; various fillers, triangle tanks, valves used by mines). It also includes the output value of equipment manufactured by subsidiary workshops.

Value–added of Construction refers to the final result of the activities of production and operation of enterprises of the construction industry in monetary terms during the reference period.

Starting from the 2004 economic census, value-added of construction is calculated by both production approach and income approach, with the figures from the income approach as the final figures. Under the income approach, calculation starts from the perspective of income and is based on the share of income derived from the production process by the relevant factors of production. Specifically, value-added of construction for the Census years is calculated in accordance with the Programme of Compilation of GDP and National Accounts for the Year of Economic Census, and value-added of construction for other years is calculated in accordance with the Programme of Compilation of GDP and National Accounts for the Non Economic Census Years.

Floor Space of Buildings Under Construction refers to floor space of buildings under construction during the reference period, including the floor space of buildings for which construction has newly started; buildings for which construction has started earlier and is continuing during the reference period, and buildings for which construction has been suspended earlier but has restarted during the reference period; buildings completed during the reference period; and buildings under construction but construction has subsequently been during the reference period.

Floor Space of Buildings Completed refers to the floor space of buildings that are completed in the reference period in accordance with the requirements of the design, up to the standard for being put into use, and having been checked and accepted by departments concerned as qualified ones.

15 运输和邮电

TRANSPORT,POSTAL AND TELECOMMUNICATION SERVICE

资料整理：齐昆峰
Data management:Ci Kunfeng

第十五部分　运输和邮电

一、简要说明

本章资料包括交通运输业和邮电通信业的基本情况，主要是交通运输工具、货物和旅客运输量、邮电业务、邮政局所及服务点等基本情况。资料由西安市统计局社会科技处根据有关部门提供资料整理。

二、主要指标

旅客周转量（亿人公里）	363.49	比上年增长	7.3%
货物周转量（亿吨公里）	674.15	比上年增长	13.1%
邮电业务总量（亿元）	247.94	比上年增长	14.7%
全社会车辆数（万辆）	186.21	比上年增长	14.0%
#民用小轿车	91.98	比上年增长	22.3%

15 TRANSPORT,POSTAL AND TELECOMMUNICATION SERVICES

Ⅰ.Brief Introduction

Data in this chapter consists of primarily basic data of communication, transportation and postal service industry, transportation facility, amount of goods and passenger transportation, basic data of postal service, post offices and service establishments of Xi'an City. Data in this chapter is compiled by Social & Science and Technology Division of the Xi'an Bureau of Statistics according to the data provided by department concerned of the municipal government.

Ⅱ.Major Indicators

		Increase over Preceding Year
Passenger-Km (100 mil. Person-km)	363.49	7.3%
Freight Ton-Km (100 mil. Ton-km)	674.15	16.3%
Amount of Postal and Telecommunication Service(100 mil. Yuan)	247.94	14.7%
Number of Vehides in the whole Sciety(10 000 unit)	186.21	14.0%
Civil Car	91.98	22.3%

15-1 主要年份各种交通线路和桥梁

Transportation Routes and Number of Bridges in Representative Years

年 份 Year	铁路营业 里程（公里） Length of Railways in Operation (km)	公路里程 （公里） Length of Highways (km)	桥 梁 （座） Bridges (seat)	桥梁长度 （公里） .ength of Bridge (km)
1978	555			
1980	555			
1981	569			
1982	569			
1983	569			
1984	569			
1985	697			
1986	697			
1987	1333			
1988	1339			
1989	1339	2563		
1990	1339	2586		
1991	1357	2785		
1992	1357	2786		
1993	1356	2801		
1994	1357	2830		
1995	1357	2852		
1996	1358	2877		
1997	1489	3026		
1998	1492	3047		
1999	1478	2789		
2000	1540	3010		
2001	1536	3298		
2002	1543	7862	629	29799
2003	1522	8360	629	29799
2004	1608	8360	629	29799
2005	202	8500	634	46973
2006	269	9530	634	46973
2007	269	9672	1319	91412
2008	269	11895	1710	151995
2009	269	12378	1856	154866
2010	269	12378	1856	154866
2011	269	12599	1863	149743
2012	269	13127	2190	214978
2013	269	13135	2213	224962

注：本表数据来自市交通局、西安铁路局，民航通航里程2013年统计口径发生较大变化。

15-1 续表 continued

年　份 Year	永久式桥梁 （座） Permanent Bridges (seat)	永久式桥梁 （公里） Length of Permanent Bridges (m)	民航通航里程 （重复航线）（公里） Length of Total Civil Aviation Routes(km)
1978			
1980			
1981			
1982			
1983			
1984			
1985			
1986			
1987			
1988			
1989			
1990			
1991			
1992			65007
1993			83215
1994			100800
1995			119753
1996			126433
1997			173010
1998			180000
1999			141284
2000			139764
2001			154614
2002	629	29799	211000
2003	629	29799	381800
2004	629	29799	386953
2005	632	46915	485749
2006	632	46915	418852
2007	1275	90716	553355
2008	1657	150980	515524
2009	1803	153850	587904
2010	1803	153850	742375
2011	1811	148810	898628
2012	2138	213985	981450
2013	2161	223970	70643568

15-2 各种交通线路里程和桥梁数（2013年）

Length of Transportation Routes and Number of Bridges（2013）

指　标	Item	2013
铁路营业里程（公里）	**Length of Railways in Operation (km)**	**269**
电气化营业里程	Length of Electrified Railways in Operation	
复线里程	Double-Tracking Length	
公路里程（公里）	**Length of Highways (km)**	**13135**
等级公路	Expressways and Class I to IV Highways	12598
高速	Expressway	471
一级	First Class	325
二级	Second Class	1466
三级	Third Class	1186
四级	Forth Class	9150
等外公路	Highways below Class IV	537
桥梁	**Bridges**	
永久式桥梁	Permanent	
座（座）	Seat (seat)	2161
长度（公里）	Length (m)	223970
民航通航里程(公里)(重复航线)	**Length of Total Civil Aviation Routes(km)**	**70643563**
国际航线（公里）		
民航航线条数（条）	**Length of Civil Aviation routes(Article)**	**242**
国际航线	International routes	13

注：本表数据来自市交通局、西安铁路局。

15-3 主要年份全社会车辆数

Possession of Civil Vehicles in Representative Years

单位：辆、台　　　　(unit)

年　份 Year	合计 Total	汽车 Motor	载客汽车 Passenget Vehicles	载货汽车 Ordinary Trucks	摩托车 Motorcycles	拖拉机 Tractors
1999	**279335**	133192	63772	44348		38023
2000	**310252**	138318	89783	44974		37177
2001	**369988**	172436	110744	55453		31355
2002	**454998**	206653	134527	64623	176960	36083
2003	**516719**	242599	163872	70781	191834	34733
2004	**512802**	276012	195524	74557	156709	34755
2005	**544586**	377628	240923	82463	131440	34741
2006	**608155**	393778	296078	89772	131449	33236
2007	**840376**	522616	360081	97614	284594	32028
2008	**875005**	595735	430472	89093	247079	30176
2009	**1012937**	754803	567326	113430	224121	31347
2010	**1253461**	961283	739038	145740	259239	29151
2011	**1445811**	1174874	928669	171649	241132	25600
2012	**1633257**	1380125	1123105	186412	224279	24458
2013	**1862063**	1634885	1372371	207058	200419	21904

注：本表数据来自市车管所

15-4 全社会车辆数（2013年）

Possession of Civil Vehicles（2013）

指 标	Item	2013
合计	**Total**	**1862063**
民用汽车（辆）	Motor(unit)	1634885
#私人汽车拥有量	Possession of Private Vehicles	1412396
载客汽车	Passenget Vehicles	1372371
#大 型	Large	15201
轿 车	Car	919757
普通载货汽车	Ordinary Trucks	207058
#重、中型	Heavy and Medium	60477
其他汽车	Others	55456
#三 轮	Three Wheelers	24633
拖拉机（台）	Tractors(unit)	21898
# 大中型	Large and Medium	12927
小 型	Small-sized	8971
摩托车（辆）	Motorcycle (unit)	200419
普通摩托车	Bicycle Motor	193799
挂车（辆）	Articulated Trailers (unit)	4790
其他类型车（辆）	Others (unit)	71

注：本表数据来自市车管所

15-5 主要年份交通运输量及周转量

Passenger Traffic and Kilometers and Freight Traffic and Ton-kilometers in Representative Years

年　份 Year	客运量 （万人次） Passenger Traffic (10 000 person-times)	旅客周转量 （万人公里） Passenger-Km (10 000 person-Km)	货运量 （万吨） Freight Traffic (10 000 tons)	货物周转量（万吨公里） Freight Ton-Km (10 000 ton-Km)
1978	1334		3723	
1980	1508		3655	
1981	1839		3379	
1982	2340		4067	
1983	3054		4225	
1984	2899		4966	
1985	2404		5681	
1986	2186		5409	
1987	3781		6294	
1988	5721		6968	
1989	6092		8742	
1990	5748		6980	
1991	4193		3389	
1992	4368		8233	
1993	8036		8406	
1994	8321		8754	
1995	9069		9590	
1996	9854		10577	
1997	8922		9358	
1998	9223		9429	
1999	10311	2130383	9766	3452383
2000	10756	2507896	10191	3691963
2001	9078	2658037	7728	4229430
2002	12527	2524444	9484	4544040
2003	11413	2596402	9392	5037684
2004	10832	3112374	14845	5850029
2005	10479	1607568	12051	1249525
2006	11245	1721217	11832	1354318
2007	12466	1753464	15124	1473182
2008	26501	2529007	27560	3490707
2009	28693	2582025	30606	3766806
2010	30294	2942957	34323	4301680
2011	33375	3223544	39239	5212010
2012	36154	3387448	44924	5958742
2013	38289	3634915	50119	6471497

注：本表数据由市交通局、西安铁路局、咸阳机场、长安航空公司、东方航空公司西北分公司提供。

15-6 交通运输量及运输周转量（2013年）

Passenger Traffic and Kilometers and Freight Traffic and Ton-kilometers（2013）

指　标	Item	2013年	2013比上年增长（%）Increase over Preceding Year
一　客运量合计（万人次）	**Passenger Traffic(10 000 person–times)**	**38289**	**5.9**
铁路	Railway	3071	4.7
公路	Highway	32614	5.6
民航	Civil Aviation	2604	11.2
二　旅客周转量合计（万人公里）	**Passenger–Km (10 000 person–Km)**	**3634915**	**7.3**
铁路	Railway	619361	1.4
公路	Highway	1804519	5.6
民航	Civil Aviation	1211036	13.2
三　货运量合计（万吨）	**Freight Traffic(lO 000 tons)**	**50119**	**11.6**
铁路	Railway	858	4
公路	Highway	49243	11.7
民航	Civil Aviation	18	2.3
四　货物周转量（万吨公里）	**Freight Ton–Kin (10 000 ton–Km)**	**6471497**	**8.6**
铁路	Railway	2292497	3.2
公路	Highway	4168694	11.8
民航	Civil Aviation	10307	4.9

注：本表数据由市交通局、西安铁路局、咸阳机场、长安航空公司、东方航空公司西北分公司提供。

15-7 主要年份邮政电信情况

年份 Year	邮电业务总量（万元） Business Volume of Postal and Telecommunication Services(10 000 yuan)	电信业务总量 Business Volume of Telecommunication Services	邮政业务总量 Business Volume of Postal Services
1978	1420		
1980	1640		
1981	1713		
1982	2154		
1983	2250		
1984	2484		
1985	2972		
1986	3244		
1987	3911		
1988	5327		
1989	5973		
1990	7843		
1991	5700		
1992	6610		
1993	36581		
1994	54034		
1995	76450		
1996	104566		
1997	124601		
1998	204927		
1999	306457		
2000	461628		
2001	367620		
2002	515259	470492	44767
2003	820943	770673	50270
2004	1027415	975045	52370
2005	1320447	1261033	59414
2006	1867560	1796533	71027
2007	2267633	2191250	76383
2008	2646662	2564524	82138
2009	2989246	2900836	88410
2010	3231059	3167750	63309
2011	2005025	1944329	60696
2012	2162065	2098273	63762
2013	2479430	2313630	165800

注：2002年及以后，邮政电信机构分离；2001—2010年邮电业务总量按2000年不变价格计算；2011年邮电业务总量按2010年不变价格计算，故与以往年份不可比。

Basic Statistic on Postal and Telecommunication Service in Representative Years

固定电话年末用户数（户） Number of Immobile Telephone at Year-end (subscriber)	农村电话用户数 Number of Telephone in Rural Areas at Year-end	移动电话用户年末数（户） Number of Mobile Phone at Year-end (subscriber)	互联网年末宽带用户数（户） Number of Broad Band Net User (subscriber)
12828	1062		
14024	1086		
14497	1125		
15357	1129		
16922	1156		
18611	1203		
21624	1239		
26373	1235		
30200	1290		
34265	1357		
39506	1498		
45267	1668		
49516	2479		
60727	2613		
101327	2671		
197398	5067		
299485	8386		
430270	13654		
573244	21202		
736998	37863		
874586	74761		
1242637	170199		
1711500	259374	1277400	17183
2095230	358803	1964200	35230
2538393	415593	2412392	160900
2934424	480276	3500900	243448
3214806	500847	4199570	339280
3159639	467526	5510720	508775
3145819	419446	6645863	586213
3068807	383869	7377575	813987
2891009	358238	11200566	1167916
2617691	335048	14230800	1461804
2703640	320189	16141463	1841027
3110176	335864	18035397	2023059
3191112	330602	21606662	2670473

注：本表数据由市邮政管理局、市邮政局，中国联通、中国电信、中国移动和中国铁通等西安分公司提供。

15-8 邮政业务及服务网点

Postal Service and Branch Post Office

指　标	Item	2011	2012	2013
一、邮政业务总量（万元）	**Business Volume of Postal Services(10 000 yuan)**	**60696**	**63077**	**165800**
二、邮政业务收入（万元）	**Gross Income of Post Services (10 000 yuan)**	**65174**	**71778**	**177100**
快递业务收入	Express delivery business income			97100
三、函件（万件）	**Number of Letters (10 000 pcs)**	**3061**	**2769**	**2856**
四、包件（万件）	**Parcels (10 000 pcs)**	**91**	**50**	**89**
五、汇票（万张）	**Money Order (10 000 pcs)**	**112**	**90**	**148**
六、报纸订销累计份数（万份）	**Accumulated Newspaper Prescribing and** Sales Volume (10 000 pcs)	**12603**	**13052**	**14495**
七、杂志订销累计份数（万份）	**Accumulated Magazine Prescribing and** Sales Volume (10 000 pcs)	**564**	**613**	**1628**
八、特快专递类业务（万件）	**Express Mail Service Volume (10 000 pcs)**	**1901**	**129**	**6896**
九、集邮业务量（万枚）	**Stamps For Collection (10 000 pcs)**	**1060**	**2312**	**1431**
十、邮政营销网点（处）	**Number of Post Office Branch Establishments (unit)**	**277**	**279**	**269**
#设在农村的局所	In it: number of post offices in rural area	50	115	110
十一、邮政信筒信箱（个）	**Number of Mailboxes(unit)**	**1108**	**1108**	**1108**

注：本表数据来自市邮政管理局和邮政局，2013年邮政数据统计口径变化。

15-9 电信业务情况

Telecommunication Service

指　标	Item	2011	2012	2013
一、电信业务总量（万元）	**Business Volume of Telecommunication Services (10 000 yuan)**	**1944329**	**2098274**	**2313630**
二、电信业务总收入（万元）	**Gross Income of Telecommunication Services (10 000 yuan)**	**1029629**	**1162257**	**1316435**
三、固定电话年末用户数（万户）	**Number of Immobile Telephone at Year-end (10 000 subscribers)**	**270.36**	**311.02**	**319.11**
#农村电话年末户数	Number of Telephone in Rural Areas at Year-end	**32.02**	**33.59**	**33.06**
四、电话交换机总容量（万门）	**Capacity (number) of Telephone Switchboard (10 000 lines)**	**441.49**	**878.27**	**835.91**
五、移动电话用户年末数（万户）	**Number of Mobile Phone at Year-end(10 000 subscribers)**	**1614.15**	**1803.54**	**2160.67**
#3G电话用户数	3G Mobile Phone Subscribers	177.37	394.97	666.36
六、互联网年末用户数（万户）	**Number of Broad Band Net User (10 000 subscribers)**	**184.10**	**202.31**	**267.05**

注：本表数据由中国联通、中国电信、中国移动和中国铁通等西安分公司提供。

主要统计指标解释

铁路营业里程 又称营业长度（包括正式营业和临时营业里程），指办理客货运输业务的铁路正线总长度。凡是全线或部分建成双线及以上的线路，以第一线的实际长度计算；复线、站线、段管线、岔线和特殊用途线以及不计算运费的联络线都不计算营业里程。铁路营业里程是反映铁路运输业基础设施发展水平的重要指标，也是计算客货周转量、运输密度和机车车辆运用效率等指标的基础资料。

公路里程 指在一定时期内实际达到《公路工程技术标准JTJ01-88》规定的等级公路，并经公路主管部门正式验收交付使用的公路里程数。包括大中城市的郊区公路以及通过小城镇街道部分的公路里程和桥梁、隧道渡口的长度，不包括大中城市的街道、厂矿、林区生产用道和农业生产用道的里程。两条或多条公路共同经由同一路段，只计算一次，不得重复计算里程长度。它是反映公路建设发展规模的重要指标，也是计算运输网密度等指标的基础资料。

民用航空航线里程 指民航运输定期班机飞行的航线长度的总和。航线长度按机场之间的距离计算，通常有两种计算方法：一是将每条航线长度相加称为重复计算航线里程；一是将两线或两条以上航线经过同一区段里程，只计算一次航线长度称为不重复计算航线里程。一般常用的是后者，它能确切反映民航运输网的规模，是表明民航事业为国民经济服务和方便人民生活程度的主要指标。

货（客）运量 指在一定时期内，各种运输工具实际运送的货物（旅客）数量。它是反映运输业为国民经济和人民生活服务的数量指标，也是制定和检查运输生产计划、研究运输发展规模和速度的重要指标。货运按吨计算，客运按人计算。货物不论运输距离长短、货物类别，均按实际重量统计。旅客不论行程远近或票价多少，均按一人一次客运量统计；半价票、小孩票也按一人统计。

货物（旅客）周转量 指在一定时期内，由各种运输工具运送的货物（旅客）数量与其相应运输距离的乘积之总和。它是反映运输业生产总成果的重要指标，也是编制和检查运输生产计划，计算运输效率、劳动生产率以及核算运输单位成本的主要基础资料。计算货物周转量通常按发出站与到达站之间的最短距离，也就是计费距离计算。计算公式为：

货物（旅客）周转量=∑货物（旅客）运输量×运输距离

民用汽车拥有量 指报告期末，在公安交通管理部门按照《机动车注册登记工作规范》，已注册登记领有民用车辆牌照的全部汽车数量。汽车拥有量统计的主要分类：根据汽车结构分为载客汽车、载货汽车及其他汽车；根据汽车所有者不同分为个人（私人）汽车、单位汽车；根据汽车的使用性质分为营运汽车、非营运汽车；根据汽车大小规格不同载客汽车分为大型、中型、小型和微型，载货汽车分为重型、中型、轻型和微型。

邮电业务总量 指以价值量形式表现的邮电通信企业为社会提供各类邮电通信服务的总数量。邮电业务量按专业分类包括函件、包件、汇票、报刊发行、邮政快件、特快专递、邮政储蓄、集邮、公众电报、用户电报、传真、长途电话、出租电路、无线寻呼、移动电话、分组交换数据通信、出租代维等。计算方法为各类产品乘以相应的平均单价（不变价）之和，再加上出租电路和设备、代用户维护电话交换机和线路等的服务收入。它综合反映了一定时期邮电业务发展的总成果，是研究邮电业务量构成和发展趋势的重要指标。计算公式为：

邮电业务总量=∑（各类邮电业务量×不变单价）+出租代维及其他业务收入

移动电话用户 是指通过移动电话交换机进入移动电话网、占用移动电话号码的电话用户。用户数量以报告期末在移动电话营业部门实际办理登记手续进入移动电话网的户数进行计算，一部移动电话统计为一户。

电话用户 指接入国家公众固定电话网，并按固定电话业务进行经营管理的电话用户。1997年以前，电话用户分为市内电话用户和农村电话用户。“市内电话用户”是指接入县城及县以上城市的电话网上的电话用户；“农村电话用户”是指接入县邮电局农话台及县以下农村电话交换点，以县城为中心（除市话用户外）联通县、乡（镇）、行政村、村民小组的用户。从1997年起，电话用户数分组调整为以用户所在区域划分为“城市电话用户”和“乡村电话用户”，与过去的按市内电话和农村电话划分方法不同。而电话用户总数、电话机总部数统计范围不变。

农村电话用户 指县城关区以下的集镇和农村接入局用交换机的电话用户数。

局用交换机容量 是指安装在本地电信运营商内用于接续本地固定电话的电话交换机容量，有倍增设备按倍增后的数量计数。包括现用和备用的人工或自动交换机的全部容量。

互联网宽带接入端口 指用于接入互联网用户的各类实际安装运行的接入端口的数量，包括xDSL用户接入端口、LAN接入端口以及其他类型接入端口等，不包括窄带拨号接入端口。

Explanatory Notes on Main Statistical Indicators

Length of Railways in Operation refers to the total length of the trunk line under passenger and freight transportation(including both full operation and temporary operation). The calculation is based on the actual length of the first line even if this line has a full or partial double track or more tracks, excluding double tracks, station sidings, tracks under the charge of stations, branch lines, special-purpose lines and the non-payable connecting lines. The length of railways in operation is an important indicator to show the development of the infrastructure for the railway transport, and also the essential data to calculate volume of passenger freight transport,traffic density and utilization efficiency of the locomotives and carriages.

Length of Highways refers to the length of highways which are built in conformity with the grades specified by the highway engineering standard formulated by the Ministry of Communications, and have been formally checked and accepted by the departments of highways and put into use. The length of highways includes that of the suburb highways at large and medium- sized cities,highways passing through streets at small cities and towns,and also the length of bridges, tunnel and ferries. It does not include the length of streets in big and medium-sized cities and highways built for the production purpose at factories, mines, forest areas and agricultural areas. If two or more highways go the same section of the way, the length of the section is only calculated for once and no duplication is allowed. The length of highways is an important indicator to show the development of the highway construction and to provide essential information to calculate the transport network density.

Length of Civil Aviation Routes refers to the length of all routes for regular civil aviation flights. There are usually two ways to calculate the distance between airports connected by the route length: one is to put the length of all air routes together, called duplicated calculation of the length of the routes; the other is not to allow the duplication in calculation when two or more routes passing the same section of aviation routes. The latter is usually used, as it can precisely show the size of the civil aviation network and indicate the extent of civil aviation serving the national economy and the people.

Freight (Passenger) Traffic refers to the volume of freight (passenger) transported with various means Freight transport is calculated in tons and passenger traffic is calculated in the number of persons. Despite the type of freight and travelling distance, the freight transport is calculated in the actual weight of the goods and despite the travelling distance and ticket price, the passenger traffic is calculated by the principle that one person can be counted only once in one travel. The passenger who travel with a half price ticket or a child ticket is also calculated as one person. The freight (passenger) traffic provides a quantitative measure to show how the transport industry serves the national economy and people, and is also an important indicator for planning the transport industry and for studying the development scale and speed of the transport industry.

Freight Ton-kilometers(Passenger-kilometers) refer to the sum of the products of the volume of transported cargo (passengers) multiplying by the transport distance, usually using ton-kilometer and passenger-kilometer as units for measurement. Normally, the shortest distance between the departure station and the destination station (i.e., the payable distance) is the basis to calculate the freight ton-kilometers. This is an important indicator to show the total results of the transport industry, to prepare and examine the transport plan and to measure the efficiency, the labour productivity and the unit cost of transport.

The formula is as follows:

Freight Ton-kilometers(Passenger-kilometers)=Σ {Freight (Passenger) Traffic × Distance of Transportation }

Measuring unit: ton-kilometer (person-kilometer)

Possession of Civil Motor Vehicles refer to the total numbers of vehicles that are registered and received vehicles license tags according to the Work Standard for Motor Vehicles Registration formulated by the Transport Management Office under the department of public security at the end of the reference period. They are divided into categories. According to the structure of motor vehicles, they are divided into passenger vehicles, trucks and others; according to ownership into private vehicles and vehicles for the unit' s use; according to kind of usage into working vehicles and non-working vehicles; and according to size of vehicles into large passenger vehicles, medium-sized passenger vehicles, small passenger vehicles and mini passenger vehicles,heavytrucks, light-heavy trucks, light trucks and mini-trucks.

Business Volume of Post and Telecommunications refers to the total amount of post and telecommunications services, expressed in value terms, provided by the post and telecommunications departments for the society. Post and telecommunication services can be classified asletters, parcels, remittance, issue of newspapers and magazines, fast mail service, express mail service, savings deposits, stamps for collection, public and individual telegraph service, facsimiles, long-distance telephone service,leasing of telephone lines, urban paging service, mobile telephone service, data transfer and transmission, etc. The accounting approach is to multiply the service products of all types with their average unit price (constant price) to get sum of business value, plus income from other services such as leasing of telephone lines and equipment, maintenance of telephone switchboards and lines on behalf of customers. This indicator reflects the overall results of post and telecommunications service during a given period, and is important to study the composition of business service and the development of post and telecommunications service.

The formula is as follows:

Business Volume of Post and Telecommunications= Σ (Transaction of Post and Telecommunication Service x Constant Price) + Income from Leasing, Maintenance and other Services

Mobile Telephone Subscribers refer to the persons who own mobile telephone numbers and are connected with the mobile telephone communication network through the mobile telephone switchboards. The number of subscribers is calculated by the subscribers who have completed registration at mobile communication business centers and entered into the mobile telephone network. One mobile telephone is taken as a subscriber.

Telephone Subscribers refer to subscribers that are connected to the public line telephone network provided with telephone services. Before 1997, telephone subscribers were classified as city subscribers and village subscribers. City subscribers referred to those connected to city telephone networks in county towns and cities, while village subscribers referred to those connected to village telephone stations at and below counties. Since 1997, the classification of telephone subscribers was modified on the basis of physical location of the subscribers as Urban telephone subscribers and rural telephone subscribers , which is different from the previous classification of categorizing local telephones and rural telephones , while the definition of total subscribers and total number of telephones remain unchanged.

Rural Telephone Subscribers refer to telephone subscribers, located at towns under county town and country, that are connected to the public line telephone network.

Capacity of Office Telephone Exchanges refers to the capacity (measured in gate) of telephone exchanges installed in the offices of local telecommunication service providers for communication between fixed telephones. It includes the capacity of both manual and automatic exchanges in use and for stand-by purpose. Equipment with expansion function is to be counted by the expanded capacity.

Broadband Connection Terminals refer to the connection terminals to internet users actually installed and put into operation, including connection terminals for xDSL, connection terminals for LAN, and other connection terminals for xDSL. N-ISDN connection terminals are not included.

16 国内贸易

DOMESTIC TRADE

资料整理：马晓庆　杨　骏　左　宇　赵琳瑛　胡树建
Data management:Ma Xiaoqing　Yang Jun　Zuo Yu　Zhao linying　Hu Shujian

第十六部分　国内贸易

一、简要说明

本章资料主要包括社会消费品零售总额，批发零售贸易业商品购、销等情况，限额以上批发零售贸易业主要商品销售情况，限额以上批发零售贸易和住宿餐饮企业财务状况、经济效益，以及交易市场情况，由西安市统计局贸易外经处提供。

二、主要指标

批发零售贸易业网点（万个）	19.53	比上年下降	11.9%
餐饮业网点（万个）	4.74	比上年增长	3.7%
社会消费品零售总额（亿元）	2580.42	比上年增长	14.0%
#批发零售贸易业零售额	2315.59	比上年增长	15.5%

16 DOMESTIC TRADE

Ⅰ.Brief Introduction

Content of this chapter consists of total retail sales of consumer goods, sails data on commodity purchasing and sails of wholesale and retail trade, sales data on primary goods exceeds quotation, financial, economic performance and market data on wholesale and retail trade and food services industry exceeds quotation. Data in this chapter is compiled and provided by Trade and Foreign Economy Division of the Xi'an Bureau of Statistics.

Ⅱ.Maior Indicators

		Increase over Preceding Year
Establishments Engaged in Whole-sale and Retail Trade(10 000 unit)	19.53	11.9%
Establishments Engaged in Catering Zndustry(10 000 unit)	4.74	3.7%
Total Retail Sales of Consumer Goods (100 mil. yuan)	2580.42	14.0%
Retail Sales of Wholesale and Retail Enterprises	2315.59	15.5%

16-1 主要年份社会消费品零售额

Total Retail Sales of Consumer Goods in Representative Years

单位：亿元　　　　(100 million yuan)

年　份 Year	社会消费品零售总额 Total Retail Sales of Consumer Goods	城镇 Urban	乡村 Village	批发和零售业 Wholesale Trades and Retail Trades	住宿和餐饮业 Accommodation and Catering Trade	其他行业 Others
1978	12.70	8.82	3.88	11.01	0.53	0.21
1979	13.94	9.88	4.06	11.88	0.60	0.21
1980	15.88	11.53	4.35	13.05	0.80	0.20
1983	20.82	15.14	5.68	16.95	1.03	0.32
1984	24.87	19.13	5.74	19.47	1.29	0.46
1985	32.92	26.09	6.83	25.04	1.69	0.48
1986	37.50	29.25	8.25	28.88	1.97	0.64
1987	43.86	34.62	9.24	33.32	2.50	0.49
1988	59.65	47.74	11.91	44.84	2.97	0.78
1989	68.05	54.60	13.45	54.41	2.98	0.76
1990	72.77	59.42	13.35	57.46	3.79	0.90
1991	81.04	66.93	14.11	60.35	4.43	1.26
1992	100.84	89.17	11.67	71.86	6.13	2.30
1993	115.38	104.41	10.97	75.99	7.49	2.71
1994	144.64	131.56	13.08	89.79	9.12	3.43
1995	186.60	165.98	20.62	115.46	11.97	3.73
1996	222.94	198.19	24.75	145.05	15.83	4.02
1997	264.47	238.17	26.30	169.08	22.12	4.17
1998	291.45	257.39	34.06	183.43	30.97	4.27
1999	323.37	283.32	40.05	207.96	34.78	4.85
2000	360.42	317.12	43.30	232.89	41.42	5.43
2001	406.21	358.97	47.24	265.25	48.87	5.86
2002	459.76	409.86	49.90	309.36	51.42	6.45
2003	502.65	449.62	53.03	440.28	53.30	9.07
2004	578.60	520.94	57.66	509.60	56.87	12.13
2005	670.56	604.63	65.93	592.77	63.59	14.20
2006	784.95	708.31	76.64	694.03	74.77	16.15
2007	936.21	845.59	90.62	828.63	89.32	18.26
2008	1176.58	1063.93	112.65	1033.00	122.90	20.68
2009	1381.12	1249.79	131.33	1222.98	134.54	23.60
2010	1637.04	1570.16	66.88	1431.23	179.82	25.99
2011	1965.98	1908.65	57.33	1725.03	210.15	30.80
2012	2263.86	2195.18	68.68	2004.90	231.16	27.80
2013	2580.42	2501.85	78.57	2315.59	232.43	32.40

注：依据2008年第二次经济普查数据，对2005-2007年数据进行调整。
2009年以前按经营单位所在地分为市和县及县以下。
2002年以前按行业分组中不包括制造业零售额和农业对非农业居民零售额。

16-2 社会消费品零售总额（2013年）

Total Retail Sales of Consumer Goods（2013）

单位：亿元 (100 million yuan)

分 类	Classify	金额 Sum
社会消费品零售总额	**Total Retail Sales of Consumer Goods**	**2580.42**
（一）按销售单位所在地分	Grouped by Region	
（1）城镇	Urban	2501.85
#城区	District	2124.72
（2）乡村	Village	78.57
（二）按行业分：	Grouped by Sector	
（1）批发业	Wholesale Enterprises	392.20
限额以上单位	Enterprises Above Designated Size	366.91
限额以下单位	Enterprises Below Designated Size and Self-employed Laborers	25.29
（2）零售业	Retail Enterprises	1923.39
限额以上单位	Enterprises Above Designated Size	1513.83
限额以下单位	Enterprises Below Designated Size and Self-employed Laborers	409.56
（3）住宿和餐饮业	Accommodation and Catering Trade	232.43
限额以下单位	Enterprises Above Designated Size	104.85
限额以上单位	Enterprises Below Designated Size and Self-employed Laborers	127.58
（4）其他行业	Others	32.40

16-3 各区县社会消费品零售总额（2013年）

Total Retail Sales of Consumer Goods by Region（2013）

单位：亿元 (100 million yuan)

区 县	Region	社会消费品零售总额 Total Retail Sales of Consumer Goods	批发零售贸易业零售额 Wholesale and Retail Trade of Retail Sales	住宿餐饮业零售额 Accommodation and Catering Trade of Retail Sales
新城区	Xincheng	450.52	423.37	21.26
碑林区	Beilin	447.04	398.10	45.95
莲湖区	Lianhu	368.29	335.96	31.64
灞桥区	Baqiao	64.12	56.50	7.40
未央区	Weiyang	361.73	342.50	18.96
雁塔区	Yanta	503.53	436.86	50.78
阎良区	Yanliang	30.08	25.21	4.64
临潼区	Lintong	62.71	55.13	6.43
长安区	Chang'an	144.15	113.51	28.32
蓝田县	Lantian	45.80	40.17	5.16
周至县	Zhouzhi	31.01	27.91	2.53
户 县	Huxian	50.18	43.47	6.36
高陵县	Gaoling	21.24	16.90	2.98

16-4 主要年份批发零售贸易业、餐饮业网点和人员

Wholesale and Retail Trade, Catering Outlets and Staff in Representative Years

单位：个、人　　　　(unit,person)

年份 Year	批发业 Wholesale Trade		零售业 Retail Trade		餐饮业 Catering Services	
	网点 Branch Shop	人员 Personnel	网点 Branch Shop	人员 Personnel	网点 Branch Shop	人员 Personnel
1978	586	22136	5862	51462	442	9043
1979	462	14002	5387	49252	815	10349
1980	1505	28320	6312	51927	1893	16297
1983	1642	32597	17130	77863	6337	28054
1984	1875	34906	27043	136852	8434	25977
1985	1247	43311	35860	223076	11907	41025
1986	1706	42270	37503	241052	11977	48335
1987	3351	44475	42484	260450	13673	51361
1988	1829	40324	44330	282911	9575	47131
1989	1638	80078	46613	229705	10223	46420
1990	1558	37077	43244	219413	9800	34561
1991	1918	45583	48171	236235	10359	36813
1992	1864	36012	48422	258491	9915	38935
1993	5177	54255	43289	226572	11804	38318
1994	6338	58154	60292	318287	14295	56502
1995	6564	63337	69623	364430	15485	68782
1996	8008	67840	76828	437655	15653	78313
1997	8414	71178	80379	468811	20259	82917
1998	10780	85420	95056	515723	22500	100862
1999	10865	86630	96516	516163	24977	118442
2000	10393	81519	93928	492083	27531	124988
2001	10534	78285	95414	497448	28219	128738
2002	12220	107352	96815	465320	29219	140623
2003	13274	117740	99764	490169	32899	150883
2004	19696	102779	106477	281221	27905	132855
2005	20392	106138	112541	298285	30156	142176
2006	21243	110595	117168	312426	31694	148317
2007	21835	114497	122810	330583	34249	161517
2008	26813	148403	164642	470886	38134	201978
2009	26403	154777	165921	507706	39515	205364
2010	27887	166735	173218	544487	41289	219793
2011	30441	253618	180782	585680	43728	232552
2012	34165	280672	187466	611561	45667	241390
2013	42226	331442	153039	572025	47356	285746

16-5 批发贸易业机构、网点、人员（2013年）

单位：个、人

分　类	Classify	合计 Total			
		法人单位 Constitutional Unit	产业活动单位 Movemental Unit	网点 Branch Shop	人员 Personnel
总计	**Total**	**14137**	**15688**	**42226**	**331442**
一、按登记注册类型分组	Grouped by Registered Kind				
内资企业	Civil Funded Enterprises	14044	15510	15851	214597
国有企业	State-owned Enterprises	199	273	270	12615
集体企业	Collective-owned Enterprises	215	232	231	2558
股份合作企业	Cooperative Enterprises	69	77	83	752
联营企业	Joint Ownership Enterprises	36	37	38	604
有限责任公司	Limited Liability Corporations	5989	6658	6910	97283
股份有限公司	Share-holding Corporations Ltd.	142	179	191	14113
私营企业	Private Enterprises	6495	7119	7180	76931
其他企业	Other Enterprises	899	935	948	9741
港澳台商投资企业	Enterprises with Funds from Hong Kong, Macao &Taiwan	42	59	59	3545
外商投资企业	Foreign Funded Enterprises	51	119	122	8189
个体经济	Individuals			26194	105111
二、按国民经济行业分组	**Grouped by Seetor**				
农、林、牧产品批发	Wholesale of Farm Produce and Livestock Products	860	871	6812	31538
食品、饮料及烟草制品批发	Wholesale of Food, Beverages and Tobaccos	1397	1618	4940	46006
纺织、服装及家庭用品批发	Wholesale of Textiles, Garments and Daily Articles	1027	1338	9368	60037
文化、体育用品及器材批发	Wholesale of Culture, Sports Articles and Equipments	707	861	1740	10662
医药及医疗器材批发	Wholesale of Medicines and Medical Appliances	762	901	1563	50531
矿产品、建材及化工产品批发	Wholesale of Mineral Products, Building Materials and Chemical Products	3306	3483	6217	60528
机械设备、五金交电及电子产品批发	Wholesale of Machinery, Hardwares, Transport Means and Electronic Equipment	4721	5071	8071	56600
贸易经济与代理	Trade Broker and Agency	324	340	368	3240
其他批发	Other Wholesales	1033	1205	3147	12300

Organizations, Establishments and Staff Engaged in Whole-sale Trade（2013）

(unit, person)

城镇 Urban								乡村 Village			
				城区 County							
法人单位 Constitutional Unit	产业活动单位 Movemental Unit	网点 Branch Shop	人员 Personnel	法人单位 Constitutional Unit	产业活动单位 Movemental Unit	网点 Branch Shop	人员 Personnel	法人单位 Constitutional Unit	产业活动单位 Movemental Unit	网点 Branch Shop	人员 Personnel
13304	**14796**	**34589**	**307980**	**12890**	**14300**	**31976**	**297268**	**833**	**892**	**7637**	**23462**
13211	14619	14937	206567	12797	14126	14461	201271	833	891	914	8030
193	258	255	12441	168	206	203	11365	6	15	15	174
190	205	204	2417	165	176	175	2105	25	27	27	141
67	73	79	720	62	63	69	657	2	4	4	32
36	37	38	604	35	35	36	490				
5947	6610	6862	96769	5874	6531	6783	95691	42	48	48	514
141	171	183	13876	135	166	178	13824	1	8	8	237
6368	6967	7005	75732	6179	6743	6798	74069	127	152	175	1199
269	298	311	4008	179	206	219	3070	630	637	637	5733
42	59	59	3545	42	59	59	3545				
51	118	119	8172	51	115	116	8127		1	3	17
		19474	89696			17340	84325			6720	15415
578	588	1776	19150	457	465	828	15768	282	283	5036	12388
951	1167	3825	40791	868	1047	3358	38561	446	451	1115	5215
1015	1311	9286	59731	972	1253	9068	59119	12	27	32	306
705	859	1722	10565	698	850	1663	10241	2	2	18	97
758	887	1474	50315	743	863	1432	49880	4	14	39	216
3260	3414	5761	59043	3183	3330	5165	56741	46	69	456	1485
4705	5055	8006	56199	4661	5001	7870	55567	16	16	55	401
320	336	360	3207	308	323	338	3151	4	4	8	33
1012	1179	2379	8979	1000	1168	2254	8240	21	26	758	3321

16-6 零售贸易业机构、网点、人员（2013年）

单位：个、人

分类	Classify	合计 Total 法人单位 Constitutional Unit	产业活动单位 Movemental Unit	网点 Branch Shop	人员 Personnel
总计	**Total**	**11288**	**15097**	**153039**	**572025**
一、按登记注册类型分组	**Grouped by Registered Kind**				
内资企业	Civil Funded Enterprises	11203	14838	14689	216257
国有企业	State-owned Enterprises	245	429	441	7913
集体企业	Collective-owned Enterprises	210	308	309	3697
股份合作企业	Cooperative Enterprises	104	163	163	1221
联营企业	Joint Ownership Enterprises	50	100	100	649
有限责任公司	Limited Liability Corporations	5081	6762	6899	108143
股份有限公司	Share-holding Corporations Ltd.	134	325	346	7647
私营企业	Private Enterprises	4645	5861	5897	81484
其他企业	Other Enterprises	734	890	534	5503
港澳台商投资企业	Enterprises with Funds from Hong Kong, Macao &Taiwan	37	97	98	11770
外商投资企业	Foreign Funded Enterprises	48	162	168	8446
个体经济	Individuals			138084	335552
二、按国民经济行业分组	**Grouped by Seetor**				
综合零售	Intergrated Retail	856	1359	21735	133227
食品、饮料及烟草制品专门零售	Retail of Food,Beverages and Tobaccos	1082	1394	28981	90402
纺织、服装及日用品专门零售	Special Retail of Textiles,Garments and Daily Consumer Articles	1109	1593	32521	94943
文化、体育用品及器材专门零售	Retail of Culture, Sports Appliances and Equipments	805	980	5439	30527
医药及医疗器材专门零售	Retail of Medicines and Medical Appliances	1188	2286	9385	32218
汽车、摩托车、燃料及零售配件专门零售	Retail of Motor Vehicles, Motorcycles, Fuel and Parts	891	1130	6452	45698
家用电器及电子产品专门零售	Special Retail of Household Electric Appliances and Electronic Products	2686	3185	12104	48006
五金、家具及室内装修材料专门零售	Special Retail of Hardware, Furniture and Decoration Materials	1504	1839	16575	43074
货摊、无店铺及其他零售业	Non-shop and Other Retail	1167	1331	19847	53930

Organizations, Establishments and Staff Engaged in Retail Trade （2013）

(unit,person)

城镇 Urban								乡村 Village			
				城区 County							
法人单位 Constitutional Unit	产业活动单位 Movemental Unit	网点 Branch Shop	人员 Personnel	法人单位 Constitutional Unit	产业活动单位 Movemental Unit	网点 Branch Shop	人员 Personnel	法人单位 Constitutional Unit	产业活动单位 Movemental Unit	网点 Branch Shop	人员 Personnel
10981	**14607**	**132698**	**524884**	**10403**	**13606**	**107004**	**466003**	**307**	**490**	**20341**	**47141**
10896	14351	14172	211831	10318	13354	13134	204683	307	487	517	4426
237	394	406	7337	194	304	308	6539	8	35	35	576
186	276	277	3169	154	208	209	2571	24	32	32	528
103	160	160	1205	98	132	132	1134	1	3	3	16
49	95	95	629	40	73	73	453	1	5	5	20
5005	6644	6759	107008	4898	6473	6575	105082	76	128	140	1135
130	293	314	7418	116	219	230	7019	4	32	32	229
4531	5701	5731	80500	4271	5316	5338	78398	114	160	166	984
655	788	430	4565	547	629	269	3487	79	102	104	938
37	97	98	11770	37	97	98	11768				
48	159	165	8367	48	155	161	8304		3	3	79
		118263	292916			93611	241248			19821	42636
810	1300	17563	125244	709	1148	13177	115111	46	59	4172	7983
1027	1324	25767	83141	931	1179	20196	71357	55	70	3214	7261
1095	1566	31237	92511	1065	1524	24978	80496	14	27	1284	2432
794	963	5034	29605	775	926	4203	27587	11	17	405	922
1157	2214	7908	27908	1055	1983	6602	24182	31	72	1477	4310
818	1002	5721	43110	733	862	5034	40929	73	128	731	2588
2657	3153	11541	46160	2587	3003	10282	42903	29	32	563	1846
1481	1805	15558	40962	1430	1737	12916	35175	23	34	1017	2112

16-7 餐饮业机构、网点、人员（2013年）

单位：个、人

分 类	Classify	合计 Total			
		法人单位 Constitutional Unit	产业活动单位 Movemental Unit	网点 Branch Shop	人员 Personnel
总计	**Total**	**1581**	**2302**	**47356**	**285746**
一、按登记注册类型分组	**Grouped by Type of Registration**				
内资企业	Domestic Funded Enterprises	1544	2024	2077	90418
国有企业	State-owned Enterprises	14	31	31	2450
集体企业	Collective-owned Enterprises	16	26	26	718
股份合作企业	Share-holding Cooperative Enterprises	4	7	7	271
联营企业	Joint Ownership Enterprises	3	4	4	61
有限责任公司	Limited Liability Corporations	544	755	773	41002
股份有限公司	Share-holding Corporations Ltd.	17	56	56	6138
私营企业	Private Enterprises	912	1091	1126	38889
其他企业	Other Enterprises	34	54	54	889
港澳台商投资企业	Enterprises with Funds from Hong Kong, Macao & Taiwan	16	170	170	7995
外商投资企业	Foreign Funded Enterprises	21	108	109	12492
个体经济	Individuals			45000	174841
二、按餐饮业行业分组	**Grouped by Sector of Catering Trade**				
正餐服务	Restaurant	1227	1628	19799	162745
快餐服务	Fast Food	91	307	3658	26080
饮料及冷饮服务	Beverages and Cold Drinks	125	192	1413	10666
其他餐饮服务	Others	138	175	22486	86255

Organizations ,Establishments and Staff Engaged in Catering Trade（2013）

(unit,person)

城镇 Urban								乡村 Village			
				城区 County							
法人单位 Constitutional Unit	产业活动单位 Movemental Unit	网点 Branch Shop	人员 Personnel	法人单位 Constitutional Unit	产业活动单位 Movemental Unit	网点 Branch Shop	人员 Personnel	法人单位 Constitutional Unit	产业活动单位 Movemental Unit	网点 Branch Shop	人员 Personnel
1514	**2222**	**41548**	**264651**	**1414**	**2094**	**35182**	**244189**	**67**	**80**	**5808**	**21095**
1477	1944	1997	88670	1377	1817	1870	85725	67	80	80	1748
13	28	28	2232	11	24	24	2013	1	3	3	218
16	26	26	718	15	21	21	391				
4	7	7	271	3	5	5	246				
3	4	4	61	3	4	4	61				
531	740	758	40476	510	714	732	39578	13	15	15	526
16	54	54	6083	15	53	53	6049	1	2	2	55
868	1041	1076	38128	802	968	1003	36885	44	50	50	761
26	44	44	701	18	28	28	502	8	10	10	188
16	170	170	7995	16	170	170	7995				
21	108	109	12474	21	107	108	12411				18
		39272	155512			33034	138058			5728	19329
1174	1566	17798	153678	1089	1459	15903	145037	53	62	2001	9067
91	305	3552	25540	89	298	3402	24777		2	106	540
123	190	1304	10049	122	189	1204	9603	2	2	109	617
126	161	18894	75384	114	148	14673	64772	12	14	3592	10871

16-8 各区县批发、零售、餐饮业机构、网点、人员（2013年）

Organizations, Branch Shops and Staff of Wholesale,Retail and Catering Trade by Region（2013）

单位：个、人 (unit，person)

分　类	Classify	法人单位 Constitutional Unit	产业活动单位 Movemental Unit	网点 Branch Shop	人员 Personnel
一、批发业	**Wholesale Trade**	**14137**	**15688**	**42226**	**331442**
新城区	Xincheng	1412	1485	11324	53665
碑林区	Beilin	1542	1703	2458	28993
莲湖区	Lianhu	2702	2972	5999	41737
灞桥区	Baqiao	758	804	1536	9740
未央区	Weiyang	3430	4059	6185	116803
雁塔区	Yanta	2809	3015	3444	41125
阎良区	Yanliang	234	243	658	3246
临潼区	Lintong	116	124	812	4846
长安区	Chang'an	198	229	953	6260
蓝田县	Lantian	145	158	3767	8102
周至县	Zhouzhi	468	481	3845	11502
户　县	Huxian	109	121	795	3023
高陵县	Gaoling	214	294	450	2400
二、零售业	**Retail Trade**	**11288**	**15097**	**153039**	**572025**
新城区	Xincheng	1146	1484	12799	49137
碑林区	Beilin	1813	2875	14395	74269
莲湖区	Lianhu	979	1355	11480	47787
灞桥区	Baqiao	638	927	10910	40477
未央区	Weiyang	2424	2821	20308	60559

16-8 续表 continued

单位：个、人 (unit, person)

分类	Classify	法人单位 Constitutional Unit	产业活动单位 Movemental Unit	网点 Branch Shop	人员 Personnel
雁塔区	Yanta	2992	3497	23553	155254
阎良区	Yanliang	156	217	4773	9531
临潼区	Lintong	176	296	9710	24218
长安区	Chang'an	328	537	14806	50740
蓝田县	Lantian	107	149	8441	16330
周至县	Zhouzhi	109	155	9512	19536
户 县	Huxian	195	304	9152	17587
高陵县	Gaoling	225	480	3200	6600
三、餐饮业	**Catering Trade**	**1581**	**2302**	**47356**	**285746**
新城区	Xincheng	105	158	2295	15088
碑林区	Beilin	250	535	3562	44038
莲湖区	Lianhu	172	318	3366	23905
灞桥区	Baqiao	67	82	4109	20499
未央区	Weiyang	157	228	5260	37540
雁塔区	Yanta	577	656	11325	78027
阎良区	Yanliang	20	25	1250	5584
临潼区	Lintong	28	43	2808	10890
长安区	Chang'an	99	129	6062	26890
蓝田县	Lantian	29	32	2377	6888
周至县	Zhouzhi	7	7	1929	5614
户 县	Huxian	29	39	2193	7453
高陵县	Gaoling	41	50	820	3330

16-9 限额以上批发零售贸易企业财务状况（2013年）

单位：万元

分 类	Classify	单位数（个）Number (unit)	资产总计 Total Assets	流动资产合 计 Circulating Funds	固定资产合 计 Total Fixed Assets
总计	**Totai**	**683**	**15263650.1**	**11146256.9**	**1389424.3**
一、批发企业	**Wholesale Enterprises**	**282**	**8058318.0**	**6414368.1**	**382462.0**
1. 按登记注册类型分组	Grouped by Category of Commodities				
内资企业	Domestic Funded Enterprises	272	6835502.0	5472699.0	369721.6
国有	State-owned Enterprises	17	1045367.9	906599.4	92002.5
集体	Collective-owned Enterprises	3	68558.6	34793.2	5282.7
股份合作	Corperative Enterprises				
联营	Joint Ownership Enterprises				
国有联营	State Joint Ownership Enterprises				
集体联营	Collective Joint Ownership Enterprises				
国有与集体联营	Joint State-collective Enterprises				
其他联营	Others Joint Ownership Enterprises				
有限责任公司	Limited Liability Corporrations	171	3812790.3	3242901.7	126466.2
国有独资公司	State Funded Corporations	7	1057343.7	780666.3	23247.7
其他有限责任公司	Other Limited Liability Corporrations	164	2755446.6	2462235.4	103218.5
股份有限公司	Other Limited Liability Corporrations	5	1007098.7	487518.5	114635.5
私营	Other Limited Liability Corporrations	73	898565.7	799466.5	29782.6
私营独资	Private-funded Enterprises	1	1655.7	1604.9	50.8
私营合伙	Private Partnership Enterprises				
私营有限责任公司	Private Limited Liability Corporations	70	865548.8	767798.0	29532.3
私营股份有限公司	Private Share-holding Corporations Ltd.	2	31361.2	30063.6	199.5
其他	Other Enterprises	3	3120.8	1419.7	1552.1
港澳台商投资	Enterprises with Funds from Hong Kong, Macao &Taiwan	4	101353.8	92806.8	7007.9
外商投资	Foreign Funded Enterprises	6	1121462.2	848862.3	5732.5
2. 按国民经济行业分组	Grouped by Sector				

Financial Stares of Enterprises above Designated Size in Wholesale and Retail（2013）

(10 000 yuan)

固定资产原价 Original Value of Fixed Assets	累计折旧 Accumulated Depreciation	负债合计 Total Liabilities	流动负债合计 Circulating Liabilities	非流动负债 Non-Circulating Liabilities	所有者权益合计 Total Owners' Equities	实收资本 Paid in Capital	营业收入 Total Revenue	主营业务收入 Revenue from Principal Business
2027850.9	**647492.8**	**11686904.3**	**11210081.2**	**487901.5**	**3576745.8**	**1975525.0**	**37857908.2**	**37477659.8**
601139.7	**222103.7**	**6563836.3**	**6435999.1**	**142653.1**	**1494481.7**	**977295.2**	**24315071.2**	**24202997.7**
584853.1	218557.5	5541286.1	5413553.5	142548.5	1294215.9	821887.2	21056230.9	20945081.7
139601.5	47599.1	635534.8	631240.3	9514.4	409833.1	48775.4	3027435.5	3003195.2
8334.5	3313.6	70950.8	43216.6	27734.2	-2392.2	4658.0	8531.5	8531.5
216967.7	93661.5	3326616.3	3253743.0	73237.9	486174.0	338860.2	12525105.9	12467635.2
37202.5	13954.8	954334.3	947563.2	6771.1	103009.4	44235.4	2405720.5	2402953.6
179765.2	79706.7	2372282.0	2306179.8	66466.8	383164.6	294624.8	10119385.4	10064681.6
158413.1	43777.6	730563.4	724615.8	5947.6	276535.3	278229.5	3379881.6	3356526.7
59373.3	30094.8	777033.3	760150.3	26114.4	121532.4	150691.5	2093321.0	2087237.7
120.7	69.9	1595.2	1595.2		60.5	50.0	4180.9	4180.9
59420.6	29892.4	753110.6	737375.3	24966.7	112438.2	141841.4	1987569.7	1981436.4
332.0	132.5	22327.5	21179.8	1147.7	9033.7	8800.1	101570.4	101570.4
1663.0	110.9	587.5	587.5		2533.3	672.6	21955.4	21955.4
8568.1	1560.2	87920.4	87920.4		13433.4	4073.6	349286.1	349286.1
7718.5	1986.0	934629.8	934525.2	104.6	186832.4	151334.4	2909554.2	2908629.9

16-9 续表1

单位：万元

分 类	Classify	营业成本 Total Cost	主营业务成本 Cost of Principal Business	营业税金及附加 Taxs and Other Changes	主营业务税金及附加 Taxs and Other Changes on Principal Business
总计	**Totai**	**34551413.6**	**34391541.3**	**245641.1**	**241977.8**
一、批发企业	**Wholesale Enterprises**	**22984542.0**	**22902546.0**	**122829.3**	**122434.9**
1. 按登记注册类型分组	Grouped by Category of Commodities				
内资企业	Domestic Funded Enterprises	19766116.2	19684630.6	122080.9	121686.9
国有	State-owned Enterprises	2715257.3	2698606.6	59312.8	59305.3
集体	Collective-owned Enterprises	6997.4	6997.4	46.3	46.3
股份合作	Corperative Enterprises				
联营	Joint Ownership Enterprises				
国有联营	State Joint Ownership Enterprises				
集体联营	Collective Joint Ownership Enterprises				
国有与集体联营	Joint State-collective Enterprises				
其他联营	Others Joint Ownership Enterprises				
有限责任公司	Limited Liability Corprorations	11841124.5	11797794.2	51913.9	51842.6
国有独资公司	State Funded Corporations	2313849.5	2311221.9	1331.9	1317.2
其他有限责任公司	Other Limited Liability Corprorations	9527275.0	9486572.3	50582.0	50525.4
股份有限公司	Other Limited Liability Corprorations	3225116.5	3205280.8	2302.8	2235.2
私营	Other Limited Liability Corprorations	1957460.7	1955791.8	8294.2	8046.6
私营独资	Private-funded Enterprises	3973.0	3973.0	1.2	1.2
私营合伙	Private Partnership Enterprises				
私营有限责任公司	Private Limited Liability Corporations	1863521.3	1861852.4	7846.3	7598.7
私营股份有限公司	Private Share-holding Corporations Ltd.	89966.4	89966.4	446.7	446.7
其他	Other Enterprises	20159.8	20159.8	210.9	210.9
港澳台商投资	Enterprises with Funds from Hong Kong, Macao &Taiwan	316795.8	316795.8	547.6	547.6
外商投资	Foreign Funded Enterprises	2901630.0	2901119.6	200.8	200.4
2. 按国民经济行业分组	Grouped by Sector				

continued 1

(10 000 yuan)

销售费用 Sale Expenses	管理费用 Management Expenses	财务费用 Financial Expenses	营业利润 Business Profits	利润总额 Total Profits	应付职工薪酬 Salary Payable	本年应交增值税 Value Added Tax Payable
1125992.3	**594095.8**	**158823.0**	**1202558.3**	**994399.1**	**544580.8**	**508200.7**
435512.1	**247919.9**	**54136.4**	**478124.9**	**442360.8**	**228739.8**	**251943.0**
406967.7	241766.8	55273.5	474205.5	435539.4	212476.0	245605.9
49816.6	51566.9	3916.5	147852.0	149665.5	41648.6	44856.6
756.2	1212.7	1.1	-139.6	155.4	539.2	11.9
233144.5	139615.0	25928.3	242803.6	230492.0	89150.9	119216.6
49141.8	32258.5	118.3	17675.0	18912.1	14649.1	7973.3
184002.7	107356.5	25810.0	225128.6	211579.9	74501.8	111243.3
85233.6	22492.9	10207.5	32305.7	31269.4	58692.4	61953.2
37763.6	26714.4	15120.3	50317.0	22890.3	21963.4	19532.4
120.9	19.3	64.4	2.1	10.5	52.8	12.6
35524.8	25973.7	14864.4	42045.9	18306.8	13797.0	19379.2
2117.9	721.4	191.5	8269.0	4573.0	8113.6	140.6
253.2	164.9	99.8	1066.8	1066.8	481.5	35.2
22840.7	2960.6	4.1	6137.3	6133.7	13813.1	5101.7
5703.7	3192.5	-1141.2	-2217.9	687.7	2450.7	1235.4

16-9 续表2

单位：万元

分 类	Classify	单位数（个）Number (unit)	资产总计 Total Assets	流动资产合计 Circulating Funds	固定资产合计 Total Fixed Assets
农、林、牧产品批发	Wholesale of Agricultural,Forestry and Animal Husbandry Products	3	77126.9	40469.1	7173.4
食品、饮料及烟草制品批发	Wholesale of food Beverages and Tobaccos	26	568241.2	441361.9	80262.3
纺织、服装及家庭服务器批发	Wholesale of Textiles, Garments and Daily Articles	23	472936.5	432864.7	29079.7
文化、体育用品及器材批发	Wholesale of Culture, Sports Applionces and Equipments	14	216988.2	128111.6	11312.5
医药及医疗器材批发	Wholesale of Medicines and Medical Appliances	42	673428.7	629294.0	8490.7
矿产品、建材及化工产品批发	Wholesale of Mineral Products, Building Materials and Chemical Products	108	4957164.1	3709544.5	217237.8
机械设备、五金产品及电子产品批发	Wholesale of Machinery, Hardware, and Electronic Equipment	61	1073316.3	1016752.3	26337.2
贸易经纪与代理	Trade Borker and Agency	2	10749.8	10051.1	356.3
其他批发	Other wholesale not Classified Elsewhere	3	8366.3	5918.9	2212.1
二、零售企业	**Retail Trade**	**401**	**7205332.1**	**4731888.8**	**1006962.3**
1. 按登记注册类型分组	Grouped by Category of Commodities				
内资	Domestic Funded Enterprises	363	5548693.2	3665553.6	857714.6
国有	State-owned Enterprises	12	171556.1	131839.3	35661.3
集体	Collective-owned Enterprises	24	13151.2	7120.3	4387.9
股份合作	Share-holding Cooperative Enterprises				
联营	Joint Ownership Enterprises	1	242.3	194.3	48.0
国有联营	State Joint Ownership Enterprises				
集体联营	Collective Joint Ownership Enterprises	1	242.3	194.3	48.0
国有与集体联营	Joint State-collective Enterprises				
其他联营	Others Joint Ownership Enterprises				
有限责任公司	Limited Liability Corporations	227	3249138.2	2180462.0	462809.2
国有独资	State Funded Corporations	4	70843.1	52246.3	18478.0

continued 2

(10 000 yuan)

固定资产原价 Original Value of Fixed Assets	累计折旧 Accumulated Depreciation	负债合计 Total Liabilities	流动负债合计 Circulating Liabilities	非流动负债 Non-Circulating Liabilities	所有者权益合计 Total Owners' Equities	实收资本 Paid in Capital	营业收入 Total Revenue	主营业务收入 Revenue from Principal Business
10713.9	3802.3	76021.4	48287.2	27734.2	1105.5	9098.0	12703.2	12703.2
119302.6	39044.9	149836.1	138027.6	11808.4	418405.1	39447.3	1585414.6	1583829.9
63765.0	34916.3	417712.4	413529.1	4183.3	55224.1	37911.4	2168276.8	2161098.9
15384.6	6554.1	133187.2	126537.2	6650.0	83801.0	44261.0	239827.5	237372.2
16712.8	8222.1	593741.4	586657.6	7448.4	79687.3	48646.4	1409063.4	1404273.5
327593.4	110355.7	4194899.5	4127877.4	76384.8	762264.6	729584.0	16744012.8	16671731.9
44383.0	18492.3	984205.1	982670.2	6623.6	89111.2	63796.0	2096815.4	2073063.4
426.0	69.7	9556.4	9236.0	320.4	1193.4	1251.1	30861.7	30834.5
2858.4	646.3	4676.8	3176.8	1500.0	3689.5	3300.0	28090.8	28090.2
1426711.2	**425389.1**	**5123068.0**	**4774082.1**	**345248.4**	**2082264.1**	**998229.8**	**13542837.0**	**13274662.1**
1212296.7	360222.3	4105140.6	3752087.4	349315.7	1443552.6	650781.8	10226972.0	10042866.3
41474.2	6426.3	132793.7	79558.0	53235.7	38762.4	4127.6	263138.1	259066.4
4566.3	970.0	11329.9	9902.3	743.8	1821.3	3489.5	112697.1	112697.1
147.6	99.6	118.5	118.5		123.8	50.0	3409.2	3409.2
147.6	99.6	118.5	118.5		123.8	50.0	3409.2	3409.2
643282.0	184118.4	2395865.7	2315942.7	77456.8	853272.5	446965.2	6843756.7	6711024.5
25545.6	8132.6	58155.9	57751.9	404.0	12687.2	4885.4	89006.0	87926.1

16-9 续表3

单位：万元

分类	Classify	营业成本 Total Cost	主营业务成本 Cost of Principal Business	营业税金及附加 Taxs and Other Changes	主营业务税金及附加 Taxs and Other Changes on Principal Business
农、林、牧产品批发	Wholesale of Agricultural,Forestry and Animal Husbandry Products	10493.1	10493.1	220.3	220.3
食品、饮料及烟草制品批发	Wholesale of food Beverages and Tobaccos	1189022.9	1189021.0	69206.3	69206.3
纺织、服装及家庭服务器批发	Wholesale of Textiles, Garments and Daily Articles	1976530.3	1973963.0	23977.9	23977.9
文化、体育用品及器材批发	Wholesale of Culture, Sports Applionces and Equipments	216745.4	216661.3	379.3	358.4
医药及医疗器材批发	Wholesale of Medicines and Medical Appliances	1333094.7	1333013.9	1980.3	1942.1
矿产品、建材及化工产品批发	Wholesale of Mineral Products, Building Materials and Chemical Products	16247998.0	16185311.6	24520.0	24185.4
机械设备、五金产品及电子产品批发	Wholesale of Machinery, Hardware, and Electronic Equipment	1957585.9	1941010.5	2514.9	2514.2
贸易经纪与代理	Trade Borker and Agency	27400.7	27400.7	2.3	2.3
其他批发	Other wholesale not Classified Elsewhere	25671.0	25670.9	28.0	28.0
二、零售企业	**Retail Trade**	**11566871.6**	**11488995.3**	**122811.8**	**119542.9**
1. 按登记注册类型分组	Grouped by Category of Commodities				
内资	Domestic Funded Enterprises	8742743.1	8676299.1	107714.5	105139.2
国有	State-owned Enterprises	227122.0	226649.6	1656.5	1640.7
集体	Collective-owned Enterprises	101768.1	101768.1	4958.2	4958.0
股份合作	Share-holding Cooperative Enterprises				
联营	Joint Ownership Enterprises	3069.9	3069.9	5.5	5.5
国有联营	State Joint Ownership Enterprises				
集体联营	Collective Joint Ownership Enterprises	3069.9	3069.9	5.5	5.5
国有与集体联营	Joint State-collective Enterprises				
其他联营	Others Joint Ownership Enterprises				
有限责任公司	Limited Liability Corporations	5830577.9	5780388.4	76398.4	73954.5
国有独资	State Funded Corporations	72708.1	72672.2	261.3	184.2

continued 3

(10 000 yuan)

销售费用 Sale Expenses	管理费用 Management Expenses	财务费用 Financial Expenses	营业利润 Business Profits	利润总额 Total Profits	应付职工薪酬 Salary Payable	本年应交增值税 Value Added Tax Payable
1035.9	1312.3	169.2	-185.0	166.1	781.5	246.7
72808.9	60955.3	4909.9	188744.4	190387.9	56585.2	41828.4
52674.3	26545.4	1245.9	87113.6	70059.1	35206.9	19201.1
11055.0	7155.3	-285.3	4288.5	4394.7	5929.6	1632.0
29533.1	19566.4	10604.6	14010.5	14334.8	17985.0	6352.3
194705.7	99925.4	34291.2	154491.0	154001.6	84246.5	159458.7
69465.9	31803.1	3092.1	28810.2	8165.5	27163.0	22859.6
2534.9	467.0	17.1	439.7	439.3	518.4	10.3
1698.4	189.7	91.7	412.0	411.8	323.7	283.9
690480.2	**346175.9**	**104686.6**	**724433.4**	**552038.3**	**315841.0**	**256257.7**
465163.1	270465.5	82785.0	567644.7	428021.7	239553.0	183159.6
13600.7	16043.4	1045.8	3989.3	3301.5	15303.6	9224.4
1415.3	3278.5	103.4	1246.4	1245.7	2133.8	568.7
243.0	79.3	0.2	11.3	9.7	85.0	50.0
243.0	79.3	0.2	11.3	9.7	85.0	50.0
311633.6	165136.9	35001.3	419897.0	294429.8	159749.9	143769.3
9388.0	6407.3	-95.3	357.6	683.4	8743.1	4911.8

16-9 续表4

单位：万元

分　类	Classify	单位数（个）Number (unit)	资产总计 Total Assets	流动资产合　计 Circulating Funds	固定资产合　计 Total Fixed Assets
其他有限责任公司	Other Limited Liability Corporations	223	3178295.1	2128215.7	444331.2
股份有限公司	Share-holding Corporations Ltd.	9	1304515.9	783535.6	263408.4
私营	Private Enterprises	88	809065.2	562024.9	91077.6
私营独资	Private-funded Enterprises	1	1209.4	491.0	88.2
私营合伙	Private Partnership Enterprises	2	1018.0	819.3	198.7
私营有限责任公司	Private Limited Liability Corporations	77	761492.5	524887.6	86042.2
私营股份有限公司	Private Share-holding Corporations Ltd.	8	45345.3	35827.0	4748.5
其他	Other	2	1024.3	377.2	322.2
港澳台商投资	Enterprises with Funds from Hong Kong, Macao &Taiwan	19	1100634.1	769998.6	72219.7
外商投资	Foreign Funded Enterprises	19	556004.8	296336.6	77028.0
2. 按国民经济行业分组	Grouped by Sector				
综合零售	Integrated Retail	93	2540453.9	1588720.5	399610.5
食品、饮料及烟草制品专门零售	Food, Beverages and Tobaccos Special Retail Trade	18	615527.4	395206.7	149899.7
纺织、服装及日用品专门零售	Special Retail of Textiles,Garments and Daily Consumer Articles	23	340971.5	113455.6	126031.4
文化、体育用品及器材专门零售	Retail of Culture,Sports Appliances and Equipments	19	219148.6	195805.0	14733.4
医药及医疗器材专门零售	Retail of Medicines and Medical Appliances	16	166220.8	157523.9	5389.8
汽车、摩托车、燃料及零配件专门零售	Retail of Motor Vehicles,Motorcycles, Fuel and Parts	160	2410899.1	1645350.3	185473.2
家用电器及电子产品专门零售	Special Retail of Household Electric Appliances and Electronic Products	37	523282.4	409640.2	42191.8
五金、家具及室内装饰材料专门零售	Special Retail of Hardware,Furniture and Decoration Materials	27	359811.3	204136.4	80397.2
货摊、无店铺及其他零售业	Non-shop and Other Retail	8	29017.1	22050.2	3235.3

continued 4

(10 000 yuan)

固定资产原价 Original Value of Fixed Assets	累计折旧 Accumulated Depreciation	负债合计 Total Liabilities	流动负债合计 Circulating Liabilities	非流动负债 Non-Circulating Liabilities	所有者权益合计 Total Owners' Equities	实收资本 Paid in Capital	营业收入 Total Revenue	主营业务收入 Revenue from Principal Business
617736.4	175985.8	2337709.8	2258190.8	77052.8	840585.3	442079.8	6754750.7	6623098.4
382930.6	119735.2	1026919.5	835005.4	191332.8	277596.4	81989.5	1061608.6	1027675.9
139465.6	48764.6	537696.3	511184.4	26505.7	271368.9	113555.0	1938478.1	1925109.0
128.5	40.3	23.5	23.5		1185.9	63.0	4179.2	4179.2
242.5	43.8	1208.8	1208.8		-190.8	130.0	5341.7	5341.7
131579.5	45537.3	503166.2	476839.3	26320.7	258326.3	108652.0	1773312.6	1759943.5
7515.1	3143.2	33297.8	33112.8	185.0	12047.5	4710.0	155644.6	155644.6
430.4	108.2	417.0	376.1	40.9	607.3	605.0	3884.2	3884.2
106506.0	34286.3	704177.3	739380.6	-35203.3	396456.8	130989.9	1775819.9	1712178.2
107908.5	30880.5	313750.1	282614.1	31136.0	242254.7	216458.1	1540045.1	1519617.6
563166.5	165397.8	1806714.7	1721612.7	85065.4	733739.2	331813.3	3096544.8	2940104.5
213970.1	64070.4	519983.6	399078.0	120898.6	95543.8	29535.9	216355.5	199506.0
170543.1	44563.5	156881.9	127777.0	28523.6	184089.6	80839.8	1071295.5	1061515.1
23209.4	9541.0	160529.1	143199.0	14864.0	58619.5	41988.1	321159.5	320041.7
9457.0	4151.8	154778.9	151931.9	2846.9	11441.9	18480.5	198434.0	196372.2
258047.6	75092.9	1838022.2	1788333.1	49689.1	572876.9	381401.8	5420387.2	5373172.4
64273.2	22096.8	217777.2	214345.4	2784.6	305505.2	57239.1	1536808.9	1513026.5
118229.1	37831.9	252142.0	212455.3	39687.5	107669.3	51140.9	1577450.3	1566151.8
5815.2	2643.0	16238.4	15349.7	888.7	12778.7	5790.4	104400.3	104271.9

16-9 续表5

单位：万元

分 类	Classify	营业成本 Total Cost	主营业务成本 Cost of Principal Business	营业税金及附加 Taxs and Other Changes	主营业务税金及附加 Taxs and Other Changes on Principal Business
其他有限责任公司	Other Limited Liability Corporations	5757869.8	5707716.2	76137.1	73770.3
股份有限公司	Share-holding Corporations Ltd.	926118.3	912480.2	4829.7	4829.0
私营	Private Enterprises	1650710.3	1648566.3	19864.4	19749.7
私营独资	Private-funded Enterprises	3433.5	3433.5	60.4	60.4
私营合伙	Private Partnership Enterprises	4986.2	4986.2	58.7	58.7
私营有限责任公司	Private Limited Liability Corporations	1520593.6	1518449.6	19109.3	18994.6
私营股份有限公司	Private Share-holding Corporations Ltd.	121697.0	121697.0	636.0	636.0
其他	Other	3376.6	3376.6	1.8	1.8
港澳台商投资	Enterprises with Funds from Hong Kong, Macao &Taiwan	1481978.0	1477782.4	9307.9	8758.3
外商投资	Foreign Funded Enterprises	1342150.5	1334913.8	5789.4	5645.4
2. 按国民经济行业分组	Grouped by Sector				
综合零售	Integrated Retail	2470731.9	2465680.2	30767.0	29359.2
食品、饮料及烟草制品专门零售	Food, Beverages and Tobaccos Special Retail Trade	186565.7	171548.2	507.3	507.2
纺织、服装及日用品专门零售	Special Retail of Textiles,Garments and Daily Consumer Articles	879546.0	873713.4	6886.4	6837.5
文化、体育用品及器材专门零售	Retail of Culture,Sports Appliances and Equipments	278519.8	278472.5	5162.2	5090.1
医药及医疗器材专门零售	Retail of Medicines and Medical Appliances	167652.0	166847.1	469.7	469.7
汽车、摩托车、燃料及零配件专门零售	Retail of Motor Vehicles,Motorcycles, Fuel and Parts	4968127.3	4959334.3	8822.4	8477.2
家用电器及电子产品专门零售	Special Retail of Household Electric Appliances and Electronic Products	1341804.6	1302080.0	21291.7	21021.6
五金、家具及室内装饰材料专门零售	Special Retail of Hardware,Furniture and Decoration Materials	1200123.9	1197519.2	48527.9	47403.2
货摊、无店铺及其他零售业	Non-shop and Other Retail	73800.4	73800.4	377.2	377.2

continued 5

销售费用 Sale Expenses	管理费用 Managenment Expenses	财务费用 Financial Expenses	营业利润 Business Profits	利润总额 Total Profits	应付职工薪酬 Salary Payable	本年应交增值税 Value Added Tax Payable
302245.6	158729.6	35096.6	419539.4	293746.4	151006.8	138857.5
44695.4	35564.7	32061.8	32146.9	33842.9	15420.2	13014.6
93305.3	50337.6	14563.1	110152.3	94990.6	46675.6	16532.6
160.9	234.9	3.2	286.3	286.3	168.8	37.6
201.6	235.6		-140.4	-75.1	298.4	74.7
87648.0	44100.1	14319.2	87886.5	72698.3	42920.0	14488.2
5294.8	5767.0	240.7	22119.9	22081.1	3238.4	1932.1
269.8	25.1	9.4	201.5	201.5	139.9	
122710.6	42535.0	13891.5	108370.1	76273.5	40403.9	45231.1
102606.5	33175.4	8010.1	48418.6	47743.1	35879.1	27867.0
297835.3	141372.5	22470.7	134594.5	130396.2	134917.0	67662.6
17846.4	10295.6	16136.8	-1087.9	912.3	5157.7	4095.6
63707.2	14673.5	2955.1	103733.8	97118.9	16945.6	10933.5
18639.1	12690.8	2897.4	3285.5	3133.3	14802.8	2977.2
19177.5	7689.4	1026.9	3145.8	3603.1	17359.3	5156.0
161405.2	94402.5	48974.8	141207.9	112343.4	87548.7	102891.7
86731.4	31768.9	1944.0	54514.0	43134.9	23805.2	32167.5
20446.3	28090.9	8148.1	264792.2	141156.9	12182.5	28610.6
4691.8	5191.8	132.8	20247.6	20239.3	3122.2	1763.0

16-10 限额以上住宿和餐饮企业主要财务状况（2013年）

单位：万元

分 类	Classify	单位数（个）Number (unit)	资产总计 Total Assets	流动资产合计 Circulating Funds	固定资产合计 Total Fixed Assets
总计	**Total**	**536**	**2543644.8**	**792428.0**	**1168548.0**
一、住宿业	**Hotel Services**	**217**	**1822741.2**	**463970.8**	**1016332.9**
1.按登记注册类型分组	Grouped by Type of Registration				
内资	Domestic Funded Enterprises	204	1565686.5	403062.8	847913.3
国有	State-owned Enterprises	31	136657.5	25566.3	69168.6
集体	Collective-owned Enterprises	3	4314.7	394.0	1611.6
股份合作	Cooperative Enterprises				
联营	Joint Ownership Enterprises				
国有联营	State Joint Ownership Enterprises				
集体联营	Collective Joint Ownership Enterprises				
国有与集体联营	Joint State-collective Enterprises				
其他联营	Others Joint Ownership Enterprises				
有限责任公司	Limited Liability Corporations	114	1198376.5	286214.3	693953.0
国有独资公司	State Sole Funded Corporations	4	58993.4	4659.9	45510.3
其他有限责任公司	Other Limited Liability Corporations	110	1139383.1	281554.4	648442.7
股份有限公司	Share-holding Corporations Ltd.	2	9206.8	1422.6	7541.4
私营	Private Enterprises	53	216805.6	89423.6	75355.3
私营独资	Private-funded Enterprises	4	1321.7	611.8	422.5
私营合伙	Private Partnership Enterprises	1	430.0	345.2	84.8
私营有限责任公司	Private Limited Liability Corporations	46	211081.3	87676.5	74820.2
私营股份有限公司	Private Share-holding Corporations Ltd.	2	3972.6	790.1	27.8
其他	Other Enterprises	1	325.4	42.0	283.4
港澳台商投资	Enterprises with Funds from Hong Kong, Macao &Taiwan	5	142690.7	30224.0	90757.5
外商投资	Foreign Funded Enterprises	8	114364.0	30684.0	77662.1
2.按国民经济行业分组	Grouped by Sector				
旅游饭店	Tourist Hotel	175	1727881.9	412302.5	994564.2
一般旅馆	Normal Hotel	36	49500.3	23718.7	14842.2
其他住宿业	Others	6	45359.0	27949.6	6926.5

Finacial Status of Catering Eenterprises Above Designated Size（2013）

(10 000 yuan)

固定资产原价 Original Value of Fixed Assets	累计折旧 Accumulated Depreciation	负债合计 Total Liabilities	流动负债合计 Circulating Liabilities	非流动负债 Non-Circulating Liabilities	所有者权益合计 Total Owners' Equities	实收资本 Paid in Capital	营业收入 Total Revenue	主营业务收入 Revenue from Principal Business
1757178.9	**593866.4**	**1939186.9**	**1427271.4**	**476946.5**	**604457.9**	**845239.8**	**1198025.3**	**1181695.9**
1479688.2	**468168.7**	**1468561.1**	**997623.1**	**438803.9**	**354180.1**	**636348.3**	**526785.0**	**519565.9**
1167945.2	324845.3	1210127.9	902717.3	275276.5	355558.6	521420.0	430543.3	425235.9
132138.9	67326.1	113134.2	54662.7	32928.2	23523.3	50434.3	61305.2	60134.9
3204.1	1592.5	1749.4	106.9	1642.5	2565.3	2311.8	3277.7	2156.2
902220.4	208683.1	925141.5	736329.9	182501.3	273235.0	377034.3	283389.0	280725.4
82291.9	36781.6	58281.5	42482.5	15799.0	711.9	29693.3	14198.2	14190.0
819928.5	171901.5	866860.0	693847.4	166702.3	272523.1	347341.0	269190.8	266535.4
10791.6	3250.2	7450.0	7450.0		1756.8	2185.5	4490.5	4490.5
119292.4	43979.0	162347.4	104142.8	58204.5	54458.2	89434.1	77932.2	77580.2
649.6	227.1	795.2	795.2		526.5	988.8	1340.9	1340.9
106.0	21.2	220.0	220.0		210.0	200.0	240.6	240.6
113491.7	43713.4	159217.3	101562.8	57654.4	51864.0	85337.2	75092.1	74740.1
45.1	17.3	2114.9	1564.8	550.1	1857.7	2908.1	1258.6	1258.6
297.8	14.4	305.4	25.0		20.0	20.0	148.7	148.7
154648.7	63891.2	95237.7	49424.7	45813.0	47453.0	56353.3	36851.7	36570.6
157094.3	79432.2	163195.5	45481.1	117714.4	-48831.5	58575.0	59390.0	57759.4
1442858.5	453063.8	1396210.0	928727.1	435629.2	331671.9	592264.4	475451.8	468301.5
23654.2	13855.9	36415.9	34770.8	1364.7	13084.4	29583.9	42536.0	42082.7
3175.5	1249.0	35935.2	34125.2	1810.0	9423.8	14500.0	8797.2	8681.7

16-10 续表1

单位：万元

分 类	Classify	营业成本 Total Cost	主营业务成本 Cost of Principal Business
总计	**Total**	**504466.8**	**498900.5**
一、住宿业	**Hotel Services**	**178373.4**	**175739.6**
1.按登记注册类型分组	Grouped by Type of Registration		
内资	Domestic Funded Enterprises	146708.3	144747.2
国有	State-owned Enterprises	26158.8	25444.2
集体	Collective-owned Enterprises	2256.5	1814.7
股份合作	Cooperative Enterprises		
联营	Joint Ownership Enterprises		
国有联营	State Joint Ownership Enterprises		
集体联营	Collective Joint Ownership Enterprises		
国有与集体联营	Joint State-collective Enterprises		
其他联营	Others Joint Ownership Enterprises		
有限责任公司	Limited Liability Corporations	87121.7	86333.7
国有独资公司	State Sole Funded Corporations	3966.1	3965.1
其他有限责任公司	Other Limited Liability Corporations	83155.6	82368.6
股份有限公司	Share-holding Corporations Ltd.	1151.6	1151.6
私营	Private Enterprises	29976.1	29959.4
私营独资	Private-funded Enterprises	751.3	751.3
私营合伙	Private Partnership Enterprises	186.2	186.2
私营有限责任公司	Private Limited Liability Corporations	28492.7	28476.0
私营股份有限公司	Private Share-holding Corporations Ltd.	545.9	545.9
其他	Other Enterprises	43.6	43.6
港澳台商投资	Enterprises with Funds from Hong Kong, Macao &Taiwan	13598.9	13457.4
外商投资	Foreign Funded Enterprises	18066.2	17535.0
2.按国民经济行业分组	Grouped by Sector		
旅游饭店	Tourist Hotel	160234.8	157609.5
一般旅馆	Normal Hotel	16438.5	16430.0
其他住宿业	Others	1700.1	1700.1

continued 1

(10 000 yuan)

营业税金及附加 Taxs and Other Charges	主营业务税金及附加 Taxs and Other Changes on Principal Business	销售费用 Sale Expenses	管理费用 Management Expenses	财务费用 Financial Expenses	营业利润 Business Profits	利润总额 Total Profits	应付职工薪酬 Salary Payable	本年应交所得税 Value Added Tax Payable
64259.7	**63690.5**	**419058.5**	**234181.6**	**27730.9**	**-49804.1**	**-44458.8**	**283688.3**	**9475.5**
28696.4	**28139.6**	**180034.6**	**162657.9**	**20406.6**	**-43688.0**	**-37769.8**	**136524.1**	**3688.5**
23725.5	23209.9	155274.3	134767.4	18389.8	-48602.9	-42693.2	115301.1	1415.2
3043.4	3043.4	16482.6	16740.5	2767.2	-3896.0	-3305.1	18520.7	783.3
174.3	131.6	197.0	355.1	15.4	279.4	372.4	504.9	78.7
16036.0	15563.1	109723.6	92298.2	12757.8	-34819.5	-30397.9	77611.3	511.3
776.3	776.3	5563.8	6973.6	1111.3	-4192.0	-3123.7	5669.7	
15259.7	14786.8	104159.8	85324.6	11646.5	-30627.5	-27274.2	71941.6	511.3
251.6	251.6	2339.2	600.0	5.0	145.3	137.3	1672.9	
4212.0	4212.0	26471.9	24728.6	2844.2	-10303.8	-9499.9	16899.8	41.4
76.5	76.5	485.2	145.9	23.8	-141.8	-145.5	596.8	2.7
5.6	5.6	13.0	18.0	8.5	9.3	9.3	60.0	2.3
4077.0	4077.0	25181.2	24349.6	2750.3	-9761.9	-8893.2	15844.9	36.1
52.9	52.9	792.5	215.1	61.6	-409.4	-470.5	398.1	0.3
8.2	8.2	60.0	45.0	0.2	-8.3		91.5	
1723.2	1723.2	10622.5	11716.2	596.7	-1423.4	-1356.0	7314.6	163.4
3247.7	3206.5	14137.8	16174.3	1420.1	6338.3	6279.4	13908.4	2109.9
25914.0	25357.2	163678.3	147133.4	19270.0	-41069.8	-37986.5	123525.5	3513.2
2294.6	2294.6	11248.1	11626.0	943.6	-27.8	70.6	10716.9	175.3
487.8	487.8	5108.2	3898.5	193.0	-2590.4	146.1	2231.7	

16-10 续表2

单位：万元

分 类	Classify	单位数（个） Number (unit)	资产总计 Total Assets	流动资产合计 Circulating Funds	固定资产合计 Total Fixed Assets
二、餐饮业	**Catering Trade**	**319**	**720903.6**	**328457.2**	**152215.1**
1.按登记注册类型分组	Grouped by Type of Registration				
内资	Domestic Funded Enterprises	304	557746.1	272561.7	102906.9
国有	State-owned Enterprises	3	5902.9	1766.6	4036.3
集体	Collective-owned Enterprises	1	174.5	75.0	29.2
股份合作	Cooperative Enterprises				
联营	Joint Ownership Enterprises				
国有联营	State Joint Ownership Enterprises				
集体联营	Collective Joint Ownership Enterprises				
国有与集体联营	Joint State-collective Enterprises				
其他联营	Others Joint Ownership Enterprises				
有限责任公司	Limited Liability Corporations	174	342153.7	173614.5	62061.5
国有独资公司	State Sole Funded Corporations	3	4785.7	1831.8	2923.3
其他有限责任公司	Other Limited Liability Corporations	171	337368.0	171782.7	59138.2
股份有限公司	Share-holding Corporations Ltd.	4	101970.3	38129.8	16174.9
私营	Private Enterprises	119	106597.2	58554.7	20438.1
私营独资	Private-funded Enterprises	13	3318.1	1090.7	918.6
私营合伙	Private Partnership Enterprises	1	174.0	5.5	141.0
私营有限责任公司	Private Limited Liability Corporations	102	102287.4	56750.0	19342.5
私营股份有限公司	Private Share-holding Corporations Ltd.	3	817.7	708.5	36.0
其他	Other Enterprises	3	947.5	421.1	166.9
港澳台商投资	Enterprises with Funds from Hong Kong, Macao &Taiwan	7	100496.3	36500.6	32181.2
外商投资	Foreign Funded Enterprises	8	62661.2	19394.9	17127.0
2.按国民经济行业分	Grouped by Sdctor				
正餐服务	Dinner	308	569753.0	277362.1	116154.6
快餐服务	Fast Food	10	113294.9	43938.9	35753.4
饮料及冷饮服务	Beverages and Cold Drinks				
其他餐饮业	Other Catering Services	1	37855.7	7156.2	307.1

continued 2

(10 000 yuan)

固定资产原价 Original Value of Fixed Assets	累计折旧 Accumulated Depreciation	负债合计 Total Liabilities	流动负债合计 Circulating Liabilities	非流动负债 Non-Circulating Liabilities	所有者权益合计 Total Owners' Equities	实收资本 Paid in Capital	营业收入 Total Revenue	主营业务收入 Revenue from Principal Business
277490.7	**125697.7**	**470625.8**	**429648.3**	**38142.6**	**250277.8**	**208891.5**	**671240.3**	**662130.0**
193472.9	90987.0	362900.8	328779.8	31385.4	194845.3	172145.8	490225.4	488702.3
4644.4	608.1	3609.1	984.8	2624.3	2293.8	2067.0	5445.5	5445.5
36.0	6.8	165.4	165.4		9.1	5.0	577.2	577.2
113454.5	51553.5	237509.1	211440.9	22207.8	104644.6	114693.3	296571.8	295374.5
4544.6	1621.3	5476.1	5476.1		-690.4	2100.0	4033.9	4033.1
108909.9	49932.2	232033.0	205964.8	22207.8	105335.0	112593.3	292537.9	291341.4
29292.5	13249.4	28814.0	27589.2	1226.0	73156.3	25754.6	49618.0	49361.7
45390.7	25081.3	91580.8	87377.1	5327.3	15016.4	29462.9	132528.3	132458.8
1645.7	727.1	2191.2	2072.3	118.9	1126.9	1232.2	6721.8	6721.6
155.0	14.0				174.0	174.0	259.5	259.5
43516.9	24303.1	88913.6	84828.8	5208.4	13373.8	27556.7	123692.7	123623.4
73.1	37.1	476.0	476.0		341.7	500.0	1854.3	1854.3
654.8	487.9	1222.4	1222.4		-274.9	163.0	5484.6	5484.6
57687.9	25507.8	70251.3	68078.0	2074.0	30245.0	28367.3	80800.6	80800.6
26329.9	9202.9	37473.7	32790.5	4683.2	25187.5	8378.4	100214.3	92627.1
221213.3	105475.4	375483.8	341708.3	30945.3	194269.2	173952.5	575615.2	574097.7
55954.7	20206.7	65335.8	60085.0	5246.1	47959.1	26939.0	92689.0	85096.2
322.7	15.6	29806.2	27855.0	1951.2	8049.5	8000.0	2936.1	2936.1

16-10 续表3

单位：万元

分 类	Classify	营业成本 Total Cost	主营业务成本 Cost of Principal Business
二、餐饮业	**Catering Trade**	**326093.4**	**323160.9**
1.按登记注册类型分组	Grouped by Type of Registration		
内资	Domestic Funded Enterprises	250250.8	249568.3
国有	State-owned Enterprises	3984.8	3984.8
集体	Collective-owned Enterprises	376.3	376.3
股份合作	Cooperative Enterprises		
联营	Joint Ownership Enterprises		
国有联营	State Joint Ownership Enterprises		
集体联营	Collective Joint Ownership Enterprises		
国有与集体联营	Joint State-collective Enterprises		
其他联营	Others Joint Ownership Enterprises		
有限责任公司	Limited Liability Corporations	153314.7	152682.3
国有独资公司	State Sole Funded Corporations	3291.7	3291.7
其他有限责任公司	Other Limited Liability Corporations	150023.0	149390.6
股份有限公司	Share-holding Corporations Ltd.	20657.9	20634.8
私营	Private Enterprises	68338.7	68311.7
私营独资	Private-funded Enterprises	3580.2	3564.4
私营合伙	Private Partnership Enterprises	143.5	143.5
私营有限责任公司	Private Limited Liability Corporations	63831.8	63820.6
私营股份有限公司	Private Share-holding Corporations Ltd.	783.2	783.2
其他	Other Enterprises	3578.4	3578.4
港澳台商投资	Enterprises with Funds from Hong Kong, Macao &Taiwan	30952.8	30952.8
外商投资	Foreign Funded Enterprises	44889.8	42639.8
2.按国民经济行业分	Grouped by Sdctor		
正餐服务	Dinner	288393.7	287711.2
快餐服务	Fast Food	37084.7	34834.7
饮料及冷饮服务	Beverages and Cold Drinks		
其他餐饮业	Other Catering Services	615.0	615.0

continued 3

(10 000 yuan)

营业税金及附加 Taxs and Other Changes	主营业务税金及附加 Taxs and Other Changes on Principal Business	销售费用 Sale Expenses	管理费用 Management Expenses	财务费用 Financial Expenses	营业利润 Business Profits	利润总额 Total Profits	应付职工薪酬 Salary Payable	本年应交所得税 Value Added Tax Payable
35563.3	**35550.9**	**239023.9**	**71523.7**	**7324.3**	**-6116.1**	**-6689.0**	**147164.2**	**5787.0**
26555.9	26543.5	165541.1	53463.8	5435.1	-8986.5	-9706.3	115686.4	3411.7
264.8	264.8	676.1	578.1	2.4	-60.7	-55.2	655.7	13.6
32.3	32.3		162.6	0.6	5.4	5.4	103.0	1.3
16561.0	16552.2	95513.3	34894.8	3870.2	-7337.3	-7625.5	69042.4	1979.0
240.0	240.0	779.9	1434.8	12.9	-1726.4	-1722.7	1835.5	
16321.0	16312.2	94733.4	33460.0	3857.3	-5610.9	-5902.8	67206.9	1979.0
2544.6	2544.6	22386.5	2502.6	173.2	3189.6	3563.4	12974.6	945.9
6997.4	6993.8	45682.4	15038.9	1375.7	-4951.3	-5762.2	32173.7	471.9
339.1	339.1	2376.3	389.5	13.0	18.7	-12.0	1698.8	12.0
12.0	12.0	21.0	13.5	4.0	65.5	72.0	78.0	
6546.6	6543.0	42480.6	14444.0	1335.9	-4987.6	-5782.0	29845.9	455.8
99.7	99.7	804.5	191.9	22.8	-47.9	-40.2	551.0	4.1
155.8	155.8	1282.8	286.8	13.0	167.8	167.8	737.0	
3954.0	3954.0	44029.1	7265.8	1770.9	-7331.0	-7026.2	13766.4	61.3
5053.4	5053.4	29453.7	10794.1	118.3	10201.4	10043.5	17711.4	2314.0
31099.4	31087.0	193480.8	63024.1	6180.5	-4543.5	-5609.1	131624.0	4826.6
4290.3	4290.3	44626.9	7719.5	1126.1	-2006.1	-1513.4	14599.9	960.4
173.6	173.6	916.2	780.1	17.7	433.5	433.5	940.3	

16-11 限额以上批发零售贸易业商品购进、销售、库存总额（2013年）

单位：个、万元

分 类	Classify	单位数 Number of Enterprises	商品购进额 Total Purchases	进口 Exports
总计	**Total**	**758**	**40064047.5**	**2559094.3**
一、批发企业	**Wholesale Enterprises**	**293**	**26178977.7**	**2344596.8**
1.按登记注册类型分组	Grouped by Type of Registration			
内资	Domestic Funded Enterprises	275	22667029.2	180137.8
国有	State-owned Enterprises	17	2899310.3	20623.5
集体	Collective-owned Enterprises	3	8172.2	
股份合作	Cooperative Enterprises			
联营	Joint Ownership Enterprises			
国有联营	State Joint Ownership Enterprises			
集体联营	Collective Joint Ownership Enterprises			
国有与集体联营	Joint State-collective Enterprises			
其他联营	Others Joint Ownership Enterprises			
有限责任公司	Limited Liability Corporations	172	13538897.4	135059.9
国有独资公司	State Sole Funded Corporations	7	2440051.9	34140.8
其他有限责任公司	Other Limited Liability Corporations	165	11098845.5	100919.1
股份有限公司	Share-holding Corporations Ltd.	7	3611262.9	
私营	Private Enterprises	73	2586418.9	24454.4
私营独资	Private-funded Enterprises	1	4301.9	
私营合伙	Private Partnership Enterprises			
私营有限责任公司	Private Limited Liability Corporations	70	2478446.4	24454.4
私营股份有限公司	Private Share-holding Corporations Ltd.	2	103670.6	
其他	Other Enterprises	3	22967.5	
港澳台商投资	Enterprises with Funds from Hong Kong, Macao &Taiwan	5	409404.1	
外商投资	Foreign Funded Enterprises	7	3045076.6	2164459.0
2.按国民经济行业分组	Grouped by Economic Sector			
农、林、牧产品批发	Wholesale of Agricultural,Forestry and Animal Husbandry Products	3	13342.0	

Total Sales of Enterprises above Designated Size in Wholesale and Retail Trades Grouped by Category of Commodities（2013）

(unit，10 000 yuan)

商品销售额 Sales Value	批发额 Wholesale Trade	出口 Exports	零售额 Retail Trade	期末商品库存额 Value of Stock at Final goods
42966228.9	**23949878.6**	**628196.7**	**19016350.3**	**1894316.2**
27249788.0	**23502718.7**	**628150.7**	**3747069.3**	**790542.0**
23696320.8	20072358.7	627889.6	3623962.1	749857.6
3292127.2	3070618.3	20272.5	221508.9	105931.5
9444.4	8458.3		986.1	975.9
14006515.4	12041823.6	178364.8	1964691.8	412414.6
2459278.9	1820594.7	4530.0	638684.2	26783.3
11547236.5	10221228.9	173834.8	1326007.6	385631.3
3982878.1	2681069.5	374435.9	1301808.6	45986.7
2382479.2	2250614.4	54816.4	131864.8	184457.9
4250.3	4250.3			220.4
2274908.3	2169028.1	54816.4	105880.2	182597.5
103320.6	77336.0		25984.6	1640.0
22876.5	19774.6		3101.9	91.0
448813.1	325719.0		123094.1	24837.2
3047196.0	3047182.9	261.1	13.1	15137.5
12711.1	12711.1			3519.4

16-11 续表1

单位：个、万元

分　类	Classify	单位数 Number of Enterprises	商品购进额 Total Purchases	进口 Exports
食品、饮料及烟草制品批发	Wholesale of Food, Beverages and Tobacco Products	28	1471668.5	
纺织、服装及家庭服务器批发	Wholesale of Textiles, Garments and Daily Articles	24	2917283.9	
文化、体育用品及器材批发	Wholesale of Culture, Sports Articles and Equipments	14	216620.5	
医药及医疗器材批发	Wholesale of Medicines and Medical Appliances	42	1472891.9	
矿产品、建材及化工产品批发	Wholesale of Mineral Products, Building Materials and Chemical Products	108	17888567.8	2266825.2
机械设备、五金产品及电子产品批发	Wholesale of Machinery, Hardwares, Transport Means and Electronic Products	63	2081132.1	76998.1
贸易经纪与代理	Trade Manage and Agent	7	82151.1	773.5
其他批发	Other Wholesales	4	35319.9	
3.按经营形式分组	Grouped by Means of Operation			
独立门店	Independent Shop	219	20341147.5	2301168.3
连锁总店	Headquarter of Chain Store	3	842342.4	
连锁门店	Chain Store	1	429998.1	
其他	Other	70	4565489.7	43428.5
二、零售企业	**Retail Trade**	**465**	**13885069.8**	**214497.5**
1.按登记注册类型分组	Grouped by Registration Status			
内资	Domestic Funded Enterprises	365	10108640.5	170765.0
国有	State-owned Enterprises	14	276380.7	
集体	Collective-owned Enterprises	24	116634.2	
股份合作	Cooperative Enterprises			
联营	Joint Ownership Enterprises	1	4118.0	
国有联营	State Joint Ownership Enterprises			
集体联营	Collective Joint Ownership Enterprises	1	4118.0	
国有与集体联营	Joint State-collective Enterprises			

continued 1

(unit，10 000 yuan)

商品销售额 Sales Value	批发额 Wholesale Trade	出口 Exports	零售额 Retail Trade	期末商品库存额 Value of Stock at Final goods
1846680.8	1672521.5	50.0	174159.3	84236.3
2538074.2	1742246.0	54816.4	795828.2	99503.9
265928.2	261965.3	7670.7	3962.9	26760.0
1614243.5	1442949.5		171294.0	114721.8
18455154.1	16246806.3	38823.4	2208347.8	288731.7
2397086.4	2003609.3	506517.7	393477.1	167884.9
82326.1	82326.1	20272.5		3296.6
37583.6	37583.6			1887.4
20793221.7	17609044.4	233181.2	3184177.3	532565.1
1128834.1	1128834.1			38189.7
536609.6	316599.7		220009.9	20360.1
4791122.6	4448240.5	394969.5	342882.1	199427.1
15716440.9	**447159.9**	**46.0**	**15269281.0**	**1103774.2**
11465537.0	327891.9	46.0	11137645.1	853770.1
299465.3	579.2		298886.1	47089.0
119603.5	1731.6		117871.9	4897.7
3998.0	9.2		3988.8	120.0
3998.0	9.2		3988.8	120.0

16-11 续表2

单位：个、万元

分　类	Classify	单位数 Number of Enterprises	商品购进额 Total Purchases	进口 Exports
其他联营	Others Joint Ownership Enterprises			
有限责任公司	Limited Liability Corporations	227	6522244.7	98697.0
国有独资公司	State Sole Funded Corporations	4	101018.6	
其他有限责任公司	Other Limited Liability Corporations	223	6421226.1	98697.0
股份有限公司	Share-holding Corporations Ltd.	9	1016818.9	71143.8
私营	Private Enterprises	88	2168443.3	924.2
私营独资	Private-funded Enterprises	1	4979.5	
私营合伙	Private Partnership Enterprises	2	6060.4	
私营有限责任公司	Private Limited Liability Corporations	77	1999339.1	924.2
私营股份有限公司	Private Share-holding Corporations Ltd.	8	158064.3	
其他	Other Enterprises	2	4000.7	
港澳台商投资	Enterprises with Funds from Hong Kong, Macao &Taiwan	19	1545282.0	43732.5
外商投资	Foreign Funded Enterprises	20	1654173.8	
2.按国民经济行业分组	Grouped by Registered Kind			
综合零售	General Retail Sales Trade	105	2879046.7	65043.2
食品、饮料及烟草制品专门零售	Retail of Food, Beverage and Tobaccos	33	258776.3	
纺织、服装及日用品专门零售	Retail of Textiles, Garments and Daily Articles	35	1292439.4	
文化、体育用品及器材专门零售	Retail of Culture, Sports Articles and Equipments	24	378400.9	
医药及医疗器材专门零售	Retail of Medicines and Medical Appliances	16	207320.3	
汽车、摩托车、燃料及零配件专门零售	Retail of Motor Vehicles, Motorcycles, Feuls and Parts	168	5541404.8	148914.3
家用电器及电子产品专门零售	Retail of Household Electronic Equipments and Products	42	1648059.8	

continued 2

(unit, 10 000 yuan)

商品销售额 Sales Value	批发额 Wholesale Trade	出口 Exports	零售额 Retail Trade	期末商品库存额 Value of Stock at Final goods
7586028.9	256754.6	46.0	7329274.3	565833.8
106731.0			106731.0	25236.8
7479297.9	256754.6	46.0	7222543.3	540597.0
1149092.0	58608.8		1090483.2	103280.4
2303465.1	10208.5		2293256.6	132432.7
5160.2			5160.2	108.9
6364.7			6364.7	668.6
2132414.9	7851.2		2124563.7	123245.0
159525.3	2357.3		157168.0	8410.2
3884.2			3884.2	116.5
1837879.0	25162.6		1812716.4	168300.4
1769670.5	50056.0		1719614.5	65317.8
3505183.0	1273.9		3503909.1	198957.7
351003.0	17430.2		333572.8	82210.9
1328082.3	56677.2		1271405.1	73392.7
391411.7	31853.9		359557.8	81187.4
231571.0	26663.6		204907.4	44423.4
5974862.4	46443.3		5928419.1	523817.3
1962053.4	233201.9		1728851.5	69323.4

16-11 续表3

单位：个、万元

分 类	Classify	单位数 Number of Enterprises	商品购进额 Total Purchases	进口 Exports
五金、家具及室内装饰材料专门零售	etail of Hardwares, Furniture and Room Decorative Building	34	1576167.2	540.0
货摊、无店铺及其他零售业	No Fixed Stores and Other Retails	8	103454.4	
3.按经营形式分组	Grouped by Means of Operation			
独立门店	Independent Shop	398	11064881.2	148914.3
连锁总店	Headquarter of Chain Store	25	802852.3	65043.2
连锁门店	Chain Store	8	596475.8	
其他	Other	34	1420860.5	540.0
4.按零售业态分组	Grouped by Retail Size			
有店铺	Retail of Shop	462	13792362.4	214497.5
食杂店	Grocery Store			
便利店	Convenience Store	3	18606.6	
折扣店	Dime Store			
超市	Supermarket	41	155156.3	
大型超市	Larget Supermarket	15	1021867.9	65043.2
仓储会员店	Warehouse Club	2	7925.8	
百货店	Department Store	61	1827323.4	
专业店	Special Store	164	4227083.6	92542.6
专卖店	Monopoly Store	133	3212259.2	56371.7
家居建材商店	Home-building Material Store	18	1234129.3	540.0
购物中心	Shopping Center	13	1684605.5	
厂家直销中心	Factory Outlet Center	12	403404.8	
无店铺零售	Retail of No-shop	3	92707.4	
电视购物	TV Shopping	2	91395.1	
邮购	Mail Order			
网上商店	Online Stores			
自动售货亭	Vending Machine			
电话购物	Tele Shopping	1	1312.3	

continued 3

(unit: 10 000 yuan)

商品销售额 Sales Value	批发额 Wholesale Trade	出口 Exports	零售额 Retail Trade	期末商品库存额 Value of Stock at Final goods
1867135.1	31477.2	46.0	1835657.9	28821.7
105139.0	2138.7		103000.3	1639.7
12249255.1	177802.4		12071452.7	758235.3
898172.8	26084.4		872088.4	88295.4
876210.2	60076.0		816134.2	82034.8
1692802.8	183197.1	46.0	1509605.7	175208.7
15622412.5	444809.8	46.0	15177602.7	1102741.6
20367.3			20367.3	1986.3
159562.5	13330.4		146232.1	22649.2
1310831.7			1310831.7	117456.6
8761.7			8761.7	775.3
2160396.4	1671.6		2158724.8	68115.2
4700838.7	122636.4		4578202.3	461470.1
3574913.3	105333.6		3469579.7	317830.5
1508581.7	30466.9	46.0	1478114.8	8898.2
1755218.4	159917.9		1595300.5	34250.8
422940.8	11453.0		411487.8	69309.4
94028.4	2350.1		91678.3	1032.6
92695.1	1316.8		91378.3	896.3
1333.3	1033.3		300.0	136.3

16-12 限额以上住宿和餐饮业经营情况（2013年）

Statistic on Hotel Services and Catering Services above Designed Size（2013）

单位：个、万元 (unit,10 000 yuan)

分 类	Classify	单位数 Number of Enterprises	营业额 Business Revenue	客房收入 From Hotel Room	餐费收入 From Meals	商品销售收入 From Commodities
总计	**Total**	**652**	**3394646**	**701580**	**2313412**	**242764**
一、住宿业	**Lodging Services**	**232**	**1332727**	**640817**	**558459**	**37215**
1. 按登记注册类型分组	Grouped by Registration Status					
内资企业	Domestic Funded Enterprises	217	1140764	540079	488300	31706
国有	State-owned Enterprises	37	254065	100856	101105	15651
集体	Collective-owned Enterprises	3	3278	2063	742	52
股份合作	Cooperative Enterprises					
联营	Joint Ownership Enterprises					
国有联营	State Joint Ownership Enterprises					
集体联营	Collective Joint Ownership Enterprises					
国有与集体联营	Joint State-collective Ownership Enterprises					
其他联营	Other Joint Ownership Enterprises					
有限责任公司	Limited Liability Corporations	119	754945	368083	335379	12913
国有独资公司	State-funded Corporations	4	14755	6537	6523	204
其他有限责任公司	Other Limited Liability Corporations	115	740190	361546	328856	12710
股份有限公司	Stock Limited Corporation	3	22746	14676	5764	522
私营	Private Enterprises	54	105581	54309	45253	2568
私营独资	Private-funded Enterprises	4	1321	560	723	38
私营合伙	Private Partnership Enterprises	1	241	208	33	
私营有限责任公司	Private Limited Liability Corporations	47	102837	52912	43969	2505
私营股份有限公司	Private Share Holding Corporations	2	1182	629	528	25
其他	Others	1	149	92	57	
港澳台商投资	Enterprises Funded by Hong Kong, Macao and Taiwan	6	130132	66748	46985	4236
外商投资	Foreign Funded Enterprises	8	59732	32939	22124	1273
2. 按国民经济行业分组						
旅游饭店	Tour Restaurant	187	1237066	595560	513059	34864
一般旅馆	Common Hotel	39	87574	40804	42234	2280
其他住宿业	Others	6	8087	4453	3166	71

16–12 续表1 continued 1

单位：个、万元						(unit, 10 000 yuan)
分　类	Classify	单位数 Number of Enterprises	营业额 Business Revenue	客房收入 From Hotel Room	餐费收入 From Meals	商品销售收入 From Commodities
二、餐饮业	**Catering Trade**	**420**	**2061919**	**60763**	**1754953**	**205549**
1. 按登记注册类型分	Grouped by Registration Status					
内资	Domestic Funded Enterprises	313	748322	38705	581322	108634
国有	State-owned Enterprises	5	89129	1588	50289	36431
集体	Collective-owned Enterprises	1	577		577	
股份合作	Cooperative Enterprises					
联营	Joint Ownership Enterprises					
国有联营	State Joint Ownership Enterprises					
集体联营	Collective Joint Ownership Enterprises					
国有与集体联营	Joint State-collective Ownership Enterprises					
其他联营	Other Joint Ownership Enterprises					
有限责任公司	Limited Liability Corporations	179	455398	31573	352571	59474
国有独资公司	State-funded Corporations	3	4026	884	2078	295
其他有限责任公司	Other Limited Liability Corporations	176	451371	30689	350492	59179
股份有限公司	Stock Limited Corporation	4	49618	1377	36479	5000
私营	Private Enterprises	120	143164	3123	132572	7171
私营独资	Private-funded Enterprises	13	6721		6346	375
私营合伙	Private Partnership Enterprises	1	260	22	204	34
私营有限责任公司	Private Limited Liability Corporations	103	134213	2989	124242	6684
私营股份有限公司	Private Share Holding Corporations	3	1971	112	1780	79
其他	Others	4	10436	1044	8834	558
港澳台商投资	Enterprises Funded by Hong Kong, Macao and Taiwan	7	81270	123	78677	1754
外商投资	Foreign Funded Enterprises	8	100214		92527	
2. 按国民经济行业分						
正餐服务	Dinner Services	396	1861313	59493	1564257	204603
快餐服务	Fast Food Services	15	129972	40	122055	251
饮料及冷饮服务	Beverage and Cold Beverage Services					
其他餐饮业	Other Catering Services	9	70634	1230	68641	685

16-13 限额以上批发和零售贸易业主要商品分类销售额（2013年）

Sale Values of Enterprises above Designated Size of Wholesale and Retail Trades by Category of Main Commodities（2013）

单位：万元 (10 000 yuan)

分 类	Classify	销售合计 Total Sales Value	批发 Wholesale Value	零售 Retail Value
总计	**Total**	**41874736.2**	**23175769.1**	**18698967.1**
粮油、食品饮料、烟酒类	Grain and Oil, Food and Beverages, Alcoholic Drinks and Tobacco	3146818.5	1660776.5	1486042
#粮油、食品类	Cereals, Oils and Foodstuffs	1111444.6	246061.7	865382.9
#粮油类	Grain and Oil	463176.2	51373.5	411802.7
肉禽蛋类	Meat, Poultry and Eggs	106182.2	22294.7	83887.5
水产品类	Aquatic Products	118950.8	5414.1	113536.7
蔬菜类	Vegetables	138478.4	85121	53357.4
干鲜瓜果类	Fresh and Dried Fruit Category	88280	30350.9	57929.1
饮料类	Beverages	699751.4	299115.1	400636.3
烟酒类	Tobacco and Liquor	1335622.5	1115599.7	220022.8
服装、鞋帽、针、纺织品类	Clothing, Shoes, Hats and Textiles	4706138	1121966.2	3584171.8
#服装类	Clothing	4047875.7	1022541.8	3025333.9
鞋帽类	Shoes and Hats	379221.9	44677	334544.9
针、纺织品类	Knitwear and Textiles	279040.4	54747.4	224293
化妆品类	Cosmetics	319729.9	52010.8	267719.1
金银珠宝类	Gold,Silver and Jewelry	489273.8	12519.1	476754.7
日用品类	Articles for Daily Use	656275.9	118824.1	537451.8
#洗涤用品类	Bathing and Washing	176029.9	79463.7	96566.2
儿童玩具类	Children's Toys	73450.4	12305.1	61145.3
五金、电料类	Hardwear and Electrical Materials	225102.4	77427.6	147674.8
体育、娱乐用品类	Sports and Recreation Articles	248594.3	60672.8	187921.5
书报杂志类	Newspapers and Magazines	205904.6	116461	89443.6
电子出版物及音像制品类	E-journal and Video Products	16174.6	2640.2	13534.4
家用电器和音像器材类	Household Appliances and Video Products	1520103.5	581048.7	939054.8
中西药品类	Traditional Chinese and Western Medicine	1732375.5	1372425	359950.5
#西药	Western Medicine	1375459.5	1048085.2	327374.3
中草药及中成药	Chinese Herbal Medicine and Traditional Chinese Medicine	135749.1	117790.3	17958.8
文化办公用品类	Cultural and Official Goods	690477.8	357855.4	332622.4
家具类	Furniture	927540.1	11356.1	916184
通讯器材类	Communication Appliances	347542.6	70569.2	276973.4
煤炭及制品类	Coal and Related Products	2458735.6	1817842.1	640893.5
木材及制品类	Wood and Wooden Products	0.2	0.2	
石油及制品类	Petroleum and Related Products	10043993	7720503.4	2323489.6
化工材料及制品类	Raw Chemical Materials	58939.1	58939.1	
#化肥类	Chemical Fertilizers	52925.2	52925.2	
金属材料类	Metal Materials	6185672.3	6185672.3	
建筑及装潢材料类	Buildings and Decoration Materials	1448118.1	367743.6	1080374.5
机电产品及设备类	Mechanical and Electrical Products	584073.9	564193.1	19880.8
#农机类	Agricultural Machinery	176.8	176.8	
汽车类	Automobile	5694873.6	791719.1	4903154.5
种子饲料类	Seeds and Feedstuff	3037.7	3037.7	
棉麻类	Cotton,Hemp	3183.7	3183.7	
其他类	Others	162057.5	46382.1	115675.4

16-14 亿元以上商品交易市场成交情况(2013年)

Basic Statistics on Commodity Exchange Markets of Transaction Value over 100 Million Yuan (2013)

分类	Classify	年末出租摊位数(个) Number of Rental Booths at Year-end (unit)	成交额(万元) Turnover (10 000 yuan)
粮油、食品饮料、烟酒类	Grain and Oil, Food and Beverages,Alcoholic Drinks and Tobacco	**5461**	**747544**
#粮油、食品类	Cereals, Oils and Foodstuffs	3438	665717
#粮油类	Grain and Oil	445	294496
肉禽蛋类	Meat, Poultry and Eggs	933	88287
水产品类	Aquatic Products	316	16378
蔬菜类	Vegetables	858	200032
干鲜瓜果类	Fresh and Dried Fruit Category	788	65844
饮料类	Beverages	1935	79345
烟酒类	Tobacco and Liquor	88	2482
服装、鞋帽、针、纺织品类	Clothing, Shoes, Hats and Textiles	7053	426626
#服装类	Clothing	4832	179249
鞋帽类	Shoes and Hats	1095	180174
针、纺织品类	Knitwear and Textiles	1126	67203
化妆品类	Cosmetics	96	2487
金银珠宝类	Gold,Silver and Jewelry	50	1100
日用品类	Articles for Daily Use	1012	23128
#洗涤用品类	Bathing and Washing	548	13580
儿童玩具类	Children's Toys	450	9240
五金、电料类	Hardwear and Electrical Materials	554	18124
体育、娱乐用品类	Sports and Recreation Articles	80	1700
书报杂志类	Newspapers and Magazines	3	40
电子出版物及音像制品类	E-journal and Video Products	103	9341
家用电器和音像器材类	Household Appliances and Video Products	128	17345
中西药品类	Traditional Chinese and Western Medicine	430	57800
#西药	Western Medicine		
中草药及中成药	Chinese Herbal Medicine and Traditional Chinese Medicine	430	57800
文化办公用品类	Cultural and Official Goods	1147	121904
家具类	Furniture		
通讯器材类	Communication Appliances	265	37490
煤炭及制品类	Coal and Related Products		
木材及制品类	Wood and Wooden Products		
石油及制品类	Petroleum and Related Products		
化工材料及制品类	Raw Chemical Materials	21	181670
#化肥类	Chemical Fertilizers		
金属材料类	Metal Materials	45	297969
建筑及装潢材料类	Buildings and Decoration Materials	625	42148
机电产品及设备类	Mechanical and Electrical Products	780	158000
#农机类	Agricultural Machinery		
汽车类	Automobile	1879	698516
种子饲料类	Seeds and Feedstuff		
棉麻类	Cotton,Hemp		
其他类	Others	194	16463

16-15 批发和零售业连锁经营情况(2013年)

Basic Statistics on Chain Business of Wholesale and Retail Trades（2013）

指　标	Item	本年合计 Total	上年合计 Total Last Year	本年直营店 Regular Chain
一、门店总数（个）	**Number of Stores(unit)**	**718**	**696**	**585**
二、年末从业人员数（人）	**Employees at Year-end(person)**	**19368**	**20195**	**17370**
三、年末零售营业面积（平方米）	**Operating Area of Retail at Year-end(sq.m)**	**854598**	**800587**	**687068**
四、连锁门店商品购进额（万元）	**Purchases Value of Chain Stores(10 000 yuan)**	**3461569**	**3147929**	**3318445**
其中：统一配送商品购进额	Centralized Purchases and Delivery	2792281	2545905	2770302
其中：自有配送中心配送商品购进额	Self Centralized Purchases and Delivery	2774766	2530079	2755272
非自有配送中心配送商品购进额	Non-self Centralized Purchases and Delivery			
五、连锁门店商品销售额（万元）	**Sales Value of Chain Store(10 000 yuan)**	**4036369**	**3719649**	**3837598**
其中：零售额	Retail Value	1819513	1659130	1620742

16-15 续表 continued

指　标	Item	上年直营店 Regular Chain Last Year	本年加盟店 Franchise	上年加盟店 Franchise Last Year
一、门店总数（个）	**Number of Stores(unit)**	**553**	**133**	**143**
二、年末从业人员数（人）	**Employees at Year-end(person)**	**18151**	**1998**	**2044**
三、年末零售营业面积（平方米）	**Operating Area of Retail at Year-end(sq.m)**	**632437**	**167530**	**168150**
四、连锁门店商品购进额（万元）	**Purchases Value of Chain Stores(10 000 yuan)**	**3029969**	**143124**	**117960**
其中：统一配送商品购进额	Centralized Purchases and Delivery	2521227	21979	24678
其中：自有配送中心配送商品购进额	Self Centralized Purchases and Delivery	2507442	19494	22637
非自有配送中心配送商品购进额	Non-self Centralized Purchases and Delivery			
五、连锁门店商品销售额（万元）	**Sales Value of Chain Store(10 000 yuan)**	**3543088**	**198771**	**176561**
其中：零售额	Retail Value	1482569	198771	176561

16-16 住宿和餐饮业连锁经营情况(2013年)

Basic Statistics on Chain Business of Hotels and Catering Services（2013）

指 标	Item	本年合计 Total	上年合计 Total Last Year
一、门店总数（个）	**Number of Stores(unit)**	**174**	**162**
二、年末从业人员数（人）	**Employees at Year-end(person)**	**11111**	**11002**
三、年末餐饮营业面积（平方米）	**Operating Area of Retail at Year-end(sq.m)**	**69084**	**66877**
四、客房总数（间）	**Guest Rooms(room)**		
五、床位数（张）	**Guest Beds(bed)**		
六、餐位数（位）	**Dining Seats(set)**	**22604**	**24562**
七、连锁门店商品购进额（万元）	**Operating Area of Catering Services at Year end(room)(10 000 yuan)**	**64142**	**86311**
其中：统一配送商品购进额	Centralized Purchases and Delivery	61738	80808
其中 自有配送中心配送商品购进额	Self Centralized Purchases and Delivery	59554	78722
非自有配送中心配送商品购进额	Non-self Centralized Purchases and Delivery		
八、连锁门店商品营业额（万元）	**Sales Value of Chain Store(10 000 yuan)**	**127188**	**126651**
其中：餐费收入	Catering Revenues	126386	126055
商品销售额	Sales Value	802	596

16-16 续表 continued

指 标	Item	本年直营店 Regular Chain	上年直营店 Regular Chain Last Year
一、门店总数（个）	**Number of Stores(unit)**	**174**	**162**
二、年末从业人员数（人）	**Employees at Year-end(person)**	**11111**	**11002**
三、年末餐饮营业面积（平方米）	**Operating Area of Retail at Year-end(sq.m)**	**69084**	**65877**
四、客房总数（间）	**Guest Rooms(room)**		
五、床位数（张）	**Guest Beds(bed)**		
六、餐位数（位）	**Dining Seats(set)**	**22604**	**24562**
七、连锁门店商品购进额（万元）	**Operating Area of Catering Services at Year end(room)(10 000 yuan)**	**64142**	**86311**
其中：统一配送商品购进额	Centralized Purchases and Delivery	61738	80808
其中：自有配送中心配送商品购进额	Self Centralized Purchases and Delivery	59554	78722
非自有配送中心配送商品购进额	Non-self Centralized Purchases and Delivery		
八、连锁门店商品营业额（万元）	**Sales Value of Chain Store(10 000 yuan)**	**127188**	**126651**
其中：餐费收入	Catering Revenues	126386	126055
商品销售额	Sales Value	802	596

16-17 成品油批发企业（单位）能源购进、销售与库存(2013年)

Purchases,Sales and Stock of Refined Oil Wholesale Enterprises（2013）

单位：吨 (ton)

指 标	Item	期初库存量 Stock at Beginning of the Year	本年购进量 Purchases This Year	其中：购自省(区、市)外 From Other Provinces (Regions,Cities)	本年销售量 Sales This Year	其中：销往省(区、市)外 For Other Provinces (Regions,Cities)	售予省内批发和零售企业 For Wholesale and Retail Trades	年末库存量 Stock at End of the Year
汽油	Gasoline	43045	4229305	204720	4254580	616608	3380498	37151
#93 ″	#93″	29340	3781293	161556	3805293	579620	3028841	28825
柴油	Diesel Oil	55614	8894699	2334595	8958727	2181695	6455777	38006
#0 ″	#0″	55475	6496411	750538	6566597	622367	5583260	32319
煤油	Kerosene	43230	888963	317903	866431	300005	10045	34156
燃料油	Fuel Oil		23295	21867	23295	20871	2424	
润滑油	Lube	455	17757	13589	17796	5050	11674	392

16-18 成品油零售企业（单位）能源商品销售与库存(2013年)

Purchases,Sales and Stock of Refined Oil Retail Enterprises（2013）

单位：吨 (ton)

指 标	Item	期初库存量 Stock at Beginning of the Year	本年销售量 Sales This Year	年末库存量 Stock at End of the Year
汽油	Gasoline	93025	1058230	17407
#93 ″	#93″	90686	859536	13646
柴油	Diesel Oil	190460	1028299	16089
#0 ″	#0″	189723	1001338	15046
煤油	Kerosene			1
燃料油	Fuel Oil			
润滑油	Lube	38	4355	49

主要统计指标解释

批发业 指批发商向批发、零售单位及其他企事业、机关单位批量销售生活用品和生产资料的活动，以及从事进出口贸易和贸易经纪与代理的活动。批发商可以对所批发的货物拥有所有权，并以本单位、公司的名义进行交易活动；也可以不拥有货物的所有权，而以中介身份做代理销售商。还包括各类商品批发市场中固定摊位的批发活动。

零售业 指百货商店、超级市场、专门零售商店、品牌专卖店、售货摊等主要面向最终消费者（如居民等）的销售活动。包括以互联网、邮政、电话、售货机等方式的销售活动，还包括在同地点，后面加工生产、前面销售的店铺（如前店后厂的面包房）。不包括：谷物、种子、饲料、牲畜、矿产品、生产用原料、化工原料、农用化工产品、机械设备（用车、计算机及通信设备等除外）等生产资料的销售（批发业）；非零售单位附带的零售活动（如汽车修理单位销售汽车零件）；商业零售单位所在商厦的物业管理（物业管理）；商业零售单位所在的商品市场、商业大厦的市场管理活动（市场管理）。

住宿业 指有偿为顾客提供临时住宿的服务活动，不包括提供长期住宿场所的活动（如出租房屋、公寓等）。

餐饮业 指在一定场所，对食物进行现场烹饪、调制，并出售给顾客主要供现场消费的服务活动。

社会消费品零售总额 指批发和零售业、餐饮业、新闻出版业、邮政业和其他服务业等，售予城乡居民用于生活消费的商品和社会集团用于公共消费的商品之总量。社会消费品零售总额包括：

一、批发和零售业企业（单位）售予城乡居民用于生活消费和社会集团用于公共消费的商品。包括：

1. 售予城乡居民的各种生活消费品；

2. 售予入境旅游的外国人、华侨、港澳台同胞的各类商品；

3. 售予行政事业单位、社会团体、军队和武警等机构的商品，以及以零售方式售予各类企业的商品。具体包括：用于非生产和社会交往的办公用品，如通讯设备、计算器具和设备、电讯网络设备、文印设备、音像、听器材和设备、纸张、本册、文具及装订文印材料、家具、日用电器、针纺织品、清洁卫生用品、文体用品、奖品、纪念品、礼品等；供内部人员乘坐的交通工具和燃料；用于办公设施修缮的各类配件、材料、工具等；用于取暖和防暑降温的设备、燃料、材料及食品等；专用于教学的用品和设备；非营利医疗机构的中、西药品、中药材和医疗设备器材；非专用的劳动保护用品；不对外营业的内部食堂用的餐具、炊具、设备、清洁卫生工具和食品、燃料等；军队、武警用于其人员生活的衣着品和个人用品；其他各类非生产性设备和用品。

二、餐饮业出售的主食、菜肴、烟酒饮料和其他商品。

三、新闻出版业、邮政业售予城乡居民、企事业单位、军队和武警等机构的书报杂志、音像制品、邮品等。

四、其他服务业出售的食品、烟酒饮料、服装鞋帽、日常生活用品、医药保健用品、艺术品、工艺美术品、玩具、殡葬用品以及其他消费品。

批发和零售业商品购进、销售、库存总额 指各种登记注册类型的批发和零售业企业（单位）以本企业（单位）为总体的，从国内、国外市场购进的商品总量，销售和出口的商品总量，库存的商品总量等情况。该指标可以反映商品流转过程中商品的购进、销售、库存之间的比例关系和存在的问题。

购进总额 指从本企业（单位）以外的单位和个人购进（包括从境外直接进口）作为转卖或加工后转卖的商品总额。它反映批发和零售业从国内、国外市场上购进商品的总量。商品购进包括：（1）从工农业生产者购进的商品；（2）从出版社、报社的出版发行部门购进的图书、杂志和报纸；（3）从各种登记注册类型的批发和零售业企业（单位）购进的商品；（4）从其他单位购进的商品，如从机关、团体、企业等单位购进的剩余物资，从住宿和餐饮业、其他服务业购进的商品，从海关、市场管理部门购进的缉私和没收的商品，从居民手中收购的废旧商品等；（5）从国（境）外直接进口的商品。不包括企业（单位）为自身经营用和未通过买卖行为而收入的商品以及销售退回、商品升溢等。

销售总额 指对本企业（单位）以外的单位和个人出售（包括对境外直接出口）的商品总额。它反映批发和零售业在国内市场上销售商品以及出口商品的总量。商品销售包括：（1）售给城乡居民和社会集团消费用的商品；（2）售给工业、农业、建筑业、运输邮电业、批发和零售业、住宿和餐饮业、其他服务业等作为生产、经营使用的商品；（3）售给批发和零售业作为转卖或加工后转卖的商品；（4）对国（境）外直接出口的商品。不包括出售本企业（单位）自用的废旧包装用品，未通过买卖行为付出的商品，经本单位介绍、由买卖双方直接结算、本单位只收取手续费的业务，购货退出的商品以及商品损耗和损失等。

库存总额 指报告期末各种登记注册类型的批发和零售业企业（单位）已取得所有权的商品。它反映批发和零售业企业（单位）的商品库存情况和对市场商品供应的保证程度。商品库存包括：（1）存放在批发和零售业经营单位（如门市部、批发站、经营处）仓库、货场、货柜和货架中的商品；（2）挑选、整理、包装中的商品；（3）已记入购进而尚未运到本单位的商品，即发货单或银行承兑凭证已到而货未到的商品；（4）寄放他处的商品，如因购货方拒绝承付而暂时存放在购货方的商品和已办完加工成品收回手续而未提回的商品；（5）委托其他单位代销（未作销售或调出）尚未售出的商品；（6）代其他单位购进尚未交付的商品。不包括所有权不属于本单位的商品、委托外单位加工生产尚未收回成品的商品、外贸企业代理其他单位从国外进口尚未付给订货单位的商品、代国家物资储备部门保管的商品等。

住宿和餐饮业营业额 指住宿和餐饮业法人企业（单位）在经营活动中因提供服务或销售商品等取得的收入。包括：客房收入、餐费收入、商品销售额和其他收入。客房收入指住宿和餐饮业法人企业（单位）在经营活动中因提供住宿服务取得的收入。餐费收入指住宿和餐饮业法人企业、（单位）因为顾客提供就餐服务取得的收入，包括经烹饪、调制加工后出售的各种食品，如主食、炒菜、凉拌菜等的收入。商品销售额指住宿和餐饮业法人企业（单位）伴随服务而出售商品所取得的收入（含增值税）。其他收入指营业收入中除客房收入、餐费收入、商品销售额以外的其他收入，包括娱乐、健身和商务服务等。

连锁企业（或称连锁店、连锁公司） 指在核心企业或总店的领导下，由分散的、经营同类商品或服务的企业或活动单位，采取共同方针，实行集中采购和分散销售的有机结合，通过规范化经营，实现规模效益的经济联合组织形式。一般连锁店应由若干个分店组成。其经营特征：（1）经营同类商品；（2）使用统一商号；（3）统一采购配送，采购与销售相分离（部分商品可根据物流合理和保质保鲜原则，由供应商直接送货到门店，其余均由总部统一配送）。

连锁门店的形式分为直营连锁和加盟连锁。

直营连锁也叫正规连锁。指连锁门店均由总部独资或控股开设，在总部的直接领导下统一经营。总部采取纵深似的管理方式，直接下令掌管所有的零售门店，零售门店也必须完全接受总部指挥。这是大型垄断商业资本通过吞并、兼并或独资、控股等途径，发展壮大自身实力和规模的一种形式。

加盟连锁包括特许连锁和自由连锁两种形式，

特许连锁指各连锁门店（被特许人）通过合同形式，取得使用总部（特许人）商标、商号、经营技术和销售总部开发的商品的特许权，各加盟连锁门店为独立法人，在总部指导下统一经营。

自由连锁也称自愿连锁。指连锁公司的门店均为独立法人，各自的资产所有权关系不变，在公司总部的指导下共同经营。各成员店使用共同的店名，与总部订阅有关购、销、宣传等方面的合同，并按合同开展经营活动。在合同规定的范围之外，各成员店可以自由活动。根据自愿原则，各成员店可自由加入连锁体系，也可自由退出。

Explanatory Notes on Main Statistical Indicators

Wholesale Trade refers to the activities of wholesaler selling at wholesale commodities for daily use and capital goods to enterprises of wholesale and retail trades and other enterprises, institutions and government offices, including the activities of wholesaler engaged in import and export and acting as a trade agent. The wholesaler may have the right of ownership over the commodities of wholesale and trade in the name of its own or a company, the wholesaler may not have the right of ownership, only acts an agent. The wholesale trade also include the activities of wholesaler at the fixed stalls of the wholesale market of different commodities.

Retail Trade refers to the activities of department store,supermarket, franchised store, brand store, retail stall and on-the-spot-making-selling store selling commodities to the final consumers (citizens) by any means including internet, post, telephone, sales machine. Retail trade excludes the activities of sales of capital goods such a grain, seed, feed, livestock, mineral products, raw material for production, industrial chemicals, chemical products for farm, machine and equipment (vehicle, computer and communication equipment), and the activities of supplementary sales of non-retailer such as the sales of spare parts of car repair business

Hotel Services refer to the activities of enterprises providing paid services of lodging to the customer, excluding the activities of providing long period of services of lodging (such as leased house and apartments).

Catering Services refer to the activities of enterprises providing on-the-spot services of selling food cooked and prepared to the customer in certain sites

Total Retail Sales of Consumer Goods refer to the sum of retail sales of commodities sold by wholesale and retail trades, catering services, publishing, post and telecommunications and other service industries to urban and rural households for household consumption and to social institutions for public consumption. Retail sales of consumer goods include:

1) Sales sold by wholesale and retail trades to urban~thA and rural households for household consumption and to social institutions for public consumption.

a) of commodities to urban and rural households;

b) of commodities to foreigners, overseas Chinese and Chinese compatriots from Hong Kong, Macao and Taiwan visiting China;

c) of commodities to government agencies, institutions, social organizations, military and armed police units, and commodities to enterprises in the form of retail sales. More specifically, they include: office facilities and articles for non-production purposes such as communications equipment, computing equipment and instruments, TV and network equipment, printing and copying equipment, audio-visual equipment and instruments, paper, notebooks, stationeries, furniture, electric appliances, knitwear, sanitation and cleaning articles, cultural and sport articles, articles for prizes, souvenirs, etc.; transport vehicles and fuels for employees; materials, spare parts and tools for the maintenance of office facilities; equipment, fuels, materials and food for winter heating or summer cooling purposes; articles and equipment for teaching purpose; Chinese and western medicines and medical equipment and facilities purchased by non profit-making medical institutes; non- specialized work safety articles; cooking utensils, tableware, equipment, cleaning articles, food and fuels purchased by in-house cafeterias; clothes and personal articles purchased by military or armed police units for their officials and soldiers; and other equipment and articles for non-production purposes.

2) Sales of stable food, cooked dishes, beverages, tobaccos and other articles by catering units.

3) Sales of books, newspapers, magazines, audio-visual products and post products by publishing, post and telecommunications departments to urban and rural households and to enterprises, institutions, military and armed police units.

4) Sales of food, beverages, tobaccos, clothing, hats, footwear, articles for daily use, medicines, medical and health articles, work of art, handicrafts, toys, funeral articles and other articles by other service industries.

Purchase, Sales and Stock of Commodities by Wholesale and Retail Trades refer to the total volume of commodities purchased, total volume of sales and exports, and the stock of commodities by wholesale and retail enterprises (establishments) of different status of registration from domestic and overseas markets. This indicator reflects the relationship among purchase, sales and stock of commodities in the circulation of goods and reveals the existing problems.

Total Purchases of Commodities refer to the total value of purchases of commodities by enterprises (establishments)from other establishments or individuals (including direct import from abroad) for the purpose of re-selling, either with or without further processing of the commodities purchased. The commodities include: (1) commodities purchased from agricultural and industrial producer, wholesaler, retailer, publishing house and other service business; (2) commodities purchased from institutions and government departments; (3) confiscated goods purchased from the customs authorities or market management agencies; (4) second-hand goods and wastes purchased from residents; The commodities exclude 1 commodities purchased by enterprises (establishments) for use in their own business operation, commodities obtained without buying or selling procedures such as materials, consumable goods of low value, office appliances, etc. 2 received goods without trading, such as goods handed over from others, borrowed goods, preserved goods for others, donated goods from others, processed and retrieved goods, etc. 3. goods of direct settlement between buyer and seller with handling fees introduced by others, 4. goods returned or refused to pay by the buyer, 5. excessive goods.

Total Sales of Commodities refer to value of commodities sold by the establishments to other establishments and individuals (including goods sold for self consumption, including the value-added tax). The commodities include: (1) commodities sold to urban and rural residents and social groups for their consumption; (2) commodities sold to establishments in all industries for their production and operation, including agriculture, industry, construction, transportation, post and telecommunications, catering services, and public utility including commodities sold to wholesale and retail establishments for re-selling, with or without further processing; and (3) commodities for direct export to abroad.Excluded are (1) extended commodities without trading, such as goods handed over to other enterprises and institutions because of the change of organizations, lent goods, returned goods preserved for others, extended processing materials and samples donated to others, (2) goods of direct settlement between buyer and seller with handling fees introduced by others, (3)goods returned after purchase, (4) damaged and spoiled goods, (5) waste and used goods of selfuse,

Total Stock of Commodities refers to total commodities possessed by wholesaler and retailer of various types of registration status at the end of the reference period, reflecting the commodity stock level of various wholesaler and retailer and the potential for market supply. It includes: (1) commodities located in storage, garages, counters, and shelves of operating places (such as sale stores, wholesale centres, and operating offices) ; (2) commodities in the process of being selected, sorted, and packed; (3) commodities not arrived but recorded as purchase in the account, i.e. commodities not arrived but payment receipts for the commodities from the sellers or the banks arrived; (4) commodities deposited in other places rather than places mentioned above, for instance: commodities in the hold of purchasers temporarily due to the refusal of payment and commodities not taken back after going through the formalities; (5) commodities entrusted to other units to sell but not sold yet; (6) commodities purchased for other units but not delivered yet. Commodities not included as stock are those not owned by the enterprises (units), commodities on commission for processing but not yet delivered, imported commodities of agency of foreign trade enterprise but not yet delivered to ordering units and finally those put in stock on behalf of the state material reserves units.

Business Revenue of Hotels and Catering Services refers to revenue received from providing services or selling commodities by corporate enterprises and establishments engaged in hotels and catering services, including income from hotels, from catering services, from selling of commodities and from other services. Income from hotels refers to income of corporate enterprises and establishments engaged in hotels and catering services by providing lodging services. Income from catering services refers to income of corporate enterprises and establishments engaged in hotels and catering services by providing catering services, including selling of cooked or prepared foods such as staple food, cooked dishes or cold dishes. Income from selling of commodities refers to income of corporate enterprises and establishments engaged in hotels and catering services by selling commodities (including value-added tax) that accompany the services they provide. Income from other activities refers to income received other than income from hotels, catering services or selling of commodities, such as income from providing recreation, fitness or business services.

Chain Head Stores (headquarter) refer to the core leading stores responsible for development, allocation, administration and utilization of resources (name of stores, brand of stores, operation model, service standard, management way, ect.) of chain stores. Chain stores refers to the stores engaged in providing homogeneous commodities or services, with the central leadership of head store and guided by common policies, conduct centralized purchase and distributed selling of commodities, in order to gain better efficiency through standardized operation. The chain stores include regular chain stores, franchise chain stores and voluntary chain stores.

Regular Chain store refers to chain stores that are invested or controlled by the headquarters. They operate under direct and unified management from the headquarters.

Franchise chain store refers to the chain stores (franchisees) which are franchised with operation resources such as trade marks, names, patent and operation know-how by the franchisors in form of contract and pay the operation fees to the franchisors.

Voluntary chain store refers the stores operate jointly on the voluntary bases while maintaining their status of independent legal entities with full ownership of their assets. They sell goods of same brand from same channel of resource to the consumers.

17 对外经济贸易和旅游

FOREIGN TRADE AND ECONOMIC COOPERATION TOURISM

资料整理：马晓庆　赵琳瑛

Data management:Ma Xiacqirg Zhao linving

第十七部分　对外经济贸易和旅游

一、简要说明

本章资料包括对外经济贸易、利用外资和旅游等方面资料，由西安市统计局贸易外经处根据西安市商务局、海关和旅游局提供资料整理。

二、主要指标

指标	数值		增长
进出口总额（亿美元）	179.85	比上年增长	38.2%
#出　口	84.78	比上年增长	16.2%
实际利用外商直接投资额（亿美元）	31.30	比上年增长	26.3%
国际旅游人数（万人次）	121.11	比上年增长	5.0%
国际旅游收入（亿美元）	8.02	比上年增长	7.1%

17 FOREIGN TRADE AND ECONOMIC COOPERATION,TOURISM

Ⅰ.Brief Introduction

Data in this chapter consists of data on foreign trade, using of foreign capital and fund and tourism. Data on foreign economy and trade and tourism are compiled and provided by Foreign Economy Division of the Xi'an Bureau of Statistics according to the data from Xi'an Bureau of Commerce, Xi'an Custom Office and Xi'an Bureau of Tourism.

Ⅱ.Major Indicators

		Increase over Preceding Year
Total Imports and Exports (USD 100 mil.)	179.85	38.2%
#Toal Exports	84.78	16.2%
Total Amount of Foreign Direst zwestment (USD 100 mil.)	31.30	26.3%
Total Number of International Tourists (10 000 persons)	121.11	5.0%
Total Foreign Exchange Earnings (USD 100 mil.)	8.02	7.1%

17-1 主要年份外资、外贸和国际旅游基本情况

Main Indicators on Foreign Investments,International Trading and International Tourism In Representative Years

指 标	Item	1990	1995	2000	2005	2007
一、利用外资签定协议项目(个)	**Number of Projects of Foreign Capital Used through the Signed Agreements and Contracts (unit)**	**11**	**184**	**135**	**157**	**135**
利用外资签定协议金额 (万美元)	Value of Foreign Capital Used through the Signed Agreements and Contracts(USD 10 000)	415	28956	54123	121499	143973
外商实际直接投资额 (万美元)	Value of Foreign Direct Investment (USD 10 000)	1154	18653	15633	57113	111567
二、进出口总额(万美元)	**Total Imports and Exports (USD 10 000)**	**38229**	**137510**	**173696**	**390146**	**536162**
#进口总额	Total Imports	9939	27347	67634	126705	189029
出口总额	Total Exports	28290	110163	106052	263441	347133
进出口差额(出口-进口)	Balance of Imports and Exports	18351	82816	38428	136736	158104
三、国际旅游者人数总计 (万人次)	**Total Number of International Tourists (10 000 person-times)**	**25.88**	**41.35**	**65.03**	**77.56**	**100.01**
#外国人	Foreigners	15.40	37.11	54.65	65.86	85.09
港、澳、台同胞	Chinese Compatriot From Hong Kong, Macao and Taiwan	10.07	4.16	10.38	11.70	14.92
四、国际旅游者人天数总计 (万人天)	**Total Number of Days of International Tourists (10 000 person/day)**	**55.03**	**84.44**	**162.69**	**224.93**	**290.02**
#外国人	Foreigners	33.48	75.71	131.44	190.99	246.76
港、澳、台同胞	Chinese Compatriot From Hong Kong, Macao and Taiwan	21.55	8.56	31.15	33.94	43.26
五、国际旅游收入(亿元)	**Earning of International Tourism (100 millon yuan)**	**1.96**	**10.38**	**22.41**	**33.54**	**42.43**
#商品收入	Income from Mercantile	0.44	2.57	7.71	11.25	15.19
劳务收入	Income from Labour Service	1.52	7.81	14.70	22.29	27.24
六、旅游者在西安人均停留天数(天)	Number of Days of Average Tourists Staying in Xi'an (day)	**2.1**	**2.0**	**2.5**	**2.9**	**2.9**

注：1990年和1995年国际旅游者中含华侨。
本表数据来源于市商务局、西安海关、市旅游局。

17-1 续表 continued

指 标	Item	2008	2009	2010	2011	2012	2013
一、利用外资签定协议项目(个)	**Number of Projects of Foreign Capital Used through the Signed Agreements and Contracts (unit)**	**100**	**65**	**82**	**99**	**87**	**152**
利用外资签定协议金额（万美元）	Value of Foreign Capital Used through the Signed Agreements and Contracts(USD 10 000)	118230	60027	119689	120083	360264	251874
外商实际直接投资额（万美元）	Value of Foreign Direct Investment (USD 10 000)	114738	121872	156653	200522	247800	312994
二、进出口总额（万美元）	**Total Imports and Exports (USD 10 000)**	**704029**	**724618**	**1039273**	**1260179**	**1301446**	**1798534**
#进口总额	Total Imports	256916	391504	507544	677517	571568	950715
出口总额	Total Exports	447113	333114	531729	582662	729878	847819
进出口差额(出口-进口)	Balance of Imports and Exports	190197	-58390	24185	-94855	158310	-102896
三、国际旅游者人数总计（万人次）	**Total Number of International Tourists (10 000 person-times)**	**63.20**	**67.29**	**84.18**	**100.23**	**115.34**	**121.11**
#外国人	Foreigners	53.58	59.09	73.21	88.63	101.40	106.89
港、澳、台同胞	Chinese Compatriot From Hong Kong, Macao and Taiwan	9.62	8.20	10.97	11.60	13.94	14.22
四、国际旅游者人天数总计（万人天）	**Total Number of Days of International Tourists (10 000 person/day)**	**162.93**	**195.14**	**241.67**	**287.09**	**334.44**	**351.11**
#外国人	Foreigners	138.72	171.36	211.48	254.78	294.90	310.26
港、澳、台同胞	Chinese Compatriot From Hong Kong, Macao and Taiwan	24.21	23.78	30.19	32.31	39.54	40.85
五、国际旅游收入（亿元）	**Earning of International Tourism (100 millon yuan)**	**28.72**	**31.05**	**42.40**	**51.28**	**59.89**	**64.16**
#商品收入	Income from Mercantile	9.74	8.94	11.87	11.38	14.19	14.69
劳务收入	Income from Labour Service	18.98	22.11	30.53	39.90	45.70	49.47
六、旅游者在西安人均停留天数(天)	Number of Days of Average Tourists Staying in Xi'an (day)	**2.58**	**2.9**	**2.9**	**2.9**	**2.9**	**2.9**

17-2 主要年份利用外资情况

Utilization of Foreign Capital In Representative Years

单位：万美元　　　　　　(USD 10 000)

年　份 Year	利用外资签订协议金额 Value of Foreign Capital Used through the Signed Agreements and Contracts	外商实际直接投资额 Direct Foreign Investment
1983	3500	800
1984	8	
1985	8361	1106
1986	19919	4010
1987	3218	5552
1988	2423	6758
1989	1645	11632
1990	415	1154
1991	591	1094
1992	24165	5200
1993	57289	8996
1994	20321	15240
1995	28956	18653
1996	35978	20510
1997	27214	22057
1998	40034	22286
1999	40390	13801
2000	54123	15633
2001	60736	17687
2002	70692	20281
2003	96380	25557
2004	78312	27595
2005	121499	57113
2006	182525	82463
2007	143978	111567
2008	118230	114738
2009	60027	121872
2010	119689	155653
2011	120083	200522
2012	360264	247800
2013	251874	312994

注：本表数据来源于市商务局

17-3 外国和港澳台地区在西安直接投资（2013年）

Direct Investments from Foreign Countries and Hong Kong, Macao and Taiwan in Xi'an（2013）

分类	Classity	新签协议情况 New-signed Agreement Circumstances		外商实际直接投资额（万美元）
		合同数（个） Number of Constracts (unit)	利用外资签定协议金额（万美元） Value of Foreign Captial Used through the Signed (USD10 000)	Value of Foreign Direct Investment (USD 10 000)
合　计	**Total**	**152**	**251874**	**312994**
一、按投资方式分	**Grouped by Investment Mode**			
1.中外合资经营企业	Joint-venture Enterprises	47	110742	84383
2.中外合作经营企业	Cooperation Enterprises	1	-4787	
3.外资企业	Wholly Foreign-owned Enterprises	104	145918	174495
4.外资企业再投资	Re-investment from Foreign-funded Enterprises			54116
二、按国民经济行业分组	**Grouped by Sector**			
1.农、林、牧、渔业	Agriculture, Forestry, Animal Husbandry and Fishery	2	-532	818
2.采矿业	Mining	1	30	
3.制造业	Manufacturing	39	103415	231247
4.电力、燃气及水的生产供应业	Production and Distribution of Electricity,Gas and Water	2	240	200
5.建筑业	Construction	4	118	
6.批发和零售业	Wholesale and Retail Trades	41	11977	16664
7.交通运输、仓储和邮政业	Traffic, Transport, Storage and Post	9	8989	109
8.住宿和餐饮业	Hotels and Catering Services	8	5609	2288
9.信息传输、软件和信息技术服务业	Information Transmission,Software and Information Technology Services	11	1054	227
10.金融业	Financial Intermediation			
11.房地产	Real Estate	12	112967	59608
12.租赁和商务服务业	Leasing and Business Services	20	5866	302
13.科学研究和技术服务业	Scientific Research and Technical Service	2	2107	636
14.水利、环境和公共设施管理业	Management of Water Conservancy,Environment and Public Facilities			886
15.居民服务、修理和其他服务业	Services to Households,Repairs and Other Services	1	5	10
16.教育	Education		30	
17.卫生和社会工作	Health and Social Work			
18.文化、体育和娱乐业	Culture, Sports and Entertainment			
19.公共管理社会保障和社会组织	Public Management ,Social Security and Social Drganizations			
20.国际组织	International Organizations			
三、按投资国别、地区分组	**Grouped by Different Countries and Regions**			
香港	Hong Kong	60	209520	148349
澳门	Macao			10
台湾省	Taiwan	3	86	2946
日本	Japan	3	714	4941
泰国	Thailand			
马来西亚	Malaysia	1	55	
新加坡	Singapore	7	17133	57659
韩国	Korea	50	3534	78271
德意志联邦国	Germany	2	348	222
意大利	Italy		-122	110
法国	France	2	493	1619
英国	United Kingdom	1	210	104
捷克共和国	Czechoslovakia			
加拿大	Canada	1	58	
美国	America	7	762	882
澳大利亚	Australia	1	776	
维尔京群岛	Virgian Islands			
其它	Other	14	18306	17882

注：本表数据来源于市商务局。

17-4 各区县、开发区外商实际直接投资

Direct Investment by Foreign Entrepreneurs by Region and Development Zone

单位：万美元 (USD 10 000)

区县及开发区	Region and Economic Zone	2009	2010	2011	2012	2013
区、县合计	**Sum of Region**	**29766**	**38855**	**49726**	**58119**	**45164**
新城区	Xincheng	3740	4900	6765	7800	5012
碑林区	Beilin	4780	5150	6273	7800	5103
莲湖区	Lianhu	3953	5471	7405	7800	5100
灞桥区	Baqiao	4300	5215	6001	7397	6124
未央区	Weiyang	3902	5023	6202	7800	6000
雁塔区	Yanta	4087	5488	6912	8190	6179
阎良区	Yanliang	675	1208	2070	2200	2200
临潼区	Lintong	970	1200	2000	2400	2400
长安区	Chang'an	1219	1680	2300	2768	3003
蓝田县	Lantian	605	950	1089	1100	1100
周至县	Zhouzhi	315	550	600	650	660
户县	Huxian	560	970	1050	1100	1110
高陵县	Gaoling	660	1050	1060	1115	1173
开发区合计	**Sum of Development Zones**	**92107**	**117798**	**150797**	**189681**	**267830**
高新区	GaoXin	40613	51130	64935	81776	132632
经开区	JingKai	33661	42608	54201	68202	81423
曲江新区	Qujiang	12589	17187	21002	26433	33870
浐灞生态区	Chanba Eco-District	2400	3070	3856	4837	7266
航空基地	Aviation Industry Base	1016	1239	1701	2072	2640
航天基地	Aerospace Base	1208	1554	2030	2403	3000
国际港务区	International Trade&Logistic Park	620	1010	1571	2082	3469
沣东新城	FengDongXinCheng			1500	1876	3530

注：本表数据来源于市商务局。

17-5 主要年份进出口总额

Total Imports and Exports In Representative Years

单位：万美元 (USD 10 000)

年 份 Year	进出口总额 Total Imports and Exports	出口总额 Total Exports	进口总额 Total Imports
1987	13596	7540	6056
1988	36750	24632	12118
1989	32715	21564	11151
1990	38229	28290	9939
1991	55356	41511	13845
1992	70467	53060	17407
1993	93330	62393	30937
1994	104752	76897	27855
1995	137510	110163	27347
1996	143187	91745	51442
1997	150668	107753	42915
1998	180589	100492	80097
1999	172919	94495	78424
2000	173696	106062	67634
2001	169914	87948	81966
2002	186966	112479	74487
2003	230932	140327	90605
2004	309295	203539	105756
2005	390146	263441	126705
2006	415403	272862	142541
2007	536162	347133	189029
2008	704029	447113	256916
2009	724618	333114	391504
2010	1039273	531729	507544
2011	1260179	582662	677517
2012	1301446	729878	571568
2013	1798534	847819	950715

注：本表数据来源于西安海关。

17-6 外贸商品进出口总额分国别和地区（2013年）

Total Value of Imports and Exports by Country and Region（2013）

单位：万美元 (USD 10 000)

国别和地区	Country and Region	进出口总额 Total Imports and Exports	出口 Exports
亚洲	**Asia**	**908377**	**446275**
#香港	Hong kong	35299	34969
台湾省	Taiwan	50254	17602
日本	Japan	23122	10336
菲律宾	Phiilippines	3576	2072
马来西亚	Malaysia	4592	3329
韩国	Korea	24980	8854
非洲	**Africa**	**71150**	**49730**
#埃及	Egypt	2341	2336
突尼斯	Tunisia	121	117
埃塞俄比亚	Ethiopia	80	80
博茨瓦纳	Botswana		
南非	South Africa	2960	2957
欧洲	**Europe**	**300152**	**120692**
#德意志联邦国	Germany	17627	4700
法国	France	8537	5782
意大利	Italy	8572	2799
荷兰	Netherland	4035	3018
英国	England	10469	7522
瑞士	Switzerland	5103	73
西班牙	Spain	863	745
俄罗斯联邦	Russia	3884	2568
拉丁美洲	**Latin America**	**69812**	**28208**
#哥伦比亚	Colombia	298	297
巴西	Brazil	7321	1384
阿根廷	Argentina	327	324
北美洲	**North America**	**392740**	**193547**
加拿大	Canada	4512	3369
美国	America	115844	52817
大洋洲及太平洋岛屿	**Oceanic and Pacific Islands**	**56296**	**9318**
#澳大利亚	Australia	20073	2535
新西兰	New Zealand	273	201

注：本表数据来源于西安海关。

17–7 主要商品分大类出口金额

单位：万美元

商品分类	HS Section and Division	2000	2004
食用蔬菜、根及块茎	Edible Vegetables, Certain,Roots amd Tubers	1095	1386
蔬菜、水果、坚果或植物其他部分的制品	Vegetables, Fruits, Nuts, or Products Made of Other Parts of Plants	2076	7786
矿砂、矿渣及矿灰	Ores,Slags and Ash	4083	30590
无机化学品；贵金属、稀土金属、放射性元素及其同位素的有机及无机化合物	Inorganic Chemicals,Organic or Inorganic Compounds of Precious Metals,of Rare Earth Metals,of Radioactive Elements or of Isotopes	3714	5806
有机化学品	Organic Chemicals	2367	4837
羊毛、动物细毛或粗毛、马毛纱线及其机织物	Wool ,Fine or Coarse Animal Hair; Horsehair Yarn and Woven Fabric	810	1640
棉花	Cotton	3197	3133
化学纤维短纤	Short Staple Chemical' Fibers	5061	1987
针织或钩编的服装及衣着附件	Articles of Apparel and Clothing Accessories, Knitted or Crocheted	6753	7465
非针织或非钩编的服装及衣着附件	Articles of Apparel and Clothing Accessories, not Knitted or Crocheted	7269	5543
其它纺织制成品；成套物品；旧衣着及旧纺织品	Other Made Up Textile Articles;Sets;Worn Clothing and Worn Textile Articles;Rags Articles	1649	2667
鞋靴、护膝和类似品及其零件	Footwear,Gaiters and The Like;Parts of Such Articles Headgear and Parts Thereof	1347	2687
玻璃及其制品	Glass and Glassware	3376	8083
钢铁	Iron and Steel	3534	5244
钢铁制品	Articles of Iron or Steel	5535	10398
铅及制品	Lead Areticles Thereof	1371	43
锌及制品	Zinc Areticles Thereof	4031	522
其他贱金属、金属陶瓷及其制品	Other Base Metals,Germets;Areticles Thereof	1066	6419
贱金属工具、器具、利口器、餐匙、餐叉及其零件	Tools,Implements,Cutlery,Spons and Forks, of Base Metal;Parts Thereof of Base Metal	2933	3406
核反应堆、锅炉、机器、机械器具及其零件	Nuclear Reactors ,Boilers, Machinery and Mechanical Appliances; and Parts Thereof	10915	24696
电机、电气设备及其零件；录音机及放声机、电视图象、声音的录制和重放设备及其零件、附件	Electrical Machinery and Equipment and Parts Thereof;Sound Recorders and Repreducers, Television Image and Sound Recordes and Repreducers,and Parts and Accessories of Such Articles	8339	19812
光学、照相、电影、计量、检验、医疗或外科仪器及设备、精密仪器及设备；上述物品的零配件、附件	Optical,Photographic,Cinematographic,Measuring, Checking,Precision Medical or Surgical Instruments and Apparatus;Parts and Accessories Thereof	2020	1847
家具、寝具、褥垫、弹簧床垫、软床垫及类似的填充制品；未列名灯具及照明装置；发光标志、发光名牌及类似品；活动房屋	Mattresses,Mattress Supports,Cushions and Similar Stuffed Furnishings;Lamps and Lighting Fittings, not Elsewhere Spcified or Included;Illumihated Signs,Illuminated	2587	4955

Export Value of Major Merchandise by Type

(USD 10 000)

2005	2006	2007	2008	2009	2010	2011	2012	2013
1190	1136	1232	1374	803	4740	2016	1961	2699
10531	15374	37426	29270	21920	41289	36763	2576	49361
63247	52046	47378	40502	6141	325	4709	1679	1685
10997	10916	16508	15882	9774	24875	11735	8911	12588
8569	11923	11182	13954	16294	982	20067	17890	28694
903	1400	1065	720	460	10133	796	562	2433
3240	3808	3255	3213	2346	98	2628	2185	5827
1471	1556	1767	1181	2217	479	2586	2375	8245
5736	5332	5345	4371	3617	3209	3366	12316	6491
5068	4078	3875	3623	2919	3394	3262	7050	4861
3000	3342	3090	3187	2813	544	2838	4412	4471
1368	216	348	380	367	150	1003	5252	6293
8576	8272	6246	6538	5574	928	8073	10995	13856
5314	4900	11366	11966	4254	18549	16681	8407	6730
13959	16903	17329	26568	11943	5998	25319	24259	33546
12	158	1650	2	1	10	2	4913	16
135	4119	2470	46	78	28545	10	11	59
11233	17695	23414	27576	11276	3556	28092	21397	24030
3052	3607	3917	4083	2777	2893	3641	5176	5992
30832	36174	47381	75911	52372	130296	99631	127795	211009
23605	22801	33393	56758	53355	136	137105	183536	327931
2341	3521	4230	6348	5255	196	11066	14908	17879
4773	5086	8301	8296	4769	5328	3860	25644	23595

17-8 主要商品分大类进口金额

Import Value of Major Merchandise by Type

单位：万美元 (USD 10 000)

商品分类	HS Section and Division	2000	2005	2006	2007	2008
无机化学品；贵金属、稀土金属、放射性元素及其同位素的有机及无机化合物	Inorganic Chemicals,Organic or Inorganic Compounds of Precious Metals,of Rare Earth Metals,of Radioactive Elements or of Isotopes	1467	317	709	1039	6001
有机化学品	Organic Chemicals	7257	15237	13521	14536	15692
塑料及其制品	Plastic and Articles Thereof	2559	4317	2889	5149	2553
钢铁	Iron and Steel	2467	752	1014	1270	3888
铜及制品	Copper and Articles Thereof	2367	689	8035	22683	11097
铝及制品	Aluminium and Articles Thereof	2652	3627	3172	3223	4767
核反应堆、锅炉、机器、机械器具及其零件	Nuclear Reactors ,Boilers, Machinery and Mechanical Appliances; and Parts Thereof	12990	38050	33065	55243	68504
电机、电气设备及其零件；录音机及放声机、电视图象、声音的录制和重放设备及其零件、附件	Electrical Machinery and Equipment and Parts Thereof;Sound Recorders and Repreducers, Television Image and Sound Recordes and Repreducers,and Parts and Accessories of Such Articles	5911	23337	21279	25164	48008
车辆及其零件、附件、铁道及电车道车辆除外	Vehicles Other Than Railway or Tramway Rolling-Stock, and Rarts and Accessories Thereof	1530	1387	1228	1529	3789
航空器、航天器及其零配件	Aircraft, Spacecraft and Parts Thereof	10443	8800	17879	2463	26148
光学、照相、电影、计量、检验、医疗或外科仪器及设备、精密仪器及设备；上述物品的零配件、附件	Optical,Photographic,Cinematographic,Measuring, Checking,Precision Medical or Surgical	3673	10424	12152	17026	17737

17-8 续表 continued

单位：万美元 (USD 10 000)

商品分类	HS Section and Division	2009	2010	2011	2012	2013
无机化学品；贵金属、稀土金属、放射性元素及其同位素的有机及无机化合物	Inorganic Chemicals,Organic or Inorganic Compounds of Precious Metals,of Rare Earth Metals,of Radioactive Elements or of Isotopes	5040	7513	19766	13329	11869
有机化学品	Organic Chemicals	14186	13949	18100	12331	12504
塑料及其制品	Plastic and Articles Thereof	3134	4091	3250	3107	8014
钢铁	Iron and Steel	2537	10949	10643	5928	1802
铜及制品	Copper and Articles Thereof	41195	43343	78482	11857	65170
铝及制品	Aluminium and Articles Thereof	6505	3116	5913	8649	11758
核反应堆、锅炉、机器、机械器具及其零件	Nuclear Reactors ,Boilers, Machinery and Mechanical Appliances; and Parts Thereof	87493	134753	135240	98802	186974
电机、电气设备及其零件；录音机及放声机、电视图象、声音的录制和重放设备及其零件、附件	Electrical Machinery and Equipment and Parts Thereof;Sound Recorders and Repreducers, Television Image and Sound Recordes and Repreducers,and Parts and Accessories of Such Articles	113034	207937	230957	257444	444407
车辆及其零件、附件、铁道及电车道车辆除外	Vehicles Other Than Railway or Tramway Rolling-Stock, and Rarts and Accessories Thereof	1798	3109	1527	2222	2966
航空器、航天器及其零配件	Aircraft, Spacecraft and Parts Thereof	13057	3620	4654	8516	9179
光学、照相、电影、计量、检验、医疗或外科仪器及设备、精密仪器及设备；上述物品的零配件、附件	Optical,Photographic,Cinematographic,Measuring, Checking,Precision Medical or Surgical	24210	37414	39317	48206	61727

注：本表数据来源于西安海关。

17–9 主要年份旅游人数及收入

Number of Tourists and Tourism Earnings In Representative Years

年份 Year	接待旅游者人数（万人次） Number of Tourists (10 000 person-times)	国际旅游人数 Number of International Tourists	旅游总收入（万元） Total Tourism Earnings (10 000 yuan)	国际旅游收入 Earning of International Tourists	国际旅游者在西安人均停留天数（天） Number of Days of Average International Tourists Staying in Xi'an(day)
1980	4.00	4.00	1757	1757	3.8
1981	6.71	6.71	2314	2314	3.4
1985	21.15	21.15	7029	7029	2.2
1986	25.78	25.78	10886	10886	2.2
1987	30.15	30.15	16588	16588	2.1
1988	36.58	36.58	21152	21152	2.0
1989	21.20	21.20	14125	14125	1.9
1990	25.88	25.88	19628	19628	2.1
1991	31.00	31.00	29051	29051	2.3
1992	40.16	40.16	40966	40966	2.2
1993	43.50	43.50	48951	48951	1.9
1994	41.49	41.49	82000	82000	2.2
1995	791.35	41.35	440000	103818	2.0
1996	925.39	45.39	470000	149400	2.6
1997	1010.53	48.53	510000	166359	2.6
1998	1105.80	47.98	560000	160244	2.6
1999	1260.40	55.41	830000	186282	2.5
2000	1567.00	65.03	1050000	224100	2.5
2001	1752.20	67.20	1130000	240700	2.4
2002	1984.13	74.13	1310000	260000	2.2
2003	1647.67	33.66	1064200	121200	2.5
2004	2149.03	65.03	1544000	273900	2.9
2005	2423.60	77.56	1785000	335380	2.9
2006	2738.70	86.73	2043000	378270	2.9
2007	3118.01	100.01	2372000	424263	2.9
2008	3232.20	63.20	2435200	287200	2.6
2009	3929.29	67.29	2974000	310500	2.9
2010	5285.18	84.18	4051800	424000	2.9
2011	6653.23	100.23	5301500	512800	2.9
2012	7978.35	115.35	6543900	598900	2.9
2013	10130.00	121.11	8114400	641600	2.9

主：本表数据来源于市旅游局。

17-10 主要年份国际旅游收入

Earning of International Tourism In Representative Years

单位：万美元 (USD 10 000)

项 目	Item	2003	2004	2005	2006	2007	2008	2009	2010	2011	2012	2013
合 计	**Total**	**14600**	**33000**	**40900**	**46700**	**54323**	**35900**	**39000**	**53000**	**64100**	**74862**	**80200**
一、长途交通费	**Long Distance Transportation**	**3109**	**8415**	**12311**	**11442**	**14286**	**10016**	**12597**	**19292**	**26153**	**26876**	**28792**
1. 飞机	Airplane	2526	7524	9407	9527	10918	7467	9438	15264	19807	20887	23579
2. 火车	Train	131	264	858	561	2009	1436	2262	2968	2692	3369	4411
3. 汽车	Highway	452	627	2046	1354	1359	1113	897	1060	3654	2620	802
二、游览	**Sightseeing**	**511**	**1155**	**2045**	**2335**	**2335**	**1831**	**2262**	**3445**	**3846**	**4641**	**5133**
三、住宿	**Accommodation**	**2044**	**4752**	**4621**	**5977**	**6573**	**4523**	**5343**	**6572**	**6859**	**9358**	**10025**
四、餐饮	**Food and Beverage**	**1489**	**2673**	**3823**	**2195**	**3804**	**2908**	**3471**	**4929**	**2436**	**3444**	**3930**
五、娱乐	**Entertainment**	**409**	**990**	**1779**	**747**	**1847**	**2046**	**1833**	**2120**	**3525**	**5240**	**5774**
六、购物	**Shopping**	**4380**	**9900**	**9897**	**17466**	**15645**	**9262**	**7761**	**9911**	**11794**	**14298**	**14436**
七、邮电通讯	**Post and Communication Services**	**512**	**957**	**2454**	**1261**	**1794**	**1652**	**1131**	**1272**	**1474**	**1572**	**1604**
八、市内交通	**Local Transportation**	**350**	**726**	**858**	**841**	**1249**	**1041**	**975**	**2120**	**2564**	**2770**	**3529**
九、其它	**Others**	**1796**	**3432**	**3112**	**4436**	**6790**	**2621**	**3627**	**3339**	**5449**	**6663**	**6977**

注：本表数据来源于市旅游局。

17-11 主要涉外星级宾馆接待海外旅游者情况

Mainly Concerning Oversea Tourists Reception in Star Hotels in Representative Years

单位 人次 (person-time)

项 目	Item	2008	2009	2010	2011	2012	2013
海外旅游者人数	**International Tourists**	**632036**	**672909**	**841819**	**1002326**	**1153469**	**1211175**
外国人	Foreigners	535837	590870	732065	886276	1014036	1068980
#日本	Japan	43017	60192	70368	61844	62238	31010
菲律宾	Philippines	1466	1708	2213	2587	2311	1630
新加坡	Singapore	6335	7570	10158	12759	12028	10832
美国	America	104742	100445	106042	117485	124490	127772
加拿大	Canada	19047	21901	28409	37511	36494	33[illegible]80
英国	England	40299	43068	41023	44386	43145	44[illegible]12
法国	France	37415	39350	42337	42114	46870	42434
德意志联邦国	Germany	32892	36371	40166	40777	45860	43365
意大利	Italy	9445	15316	15868	19737	20770	17091
瑞士	Switzerland	3763	4479	5528	5933	7006	8354
澳大利亚	Australia	24784	26349	30507	34411	38180	37021
新西兰	New Zealand	4027	4238	5005	5248	5399	6782
港、澳、台同胞	Chinese Compatriots from Hong Kong,Macao and Taiwan	96199	82039	109754	116050	139433	142195
#台湾省同胞	Taiwan	44552	37464	54119	58197	70051	7[illegible]408

注：本表数据来源于市旅游局。

17-12 主要年份旅行社及A级景点

Statistics of Travel Agencies and Level-A Scenic Spots in Representative Years

项 目	Item	2007	2008	2009	2010	2011	2012	2013
旅行社数（个）	Number of Travel Agencies (unit)	262	271	303	334	365	344	360
旅行社营业收入（亿元）	Revenue of Travel Agencies (100 million yuan)	26.48	17.85	21.34	31.22	44.31	49.49	57.93
旅游A级景点数（个）	Number of Level-A Scenic Spots(unit)	23	23	24	34	43	55	61
旅游A级景点年接待游客人次（万人次）	Number of Tourists Received at Level-A Scenic Spots (10 000 person times)	1410	1420	1504	2726.20	4295[illegible]	5306	7163[illegible]

注：本表数据来源于市旅游局。

主要统计指标解释

进出口总额 指实际进出我国国境的货物总金额。包括对外贸易实际进出口货物，来料加工装配进出口货物，国家间、联合国及国际组织无偿援助物资和赠送品，华侨、港澳台同胞和外籍华人捐赠品，租赁期满归承租人所有的租赁货物，进料加工进出口货物，边境地方贸易及边境地区小额贸易进出口货物（边民互市贸易除外），中外合资企业、中外合作经营企业、外商独资经营企业进出口货物和公用物品，到、离岸价格在规定限额以上的进出口货样和广告品（无商业价值、无使用价值和免费提供出口的除外），从保税仓库提取在中国境内销售的进口货物，以及其他进出口货物。该指标可以观察一个国家在对外贸易方面的总规模。我国规定出口货物按离岸价格统计，进口货物按到岸价格统计。

商品经营单位所在地进、出口额 指在所在地海关注册登记的有进出口经营权的企业实际进、出口额。

商品目的地进口额和商品货源地出口额 目的地进口额指进口货物的消费、使用或最终抵运地的实际进口额；货源地出口额指出口货物的产地或原始发货地的实际出口额。

利用外资 指我国各级政府、部门、企业和其他经济组织通过对外借款、吸收外商直接投资以及用其他方式筹措的境外现汇、设备、技术等。

外商直接投资 指外国企业和经济组织或个人（包括华侨、港澳台胞以及我国在境外注册的企业）按我国有关政策、法规，用现汇、实物、技术等在我国境内开办外商独资企业、与我国境内的企业或经济组织共同举办中外合资经营企业、合作经营企业或合作开发资源的投资（包括外商投资收益的再投资），以及经政府有关部门批准的项目投资总额内企业从境外借入的资金。

旅游人数：

（1）入境旅游人数：指报告期内来我国观光、度假、探亲访友、就医疗养、购物、参加会议或从事经济、文化、体育、宗教活动的外国人、港澳台同胞等入境游客。统计时，外国人、港澳台同胞每入境一次统计1人次。

（2）出境人数：指中国（大陆）居民因公或因私出境前往其他国家、中国香港特别行政区、澳门特别行政区和台湾省观光、度假、探亲访友、就医疗养、购物、参加会议或从事经济、文化、体育、宗教活动的人数，即出境游客。统计时，按每出境一次统计1人次。

（3）国内旅游人数：指在报告期内在中国（大陆）观光游览、度假、探亲访友、就医疗养、购物、参加会议或从事经济、文化、体育、宗教活动的中国（大陆）居民人数，其出游的目的不是通过所从事的活动谋取报酬。统计时，国内游客按每出游一次统计1人次。

国际旅游（外汇）收入 指入境游客在中国（大陆）境内旅行、游览过程中用于交通、参观游览、住宿、餐饮、购物、娱乐等全部花费。

国内旅游收入 又称旅游总花费指国内游客在国内旅行、游览过程中用于交通、参观游览、住宿、餐饮、购物、娱乐等全部花费。

国际旅行社 指经营业务范围包括入境旅游业务、出境旅游业务和国内旅游业务的旅行社。

国内旅行社 指经营范围仅限于国内旅游业务的旅行社。

星级饭店 指设备、设施、服务符合《旅游饭店星级的划分与评定》（CB/T14308—2003），通过相关旅游管理部门评定，并取得星级饭店称号的饭店（含预备星级饭店）。

Explanatory Notes on Main Statistical Indicators

Total Imports and Exports at Customs refer to the real value of commodities imported and exported across the border of China. They include the actual imports and exports through foreign trade, imported and exported goods under the processing and assembling trades and materials, supplies and gifts as aid given gratis between governments and by the United Nations and other international organizations, and contributions donated by overseas Chinese, compatriots in Hong Kong and Macao and Chinese with foreign citizenship, leasing commodities owned by tenant at the expiration of leasing period, the imported and exported commodities processed with imported materials, commodities trading in border areas (excluding mutual exchange goods), the imported and exported commodities and articles for public use of the Sino-foreign joint ventures, cooperative enterprises and ventures with sole foreign investment. Also included is import or export of samples and advertising goods for which CIF or FOB value are beyond the permitted ceiling (excluding goods of no tracing or use value and free commodities for export), imported goods sold in China from bonded warehouses and other imported or exported goods. The indicator of the total imports and exports at customs can be used to observe the total size of external trade in a country. In accordance with the stipulation of the Chinese government, imports are calculated at CIF, while exports are calculated at FOB.

Import Export Value by Location of China's Foreign Trade Managing Units refers to actual value of imports and exports carried out by corporations which have been registered by the local Customs house and are vested with right to run import export business.

Import Value of Commodities by Place of Destination and Export Value of Commodities by Place of Origin in China The former indicator refers to the value of import commodities of the places of their consumption, utilization or the places of their final destination. The latter indicator refers to the value of export commodities of the places of their origin or the places of the commodities dispatched.

Utilization of Foreign Capitals refers to remittance, equipment and technology financed from abroad, by loans, foreign direct investment and other forms undertaken by the Chinese governments at all levels, by various departments, enterprises and other economic units.

Foreign Borrowings refer to funds borrowed from abroad through formal signing of borrowing agreements with foreign institutions, including loans of foreign governments, loans of international financial institutions, commercial loans of foreign banks, export credit, and funds raised by Chinese bonds (and shares before 1996) issued abroad. It is an important part of China's utilization of foreign capitals.

Foreign Direct Investment refers to the investments inside China by foreign enterprises and economic organizations or individuals (including overseas Chinese, compatriots from Hong Kong, Macao and Taiwan, and Chinese enterprises registered abroad), following the relevant policies and laws of China, for the establishment of ventures exclusively with foreign own investment, Sino-foreign joint ventures and cooperative enterprises or for co-operative exploration of resources with enterprises or economic organizations in China.

Number of Tourists

(1) Visitor arrivals refer to the number of foreigners,Chinese compatriots from Hong Kong, Macao and Taiwan Chinese (mainland) who come to China (mainland) for sight-seeing,vacation,visiting relatives, medical treatment, shopping, attending conference, or to engage in economic, cultural, sports and religious activities. In compiling statistics, each time of entering China is counted as one person-time.

(2) Number of Chinese residents going abroad refer to the number of Chinese (mainland) residents going to other countries, Hong Kong Special Administrative region, Macao Special Administrative region and Taiwan for on official or private purposes, for sight-seeing, vacation, visiting relatives, medical treatment, shopping, attending conference, or to engage in economic, cultural, sports and religious

activities. In compiling statistics, each time of leaving is counted as one person-time.

(3) Number of domestic tourists refers to the number of Chinese (mainland) residents who travel within China (mainland) for sight-seeing, vacation, visiting relatives, medical treatment, shopping, attending conference, or to engage in economic, cultural, sports and religious activities. In compiling statistics, each time of travelling is counted as one person-time.

Foreign Exchange Earnings from International Tourism refer to the total expenditure of foreigners, overseas Chinese,Chinese compatriots from Hong Kong,Macao and Taiwan during their stay in the mainland of China on transportation,sighting,accommodation, food,shopping and entertainment.

Income from Domestic Tourism refer to expenditure of domestic tourists on transportation,sighting, accommodation, food, shopping and entertainment while they travel.

International Travel Agencies refer to travel agencies engaged in tourism entering China, Chinese residents going abroad and domestic tourism.

Domestic Travel Agencies refer to travel agencies only engaged in domestic tourism.

Star–rated Hotels refer to hotels rated with stars as assessed by the relevant tourism authorities according to GB/T14308-2003 standard with reference to their infrastructure, facilities and service levels.

18 金融业

FINANCIAL INTERMEDIATION

资料整理：刘　婷
Data management:Liu Ting

第十八部分　金融业

一、简要说明

本章资料包括金融、证券和保险业情况，由西安市统计局综合处根据人民银行西安分行营业管理部和市金融办提供资料整理。

二、主要指标

金融机构人民币（含外资）存款余额（亿元）	13763.19	比上年增长	13.5%
金融机构人民币（含外资）贷款余额（亿元）	10023.63	比上年增长	16.1%
保费收入（亿元）	202.41	比上年增长	16.9%

18　FINANCIAL INTERMEDIATION

Ⅰ.Brief Introduction

This chapter includes information of the financial, securities and insurance, compiled by Integration Division of the Xi'an Bureau of Statistics, according to data from Xi'an Branch Management Department of the People's Bank of China, Provincial Banking Bureau and Xi'an Financial Office.

Ⅱ.Major Indicators

		Increase over Preceding Year
Deposit in Financial Institution(100 mil. Yuan)	13763.19	13.5%
Loans in Financial Institutions(100 mil. Yuan)	10023.63	16.1%
Premiums(100 mil. Yuan)	202.41	16.9%

18-1 西安银行系统机构、人员数

Number of Institution and Employed Person in Finance System in Xi'an

机构名称	Name of Institution	2012		2013	
		机构数（个）Number of Institution (unit)	年末人数（人）Number of Staff and Workers (person)	机构数（个）Number of Institution (unit)	年末人数（人）Number of Staff and Workers (person)
合　计	**Total**	**1803**	**33478**	**1849**	**35577**
1.人民银行西安分行营业管理部	Management Department of the People's Bank of China Xi'an Branch	1	396	1	389
2.中国工商银行西安分行	Industrial and Commercial Bank of China Shaanxi Branch	193	4959	193	4937
3.中国农业银行西安分行	Agricultural Bank of China Shaanxi Branch	165	3160	169	3200
4.中国银行西安分行	Bank of China Xi'an Branch	122	3309	124	3382
5.中国建设银行西安分行	Construction Bank of China Shaanxi Branch	179	4059	189	4132
6.国家开发银行西安分行	National Development Bank Xi'an Branch	1	179	1	183
7.中国农业发展银行西安分行	Agricultural Development Bank of China Xi'an Branch	10	253	10	263
8.中国进出口银行	Export Import Bank of Xi'an Branch	1	80	1	74
9.交通银行西安分行	Bank of Communication Xi'an Branch	50	1197	49	1204
10.中信实业银行西安分行	CITIC Industrial Bank Xi'an Branch	20	774	22	855
11.中国光大银行西安分行	China Everbright Bank Xi'an Branch	20	711	21	773
12.华夏银行西安分行	China Huaxia Bank Xi'an Branch	11	347	13	393
13.招商银行西安分行	China Merchants Bank Xi'an Branch	25	1102	26	1161
14.上海浦东发银行西安分行	Pufa Bank Xi'an Branch	13	612	15	623
15.兴业银行西安分行	Fujian Industrial Bank Xi'an Branch	15	876	16	870
16.民生银行西安分行	China Minsheng Banking Corp., Ltd Xi'an Branch	17	863	18	1044
17.浙商银行西安分行	China Zheshang Bank Xi'an Branch	3	191	5	255
18.恒丰银行西安分行	Evergrowing Bank Xi'an Branch	2	84	4	126
19.中国邮政储蓄银行西安分行	The postal savings bank branch in Xi'an	280	762	281	848
20.西安银行	Bank of Xi'an	115	2249	115	2545
21.重庆银行西安分行	Bank of Chongqing, Xi'an Branch	2	132	4	150
22.北京银行西安分行	Bank of Beijing,Xi'an Branch	7	367	10	455
23.长安银行	Bank of Changan	6	213	8	293
24.昆仑银行西安分行	Kunlun Xi'an Branch Bank	3	243	5	317
25.齐商银行西安分行	Qi Commercial Bank Xi'an Branch	3	83	5	168
26.成都银行西安分行	Bank of Chengdu, Xi'an Branch	2	114	4	143
27.宁夏银行西安分行	Bank of Ningxia Xi'an Branch	3	134	4	184
28.农村信用社联合社	Rural Credit Cooperatives Association	522	5623	523	5869
29.东亚银行西安分行	Dongya Bank Xi'an Branch	7	290	7	334
30.汇丰银行西安分行	Huifeng Bank Xi'an Branch	3	51	3	60
31.渣打银行西安分行	British Standard Chartered bank Xi'an Branch	1	40	1	41
32.西安高陵阳光村镇银行	Xi'an Gaoling sunshine village bank	1	25	1	25
33.平安银行西安分行	Ping'an Bank Xi'an Branch			1	276

注：本表数据来源于人民银行西安营管部

18-2 金融机构（含外资）本外币存贷款年末余额（2013年）

Financial institution Including Foreign-funded Balance of Bisic Currency and Foreign Currency at Year-end（2013）

单位：万元 (10 000 yuan)

指 标	Item	2013	比年初增加额 Increase or decrease compared with the beginning of the Year
存款余额合计（汇率：6.0969）	**Total Deposit (Exchange Rate: 6.0969)**	**138927748**	**15977705**
一、单位存款	**Company Deposit**	**78393000**	**7951427**
#活期存款	Demand Deposits	37086364	627212
定期存款	Time Deposits	21343762	4504375
二、个人存款	**Personal Deposits**	**57063744**	**7426518**
#储蓄存款	Savings Deposits	53988813	5794850
三、财政性存款	**Fiscal Deposits**	**564390**	**53851**
四、临时性存款	**Temporary Deposit**	**297176**	**3221**
五.委托存款	**Consignment Deposits**	**867442**	**681542**
六.其他存款	**Other Deposits**	**1741995**	**-138854**
贷款余额合计（汇率：6.0969）	**Total Loans (Exchange Rate: 6.0969)**	**102147818**	**14026605**
一、境内贷款	**Domestic Loans**	**101986742**	**14047463**
短期贷款	Short-term Loans	24071524	4078820
中长期贷款	Medium-term and Long-term loans	74754958	10234167
融资租赁	Financial Leasing	2764	-8066
票据融资	Bill Financing	3106469	-261448
各项垫款	Various Advance Funds	51026	3990
二、境外贷款	**Foreign Loans**	**161076**	**-20857**

注：本表数据来源于人民银行西安营管部

18-3 金融机构（不含外资）本外币存贷款年末余额（2013年）

Domestic Funded Financial institution balance of Bisic Currency and Foreign Currency at Year-end (2013)

单位：万元 (10 000 yuan)

指　标	Item	2013	比年初增加额 Increase or decrease compared with the beginning of the Year
存款余额合计	**Total Deposit**	**137881852**	**15870388**
一、单位存款	**Company Deposit**	**77660805**	**7874933**
#活期存款	Demand Deposits	36896796	683406
定期存款	Time Deposits	21249469	4642780
二、个人存款	**Personal Deposits**	**56832817**	**7423365**
#储蓄存款	Savings Deposits	53830084	5755200
三、财政性存款	**Fiscal Deposits**	**564390**	**58927**
四、临时性存款	**Temporary Deposit**	**294410**	**455**
五、委托存款	**Trusted Deposits**	**867442**	**681542**
六、其他存款	**Other Deposits**	**1661987**	**-168834**
贷款余额合计	**Total Loans**	**101184545**	**13855382**
一、境内贷款	**Domestic Loans**	**101024022**	**13376387**
短期贷款	Short-term Loans	23778666	3957992
中长期贷款	Medium-term&Long-term Loans	74096280	10135790
融资租赁	Financial Leasing	2764	-8066
票据融资	Bill Financing	3096269	-213319
各项垫款	Various Advance Funds	50043	3990
二、境外贷款	**Foreign Loans**	**160523**	**-21004**

注：本表数据来源于人民银行西安营管部

18-4 主要年份金融机构（含外资）人民币存款年末余额

Year-end Balance of Deposit in Financial Institutions Including Foreign-funded in Representative Years

单位：亿元 (100million yuan)

年 份 Year	合计 Total	其 中：Among 单位存款 Company Deposit	储蓄存款 Savings Deposits
1978	12.82		3.72
1980	20.99		5.48
1985	40.68		16.70
1990	112.37	31.10	62.23
1995	359.51	114.54	230.63
1996	619.98	199.85	394.02
1997	602.50	227.61	358.78
1998	799.54	245.44	499.68
1999	1014.27	347.49	586.40
2000	1335.63	540.19	675.83
2001	1629.72	674.49	800.86
2002	2191.47	884.69	988.04
2003	2665.87	1041.43	1210.56
2004	3061.66	1159.98	1432.86
2005	3599.70	1237.37	1716.76
2006	4066.16	1374.91	1950.53
2007	4582.71	1702.12	2002.38
2008	5749.35	2213.67	2513.70
2009	7522.08	3077.99	3084.20
2010	8933.23	3556.78	3641.09
2011	10430.27	5997.60	4155.65
2012	12125.53	6927.84	4787.03
2013	13763.19	7759.61	5357.05

注：本表数据来源于人民银行西安营管部

18-5　主要年份金融机构（含外资）人民币贷款年末余额

Year-end Balance of Loans in Financial Institutions Including Foreign-funded in Representative Years

单位：亿元　　(100 million yuan)

年　份 Year	合计 Total	其　中：Among 短期贷款 Short-term Loans	中长期贷款 Medium-term&Long-term Loans
1978	23.56		
1980	26.40		
1985	48.60		
1990	131.67	101.13	23.78
1995	334.50	252.30	73.32
1996	477.97	333.88	90.12
1997	443.76	342.79	87.27
1998	597.34	448.74	118.42
1999	786.20	589.52	150.64
2000	972.51	652.00	241.27
2001	1185.97	666.41	387.82
2002	1598.42	780.69	502.03
2003	1954.18	946.64	743.72
2004	2052.33	950.50	850.01
2005	2158.10	830.68	1013.32
2006	2344.77	812.33	1310.57
2007	2683.77	883.32	1593.37
2008	3275.12	1031.62	1905.08
2009	4482.63	1155.83	2908.75
2010	6482.28	1097.60	5075.93
2011	7564.93	1431.29	5776.48
2012	8635.22	1917.51	6378.88
2013	10023.63	2326.63	7385.37

注：本表数据来源于人民银行西安营管部

18-6 金融机构（含外资）人民币存贷款年末余额（2013年）

Year-end Balance of Deposit and Loans in Financial Institutionst Including Foreign-funded（2013）

单位：万元　　　　(10 000 yuan)

指　标	Item	2013	比年初增加额 Increase or decrease compared with the beginning of the Year
存款余额合计	**Total Deposit**	**137631895**	**16289264**
一、单位存款	**Company Deposit**	**77596140**	**8310980**
#活期存款	Demand Deposits	36544905	1023439
定期存款	Time Deposits	21257944	4466198
二、个人存款	**Personal Deposits**	**56631184**	**7405877**
#储蓄存款	Savings Deposits	53570459	5773257
三、财政性存款	**Fiscal Deposits**	**564390**	**53851**
四、临时性存款	**Temporary Deposit**	**231456**	**-23518**
五、委托存款	**Trusted Deposits**	**867193**	**681366**
六、其他存款	**Other Deposits**	**1741533**	**-139293**
贷款余额合计	**Total Loans**	**100236266**	**13843756**
一、境内贷款	**Domestic Loans**	**100231260**	**13843208**
（一）短期贷款	Short-term Loans	23266330	4051867
1. 个人贷款及透支	Individual Loans and Overdrafts	3162699	1180268
2. 单位贷款及透支	Unit Loans and Overdrafts	18535300	2453689
3. 普通并购贷款	Ordinary Merging Loans		
4. 银团贷款	Syndicated Loans	123030	48981
5. 贸易融资	Trade Finance	1445301	368929
（二）中长期贷款	Medium-term&Long-term Loans	73853657	10064858
1. 个人贷款	Individual Loans and Overdrafts	18725579	2793652
2. 单位贷款	Unit Loans and Overdrafts	45520169	5606595
3. 普通并购贷款	Ordinary Merging Loans	319130	-170
4. 贸易融资	Syndicated Loans	18905	16591
5. 银团贷款	Trade Finance	9269873	1648190
（三）融资租赁	Financial Leasing	2764	-8066
（四）票据融资	Bill Financing	3106462	-261455
（五）各项垫款	Various Advance Funds	2047	-3995
二、境外贷款	**Foreign Loans**	**5006**	**547**

注：本表数据来源于人民银行西安营管部

18-7 金融机构（不含外资）人民币存贷款年末余额（2013年）

Year-end Balance of Deposit and Loans in Financial Institutions Not Including Foreign-funded（2013）

单位：万元　　　　(10 000 yuan)

指　标	Item	2013	比年初增加额 Increase or decrease compared with the beginning of the Year
存款余额合计	**Total Deposit**	**136658898**	**16186794**
一、单位存款	**Company Deposit**	**76921127**	**8239870**
#活期存款	Demand Deposits	36382770	1071771
定期存款	Time Deposits	21191737	4618760
二、个人存款	**Personal Deposits**	**56415974**	**7402138**
#储蓄存款	Savings Deposits	53427447	5743213
三、财政性存款	**Fiscal Deposits**	**564390**	**58927**
四、临时性存款	**Temporary Deposit**	**228689**	**-26284**
五、委托存款	**Trusted Deposits**	**867193**	**681366**
六、其他存款	**Other Deposits**	**1661525**	**-169273**
贷款余额合计	**Total Loans**	**99300373**	**13667286**
一、境内贷款	**Domestic Loans**	**99295705**	**13666894**
（一）短期贷款	Short-term Loans	22977997	3924382
1. 个人贷款及透支	Individual Loans and Overdrafts	3140131	1170481
2. 单位贷款及透支	Unit Loans and Overdrafts	18280780	2330098
3. 普通并购贷款	Ordinary Merging Loans		
4. 银团贷款	Syndicated Loans	123030	48981
5. 贸易融资	Trade Finance	1424057	374822
（二）中长期贷款	Medium-term&Long-term Loans	73217617	9967899
1. 个人贷款	Individual Loans and Overdrafts	18575237	2780239
2. 单位贷款	Unit Loans and Overdrafts	45034472	5523050
3. 普通并购贷款	Ordinary Merging Loans	319130	-170
4. 贸易融资	Trade Finance	18905	15591
5. 银团贷款	Syndicated Loans	9269873	1643190
（三）融资租赁	Financial Leasing	2764	-8066
（四）票据融资	Bill Financing	3096262	-213326
（五）各项垫款	Various Advance Funds	1064	-3995
二、境外贷款	**Foreign Loans**	**4668**	**392**

注：本表数据来源于人民银行西安营管部

18-8 保险业务情况

Indicators of Insurance Business

指　标	Item	2011	2012	2013
保险金额（亿元）	**Amount Insured(100 million yuan)**	**44511**	**35199**	**42596**
保费收入（万元）	**Premiums(10 000 yuan)**	**1625666**	**1732088**	**2024067**
一、财产险	**Property Insurance**	**449625**	**521619**	**629947**
（一）财产保险	Property Insurance	422739	484476	576666
1. 机动车辆及第三者责任	Motor Vehicle and Outside Person Liability	364585	431460	513634
2. 企业财产险	Enterprise Property Insurance	37452	41398	41140
3. 货物运输险	Freight Transport Insurance	4208	4312	3944
4. 家庭财产险	Family Property Insurance	365	323	296
5. 建工及安工保险及其责任险	Construction and Installation Projects Insurance and Related Libility Insurance	15004	5938	16133
6. 其他	Others	1124	1045	1519
（二）责任保险	Liability Insurance	8988	10719	13393
（三）信用保险	Export Credit Insurance	8188	8257	8648
（四）保证保险	Guarantee Insurance	8798	15421	21588
（五）农业保险	Agriculture Insurance	913	2747	9653
二、人身险	**Personnel Insurance**	**1176041**	**1210469**	**1394120**
（一）人寿保险	Life Insurance	1072364	1077710	1221975
1. 非分红保险	Non Dividend Insurance	95292	99073	109810
2. 分红保险	Dividend Insurance	966024	967751	1099986
3. 投资连接保险	Insurance Connection Insurance	362	346	330
4. 万能保险	Universal Insurance	10687	10541	11849
（二）意外伤害险	Unforeseen Injury Insurance	37064	40433	49541
（三）健康保险	Health Insurance	66613	92326	122604
赔款支出和各项给付(万元)	**Indemnity and Other Expenditure(10 000 yuan)**	**371421**	**475483**	**664905**
一、财产险	**Property Insurance**	**199915**	**274285**	**339004**
（一）财产保险	Property Insurance	192900	263917	325128
1. 机动车辆及第三者责任	Motor Vehicle and Outside Person Liability	163878	235665	291390
2. 企业财产险	Enterprise Property Insurance	15151	18805	24870
3. 家庭财产保险	Freight Transport Insurance	130	66	93
4. 货物运输保险	Family Property Insurance	1342	1148	1224
5. 建工及安工保险及其责任险	Construction and Installation Projects Insurance and Related Libility Insurance	11345	7893	6480
6. 其他	Others	1054	340	1070
（二）责任保险	Liability Insurance	3114	4713	5192
（三）信用保险	Export Credit Insurance	2324	5357	5414
（四）保证保险	Guarantee Insurance	579	-581	1450
（五）农业保险	Agriculture Insurance	999	878	1820
二、人身险	**Personnel Insurance**	**171505**	**201198**	**325900**
（一）人寿保险	Life Insurance	140240	167146	268455
1. 非分红保险	Non Dividend Insurance	40017	50929	48680
2. 分红保险	Dividend Insurance	98169	113557	216911
3. 投资连接保险	Insurance Connection Insurance	595	327	32
4. 万能保险	Universal Insurance	1459	2334	2832
（二）意外伤害险	Unforeseen Injury Insurance Health Insurance	7572	9013	10685
（三）健康保险	Health Insurance	23693	25039	46760
退保金（万元）	**Withdrawal(10 000 yuan)**	**90546**	**107665**	**167446**
#人寿保险	Life Insurance	89150	105909	165303
1. 非分红保险	Ordinary Life Insurance	4302	5514	6192
2. 分红保险	Dividend Insurance	84804	100373	159077
3. 投资连接保险	Insurance Connection Insurance	2		9
4. 万能保险	Universal Insurance	43	21	24

注：本表数据来源于市金融办

18-9 西安地区证券期货系统机构、人员数

Number of Institution and Employed Person in Securities and Futures System in Xi'an

机构名称	Name of Institution	2012年		2013年	
		机构数（个）Number of Institution (unit)	年末人数（人）Number of Staff and Workers (person)	机构数（个）Number of Institution (unit)	年末人数（人）Number of Staff and Workers (person)
证券经营机构	**Securities Company and the Sales Department**				
一、证券公司	**Securities Company**				
西部证券股份有限公司	Western Securities Company Ltd.	62	2130	71	2025
陕西开源证券经纪有限责任公司	KaiYuan Securities Company Ltd.	16	413	22	463
西安华弘证券经纪有限责任公司	Xi'an Huahong Securities Brokerage Co., Ltd.	10	291	8	293
二、证券营业部（含外地公司在西安营业部）	**Sales Department (include Xi'an departments of nonlocal companies.)**	**68**	**5946**	**73**	**2533**
期货经纪公司	**Futures Company**	**3**	**377**	**3**	**402**
迈科期货经纪有限公司	Maike Futures Company Ltd.	1	184	1	194
陕西长安期货经纪有限公司	Shanxi ChangAn Futures Company Ltd.	1	89	1	92
西部期货经纪有限公司	Western Futures Brokerage Co., Ltd.	1	104	1	116

注：证券公司包括三家公司及其在西安和外地的营业部。
本表数据来源于市金融办

18-10　证券期货市场基本情况（2013年）

Basic Facts on Securities and Futures Markets（2013）

指　标	Item	2013
一、上市证券公司情况	**Listed Securities Companies**	
拥有上市股份公司（个）	Number of Listed Share-holding Companies(unit)	29
上市股份公司总股本（亿股）	Total Capital of Listed Share-holding Companies (100 millon shares)	237
#流通股(亿股)	Negotiable Shares(100 million shares)	202
总市值（亿元）	Total Market Capitalization(100 million yuan)	1909
累计证券市场筹措资金（亿元）	Accumulated Capital Raised by Securities Markets(100 millon yuan)	625
二、证券经营机构情况	**Securities Trading Organizations**	
拥有证券公司（个）	Number of Securities Companies(unit)	3
证券营业部（个）（含外地公司在西安营业部）	Number of Securities Business Departments(unit)	73
投资者开户数（万户）	Number of Investors Who have Opened an Account(10 000 accounts)	175
证券交易总额（亿元）	Total Turnover(100 million yuan)	12845
三、期货市场情况	**Futures Market**	
拥有期货经纪公司（个）	Number of Futures Business Management Companies(unit)	3
期货营业部（个）	Number of Futures Business,Departments(unit)	20
期货代理交易额（亿元）	Total Transaction Value in Futures Commissioning (100 million yuan)	36876
每个经纪公司平均拥有注册资金（万元）	Average Registered Capital of Each Business Management Company(10 000 yuan)	2

注：本表数据来源于市金融办

主要统计指标解释

信贷资金 指金融机构以信用方式积聚和分配的货币资金。金融机构信贷资金的来源有各项存款、金融债券、对国际金融机构负债、流通中现金、其他项目等；信贷资金的运用有各项贷款、有价证券及投资、金银占款、外汇占款、财政借款及在国际金融机构中的资产等。

存款 指企业、机关、团体或居民根据资金必须收回的原则，把货币资金存入银行或其他信贷机构保管并取得一定利息的一种信用活动形式。根据存款对象或性质的不同可划分为企业存款、财政存款、机关团体存款、城乡储蓄存款、农业存款、信托及委托类存款、其他存款等科目。它是银行信贷资金的主要来源。

贷款 指银行或其他信贷机构根据资金必须归还的原则，按一定利率，为企业、个人等提供资金的一种信用活动形式。我国银行贷款分为短期贷款、委托及信托类贷款、其他类贷款等。

保险公司 在中国境内的、经过保险监督管理部门批准设立，并依法登记注册的各类商业保险公司。

保险金额 指保险人承担赔偿或者给付保险金责任的最高限额。

保费 指投保人为取得保险人在约定范围内所承担赔偿责任而支付给保险人的费用。

赔款指保险人根据保险合同的规定，向被保险人支付的赔偿保险责任损失的金额。

给付 包括死伤医疗给付和满期给付。死伤医疗给付是指保险人根据人寿保险及长期健康保险合同的规定，因被保险人在保险期内发生保险责任范围内的保险事故支付给被保险人（或受益人）的金额。满期给付是指被保险人生存期满，保险人按人寿保险合同规定支付给被保险人的满期保险金额。

Explanatory Notes on Main Statistical Indicators

Credit Funds refer to the monetary funds accumulated and distributed in the means of credit by the financial institutions. The sources of credit funds include various deposits, financial bonds, liabilities to international financial institutions, currency in circulation, other items. The uses of credit funds include loans, securities and investment, position for bullion and silver purchase, position for foreign exchange purchase, advances to treasury, and assets with international financial institutions..

Deposit is a form of credit by which enterprises, institutions, organizations or households can put money into banks and other credit institutions for safekeeping and interest earning under the principle of free withdrawal. According to different depositors, deposits are divided into enterprise deposits, fiscal deposits, deposits of government agencies and organizations, savings deposits of rural and urban households, agricultural savings deposits, entrusted deposits and other deposits. Deposits are major sources of the credit funds of banks.

Loan is a form of credit by which banks and other credit institutions provide funds at certain interest rate to enterprises and individuals in the light of the principle of unconditional repayment. Loans from Chinese banks include short-term loan, medium- term and long-term loans, entrusted loans, and other loans.

Insurance Companies refer to commercial insurance companies of various forms registered by law and established in China with the approval of insurance regulatory agencies.

Amount Insured refers to the maximum that the insurant will get for the claim of the case insured.

Premium is the fee paid by the insurant to the insurer to obtain the obligation of compensation from the insurance within the agreed terms.

Settled Claim is the compensation paid by the insurer to the insurant in accordance with the insurance contract.

Payment includes payment for death, injury or medical treatment and payment at maturity. Payment for death, injury or medical treatment refers to the money paid to the insurant (or the beneficiary) in accordance with the life or health insurance contract when the insurant encounters accidents within the insured period covered in the contract. Payment at maturity refers to the payment to the insurant in accordance with the life insurance contract at the end of the insured period.

19 教育和科技

EDUCATION,SCIENCE AND TDCHNOLOGY

资料整理：郝　静　齐昆峰　陈春光

Data management:Hao Jing Qi Kunfenc Chen Chunguang

第十九部分　教育和科技

一、简要说明

本章资料包括教育事业、科技事业基本情况，由西安市统计局社会科技处根据西安市教委等有关部门提供资料整理。

二、主要指标

普通高等学校数（所）	63	比上年增加	1所
普通高等学校（本专科）在校学生（万人）	75.27	比上年增加	2.87万人
高等学校研究生在校人数（万人）	8.56	比上年增加	0.23万人

19 EDUCATION,SCIENCE AND TECHNOLOGY

Ⅰ.Brief Introduction

Data in this chapter consists of primarily data of educational undertakings, science and technology Activities of Xi'an city, compiled by Social & Science and Technology Division of the Xi'an Bureau of Statistics according to data from Xi'an Municipal Government Departments concerned.

Ⅱ Major Indicators

		Increase over Preceding Year
Number of Schools Regular Institutions of Higher Education(unit)	63	1
Student Enrollment of Regular Institutions of Higher Education(10 000 persons)	75.27	2.87
Postgraduates(10 000 persons)	8.56	0.23

19-1 主要年份各类普通教育基本情况

Basic Statistics on Regular Eduction in Representative Years

指　标	Item	2006	2007	2008	2009	2010	2011	2012	2013
学校数（所）	**Number of Schools (units)**								
普通高等学校	Regular Institutions of Higher Education	47	48	48	49	50	61	62	63
普通中等专业学校	Regular Specialized Secondary Schools	31	30	29	28	28	24	24	22
普通中学	Regular Secondary School	457	453	442	439	436	423	419	418
小学	Primary Schools	1929	1872	1781	1666	1531	1424	1322	1291
幼儿园	Kindergarten	863	830	905	896	1004	1122	1239	1295
毕业生人数（万人）	**Graduates (10 000 persons)**								
普通高等学校	Regular Institutions of Higher Education	13.0	15.8	17.6	16.9	18.3	19.7	20.9	20.2
普通中等专业学校	Regular Specialized Secondary Schools	1.8	2.0	2.6	2.7	2.5	2.3	2.1	1.9
普通中学	Regular Secondary School	18.0	18.4	18.0	17.8	17.0	16.4	15.6	15.2
小学	Primary Schools	11.5	11.4	10.6	10.0	9.6	8.9	8.9	8.5
幼儿园	Kindergarten						6.4	7.6	8.4
招生数（万人）	**New Enrollment (10 000 persons)**								
普通高等学校	Regular Institutions of Higher Education	17.1	19.0	21.5	21.3	21.7	23.1	25.2	23.9
普通中等专业学校	Regular Specialized Secondary Schools	2.6	2.9	2.6	2.2	2.1	2.0	1.7	1.4
普通中学	Regular Secondary School	18.6	18.0	17.2	16.6	16.2	15.4	15.0	14.5
小学	Primary Schools	9.2	8.7	8.3	7.8	8.6	8.8	8.9	9.6
幼儿园	Kindergarten	6.9	6.7	7.7	7.2	8.4	10.0	11.6	11.0
在校学生数（万人）	**Total Enrollment (10 000 persons)**								
普通高等学校	Regular Institutions of Higher Education	57.1	62.3	66.7	70.3	73.3	76.6	80.7	83.8
普通中等专业学校	Regular Specialized Secondary Schools	7.3	8.0	8.1	7.4	6.8	6.1	5.4	4.7
普通中学	Regular Secondary School	56.1	54.7	52.8	50.6	48.9	47.2	45.3	43.7
小学	Primary Schools	59.3	56.8	54.7	52.5	51.6	51.4	50.9	51.95
幼儿园	Kindergarten	13.4	14.1	15.5	16.3	18.4	24.0	27.1	28.6
教职工数（人）	**Staff and Teachers (persons)**								
普通高等学校	Regular Institutions of Higher Education	61414	65624	69048	70818	72247	72739	74041	74993
普通中等专业学校	Regular Specialized Secondary Schools	3621	3548	3417	2965	3249	2868	2733	2599
普通中学	Regular Secondary School	39341	39171	39088	39002	39207	41135	41197	41003
小学	Primary Schools	34460	34901	34653	34389	34118	32457	32208	31863
幼儿园	Kindergarten	12335	13468	14932	15928	18710	23680	27735	31989
专任教师（人）	**Number of Full-time Teachers (persons)**								
普通高等学校	Regular Institutions of Higher Education	32891	36717	38926	40605	42098	42734	44487	46436
普通中等专业学校	Regular Specialized Secondary Schools	2014	2011	1904	1720	1845	1723	1595	1474
普通中学	Regular Secondary School	31203	31373	31425	31415	31506	33122	31526	31419
小学	Primary Schools	30018	30533	30382	30334	29944	28453	29651	29421
幼儿园	Kindergarten	7106	7951	8704	9240	10638	12577	14293	16238

注：本表数据来源于市教育局。

本表中普通高等学校毕业生、招生、在校生数含研究生及普通高等学校中普通本、专科学生数。

本表中小学的学校数是指独立小学个数，其在校生、教职工等指标均为普通初等教育；幼儿园的校数是指独立的幼儿园个数，其在校生、教职工等指标均为学前教育。（下表同）。

19-2 各级各类学校校数、教职工、专任教师数（2013年）

Basic Facts on Regular Education Teacher by School Type（2013）

指　标	Item	学校数（所）Number of Schools (units)	教职工数（人）Number of Staff and Teachers (persons)	专任教师数（人）Full-time Teachers (persons)
一、高等教育	**Higher education**	**76**	**77552**	**47965**
（一）研究生培养机构	Postgraduate training institutions	(46)		
1、高等学校	Institutions of Higher Schools	(22)		
2、科研机构	Scientific Research Institution	(24)		
(二)普通高等学校	Regular Institutions of Higher Schools	63	74993	46436
1、 本科院校	Universities and Colleges of Undergraduate Course	41	63742	39493
其中：独立学院	Non-university Tertiary	11	7017	4565
2、专科院校	Higher Vocational Colleges	22	11251	6943
其中：高等职业学校	Higher Vocational College	20	9344	5979
(三)成人高等学校	Adult Higher Schools	13	2559	1529
二、中等职业教育	**Secondary Occupation Education**	**207**	**16254**	**11620**
1、普通中等专业学校	Regular Specialized Secondary Schools	22	2599	1474
2、成人中等专业学校	Adult Secondary Specialized Schools	6	1269	709
3、职业高中学校	Vocational Hight Schools	75	4854	3150
4、技工学校	Technical Schools	104	7532	6287
其中：市属	Municipal schools	41	1935	1866
三、基础教育	**Elementary Education**	**3013**	**105233**	**77341**
（一）普通中等教育	Regular Institutions Education	418	41003	31419
1、高中	Senior High Schools	167		11978
完全中学	Complete Secondary Schools	101	13011	5304
高级中学	Senior Secondary Schools	51	7771	6254
十二年一贯制学校	Twelve-year Consistency Schools	15	2313	420
2、初中	Junior Middle Schools	251		19441
初级中学	Junior Middle Schools	222	15735	12868
九年一贯制学校	Nine-year Consistency Schools	29	2173	863
完全中学	Complete Secondary school	(101)		5030
十二年一贯制学校	Twelve-year Consistency schools	(15)		680
附设普通初中班的学校	Senior Secondary Schools with Regular Junior Secondary Classes	(2)		
（二）普通初等教育	Regular Primary Education	1291	31863	29421
独立小学	Independent Primary Schools	1291		27954
教学点	Teaching Points	(119)		
九年一贯制学校	Nine-year Consistency schools	(29)		885
十二年一贯制学校	Twelve-year Consistency schools	(15)		582
附设小学班的学校	Schools with Primary Classes	(3)		
（三）特殊教育	Special Education Schools	8	338	243
特殊教育学校	Special Education Schools	8	338	243
附设特教班的学校	Schools with Special Edution Classes	(1)		(1)
（四）工读学校	Reformatory Schools	1	40	20
（五）学前教育	Preschool Education	1295	31989	16238
幼儿园	Kindergarten	1295	31989	16238
附设幼儿班的学校	Schools with Nursery Classes	(314)		
另有：成人中小学	Adult Junior Secondary schools and Adult Primary Schools	23	66	44
另有：技术培训机构	Technique Training Institution	72	1632	1042

注：本表数据来源于市教育局。
本表为西安市行政区划内各级各类学校全口径数据（不含军事院校、党校）。
技工学校数据由西安市人力资源和社会保障局提供。
按照事业统计主体校原则，完全中学、十二年一贯制学校的学校数计入普通高中，九年一贯制学校的校数计入普通初中。
教职工数按照办学类型划分，为使用方便，专任教师同时按照办学层次列出。
( ) 内数据不计入总计，下表同。

19-3 各级各类教育学生情况（2013年）

Basic Facts on Education Student by School Type（2013）

单位：人 (persons)

指标	Item	毕业生数 Number of Graduates	招生数 New Enrollment	在校学生数 Total Enrollment	女生 Female Students
一、高等教育	**Higher education**	**303467**	**356805**	**1113671**	**540203**
(一)研究生	Postgraduates	24778	28786	87002	38906
1、高等学校	Institutions of Higher Schools	24385	28333	85570	38513
2、科研机构	Scientific Research Institution	393	453	1432	393
(二)普通高等教育	Regular Institutions of Higher Schools	177318	210495	752682	379114
1、本科	Universities Course Schcols	103525	130537	518471	259844
2、专科	Junior Colleges	73793	79958	234211	119270
(三)成人高等教育	Higher Vocational Colleges	55956	44997	144675	51839
其中：成人高等学校	Contains:Adult Higher Education	7433	5548	18139	10054
(四)网络本专科生	Network Undergraduate and clooege students	45415	72527	129312	60344
1、本科	Universities Course Schools	20217	30889	55115	27425
2、专科	Junior Colleges	25198	41638	74197	32919
二、中等职业教育	**Secondary Occupation Education**	**89738**	**68289**	**211480**	**60889**
1、普通中等专业学校	Regular Specialized Secondary Schools	19290	13547	46552	24969
2、成人中等专业学校	Adult Secondary Specialized Schools	2895	1477	7104	2236
3、职业高中学校	Vocational high Schools	22139	23484	63788	33684
其中：市属	Municipal schools	21243	23043	61968	32425
4、技工学校	Technical Schools	45414	29781	94036	
其中：市属	Municipal schools	11781	8534	25402	
三、基础教育	**Elementary Education**	**321925**	**350524**	**1243577**	**576869**
(一)普通中等教育	Regular Institutions Education	152438	144734	437292	204163
1、高中	Senior High Schools	60125	57842	173443	85393
完全中学	Complete Secondary Schools	25822	25236	74849	37732
高级中学	Senior Secondary Schools	32589	30743	93399	45160
十二年一贯制学校	Twelve-year Consistency schools	1714	1863	5195	2501
2、初中	Junior Middle Schools	92313	86892	263849	118770
初级中学	Junior Middle Schools	54442	46142	144844	64635
九年一贯制学校	Nine-year Consistency Schools	3982	4435	12582	5679
十二年一贯制学校	Twelve-year Consistency Schools	3285	4100	11339	5027
完全中学	Complete Secondary school	30604	32215	95084	43379
(二)普通初等教育	Regular Primary Education	85079	95604	519490	237835
小学	Pricmary Schools	78995	89133	484196	221629
九年一贯制学校	Nine-year Consistency schools	3605	4145	21583	9964
十二年一贯制学校	Twelve-year Consistency Schools	2479	2325	13711	6242
(三)特殊教育	Special Education Schools	194	212	1174	433
1、特殊教育学校	Special Education Schools	122	147	760	293
2、小学附设特教班	Primary Schools with Special Education Classes		3	7	1
3、小学随班就读	Elementary Inclusive	49	44	359	121
4、初中随班就读就读	Junior Mainstreaming	23	18	48	18
(四)工读学校	Reformatory Schools	10	13	42	12
(五)学前教育	Preschool Education	84204	109961	285579	134426
1、独立幼儿园	Independent Kindergartens	76705	101368	274359	129115
2、附设幼儿园	Attached Kindergartens	7499	8595	11210	5311
另有：成人中小学	Adult Junior Secondary schools and Adult Primary Schools	27		457	267
另有：职业技术培训机构	Vocational and Technical Institutions	422834		513382	

注：本表数据来源于市教育局。

19-4 主要年份普通高等学校和科研机构研究生情况

Basic Statistics on Regular Institutions Schools and Post-graduates of Scientific Research Institution in Representative Years

单位：人 (person)

年份 Year	毕业生数 Number of Graduates	高等学校 Higher Schools	招生数 New Enrollment	高等学校 Higher Schools	在校学生数 Total Enrollment	高等学校 Higher Schools
1978					232	232
1980					651	651
1985					4799	4799
1990	2051	2051	1662	1662	5275	5275
1995	1769	1769	2712	2712	7974	7974
1998	2316	2316	3888	3888	10833	10833
1999	2903	2903	5020	5020	12986	12986
2000	3236	3236	6924	6924	16620	16620
2001	3881	3770	9274	8966	22564	21855
2002	4103	3952	11282	10882	28446	27471
2003	5971	5765	14322	13882	36936	35790
2004	8384	8127	17310	16871	45402	44169
2005	10416	10127	18583	18106	52699	51310
2006	12914	12552	19581	19105	58433	56951
2007	15506	15124	20570	20167	64137	62801
2008	17234	16788	21892	21443	67296	65834
2009	19025	18574	24879	24400	72366	70908
2010	19526	19129	25971	25477	76993	75483
2011	20965	20605	26686	26256	81696	80332
2012	22963	22578	28065	27618	84712	83306
2013	24778	24385	28786	28333	87002	85570

注：本表数据来源于市教育局。

19-5 主要年份普通高等学校基本情况

Baisc Statistics on Regular Higher Education in Representative Years

单立：所、万人　　　　(units 10 000 persons)

年份 Year	学校数 Number of Schools	毕业生数 Number of Graduates	招生数 New Enrollment	在校学生数 Total Enrollment	教职工数 Number of Staff and Teachers	专任教师数 Full-time Teachers
1978	21	0.60	1.31	2.88	2.24	0.87
1980	24	0.21	1.08	4.17	2.55	0.97
1985	28	1.17	2.28	6.49	3.40	1.28
1990	31	2.11	2.00	7.50	4.15	1.56
1995	32	2.87	3.13	10.07	4.21	1.59
1998	29	2.61	3.30	11.58	3.91	1.50
1999	29	2.84	5.12	13.79	3.95	1.52
2000	25	2.71	6.79	17.75	3.81	1.57
2001	32	3.31	8.31	23.24	4.30	1.75
2002	35	3.82	10.75	30.15	4.67	2.06
2003	37	5.89	12.21	36.42	4.92	2.21
2004	41	7.66	13.17	40.29	5.45	2.69
2005	44	10.08	14.68	47.79	5.73	2.95
2006	47	11.75	15.15	51.40	6.14	3.29
2007	48	14.33	16.96	56.03	6.56	3.67
2008	48	15.82	19.31	60.10	5.90	3.39
2009	49	15.04	18.84	63.22	7.08	4.06
2010	50	16.33	19.16	65.74	7.22	4.21
2011	61	17.68	20.52	68.52	7.27	4.27
2012	62	18.64	22.46	72.40	7.40	4.45
2013	63	17.73	21.05	75.27	7.50	4.64

注：本表数据来源于市教育局。
本表仅包括本、专科。
历史年份个别数据有调整，以此表数据为准。

19-6 主要年份普通中等专业学校基本情况

Baisc Statistics on Regular Specialized Secondary Schools in Representative Years

年 份 Year	学校数（所） Number of Schools (units)	毕业生数（万人） Number of Graduates (10 000 persons)	招生数（万人） New Enrollment (10 000 persons)	在校学生数（万人） Total Enrollment (10 000 persons)	教职工数（人） Number of Staff and Teachers(person)	专任教师数（人） Full-time Teachers(person)
1978	19	0.19	0.45	0.82	3937	1110
1980	31	0.18	0.42	1.50	3895	1474
1985	37	0.43	0.76	1.70	6071	2363
1990	44	0.56	0.68	2.09	7136	2891
1995	46	0.97	1.37	3.74	5903	2533
1996	47	1.15	1.61	4.18	5940	2573
1997	47	1.20	1.65	4.63	6124	2731
1998	47	1.26	1.62	5.08	6181	2840
1999	46	1.42	2.11	5.75	6385	2865
2000	47	1.63	1.90	6.02	6964	3172
2001	47	1.70	1.58	5.63	5252	2467
2002	46	1.60	1.69	5.57	5170	2508
2003	34	1.62	1.80	5.28	4562	2302
2004	35	1.40	2.09	5.71	4676	2388
2005	32	1.44	2.26	6.16	3924	2130
2006	31	1.84	2.61	7.30	3621	2014
2007	30	2.03	2.91	7.97	3548	2011
2008	29	2.58	2.55	8.06	3278	1814
2009	28	2.70	2.15	7.44	2965	1720
2010	28	2.45	2.08	6.75	3249	1845
2011	24	2.34	1.96	6.11	2868	1723
2012	24	2.15	1.67	5.43	2733	1595
2013	22	1.93	1.35	4.66	2599	1474

注：本表数据来源于市教育局。
历史年份个别数据有调整，以此表数据为准。

19–7 主要年份普通中学基本情况

Baisc Statistics on Regular Secondary Schools in Representative Years

年份 Year	学校数（所） Number of Schools (units)	毕业生数（万人） Number of Graduates (10 000 persons)	招生数（万人） New Enrollment (10 000 persons)	在校学生数（万人） Total Enrollment (10 000 persons)	教职工数（人） Number of Staff and Teachers(person)	专任教师数（人） Full-time Teachers(person)
1978	962			44.16	27380	20660
1980	1002	12.33	14.03	44.08	29867	22530
1985	563	10.72	13.05	38.24	30063	22050
1990	518	9.11	10.49	30.03	30739	22385
1995	485	8.13	12.40	32.32	30423	21984
1996	462	8.67	13.03	35.25	30902	22473
1997	466	9.96	13.83	37.16	31682	23129
1998	467	10.64	15.00	39.79	32371	23884
1999	469	11.21	16.58	43.49	33387	25114
2000	466	12.01	17.88	48.31	34385	26230
2001	470	13.85	18.98	52.50	35442	27190
2002	467	15.76	19.68	55.36	36706	28335
2003	467	16.76	18.78	56.44	38252	29887
2004	461	18.01	18.85	56.54	39121	30600
2005	460	18.82	18.83	55.74	39455	31094
2006	457	18.04	18.61	56.11	39341	31203
2007	453	18.37	17.96	54.68	39171	31373
2008	442	17.99	17.16	52.83	39088	31425
2009	439	17.80	16.57	50.63	39002	31415
2010	436	17.01	16.15	48.89	39207	31506
2011	423	16.44	15.42	47.20	41135	31675
2012	419	15.64	14.98	45.33	41197	31526
2013	418	15.24	14.47	43.73	41003	31419

注：本表数据来源于市教育局。

19-8 各区县普通中学基本情况（2013年）

Baisc Statistics on Regular Secondary Schools by Region（2013）

单位：所、人 (unit, person)

区 县	Region	学校数 Number of Schools	毕业生数 Number of Graduates	高中 Senior	招生数 New Enrollment	高中 Senior	在 校 学生数 Total Enrollment	女生 Female Students	高中 Senior	教职工数 Number of Staff and Teachers	专任教师数 Full-time Teachers
合 计	**Total**	**418**	**152438**	**60125**	**144734**	**57842**	**437292**	**204163**	**173443**	**41003**	**31419**
新城区	Xincheng	25	12195	4222	12088	3991	36019	17287	11990	2631	1974
碑林区	Beilin	35	15632	6546	15708	6396	47283	22035	18960	3834	2898
莲湖区	Lianhu	20	11801	4341	11682	3976	34602	16718	11682	2912	2118
灞桥区	Baqiao	28	7504	2639	8018	2545	22781	11044	7522	2307	1701
未央区	Weiyang	28	9441	4551	10581	4535	30423	14979	13308	3223	2050
雁塔区	Yanta	43	15855	5371	16219	5456	47934	22676	16234	4640	3174
阎良区	Yanliang	12	4483	1852	3957	1621	12191	6018	4957	1164	951
临潼区	Lintong	32	13068	4826	11092	4585	35356	17390	14358	3429	2899
长安区	Chang'an	48	15927	7248	14159	6408	43142	19912	19480	4214	3535
蓝田县	Lantian	46	12525	4757	11638	5233	35122	16748	14741	3391	2640
周至县	Zhouzhi	35	13890	5713	11757	5406	37154	14537	16928	3623	2761
户 县	Huxian	39	12485	5293	10698	5056	33781	14588	15390	3292	2818
高陵县	Gaoling	15	4295	1820	3539	1445	11457	5624	4863	1206	1008
沣东新城	Fengdongxincheng	12	3337	946	3598	1189	10047	4607	3030	1137	892

注：本表数据来源于市教育局。
本表中教职工数按照办学类型划分，专任教师数按照办学层次划分。

19-9 主要年份职业高中基本情况

Baisc Statistics on Vocational Secondary Schools in Representatove Years

单位：所、人 (unit, person)

年份 Year	学校数 Number of Schools	毕业生数 Number of Graduates	招生数 New Enrollment	在校学生数 Total Enrollment	教职工数 Number of Staff and Teachers	专任教师数 Full-time Teachers
1985	40	1661	8346	17621	1375	868
1990	58	5936	8095	20151	2674	1574
1995	71	8976	12490	32673	2394	1877
1996	67	9235	10563	25955	3098	1735
1997	73	8756	13390	29068	2993	1709
1998	89	7753	13949	31264	3152	1823
1999	91	8480	13062	31973	3217	1908
2000	95	9949	13903	32188	3311	1997
2001	85	10300	15591	34336	3517	2113
2002	78	8659	17231	39428	3461	2192
2003	87	10755	17310	44033	4035	2458
2004	83	12177	17865	46358	4101	2515
2005	91	15092	20603	51766	4750	2892
2006	96	14887	21158	53828	5193	3126
2007	86	14881	24434	56012	4899	3064
2008	84	15813	30201	62963	4878	3008
2009	84	14691	31042	72388	5129	3179
2010	84	18100	30042	78244	5222	3178
2011	78	22493	27641	75108	4849	3173
2012	77	24048	24995	67969	4775	3148
2013	74	21243	23043	61968	4699	3085

注：本表数据来源于市教育局。
本表仅包括市属部分。

19–10 各区县职业高中基本情况（2013年）

Basic Statistics on Vocational Secondary Schools by Region (2013)

单位：所、人 (unit, person)

区 县	Region	学校数 Number of Schools	毕业生数 Number of Graduates	招生数 New Enrollment	在校学生数 Total Enrollment	女生 Female Students	教职工数 Number of Staff and Teachers	专任教师数 Full-time Teachers
合 计	**Total**	**74**	**21243**	**23043**	**61968**	**32490**	**4699**	**3085**
新城区	Xincheng	10	3113	4582	11175	6309	766	454
碑林区	Beilin	7	1067	2893	7405	2644	548	336
莲湖区	Lianhu	6	2275	2855	7788	4279	538	308
灞桥区	Baqiao	10	1300	1271	3676	2705	432	214
未央区	Weiyang	7	2028	1148	4142	3024	309	199
雁塔区	Yanta	10	2298	2284	6068	2669	547	339
阎良区	Yanliang	1	402	843	1731	772	111	89
临潼区	Lintong	5	2255	2049	3622	1717	288	225
长安区	Chang'an	6	2085	2068	6106	3456	505	365
蓝田县	Lantian	1	498	604	1542	778	17	13
周至县	Zhouzhi	5	2261	960	4411	2319	311	254
户 县	Huxian	5	614	796	2144	969	256	224
高陵县	Gaoling	1	1047	690	2158	849	71	65
沣东新城	Fengdongxincheng							

注：本表数据来源于市教育局。
本表仅包括市属部分。

19-11 主要年份小学基本情况

Basic Statistics on Primary Schools in Representative Years

年 份 Year	学校数（所） Number of Schools (units)	毕业生数（万人） Number of Graduates (10 000 persons)	招生数（万人） New Enrollment (10 000 persons)	在校学生数（万人） Total Enrollment (10 000 persons)	教职工数（人） Number of Staff and Teachers(person)	专任教师数（人） Full-time Teachers(person)
1978	2667	13.07	14.10	74.03	29744	26428
1980	2337	11.91	12.57	73.36	31770	28360
1985	2337	11.21	9.57	62.16	31075	26430
1990	2343	8.67	10.85	61.87	37783	29090
1995	2360	9.93	14.09	79.36	35568	30270
1996	2362	10.48	13.63	81.81	35821	30267
1997	2368	10.98	12.48	82.67	35767	30117
1998	2361	12.18	11.88	82.03	35576	30089
1999	2354	13.65	11.61	79.81	35639	30196
2000	2323	13.83	11.51	77.81	35336	30215
2001	2277	14.20	11.07	74.51	34257	29281
2002	2137	13.89	10.13	70.78	34143	29428
2003	2084	12.97	9.28	66.78	34080	29531
2004	2016	12.37	9.12	63.75	33794	29367
2005	1980	11.92	8.47	60.47	33907	29674
2006	1929	11.53	9.16	59.33	34460	30018
2007	1872	11.38	8.67	56.83	34901	30533
2008	1781	10.58	8.33	54.66	34653	30382
2009	1666	9.96	7.84	52.52	34389	30334
2010	1531	9.61	8.64	51.56	34118	29944
2011	1424	8.92	8.77	51.39	32457	29900
2012	1322	8.88	8.88	50.85	32208	29651
2013	1291	8.51	9.56	51.95	31363	29421

注：本表数据来源于市教育局。

19-12 各区县小学基本情况（2013年）

Basic Statistics on Primary Schools by Region (2013)

单位：所、人 (unit, person)

区 县	Region	学校数 Number of Schools	毕业生数 Number of Graduates	招生数 New Enrollment	在校学生数 Total Enrollment	女生 Female Students	教职工数 Number of Staff and Teachers	专任教师数 Full-time Teachers
合 计	**Total**	**1291**	**85079**	**95604**	**519490**	**237835**	**31863**	**29421**
新城区	Xincheng	34	6578	6285	37121	17088	1840	1718
碑林区	Beilin	43	6563	7710	40391	18836	2227	1895
莲湖区	Lianhu	47	7446	9022	47213	22170	2439	2196
灞桥区	Baqiao	75	5464	7281	36658	16950	1962	1631
未央区	Weiyang	53	7119	10417	51232	23555	1748	2027
雁塔区	Yanta	69	11198	14355	73857	33945	3424	3436
阎良区	Yanliang	22	2385	2413	13439	6488	1032	908
临潼区	Lintong	153	7090	6189	36867	17071	3222	2966
长安区	Chang'an	165	7439	9503	49233	22770	3743	3122
蓝田县	Lantian	226	6513	4867	32257	14992	2872	2737
周至县	Zhouzhi	145	6471	5562	35063	14271	2681	2477
户 县	Huxian	126	5834	5124	30762	13439	2095	2033
高陵县	Gaoling	86	2198	2953	14644	6938	1490	1324
沣东新城	Fengdongxincheng	47	2781	3923	20753	9322	1088	951

注：本表数据来源于市教育局。
本表中教职工数按照办学类型划分，专任教师数按办学层次划分。

19-13 主要年份幼儿园基本情况

Basic Statistics on Kindergartens in Representative Years

年 份 Year	幼儿园（所） Number of Kindergartens (units)	班数（个） Number of Class (unit)	在园幼儿人数（万人） Student Enrollment (10000 persons)	教职工数（人） Number of Staff and Teachers(person)	专任教师数（人） Full-time Teachers(person)
1978	363		4	3568	1315
1980	186		10	5525	2657
1985	310	3135	10	6887	2770
1990	256	3816	14	6123	2058
1995	257	4464	16	6173	2659
1996	244	4313	15	5913	2661
1997	228	4243	15	6065	2748
1998	235	4195	13	6272	2910
1999	234	4222	13	6329	2982
2000	367	4142	13	6346	2995
2001	366	4306	12	6224	3069
2002	378	4186	12	6541	3397
2003	610	4470	12	8959	4853
2004	660	4507	12	9870	5577
2005	737	4712	13	10523	5959
2006	863	5037	13	12335	7106
2007	830	5081	14	13468	7951
2008	905	5506	15	14932	8704
2009	896	5710	16	15928	9240
2010	1004	6420	18	18710	10638
2011	1122	8010	24	23680	12577
2012	1239	8729	27.1	27735	14293
2013	1295	9408	28.56	31939	16238

注：本表数据来源于市教育局。
幼儿园在园人数中包括学前班。

19-14 主要年份特殊教育基本情况

Basic Statistics on Special Education in Representative Years

单位：所、人 (unit, person)

年 份 Year	学校数 Number of Schools	毕业生数 Number of Graduates	招生数 New Enrollment	在校学生数 Total Enrollment	教职工数 Number of Staff and Teachers	专任教师数 Full-time Teachers
1978						
1980	1	48	64	315	66	43
1985	2	14	36	318	94	59
1990	5	35	111	451	142	96
1995	5	27	147	1363	204	141
1996	5	60	164	1520	210	150
1997	5	153	164	1655	210	148
1998	5	266	140	2145	232	157
1999	5	349	115	1912	235	160
2000	5	269	145	1880	230	156
2001	5	237	209	1915	238	162
2002	5	216	148	1661	232	157
2003	5	156	161	1380	237	166
2004	5	137	142	1290	236	167
2005	5	184	182	1445	240	169
2006	6	171	143	1425	254	178
2007	6	169	114	1342	259	190
2008	6	83	96	1286	259	190
2009	7	311	202	1523	335	234
2010	8	214	402	1529	340	235
2011	8	280	222	1393	343	231
2012	8	197	220	1392	352	248
2013	8	194	212	1174	338	243

注：本表数据来源于市教育局。
包括盲、聋、哑、弱智儿童教育在内。

19-15 基础教育监测评价情况（2013年）

Monitoring and Evaluation of Basic Education(2013)

指　标	Item	2013
入学率(%)	Enrollment Rate(%)	
小学	Primary Schools	99.98
初中	Junior Middle Schools	99.71
重读率(%)	Restduy-Rate(%)	
小学	Primary schools	0.06
初中	Junior Middle Schools	0.02
巩固率(%)	The Consolidation Rate (%)	
小学(六年)	Primary Schools (six years)	98.15
初中(三年)	Junior Middle Schools (three years)	93.76
毕业率(%)	The Graduate Rate(%)	
小学	Primary school	99.82
初中	Junior middle school	99.27
专任教师学历合格率(%)	Qualified Rate Of Full-time Teacher Education (%)	
小学	Primary Schools	99.95
初中	Junior Middle Schools	99.42
高中	Senior Middle Schools	97.60
幼儿园	Kindergartens	98.92
小学教师专科以上学历达到率(%)	Rate of Primary School Teachers with College degree or Above (%)	92.69
初中教师本科以上学历达到率(%)	Rate of Junior Middle SchoolTeachers with Bachelor degree or Above (%)	86.02
高中教师研究生以上学历达到率(%)	Rate of Senior Middle School Teachers with Postgraduate degree or Above (%)	12.15

注：本表数据来源于市教育局。

19-16 主要年份平均每万人口在校学生数及构成

单位：人、%

年 份 Year	平均每万人 高等学校在校学生 Per 10000 people on average Hight Education Students in the school	平均每万人 高中阶段在校学生 Per 10000 people on average Number of Senior high School Students in the school	平均每万人 初中在校学生 Per 10000 people on average Number of Junior Secondary School Students in the school
1978	58		
1980	84		
1985	117		
1990	123		
1995	168		
1996	177		
1997	180		
1998	189		
1999	224		
2000	282		
2001	366		
2002	470		
2003	560		
2004	618	463	517
2005	715	492	489
2006	760	534	484
2007	817	543	466
2008	863	571	444
2009	901	619	413
2010	939	635	361
2011	1090	576	337
2012	1132	541	319
2013	1146	448	307

注：本表数据来源于市教育局。

The Number of Students in the School in Major Years Per 10000 Pepole on Average

(persons,%)

平均每万人 小学在校学生 Per 10000 people on average Number of Primary School Students in the school	普通高等学校在校学生 占学生总数比重 Senior high School Students in the school in accounting for the proportion of the total number of students	中等学校在校学生 占学生总数比重 Junior Secondary School students in the school in accounting for the proportion of the total number of students	小学在校学生 占学生总数比重 Primary School students in the school in accounting for the proportion of the total number of students
1486	2.3	34.9	58.6
1434	3.1	33.2	55.3
1124	5.3	31.3	50.9
1016	6.7	25.1	51.7
1224	7.3	28.0	53.6
1249	7.6	28.8	53.5
1249	7.6	29.8	53.1
1228	8.0	31.3	52.0
1183	9.3	33.2	49.2
1131	11.5	34.8	46.0
1072	14.6	35.9	42.6
1007	18.2	36.4	39.[illegible]
932	20.1	33.8	33.5
879	22.2	35.2	31.5
815	26.4	36.2	30.1
788	27.7	37.1	28.7
744	29.3	36.3	26.7
708	30.8	36.1	25.2
672	31.8	36.5	23.7
660	33.0	35.0	23.2
604	29.8	30.1	19.9
595	31.0	28.2	19.5
605	32.6	25.3	20.2

19-17 民办教育情况（2013年）

Private Education Situation (2013)

单位：所、人 (unit, person)

指 标	Item	学校数 Number of Schools	毕业生数 Number of Graduates	招生数 New Enrollment
一、民办高等教育(民办高校）	**Private higher Education (Institutions)**	**16**	**64733**	**77243**
二、民办中等教育	**Private Secondary Education**	**91**	**38578**	**42590**
民办普通高中	Ordinary High School	30	5958	6577
民办中等专业学校	Specialized Secondary School	1	2161	839
民办职业高中	Vocational hight school	42	9518	11120
民办普通初中	Ordinary Junior middle school	18	18333	20490
民办的附设中职班	Private primary school class	(9)	2608	3564
三、民办普通小学	**Private Primary School**	**41**	**7627**	**10522**
四、民办幼儿园	**Private kindergarten**	**1040**	**54819**	**75777**
另有：民办培训机构（不计校数）	Private Training Institutions (Not included in the totals number of schools)	**559**	**198488**	

19-17 续表 continued

单位：所、人 (unit, person)

指 标	Item	在校学生数 Total Enrollment	教职工数 Number of Teachers and Staff	专任教师 Full-time Teachers	聘请外校教师 Teachers hired from Outside Schools
一、民办高等教育(民办高校）	**Private higher Education (Institutions)**	**277462**	**21249**	**13183**	
二、民办中等教育	**Private Secondary Education**	**118222**	**2511**	**1396**	**423**
民办普通高中	Ordinary High School	18458			
民办中等专业学校	Specialized Secondary School	3905	266	106	
民办职业高中	Vocational hight school	27530	2245	1290	423
民办普通初中	Ordinary Junior middle school	59119			
民办的附设中职班	Private primary school class	9210			
三、民办普通小学	**Private Primary School**	**52280**	**2460**	**1942**	**27**
四、民办幼儿园	**Private kindergarten**	**202727**	**24205**	**11941**	**336**
另有：民办培训机构（不计校数）	Private Training Institutions (Not included in the totals number of schools)	**272925**	**8262**	**4903**	**4753**

注：本表数据来源于市教育局。
毕业生数中幼儿园为离园人数。
民办高等教育在校生为民办高校普通、成人本专科学生数。
聘请校外教师中，小学、中学、幼儿园为代课教师和兼任教师之和。
民办普通高中含完全中学17所、12年一贯制8所；民办普通初中含9年一贯制7所。

19-18 研究与试验发展（R&D）情况

Research and Experiment Development Facts

指 标	Item	2012	2013
一、单位数（个）	**Number of Units(unit)**	**1631**	**1684**
#科研单位	Units of Scientific Research	81	80
高等院校	Institutions of Higher Education	48	46
规模以上工业企业	Industrial Enterprises above Designated Size	971	1061
#有R&D 活动单位数	Number of Units with R&D Activities	387	403
科研单位	Units of Scientific Research	49	48
高等院校	Institutions of Higher Education	48	46
规模以上工业企业	Industrial Enterprises above Designated Size	208	244
二、科技活动人员（人）	**Personnel Eagaged in Scientific and Technical Activities (person)**	**162232**	**161004**
科研单位	Units of Scientific Research	35430	33423
高等院校	Institutions of Higher Education	42652	40454
规模以上工业企业	Industrial Enterprises above Designated Size	64375	65132
三、R&D经费内部支出（万元）	**Interier Expenditures for R&D(10 000 yuan)**	**2294743**	**2567704**
科研单位	Units of Scientific Research	1117292	1350092
高等院校	Institutions of Higher Education	289010	304608
规模以上工业企业	Industrial Enterprises above Designated Size	795919	800038
四、R&D项目（课题）（个）	**Number of Projects of R&D(item)**	**30155**	**30627**
科研单位	Units of Scientific Research	1797	2016
高等院校	Institutions of Higher Education	24042	24575
规模以上工业企业	Industrial Enterprises above Designated Size	3465	3629

注：本表数据来源于省教育厅、省统计局、市科技局。本表单位数含规模以上工业企业、非工业企业和事业单位。

19–19 科研院所研究与试验发展（R&D）情况

Research and Experiment Development Facts in Scientific Research Institutions

指　标	Item	2012	2013
一、基本情况	**Basic Facts**		
单位数（个）	Number of Unit(unit)	81	80
#有R&D活动的单位数	Number of Units with Scientific and Technical Activities	49	48
科技活动人员（人）	Number of Personnel Engaged in Scientific Research (person)	36430	38423
# R&D人员	R&D Personnel	26201	28004
其中：女性	Female	8155	8663
其中：博士毕业	Doctor	978	1151
硕士毕业	Master	6542	8055
本科毕业	Undergraduate	10650	11198
二、R&D人员折合全时当量（人/年）	**Full Time Equivalent of R&D Personnel (person/year)**	**24400**	**25902**
其中：研究人员	Personnel Engaged in Research	14831	17978
其中：基础研究	Basic Research	1665	2077
应用研究	Applied Research	6941	7972
试验发展	Experiment Development	15794	15853
三、R&D经费内部支出（万元）	**Raising and Use of Funds for Scientific and(10 000 yuan) Technical Activities**	**1117292**	**1350092**
在支出中：1、基础研究	Expenditure on: Basic Research	47905	52265
2、应用研究	Applied Research	205908	310187
3、试验发展	Experiment Development	863479	987640
在支出中：1、日常支出	Expenditure on: Daily Expenditure	852894	1045884
#人员劳务费	Service Fees of Personnel	181420	214742
2、资产性支出	Assets Expenditure	264399	304208
#仪器和设备	Instruments and Equipment	114090	138702
在支出中：1、政府资金	Expenditure on: Government Funds	1017985	1203551
2、企业资金	Enterpreises Funds	24233	13085
3、境外资金	Overseas Funds		
4、其他资金	Others	75076	133456
四、R&D产出	**Achievements of R&D**		
专利申请数（个）	Number of Patent Applications (item)	1608	2205
#发明专利	Number of Invention Patents	1149	1626
专利授权数（个）	Number of Patents Awarded (item)	738	1138
#发明专利	Number of Invention Patents	431	599
有效发明专利数（件）	Number of Effective Invention Patents (item)	1397	2135
发表科技论文（篇）	Scientific and Technical Thesis (piece)	5406	5663
出版科技著作（种）	Scientific and Technical Works Published (book)	77	87

注：本表数据来源于市科技局。

19-20 大专院校研究与试验发展（R&D）情况

Research and Experiment Development Facts in Universities

指　标	Item	2012	2013
一、基本情况	**Basic Facts**		
单位数（个）	Number of Unit(unit)	48	46
#有R&D活动的单位数	Number of Units with Scientific and Technical Activities	48	46
科技活动人员（人）	Number of Personnel Engaged in Scientific Research (person)	42652	40454
# R&D人员	R&D Personnel	17979	17395
其中：女性	Female	5720	5806
其中：博士毕业	Doctor	5426	5689
硕士毕业	Master	6078	5931
本科毕业	Undergraduate	5086	4717
二、R&D人员折合全时当量（人/年）	**Full Time Equivalent of R&D Personnel (person/year)**	**8968**	**8497**
其中：研究人员	Personnel Engaged in Research	7868	7462
其中：基础研究	Basic Research	3935	3837
应用研究	Applied Research	3939	3694
试验发展	Experiment Development	1093	966
三、R&D经费内部支出（万元）	**Raising and Use of Funds for Scientific and Technical Activities (10 000 yuan)**	**289010**	**304608**
在支出中：1、基础研究	Expenditure on: Basic Research	88080	93418
2、应用研究	Applied Research	128323	132607
3、试验发展	Experiment Development	72608	78584
在支出中：1、日常支出	Expenditure on: Daily Expenditure	252036	256710
#人员劳务费	Service Fees of Personnel	35901	31197
2、资产性支出	Assets Expenditure	36975	47889
#仪器和设备	Instruments and Equipment	24640	29573
在支出中：1、政府资金	Expenditure on: Government Funds	180089	186527
2、企业资金	Enterpreises Funds	99593	109480
3、境外资金	Overseas Funds	885	1226
4、其他资金	Others	8343	7375
四、R&D产出	**Achievements of R&D**		
专利申请数（个）	Number of Patent Applications (item)	5390	6153
#发明专利	Number of Invention Patents	3453	4180
专利授权数（个）	Number of Patents Awarded (item)	3748	4301
#发明专利	Number of Invention Patents	2075	2111
有效发明专利数（件）	Number of Effective Invention Patents (item)	6060	7283
发表科技论文（篇）	Scientific and Technical Thesis (piece)	41498	37542
出版科技著作（种）	Scientific and Technical Works Published (book)	991	891

注：本表数据来源于省教育厅。

19–21 规模以上工业企业研究与试验发展（R&D）情况

Research and Experiment Development Facts in Large-size and Medium-size Industrial Enterprises

指　标	Item	2012	2013
一、基本情况	**Basic Facts**		
单位数（个）	Number of Unit(unit)	971	1061
有（R&D）活动的单位数	Number of Units with Scientific and Technical Activities	208	244
从事科技活动人员（人）	Number of Personnel Engaged in Scientific Research (person)	64375	65132
#（R&D）人员	R&D Personnel	39265	42229
其中：女性	Female	11131	11432
二、R&D人员折合全时当量（人/年）	**Full Time Equivalent of R&D Personnel (person/year)**	**24786**	**28715**
其中：研究人员	Personnel Engaged in Research	12125	8586
其中：基础研究	Basic Research	21	26
应用研究生	Applied Research	1224	895
试验发展	Experiment Development	23541	27794
三、R&D经费内部支出（万元）	**Raising and Use of Funds for Scientific and Technical Activities(10 000 yuan)**	**795919**	**800038**
在支出中：1、基础研究	Expenditure on: Basic Research	183	501
2、应用研究	Applied Research	53307	50533
3、试验发展	Experiment Development	742429	749004
在支出中：1、日常支出	Expenditure on: Daily Expenditure	715219	703539
#人员劳务费	Service Fees of Personnel	142301	153624
2、资产性支出	Assets Expenditure	80700	96498
#仪器和设备	Instruments and Equipment	77336	90290
在支出中：1、政府资金	Expenditure on: Government Funds	174911	188566
2、企业资金	Enterpreises Funds	611552	602911
3、境外资金	Overseas Funds		62
4、其他资金	Others	9455	8500
四、R&D产出	**Achievements of R&D**		
专利申请数（个）	Number of Patent Applications (item)	3613	4836
#发明专利	Number of Invention Patents	1492	2149
专利授权数（个）	Number of Patents Awarded (item)		
#发明专利	Number of Invention Patents		
有效发明专利数（件）	Number of Effective Invention Patents (item)	3796	4017
发表科技论文（篇）	Scientific and Technical Thesis (piece)	2831	2821
出版科技著作（种）	Scientific and Technical Works Published (book)		

注：2012年大中型工业企业科技年报为省统计局反馈数据，包括5家省直报单位。

19-22 主要年份企事业单位知识产权情况

Intellectual Property Right of Enterprises and Institutions in Representative Years

指 标	Item	2007	2008	2009	2010	2011	2012	2013
一 科技活动情况	**Science and technology activities**							
科技活动人员（人）	People involved into activities(person)	87095	91994	137934	128559	147814	162232	161004
科技活动机构数（个）	units involved into activities(unit)	380	411	569	490	625	616	634
二、知识产权拥有量情况	**Number of IPR**							
1. 专利情况（件）	Patents(item)							
（1）累计申请专利	Accumulated patent applications	32852	42436	55208	74694	1024[illegible]1	139290	185401
当年申请专利	Patent applictions in this year	6768	9584	12772	19486	27717	36983	47111
#发明专利	Invention patents	1886	3049	5014	7176	11639	15029	23534
（2）累计授权专利	Accumulated patents awarded	15971	19256	23962	31999	41273	53118	69368
当年授权专利	Patents awarded in this year	2529	3285	4706	8037	9274	11862	16250
#发明专利	Invention patents	595	749	1121	1651	2738	3475	3708
2. 商标情况（件）	Trade marks(item)							
（1）当年注册商标申请	Trade mark registration claimed in this year	5559	7613	8972	21562	15620	18230	12372
（2）累计注册商标	Accumulated trade mark registrations	22860	26386	23078	52387	39381	65733	59915
#当年注册商标	Trade mark registrations in this year	2052	3526	5278	18107	12278	12120	8850
三、民事知识产权维权情况（件）	**IPR controversy(item)**	**131**	**212**	**427**	**241**	**512**	**631**	**475**
1. 专利纠纷	Patent controversies	44	47	37	69	104	107	77
2. 商标纠纷	Trade mark controversies	32	51	42	29	49	107	209
3. 著作权纠纷	Copyright controversies	36	91	319	110	315	365	141
4. 技术合同纠纷	Technological contract controversies	3	3	9	6	15	9	16
5. 发现权与发明权纠纷	Discover and invention controversies							
6. 其他知识产权纠纷	Others IPR controvers	16	20	20	27	29	43	33

注：本表数据由市科技局、陕西省工商局、陕西省新闻出版局、西安市中级人民法院等提供。

19–23 主要年份高新技术产业开发区情况

Basic Statistics of Hi-Tech Development Zone in Representative Years

指　标	Item	2007	2008	2009	2010	2011	2012	2013
1. 高新技术企业数（个）	Number of High-tech Enterprises(unit)	1311	1324	592	672	774	690	822
2. 年末从业人员（人）	Number of Persons Employed at year-end (person)	368757	388644	275141	287140	296723	320259	328707
从事技术开发人数（人）	Number of Persons Engaged in Technology Development	39248	48355	64212	67708	78636	81787	88179
3. 技术开发经费支出总额（万元）	Expenditures on Technology Development(10 000 yuan)	705066	777516	756767	1031223	1322923	1768282	1926100
研究与发展支出	Expenditures on Research and Development	533924	581716	585449	669083	831822	1273311	1666389
4. 利润总额（万元）	Total Profits (10 000 yuan)	1087311	1231146	1308432	1707925	2224850	2905877	3539526
5. 上缴税费总额（万元）	Sum of tax (10 000 yuan)	1394194	1576472	1486556	1964820	2586712	3383678	4465587
6. 出口创汇总额（千美元）	Foreign Exchange Earnings of Exports(USD 1 000)	1927114	2188721	1177000	4951265	6447050	6591977	7880206

19–24 高新技术产业开发区发展规模（2013年）

Development Status of Hi-Tech Development Zone (2013)

指　标	Item	合计 Total	新建区 Newly constructed Zone
累计已开发面积（平方公里）	Accumulated Areas Developed (sq.km)	50	50
高新区工商注册（个）	Registered Enterprises in Hi-tech Zones (unit)	19771	19771
#工业型技术开发技术服务型企业数	Number of industrial technology developing enterprises	9314	9314
#三资企业数	Enterprises of Joiut Venture,Cooperation and Foreign-funded	1105	1105
已认定的高新技术企业数（个）	Hi-tech Enterprises Designated	822	822

注：本表数据来源于西安市高新技术开发区。

19-25 主要年份高新技术产业开发区建设与集资情况

Capital Construction and Funds-Raising of Hi-Tech Development Zone in Representative Years

指 标	Item	2007	2008	2009	2010	2011	2012	2013
一、基建投资（亿元）	Investment on Capital Construction (100 million yuan)							
本年基建投资	Investment on Capital Construction of this year	132.17	159.78	196.9	255.57	266.51	350.88	432.38
二、开发面积	Area Developed							
新建区累计开发土地面积（平方公里）	Accumulated Area Developed in Newly Constructed Zone (sq.km)	35	35	35	35	35	40	50
#当年新开发土地面积	Area Developed in this year						5	10
累计竣工建筑面积（万平方米）	Accumulated Floor Space Completed (10 000 sq.m)	1558.7	1782.4	2085.7	2419.9	2743.1	3095.1	3433.9
#当年竣工建筑面积	Floor Space Completed in this year	232.70	223.76	303.23	334.20	328.22	347.00	338.80
三、吸引外资（亿美元）	**Foreign Investment(100million USB)**							
年末累计境外客商协议投资额	Contracted Foreign Investment Accumulated at Year-end	32.35	36.26	43.76	52.76	56.71	74.11	150.61
年末累计境外客商实际投资额	Actual Foreign Investment	16.08	20.29	24.63	29.75	35.24	45.02	58.28
#当年实际投资额	Actual Investmen in this year	3.90	4.21	4.34	5.11	6.49	8.18	13.26

注：本表数据来源于西安市高新技术开发区。

主要统计指标解释

普通高等学校 指按国家规定的设置标准和审批程序批准举办的，通过全国普通高等学校统一招生考试，招收高中毕业生为主要培养对象，实施高等学历教育的全日制大学、独立设置的学院和高等专科学校、高等职业学校及其他机构（独立学院和分校、大专班）。

大学、独立设置的学院主要实施本科层次以上教育。高等专科学校、高等职业学校实施专科层次教育。其他机构是承担国家普通招生计划任务不计校数的机构，包括独立学院、普通高等学校分校、大专班和批准筹建的普通高等学校等。独立学院指由普通本科高校按新机制、新模式举办的本科层次的二级学院，一些普通本科高校按公办机制和模式建立的二级学院，“分校”或其他类似的二级办学机构不属此范畴。

成人高等学校 指按照国家规定的设置标准和审批程序批准举办的，通过全国成人高等教育统一招生考试，招收具有高中毕业或同等学历的人员为主要培养对象，利用函授、业余、脱产等多种形式对其实施高等学历教育的学校。包括职工高等学校、农民高等学校、管理干部学院、教育学院、独立函授学院、广播电视大学、其他机构等。其他机构是承担国家成人招生计划任务不计校数的机构。

小学学龄儿童净入学率 指调查范围内已入小学学习的学龄儿童占校内外学龄儿童总数（包括弱智儿童，不包括盲聋哑儿童）的比重。计算公式为：

小学学龄儿童净入学率（%）=已入学的小学学龄儿童数／校内外小学学龄儿童总数×100%

研究与试验发展（R&D） 指在科学技术领域，为增加知识总量，以及运用这些知识去创造新的应用进行的系统的创造性的活动，包括基础研究、应用研究、试验发展三类活动。国际上通常采用R&D活动的规模和强度指标反映一国的科技实力和核心竞争力。

基础研究 指为了获得关于现象和可观察事实的基本原理的新知识（揭示客观事物的本质、运动规律，获得新发现、新学说）而进行的实验性或理论性研究，它不以任何专门或特定的应用或使用为目的。其成果以科学论文和科学著作为主要形式。用来反映知识的原始创新能力。

应用研究 指为获得新知识而进行的创造性研究，主要针对某一特定的目的或目标。应用研究是为了确定基础研究成果可能的用途，或是为达到预定的目标探索应采取的新方法（原理性）或新途径。其成果形式以科学论文、专著、原理性模型或发明专利为主。用来反映对基础研究成果应用途径的探索。

试验发展 指利用从基础研究、应用研究和实际经验所获得的现有知识，为产生新的产品、材料和装置，建立新的工艺、系统和服务，以及对已产生和建立的上述各项作实质性的改进而进行的系统性丁作。其成果形式主要是专利、专有技术、具有新产品基本特征的产品原型或具有新装置基本特征的原始样机等。在社会科学领域，试验发展是指把通过基础研究、应用研究获得的知识转变成可以实施的计划（包括为进行检验和评估实施示范项目）的过程。人文科学领域没有对应的试验发展活动。主要反映将科研成果转化为技术和产品的能力，是科技推动经济社会发展的物化成果。

R&D人员 指参与研究与试验发展项目研究、管理和辅助工作的人员，包括项目（课题）组人员，企业科技行政管理人员和直接为项目（课题）活动提供服务的辅助人员。反映投入从事拥有自主知识产权的研究开发活动的人力规模。

R&D人员全时当量 指全时人员数加非全时人员按工作量折算为全时人员数的总和。例如：有两个全时人员和三个非全时人员（工作时间分别为20%、30%和70%），则全时当量为2+0.2+0.3+0.7=3.2人年。为国际上比较科技人力投入而制定的可比指标。

R&D经费内部支出 合计指调查单位用于内部开展R&D活动（基础研究、应用研究和试验发展）的实际支出。包括用于R&D项目（课题）活动的直接支出，以及间接用TR&D活动的管理费、服务费、与R&D有关的基本建设支出以及外协加工费等。不包括生产性活动支出、归还贷款支出以及与外单位合作或委托外单位进行R&D活动而转拨给对方的经费支出。

R&D经费内部支出中政府资金 指R&D经费内部支出中来自各级政府部门的各类资金，包括财政科学技术拨款、科学基金、教育等部门事业费以及政府部门预算外资金的实际支出。

R&D经费内部支出中企业资金 指R&D经费内部支出中来自本企业的自有资金和接受其他企业委托而获得的经费，以及科研院所、高校等事业单位从企业获得的资金的实际支出。

R&D项目（课题）数 指在当年立项并开展研究工作、以前年份立项仍继续进行研究的研发项目（课题）数。包括当年完成和年内研究：工作已告失败的研发项目（课题），但不包括委托外单位进行的研发项目（课题）数。

R&D项目（课题）人员全时当量 指实际参加研发项目（课题）活动人员折合的全时当量。

R&D项目（课题）经费内部支出 指调查单位内部在报告年度进行研发项目（课题）研究和试制等的实际支出。包括劳务费、其他日常支出、固定资产购建费、外协加工费等，不包括委托或与外单位合作进行项目（课题）研究而拨付给对方使用的经费。

新产品产值 指报告期企业生产的新产品的产值。新产品是指采用新技术原理、新设计构思研制、生产的全新产品，或在结构、材质、工艺等某一方面比原有产品有明显改进，从而显著提高了产品性能或扩大了使用功能的产品。新产品产值、新产品销售收入既包括经政府有关部门认定并在有效期内的新产品，也包括企业自行研制开发，未经政府有关部门认定，从投产之日起一年之内的新产品。

新产品销售收入 指报告期企业销售新产品实现的销售收入。

专利 是专利权的简称，是对发明人的发明创造经审查合格后，由专利局依据专利法授予发明人和设计人对该项发明创造享有的专有权。包括发明、实用新型和外观设计。反映拥有自主知识产权的科技和设计成果情况。

发明（专利） 指对产品、方法或者其改进所提出的新的技术方案。是国际通行的反映拥有自主知识产权技术的核心指标。

实用新型（专利） 指对产品的形状、构造或者其结合所提出的适于实用的新的技术方案。反映具有一定技术含量的技术成果情况。

外观设计（专利） 指对产品的形状、图案、色彩或者其结合所作出的富有美感并适于工业上应用的新设计。反映拥有自主知识产权的外观设计成果情况。

工业企业R&D投入强度 指研究与试验发展经费内部支出与主营业务收入的比值。

Explanatory Notes on Main Statistical Indicators

Regular Institutions of Higher Education refer to educational establishments set up according to the government evaluation and approval procedures, recruiting graduates from senior secondary schools as the main target by National Matriculation TEST. They include full-time universities, colleges, institutions of higher professional education, institutions of higher vocational education, institutions of higher vocational education and others (non-university tertiary, branch schools and undergraduate classes) .

Universities and colleges primarily provide undergraduate courses; institutions of higher professional education and institutions of higher vocational education primarily provide professional trainings; and others refer to educational establishments, which are responsible for enrolling higher education students under the State Plan but not enumerated in the total number of schools, including: branch schools of universities and colleges, and universities and colleges that have been approved and under plan for construction. Non-university tertiary refers to the regular undergraduate branch college which is running in new mechanism and mode, excluding the branch schools and other similar branches of educational institutions.

Institutions of Higher Education for Adults refer to educational establishments, set up in line with relevant rules approved by the government, enrolling staff and workers with senior secondary school or equivalent education, and providing higher education courses in many forms of correspondence, spare time, or full time for adults. Professionals thus trained receive a qualification equivalent to graduates studying regular courses at regular universities, colleges and professional colleges. Institutions of higher learning for adults include schools of higher education for staff and workers, schools of higher education for peasants, colleges for management cadres, pedagogical colleges, independent correspondence colleges, Radio and TV universities and other educational establishments. Other educational establishments have undertakings to enrol adult students but not enumerated in the schools under the State Plan.

Net Enrolment Ratio of Primary Schools refers to the proportion of school age children enrolled at schools to the total number of school age children both in and outside schools (including retarded children, but excluding blind, deaf and mute children) . The formula is:

$$\text{Net Enrolment Ratio Of Primary Schools} = \frac{\text{Total Primary School-age Children at Schools}}{\text{Total Primary School-age WnerdlihChether or Not Attending School}} \times 100\%$$

Research and Development (R&D) refers to systematic and creative activities in the field of science and technology aiming at increasing the knowledge and using the knowledge for new application. R&D includes 3 categories of activities: basic research, applied research and experimentation for development. The scale and intensity of R&D are widely used internationally to reflect the strength of S&T and the core competitiveness of a country in the world.

Basic Research refers to empirical or theoretical research aiming at obtaining new knowledge on the fundamental principles regarding phenomena or observable facts to reveal the intrinsic nature and underlying laws and to acquire new discoveries or new theories. Basic research takes no specific or designated application as the aim of the research. Results of basic research are mainly released or disseminated in the form of scientific papers or monographs. This indicator reflects the innovation capacity for original knowledge.

Applied Research refers to creative research aiming at obtaining new knowledge on a specific objective or target. Purpose of the applied research is to identify the possible uses of results from basic research, or to explore new (fundamental) methods or new approaches. Results of applied research are expressed in the form of scientific papers, monographs, fundamental models or invention patents. This indicator reflects the exploration of ways to apply the results of basic research.

Experiments and Development refer to systematic activities aiming at using the knowledge from basic and applied researches or from practical experience to develop new products, materials and equipment, to establish new production process, systems and services, or to make substantial improvement on the existing products, process or services. Results of experiment and development activities are embodied in patents, exclusive technology, and monotype of new products or equipment. In social sciences, experiment and development activities refer to the process of converting the knowledge from basic or applied researches into feasible programmes (including conduct of demonstration projects for assessment and evaluation). There are no experiment and development activities in the science of humanities. This indicator reflects the capability of transferring the results of S&T into technique and products, and measures the realization of S&T in spearheading the economic and social development.

R&D Personnel refer to persons engaged in research, management and supporting activities ofR & D, including persons in the project teams, persons engaged in the management of S&T activities of enterprises and supporting staff providing direct service to the research projects. This indicator reflects the size of personnel engaged in R&D activities with independent intellectual property.

Full-time Equivalent of R&D Personnel refers to the sum of the full-time persons and the full-time equivalent of part-time persons converted by workload. For instance, if there are 2 full-time persons and 3 part-time workers (20%, 30% and 70% of working hours respectively on R&D activities), the full-time equivalent are 2+0.2+0.3+0.7=3.2 person-years. This is an internationally comparable indicator of S&T manpower input.

Total Internal Expenditure of Funds on R&D refers to the real expenditure of surveyed units on their own R&D activities (basic research, application study, test and development) including direct expenditure on R&D activities, indirect expenditure of management and services on R&D activities, expenditure on capital construction and material processing by others. Excluding the expenditure on production activities, return of loan, and fees transferred to cooperated and entrusted agencies on R&D activities.

Internal Expenditure of Government Funds refersto the expenditure of funds on R&D activities from government agencies at different levels, including appropriate funds on science and technology from financial departments, scientific funds, operating expenses from education departments and the real expenditure of extra budgetary funds from government agencies.

Internal Expenditure of Funds of Enterprises refers to the expenditure of funds on R&D activities from self-raised funds of enterprises and funds from other enterprises through entrustment, and the expenditure of funds of institutions, such as institution of scientific research and universities, from enterprises.

Number of R&D Projects (subjects) refers to the number of R&D projects (subjects) set up and implemented at the reference year, and the number of R&D projects (subjects) set up in former years and under implementation, including the projects (subjects) finished and failed at the reference year, excluding the projects (subjects) implemented by others through entrustment.

Full-time Equivalent of R&D Personnel refers to the full-time equivalent of persons actually engaged in R&D projects. (subjects)

Internal Expenditure of Funds on R&D Projects (subjects) refers to the real expenditure of internal funds of the surveyed units on research and test of R&D projects (subjects) at the reference year, including service fee, other daily expenditure, cost for capital goods, cost of external process; excluding expenditure of funds transferred to other cooperated and entrusted units of the projects.

Output Value of New Products refers to the output value of new products during the reporting period. The new products refer to brand new products produced with new technology and new design, or product that represent noticeable improvement in terms of structure, material, or production process for improving significantly the character of function of the older versions. The output value and sales income of the new products include those of new products certified by relevant government agencies within the period of certification, as well as new procucts designed and produced by enterprises within a year without certification by government agencies.

Sales Income of New Products refers to the real sales income of new products of the enterprises at the reporting period.

Patent is an abbreviation for the patent right and refers to the exclusive right of ownership by the inventors or designers for the creation or inventions, given from the patent offices after due process of assessment and approval in accordance with the Patent Law. Patents are granted for inventions, utility models and designs. This indicator reflects the achievements of S&T and design with independent intellectual property.

Patented Inventions refer to new technical proposals to the products or methods or their modifications. This is universal core indicator reflecting the technologies with independent intellectual property.

Patented Utility Models refer to the practical and new technical proposals on the shape and structure of the product or the combination of both. This indicator reflects the condition of technological results with certain technical content.

Designs refer to the aesthetics and industrially applicable new designs for the shape, pattern and colour of the product, or their combinations. This indicator reflects the appearance design achievements with independent intellectual property.

Intensity of Input into R&D of Industrial Enterprises refers to the percentage of main operation income spent on R&D activities by industrial enterprises.

20 文化、体育、卫生、社会福利和其他

CULTURE,SPORTS,PUBLIC HEALTH,SOCIAL WELFARE INSTITUTIONS AND OTHER SOCIAL ACTIVITIES

资料整理：郝　静

Data management:Hao jing

第二十部分　文化、体育、卫生、社会福利和其他

一、简要说明

本章资料主要包括文化、卫生、民政、体育、计划生育、共青团、妇联以及公检法等方面的内容，由西安市统计局社会科技处根据西安市文广新局、卫生局、民政局、体育局、妇联、共青团市委、计划生育委员会以及公安局、检察院、法院等部门提供资料整理。

二、主要指标

图书馆总藏量（千册件）	6646.6	比上年增加	523.6千册件
医院数（个）	281	比上年增加	5个
医院床位数（万张）	4.28	比上年增加	3540张

20　CULTURE,SPORTS,SANITATION,SOCIAL WELFARE INSTITUTIONS AND OTHER SOCIAL ACTIVITIES

Ⅰ.Brief Introduction

Data in this chapter primarily consists of data of culture, sanitation, civil administration, physical education, family planning, Communist Youth League, the Women's Federation, public security organs, procuratorial organs and people's court, compiled by Social Science & Technology Division of Xi'an Bureau of Statistics according to data from Xi'an Bureau of Cuture, Bureau of Sanitation, Bureau of Civial Adnimistration, Bureau of PE, the Women's Federation, Municipal Committee of Communist Youth League, Committee of Family Planning, Bureau of Public Security, Procuratorate, People's Court and other department concerned.

Ⅱ.Major Indicators

		Increase over Preceding Year
Number of Collections in Libraries(1 000 vol.)	6646.6	523.6
Number of Hospitals(unit)	281	5
Number of Beds(10 000 units)	4.28	3540 units

20-1 文化事业机构和人数（2013年）

Number of Institutions and Personnel in Culture and Art（2013）

项 目	Item	机构数（个） Number of Institutions (unit)	人员数（人） Number of Personnel (person)
一、电影事业	**Career of Film**		
制片厂	Studio	1	
发行放映管理机构	Number of Film Projection and Publication Administrating Institutions	2	8
电影放映单位	Unit of Film shows	163	1580
#电影院	Cinema	32	1368
影剧院	Theaters	5	65
放映队	Film Projection Team	126	147
二、艺术事业	**Art**		
艺术表演团体	Art Performance Troupes	18	2336
艺术表演场所	Art Centers	17	362
三、艺术科研机构	**Art Scientific Research Institution**	**2**	**65**
四、图书馆事业	**Libraries**	**15**	**535**
五、群众文化事业	**Mass Culture**		
群众艺术馆	Activities of Mass Art Centres	2	125
文化馆	Cultural Centers	14	253
文化站	Culture Stations	182	703
农村文化室	Rural Cultural Center	2377	
六、文化部门教育机构	**Educations Institution of Culture Department**	**2**	**126**

注：本表数据来源于市文广新局。

20-2 文化事业发展情况（2013年）

Basic Statistics on Culture Development（2013）

指 标	Item	2013
电影放映场数（千场）	Number of Film Shows (1 000 shows)	345.02
电影观众人数（千人次）	Number of Spectators (1 000 person-times)	12238.6
电影票房收入（万元）	Box-office Receipts(10 000 yuan)	41950.9
艺术表演团体演出场次（场）	Number of Art Performance Troupes Performers (shows)	6299
#国内演出场次	Number of domestic Performance	6261
艺术表演观众人次（千人次）	Number of Spectators(1 000 person-times)	9157
图书馆总藏量（千册件）	The total reserves of the library(1 000 pieces)	6646.6
书刊文献外借人次（千人次）	Books, Journals and Documents Borrowing (1 000 person-times)	898
书刊文献外借册次（千册次）	Books, Journals and Documents Borrowing (1 000 Volume-time)	2320
县以上公共图书馆购书经费（万元）	Book-purchase Fund of Public Library above the County Level(1 000yuan）	1404.6

注：本表数据来源于市文广新局。

20-3 主要年份群众艺术馆、文化馆（站）活动情况

Basic Statistics on Activities of Mass Art Centers and Cultural Centers in Representative Years

指 标	Item	2008	2009	2010	2011	2012	2013
机构数（个）	Number of Insititutions (units)	197	197	197	196	197	198
举办展览个数（个）	Number of Exhibitions (units)	520	716	705	592	652	658
举办展览参观人次（千人次）	Number of Exhibition Visitors(1 000 person-times)				375	416	1201
组织文艺活动次数 （次）	Art Performances and Story-telling Sessions (times)	2378	3158	3729	4544	3273	4114
组织文艺活动参加人次（千人次）	Number of Culture Activities attendees (1 000 person-times)				1778	1377	1633
举办训练班班次（个）	Number of Training Courses (units)	1109	1467	3018	2224	1798	1616
举办训练班结业人次（千人次）	Number of Certificate Trained Persons (1 000 person-times)	87	96	133	115	143	155
组织各类理论研讨和讲座次数(次)	Number of Theoretical Discussion and Seminars(1 000 person-times)				106	78	122
组织各类理论研讨和讲座参加人次（千人次）	Number of Persons in Theoretical Discussion and Seminars(1 000 person-times)				15	14	19
本年收入（千元）	Income of this year (1 000 yuan)	22571	40891	42937	55367	88475	101365
本年支出（千元）	Expenditure of this year (1 000 yuan)	22458	42826	45160	62368	84522	93485

注：本表数据来源于市文广新局。

20-4 文物保护业基本情况（2013年）

Basic Statistics on Cultural Relics Protection（2013）

指 标	Item	机 构（个）Insitituion (unit)	人 员（人）Personnel (person)	文物藏品 实际数量（件）Factual Number of Collections(piece)	一级品 Grade One	举办陈列展览次数(次) Times of exhibition(times)	参观人员（千人次）Number of Visitors (1000 person-times)
总 计	**Total**	**156**	**4129**	**988838**	**5470**	**504**	**18985**
文物行政管理机关	Protection and Management Agencies	16	226				
文物保护管理机构	Cultural Relics administrative Departments	29	514	29228	32	17	1517
其他文物机构	Other Agencies	8	168	40219			
博物馆	Museums	100	2994	886449	5252	487	17468
文物商店	Cultural Relics Agencies						
文物科研机构	Scientific Research of Historical Relics Preservation	3	227	32942	186		

注：本表数据来源于市文物局。

2010年前为省市直属文物单位数据，2011年及以后为全口径数据(含民营、院校等)。

20-5 主要年份广播电台及节目制作情况

Basic Statistics of Broadcasting Stations and Program Production in Representative Years

指 标	Item	2008	2009	2010	2011	2012	2013
省、地广播电台（座）	Broadcasting Stations at the Province and District Level(set)	2	2	2	1	1	
省、地广播电视台（座）	Broadcasting Station at Province and District Level(set)				1	1	2
县级广播电视台（座）	Number of Wire Broadcasting Stations and TV Relaying Stations(set)	6	6	6	6	6	6
中短波、调频发射台及转播台（座）	Medium/Short Ware and FM Broadcast Transmission Stations and Relaying Stations(set)	46	51	55	54	59	57
节目套数（套）	Number of Programs(set)	17	18	18	19	20	20
全年播出时间(时：分)	Broadcasting Hours annually(hour)	113880	123005	124100	121723	129856	138278
广播节目综合人口覆盖率（%）	Broadcasts comprehensive population coverage	99.37	99.37	99.40	99.42	99.45	99.47
制作广播节目(时：分)	Productions of Broadcasting(hour)	103328	110455	110639	83368	104300	106554
#新闻资讯类	News Programs			13786	13821	14025	14355
专题服务类	Special Subject Programs			24451	16318	21891	30181
综艺类	Variety Programs			37720	28679	28096	24516
广播剧类	Literature Programs			2406	2014	1720	3083
广告类	Advertisements			28339	14202	19547	20552
其他类	Service Programs			3937	8334	19021	13867

注：本表数据来源于市文广新局。

2010年制作广播节目时间分类发生变化，故2009年及以前无数据。

20-6 主要年份电视台及节目制作情况

Basic Statistics of TV Stations and Production of TV Program in Representative Years

指　　标	Item	2008	2009	2010	2011	2012	2013
电视台（座）	Number of Television Stations (set)	2	2	2	1	1	
发射台及转播台（座）	Number of Television Transmission Stations and Relaying Stations (set)	8	10	10	10	11	11
无线电视节目（套）	Program Productions of Non-cable television Stations (set)	5	7	6	6	6	6
有线电视节目（套）	Program Productions of cable television Stations (set)	17	15	16	16	16	16
全年播出时间（时：分）	Broadcasting Hours annually(hour)	140608	138372	141856	147003	137936	140927
电视节目综合人口覆盖率（%）	TV shows comprehensive population coverage	98.35	98.41	98.57	98. 60	98.83	98.84
制作电视节目（时：分）	Earth Stations of Satellite TV (set)	26097	27131	29626	43925	30091	46614
#新闻资讯类	News and Information Programs			8930	10656	11169	13360
专题服务类	Special Subject Programs			7762	19191	7689	7751
综艺类	Variety Programs			3942	5202	5458	6508
广播剧类	Literature Programs			1729	3781	113	1820
广告类	Advertisement			3313	3200	3663	8066
其他类	Service Programs			3950	1894	1997	9109
有线电视用户（万户）	Users of Cable television Stations (10 000 households)	138.79	146.84	164.64	179.29	188.71	207.48
有线广播电视干线网总长度(公里)	The total length of cable broadcasting and television arteries of communication(km)				62494	62494	37126
有线电视入户率(%)	The Rate of Cable Television(%)				79.08	80.53	86.62

注：本表数据来源于市文广新局。
2010年制作电视节目时间分类发生变化，故2009年及以前无数据。

20-7 体育事业基本情况（市属）（2013年）

The Basic Situations of Sport（Under Municipality）（2013）

单位：人、枚　　(person, unit)

指　　标	Item	2012	2013
一、体育部门职工人数	**Number of Staffs and Workers in Physical Education System**	**1300**	**1258**
#运动员	Athletes	860	850
教练员	Coaches	131	140
二、等级裁判员发展人数	**Number of the Development of Grade Referees**	**216**	**457**
三、等级运动员发展人数	**Number of the Development of Grade Athletes**	**195**	**434**
四、全年获得奖牌数	**Number of Full-year Medals**	**420**	**502**
#国家级金牌	National Gold	12	19
国家级银牌	National Silver	11	10
省级金牌	Provincial Gold	182	140
省级银牌	Provincial Silver	138	153

注：本表数据来源于市体育局。

20-8 少年儿童分项业余体校情况（市属）（2013年）

Basic Statistics of Youth Part-time Physical Training School（2013）

单位：人　　(person)

指　　标	Items	2013
一、在课学生数	**Total Enrollment**	**6953**
田径	Track and Field	1800
游泳	Swimming	1100
体操	Gymnastics	75
举重	Weightlifting	60
国际式摔跤	Wrestling	80
柔道	Judo	60
射击	Shooting	260
射箭	Archery	180
足球	Football	270
篮球	Basketball	1620
排球	Volleyball	200
乒乓球	Table Tennis	650
拳击	Boxing	23
武术	Wu Shu	390
跆拳道	Kickboxing	50
跳水	Diving	65
棒球	Baseball	70
二、职工数	**Number of Staff and Workers**	**1258**

注：本表数据来源于市体育局。

20-9 群众体育事业（2013年）

Mass Sports（2013）

指　　标	Items	2012	2013
社会体育指导员（人）	Social Sports Instructor(persons)	8600	9689
晨晚健身站点（个）	Morning and Evening Fitness sites(units)	1600	1650
社区建有体育组织比重（%）	The community has a sports organization proportion (%)	89	90
全国、全省体育先进社区（个）	National, provincial advanced sports community (units)	25	25
体育人口(万人)	Sports population(10 000 persons)	420	450

注：本表数据来源于市体育局。

20-10 主要年份卫生机构、床位、人员情况

Number of Health Care Institutions, Beds and Employed Persons in Health Care Institutions in Representative Years

年份 Year	卫生机构数（个） Number of Health Care Institutions (unit)	医院数（个） Number of Health Care Hospital (unit)	卫生机构床位数(张） Number of Health Care Bed (unit)	医院床位数(张） Number of Hospital Bed (unit)	卫生技术人员数(人） Number of Medical Technical Personnel (person)
2008	2239	276	34618	30582	47433
2009	2162	261	36849	32371	51641
2010	2385	258	39407	34274	56579
2011	5554	268	41010	35976	61281
2012	5576	276	44239	39213	66399
2013	5503	281	47867	42753	71134

注：本表数据来源于市卫生局。
　　2008年及以后为新的统计口径、分类。

20-11 卫生机构、床位及人员情况（2013年）

卫生机构	Health Care Institutions	机构数（个）Number of Institutions (unit)	床位数（张）Number of Beds (unit)
总计	**Total**	**5503**	**47867**
一、医院	**Hospitals**	**281**	**42753**
综合医院	General Hospitals	211	33592
中医医院	Hospitals Specialized in Traditional Chinese Medicine	37	4211
中西医结合医院	Hospitals Integrating Traditional Chinese Medicine with Western Therapeutics in Practice	2	90
民族医院	Nationalities Hospitals		
专科医院	Specialized Hospitals	31	4860
护理院	Nursing Centets		
二、基层医疗卫生机构	**Commuting health care service centre**	**5147**	**3307**
社区卫生服务中心(站)	Community Health Care Center(Station)	202	1823
社区卫生服务中心	Community Health Care Center	130	1823
社区卫生服务站	Community Health Care Station	72	
卫生院	Health Center	100	1437
街道卫生院	Urban Health-center	5	53
乡镇卫生院	Rural Health-center	95	1384
村卫生室	Village clinics	2981	
门诊部	Outpatient department	169	47
诊所、卫生所、医务室	Clinic, health center, Infirmary	1695	
三、专科公共卫生机构	**College of public health institutions**	**52**	**1685**
疾病预防控制中心	Center for Disease Control and Prevention	17	
专科疾病防治院（所、站）	Specialized disease prevention and cure center (place, station)	1	700
健康教育所（站、中心）	Health Education Institute (station, center)	2	
妇幼保健院（所、站）	Maternal and Child Health Hospital (Station)	15	985
急救中心（站）	Emergency Center	1	
采供血机构	Blood Collection Agencies	1	
卫生监督所（中心）	Health Supervision Agencies (Center)	15	
四、其他卫生机构	**Other Health Institution**	**23**	**122**
疗养院	Nursing Centres	1	122
卫生监督检验(监测、检测)所(站)	Health Supervision and inspection Agencies		
医学科学研究机构	Medical scientific research institutions	3	
医学在职培训机构	Medical training institutions	4	
临床检验中心（所、站）	Clinical testing center (place, station)	0	
其他	other	14	

注：本表数据来源于市卫生局。

Number of Health Care Institutions, Beds and Employed Persons in Health Care Institutions（2013）

人员合计（人）Total Number of Employed Persons (person)	卫生技术人员 Medical Technical Personnel	执业(助理)医师数 Licensed (Assistant) Doctors	#执业医师 Chartered Doctors
90129	**71134**	**23885**	**21205**
63303	**51368**	**15785**	**14916**
51207	41959	12956	12314
5458	4426	1412	1273
85	76	30	24
6553	4907	1387	1305
21358	**15738**	**7007**	**5312**
5461	4469	1489	1096
4864	3944	1283	923
597	525	206	173
2761	2265	584	355
87	73	21	15
2674	2192	563	340
4768	960	803	277
2420	2186	976	830
5948	5858	3155	2754
4801	**3669**	**960**	**853**
1066	814	289	251
432	324	82	79
70	28	5	5
2399	1905	540	477
122	49	28	26
149	96	16	15
563	453		
667	**359**	**133**	**124**
77	42	14	14
160	90	53	52
178	70	6	6
246	157	60	52

20-11 续表1

卫生机构	Health Care Institutions	人员合计	
		卫生技术人员中（人）	
		注册护士 Registered Nurses	药师（士） Junior Paramedics
总计	**Total**	**29967**	**3551**
一、医院	**Hospitals**	**23894**	**2505**
综合医院	General Hospitals	19539	1896
中医医院	Hospitals Specialized in Traditional Chinese Medicine	1775	375
中西医结合医院	Hospitals Integrating Traditional Chinese Medicine with Western Therapeutics in Practice	34	5
民族医院	Nationalities Hospitals		
专科医院	Specialized Hospitals	2546	229
护理院	Nursing Centets		
二、基层医疗卫生机构	**Commuting health care service centre**	**4909**	**931**
社区卫生服务中心(站)	Community Health Care Center(Station)	1455	334
社区卫生服务中心	Community Health Care Center	1228	294
社区卫生服务站	Community Health Care Station	227	40
卫生院	Health Center	477	139
街道卫生院	Urban Health-center	15	5
乡镇卫生院	Rural Health-center	462	134
村卫生室	Village clinics	157	
门诊部	Outpatient department	720	190
诊所、卫生所、医务室	Clinic, health center, Infirmary	2100	268
三、专科公共卫生机构	**College of public health institutions**	**1084**	**104**
疾病预防控制中心	Center for Disease Control and Prevention	52	15
专科疾病防治院（所、站）	Specialized disease prevention and cure center (place, station)	173	12
健康教育所（站、中心）	Health Education Institute (station, center)	1	
妇幼保健院（所、站）	Maternal and Child Health Hospital (Station)	820	70
急救中心（站）	Emergency Center	10	1
采供血机构	Blood Collection Agencies	28	6
卫生监督所（中心）	Health Supervision Agencies (Center)		
四、其他卫生机构	**Other Health Institution**	**80**	**11**
疗养院	Nursing Centres	19	3
卫生监督检验(监测、检测)所(站)	Health Supervision and inspection Agencies		
医学科学研究机构	Medical scientific research institutions	13	4
医学在职培训机构	Medical training institutions		1
临床检验中心（所、站）	Clinical testing center (place, station)		
其他	other	48	3

continued 1

Total Number of Employed Persons (person)					
Among:Medical Technical Personnel			其他技术人员 Other Technical Personnel	管理人员 Administrative Personnel	工勤技能人员 Logistics Technical Workers
技师（士） Technicians	#检验师 Laboratory Technicians	其他 Other			
4089	**2974**	**9642**	**590**	**7160**	**7437**
2934	**2091**	**6250**	**454**	**5696**	**5785**
2372	1723	5196	354	4363	4531
276	160	588	72	477	483
6	5	1		7	2
280	203	465	28	849	769
686	**457**	**2205**	**9**	**696**	**1107**
284	197	907	1	420	571
261	176	878	1	381	538
23	21	29		39	33
187	106	878	8	276	212
6	4	26		10	4
181	102	852	8	266	208
163	113	137			234
52	41	283			90
426	**390**	**1095**	**48**	**620**	**464**
221	212	237	10	143	99
22	19	35	0	59	49
		22	22	18	2
148	124	327	5	253	226
		10		40	33
35	35	11	3	40	10
		453	8	57	45
43	**36**	**92**	**79**	**148**	**81**
2	2	4		16	19
18	14	2	13	34	23
2	2	61	48	45	15
21	18	25	14	51	24

20-12 各区县卫生机构、床位及人员情况（2013年）

Number of Health Care Institutions, Beds and Employed Persons in Health Care Institutions By Region（2013）

区 县	Region	机构（个）Number of Health Care Institutions (unit)	床位（张）Number of Beds (unit)	人员合计（人）Total Number of Employed Persons (person)	#卫生技术人员（人）Total Number of Medical Technical Personnel
合 计	**Total**	**5503**	**47867**	**90129**	**71134**
新城区	Xincheng	280	6988	14130	11248
碑林区	Beilin	360	7202	13451	11105
莲湖区	Lianhu	336	5972	11341	9313
灞桥区	Baqiao	483	2621	5005	4129
未央区	Weiyang	278	3330	6094	4984
雁塔区	Yanta	474	8508	15331	12347
阎良区	Yanliang	163	1401	2482	1960
临潼区	Lintong	485	2221	3624	2454
长安区	Chang'an	779	3349	6122	4526
蓝田县	Lantian	589	1127	2305	1565
周至县	Zhouzhi	474	1276	3579	2543
户 县	Huxian	591	2612	4395	3195
高陵县	Gaoling	211	1260	2270	1765

注：本表数据来源于市卫生局。

20-13 主要年份卫生机构各类人员情况

Number of Employed Persons in Health Care Institutions in Representative Years

单位：人 (person)

指　标	Item	2008	2009	2010	2011	2012	2013
人员合计	**Total**	**59934**	**65003**	**71230**	**79999**	**86096**	**90129**
卫生技术人员	Medical Technical Personnel	47433	51641	56579	61281	66899	71134
执业（助理）医师	Licensed (Assistant) Doctors	18066	19284	18763	21551	23051	23885
#执业医师	Chartered Doctors	15975	17286	16613	18904	20414	21205
注册护士	Registered Nurses	17186	20167	22640	25043	27837	29967
药师（士）	Junior Paramedics	2721	2814	3030	3127	3380	3551
技师（士）	Technicians	3168	3350	4589	3622	3953	4089
#检验师	Laboratory Technicians	2204	2290	2439	2622	2830	2974
其他	Other	6292	6026	7557	7938	8678	9642
其他技术人员	Other Technical Personnel	1051	1325	1156	895	633	590
管理人员	Administrative Personnel	6007	6067	6416	6769	6939	7160
工勤技能人员	Logistics Technical Workers	5443	5970	7079	6789	7555	7437

注：本表数据来源于市卫生局。
本表2011年人员合计中包括乡村医生3356人和卫生员409人；2012年人员合计中包括乡村医生3611人和卫生员459人。
2013年人员合计中包括乡村医生3477人和卫生员331人。

20-14 医疗卫生机构门诊、住院及病床使用情况（2013年）

指　标	Item	总诊疗人次数 总计 Total
总计	**Total**	**51155482**
一、医院	**Hospitals**	**26398431**
综合医院	General Hospitals	21565232
中医医院	Hospitals Specialized in Traditional Chinese Medicine	2187973
中西医结合医院	Hospitals Integrating Traditional Chinese Medicine with Western Therapeutics in Practice	23661
民族医院	Nationalities Hospitals	
专科医院	Specialized Hospitals	2621565
护理院	Nursing Centets	
二、基层医疗卫生机构	**Commuting health care service centre**	**23113777**
社区卫生服务中心（站）	Community Health Care Center(Station)	3954991
社区卫生服务中心	Community Health Care Center	3288525
社区卫生服务站	Community Health Care Station	666466
卫生院	Health Center	1191717
街道卫生院	Urban Health-center	37401
乡镇卫生院	Rural Health-center	1154316
村卫生室	Village clinics	10612360
门诊部	Outpatient department	1646724
诊所、卫生所、医务室	Clinic, health center, Infirmary	5707985
三、专业公共卫生机构	**College of public health institutions**	**1640551**
专科疾病防治院（所、站）	Specialized disease prevention and cure center (place, station)	29131
妇幼保健院（所、站）	Maternal and Child Health Hospital (Station)	1492331
急救中心（站）	Emergency Center	119089
四、其他卫生机构	**Other Health Institution**	**2723**
疗养院	Sanatorium	2723

注：本表数据来源于市卫生局。

Medical and Health Institutions Outpatient, Inpatient and Utilization of Beds(2013)

Total Number of Clinics (person time)				观察室 Observation Room	
门.急诊人次数				留观病例数（人次）	死亡人数（人）
	门诊人次数	急诊人次数	死亡人数（人）		
Number of Outpatient and Emergency	Number of Outpatients	Number of Emergency	Number of Deaths (person)	Number of Patients Receiving (person time)	Number of Deaths (persons)
50075576	**47403144**	**2672432**	**2823**	**28726**	**32**
26238587	**23897051**	**2341536**	**2791**	**25403**	**32**
21424716	19459658	1965058	2731	25189	29
2181021	2115333	65688	30	35	1
23661	23641	20			
2609189	2298419	310770	30	179	2
22193715	**22044103**	**149612**	**30**	**3268**	
3810569	3693835	116734	30	845	
3166808	3064962	101846	4	845	
643761	628873	14888	26		
1187377	1154499	32878		2423	
37336	35971	1365			
1150041	1118528	31513		2423	
9919839	9919839				
1622333	1622333				
5653597	5653597				
1640551	**1459267**	**181284**	**2**	**55**	
29131	29088	43			
1492331	1430179	62152	2	55	
119089		119089			
2723	**2723**				
2723	2723				

20-14 续表1

指 标	Item	急诊死亡率（%） Emergency Mortality (%)	入院人数合计（人） Total Number of Admission Patients (person)
总计	**Total**	**0.11**	**1462336**
一、医院	**Hospitals**	**0.12**	**1337645**
综合医院	General Hospitals	0.14	1117278
中医医院	Hospitals Specialized in Traditional Chinese Medicine	0.05	97069
中西医结合医院	Hospitals Integrating Traditional Chinese Medicine with Western Therapeutics in Practice		717
民族医院	Nationalities Hospitals		
专科医院	Specialized Hospitals	0.01	122581
护理院	Nursing Centets		
二、基层医疗卫生机构	**Commuting health care service centre**	**0.02**	**66077**
社区卫生服务中心（站）	Community Health Care Center(Station)	0.03	39892
社区卫生服务中心	Community Health Care Center		39892
社区卫生服务站	Community Health Care Station	0.17	
卫生院	Health Center		25174
街道卫生院	Urban Health-center		559
乡镇卫生院	Rural Health-center		24615
村卫生室	Village clinics		
门诊部	Outpatient department		1011
诊所、卫生所、医务室	Clinic, health center, Infirmary		
三、专业公共卫生机构	**College of public health institutions**		**57144**
专科疾病防治院（所、站）	Specialized disease prevention and cure center (place, station)		5687
妇幼保健院（所、站）	Maternal and Child Health Hospital (Station)		51457
急救中心（站）	Emergency Center		
四、其他卫生机构	**Other Health Institution**		**1470**
疗养院	Sanatorium		1470

continued 1

出院人数合计 (人) Total Number of Discharge Patients (person)	死亡人数 (人) Number of Hospital Csualty (person)	病床周转次数 (次) Nnumber of Bed Rumover (time)	病床使用率 (%) Bed occupancy rate (%)	出院者平均住院日 (天) Average Stay Days in Hospital (day)
1455947	**7984**	**31.3**	**85.35**	**9.9**
1332356	**7938**	**32.1**	**88.10**	**9.9**
1110877	7276	33.7	87.61	9.4
99458	297	25.8	86.87	12.3
717		8.0	40.98	9.3
121304	365	26.0	93.45	12.9
65299	**16**	**20.2**	**48.59**	**8.7**
39576	16	22.0	51.84	8.5
39576	16	22.0	51.84	8.5
24712		17.3	44.50	9.3
556		10.5	18.79	6.5
24156		17.5	45.48	9.3
1011				
56834	**30**	**34.2**	**90.76**	**9.7**
5440	21	7.8	100	47.4
51394	9	53.2	84.08	5.7
1458		**12.0**	**49.93**	**13.8**
1458		12.0	49.93	13.8

20-15 社会福利事业单位基本情况（2013年）

Basic Statistics on Social Welfare Insititutions (2013)

指 标	Item	机构数（个）Number of Institutions	年末职工人数（人）Number of Staff at the Year End	床位数（张）Number of Beds	年末在院人数（人）Number of Persons Housed at the Year-end
社会福利院情况	**Statistics on Social Welfare**				
1. 社会福利院	Social Welfare Homes	4	89	1285	897
2. 儿童福利院	Baby Welfare Homes	1	77	900	591
3. 社会福利医院	Social Welfare Hospitals	1	147	500	425
4. 收养性老年福利机构	Welfare Units Adopting the Elderly	75	1665	12409	7503
城镇	Urban	49	1322	9279	6174
农村	Rural	26	343	3130	1329

注：本表数据来源于市民政局。

20-16 主要年份社会福利事业单位机构、人员情况

Number of Social Welfare Institutions and Employed Persons

单位：个、人 (unit, person)

指 标	Item	2008	2009	2010	2011	2012	2013
一、机构	**Insititutions**						
烈士纪念建筑物管理单位	Institutions Managing Memorial Buildings of Martyrs	2	2	2	2	2	2
救助类单位	Units Providing Assistance	8	8	8	8	8	8
殡仪服务单位	Funeral Service Units	20	20	22	21	22	25
殡仪馆	Funeral Homes	4	4	4	5	4	4
公墓	Cemeteries	12	12	14	12	12	15
殡葬管理单位	Funeral Management Units	4	4	4	4	6	6
二、人员	**Staff**						
烈士纪念建筑物管理单位	Institutions Managing Memorial Buildings of Martyrs	39	39	37	38	40	42
救助类单位	Units Providing Assistance	110	118	116	119	130	137
殡仪服务单位	Funeral Service Units	1015	1046	1371	1313	1400	1430
殡仪馆	Funeral Homes	220	218	375	408	442	491
公墓	Cemeteries	745	776	939	838	869	855
殡葬管理单位	Funeral Management Units	50	52	57	67	89	84

注：本表数据来源于市民政局。

20-17 全市及各区县福利企业单位基本情况（2013年）

Basic Statistics on Social Welfare Insititutions (2013)

单位：个、人 (unit, person)

区 县	Region	单位数 Number of Enterprise	年末职工人数 Number of Staff and Workers at the end of year	年末残疾职工人数 Number of Disabled Staff and Workers at the end of year	女性 Female
合 计	**Total**	**96**	**5648**	**2221**	**828**
市本级	City Level	13	833	351	94
新城区	Xincheng	10	374	188	66
碑林区	Beilin				
莲湖区	Lianhu	13	968	410	138
灞桥区	Baqiao	20	1257	471	248
未央区	Weiyang	9	431	169	80
雁塔区	Yanta	2	114	11	8
阎良区	Yanliang	3	141	68	16
临潼区	Lintong	1	93	23	10
长安区	Chang'an	10	564	221	55
蓝田县	Lantian	2	158	64	18
周至县	Zhouzhi	2	108	38	10
户 县	Huxian	11	607	207	85
高陵县	Gaoling				
沣东新城	Fengdongxincheng				

注：本表数据来源于市民政局。

20-18 社会保险基本情况

Basic Sitiation of Social Insurance

单位：万人 (10 000 persons)

指 标	Item	2013
基本养老保险参保人数	Number of Basic Old-age Insurance	540.55
1. 城镇企业职工养老保险参保人数	Number of Town Enterprise Worker Old-age Insurance	264.36
2. 机关事业单位养老保险参保人数	Number of Institution Old-age Insurance	27.98
3. 城乡居民养老保险参保人数	Number of Rural Residents Old-age Insurance	248.21
城镇基本医疗保险参保人数	Number of urban basic medical insurance	416.63
失业保险参保人数	Number of unemployed insurance	145.58
生育保险参保人数	Number of Maternity insurance	98.20
工伤保险参保人数	Number of industrial injury insurance	138.85

注：本表数据来源于市人社局。

20-19 全市及各区县新型农村合作医疗情况（2013年）

Situation of the New Rural Cooperative Medical Care of the Whole City and Area County（2013）

区　县	Region	参加新型农村合作医疗人数(万人) Participate in the new rural cooperative medical Population (10 000 persons)	新型农村合作医疗参合率(%) Participate in the new rural cooperative medical care ration (%)
合　计	**Total**	**402.88**	**99.15**
新城区	Xincheng		
碑林区	Beilin		
莲湖区	Lianhu		
灞桥区	Baqiao	29.18	99.91
未央区	Weiyang	19.25	100
雁塔区	Yanta	16.47	100
阎良区	Yanliang	16.62	99.86
临潼区	Lintong	55.91	99.88
长安区	Chang'an	82.34	99.61
蓝田县	Lantian	56.02	98.25
周至县	Zhouzhi	57.52	99.52
户　县	Huxian	46.97	96.43
高陵县	Gaoling	22.60	100

注：本表数据来源于市卫生局。

20-20　全市及各区县优抚对象人员情况（2013年）

Statistics on Persons Enjoying Favoured Treatment by Region (2013)

单位：人　　　　(persons)

区　县	Region	革命伤残人员 Number of Disabled Veterans	烈军属人员 Number of Family Members of Martyrs and Soldiers	在乡红军老战士 Old Red Army Men in Hometown	在乡复员军人 Demobilized Soldiers in Hometown	在乡退伍军人 Veterans in Hometown
全　市	**Total**	**5015**	**1210**	**2**	**5817**	**2562**
市本级	City Level	72				
新城区	Xincheng	692	67		16	
碑林区	Beilin	625	47	1	12	6
莲湖区	Lianhu	705	88	1	35	5
灞桥区	Baqiao	284	86		590	254
未央区	Weiyang	174	35		98	13
雁塔区	Yanta	735	65		240	584
阎良区	Yanliang	94	46		285	56
临潼区	Lintong	271	124		932	270
长安区	Chang'an	349	98		550	123
蓝田县	Lantian	216	126		746	306
周至县	Zhouzhi	339	245		949	213
户　县	Huxian	288	84		598	127
高陵县	Gaoling	102	66		562	155
沣东新城	Fengdongxincheng	69	33		204	450

注：本表数据来源于市民政局。

20-21 全市及各区县计划生育和婚姻登记情况（2013年）

Conditions of Birth Control and Marriage Registration by Region (2013)

区 县	Region	晚婚率（%） Late Marriage Rate(%)	计划生育率（%） Family Planning Rate(%)	综合节育率（%） Contraceptive Rate(%)
合 计	**Total**	**75**	**96**	**90**
新城区	Xincheng	100	98	84
碑林区	Beilin	100	98	90
莲湖区	Lianhu	99	98	90
灞桥区	Baqiao	82	96	90
未央区	Weiyang	90	97	91
雁塔区	Yanta	73	96	89
阎良区	Yanliang	80	96	88
临潼区	Lintong	78	95	93
长安区	Chang'an	74	95	93
蓝田县	Lantian	61	95	91
周至县	Zhouzhi	57	94	93
户 县	Huxian	67	96	93
高陵县	Gaoling	61	96	90
沣东新城	Fengdongxincheng	78	95	93

注：本表数据来源于市计生委、市民政局、市法院。

20-21 续表1 continued 1

区 县	Region	独生子女领证率（%） Only-child Certificate Rate	结婚对数（对） Marriages (couple)	再婚人数（人） Remarriages(person)	离婚对数（对） Divorced Couple (couple)
合 计	**Total**	**47**	**89136**	**25313**	**20304**
新城区	Xincheng	51	5274	2017	1699
碑林区	Beilin	59	10509	2778	2220
莲湖区	Lianhu	62	7085	2533	2155
灞桥区	Baqiao	50	5707	1667	1190
未央区	Weiyang	64	4989	1603	1630
雁塔区	Yanta	60	9288	3008	2750
阎良区	Yanliang	47	3193	1206	867
临潼区	Lintong	29	7260	1527	1353
长安区	Chang'an	36	12103	3395	2421
蓝田县	Lantian	23	5987	1288	1018
周至县	Zhouzhi	14	7316	1296	1010
户 县	Huxian	30	6417	1555	1008
高陵县	Gaoling	42	3915	1416	904
沣东新城	Fengdongxincheng	54	93	24	79

20-22 全市及各区县妇幼卫生保健情况（2013年）

Care Health Conditions of Women and Child by Region(2013)

区 县	Region	5岁以下儿童死亡率（‰）Mortality rate of Children under 5-year-old（‰）	新生儿死亡率（‰）Infant Mortality Ratio in 2012（‰）	婴儿死亡率 Neonata Mortality Ratio（‰）
合 计	**Total**	**3.77**	**2.12**	**3.01**
新城区	Xincheng	1.62	1.62	1.62
碑林区	Beilin	3.68	2.57	2.57
莲湖区	Lianhu	4.42	1.61	4.42
灞桥区	Baqiao	1.17	0.47	0.93
未央区	Weiyang	2.34	1.84	2.34
雁塔区	Yanta	2.66	1.95	2.13
阎良区	Yanliang	6.05	3.46	5.18
临潼区	Lintong	2.52	1.73	2.21
长安区	Chang'an	5.07	2.46	3.88
蓝田县	Lantian	5.12	2.93	3.66
周至县	Zhouzhi	4.96	2.63	3.5
户 县	Huxian	2.11	0.96	1.92
高陵县	Gaoling	6.10	3.35	4.88

注：本表数据来源于市卫生局。

20-22 续表1 continued 1

区 县	Region	孕产妇死亡率（1/10万）Maternal Mortality Ratio (one in hundred thousandth)	产妇住院分娩比例（%）Proportion of maternal Hospital Births (%)
合 计	**Total**	**12.29**	**99.95**
新城区	Xincheng		100
碑林区	Beilin		100
莲湖区	Lianhu	40.14	100
灞桥区	Baqiao		100
未央区	Weiyang		100
雁塔区	Yanta	17.72	100
阎良区	Yanliang	43.20	99.96
临潼区	Lintong		99.93
长安区	Chang'an	15.84	100
蓝田县	Lantian	36.58	99.93
周至县	Zhouzhi		99.61
户 县	Huxian	19.16	100
高陵县	Gaoling		100

20-23 主要年份律师、公证及调解情况

Basic Statistics on Lawyer, Notaries and Mediation in Representative Years

指 标	Item	2008	2009	2010	2011	2012	2013
一、律师工作	**Lawyers**						
律师事务所（个）	Number of Law Offices (unit)	73	79	95	97	105	116
律师（人）	Lawyers(person)	940	1058	1202	1347	1522	1639
专职	Full-time	865	1001	1139	1275	1439	1560
兼职	Part-time	66	55	63	68	73	77
二、公证工作	**Notarization**						
公证处（个）	Number of Notary Offices (unit)	14	14	14	14	14	14
公证人员（人）	Notarial Personnel (person)	189	194	202	233	235	222
#公证员	Notaries	100	102	112	118	116	115
办理公证件数（件）	Number of Notarized Documents Issued (case)	74440	88637	106491	108120	119605	136471
国内	Domestic	43640	57190	72670	68239	79167	99027
民事	Civil	15782	22337	24813	24356	32442	32940
经济	Economics	27858	34853	47857	43883	46725	66087
涉外	Foreign-related	30481	31082	33410	39545	39888	37444
港澳台	Hong Kong. Macao and Taiwan related	319	365	411	336	550	
三、人民调解工作	**Number of People Mediations**						
已建调委会数（个）	Number of Mediation Committees (unit)	3961	3961	3911	4031	4053	4040
调节人员数（人）	Number of Mediators (person)	15424	17198	15717	12848	15080	15240
调解纠纷数（件）	Number of Civil Disputes Mediated (case)	12223	23185	22247	33851	39230	33651
#调节成功数	Number of Cases Successfully Mediated	11201	21373	22164	32109	37510	32368

注：本表数据来源于市司法局。
案件数从2013年开始港澳台并入国内。

20-24 主要年份共青团组织情况

Basic Facts on Communist Youth League in Representative Years

单立：个、人 (unit, person)

指 标	Item	2000	2005	2008	2009	2010	2011	2012	2013
一、基层团组织	**Grass-root Youth League Organisations**	**10323**	**7726**	**10985**	**9054**	**7006**	**11248**	**9097**	**10770**
二、共青团员	**Youth League Members**	**278165**	**344035**	**348141**	**324785**	**308141**	**345682**	**336156**	**344096**
#女团员	Female Youth League Members	134289	153493	145777	144027	142379	159725	157924	158287
三、专职团干部	**Full-time Youth League Cadre**	**845**	**537**	**601**	**387**	**311**	**270**	**680**	**737**

注：本表数据来源于共青团西安市委员会。

20-25 妇联组织情况（2013年）

Women's Organizations Status (2013)

单位：个 (unit)

指 标	Item	2013
一、妇联组织	**Women's Organizations**	
市级妇联	Municipal Women's Federation	1
街道妇联	Street Women's Federation	107
社区妇联	Community Women's Federation	700
县（区）妇联	County (district) Women's Federation	13
乡（镇）妇联	Township (town) Women's Federation	68
村妇代会	Village Women's Representative Conference	2891
二、非公有制经济组织中妇女组织	**Women's Organizations in Non-public Economic Organizations**	
个体劳动者协会中的妇女组织	Women's Organizations in Association of Individual Workers	3
专业市场中的妇女组织	Women's Organizations in the Professional Market	5
私营企业中的妇女组织	Women's Organizations in the Private Sector	15
三资企业中的妇女组织	Foreign-funded Enterprises in the Women's Organizations	27
三、机关事业单位妇女组织	**Women's Organizations in Government Departments and Institutions**	
直属机关妇委会（妇工委）	Women's Committee of Direct-affiliated Departments	60
部门机关妇委会（妇工委）	Women's Committee of Affiliated Departments	279
事业单位妇委会（妇工委）	Women's Committee of Government Institutions	54
四、民主党派妇女组织	**Women's Organizations of Democratic Parties**	
民主党派妇委会	Women's Committee of Democratic Parties	7
五、团体会员	**Members of Organisation**	
工会女职工委员会	Women Staff Committee of Labor Unions	2972
民政部门登记注册的妇女社团	Women's Communities Registered at Civil Administration Departments	5

注：本表数据来源于市妇联。

20–26 妇联工作情况（2013年）

Basic Facts on Women's Federation (2013)

单位：个、人 (unit, person)

指　标	Item	2013
一、双学双比活动	**Double Learning and Double Competition Activities**	
（一）科技培训	Scientific and Technical Training	
接受技术培训人数	Number of People Receiving Technical Training	14268
获得绿色证书人数	Number of People Gaining Green Certificates	271
女农民技术员人数		150
妇代会主任中农民技术员数	Number of Farmer in Women's Head Technicians	134
（二）巾帼扶贫	Women Aid-the-poor Project	
脱贫户数	Households out of Poverty	955
扶贫项目数	Number of Poverty Alleviation Projects	8
二、巾帼建功活动	**Women Make Achievements**	
（一）巾帼建功	Women Make Achievements	
评选巾帼建功标兵数	Number of Pacemakes	141
巾帼建功先进工作者数	Number of Advanced Workers	55
巾帼建功先进协调单位数	Number of Advanced Supporting Units	56
巾帼文明示范岗数	Number of Model Workers	118
（二）下岗失业妇女再就业	Re-employment of Laid-off and Unemployed Women	
妇女就业服务机构数	Number of Institutions for Women's Employment Services	
妇联主办的劳务市场	Labor Markets Sponsored by Women's Federation	6
三、三八红旗手	**Models of Women**	**144**
四、三八红旗集体	**Models of Women Group**	**62**
五、实施春雷计划	**Carrying out of CHUNLEI Project**	
资助女童入学或返校数	Helping Women Children Enter School or Back School	109
社会捐资总额（万元）	Amount of Money That Social Attributes (10 000yuan)	34
六、来信来访情况	**Conditions of Letters and Visits(case)**	
女职工劳动保护信访案件(件)	Cases about Labor Protection of Employed Women through Letters and Visits	169
侵犯妇女财产权利信访案件(件)	Cases about Encroachment of Women's Property through Letters and Visits	169

注：本表数据来源于市妇联。

20-27 主要年份交通、火灾及安全生产情况

Transportation, Fire and Safety Production in Representative Years

指　标	Item	2008	2009	2010	2011	2012	2013
全市合计	**Sum of Entire City**						
事故数(起)	Number of Cases (case)	4138	4225	4173	4199	5029	6329
死亡人数（人）	Number of Deaths (person)	591	586	568	566	553	505
受伤人数（人）	Number of Injuries (person)	2472	2264	2529	2271	2492	2223
损失（万元）	Economic Loss (10 000 yuan)	2802.0	3128.9	3666.8	2780.5	4524.8	4432.8
道路交通事故	**Road Accidents**						
事故数(起)	Number of Traffic Accident (case)	2576	2702	2323	2264	2446	2252
死亡人数（人）	Number of Deaths (person)	551	531	531	531	516	460
受伤人数（人）	Number of Injuries (person)	2464	2247	2520	2260	2486	2217
损失（万元）	Economic Loss (10 000 yuan)	522.8	851.7	736.6	611.9	1011.1	1143.9
火灾事故	**Fire Accidents**						
事故数(起)	Number of Cases (case)	1537	1485	1825	1920	2568	4062
死亡人数（人）	Number of Deaths (person)	11	17	13	3	16	26
受伤人数（人）	Number of Injuries (person)	4	3	7	3	4	6
损失（万元）	Economic Loss (10 000 yuan)	1907.7	1850.6	2224.2	1587.2	2793.7	3011.9
农机事故	**Farm Machinery Accidents**						
事故数(起)	Number of Cases (case)	2	11	5		2	1
死亡人数（人）	Number of Deaths (person)	1				2	1
受伤人数（人）	Number of Injuries (person)	1	2	2			
损失（万元）	Economic Loss (10 000 yuan)		1.1	3.1		12.4	7.0
工矿商贸事故	**Accidents in Industry,Mine,Business and Trade**						
事故数(起)	Number of Cases (case)	22	27	20	15	13	14
死亡人数（人）	Number of Deaths (person)	27	38	24	27	19	18
受伤人数（人）	Number of Injuries (person)	3	12		8	2	
损失（万元）	Economic Loss (10 000 yuan)	366.5	425.5	703.0	581.5	707.7	270.0
特种设备	**Special Accidents**						
事故数(起)	Number of Cases (case)	1					
死亡人数	Number of Deaths (person)	1					
受伤人数	Number of Injuries (person)						
损失（万元）	Economic Loss (10 000 yuan)	5.0					

注：本表数据来源于市安监局。其中交通、火灾数据2011年及以前年份来自于市安监局，2012—2013年数据来自于市公安局。
2006年及以前道路交通数据不含高速公路数据。
2009年及以后工矿商贸事故数据含特种设备数据。

20–28 主要年份刑事案件情况

Data on Criminal Cases in Representative Years

指　标	Item	2008	2009	2010	2011	2012	2013
一、案件数情况	**Data on Number of Cases**						
立案数（起）	Number of Registered Cases(case)	41811	42321	48566	71499	61071	72611
破案数（起）	Number of Cleared up Cases(case)	19284	21921	18906	17585	20788	26587
破案率（%）	Percent of Cleared up Cases(%)	46.1	51.8	38.9	24.6	34.0	36.6
抓获作案成员(人)	Number of Criminals Caught(person)	12364	11870	13104	14672	16980	14255
二、查获犯罪集团情况	**Data on Hunted down and Seized** Criminal Gangs						
查获犯罪集团个数（个）	Number of Hunted down and Seized Criminal Gangs (person)	211	154	186	209	853	695
查获犯罪集团人数（人）	Number of Members of Hunted down and Seized Criminal Gangs (person)	916	663	939	970	3332	2632
涉及案件（起）	Number of Cases Involved(case)	1328	622	1172	485	2039	2439
三、涉枪案件情况	**Data on Cases with Guns Involved**						
立案数（起）	Number of Registered Cases(case)	11	25	16	13	30	17
破案数（起）	Number of Cleared up Cases(case)	9	24	11	10	25	16
破案率（%）	Percent of Cleared up Cases(%)	81.8	96.0	68.8	76.9	83.3	94.1

注：本表数据来源于市公安局。

20–29 主要年份治安案件情况

Data on Public Order Cases in Representative Years

指　标	Item	2008	2009	2010	2011	2012	2013
受理数（起）	Number of Accepted Cases(case)	45226	45925	58968	63289	60747	94853
查处数（起）	Number of Investigated and Prosecuted Cases(case)	44202	45871	57151	62647	59949	93546
查处率（%）	Percent of Investigated and Prosecuted Cases(%)	97.7	99.9	96.9	99	98.7	98.6
查处违法人数（人）	Number of Investigated and Prosecuted Law-breakers and Crime Committer(person)	38606	39214	45856	44199	34346	46253

注：本表数据来源于市公安局。

20-30 各区县刑事、治安案件情况（2013年）

Data on Criminal Cases and Public Order Cases Grouped by Region (2013)

单位：起 (case)

区 县 Region	刑事案件 Criminal cases			治安案件 Public order cases		
	立案数 Number of Registered Cases	破案数 Number of Cleared up Cases	破案率（%） Percent of Ceared up Cases (%)	受理数 Number of Accepted Cases	查处数 Number of Investigated and Prosecuted Cases	查处率（%） Percent of Investigated and Prosecuted Cases(%)
新城区 Xincheng	7232	2366	32.7	10382	10392	100.1
碑林区 Beilin	6631	4710	71.0	12192	12187	100
莲湖区 Lianhu	8607	4058	47.1	8208	7954	96.9
灞桥区 Baqiao	4027	1517	37.7	7193	7193	100
未央区 Weiyang	7034	2521	35.8	6183	5821	94.1
雁塔区 Yanta	11784	4292	36.4	17754	17722	99.8
阎良区 Yanliang	741	380	51.3	1124	1070	95.2
临潼区 Lintong	2420	783	32.4	4298	3973	92.4
长安区 Chang'an	4449	851	19.1	3606	3589	99.5
蓝田县 Lantian	1538	547	35.6	1124	1005	89.4
周至县 Zhouzhi	1503	503	33.5	1031	1031	100
户 县 Huxian	1602	698	43.6	3452	3395	98.3
高陵县 Gaoling	1126	436	43.2	1011	1004	99.3

注：本表数据来源于市公安局。

20-31 主要年份西安市人民检察院案件办理情况

Data on Acceptance of Cases of Xi'an People's Procuratorate

指 标	Item	2007	2008	2009	2010	2011	2012	2013
一、贪污贿赂案件立案人数（人）	**Number of Persons Invovled in Case about Corporation and Bribery(person)**	**166**	**177**	**176**	**184**	**166**	**175**	**172**
二、渎职侵权案件立案人数（人）	**Number of Persons Invovled in Case about Misprison and Toetious(person)**	**35**	**40**	**32**	**40**	**33**	**38**	**42**
三、审查逮捕案件受理件数（件）	**Examination and Arresting(case)**	**3497**	**3835**	**3656**	**4229**	**5741**	**5024**	**5748**
四、逮捕各类案件人数（人）	**Arresting of Criminals of each kind(person)**	**5012**	**5817**	**5429**	**6183**	**8787**	**7168**	**7177**
决定逮捕贪污贿赂犯罪嫌疑人（人）	Suspects of Corporation and Bribery to be Arrested (person)	73	104	97	51	34	43	49
决定逮捕渎职、侵权犯罪嫌疑人（人）	Suspects of Misprision and Tortious to be Arrested (person)	4	11	11	2		6	
批准逮捕刑事犯罪嫌疑人（人）	Suspects of Criminal to be Arrested (person)	4935	5702	5321	6130	8753	7119	7128
五、刑事立案监督、侦察活动监督（件）	**Supervision of Acceptance of Criminal** Cases and Investigation (case)	**204**	**222**	**173**	**623**	**89**	**263**	**368**
六、审查起诉案件受理件数（件）	**Examination and Prosecution (case)**	**3805**	**4325**	**4242**	**4662**	**6298**	**6747**	**6371**
七、起诉各类案件人数（人）	**Prosecution of Criminals of each kind(person)**	**5096**	**5608**	**5614**	**5946**	**8276**	**7307**	**7615**
起诉贪污贿赂犯罪被告人（人）	Prosecution of Criminals of Corruption and Bribery to be Defendants(person)	126	158	159	163	129	157	151
起诉渎职、侵权犯罪被告人（人）	Prosecution of Misprision and Tortious to be Defendants (person)	23	15	11	22	13	29	24
起诉刑事犯罪被告人（人）	Prosecution of Criminal to be Defendants (person)	4947	5435	5444	5761	8134	7121	7440

注：本表数据来源于市检察院。
本表对往年个别数据做了调整。

20–32 西安市中级人民法院案件基本情况（2013年）

Xi'an Intermediate People's Court Basic Data of the Law Cases (2013)

单位：件、万元 (case,10 000 yuan)

指 标	Item	合 计 Total		中级人民法院 the Intermediate People's Court	
		结案 Number of Case	诉讼标的总金额 Subject Matter of Litigation the Total Amount	结案 Number of Case	诉讼标底总金额 The Intermediate People's Court Litigation Total Amount
合 计	**Total**	**79568**	**1358284**	**9229**	**697138**
一、刑事	**Criminal**	**5999**	**14106**	**844**	**6620**
二、民商事	**Civil and Commercial Matters**	**49764**	**742967**	**6837**	**357828**
三、行政	**Administration**	**3960**		**207**	
四、申诉、申请再审	**Appeals, Apply for Retrial**	**305**	**24**	**280**	
五、司法赔偿	**Judicial Indemnification**	**6**	**29**	**4**	**29**
六、执行	**Execution**	**19534**	**601158**	**1057**	**332663**

20–32 续表 continued

单位：件、万元 (case,10 000 yuan)

指 标	Item	基层人民法院 the Basic People's Court		人民法庭 People's Tribunal	
		结案 Number of Case	诉讼标的总金额 Litigation Total Amount	结 案 Number of Case	诉讼标的总金额 Total Number of Litigation
合 计	**Total**	**70339**	**661145**	**15189**	**64707**
一、刑事	**Criminal**	**5155**	**7487**		
二、民商事	**Civil and Commercial Matters**	**42927**	**385139**	**15189**	**64707**
三、行政	**Administration**	**3753**			
四、申诉、申请再审	**Appeals, Apply for Retrial**	**25**	**24**		
五、司法赔偿	**Judicial Indemnification**	**2**			
六、执行	**Execution**	**18477**	**268495**		

注：本表数据来源于市中级人民法院。

主要统计指标解释

艺术表演团体 指由文化部门主办或实行行业管理（经文化行政部门审批并领取营业性演出许可证），专门从事表演艺术等活动的各类专业艺术表演团体，含民间职业剧团。（不包括群众业余文艺表演团队）

艺术表演场馆 指由文化部门主办或实行行业管理（向文化行政部门备案或领取合资（合作）演出场所许可证），有观众席、舞台、灯光设备，公开售票、专供文艺团体演出的文化活动场所。附属于文化部门机构内非独立核算的剧场、排演场，公开营业的也应单独统计。

图书馆 指各类图书馆的管理与服务（对文献和信息的搜集、整理、存储、利用和管理，向社会公众开放并提供科学、文化等各种知识普及教育）。包括公共图书馆和各类机构内部举办的或单独举办的图书馆的管理与服务。不包括部队系统以及文化馆（文化中心、群众艺术馆）、文化站内设的图书室。

群众文化活动 指开展群众文化活动的场所的管理和组织活动。包括文化馆（含综合性文化中心、群众艺术馆）、文化站、文化宫、少年宫等群众文化活动。在本制度中，目前暂不统计文化部门以外的文化宫和少年宫。

文化馆 （含综合性文化中心、群众艺术馆）、文化站：指专门从事群众文化活动的群众文化场馆。不包括临时抽调人员组成、没有编制的农村和街道文化工作队、服务站等。

广播节目综合人口覆盖率 根据国家广电总局制定的《广播电视人口覆盖率统计技术标准和方法》进行统计调查的，分别反映中央、省级、地市级、县级广播节目在本行政区域的综合覆盖情况，反应以无线方式传输的广播节目综合覆盖情况，综合反映广播公共服务覆盖的规模、能力、水平。

电视节目综合人口覆盖率 根据国家广电总局制定的《广播电视人口覆盖率统计技术标准和方法》进行统计调查的，分别反映中央、省级、地市级、县级电视节目在本行政区域的综合覆盖情况，反应以无线方式传输的电视节目综合覆盖情况，综合反映广播公共服务覆盖的规模、能力、水平。

博物馆 指为了研究、教育、欣赏的目的，　藏、保护、展示人类活动和自然环境的见证物，向公众开放，非盈利性、永久性社会服务机构，包括以博物馆（院）、纪念馆（舍）科技馆、陈列馆等专有名称开展活动的单位。

等级运动员人数 指经考核正式批准授予等级运动员称号的人数。运动员等级分为国际级运动健将、运动健将、一级运动员、二级运动员、三级运动员、少年级运动员。

等级裁判员人数 指经考核正式批准授予等级裁判员称号的人数。裁判员等级分为国际裁判、国家级裁判、一级裁判、二级裁判、三级裁判。

卫生机构 指从卫生行政部门取得《医疗机构执业许可证》，或从民政、工商行政、机构编制管理部门取得法人单位登记证书，为社会提供医疗保健、疾病控制、卫生监督服务或从事医学科研和教育等工作的单位。卫生机构包括医院、疗养院、社区卫生服务中心（站）、卫生院、门诊部、诊所（卫生所、医务室）、急救中心（站）、采供血机构、妇幼保健院（所、站）、专科疾病防治院（所、站）、疾病预防控制中心（防疫站）、卫生监督所、卫生监督监测机构、医学科研机构、医学在职培训机构、健康教育所（站）等其他卫生机构。

社区卫生服务中心（站） 指为本社区居民提供预防、医疗、保健、康复、健康教育、计划生育技术服务等的基层卫生机构。包括社区卫生服务中心和社区卫生服务站。

卫生人员 指在医疗、预防保健、医学科研和在职教育等卫生机构工作的职工，包括卫生技术人员、其他技术人员、管理人员和工勤人员。

卫生技术人员 包括执业（助理）医师、注册护士、药师（士）、检验和影像人员等卫生专业人员。不包括从事管理工作的卫生技术人员。

执业医师 指《医师执业证》“级别”为“执业医师”且实际从事医疗、预防保健工作的人员，不包括实际从事管理工作的执业医师。执业医师类别分为临床、中医、口腔和公共卫生四类。

执业助理医师 指《医师执业证》“级别”为“执业助理医师”且实际从事医疗、预防保健工作的人员，不包括实际从事管理工作的执业助理医师。执业助理医师类别同样分为临床、中医、口腔和公共卫生四类。

死亡率（疾病） 指在一定时期内，在一定人群中，死于某病的频率。

死亡率=某期间内（因某病）死亡总数／同期平均人口数1　00%

社会福利企业 指以集中安置有一定劳动能力的残疾人员就业为目的（残疾职工占生产人员10%以上）、带有社会福利性质的企业总称。主要包括福利工厂、假肢厂和其他福利企业。

公证人员 指在国家公证机关依法办理公证事务的司法人员，包括公证员、助理公证员和在公证处工作的其他人员。

办理公证文书 指公证处在一定时期内办结的公证文书件数。公证文书按司法部规定或批准的格式制作，包括国内公证和涉外公证两部分。国内公证分为经济合同公证和民事法律关系公证两大类。

调解人员 指在人民调解委员会担负调解民间一般民事纠纷和轻微违法行为引起纠纷的工作人员，包括调解委员会的委员和调解小组的调解员。

立案 指检察机关对犯罪线索进行初步调查后，认为存在职务犯罪事实并需要追究刑事责任时，依法决定作为刑事案件进行侦查的诉讼活动，是追究犯罪的开始。

Explanatory Notes on Main Statistical Indicators

Arts Performance Troupes refer to the various professional performing arts groups, which sponsored by the cultural sectors or guided by the cultural society (Receive commercial performance license approved by the cultural administration authority),including non-governmental troupes. (The mass amateur arts performance troupes are not included.)

Arts Performance Places refer to the various sites for cultural activities, which sponsored by the cultural sectors or guided by the cultural society (approved by the cultural market administration, or receive joint/cooperative venues permit), with the facility of auditorium, stage and lighting, and selling tickets in public, including the opera halls and rehearse sites, etc. which are affiliated to the culture sectors without independent financial accounts and open to the public.

Library refers to all types of library management and services(collection, collation, storage, use and management of literature and information, open and provide scientific, cultural and other literacy education to the public). Including the management and services of public libraries and the libraries internally or separately organized by various sectors. Excluding the libraries in troops system and cultural palaces (cultural centers, mass art centers),cultural stations.

Mass Culture Center refers to the management and organization of the places where mass culture activities hold. Including cultural palace (cultural center ,mass art center), cultural stations, cultural palaces ,youth palaces and other mass cultural activities. In this system ,cultural palaces and youth palaces beyond cultural sectors are not counted at present.

Cultural Palaces (Cultural Centers, Mass Art Centers),Cultural Stations refers to the mass cultural venues specialized in mass cultural activities. Excluding rural and street cultural teams, service stations which made up by temporary without authorized strength.

Radio Coverage of Population refers to the comprehensive coverage which respectively reflected central ,province, city, prefecture and county radio programs by wireless in the administrative region, and comprehensively reflect the size, capacity, level of the public broadcasting services, according to Statistical Standard and Method on Television and Radio Coverage of Population established by the State Administration of Broadcasting ,Film and Television

Television Coverage of Population refers to the comprehensive coverage which respectively reflected central, province, city, prefecture and county television programs by wireless in the administrative region, and comprehensively reflect the size, capacity, level of the public broadcasting services, according to Statistical Standard and Method on Television and Radio Coverage of Population established by the State Administration of Broadcasting , Film and Television

Museum refers to the non-profit, permanent society service sectors which collect ,protect ,show human activities and the witnesses of natural environment, including the units that organize activities with the proper name such as museum, memorial hall , science and technology museum, exhibition hall, etc.

Number of Athletes in Grades refers to the number of athletes who have been given titles through examination. The titles of athletes include international masters of sports, masters of sports, first-grade, second-grade and third-grade sportsmen and young athletes.

Number of Referees in Grades refers to the number of referees who have been given titles after examination. They are classified as international referees, national referees and referees of the first, second and third grades.

Health Care Institutions refer to the units which have been qualified the Certification of Health Care Institution by the administration of public health, or qualified the Certification of Corporate Unit by the civil affairs, administration for industry and commerce, commission office for public sector reform, and engaging in medical care, disease prevention and control, health supervision and inspection, medicine research and health education, etc., including: hospitals, sanatoriums, community health service centers （stations）, health centers, clinics (health stations and infirmaries), first-aid centres (stations), blood gathering and supplying institutions, women and children care agencies (centres and stations), special disease prevention and curing agencies (centres and stations), disease prevention and control centres (epidemic prevention stations), health supervision and inspection agencies, sanitary inspection institutions, medicinal scientific research and on-job training institutions, health education centres and so on.

Community Health Service Centres (stations) refer to the primary units that provide the health care for community residents, such as disease prevention and control, medical treatment, health care, rehabilitation, health education, family planning technical services, including community health service centres and community health service stations.

Health Care Employee refer to all employee engaged in the health care institutions, such as medical organizations, disease prevention and control centres, health care agencies, medicinal scientific research and on-job training institutions, including medical technical personnel, other technical personnel, manager and labour.

Medical Technical Personnel refer to the professional staff engaged in health care, including licensed (assistant) doctors, registered nurse, pharmacists, laboratory technician, and imaging staff, excluding the medical technical personnel engaged in management job.

Licensed Doctors refer to the medical workers who have obtained the licenses of qualified doctors and are employed in medical treatment, disease prevention or healthcare institutions, excluding the licensed doctors engaged in management job. The licensed doctors are divided into 4 categories: clinician, Chinese medicine physicians, dentist and public health physicians.

Licensed Assistant Doctors refer to the medical workers who have obtained the licenses of qualified assistant doctors and are employed in medical treatment, disease prevention or healthcare institutions, excluding the licensed assistant doctors engaged in management job. The classification of licensed assistant doctors is cliniciam Chinese medicine, dentist and public health.

Mortality Rate refers to the ratio of deaths causedby diseases at reference period to the certain group of population.

Mortality Rate = total deaths (caused by diseases) at reference period/average population at same period × 100%.

Social Welfare Enterprises refers to those welfare-oriented enterprises employing a significant number of handicapped people with certain labour ability (handicapped employees shall exceed 10% of the production staff), including welfare factories, artificial limb plants as well as other welfare enterprises.

Notary Personnel refers to judicial workers of the state notary offices handling notarization work according to law. They include notaries, assistant notaries, and other people working for notary offices.

Notarized Documents refer to the documents settled by notary offices in a year. The notary documents are drawn up in accordance with the regulations of the Ministry of Justice, including domestic documents and foreign-related documents. Domestic documents are divided into two major categories, documents on economic contracts and documents on civil legal relations.

Mediators refer to workers on peoples mediation committees responsible for mediating in civil disputes and cases of slight infraction of the law. They include members of the mediation committees and mediators of mediation groups.

Acceptance of Case refers to the decision made by the procurators office to confirm the act of crime after initial investigation and to start legal proceedings of the case as criminal case.

21

企业调查

ENTERPRISES INVESTIGATION

资料整理：薛　燕
Data management:Xue Yan

第二十一部分　企业调查

一、简要说明

本章资料主要包括各行业企业景气调查指数和企业家信心指数等，由西安市统计局社会经济调查中心提供。

二、主要指标

企业景气指数（第四季度）	115.1
企业家信心指数（第四季度）	116.9

21　ENTERPRISES INVESTIGATION

Ⅰ.Brief Introduction

Data in this chapter consists prosperity survey indices of various industries and Entrepreneur Expectation Indicator, provided by Xi'an Municipal Bureau of Statics .

Ⅱ.Major Indicators

Business Climate Index （Fourth Quarter）	115.1
Entrepreneur Expectation Indicator（Fourth Quarter）	116.9

21-1 企业景气指数（2013年）

Business Climate Index（2013）

指　标	Item	一季度 First Quarter	二季度 Second Quarter	三季度 Third Quarter	四季度 Fourth Quarter
企业景气指数	**Business Climate Index**	**132.4**	**129.8**	**127.8**	**115.1**
按行业门类分	Grouped by Sector				
工业	Industry	133.5	132.7	133.5	127.3
建筑业	Construction	144.1	129.7	131.8	131.3
交通运输、仓储及邮政业	Transport, Storage and Post	119.1	128.7	117.4	104.3
批发和零售业	Wholesale and Retail Sales	108.1	115.3	109.2	106.2
房地产业	Real Estate	120.0	113.0	120.0	101.7
社会服务业	Social Services	145.0	145.8	135.8	107.5
信息传输、计算机服务和软件业	Information Transmission, Computer Service and Safeware Service	144.0	122.0	136.0	118.0
住宿和餐饮业	Hotels and Catering Services	96.3	88.8	86.9	60.0
按企业(单位)登记注册类型分组	Grouped by Registration				
国有企业	State-owned Enterprises	137.9	133.5	137.8	124.2
集体企业	Collective-owned Enterprises	103.7	95.0	102.5	98.8
股份合作企业	Share-holding Cooperative Enterprises	126.4	139.0	139.0	126.9
联营企业	Joint Ownership Enterprises	100.0	100.0	100.0	100.0
有限责任公司	Limited Liability Corporations	132.9	131.0	129.7	113.3
股份有限公司	Share-holding Corporations Ltd.	136.1	123.3	123.0	114.8
私营企业	Privately Owned Enterprises	119.2	110.4	102.8	105.6
港澳台商投资企业	Enterprises Invested by Foreigners or Investors from Hongkong,Macro and Taiwan	120.1	114.3	101.4	80.7
外商投资企业	Foreign Funded Enterprises	112.0	124.4	109.4	97.9
按企业规模分	Grouped by Size of Enterprises				
大型企业	Large-size	145.9	141.6	145.6	130.4
中型企业	Medium-size	124.6	134.5	125.5	113.3
小型企业	Small-size	124.4	117.6	112.5	102.8

21-2 企业家信心指数（2013年）

Entrepreneur Expectation Indicator（2013）

指　标	Item	一季度 First Season	二季度 Second Season	三季度 Third Season	四季度 Fourth Season
企业景气指数	**Entrepreneur Expectation Indicator**	**124.7**	**120.6**	**119.7**	**116.9**
按行业门类分	Grouped by Sector				
工业	Industry	122.8	118.8	126.2	123.3
建筑业	Construction	133.3	121.5	117.9	123.6
交通运输、仓储及邮政业	Transport, Storage and Post	114.8	115.7	108.7	105.2
批发和零售业	Wholesale and Retail Sales	111.2	103.1	112.5	110.3
房地产业	Real Estate	89.6	84.3	95.7	92.2
社会服务业	Social Services	137.5	141.7	125.8	121.7
信息传输、计算机服务和软件业	Information Transmission, Computer Service and Safeware Service	156.0	134.0	140.0	124.0
住宿和餐饮业	Hotels and Catering Services	99.4	98.1	81.3	73.1
按企业(单位)登记注册类型分组	Grouped by Registration				
国有企业	State-owned Enterprises	121.2	128.0	125.3	123.2
集体企业	Collective-owned Enterprises	98.0	104.8	104.8	105.1
股份合作企业	Share-holding Cooperative Enterprises	136.9	134.5	136.9	129.7
联营企业	Joint Ownership Enterprises	100.0	100.0	100.0	100.0
有限责任公司	Limited Liability Corporations	127.8	119.5	118.2	115.1
股份有限公司	Share-holding Corporations Ltd.	131.7	119.9	125.4	121.8
私营企业	Privately Owned Enterprises	109.1	122.3	101.5	116.3
港澳台商投资企业	Enterprises Invested by Foreigners or Investors from Hongkong,Macro and Taiwan	82.8	67.0	82.0	88.9
外商投资企业	Foreign Funded Enterprises	112.0	101.9	109.9	107.9
按企业规模分	Grouped by Size of Enterprises				
大型企业	Large-size	140.7	135.2	139.0	129.7
中型企业	Medium-size	127.1	116.0	123.8	115.1
小型企业	Small-size	113.1	116.5	112.1	109.1

主要统计指标解释

企业景气指数：是根据企业家对本企业综合生产经营情况所作的判断与预期（通常是对“良好”、“一般”、“不佳”的选择）而编制的指数，用以综合反映企业的生产经营状况。企业景气指数也称“企业综合生产经营景气指数”。

企业家信心指数：是根据企业家对企业外部市场经济环境与宏观政策的认识、看法判断和预期（通常是对“乐观”、“一般”、“不乐观”的选择）而编制的指数，用以综合反映企业家对宏观经济环境的感受与信心。企业家信心指数也称“宏观经济景气指数”。

景气指数的表示方式：景气指数的表示范围在0～200之间，其含义：100为景气指数的临界值，表明景气状况变化不大；100～200为景气区间，表明景气状况趋于上升或改善，越接近于200，状况越景气；0～100为不景气区间，表明经济状况趋于下降或恶化，越接近于0，状况越不景气。

Explanatory Notes on Main Statistical Indicators

Business Climate Index it is an index worked out according to the judgment and anticipation (normally a choice from good, ordinary, not good) of entrepreneurs made based on synthetic productive and operational situation of the enterprise. It is used to reflect synthetically the productive and operational situation of the enterprise. It is also referred to as synthetic and productiveoperational prosperity index of enterprise.

Confidence index of entrepreneur it is an index worked out according to the judgment and anticipation (normally a choice from optimistic , ordinary , not optimistic) of entrepreneurs made based on their understandings and views of the market and economic environment outside the enterprise and the macro policies. It is used to reflect synthetically the confidence and feelings of the entrepreneurs to the macro economic environment. It is also referred to as macro-economy prosperity index.

The way to express prosperity index the range of prosperity index is from 0 to 200; 100 is the critical value, and means economic situation didn't change largely; from 100 to 200 is the interval of prosperity; and from 0 to 100 is the interval of not prosperity, meaning economic situation is going down or worse, the closer to 0, the worse the economic situation.

中国统计出版社最新图书简目

（仅供参考，以最后出书为准）

统计资料

综合类：中国统计年鉴　中国统计摘要　中国发展报告

国际资料类：国际统计年鉴　金砖国家联合统计手册　世界能源资源年鉴

区域资料类：中国区域经济统计年鉴　中国县域统计年鉴　中国城市统计年鉴

中国农村统计年鉴　中国地区经济监测报告

经贸与投资类：中国贸易外经统计年鉴　中国对外直接投资统计公报　中国商品交易市场统计年鉴

大中型批发零售和住宿餐饮企业统计年鉴　中国零售和餐饮连锁企业统计年鉴

住户与物价类：中国住户调查年鉴　中国价格统计年鉴　中国农产品价格调查年鉴

全国农产品成本收益资料汇编

资源与环境类：中国环境统计年鉴　中国能源统计年鉴

产业类：中国工业统计年鉴　中国建筑业统计年鉴　中国房地产统计年鉴

中国第三产业统计年鉴　中国证券期货统计年鉴

科技类：中国科技统计年鉴　中国高技术产业统计年鉴　工业企业科技活动资料

人口与就业类：中国劳动统计年鉴　中国人口和就业统计年鉴　中国人才资源统计报告

社会与文化类：中国社会统计年鉴　中国文化及相关产业统计年鉴

公共管理类：中国民政统计年鉴　中国民族统计年鉴　中国乡镇街道行政区域简册

省级综合统计年鉴系列

北京 天津 河北 山西 内蒙古 辽宁 吉林 黑龙江 上海 江苏 浙江 安徽 福建 江西 山东
河南 湖北 湖南 广东 广西 海南 重庆 四川 贵州 云南 西藏 陕西 甘肃 青海 宁夏 新疆
新疆生产建设兵团

市（县）级综合统计年鉴系列

天津滨海新区 石家庄 唐山 邯郸 太原 大同 阳泉 长治 晋城 朔州 晋中 运城 忻州 临汾 呼和浩特
鄂尔多斯 包头 沈阳 大连 长春 吉林市 四平 哈尔滨 黑龙江垦区 上海浦东新区 南京 无锡 徐州
常州 苏州 南通 连云港 淮安 盐城 扬州 镇江 泰州 宿迁 江阴 丹阳 杭州 宁波 温州 嘉兴 绍兴 金华
衢州 舟山 台州 丽水 合肥 福州 厦门 宁德 福州经济技术开发区 南昌 济南 青岛 郑州 洛阳 平顶山
三门峡 南阳 武汉 十堰 荆州 宜昌 荆门 咸宁 长沙 广州 深圳 惠州 东莞 南宁 柳州 桂林 来宾 海口
三亚 成都 贵阳 昆明 西安 兰州 庆阳 银川 乌鲁木齐 兵团一师 兵团十师

调查年鉴系列

山西 内蒙古 吉林 辽宁 上海 福建 湖北 广西 重庆 四川 云南 甘肃 宁夏 新疆 南宁 桂林

“十二五”规划教材

统计学（经济管理类专业本科适用，单薇 等）　抽样调查理论与方法（冯士雍 等）

贝叶斯统计（茆诗松 等）　统计学（黄良文 等）　试验设计（茆诗松 等）

统计学：从数据到结论（吴喜之）　医学统计学（于浩）　统计学（经济、管理类专业基础教材，张小斐）

概率论与数理统计三十三讲（魏振军）　概率论与数理统计三十三：学习指导与习题解答（魏振军）

非参数统计（吴喜之 等）　统计学：经济与管理中的数据分析（李慧云 等）

卫生管理统计学（新编医学院校基础课教材，尚磊）医院统计学（新编医学院校基础课教材，徐天和 等）

社会统计学（蒋萍 等）　现代金融投资统计分析（李腊生 等）

国民经济核算初级教程（经济类、统计类、管理类专业适用，蒋萍 等）

重点图书

新中国65年　新编英汉汉英统计大词典　中华医学统计百科全书

挑大学选专业2014—考研择校指南　挑大学选专业2014—高考志愿填报指南